I0754645

NOCTES AMBROSIANÆ

BY THE LATE

JOHN WILSON

PROFESSOR OF MORAL PHILOSOPHY IN THE UNIVERSITY OF EDINBURGH, EDITOR OF BLACKWOOD'S MAGAZINE, AUTHOR OF "THE ISLE OF PALMS," ETC.

AND

WM. MAGINN, LL.D. J. G. LOCKHART, JAMES HOGG, &c.

WITH

MEMOIRS AND NOTES

BY R. SHELTON MACKENZIE, D.C.L.

EDITOR OF SHEIL'S "SKETCHES OF THE IRISH BAR"

VOL. I

AUGUST, 1819—AUG. 1824

REDFIELD

110 AND 112 NASSAU STREET, NEW YORK.

1854.

EDITOR'S PREFACE.

Additional interest is given, by the recent death of Professor Wilson, to the present work. A complete edition of the Noctes Ambrosianæ (with notes and illustrations, necessary to a true understanding of the allusions with which the work is crowded, and the personal satire it contains) cannot be published in England for many years. In the lapse of time since the original appearance of "The Noctes" in Blackwood's Magazine, persons, localities, and circumstances therein mentioned or glanced at, have been so forgotten, altered, or obscured, as to require brief but sufficient explanations. A literary life, the greater part of which was passed in England and Scotland, has given me familiar acquaintance with most of the individuals and events treated of in this work, and has qualified me, I think, for the editorship which I have assumed.

Besides a History of Blackwood's Magazine, I have written memoirs of Wilson, Lockhart, Hogg and Maginn, the accredited authors of The Noctes. The engravings consist of a fine portrait of Wilson, (after Sir J. Watson Gordon, President of the Royal Scottish Academy,) with characteristic full-length sketches, by Maclise and Skillin, of the other writers. There is also the fac-simile of a page of The Noctes in Professor Wilson's own writing.

I have endeavored to render this edition complete, by introducing the celebrated Chaldee Manuscript, full of satire and libel, which first brought Blackwood's Magazine into notoriety—was suppressed as soon as published—was afterwards boasted of as a brilliant *jeu d'esprit,*—and has been so scarce that the only copy I have ever seen, and I have long sought for it, was that from which I make the present reprint.

In August and September, 1819, nearly two years antecedent to the first of The Noctes, (which commenced in March, 1822, and closed in February, 1835,) there appeared a series of articles entitled "Christopher in the Tent," never before presented in this country, in any shape, which I have here introduced as properly prefatory, because the interlocutors in The Tent include the greater number of those who afterwards appeared in The Noctes. I have also inserted a satirical poem entitled "Metricum Symposium Ambrosianum," (originally intended as an addendum to No. III. of The Noctes,) in which there is a notice of every living British author of note, in the year 1822. This has never been reprinted in America, and I have copiously annotated it. The whole work has been very carefully revised from the original issue in the Magazine, whereby Wilson's peculiarities of composition and punctuation are fully preserved.

It only remains for me to tender my grateful acknowledgments, for access to and loan of books of reference, to Messrs. Harpers, Appletons, and Evans & Dickerson, publishers in New-York;—to Messrs. Evert A. and George L. Duyckinck, for having kindly placed their valuable private library at my service;—to Mr. Philip J. Forbes, of the Society Library, for access to books, and for information;—to my good friends Messrs. Deans & Howard, (of the *New-York Sunday Times*,) for the use of a variety of publications, in their possession, which I had occasion to consult;—to Dr. Robert Tomes, of New-York, to Dr. Henry Abbott, (of the Collection of Egyptian Antiquities,) to Dr. John W. Francis, of New-York, and to Mr. William Wilson, of Poughkeepsie, for facts, anecdotes, and references.

Let me conclude with a story and a moral:—In Ireland, during one of the agrarian insurrections of the last century, a banker in Galway, named French, was particularly disliked by the laboring classes. The Peep-o'-Day Boys, as "these sons of night" called themselves, resolved to ruin "that double-distilled villain, ould French." To do this effectually, whenever they visited the houses of the farmers and gentry, besides demanding arms and ammunition, they insisted on the surrender of such of French's bank-notes as were on hand. To show that it was not from a mere predatory motive, they used solemnly to burn the notes before the late possessors, exclaiming, as they were converted into ashes, "There—there's more ruin for ould French; we'll burn every note of his that's above ground, and not leave the villain a brass farthing." They pursued this vindictive game so successfully that, in the course of a year or two, Mr. French was some £4,000 richer—by the destruction of notes which he otherwise must have taken up and paid.

MORAL.

Most gentle public, have no hesitation in following this Peep-o'-Day example. Buy up all copies of THE NOCTES which may get into the market. Loan them not, so that others will be compelled to purchase also. If you clear away the whole of our large impression, believe that publisher and editor will submit to *such* "ruin," with the exemplary patience of martyrs.

R. S. M.

112 NASSAU STREET, NEW-YORK, July 25, 1854.

HISTORY

OF

BLACKWOOD'S MAGAZINE.

BY DR. SHELTON MACKENZIE.

WILLIAM BLACKWOOD, founder and proprietor of the Magazine which has borne his name " to the uttermost parts of the earth," died at his house in Edinburgh, on the 16th September, 1834, in the fifty-eighth year of his age. His parents, who were in an humble station of life, placed him as apprentice with Bell & Bradfute, well known booksellers and publishers, in Edinburgh, in the latter part of the eighteenth and the earlier years of the nineteenth century. In their employment he read a great variety of books, but Scottish History and Antiquities more particularly engaged his attention. He was known to have closely studied and largely mastered these subjects, and, when he established himself in business, his accomplishments soon attracted the notice of persons whose good opinion was distinction. For many years he was content with being extensively engaged in the sale of classical and antiquarian works, and was considered one of the best informed booksellers of that class in Great Britain.

Even as late as forty years ago, what is called the New Town of Edinburgh was regarded with dislike and distrust by the Old. In the latter place, the Castle, the University, the Courts of Law, the Advocates' Library, the Signet Library, the Royal Exchange, the College of Surgeons, Heriot's and Watson's Hospitals, the principal churches, the Assembly Hall, and even the Palace of Holyrood, were distinguishing features. There, too, were the book-shops, the printing-offices, and the publishers' places of business. In the New Town, there were few shops. The gentry, it is true, had domiciles there. But the idea of any publisher moving thither would have been looked upon as the height of folly, half a century since.

Mr. Blackwood was a man of much sagacity. He saw that the rich, who are naturally purchasers of books, lived in the New Town. He sold off his large stock, chiefly consisting of old books,—moved to a large and airy suite of rooms in Prince's street, which had formerly been occupied by a notable confectioner, and was therefore well known to the public, and prepared to be to Edinburgh what John Murray, of Albemarle street, was among the publishers of London. The "trade" in the Old Town ominously shook their heads, and sagaciously predicted ruin. Blackwood did not mind them very much, but moved to the immortal No. 17 Prince's street, in the year 1816, and applied himself to the disposal of general literature and the business of a popular publisher. In April, 1817, he brought out No. 1 of BLACKWOOD'S EDINBURGH MAGAZINE.

It is necessary now to go back a little. The first Number of the Edinburgh Review had appeared on the 25th October, 1802 ; precisely at the period when Pitt, yielding to the general desire for peace, had retired from office, in order that Addington (afterwards Lord Sidmouth) might make a treaty with France for that purpose. Then followed Pitt's return to office in 1804 ; the prosecution of the war with France with redoubled energy ; the splendid victories on land, with which Napoleon dazzled the world ; the battle of Trafalgar, where triumph was dearly purchased by the death of Nelson ; the death of Pitt, in January, 1806 ; the succession of Fox to office, with his tenure of it lamentably abridged by death ; the continued successes of Napoleon ; the annexation of Spain and Portugal to the French empire ; and the determination of England, carried into effect by Wellington, to rescue the Peninsula from the usurpation of France. All these occurrences intervened in the seven years between 1802 and 1809, and afforded a vast supply of materials for discussion in the Edinburgh Review. Meanwhile, that periodical was successful beyond all hope and precedent, but it inculcated the idea—which was really entertained by Jeffrey—that resistance to the far-spreading power of Napoleon was and would be useless, and that peace with France, on any terms, was the only means by which the political existence of England could possibly be preserved.

The English and Scottish Tories and Anti-Gallicans held different and (as the event has proved) wiser opinions. They determined to oppose the Edinburgh Review—whose circulation was 9,000 a number at this time, with the influence which such extensive publicity gave it. The literary criticism, which was very good, carried it into quarters where the political articles, of themselves, might have tabooed it. In February, 1809, with John Murray as its publisher, and William Gifford as its editor, the first number of the Quarterly Review came before the world. With such contributors as Scott, George Ellis, Canning, Frere, Croker, Southey, and other men of repute and intellect, the Quarterly immediately took the high stand which it has since maintained. John Ballantyne, the nominal head of Scott's publishing house, was Murray's Edinburgh agent. After some time, Blackwood was placed in that lucrative position. When Scott quarrelled with Constable, the Edinburgh publisher, in 1816, Murray and Blackwood gladly became publishers of the next of the Waverley Novels, which happened to be the first series of "Tales of My Landlord." This was immediately before Blackwood had gone to the New Town, and when he was known only as an intelligent antiquarian bookseller, and agent to Murray

Removed to the New Town, in 1816, Blackwood appears to have contemplated the idea of exalting the character of magazine literature, then fallen very low indeed. At this time he was forty years old. In Peter's Letters, (by Lockhart,) he was described as "a nimble active-looking man of middle age, and moves about from one corner to another, with great alacrity, and apparently under the influence of high animal spirits. His complexion is very sanguineous, but nothing can be more intelligent, keen, and sagacious, than the expression of the whole physiognomy; above all, the gray eyes and eyebrows, as full of locomotion as those of Catalani. The remarks he makes are, in general, extremely acute—much more so, indeed, than those of any member of the trade I ever heard speak upon such topics."

Some time before this, James Hogg had conducted a weekly literary journal in Edinburgh called "The Spy." It failed, but Hogg, who was full of projects, got the idea that a monthly periodical would succeed. There was none in Edinburgh, at that time, except a miserable periodical entitled "The Scots' Magazine." Hogg spoke on the subject to the late Thomas Pringle, who, it appeared, had simultaneously entertained a similar idea. Then Blackwood was spoken to, and he, also, had not only thought of, but was actually preparing for such publication. It is evident, then, that Blackwood had not derived the idea from Hogg, as it had previously been a creation of his own mind.

Blackwood, sagacious even beyond the sagacity of "canny Scotchmen," had noted two points,—that the Edinburgh Review, with its light flying artillery of wit, personality, and sarcasm, was a more important assailant than the Quarterly, with its heavy ordnance; and that the Quarterly had a limited circulation in Scotland, wherein lay the greatest sale of the Edinburgh Review. Blackwood was a decided party-man. He belonged to the Tory side, and hated all that was Whig. From the first, he determined to make his Magazine the assailant of the Edinburgh Review and its party.

On the first of April, 1817, the first number of "BLACKWOOD'S EDINBURGH MAGAZINE" was published. It was edited by Messrs. Pringle and Cleghorn,—both of whom, curiously enough, were much deformed in person. Truth to say, the words "dull and decent" would truly characterize this opening number. There were "Notices concerning the Scottish Gipsies," written by Scott, (who occasionally wrote for it until illness wholly prostrated him)—there was a story of Pastoral Life, by Hogg—there were some antiquarian articles, probably selected by Blackwood—there was some poetry—there were a few reviews—there was a monthly chronicle of events, reports on agriculture and commerce, and lists of births, deaths, and marriages.

Such a publication, though Henry Mackenzie and others speedily came into it, as contributors, was not what the times required—nor Mr. Blackwood. He speedily felt, and lamented, its want of a distinctive character. By the time the fourth number was published, he and his editors had quarrelled: the wonder is how they ever agreed, they being bitter Whigs, while he was a decided Tory. Pringle and Cleghorn went over to Constable, the publisher, conveying with them the list of subscribers to the Magazine, which, they said, belonged to them. Constable, wroth with Blackwood for having obtained, out of his hands, the publication of the Waverley Novels, received the deserters with open arms, installing them in the Editorship of the "Scot's," henceforth, for the brief time of its future existence, to be known as "Constable's Edinburgh Magazine."

Blackwood was thrown on his own resources, which did not fail him. He undertook to be his own Editor, and so he continued, for the remaining seventeen years of his life. He looked about for assistants, and found them. There was James Hogg, whose Queen's Wake had placed him, not long before, in a station, among Scottish poets, inferior only to Robert Burns and Walter Scott. There was John Wilson, then in the spring of intellect and flush of young manhood. There was John Gibson Lockhart, eminently gifted by nature and largely improved by education. There was Robert Pierce Gillies, (afterwards the Kempferhausen of "The Noctes,") whose admirable notices of the dramatic literature of Germany and Scandinavia speedily gave the Magazine a peculiar and inimitable character. There were others, of less note,—but these were enough at the time.

In *Blackwood* for October, 1817, appeared an article occupying nearly eight pages, and entitled "Translation from an Ancient Chaldee Manuscript," which took the shape of a book of Holy Writ, being couched in biblical language, and divided into chapter and verse. In reality, this was a sharp and pregnant satire upon Constable, Jeffrey, Pringle, Cleghorn, and the most noted members of the Whig party in Edinburgh. There is no room to doubt that the main authorship of this literary Congreve rocket (for so it was) must be credited to James Hogg, though the wits of Maga used to sneer at the idea. His own account, published in each of his *five* autobiographies, (all of which appeared in William Blackwood's lifetime,) was simply this,—that he wrote the "Chaldee Manuscript," and sent to Mr. Blackwood, from Yarrow; that, on first reading it, Blackwood did not think of publishing it; that "some of the rascals to whom he showed it, after laughing at it, by their own accounts, till they were sick, persuaded him, nay almost forced him to insert it; for some of them went so far as to tell him, that if he did not admit that inimitable article they would never speak to him as long as they lived,"—and that they interlarded it "with a good deal of deevilry of their own," which Hogg had never thought of. Hogg saw nothing objectionable in the article, and would not have scrupled to have shown it to Constable, (therein described as "the Crafty,") nor to Pringle—who, with Cleghorn, figured in it, as one of "the Beasts." All that Hogg meant was to give a "sly history of the transaction, [Pringle's quarrel with Blackwood,] and the great literary battle that was to be fought." Hogg's own portion of the "Chaldee Manuscript" consisted of the first two chapters, part of the third, and part of the last. He suspected Lockhart, who was eminently sarcastic and personal, of having *thrown in the pepper.*

Words cannot adequately describe the dismay, astonishment, wrath and hatred which greeted the seventh number of Blackwood, containing the Chaldee Manuscript. There was a wild outcry, all through Edinburgh, before the Magazine had been one hour published. Not alone was the accusation of personality made, but it was declared that the interests of religion and society demanded the prosecution, with a view to the heavy punishment, of Mr. Blackwood, for having published "a ribald and profane parody upon the Bible." Greatly alarmed, Blackwood determined to withdraw the offensive article. He had actually issued only two hundred numbers of the Magazine. Every other copy that went out, was *minus* the "Chaldee," and, in the next number, which was published in November, 1817, there appeared the following very humble apology :—

"The Editor has learned with regret, that an article in the first edition of last number, which was intended merely as a *jeu d'esprit,* has been construed so as to give offence to individuals justly entitled to respect and regard; he has on that account withdrawn it in the second edition, and can only add, that if what has happened could have been anticipated, the article in question certainly never would have appeared."

Some prosecutions were commenced, and Blackwood had to pay £1000, in costs and damages, in two years. More were threatened. The result was that, henceforth, Blackwood's Magazine became looked for, month after month, in the expectation of some other group of personalities. In due season, it must be confessed, this expectation duly obtained remarkable fruitage.

At this distance of time, when thirty-seven years have elapsed between the original publication of the Chaldee Manuscript and this notice of it, difficult would it be to point out a tithe of the personalities with which it literally abounded. To obtain even a sight of the article has been difficult. I searched all the national and public libraries in England and Scotland, where sets of *Blackwood* are kept, and never succeeded in meeting one containing the first (and suppressed) edition of No. VII., containing The Chaldee. A short time since, in New-York, I discovered a set of *Blackwood* containing the desiderated article,* and, as it is in itself, not only a literary curiosity, but is repeatedly referred to

* It was Mr. Evans, (of the firm of Evans & Dickerson, New-York,) who informed me that he possessed a complete set of *Blackwood*, with this suppressed article. On examination, I found that it was even as he said. Eventually, I purchased this set, but am not the less obliged to the polite courtesy of the vendors, which permitted me to make a copy of the article, some weeks before I had determined to obtain ownership of the valuable series.—M.

in The Noctes, I shall reprint it, at the end of this narrative, with notes sufficient to indicate the principal persons therein referred to.

Soon after the publication of the Chaldee Manuscript, Wilson, Lockhart, Gillies and Hogg entered into very intimate relations with Blackwood. This list was speedily augmented. In 1818, the late Major Thomas Hamilton (subsequently known as author of "The Youth and Manhood of Cyril Thornton," and "Men and Manners in America") entered the corps as a volunteer. The following year witnessed the adhesion of Dr. Maginn, afterwards known, in *Blackwood*, as Morgan Odoherty. John Galt, the novelist, soon joined the band, and a very young versemaker (the late David Macbeth Moir) wrote a great deal for it under the Greek signature of Δ. But the actual conduct of the Magazine, which included correspondence with contributors, was wholly in Blackwood's hands. He was an excellent man of business, and the Magazine owed much of its success to him.

As early as February, 1818, probably induced by the bold personalities of the Chaldee Manuscript, the Magazine obtained an able, constant, and powerful contributor in the person of Timothy Tickler,—who figures, very extensively, as one of the *dramatis personæ* of the Noctes. The real name of this writer was Robert Syme. John Wilson's mother was his sister. He was a Writer of the Signet, in extensive practice at Edinburgh, had considerable property, lived in a grand house in George's Square, and was, if all accounts be true, one of the greatest Tories in all broad Scotland. Hogg describes him as "an uncommonly fine-looking elderly gentleman, about seven feet high, and as straight as an arrow." He was a good violinist, also,—which strongly recommended him to Hogg. He wrote on a variety of topics in the Magazine, and always with marked ability.

At one time, it was a habit to review, in *Blackwood*, books which never had been published. In February, 1819, a notable instance of this occurred. There was a review, critical enough and rich in extracts, of a book professing to have been printed in Aberystwith, (a small watering-place in Wales,) and entitled "Peter's Letters to his Kinsfolk, being the Substance of some familiar Communications concerning the present State of Scotland, written during a late Visit to that Country." A certain Dr. Peter Morris, of Pensharpe Hall, Aberystwith, was invented as the letter-writer. The extracts were piquant enough, and the allusions to persons and things said to be noticed in the book, were abundantly provoking. In the next *Blackwood* there was a further and fuller review. The result was that Lockhart was induced to complete "Peter's Letters," which Blackwood published, (as a *second* edition!) and it soon reached a third. Caustic, witty, earnest, personal, and fearless, "Peter's Letters" attracted great attention, and no slight animadversion. The author's name got known, and the Magazine gained much credit for having introduced Dr. Morris to the world.

Among the early contributors, in prose or verse, were Sir Thomas Dick

Lauder, who afterwards wrote a graphic account of the Great Morayshire Floods in 1829; Dr. McCrie, the biographer of John Knox and Andrew Melvil; Sir David Brewster; Wordsworth, the poet; Dr. Anster, of Dublin, whose translation of "Faust" is probably the best yet published; Coleridge; Galt, the Scottish novelist; the late William Gosnell, of Cork, author of "Daniel O'Rourke;" J. J. Callanan, and J. D. Murphy, also natives of Cork, the first of whom will be remembered by his ballad of "Gougane Barra;" Bowles, the poet; Crofton Croker, author of "Irish Fairy Legends;" Richard B. Peake, the dramatist, whose "Magic Lay of the One Horse Chay" first appeared in Maga; Barry Cornwall; Gleig, author of "The Subaltern;" Professor George Dunbar, of Edinburgh University; Tennant, the Oriental scholar, author of "Anster Fair;" and Mr. Townshend, of Cork, who was garrulous and anecdotal under the signature of "Senex." I knew him in my youth, and regret that he did not publish his Recollections *in extenso.*

The first actual and out-of-the-ordinary article which showed that a new power had begun to breathe itself into the Magazine, appeared in the number for August, 1819, and was the commencement of the Ante-Noctes series called "Christopher in the Tent." It affected to describe the sayings and doings of the Editor and his contributors, while encamped, on the commencement of the shooting season, at the head of the river Dee, among the mountains of Aberdeenshire. A variety of fictitious, with a few actual personages, were introduced. There were Dr. Morris, Mr. Wastle, Odoherty, the Ettrick Shepherd, Tickler, Kempferhausen, and others, including Buller and Seward, (representatives of the two English Universities,) with Price and Tims, a couple of Cockney tourists. Nearly all these were creations of and in the Magazine. Not so, Dr. Scott, the Odontist of Glasgow, who is entitled to a distinct paragraph, as one of the Curiosities of Literature.

James Scott was a reality, described by Hogg as "a strange-looking, bald-headed, bluff little man, practising as a dentist in Edinburgh and Glasgow; keeping a good house and hospitable table in both, and considered skilful." Of literature he was wholly ignorant, but Lockhart and others perpetually mystified him, publishing ballads and songs in his name, which, at last, he used to sing as his own, whenever he could get auditors. Pet phrases, allusions to particular incidents and persons, were so adroitly introduced into these pieces, that—while his friends marvelled how he had contrived to appear a dull man for the preceding fifty years of his life—nobody discredited his claims to authorship. "The Lament for Captain Paton," one of Lockhart's best ballads, was put into Dr. Scott's mouth, in The Tent, and gained him so much reputation, that, on a visit to Liverpool, soon after, the Odontist actually was entertained at a public dinner, on the strength of his reputed connection with *Blackwood!* The wits of the Magazine even went to the length of announcing, among forthcoming works, "Lyrical Ballads, with a Dissertation on some popular corruptions of Poetry; by James Scott, Esq. Two small volumes 12mo." He was anxious for the publication, and had even sat for his portrait, as a frontispiece.

The first section of "The Tent" was so popular, that the whole of the succeeding number (for September, 1819) was devoted to the continuation and conclusion, in two parts. Among the characters, real and imaginary, now brought forward, in addition to those already named, were Blackwood, John Ballantyne, (hit off to the life,) Francis Jeffrey, Professor McCulloch, Pringle and Cleghorn, (ex-editors of *Blackwood*,) Mrs. McWhirter and her husband, the erudite Dr. Parr, the Earl of Fife, the Duke and Duchess of Gordon, and Prince Leopold, now King of the Belgians! In fact, nearly three years before the actual commencement of the Noctes Ambrosianæ, *here* was the overture to that renowned series where wit and wisdom found a voice. As such, I have included it in this collection, of which it properly is at once an initiatory and integral portion. No part of Christopher in the Tent has ever before been published in America: as Coleridge would (and did) say, "It is as good as manuscript."

In October, 1830, in an article called "The Moors," there are some reminiscences of the imaginary proceedings in The Tent, in August and September, 1819. Wilson here lamented the death of the Odontist—paid a tribute to the evanished glory of Dr. Parr's wig—declared that Odoherty had been gathered to his fathers, and that his widow (Mrs. McWhirter) had applied for a pension, which the Wellington Ministry were likely to refuse, but which their successors would certainly grant,—and that Tims, though puny, was far from unwell, "and still engaged in polishing tea-spoons, and other plated articles, at a rate cheaper than travelling gipsies do horn." Wilson repeatedly writes from "The Tent," as witness his earliest and his latest articles in Maga.

There is something characteristic of his love of external nature, a passion which filled his mind while yet a boy, in the pertinacity with which, in his writings, he delights to traverse mountain and valley, to breast the deep waters of the dark and lonely tarn, to speed across the heathery moors, to follow the rapid river to its small source among the hills, to claim and make acquaintance with the free denizens of earth and air, to hold companionship with the humble shepherd in his turf-built shieling, far up among the clouds and sunshine, in the extensive tracks where thousands of sheep found food, and, at all times and seasons, to

"Look through Nature up to Nature's God."

If it be noticed that Christopher North—clarum et venerabile nomen!—is not actually designated as such, under "The Tent," my reply is the very sufficient one that, up to this time, the name had not been invented. The conductor of *Blackwood* had hitherto been represented as a sort of "stat nominis umbra," and was spoken of as "the veiled Editor." No doubt, the inconvenience of this want of individuality was felt. Therefore, on the back of the contents-page of *Blackwood* for September, 1819, appeared the following announcement among a variety of other (imaginary) "Books preparing for Publication," by Blackwood, of Edinburgh, and Cadell & Davies, of London :

THE AUTOBIOGRAPHY of CHRISTOPHER NORTH, Esq., Editor of Blackwood's Edinburgh Magazine, in 3 vols 8vo, with numerous engravings of men and things.

"Had any man the courage to write a full, candid, and unaffected account of what he himself has seen and thought—he could not fail to make the most interesting and instructive book in the world." KANT.

In the first volume of this work will be found a copious account of all the extraordinary scenes which occurred in Paris at the commencement of the Revolution, and of the wonderful escape of the Author shortly after the martyrdom of King Louis. The second is chiefly occupied with the political state of Scotland in the years immediately succeeding—and sketches of the many singular characters first about that time developed in this part of the island. The Author's travels into various countries of Europe, particularly Spain, Sicily, Germany, and Ireland—his return to Britain—and final establishment in the metropolis of Scotland—together with free and plain strictures on some recent transactions of a very uncommon nature, will bring the third volume to a conclusion.

The Author is not insensible to the very great boldness of the Work which he has thus undertaken to prepare for the public eye. The nature of those clamours which cannot fail to precede, attend, and follow, the publication of his Memoirs has been abundantly contemplated by him, and he has fairly made up his mind to endure them all. The age at which he has arrived is such as to convince him of the folly of either fearing or hoping much for himself. His only object and ambition is to produce an impartial narrative—and if he does so, he sees no reason to doubt that that narrative will be a KTHMA ΕΣ AEI.

From this period, the *eidolon* called CHRISTOPHER NORTH, was the recognised editor of *Blackwood.* Here he alluded to his age as being far advanced. Judging from a subsequent statement in the Noctes, immortal North was born in December, 1755, which would make him 64, in The Tent; 67, when the Noctes commenced; and 80, when they were concluded. Of course, then, in June, 1849, when the Dies Boreales were commenced, North must have been 94, and must have reached the ripe age of 97, when the last was penned, in September, 1852.*

The first of the Noctes Ambrosianæ was published in March, 1822. The interlocutors were North and Odoherty. In the preceding June, Dr. Maginn, who had become one of the most prolific, as he certainly was the most learned,

* Vide the article in *Blackwood*, for May, 1854, which gives this as the date of Wilson's last contribution.—M.

of all the contributors, had visited Blackwood, at Edinburgh, and made intimate acquaintance with Wilson, Lockhart, Hogg, Hamilton, Gillies, and the rest of his collaborateurs. I am much disposed to attribute the first of the Noctes wholly to his pen, and I am confident that No. IV., (July, 1822,) in which Byron and Odoherty are the only speakers, could have been written by none other than "The Doctor."

The famous Greek motto, with the (very) free translation, which used to head each of the Noctes, was not introduced until No. VI. It was written by Maginn, and runs as follows:

ΧΡΗ Δ'ΕΝ ΣΥΜΠΟΣΙΩ ΚΥΛΙΚΩΝ ΠΕΡΙΝΙΣΣΟΜΕΝΑΩΝ
ΗΔΕΑ ΚΩΤΙΛΛΟΝΤΑ ΚΑΘΗΜΕΝΟΝ ΟΙΝΟΠΟΤΑΖΕΙΝ.

Phoc. *ap. Ath.*

[*This is a distich by wise old Phocylides,*
An ancient who wrote crabbed Greek in no silly days;
Meaning, "'Tis right for good winebibbing people,
Not to let the jug pace round the board like a cripple;
But gaily to chat while discussing their tipple."
An excellent rule of the hearty old cock 'tis—
And a very fit motto to put to our Noctes.]

C. N. *ap. Ambr.*

Whoever began the Noctes, or whatever pens were first employed upon them, there can be no doubt that, very speedily, Wilson's was the master-mind which pressed the individuality of genius into them. Was it wonderful, then, if they bore the marks of his authorship? Peculiar turns of expression, and particular trains of thought, such as only he indulged in, enabled his friends to trace his pen through the series, month after month, year after year. From March, 1822, until February, 1835, when the series closed, having extended to Seventy-One Numbers, no Magazine articles won more attention or favor.

Great as was their popularity in England, it was peculiarly in America that their high merit and undoubted originality received the heartiest recognition and appreciation. Nor is this wonderful, when it is considered that for one reader of *Blackwood's Magazine* in the old country, there cannot be less than fifty in the new. There was a strong desire among the more cultivated minds of Great Britain, to have the series collected, and I have understood that the subject was seriously discussed, by Wilson and the Messrs. Blackwood; but it was considered that, abounding in literary and political personalities, as each of the Noctes did, it would be wholly impossible to make a collective republication without such omissions as would virtually destroy the original character of the articles. It was considered that a period of five-and-twenty or thirty years must pass, before the Noctes, unmutilated, and made clear by biographical, literary, political, and general notes, could be presented, as a whole, to the British public.

On this side of the water, no such reasons for delay existed, and the republication of The Noctes Ambrosianæ took place in 1843. They formed four closely-printed volumes, and I shall only say of them, that they were distinguished by two faults, one of omission, the other of commission. In the first place, no date having been given in any instance, the reader was left wholly in the dark as to the *time* of each dialogue; in the second, the whole of Wilson's peculiar mode of personifying things (which he largely did, by the abundant use of capital letters in nouns) was altered, and wherever a word commenced with a capital—thus giving it a sort of brevet title on the page—it was reduced to the [lower-case] ordinary rank-and-file. It is clear that if a writer make it part of his system to have certain words commence with a particular description of letter, (as Wilson did and as Carlyle does,) it marks his style, and should be preserved. A great deficiency in the first American edition of the Noctes was the want of an Index. It will be perceived that I have remedied, in the present edition, all that is complained of. The new matter now added makes the series as complete, so far as the text is in question, as I can make it. What else I have done, in illustration, may speak for itself.

Meanwhile, though Blackwood never relinquished the actual business conduct of the Magazine, Wilson gradually became the virtual editor. As one of the Professors in Edinburgh University, he had station; and years, as they glided on, brought soberer thought. In 1826, Lockhart went to London, to conduct the *Quarterly Review*, and with him departed much of the personal and caustic sarcasm of Maga. The more generous impulses of Wilson became lords of the ascendant. The onslaught upon the Cockney School of Literature was laid aside, and every man of genius who chose to write for Maga could

"Claim kindred there and have his claim allowed."

It would be a long task even to enumerate all who, from that time, contributed to *Blackwood*. To the last, Hogg and Hamilton, Aird and Sym continued in that band. There Maginn, for over twenty years, poured out the treasures of his learning, wit, and fancy. There, some of Lockhart's most brilliant essays and poems first met the public eye. There, Thomas Doubleday, a poet then, and only a political economist now, delighted to luxuriate. There, the delicate fancy of Charles Lamb was allowed its full range. There, Caroline Bowles was ever welcome, whether in her prose "Chapters on Churchyards," or in her simple and touching lyrics. There, after many and notable failures in other departments of letters, Galt discovered that his power lay in the delineation of familiar Scottish life. There, "Delta" flooded the land with many thousand lines of unreadable "poetry," and showed, by his "Autobiography of Mansie Wauch, tailor at Dalkeith," that not in sentiment but in humor was his real strength, in which, had he pleased, he might have surpassed Galt himself. There, Allan Cunningham gave "prose by a poet," in the adventures of Mark Macrobin, the Cameronian. There, De Quincey poured out his subtlety, which, were it less diffuse, would have been more valuable. There, Coleridge, a greatly superior mind, occasionally laid his thoughts before the public. And there, a star among them, Mrs. Hemans occasionally occupied a page or two with some noble lyric. Her "Aspiration and Despondency" was first given to the world in *Blackwood*.

Great political changes took place during this time;—the brief premiership of Canning—the incapacity of Lord Goderich, his successor—the iron grasp of power by "the Duke'—the election for Clare, which sent O'Connell to Parliament—the granting of Catholic Emancipation, by a Ministry whose lives had been spent in resisting it—the consequent branding Wellington and Peel as traitors (to party)—the death of George the Fourth—the outcry for Parliamentary Reform, under his successor—the contest for "the Bill"—the downfall of the Tories—the uprise of the Whigs,—all of these were fruitful topics, and were discussed in the articles in Maga, as well as at the Noctes.

Among the literary papers which now appeared may be noticed the continuation of, scarcely inferior to, Swift's History of John Bull, written by Professor George Moir, also author of the beautiful series entitled "Shakspeare in Germany."

Nor should there be omitted, in this rapid enumeration, the finest nautical fictions of the age, ("Tom Cringle's Log," and the "Cruise of the Midge,") written by one whose very name—Michael Scott—was ever unknown to Mr. Blackwood. In September, 1834, "Ebony," as he loved to be called, (the Chaldee Manuscript gave him the title,) "shuffled off this mortal coil," ignorant of the identity of Michael Scott, who followed him, in the next year.

In *Blackwood*, after this, appeared Sir Daniel K. Sandford's admirable papers (adapted from the German of Meissner) on the Youth and Manhood of Alcibiades. There, too, after six English periodicals had peremptorily rejected them, were published Samuel Warren's "Passages from the Diary of a late Physician," which literally took the world of letters by storm, and were succeeded by the yet more attractive novel—alas! that it should be a caricature from first to last—of "Ten Thousand a Year."

So great was the catholic spirit of Maga now, that the "Men of Character" of republican Douglas Jerrold appeared under the same cover with a biography of Burke, and the historical romance of "Marston," by Croly, the Tory. Macnish, the Glasgow doctor, was allowed to make his eccentric but often dull appearance as "The Modern Pythagorean." Ingoldsby (our genial friend Barham) introduced "My Cousin Nicholas" to the world. And, specially invited by Wilson, the late John Sterling contributed his delightful "Literary Lore." There, too, was the late M. J. Chapman, with his translations from the plays of Æschylus. There was William Hay, not translating, but actually transfusing the Greek Anthology into English poetry. There, Walter Savage Landor spoke out, as familiar with the illustrious of past centuries, in his

"Imaginary Conversations." There, Professor H. H. Wilson, of Oxford, gave Specimens of the Hindu Drama. There, James Ferrier (now Professor of Moral Philosophy in the University of St. Andrew's) produced his eloquent and thoughtful Introduction to the Philosophy of Consciousness. And there, while yet a youth, William E. Aytoun (afterwards Wilson's son-in-law) gave trochaic versions of Homer, such as have not yet been surpassed.

After Blackwood's death, the Magazine came more under Wilson's *surveillance* than it formerly had been. He lost no time in inviting Bulwer to contribute—and to this we owe some spirited translations of Schiller, and the two prose fictions ("The Caxtons," and "My Novel") which are admitted to be the best productions of the greatest living author of England. Monckton Milnes (who certainly wants common sense, or he would not have published a volume of "Poetry for the People," and charged two dollars for the book!) was allowed to spread his elegant fancies over occasional pages of Maga. Here were welcomed the lofty strains of Elizabeth Barrett Barrett, the greatest of living female poets. Here, Charles Mackay, the lyrist of humanity and progress, earnestly poured out heart-poetry. It was here that the late Bartholomew Simmons, a young Irish poet, who "died too soon," gave his exquisite lyrics to the public. And here, also, did Samuel Phillips, now the literary critic on the "Times" newspaper in London, first make a direct and successful challenge, on the universal mass of readers, in his powerful life-novel called "Caleb Stukely." Nor should I here omit to state that some of the most powerful articles, (chiefly on American politics and literature,) ever dashed off by John Neal, appeared in Maga. At a later period, here was also published the earnest poetry of Albert Pike, breathing the true spirit of old mythology, and the brilliant prose-fictions of Ruxton.

Ten years after Blackwood's death, during which the sceptre had virtually been in Wilson's hands, "the Professor" (as he was always called) gradually began to yield the power into other and younger hands. One of his oldest friends had been old Roger Aytoun, W. S. in Edinburgh.* A son of his, William Edmonstone Aytoun, had become a dear friend of Wilson's—a yet dearer of Wilson's daughter, whom he married. The elder Aytoun was a fierce little Whig: the younger, a staunch Tory; able, eloquent, witty, and laborious—which last was proven by his researchful Life of Richard the Lion-hearted, in Murray's Family Library. He became a liberal contributor, in prose and verse, to *Blackwood.* Station he did not lack, for he was Professor of Rhetoric and Belles Lettres in his Alma Mater, the University of Edinburgh. And so, Wilson's son-in-law and intimate friend, he may be said to have glided into Wilson's place in the Magazine. Under him, old contributors became more industrious:—what *Blackwood* is there now, without an article

* The lawyers, in Edinburgh, between the actual counsellors, who plead, and the mere attorneys, are Writers to the Signet.—M.

from Alison, the historian? Aytoun's own force has been further developed in satiric fiction—who can forget his railway novelettes, "My First Spec in the Bogglesw ades," and "How we got up the Glenmutchkin Railway, and how we got out of it"?—but his Lays of the Scottish Cavaliers show his vein of poetry to be rich and original. His powers of satire are great—though, as yet, he has used them very rarely.

So, as I have said, Aytoun gradually glided into the editorship of Maga. Nor did Wilson at once retire. He commenced, and completed, a series of critical articles, in his own style, called "Specimens of the British Classics." After this, the old man eloquent flashed out in his "Dies Boreales,"—the last of which was his latest composition.

Beyond this need the record be carried on? Wilson self-deposed, sparkling to the last, and then—a half unconsciousness between him and the grave. Aytoun, educated, as it were, into the management of Maga. Here join the Past and the Present.

To this, as fitting appendix, I subjoin The Chaldee Manuscript. The notes which I append, merely indicate the principal persons and things alluded to: at the lapse of thirty-seven years, it is impossible to do more. No doubt every sentence had its proper barb, when written:

TRANSLATION

FROM AN

ANCIENT CHALDEE MANUSCRIPT.

[The present age seems destined to witness the recovery of many admirable pieces of writing, which had been supposed to be lost for ever. The Eruditi of Milan are not the only persons who have to boast of being the instruments of these resuscitations. We have been favored with the following translation of a Chaldee MS. which is preserved in the great Library of Paris, (Salle 2d, No. 53, B. A. M. M.,) by a gentleman whose attainments in Oriental Learning are well known to the public. It is said that the celebrated Silvester de Lacy is at present occupied with a publication of the original. It will be prefaced by an Inquiry into the Age when it was written, and the name of the writer.]

CHAPTER I.

AND I saw in my dream, and behold one like the Messenger of a King came toward me from the East, and he took me up and carried me into the midst of the great city that looketh toward the north and toward the east,* and ruleth over every people, and kindred, and tongue, that handle the pen of the writer.

2 And he said unto me, Take heed what thou seest, for great things shall come of it; the moving of a straw shall be as the whirlwind, and the shaking of a reed as the great tempest.

* The city of Edinburgh.—M.

3 And I looked, and behold a man clothed in plain apparel stood in the door of his house: and I saw his name, and the number of his name; and his name was as it had been the color of ebony, and his number was the number of a maiden, when the days of the years of her virginity have expired.*

4 And I turned mine eyes, and behold two beasts† came from the land of the borders of the South; and when I saw them I wondered with great admiration.

5 The one beast was like unto a lamb, and the other like unto a bear; and they had wings on their heads; their faces also were like the faces of men, the joints of their legs like the polished cedars of Lebanon, and their feet like the feet of horses preparing to go forth to battle; and they arose and they came onward over the face of the earth, and they touched not the ground as they went.

6 And they came unto the man who was clothed in plain apparel, and stood in the door of his house.

7 And they said unto him, Give us of thy wealth, that we may eat and live, and thou shalt enjoy the fruits of our labors for a time, times, or half a time.

8 And he answered and said unto them, What will you unto me whereunto I may employ you?

9 And the one said, I will teach the people of thy land to till and to sow; to reap the harvest, and gather the sheaves into the barn; to feed their flocks, and enrich themselves with the wool.

10 And the other said, I will teach the children of thy people to know and discern betwixt right and wrong, the good and the evil, and in all things that relate to learning, and knowledge, and understanding.

11 And they proffered unto him a Book;‡ and they said unto him, Take thou this, and give us a piece of money, that we may eat and drink, that our souls may live.

12 And we will put words into the Book that shall astonish the children of thy people; and it shall be a light unto thy feet, and a lamp unto thy path; it shall also bring bread to thy household, and a portion to thy maidens.

13 And the man hearkened to their voice, and he took the Book and gave them a piece of money, and they went away rejoicing in heart. And I heard a great noise, as if it had been the noise of many chariots, and of horsemen passing upon their horses.

14 But after many days they put no words into the Book, and the man was astonied and waxed wroth, and he said unto them, What is that you have done unto me, and how shall I answer those to whom I am engaged? And they said, What is that to us? see thou to that.

15 And the man wist not what for to do: and he called together the friends of his youth, and all those whose heart was as his heart, and he entreated them, and they put words into the Book, and it went forth abroad, and all the world wondered after the Book, and after the two beasts that had put such amazing words into the Book.

16 Now in those days, there lived also a man who was crafty§ in counsel, and cunning in all manner of working:

* William Blackwood, (*Ebony*,) whose then place of business was at 17 Prince's street. In 1830 he removed to 45 George street, where Maga continues to be published.—M.

† Pringle and Cleghorn, the original editors of *Blackwood's Magazine*, were "the two beasts." Both were deformed in person. They had gone over to Constable, the publisher of the *Edinburgh Review*, and of the old *Scots' Magazine*, and the satire of the Chaldee MS. was elicited by this defection. In one of Scott's letters, in February, 1818, four months after the Chaldee appeared, he says: "Blackwood is in rather a bad pickle just now—sent to Coventry by the trade, as the booksellers call themselves, and all about the parody of the two beasts."—M.

‡ *Blackwood's Magazine* was "the Book."—M.

§ Archibald Constable, the celebrated Edinburgh publisher, had obtained the sobriquet of

17 And I beheld the man, and he was comely and well-favoured, and he had a notable horn in his forehead wherewith he ruled the nations.

18 And I saw the horn,* that it had eyes, and a mouth speaking great things, and it magnified itself even to the Prince of the Host, and it cast down the truth to the ground, and it grew and prospered.

19 And when this man saw the Book, and beheld the things that were in the Book, he was troubled in spirit, and much cast down.

20 And he said unto himself, Why stand I idle here, and why do I not bestir myself? Lo! this Book shall become a devouring sword in the hand of mine adversary, and with it will he root up or loosen the horn that is in my forehead, and the hope of my gains shall perish from the face of the earth.

21 And he hated the Book, and the two beasts that had put words into the Book, for he judged according to the reports of men; nevertheless, the man was crafty in counsel, and more cunning than his fellows.

22 And he said unto the two beasts, Come ye and put your trust under the shadow of my wings, and I will destroy the man whose name is as ebony, and his Book.

23 And I will tear it in pieces, and cast it out like dung upon the face of the earth.

24 And we will tread him down as the dust of the streets, and trample him under our feet; and we will break him to pieces, and grind him to powder, and cast him into the brook Kedron.

25 And I will make of you a great name; and I will place you next to the horn that is in my forehead,† and it shall be a shelter to you in the day of great adversity; and it shall defend you from the horn of the unicorn and from the might of the Bulls of Bashan.

26 And you shall be watchers and guard unto it from the emmet and the spider, and the toad after his kind;

27 And from the mole that walketh in darkness, and from the blow-fly after his kind, and the canker-worm after his kind, and the maggot after his kind.

28 And by these means you shall wax very great, for the things that are low shall be exalted.

29 And the two beasts gave ear unto him; and they came over unto him, and bowed down before him with their faces to the earth.

30 ¶ But when the tidings of these things came to the man who was clothed in plain apparel, he was sore dismayed and his countenance fell.

31 And it repented him that he had taken the Book, or sent it forth abroad; and he said, I have been sore deceived and betrayed; but I will of myself yield up the Book, and burn it with fire, and give its ashes to the winds of heaven.

32 But certain that were there present said unto him, Why art thou dismayed? and why is thy countenance fallen? Go to now; gird up thy loins like a man, and call unto thee thy friends, and the men of thy household, and thou shalt behold and see that they that are for thee are more

"The Crafty," several years before it was given to him in the Chaldee MS. The title, which stuck to him, annoyed him very much—the more so, perhaps, as he was fond of conferring nicknames upon others. Murray, the London publisher, he called *The Emperor of the West;* he dubbed himself *The Czar of Muscovy;* facetious John Ballantyne was *The Dey of Alljeers;* and Longman & Co., of London, were *The Divan*, in his nomenclature. One of Longman's firm dined with him at his country-house, and noticed what appeared to be a group of swans in the pond. "Swans!" cried Constable: "they are only geese, man. There are just five of them, and their names are Longman, Hurst, Rees, Orme, and Brown." The Londoner did not relish the jest.—M.

* By the horn, which ruled the nations, the *Edinburgh Review* was indicated.—M.

† Constable spared no cost to make *his* Edinburgh Magazine superior to Blackwood's, but did not succeed.—M.

and mightier than those that be against thee.

33 And when the man whose name was as ebony, and whose number was the number of a maiden, when the days of the years of her virginity have expired, heard this saying, he turned about;

34 And he took from under his girdle a gem of curious workmanship of silver, made by the hand of a cunning artificer, and overlaid within with pure gold; and he took from thence something in color like unto the dust of the earth, or the ashes that remain of a furnace, and he snuffed it up like the east wind, and returned the gem again into its place.*

35 Whereupon he opened his mouth, and he said unto them, As thou hast spoken, so shall it be done.

36 Woe unto all them that take part with the man who is crafty in counsel, and with the two beasts!

37 For I will arise and increase my strength, and come upon them like the locust of the desert, to abolish and overwhelm, and to destroy, and to pass over.

38 So he called together the wise men of the city, both from the Old City, and from the city which is on this side of the valley, even the New City, which looketh toward the north; and the wise men came.

39 And lo! there stood before him an aged man, whose hair was as white as snow, and in whose hand there was a mirror, wherein passed to and fro the images of the ancient days.†

40 And he said, Behold, I am stricken in years, mine eyes are dim. What will ye that I do unto you? Seek ye them that are young.

41 And all the young men that were there lifted up their voice and said, We have sat at thy feet all the days of the years which we have lived upon the earth; and that which we know is thine, and our learning is thine; and as thou sayest, even so will we do.

42 And he said unto them, Do ye what is meet in this thing, and let not our friend be discomfited, neither let the man which is crafty rejoice, nor the two beasts.

43 And when he had said this, he arose and went away; and all the young men arose up, and humbled themselves before him when he went away.

44 Then spake the man clothed in plain apparel to the great magician who dwelleth in the old fastness, hard by the river Jordan, which is by the Border.‡ And the magician opened his mouth, and said, Lo! my heart wisheth thy good, and let the thing prosper which is in thy hands to do it.

45 But thou seest that my hands are full of working, and my labour is great. For, lo, I have to feed all the people of my land, and none knoweth whence his food cometh;§ but each man openeth his mouth, and my hand filleth it with pleasant things.

46 Moreover, thine adversary also is of my familiars.

47 The land is before thee: draw thou up thy hosts for the battle in the place of Princes, over against thine adversary, which hath his station near the mount of the Proclamation; quit ye as men, and let favour be shown unto him which is most valiant.

48 Yet be thou silent: peradventure will I help thee some little.

49 So he made request also unto a wise man‖ which had come out of Joppa, where the ships are, one that

* This description of a snuff-box is one of the best hits in the Chaldee MS., and was greatly admired by Scott, as orientalizing a common and familiar object.—M.

† The aged man was Henry Mackenzie, and the *mirror* in his hand alluded to his periodical, "The Mirror," formerly conducted by him with ability and spirit. He was one of the earliest contributors to Maga.—M.

‡ Sir Walter Scott, "the great Magician of the North," whose residence, Abbotsford, was situated in a border county, by the river Tweed.—M.

§ At this time, the authorship of the Waverley Novels was unacknowledged.—M.

‖ The late Professor Jameson, (died 1854,) of Edinburgh University.—M.

had sojourned in far countries, whose wisdom is great above all the children of the east, one which teacheth the sons of the honourable men, and speaketh wonderful things in the schools of the learned men:

50 One which speaketh of trees and of beasts, and of fowl and of creeping things, and of fishes, from the great Leviathan that is in the deep sea even unto the small muscle which dwelleth in the shell of the rock;

51 Moreover, of all manner of precious stones, and of the ancient mountains, and the moving of the great waters:

52 One which had been led before the Chief Priests, and lauded of them for smiting a worshipper of Fire in the land, which being interpreted, signifieth bread.

53 And he said, Behold, here is a round stone, set thou that in a ring, and put the ring upon thy finger, and behold, while the ring is upon thy finger, thou shalt have no fear of the man which is crafty, neither of the two beasts.

54 Then the man spake to a wise man which had a light in his hand and crown of pearls upon his head, and he said, Behold, I will brew a sharp poison for the man which is crafty, and the two beasts. Wait ye till I come. So he arose also and went his way.

55 Also to a wise young man, which is learned in the law, even as his father was learned,* and who lifteth up his voice in the courts of the treasury of our Lord the King, with his fellow, who is one of the sons of the Prophets.

56 He spake also to a learned man who sendeth all the King's messengers to the four corners of the great city, each man clothed in scarlet, and bearing a bundle of letters, touching the affairs of men, in his right hand.†

57 He spake also unto a sweet singer, who is cunning to play all stringed instruments, who weareth a charm upon his bosom, even a stone, whereon is engraved ancient writing. And he framed songs, and waxeth very wroth against the horn which is in the forehead of the man which is crafty.

58 Also to one who had been a physician in his youth, and who had dwelt with the keeper of the gates of the wise men:

59 But he was now a dealer in wine and oil, and in the fishes which are taken in the nets of the people of the west;

60 Also in strong drink.

61 Then sent he for one cunning in sharp instruments and edged tools, even in razors; but he had taken unto himself a wife, and could not come.

62 But, behold, while they were yet speaking, they heard a voice of one screeching in the gate, and the voice was a sharp voice, even like the voice of the unclean bird which buildeth its nest in the corner of the temple, and defileth the holy places.

63 But they opened not the door, neither answered they a word to the voice of its screaming. So the unclean thing flew away, neither could they find any trace of its going.

64 And there was a silence in the assembly. And, behold, when they began to speak, they were too many, neither could the man know what was the meaning of their counsel, for they spake together, and the voice of their speaking was mingled.

65 So the man was sore perplexed, and he wist not what for to do.

CHAPTER II.

NOW, behold, as soon as they were gone, he sat down in his inner

* John Hope, afterwards one of the Lords of Session, (or Supreme Judges of Scotland,) whose father, Charles Hope, was then Lord President of the Court of Session.—M.

† The Postmaster-General of Scotland. The coachmen, guards, and letter-carriers then wore an uniform, of which a scarlet coat was the most remarkable portion.—M.

chamber, which looketh toward the street of Oman, and the road of Gabriel, as thou goest up into the land of Ambrose,* and the man leaned with his face upon his hand.

2 And while he was yet musing, there stood before him a man clothed in dark garments, having a veil upon his head;† and there was a rod in his hand.

3 And he said, Arise, let not thine heart be discouraged, neither let it be afraid.

4 Behold, if thou wilt listen unto me, I will deliver thee out of all thy distresses, neither shall any be able to touch a hair of thy head.

5 And when the man heard the voice of his speaking, behold, there was in his voice courage, and in his counsel boldness. And he said unto him, Do thou as it seemeth good unto thee; as thou sayest even so will I do.

6 And the man who had come in answered and said, Behold, I will call mighty creatures which will comfort thee, and destroy the power of thy adversary, and will devour the two beasts.

7 So he gave unto the man in plain apparel a tablet, containing the names of those upon whom he should call. And when he called, they came; and whomsoever he asked, he came.

8 And the man with the veil stood by, but there was a cloud about him, neither could they which came see him, nor tell who it was that compelled their coming.

9 And they came in the likeness of living things, but I knew not who were they which came.

10 And the first which came was after the likeness of the beautiful leopard, from the valley of the palm trees, whose going forth was comely as the greyhound, and his eyes like the lightning of fiery flame.

11 And the second was the lynx that lurketh behind the white cottage in the mountains.

12 There came also, from a far country, the scorpion, which delighteth to sting the faces of men, that he might sting sorely the countenance of the man which is crafty, and of the two beasts.

13 Also the great wild boar from the forest of Lebanon, and he roused up his spirit, and I saw him whetting his dreadful tusks for the battle.‡

14 And the griffin came with a roll of the names of those whose blood had been shed between his teeth; and I saw him standing over the body of one that had been buried long in the grave, defending it from all men; and behold there were none which durst come near him.

15 Also the black eagle of the desert, whose cry is as the sound of an unknown tongue, which flieth over the ruins of the ancient cities, and hath his dwelling among the tombs of the wise men.

16 Also the stork which buildeth upon the house-top, and devoureth all manner of unclean things, and all beetles, and all manner of flies, and much worms.

17 And the hyæna which escheweth the light, and cometh forth at the evening tide to raise up and gnaw the bones of the dead, and is as a riddle unto the vain man.

18 And the beagle and the slowhound after their kind, and all the beasts of the field, more than could be numbered, they were so many.

* Oman kept a hotel in Edinburgh. Ambrose's Tavern was situated at the back of Princes Street, in a place called Gabriel's Road, from a murder committed there by a tutor named Gabriel, on two of his pupils. He was caught in the act, ("red-handed,") and, by power of an ancient law, was hanged on the spot, with the bloody knife around his neck.—M.

† This man, thus mysteriously veiled, was the unknown Editor of *Blackwood*. The personality of Christopher North was not invented until September, 1819.—M.

‡ Wilson was the leopard. Robert Sym (afterwards Timothy Tickler of "The Noctes") was the hyæna. Lockhart was the scorpion. Hogg, of course, was "the great wild boar from the forest." Gillies lived at "the white cottage in the mountains."—M.

19 ¶ And when they were all gathered together, the man which was clothed in plain apparel looked about, and his heart was right merry when he saw the mighty creatures which had come in unto him, and heard the tumult of their voices, and the noise of the flapping of their wings.

20 And he lifted up his voice, and shouted with a great shout, and said, Behold, I am increased greatly, and I will do terrible things to the man who is crafty and to his two beasts.

21 And he sent away a swift messenger for a physician, which healeth all manner of bruises, and wounds, and putrefying sores, lest that he should go forth to heal up the wounds of the man that is crafty, or of his two beasts.

22 (Now this physician was a mild man, neither was there any gall within him, yet he went near.

CHAPTER III.

AND while these things were yet doing, I heard a great rushing, and the sound as of a mighty wind: and I looked over the valley into the old city, and there was a tumult over against the mount of Proclamation.*

2 For when tidings of these things came to the man which was crafty, his heart died within him, and he waxed sore afraid.

3 And he said unto himself, What is this? Behold mine adversary is very mighty, neither can I go forth to fight him: for whom have I save myself only, and my two beasts?

4 And while he was yet speaking, the two beasts stood before him.

5 And the beast which was like unto a bear said, Behold, it is yet harvest, and how can I leave my corn which is in the fields? If I go forth to make war upon the man whose name is as ebony, the Philistines will come into my farm, and carry away all the full sheaves which are ready.

6 And the beast which was like unto a lamb† answered and said, Lo! my legs are weary, and the Egyptians which were wont for to carry me are clean gone; and wherewithal shall I go forth to make war upon the man whose name is as ebony?

7 Nevertheless will I put a sweet song against him into thy Book.

8 But the man which was crafty answered and said, Unprofitable generation! ye have given unto me a horn which is empty, and a horse which hath no feet. If ye go not forth to fight with mine adversary, deliver me up the meat which I have given unto you, and the penny which ye have of me, that I may hire others who will fight with the man whose name is as ebony.

9 And the beasts spake not at all, neither answered they him one word.

10 But as they sat before him, the beast which was like unto a bear took courage; and he opened his mouth and said,

11 O man, thou hast fed me heretofore, and whatever entereth into thy lips is thine. Why now should we fall out about this thing?

12 Call unto thee thy counsellors, the spirits, and the wise men, and the magicians, if haply they may advise thee touching the man whose name is as ebony, and the creatures which are within his gates. Whatsoever they say, that shall be done.

13 Yet the man was not pleased, neither was his countenance lightened: nevertheless, he did even as the beast said.

14 So he called unto him a familiar spirit, unto whom he had sold himself.‡

15 But the spirit was a wicked spirit and a cruel: so he answered and

* The mount of Proclamation was a part of the Old Town of Edinburgh, on which, while the Stuarts reigned, heralds and criers used to read royal mandates and proclamations.—M.

† Cleghorn was the bear, and Pringle the lamb.—M.

‡ Francis Jeffrey was Constable's "familiar spirit."—M.

said, Lo, have I not put great might into the horn which is in thy forehead? What more said I ever that I would do unto thee? Thy soul is in my hands: do as thou listest in this thing.

16 But the man entreated him sorely, yet he listened not: for he had great fear of the vision of the man who was clothed in dark garments, and who had a veil upon his head;

17 (For he was of the seed of those which have command over the devils.)

18 And while the beasts were yet looking, lo, he was not;

19 For even in the twinkling of an eye he was present in the courts of the palace, to tempt the souls of the chief priests, and the scribes, and all those which administer the law for the King, and to deliver some malefactors which he loved out of their hand.

20 ¶ Then the man called with a loud voice on some other spirits in whom he put his trust.

21 And the first was a cunning spirit, which hath its dwelling in the secret places of the earth, and hath command over the snow and the hail, and is as a pestilence to the poor man: for when he is hungry he lifteth up the lid of his meal-garnel, to take out meal, and lo! it is full of strong ice.

22 And the second was a little blind spirit, which hath a number upon his forehead; and he walketh to and fro continually, and is the chief of the heathen which are the worshippers of fire. He is also of the seed of the prophet, and ministered in the temple while he was yet young; but he went out, and became one of the scoffers.

23 But when these spirits heard the words of the man, and perceived his trouble, they gave no ear unto his outcry, neither listened they to the voice of his supplication.

24 And they laughed at the man with a loud laughter, and said unto him, Lo, shall we leave our digging into the bowels of the earth, or our ice, or our fire, with which we deceive the nations, and come down to be as it were servants unto thee and these two beasts, which are lame beasts, and unprofitable? Go to, man, seek thou them which are thy fellows.

25 And they vanished from his sight: and he heard the voice of their laughter, both he and his two beasts.

26 ¶ But when the spirits were gone, he said unto himself, I will arise and go unto a magician which is of my friends: of a surety he will devise some remedy, and free me out of all my distresses.

27 So he arose and came unto that great magician which hath his dwelling in the old fastness, hard by the river Jordan, which is by the Border.

28 And the magician opened his mouth and said, Lo! my heart wisheth thy good, and let the thing prosper which is in thy hands to do it:

29 But thou seest that my hands are full of working, and my labour is great. For, lo, I have to feed all the people of my land, and none knoweth whence his food cometh; but each man openeth his mouth, and my hand filleth it with pleasant things.

30 Moreover, thine adversary also is of my familiars.

31 The land is before thee: draw thou up thine hosts for the battle on the mount of Proclamation, and defy boldly thine enemy, which hath his camp in the place of Princes; quit ye as men, and let favour be shown unto him which is most valiant.

32 Yet be thou silent: peradventure will I help thee some little.

33 But the man which is crafty saw that the magician loved him not. For he knew him of old, and they had had many dealings; and he perceived that he would not assist him in the day of his adversity.

34 So he turned about, and went out of his fastness. And he shook the dust from his feet, and said, Behold, I have given this magician much money, yet see now, he hath utterly deserted me.* Verily, my fine gold hath perished.

* Scott and Constable long had intimate relations, as author and publisher; but, taking

35 But when he had come back unto his house, he found the two beasts which were yet there; and behold the beasts were gabbling together, and making much noise. And when he looked in, behold yet another beast; and they were all gabbling together.

36 Now the other beast was a beast which he loved not. A beast of burden which he hath in his courts to hew wood and carry water, and to do all manner of unclean things. His face was like unto the face of an ape, and he chattered continually, and his nether parts were uncomely. Nevertheless, his thighs were hairy, and the hair was as the shining of a satin raiment, and he skipped with the branch of a tree in his hand, and he chewed a snail between his teeth.

37 Then said the man, Verily this beast is altogether unprofitable, and whatsoever I have given unto him to do he has spoiled: he is a sinful thing, and speaketh abominably: his doings are impure, and all people are astonished that he abideth so long within my gates.

38 But if thou lookest upon him and observest his ways, behold he was born of his mother before yet the months were fulfilled, and the substance of a living thing is not in him, and his bones are like the potsherd which is broken against any stone.

39 Therefore my heart pitieth him, and I wish not that he utterly famished; and I give unto him a little bread and wine that his soul may not faint; and I send him messages unto the towns and villages which are round about; and I give him such work as is meet for him.

40 But if we go forth to the battle, let him not go with us.

41 For behold the griffin hath heretofore wounded him, and the scorpion hath stung him sorely in the hips and the thighs, and also in the face.

42 Moreover, the eagle of heaven also is his dread, and he is terrified for the flapping of his huge wings, and for his cry, which is like the voice of an unknown tongue, also his talons, which are sharper than any two-edged sword.

43 And if it cometh to pass that he seeth them in the battle, he will not stand, but surely turn black and flee.

44 Therefore let us not take him with us, lest he be for an ensample unto the simple ones.

45 And while he was yet speaking, behold he heard a knocking upon the stair, as if yet another beast had been stirring.

46 And lo, it was even so.

47 And another beast came in, whose disease was the murrain, who had eyes yet saw not, and whose laughter was like the laughter of them whose life is hidden, and which know not what they do.

48 And I heard a voice cry, Alas! alas! even as if it were Heu! heu!

46 Now the man was sick at heart when he perceived that he was there with the four beasts,* and he said, Wretched man that I am, who shall deliver me from the weight of beasts which presseth sore upon me?

50 Then the four beasts waxed very wroth, and they all began for to cry out against the man which is crafty.

51 And he said, O race of beasts, be ye still, and keep silence until I consider what shall be done in this matter.

52 And while he spake, it seemed as if he trembled and were afraid of the four beasts and of the staves wherewith they skipped.

CHAPTER IV.

BUT while he was yet trembling, lo, there came in one which was his

offence at some expression of Constable's partner, Scott employed Blackwood as his publisher greatly to the annoyance and loss of "The Crafty." After a time, Constable resumed his relations with Scott, and they were continued, until the Panic of 1825 caused Constable's bankruptcy and Scott's ruin.—M.

* I am unable to say who were the two other "beasts" here introduced.—M.

familiar friend from his youth upwards, who keepeth the books of the scribes, and is hired to expound things which he knoweth not, and collecteth together the remains of the wise men.

2 And he opened his mouth and said, Lo, I have come even this hour from the camp of the enemy, and I have spoken with the man whose name is as ebony.

3 And while I was speaking with him kindly, lo, some of the creatures which are within his gates took notice of me, and they warned him. So he put no faith nor trust in me.

4 But take thou good heed to thyself, for they that are against thee are mighty, and I have seen their numbers.

5 Now when the man heard this, he waxed yet more fearful.

6 Then there came into his chamber another of his friends, one whose nose is like the beak of a bird of prey, whose mouth is foul, and his teeth reach from the right ear even unto the left; and he said, For why art thou so cast down? be of good cheer; behold I have an old breastplate which I will put on, and go forth with thee unto the battle.

7 And further, he began to speak of the north, and the great men of the north, even the giants, and the painted folk, but they stopped him, for of his speaking there is no end.

8 Then there came into his chamber a lean man, which hath his dwelling by the great pool to the north of the New City;*

9 Which had been of the familiars of the man in plain apparel while they were yet youths, before he had been tempted of the man which is crafty;

10 Whose name had gone abroad among the nations on many books, even as his father's name had gone abroad:

11 One which delighteth in trees, and fruits, and flowers; the palm-tree and the olive, the pomegranate and the vine, the fig and the date, the tulip and the lily;

12 Which had sojourned in far lands, gathering herbs for the chief position.

13 And he had a rotten melon on his head, after the fashion of an helmet.

14 And the man which is crafty began to take courage when his friends were gathered unto him, and he took his trumpet with boldness, and began to blow for them over which he had power.

15 But of them which listened to him, their limbs were weak, and their swords blunt, and the strings of their bows were moist.

16 Nevertheless he made an assemblage of them over against the mount of Proclamation: and these are the names of his host, and the number of his banners, whom he marshalled by the mount of Proclamation the day that he went forth to make war upon the man whose name is as ebony.

17 Now behold the four beasts were in the first band, yet they trembled, and desired not to be in the front of the host.

18 And in the second band was one which teacheth in the schools of the young men, and he was clad in gray garment whereof one-half his wife had weaved.

19 Also, Samuel, a vain young man, and a simple, which sitteth in the King's Courts, and is a tool without edge in the hands of the oppressors.

20 Also, John, the brother of James, which is a man of low stature, and giveth out merry things, and is a lover of fables from his youth up.

21 Also, James, the young man which cometh out of the west country, which feareth God, and hateth all manner of usury; who babbleth of many things, and nibbleth the shoe-latchets of the mighty; one which darkeneth counsel with the multiplying of vain words;

22 To whose sayings no man taketh heed.

23 And in the third band were a grave man, even George, the chief of the synagogue, a principal man, yea, the leader of the doctors, whose beard reacheth down unto his girdle;

* This "lean man" was Peter Hill, a bookseller in Edinburgh.—M.

24 And one David, which dwelleth at the corner as thou goest up to the place of the old prison-house, which talketh touching all manner of pictures and graven images; and he came with a feather on his head.*

25 And Andrew the chief physician, and Andrew his son,† who is a smooth man, and one which handleth all wind instruments, and boweth himself down continually before the horn which is in the forehead of the man which is crafty, and worshippeth it.

26 With James, the baker of sweet breads, which weareth a green mantle, which inhabiteth the dwelling of the nobles, and delighteth in the tongue of the strange man.

27 And Peter, who raileth at his master.

28 And in the fourth band I saw the face of Samuel,‡ which is a mason, who is clothed in gorgeous apparel, and his face was as the face of the moon shining in the north-west.

29 The number of his bands was four; and in the first band there were the four beasts,

30 And in the second band there were nine men of war, and in the third six, and in the fourth ten.

31 And the number of the bands was four: and the number of them which were in the bands was twenty and nine; and the man which was crafty commanded them.

32 And the screaming bird sat upon his shoulder.

33 And there followed him many women which know not their right hand from the left, also some cattle.

34 And John the brother of Francis,§ and the man which offered Consolation to the man which is crafty.

35 Also seven young men, whereof no man could tell by what name they were called.‖

36 But when I saw them all gathered together, I said unto myself, Of a truth the man which is crafty hath many in his host, yet think I that scarcely will these be found sufficient against them which are in the gates of the man who is clothed in plain apparel.

37 And I thought of the vision of the man which was clothed in dark garments, and of the leopard, and the lynx, and the scorpion, and the eagle, and the great boar of Lebanon, and the griffin;

38 The stork, and the hyæna, and the beagle, and all the mighty creatures which are within the gates of the man in plain apparel.

39 Verily, the man which is crafty shall be defeated, and there shall not escape one to tell of his overthrow.

40 And while I was yet speaking, the hosts drew near, and the city was moved; and my spirit failed within me, and I was sore afraid, and I turned to escape away.

41 And he that was like unto the messenger of a king, said unto me, Cry. And I said, What shall I cry? for the day of vengeance is come upon all those that ruled the nations with a rod of iron.

42 And I fled into an inner chamber to hide myself, and I heard a great tumult, but I wist not what it was.

* Who was meant by Samuel, John, James, and George, I cannot say—the allusions are so entirely personal and local. David was Mr. Brydges, a cloth merchant in the Old Town, who was a very good judge of pictures, and had made a fine collection.—M.

† The two Andrew Duncans, father and son, were eminent physicians in Edinburgh at this time. The younger was author or compiler of "The Edinburgh Dispensatory."—M.

‡ This was Samuel Anderson, high among the Freemasons of Scotland. He was a wine-merchant, but, in Brougham's Chancellorship, received the lucrative appointment of Registrar of the English Court of Chancery. He figures in "The Noctes," as one of North's guests.—M.

§ John Jeffrey, younger brother of the critic.—M.

‖ Nobody knew who "the seven young men" were. They are often mentioned through the Magazine, and at "The Noctes," but there is no clue to their identity—if any.—M.

Christopher in the Tent.

No. I.—AUGUST, 1819.

We have just returned from the Moors;* and as many erroneous reports of our proceedings must doubtlessly have been put into circulation, we do not see how we can do better than fill our last sheet with an account of our shooting excursion. Sir John Sinclair remarks, that he has a more numerous family than generally falls to the lot of literary men.† Now, though we can boast of no such achievements, being to a man bachelors, yet we really believe that for literati we are most extraordinary shots—and we hereby challenge all Scotland for a dinner at Young's, and a hundred pounds to the erection of the National Monument.‡

Immediately after the publication of our last number, an unusual stir and bustle was observable among the members of our conclave. At our monthly dinner at Ambrose's, the conversation could not be confined within its wonted channel—and a continual fire was kept up, blazing away right and left, much to the astonishment of our worthy

* The first part of this article, entituled "The true and authentic Account of the Twelfth of August, 1819," was the concluding paper in No. XXXIX of Blackwood's Magazine. It is curious to find how early Wilson took up the idea (carried out to the last in his "Dies Boreales, or Christopher under Canvas") of holding colloquies in a Tent. It may be necessary to add, in explanation of a particular day and month being singled out, that by the British game laws, grouse shooting does not commence until the 12th August, partridge shooting on 1st September, and pheasant shooting on the 1st October, in each year.—M.

† Sir John Sinclair, the greatest rural economist, perhaps (because the most practical), that Great Britain can boast of, was partly author and wholly editor of the Statistical Account of Scotland, the most minute account of a kingdom ever published. His writings on agricultural and financial science, extending over sixty years (he died, aged 82, in 1835), were distinguished for their good sense. His family was numerous—thirteen children surviving him. In his Hints on Longevity, he mentions one fact as the result of his inquiries among aged people—that whether they went to bed sober or drunk, at early even-tide, or long past the small hours, all the long-lived persons whom he knew, male or female, had invariably been early risers.—M.

‡ Young's Tavern, in High-street, Edinburgh. The locale was by no means a pleasant one, but most of the young wits of the city, including the Society called the Dilettanti, used to frequent it. The Dilettanti, in 1819, had John Wilson for their president, and among the members were Allan, Schetky, Nicholson and Baxter, artists; Lockhart, Peter Robertson, now a Scottish Judge, and many more, then in early manhood, who have since attained eminence. Young's was such a small, smoky, dingy place, that it was commonly called "The Coffin-Hole." Lockhart denounced it, in "Peters' Letters," as "situated in one of the filthiest closes in the city of Edinburgh," where visitors had to "brave with heroic courage the risk of an impure baptism from the neighboring windows." What is called the National Monument stands on Calton Hill, Edinburgh, and is an unfortunate attempt to imitate the Parthenon of Athens. It is unfinished. The part erected consists of thirteen columns, on the west side, each of which cost £1,000. They were put up between 1824 and 1830, and are not deficient in picturesque grace. The object of the monument was to commemorate those Scotchmen who had fallen in battle during the war with Napoleon.—M.

publisher, who generally graces by his presence these our lunar orgies. Not a word was uttered about "Articles." Don Juan was (for the time) silently sent to the devil*—cold water was thrown in a moment on all the Lake Poets—and a motion was put from the chair, and carried by acclamation, that the first man who smelt of the shop should undergo a tumbler of salt and small beer. Ambrose was astonished!!!

About midnight it was decided, that a letter should be written by the editor to Lord Fife,† requesting a week's shooting for himself and the eight principal supporters of Blackwood's Magazine, with permission to pitch a Tent on the Twelfth on his Lordship's moors, at the head of the Dee. As from his Lordship's well-known liberality, no doubt could be felt on that score, it was resolved, that we should all meet on the evening of the 11th at Braemar, whither our tent and assistants should be sent a day or two previous, that all might be in good order on our arrival. A letter was also written to Dr. Peter Morris of Aberystwith, and Mr. Jarvie, Saltmarket, Glasgow, ordering their attendance.‡

For the next fortnight, all was preparation. If a Contributor showed his face in No. 17, Prince's Street,|| it was but for a moment, and "with a short uneasy motion," that proved "he had no business there." Our visits were indeed like those of angels, "few and far between." Before the end of the month, Mr. Wastle entered the shop, like an apparition, in a pair of old buckskin breeches furbished up for the nonce—leather gaiters, in which his spindle-shanks looked peculiarly gentlemanly—and a jean jacket, with pockets "number without number," and of all sizes—the main inside one, like the mouth of a sack, and cunningly intended to stow away roe or the young of the red deer. Tickler was excellent. A man of six feet

* The two opening cantos of Don Juan, which did "fright the isle from its propriety," appeared in July, 1819. Murray, who had purchased them, was afraid to let his name appear on the title-page, as publisher, and only the printer's name ("Thomas Davison, Whitefriars") was placed thereon.—M.

† James Duff, Earl of Fife, was a wealthy man in 1819, with vast landed estates, in the Scottish counties of Banff, Moray, and Aberdeen. His principal residence (for he had several, including two castles) was Duff House, near the town of Banff, only part of which is built, on a plan supplied by Inigo Jones. Lord Fife served with distinction in the Peninsular War, and is a general in the Spanish army, as well as a grandee of Spain. At one time he was on most intimate terms with George IV., to whom he lent vast sums, which have never been repaid. The result of this, and of extravagant expenditure on handsome ballet-dancers of the opera-house, so nearly ruined him, that he had to retire from high life, to place his estates in the hands of trustees (in payment of his debts), and to live on £4,000, which they allow him. The trustees have done several harsh things in his name, one of the most notorious being their illegal caption of the original portrait of Charles the First, painted by Velasquez, at Madrid, in 1623, which formerly belonged to the Earl's father, and had been purchased at a sale by Mr. Snare, a bookseller in Reading. The Scottish judges declared that the picture belonged to Mr. Snare, who brought it to New York, in 1852, where it now is. All through Blackwood Lord Fife is called "The Thane." The source of the Dee (a river famous for its salmon, which runs into the sea by the city of Aberdeen) is near Mar Lodge, on Lord Fife's property.—M.

‡ Dr. Morris was the pseudo-writer of "Peter's Letters to his Kinsfolk" (Lockhart's Satire on the Whigs of Edinburgh and Glasgow), and Mr. Jarvie (a pretended grandson of Bailie Nicol Jarvie, of "Rob Roy") had written some sarcastic letters to Maga, as if from Glasgow.—M.

|| Blackwood's shop, where Maga was then published.—M.

and a half looks well in a round blue jacket—and if to that you add a white waistcoat with a red spot—a large shirt-ruffle—corduroy breeches very short at the knees—grey worsted stockings of the sort in Scotland called "rig and fur," and laced quarter boots, you unquestionably have before you the figure of a finished Contributor.* The Ettrick Shepherd condescended to show himself in the shop only once between the 20th of last month and the 6th of August, on which occasion, he was arrayed in white raiment from top to toe—his hat being made of partridge feathers, and his shoes of untanned leather. He was accompanied by a couple of very alarming animals, not unapparently of the canine race—one of which commenced an immediate attack on an old harmless Advertiser, while the other began rather unadvisedly to worry the Scotsman†—the consequence of which, as was foreseen, has been hydrophobia, and the brute is now chained up. Mr. Odoherty alone went in his usual way—and could not help smiling at the Editor, who came strutting into the front shop as boldly as his rheumatism would permit, with a dog-whip looking out of his pocket, and a call hung round his neck like a boatswain's whistle.‡ As after a few minutes' confabulation with Ebony, he hobbled off with Daniel's Rural Sports beneath his arm,—it is understood, that Odoherty applied for his situation, alleging that the man would be for ever spoiled as an editor by the mountain-dew of Braemar—and that it was indeed the Edinburgh Review to Constable's Magazine, or Lord Bacon to Macvey Napier, that he would not "come to time." But it would be quite endless to describe the appearance of each man in the regiment, before we entered on actual service—so suffice it to say, that it is now the evening of the 11th of August, and that our arrival is anxiously expected at the Inn of Braemar.‖

* William Wastle, of that Ilk (which means "Wastle of Wastle"), was supplying Maga at this time with a satirical and *de omnibus rebus* poem, called "The Mad Banker of Amsterdam," in the Don Juan metre. In the second of "Peter's Letters" he is noticed very fully as a living person, with close descriptions of his dress, features, and habits, but was only a creation of the brain—one of the many mystifications of Blackwood's Magazine. He is supposed to have represented Lockhart. Timothy Tickler was an Edinburgh lawyer, named Sym, and was Professor Wilson's maternal uncle.

† The Scotsman, then edited by J. R. McCulloch (the political economist and Edinburgh reviewer, who contended that Absenteeism was *not* injurious to the country whence it drew immense rents, inasmuch as it did not matter *where* the money was spent, so that it was disbursed somewhere !) was a newspaper, which was assumed to be the organ of the whig party in Edinburgh. It was heavy, but clever, at that time, and much ridiculed in Maga.—M.

‡ Ensign and Adjutant Morgan Odoherty was the well-known Dr. William Maginn, who contributed largely to Blackwood, from 1818 to 1830, and from that time to his death, in 1842, was the leading contributor to Fraser's Magazine. He was introduced to the Tent by anticipation, as he did not visit Scotland until June, 1821. Maginn was one of the most versatile and fertile writers of modern times.—M.

‖ Braemar is a village in Aberdeen-shire, not far from Loch-na-gar, the mountain celebrated by Byron, in his earliest and his latest poems—Hours of Idleness and Don Juan. He describes it (erroneously) as "the highest mountain, perhaps, in Great Britain," and with eternal snow upon its summit. In 1838–'39 I ascended this mountain repeatedly, and saw no snow. On the summit is a spring of ice-cold water. On a clear day, from this height, may be seen the waters of the Atlantic on the west, and of the German Ocean on the east. From the source of the Dee the ascent is difficult and tedious ; but so gradual is the slope from the summit to Braemar that a pony can easily ride it. In this manner Queen Victoria, whose seat of Balmoral is adjacent, reached the top of Loch-na-gar, in 1853.—M.

Notwithstanding our rheumatism, we arrived first at the place of rendezvous, having gone direct to Aberdeen on the top of the mail, and thence, on the dicky of a friend's chariot, to Pannanich Wells, from which we contrived to pad the hoof to Braemar, attended by our old bitch, than which a better never was shot over, but which we now took with us chiefly for companionship-sake. We did not encumber ourselves with a gun, trusting to Mr. Kempferhausen being soon knocked up, and being besides, under the necessity, on the twelfth, of looking over our "Contributors' Box," which Mr. Wastle was good enough to promise to bring in his dog-cart. We had just dined and finished half a mutchkin of whisky-toddy, when, looking out of the window, we beheld beneath us the Ettrick Shepherd, mounted on a tall brown horse with four white feet, and a countenance equally so, who, on our throwing up the window, turned up his large wall-eyes, with a placid expression, that showed at once he was a steed quite above starting at trifles. The Poet's dog, something between a Newfoundland and a colley, was not equally pacific—but went to work on an old turnspit belonging to the house, which was with difficulty rescued from his jaws.

During this temporary disturbance the sound of wheels was heard, and the Shepherd, running to the gabel-end of the house, exclaimed, "A Morris! A Morris!" and there, in good truth, was the worthy Doctor in his shandrydan, with his man John, both looking extremely well, and formidably appointed.* The clock in the kitchen struck six. "Wastle will be here in ten minutes," quoth the Doctor, "if he be a man of his word, as I trow he is." While he spake the sound of a bugle-horn was heard, and in a few minutes up drove Wastle, in high style, in his dog-cart, tandemwise, and making a sweep round the court, he pulled up at the hall-door to an inch. We want nothing but Tickler and Odoherty, cried the Shepherd; and, extraordinary as it may seem, it is nevertheless true, that the words were scarcely out of his mouth, when Tickler rose up before us, on a pony under twelve hands, so that he absolutely seemed as if he had been mounted on a velocipede. Behind him came the Standard-bearer, on a white horse, once the property of Marshal Soult, but which fell into the Adjutant's hands on the evening of Albuera's bloody day. He came into the court-yard, side foremost, under the insidious left heel of his heroic master; and when Odoherty dismounted, it is impossible to tell what life and spirit was struck into the scene and company around from the clanging of his fixed spurs. No symptoms yet of Kempferhausen,† Mullion, and Bailie Jarvie, who were to travel to-

* Dr. Morris's shandrydan was a high two-wheeled gig, drawn by a single horse, and with a seat for two persons.—M.

† Kempferhausen was the name assumed by a contributor who wrote letters from the Lakes, descriptive of Wordsworth and Southey. Robert Pearce Gillies, whose poem of Childe Alarique obtained more attention than sale, in 1813, was the author of Horæ Germanicæ and Horæ Dani-

gether in a jaunting car of the Bailie's, which had been left on his hands by an Irish gentleman from Belfast, a dealer in linens, in part payment of a bad debt. The Shepherd laughed at the idea of expecting them for several days—as "give Kempferhausen his pipe," said he, "and the ither twa their plotty,* and deevil an inch will they budge frae the first change-house they speer at in the Highlands."

However, here were we assembled in great force—Editor, Wastle, Morris, Tickler, Ettrick Shepherd, and Odoherty. As we perceived that only the first of these gentlemen had dined, we kept our thumb on that circumstance, and joined the dinner-party as if nothing had happened, being indeed, in spite of a weakish constitution and confirmed rheumatism, a sure card on such occasions. A gallon of hodge-podge—the turkey-cock roasted—five or six dozen of poached eggs—and some chops of rather a problematical character (though we shrewdly suspect them to have been pork, in direct opposition to Odoherty, who swore they were bull-beef) assuaged the fames, or rather rabies edendi—and by eight o'clock we were ready to start for the Linn of Dee,† near which our Tent had, as we were informed, already been pitched for two days, through the accustomed kindness of the Thane, who had ordered his steward, Mr. Harden, to get it up with all suitable accommodations.

As, with Wastle's and Morris' servants, we were only eight in all, dog-cart and shandrydan took us up, out, and in, very comfortably, and with room to spare; and, as the nags were in high condition, we made the tent under the hour, being received with three hearty cheers, and "the clans are coming," from a pair of bagpipes, whose drones were assuredly far from idle ones. We returned the cheers with spirit, and Wastle, who plays the bugle in a way worthy of the late Leander himself, with a sudden blast startled the grouse and the red deer through all the mountains and forests of Mar.

We found our Tent pitched on a smooth greensward, that looked as if it had been artificially formed among the tall heather that encircled it. It was placed on the confluence of several valleys, so that on whatever side the canvas was raised, we had before our eyes a long reach of the most magnificent mountain scenery. The clear

cæ in Maga, which first made England and America acquainted with the dramatic writers of Germany and Scandinavia. He was a great sonnet-writer, and had the honor of having a sonnet specially addressed to him by Wordsworth, in 1814. He was the first editor of the Foreign Quarterly Review (commenced in 1827), wrote Recollections of Sir Walter Scott in Fraser's Magazine, 1835–'36, and published his own Memoirs of a Literary Veteran in 1851.—M.

* Plotty is mulled, or rather burnt port wine, delectable (as a night-cap) in the cold nights of winter. Claret, so treated, is not a bad substitute, but a double dose of it is requisite.—M.

† The Linn of Dee is a deep circular cavity in the hard black rock into which the waters fall, from the source, and whirl round and round—a miniature maelstrom. Much of Byron's childhood was passed close to this, and, while yet a very young boy, he used to lie in the sun, on the steep bank which sloped down to the Linn. On one occasion he rolled down this slope, to the horror of the hand-maiden who attended him, and expected to see him killed in "the hell of waters" far below; but a small shrub caught his dress as he was passing, and saved him. The shrub remains—when I saw it, *a tree* would have been the better name.—M.

waters of the Dee murmured not twenty yards off—and one of those little springs, so pleasant to the Shepherd, welled out from its hillock yet closer to the tent. Here we found that excellent fisher Walter Ritchie from Peebles, and that trusty caddy John Mackay, Frederick Street, Edinburgh, who had escorted the Adjutant's tent, and many et ceteras, in an old baggage-wagon purchased at Jock's Lodge, on the departure of the Enniskillen Dragoons, and made as good as new at the magical coach-yard of Crichton.* With Walter and John we were now ten in number, while the Thane's three kilted gillies and John of Sky,† whom the MIGHTY MINSTREL had kindly sent to enliven our festivities, made precisely the devil's dozen.

"Haud mora," there was no delay. The shandrydan and dog-cart were emptied in a trice, and we ourselves were particularly anxious to see "The Contributors' Box" safely stowed away among our own furniture. Busy as we all were, each with his own concerns, none of us could help smiling at the Ettrick Shepherd, who immediately, on entering the Tent, had got astride on a pretty corpulent cask of whisky, and was filling a jug on which he had instinctively laid his hands. "It's no canny to sleep here a' nicht for fear of the fairies without saining‡ ourselves, so we'll e'en pit round the jug, and pour out a drappoch‖ to King Lu!" In a short time the Tent was in fair array—while Odoherty proposed that we should see that our pieces were all in good order, and to ascertain their comparative excellence, and the skill of the owners, that we should fire at a mark. We accordingly assembled our forces for that purpose.

By some accident or other which will probably never be explained, a copy of the last part of the Transactions of the Royal Society was found lying in the tent. Whether Wastle had brought it in his dog-cart——but the thing is inexplicable, so let it pass. The volume was opened by chance somewhere about the middle, and set up at forty yards' distance to be fired at by the contributors. The following scale will show the result of the trial.

* Ritchie has been repeatedly mentioned in Wilson's writings. The caddies are a race peculiar to Edinburgh, coming from the wilds of Lochaber and Braemar, whence the stock is re-inforced. They are dying out, but, even as late as twenty years ago, were the only trusted and recognized message-bearers in Auld Reekie, knowing every man, woman, and child there,—every street, lane, and close,—every shop, house, and staircase. Mackay, above mentioned, was a real personage, and mightily elevated of course, by this notice in Blackwood. In "Peter's Letters," Lockhart has done full justice to the caddies.—M.

† John of Sky was a tall and stalwart bag-piper, who formed one of Scott's household at Abbotsford. His name was John Bruce, and attired in full Highland costume, he used to play on the pipes, stalking up and down in front of the house, when Scott gave a set dinner, coming in at the close, to receive a *quaigh* (or Celtic wooden drinking vessel) of Glenlivet, from Scott's hand. Saluting the company, he would drink off the contents, about a quarter-pint of strong raw spirits, at a gulp, without moving a muscle of his face, and resume his out-of-door pibrochs, which he continued until after twilight had set in.—M.

‡ Blessing ourselves.—Dr. Jamieson.

‖ As *drappie* means a little drop, it is probable that the Shepherd's *drappoch* has a like signification.—M.

Trial on the 11th at 40 yards' distance, all shooting with No. 4, at an expanded volume of the Transactions of the Royal Society.

	Wadding.	Shot. Oz.	Grains put in.	Leaves pierced.
Wastle,..................	Hat.	1½	78	40
Tickler,..................	Card.	1¾	65	30
Morris,..................	Unknown.	1½	65	32
Odoherty,...............	Hat.	1¾	30	25
Ettrick Shepherd,........	Wool.	4	0	0
Editor,..................	MSS. Article.	2	20	90

A very remarkable phenomenon, and one well worthy the attention of the Royal Society, was observed on this occasion. While the left hand page, 372, was riddled to pieces,—the right hand page did not exhibit a single shot. The cause of this, we who are no philosophers are not able to explain; but such is the fact; and on the page thus miraculously unhurt, were written the following words, "an Essay on the Scope and Tendency of the Philosophical Writings of Lord Bacon, by Macvey Napier, Esq." Such impenetrable stuff was it proved to be.*

By this time it had become rather darkish, and John of the Isles began playing so sleepy an air, that it reminded us of the house of rest. In about an hour we were all fourteen stretched upon our backs with our feet meeting, in the true campaign fashion, in the centre of the tent. The last observation that was uttered came from Dr. Morris, who lamented much that Kempferhausen had not arrived, as the moon would soon rise, and the young poet might have had an opportunity of addressing a sonnet to her in High Dutch. Wastle indistinctly muttered something in reply, for the hand of Morpheus was passing over his mouth. For our own part, we were unable to close an eye, thinking of the Magazine, for, when we left Edinburgh, only two half-sheets had gone to press, and Mr. Blackwood looked unutterable things.

While considering what ought to be the opening article, such a noise arose as might have passed in America, for a frog concert. What a snore! not one of the fourteen noses, Lowland or Highland, Scotch, Irish, or Welsh, lay idle. The sum total was tremendous. By degrees our ears got somewhat accustomed to the sound, and we could distinguish the characteristic snore of every sleeper. Above all the menial and plebeian rhoncus rose the clear silver-nosed trumpet of Tickler, playing its bold reveillé—there was heard the equable, but not monotonous, and most gentlemanly snore of Wastle

* Macvey Napier, who edited the Encyclopedia Britannica, and succeeded Jeffrey as conductor of the Edinburgh Review, in 1829, was also one of the principal clerks of the Scottish Court of Session, and Professor of Conveyancing in Edinburgh University. He had perpetrated an article on Lord Bacon, which the Blackwood writers greatly ridiculed. He was a very decided Whig,—which may account for these Tory sneers. Macvey latterly occupied the house 39 North Castle-street, Edinburgh, in which Scott lived, from 1798 to July, 1826, and died in 1847.—M.

—Dr. Morris snored in such a manner as he did mock himself, and ever and anon ceased, as if he were listening, and then after a little uncertain sniffling as if tuning his instrument to concert-pitch, broke out again into full possession of his powers—Odoherty betrayed a good deal of the nasal brogue of his country, for sleeping or waking the Adjutant is a true Milesian, snoring by fits and starts in a hurried and impassioned manner like a man dreaming of Feuntes D'Onore or Donnybrook Fair*—while, from the breast, neck, shoulders, head and nose of the Ettrick Shepherd came a deep, hollow, grunting-growl, like that of the royal tiger, so admirably described by Lady H. in the last number of the Literary and Scientific Journal. When this had lasted for a couple of hours, sometimes one performer leading the band, and sometimes another, we felt that the drum of our ear could bear it no longer—so we picked our way out of the tent over limbs of Celt and Saxon, and retired from the concert-room, to hear the music "by distance made more sweet." Nearly half a mile off, we heard the

"Solemn hum,
Voice of the desert never dumb,"

and through its multitudinous murmur were distinctly audible the majestic base of the author of the above lines, and the pure tenor of Tickler—the first resembling a subterranean grumble, and the latter striking on the ear like the sound of iron against rock in a frost. During all this time, the moon was sitting in Heaven, "apparent queen," not with a stoical indifference, as Mr. Southey reports of her on the night after Prince Madoc had defeated the Mexicans, but evidently much pleased with the scene below her—both with what she saw and what she heard. We shortly after returned to the Tent; and "joining at last the general troop of sleep," we no doubt added one instrumental performer more to the grand chorus of this Musical Festival.

We do not pretend to conceal the fact, that we felt ourselves carried in a dream to the back shop, the sanctum sanctorum of No. 17 Prince's Street; and that we never thought Mr. Blackwood so beautiful as in that vision. But just as he had given us a proof to correct, it seemed as if the roof had fallen in and crushed us in the ruins. We awoke—and found that Odoherty had fired the morning-gun, as a signal. We buckled on our armor in less than no time, and the adjutant was pleased to say, that he had never seen men sharper at an alarm through the whole course of the Peninsular war. "No fear lest breakfast cool"—for in ten minutes each man had

* "Who e'er has the luck to see Donnybrook Fair,
An Irishman all in his glory is there,
With his sprig of shillelah and shamrock so green."—M.

housed half a pound at least of mutton-ham, and a dash of the dew. Early as the hour was, there was nothing like squeamishness—and it must not be omitted, that each Contributor, like a good soldier and good citizen, after an appropriate address by Odoherty, emptied his quech to the health of the Prince Regent.*

Dr. Morris, Wastle, and Odoherty, each attended by a Highland guide, provided for them, as we have said, by the munificence of the Thane, took their departure to the mountains; the Dr. ascending the pass of the Geonly Water, with a view to the ground towards the head of Glen Tilt,—Wastle taking up the glen of the source of the Dee, and the Adjutant meditating a cast or two with our own favorite bitch, over the ground behind Mar-Lodge. Tickler, who had never seen a red Deer, went to the forest with John of the Isles, and small Donald Dhu of Invercauld, having, ere he parted, fixed his bayonet at the mouth of the tent. The Ettrick Shepherd, apparently discouraged by his last night's discomfiture in shooting at the Transactions, accompanied Walter Ritchie to the Dee, to try for a salmon; while we ourselves, along with John Mackay, remained at home in the tent, to overhaul the "Contributors' Box," and if necessary, to write a leading article.

Our friends were now all gone, and we were left alone in the silence of the morning. Many years had elapsed, since our health had permitted us to be among the mountains, though in our youth, we could have "trodden the bent," with the best man in Scotland. Our heart leapt within us, as we gazed on the sea of mountains, emerging from the soft mists in which they had been shrouded during the night. The wide and sunny silence was like the bright atmosphere of former days. And when the Eagle sailed away on his broad vans, from that magnificent cliff above the Linn of Dee, we recollected our own strength, which we once thought nothing could have tamed; and which used to carry us, as on wings, unwearied and exulting, over heights that we could now travel only in the dream of fancy. Here a twinge of the rheumatism made us sensibly feel the truth of these reflections, and we hobbled into our tent with a sigh; but the comfortable arrangement of the interior, and above all the jolly cask of whisky, soon awakened us to a sense of the extreme folly of repining retrospection, and we could not help thinking, that the Editor in his camp, had greatly the advantage over his Contributors, now out in all directions on foraging parties.†

* George, Prince of Wales, was Regent, from February, 1811, (when the confirmed madness of George III., was indisputable), until January, 1820, when he became King, by succession.—M.

† In Peter's Letters to his Kinsfolk, we, the Editor are spoken of as an obscure man, a martyr to rheumatism, and one who only draws plans which others execute. That we are not so luminous a body as Dr. Morris, we admit—and that we are a martyr to rheumatism, is unfortunately true, in spite of the well-known skill of our townsman, Dr. Balfour—but we beg leave to contradict the illustrious Physician of Aberystwith on the last charge. We both plan and execute—and flatter ourselves that there is a something in our articles that betrays the hand

On opening the Box, it was found to be rich in various matter—and we amused ourselves for a couple of hours with an excellent article on the National Monument—one on Bait-Fishing—and another "on the Mechanism of the Foot and Leg."* While reading the last, we heard the noise of wings, and going to the mouth of the tent, saw a numerous pack of grouse sit down close to the little spring already mentioned. We are no poachers—but it must not be expected that a martyr to rheumatism is to be bound by the same rules with sportsmen who have the free use of their limbs. We accordingly took up Hogg's double barrel, and let fly at the pack as they were all sitting together in a snug family-party—and before they could recover from their confusion, we repeated the salutation. John Mackay went leisurely forward—and returned with five brace and a half of as fine young birds as might be looked at—and the old cock. We maintain that no man is entitled to form an opinion of our conduct in this, who has not suffered under confirmed rheumatism for ten years at least, or, which is as well, under the gout for five.†

John Mackay had scarcely got the birds hung up by the legs, when we were considerably alarmed by loud shouts or yells from the river side, which we knew to be from the Shepherd—and running down as expeditiously as our knee would permit, we found that the Bard had hooked a Fish. There was he capering along the somewhat rugged banks of the Dee, with his hair on end, and his eyes sticking out of his head, holding the butt-end of his rod with both hands in perfect desperation.

"Fit statue for the court of fear!"

Walter Ritchie ever and anon "his soul-subduing voice applied" close to his ear, instructing him how to act in this unexpected emergency; and above all things, imploring him to get the better of his fright! Unluckily the Shepherd's reel-line was too short, so, to prevent the salmon from running it out, he was under the necessity of following him up close at the heels. At every plunge the fish

of the Editor. Dr. Morris, who had never seen us when he published his "Letters," has since apologised to us in the handsomest manner, both for his unfounded charge of obscurity and incapacity, but we wish also that the world should know it. We hear that several other persons, equally opaque as ourselves, have taken it grievously to heart, that the Doctor has overlooked them altogether, and attempt to carry their heads very *high* when his name is mentioned. Such persons may be said to belong to the High School.—See Gray's Elegy,

"And leave the world to darkness and to me."—C. N.

* These articles actually did appear in the current No. of Blackwood. The first strongly urged that the suggested National Monument on Calton Hill, should consist of a restoration of the Parthenon. The second, professedly written by one Peter McFinn, was a graphic account of a fishing excursion in Dumfrieshire, with remarks on bait-fishing. The third was a very amusing review of Dr. John Cross's book On the Mechanism and Mctions of the Human Leg and Foot.—M.

† We have been so long out of the sporting world that we scarcely know what the public feeling is on subjects of this kind. We remember an old gentleman long ago, when we had a shooting box in Northamptonshire, who always shot hares sitting, on the principle that it was *more difficult* to shoot them in that situation! We despise all such sophistry.—C. N.

made—at every rush he took, the Shepherd was fearfully agitated—and floundered, stumbled, fell and recovered himself again among the large round slippery stones, in a manner wondrous to behold. For a man of his years, his activity is prodigious. "Look there, Mr. Editor! There is a LEADING ARTICLE for you!" Scarcely had he spoken, when the fish took a sullen fit, and sinking to the bottom, lay there like a log,

"Rolled round in earth's diurnal course
With rocks and stones and trees!"

The Shepherd seemed truly thankful for this short respite from toil, and helping himself cautiously to a pinch of snuff, handed over the mull* to us with that air of courteous generosity observable on such occasions. At length he became desirous of another heat, but the salmon would not budge, and the Shepherd, forgetting how much he stood in awe of the monarch of the flood when he was in motion, began insulting him in the grossest manner in his repose. Finally, he proposed to us to strip and dive down to alarm him, some fifteen or twenty feet—a modest proposal to a man of fifty†—an editor—and a martyr to the rheumatism. Here the fish darted off like lightning, and then threw a somerset many feet in the air. Though this was what the Shepherd had wished, it seemed not to be what he had expected, and the rod was twitched out of his grasp, as neatly as at a match of single stick. Walter Ritchie, however, recovered the weapon, and returned it to its master yet standing in blank discomfiture. His pride did not allow him to decline it—though it was apparent that he would have exchanged situations with Mazeppa or John Gilpin.

But why prolong the agitating narrative? Suffice it to say, that after a chase of two miles down the Dee, and from an observation of the sun's altitude of two hours' duration, the salmon gave in—and came unexpectedly to shore. There, on the green turf, lay salmon and Shepherd, both quite exhausted, and with scarcely any symptoms of life. They reminded us of one of those interesting scenes in Border History, where two gallant foemen lie side by side—or like one of those no less interesting scenes in coursing, where greyhound and hare are stretched gasping together on the wold. The Fish gave his last convulsive bound from the sod, and the shepherd, with a faint voice, cried, "take care o' yoursels or he'll lame some o' you"—but his fears were groundless, for Waltar Ritchie had already given him

* A *mull* is a Scotch snuff-box, made out of a ram's-horn, polished, and fitted with a cover, often embellished with a silver setting, on which is fixed a cairn-gorm, or Scotch topaz.—M.

† At this time, the Editor of Blackwood had neither assumed the name of CHRISTOPHER NORTH, nor quite decided what his age should be. A man of 50, in 1818, would have been born in 1769. Subsequently, the year 1754 was given as the actual date, which would have made Kit North 65, at the time he and his colleagues were at Braemar. Throughout the "Noctes," he is represented as in venerable old age, and must have been 81 when they closed, in 1835.—M.

the coup de grace, and holding him up by the gills, pronounced his eulogy with a simple pathos, worthy of better times, "a brave fish! de'el tak me ginna he binna twenty pun weight!"

The first thing the shepherd said, on coming to himself, was, "gude save us, I wou'd gie half a croon for a gill o' whusky!" The sun, however, had dissolved the mountain-dew—so we had to return (a distance of nearly three miles) to our tent, within the coolness of whose shadow we knew some of the "tears of the morning" were to be found.

On entering the tent, only judge of our surprise when we found Kempferhausen, Mullion, and Jarvie, tearing away tooth and nail at the "Branxy,"* and gulping down the aqua vitæ as if it had been small beer! The swallow of the young German, in particular, was prodigious; and much must he have astonished the Westmoreland peasantry, when in training to write his celebrated letters from the Lakes. He assured us that he had ate little or nothing for three days, which seemed to us but a partial avowal of the truth, for his present voracity could only have been satisfactorily accounted for on the theory of a fast for three weeks. That excellent actor Jones, in Jeremy Diddler, was a mere joke to him.† Mullion made a masterly meal of it; while of Jarvie it is sufficient to say, that he upheld the high character of a citizen of Glasgow. We introduced the Shepherd to Kempferhausen and Jarvie (Mullion being an old acquaintance), and nothing could be more amusing than the contrast of the Glasgow and the Hamburgh *manner*. Jarvie got into such glee, that he absolutely began to "trot"‡ the shepherd round the room; but James was soon up to him, and played off in his turn upon the bailie, asserting with meritorious gravity of face, that he had shot the salmon with a single ball, at the distance of half a mile, as he was rashly attempting, with his tail in his mouth, to leap the Linn of Dee.

It was now wearing on to two o'clock, and it is not to be denied, that though "no that fou," we had got "a drappy in our ee,"—though

* *Branxy* is the name given to mutton hams made from the sheep that have died of their own accord, or met with some fatal accident among the mountains. It is quite superior to any other, both in flavor and nutriment. It is a perquisite of the shepherds; and in this instance we had it warranted sound by the head of Lord Fife's pastoral establishment. The best we ever ate was at Dugald Campbell's, Esq. of Achlian, Argyllshire.—C. N.

† Richard Jones, commonly called "Gentleman Jones," was a great favorite at the Edinburgh theatre, as comedian, and finally settled in London, where he died a few years ago, after having realized a large fortune as a teacher of elocution.—M.

‡ To *trot* means to hoax. It used to be much practised in Glasgow, and also at Bolton, in Lancashire. A famous Bolton trot was the wager with one "in verdure clad," that he would not put one of his feet into hot water, and keep it therein as long as a certain Boltonian who was present. The trial was made, then and there. Both plunged a stocking-covered leg into a tub of boiling water. The "Bolton fellow" appeared entirely unaffected by the increased temperature: the other instantaneously withdrew his *pin*, dreadfully scalded, and paid the dozen of wine which he had lost. When the party were on the last bottle, the green young gentleman was informed and shown, that it was his opponent's *cork* leg which had competed with his own, of flesh and bone. This was a thorough *trot*—equivalent to a modern *sell!* In Lancashire, by the way, the inhabitants of certain towns are characteristically designated as "Liverpool gentlemen, Manchester men, Wigan chaps, and Bolton fellows."—M.

it was more owing to the heat of the sun and the salmon-hunt than anything else, that we found any difficulty in preserving our equilibrium. Kempferhausen and Hogg were prodigiously great, and we overheard the foreigner vowing that he would publish a German translation of the Queen's Wake; while, in another corner of the Tent, and with the whisky quech placed before us on the Contributors' box, we and Jarvie were "unco kind and couth thegither," and the Bailie solemnly promised us before winter, his article entitled "The devil on Two Sticks, on the Top of the Ram's Horn."*

While matters were thus going on, Walter Ritchie came hastily into the Tent, and let us know that "four strange gentlemen" were making the best of their way towards us, over the large stones and loose rocks of a heathery hill behind. In a few minutes he ushered two of them in. They were a brace of smart springals enough, with no small portion of self-assurance and nonchalance. "My name," quoth the tallest, "is Seward of Christchurch, and this is Buller of Brazennose."† We had heard something of Oxford ease and affluence, and indeed reckon more than one Oxonian among our contributors; but without seeing it, we could not have credited the concentration of so much self-satisfaction in any one individual of the species as in this avowed Seward of Christchurch. "Cursed comfortable marqué, Buller, and plenty of prog;—come, my old boy, tip us a beaker of your stingo." "Pray," replied we, "may I ask which of you is the Brazennose man?" "Ha! Buller, to be sure, Buller of Brazennose!—first-class-man, sir—devilish clever fellow;—allow me to introduce him to you more particularly, sir:—This, sir, is Bob Buller of Brazennose—first-class-man, sir, both in Litt. Hum. and Class. Phys.—their crack-man, sir, since the days of Milman.‡ But pray, sir, may I ask to whom I have the honor of addressing myself?" "Why," replied we politely, but with dignity, "Mr. Seward, we are the veiled Editor of Blackwood's Magazine!" "The veiled Editor of Blackwood's Magazine! By the scythe of Saturn and all that is cutting! my worthy old cock! Lend me your feelers, Buller—isn't he as like old Gaisford as two pigs? Mr. Editor, you know Gaisford—damned good fellow—one of the well-booted Greeks."—"It is my misfortune, sir, never to have seen Mr. Gaisford, but I have a copy of his Hephæstion."|| Here we chanced

* The "Ram's Horn" is the name of a church in Glasgow, from the top of whose spire the Devil on Two Sticks would unquestionably have a commanding bird's-eye view of that city.—C. N.

† Buller, of Brazennose College, Oxford, was John Hughes, (who really belonged to Oriel,) and author of an Itinerary of the Rhone. He was a great friend of Ainsworth, the novelist, Thomas Ingoldsby (the Rev. Richard Harris Barham, a member of the same college), and Theodore Hook. There was no representative, to my knowledge, of Seward.

‡ When a student at Oxford wins the highest honors, at the degree-examination, in classics and science, he is called "a double first"—as conqueror in both. The late Sir Robert Peel was so distinguished. The Rev. Henry Hart Milman here mentioned, was a Brazennose man, and is now Dean of St. Paul's Cathedral, London. He has written much in prose and verse—chiefly dramatic in the latter, of which his play of "Fazio" is the only one on the stage.—M.

|| The Rev. Dr. Thomas Gaisford, Dean of Christchurch, Oxford, since 1831, was appointed Regius Professor of Greek in 1811.—M.

to look around us, and saw the faces of the Shepherd, Mullion, and Jarvie, close to each other, and all fixed with various expressions of fear, wonder, and astonishment on Mr. Seward of Christchurch! They kept cautiously advancing towards him inch by inch, somewhat in the style of three Arctic Highlanders towards Captain Ross on his supposed descent from the moon; Jarvie bent down in a crouching attitude, with his hands on his knees, like a frog ready to make a spring; Mullion, with one fist on his chin, and the other unconsciously clawing his head, while his broad purple face was one gleam or rather "glower" of curiosity; and the Shepherd with his noble buck teeth, displayed in all their brown irregularity, like a seer in a fit of second sight. "Whare the deevil cum ye frae?" quoth the Shepherd. "Ha, ha! Buller, here is a rum one to go." On this we introduced the Shepherd to the Oxonians, as the author of the Queen's Wake, Pilgrims of the Sun, &c., and in return, with some difficulty explained to him in what part of the globe Oxford stood, and to what purpose it was dedicated, though on this latter point we did not seem to make ourselves very intelligible. "Weel, weel, gentlemen," continued the Shepherd, "I'se warrant your twa big scholars, but hech sers, there's something about you baith that is enough to mak ane split their sides with laughing. Buller o' Brazennose, I ne'er heard the like o' sic an a name as that in a' my born days, except it were the Bullers o' Buchan."* Then the Shepherd put his hands to his sides, and burst into a long loud triumphant guffaw.

Meanwhile, we had wholly forgotten the other two "strange gentlemen," and found that they were sitting outside the tent. Wastle very politely asked them in; one was a dapper little fellow, but as pale as death; and had his left hand wrapt up in a handkerchief. The other was tall and lusty, but with a face of vulgar effeminacy, and altogether breathing rather offensively of a large town. "My name is Tims," piteously uttered the small pale dapper young man; and my two-barrelled gun has cracked, and carried away my little finger, and a ring that was a real diamond. I bought it at Rundle and Bridges."† "They calls me Price," said the dandy; "a nephy of the late Sir Charles Price, that was o' Lunnun; and I am come down into Scotland here to shoot in these hereabout parts."

* The Bullers of Buchan, in Aberdeenshire, are among the wonders of Scotland. They are near Slaine's Castle, the residence of the Earl of Errol, and are remarkable for the noise and force with which, at a certain state of the tides, the sea-water is driven up through a sort of well-like cavity in a rock. When Dr. Johnson was in Scotland, the Bullers especially attracted his attention.—M.

† Originally, this Mr. Tims was as much a real character as Wastle or Mullion, but on the appearance. (as a translation from the French of Viscount Victoire de Soligny,) of a tour in England, the wits of Blackwood insisted that their own cockney, Tims, had written it, and ever afterwards, in the "Noctes," and out of it, spoke of Tims, as "the Wicount Wictoire." The jewellers, Rundell and Bridges, whom he names, were the leading jewellers in London for many years, (their shop was on Ludgate Hill, near St. Paul's Cathedral,) and the wife of Mr. Rundell was authoress of the famous cooking-book, of which, between 1811 and 1854, about five million copies have been sold. Sir Charles Price was a London banker.—M.

During this explanation, the Oxonians did not deign to look towards the Cockneys, but Seward kept humming "the bold dragoon," and the "first class man both in Litt. Hum. and Class Phys.," whose voice we had not yet heard, was peeping somewhat inquisitively into the quechs, jugs, and bottles, and occasionally applying one or other of them to his mouth, without meeting any suitable return to his ardor.

We at length found that the Oxonians and the Cockneys had left the Spittal of Glenshee by sunrise, in two totally distinct parties. But that the geography of so wild a country as Scotland, not being much known either in Oxford or the City, both had got bewildered among the everlasting hills and valleys, till, as their good luck would have it, they had joined forces within half a mile of our Tent. A bumper of whisky gave a slight tinge of red to the cadaverous phiz of Tims; and Price got quite jaunty, pulling up the collar of his shirt above his ears, which, you may well believe, were none of the shortest. Nothing could be more amusing to us, than the ineffable contempt with which Christchurch and Brazennose regarded Cheapside and Ludgate Hill; though, to say the truth, the two former seemed just as much out of place as the latter, among the wilds of Braemar; while, in spite of all we could do, to divert the conversation from such subjects, Seward kept perpetually chattering of Jack Ireland, little Jenkins of Baliol, the Dean, the great Tom of Christchurch, and other literary characters of credit and renown.

The Shepherd, eager to put a stop, if possible, to these mystical allusions, requested to see what the gentlemen had got in their bags, and Messrs. Tims and Price silently submitted theirs to the scrutiny. James put his hand boldly in—as well he might—for the lean sides of the wallet plainly showed that there was no danger of his being bitten, and it was seen by the expression of his face, on withdrawing his arm, how truly nature abhors a vacuum. Mr. Tims stood on high ground, for he had burst his gun the first fire, and Mr. Price declared, that though in other respects a finished sportsman, he had never till that day fired a shot. Mr. Seward then called on his man, by the facetious appellation of "Katterfelto," "to bring the spoil," and a knowing knave immediately emptied a huge bag containing two brace of "chirpers" (pouts evidently taken by the hand), and, to the petrifaction of the spectators, an enormous Fox. Tims and Price eyed the animal with intense curiosity, and on hearing its name, the latter declared that though he had now hunted with the Surrey-hounds for six years, he had never caught a view of reynard, and would think his journey to Scotland well repaid by the sight of an animal which he had long given up all hopes of ever beholding on this side of the grave. Seward told him, (it was the first time he had ever deigned to address the Cockney) that he was welcome to

Mr. Fox, only he begged leave to retain the brush; and Price leapt at the offer, declaring he would have him stuffed, and placed at the winder of his Box at Hampstead.

"That's the Captain's lauch," quoth the Shepherd, and forthwith entered Odoherty, picturesquely ornamented with moorfowl, snipes, and flappers, all dangling round his waist, as one might suppose as many scalps round an Indian warrior. His fine features were stained with gunpowder and blood, and Mr. Tims had nearly fainted away. "Allow me, gentlemen, to introduce Timothy Tickler, Esq.," said the Standard-bearer, and in a trice he stood before us in all his altitude. His musket, with the bayonet fixed, was in his hand, and over his shoulders hung a young roe which he had slain in the forest. Even Seward of Christchurch, and Buller of Brazennose, stood astounded at the apparition. "By the ghost of Dinah Gray, Buller, there are more things in heaven and earth than are dreamt of in Aristotle's philosophy." "There, Mr. Editor," quoth Tickler, "is John Roe—Richard Doe has escaped mortally wounded;" and with that, he threw down the creature at our feet. At that moment was heard the bugle-horn of Wastle; and by the time "that a man with moderate haste might count a thousand," he and the physician were in the tent. "My dear friend, Dr. Morris!" "What, Buller of Brazennose!" The meeting was most cordial; but the heat of the tent was quite insupportable, being about 96 of Henry Watson's thermometer—so it was proposed by Tickler to adjourn to the antechamber, whose dimensions could not easily have been aken. We mustered very strong—Editor,[1] Wastle,[2] Morris,[3] Tickler,[4] Odoherty,[5] Shepherd,[6] Jarvie,[7] Mullion,[8] Kempferhausen,[9] Seward of Christchurch,[10] Buller of Brazennose,[11] Tims,[12] Price,[13] John of Sky,[14] Lord Fife's three gillies,[17] Walter Ritchie,[18] John Mackay,[19] Katterfelto,[20] Buller's valet,[21] the Cockney's Londoner,[22] four Highlanders from the Spittal of Glenshee,[26] Peter's man John,[27] Wastle's man Thomas.[28]

It was altogether a most animating scene; and it is incredible in how short a time one kind and genial spirit seemed transferred through so great a body of men. "It's all the world like the coffee-room o' Glasgow about four o'clock," said Jarvie; "but, ochone, they'll be no punch—none o' Provost Hamilton's best here." John Mackay informed us, that he and his assistants were all at work, and that in an hour and a half dinner would be on the table. "But hae ye killed ony thing, doctor," quoth the Shepherd. Here Peter's man John, and Walter Ritchie, came forward, dragging several bags along with them, which disembogued a brown flood of grouse, that overflowed many yards of the sod. Mr. Tims could not believe his eyes, when he saw, counted before them, thirty-seven brace. "There are thirty brace mair o' them," said Watty Ritchie, "scouring for the pan." So much for Wastle and Morris.

The whole party now retired to their toilette, and most of us performed our ablutions in the limpid Dee. We, the Contributors, had greatly the advantage over the Oxonians and the Cockneys, whose wardrobe was at the Spittal of Glenshee; and we could not help observing, that when we ourselves returned to the tent in a full suit of black, little the worse for the gentle wear of three years Sundays, we were looked at with a pleasant surprise, and, if possible, an increased admiration, not only by Tims and Price, but also by Seward of Christchurch, and Buller of Brazennose.

When we all assembled again, furbished and figged up, we made a splendid figure on the mountain-side; and rarely had the heather waved over a finer body of men since the days of Fingal. It is true, that most of us were too sharp-set fully to enjoy the magnificence of the prospect. Yet it made itself be felt. Many hundred stupendous mountains towered up into the cloud-piled sky over a wide horizon—nor was it easy to distinguish earth from heaven as they lay blended together in that sublime confusion. The dark pine-forests of Mar stretched off into the dim and distant day, overshadowing rock and precipice; and in the blue misty hollows of the hill, we knew that unseen tarns and lakes were lying in their solitary beauty. Scarce visible in the dark blue sky, an eagle was heard yelling in wild and sullen fits; and when one gazed up to his flight, it was a grand feeling to imagine the boundless expanse of earth, sea, and sky, that must then have been submitted to the ken of the majestic Bird.

Our readers will observe, that the above little bit of description is not our own, but copied out of Kempferhausen's journal; and we think it not so much amiss, considering that it was pencilled under a severe fit of the toothache. One hour in the drawing-room before dinner is longer than three in the dining-room after it, and this we all experienced, while lying on the greensward before our tent. Even the unwearied wit of Tickler, who lay stretched "many a rood" among the heather, was beginning to lose its charm, when Wastle's man Thomas, a comely varlet about his master's age, advanced with the ceremonious air of a true butler of the old school, and announced that dinner was on the table. Never did thunder follow the lightening so instantaneously, as we all leapt up on this enunciation; and on looking round, we found ourselves in the chair, supported by Wastle and Morris—while Tickler was seated croupier,* supported by

* *Croupier*,—vice-chairman. Probably derived from two men riding on a horse, in which case one must sit on the croup, or loins of the animal, *i. e.* occupy a secondary or infirm position.

Odoherty and Buller of Brazennose. A principle of the most beautiful adaptation and fitness of parts seemed undesignedly to regulate the seating of the whole party; and we especially observed how finely the High-street face of Seward of Christchurch contrasted itself with the Cowgate face of the Shepherd on the one hand, and the Saltmarket one of Jarvie on the other—while that of Tims looked quite pale and interesting between the long sallow countenance of Kempferhausen and the broad rubicundity of Mullion.

By what magical process the dinner had been cooked we know not; but a fine cut of salmon lay before the chair; while Tickler cried, with a loud voice, "Dr. Morris, shall I help you to some roe-soup?" On the middle of the table, midway between Mullion and Jarvie, was an immense tureen of grouse soup, composed, as Peter's man John declared, with uplifted hands and eyes, of fifteen brace of birds! Placed at judicious intervals, smoked trenchers of grouse roasted, stewed, and grilled—while a haunch of John Doe gave a crown and consummation to a feast fit for the Immortal Gods.

The party had just been helped to grouse or roe-soup, when a card was handed to the Chairman (we shall henceforth substitute Chairman in place of Editor) with the single word, A CONTRIBUTOR, written upon it in large characters. We left our seat for an instant to usher in the GREAT UNKNOWN. IT WAS DR. SCOTT, THE CELEBRATED ODONTIST OF GLASGOW.* He was still seated on his famous white trotting pony, with his legs boldly extended in ultra-dragoon fashion from its sides, and his armed heels so much depressed, that his feet stood perfectly perpendicular with elevated toes, and exposed to our gaze those well-known broad and formidable soles which could belong to no other living man but the doctor. On his head was a hat white as snow, and in circumference wide as a fairy-ring on a hill-side—his portly frame was shrouded in a light-drab surtout, and his sturdy limbs in trowsers of the purest milled cord, which, by the action of riding, had been worked up to his knees, and considerately suffered the eye to rest on a pair of valuable top-boots spick and span new for the occasion—no unworthy successors they to those of the Ettrick Shepherd, now no more. A green silk umbrella was gorgeously expanded over the illustrious Odontist, who, having remained a full minute in all his pride of place, that we might have leisure to contemplate the fulness of his perfections, furled his banner in a style worthy of the Adjutant himself; and shouldering it as if he had been serving in the Scotch Fusileers, exclaimed, "You didna ask me to your tent, ye deevil, but here I am, in spite of your teeth. I heard o' you at Gordon Castle,† and I hae just come up to keep ye a' right

* This Scott, whom it pleased North to call Doctor, and pass off as a miracle of wit and learning, was an obese odontist (or dentist) in Glasgow, eminent for nothing beyond tooth-drawing, except punch-drinking.

† In Aberdeenshire. It was the seat of the Duke of Gordon; and Willis, who visited it, has described it in his Pencillings by the Way.—M.

and tight, ye nest o' veepers." We assured the Doctor that his honest face was always a welcome contribution to us, and that we had not asked him to join the party, solely from a feeling of compassion to his patients. The doctor's boy now ran up to assist his respected master to dismount, in a livery of blue and red, and a smart cockade; for the doctor had been a soldier in his youth, and performed many signal acts of valor in the green of Glasgow, along with the Anderston Volunteers, when that fine body of operatives were commanded by the gallant Colonel Geddes, and the invincible Major Cross. "Gentlemen, Dr. Scott from Glasgow,"—when such a shout arose as can only be described to those not present by its effects.

> "So far was heard the mighty knell,
> The stag sprung up upon the fell,
> Spread his broad nostril to the wind,
> Listed, before, aside, behind—
> Then couched him down beside the hind—
> And quaked among the mountain fern,
> To hear that sound," &c.

The Doctor was soon seated; and the drab surtout being felt rather close, he imitated the fashion of Lady Heron in Marmion, and

> "It all for heat was laid aside."

"Hoo are a' the people o' the West?" quoth Jarvie, delighted to see a Glasgow face in so high a northern latitude. "Just as you left them, Bailie—a' breaking clean aff by the stump—There's scarcely a house I wad uphald langer than a loose tooth—it's just a' ae general *squabash!*"

A short pause succeeded; and in the silence of the tent nothing was heard, save the clattering of knives and forks—the clashing of trenchers—the smacking of lips—and occasionally those long deep sighs of full and perfect enjoyment, that, be our theoretical creed what it may concerning the summum bonum, are ever felt to breathe out the very inmost soul of all earthly felicity.

Just then arose outside of the tent such a throttling noise of unnumbered dogs, that had Earl Walter, the wild huntsman, been a daylight vision, we must have expected to see him now realized. Amidst the savage growl were heard the loud curses of Celt and Sassenach, maddening the fray which they sought to assuage. "Demme if the Highland curs be not murdering my Juno," exclaimed Mr. Seward of Christchurch, "I would not lose her for the Indies—she was bred by Jack Burton!" We had our own suspicion that Mr. Constable's brown bitch was at the bottom of all this disturbance—but we found it impossible to discover, in this general "*colleshangy*"* its

* See again Dr. Jamieson.

prime mover. Mr. Price declared himself at ease about the issue of this conflict, as he had purchased his dog Randal from Bill Gibbons,* and a better never entered a ring. The Shepherd did not allow this bravado to pass unnoticed—and we are almost confident that we heard him through the din offering to fight his Hector against the "Southron dog, for a gallon o' whisky and a haggis!" Meanwhile almost a score of dogs were fiercely at work among the heather —nor could we help contrasting with the agitated action of the rest of the party, the cool composure of Morris, the calm curiosity of Wastle, and the eager ecstasy of Tickler, who, standing together on a rock elevated above the scene of action, might, perhaps, be compared to Bonaparte and his staff witnessing the Great Battle from the observatory on the heights of Mont St. Jean.

Order was at last restored—and all the dogs came shaking their ears close to the heels of their respective masters—some of them piteously limping, and others licking their wounds, which were so numerous that it would have required Monsieur Larrey† himself to bind them all up on the field of battle. But a scene, if possible, of yet greater confusion was at hand. A strong body of Celts, collected among the mountains towards the Spittal of Glenshee, advanced, with a most hostile demonstration, to the tent, and demanded £20 for the slaughter committed among their flocks by the outlandish dogs of the four English Gentlemen. We drew up our forces in battle array, to repel the threatened charge of these fierce mountaineers—ourselves commanding in the centre, Odoherty on the right wing, and Dr. Scott on the left. On seeing this, the enemy took up a position in our rear, as if wishing to cut off our retreat to Braemar. Being averse to the unnecessary effusion of blood, we sent off, with a flag of truce, (a sprig of heather in a bottle of whisky) a deputation to the enemy's camp, consisting of the Shepherd and Walter Ritchie as Assessors, and John Mackay as Interpreter, to estimate the damage. On the return of the deputation we found that only one sheep had been worried, and an old tup severely wounded. The fact seemed to be clearly brought home to Mr. Price's dog Randal, and to Mr. Tim's dog Flash—and "as, by the laws of this and every other well-governed realm, the crime of murder, more especially when aggravated, &c., is, &c.," preparations were instantly made for carrying the law into effect. Indeed, no other expiation but blood for blood seemed likely to pacify the exasperated Highlanders. Tickler, however, interceded for the lives of both culprits, maintaining, in favor of Randal, that he was born and bred a fighting dog, and that, therefore, to put him to death for such an offence as this now laid to his charge, would be to fly in the very face of nature. His defence of Flash was not equally successful—and indeed it terminated with be-

* A London pugilist of some notoriety.—M. † Napoleon's favorite surgeon.—M.

seeching the jury to recommend him to mercy. But he took occasion, at the same time, to observe, that, in point of law, Mr. Tims might recover the price from Haggart. Here Mr. Odoherty expressed some doubts as to Mr. Tim's success before the Sheriff, maintaining that a dog-seller is not liable to repayment of the price on a dog's fondness for mutton being discovered, unless special warrandice from that particular vice is expressly given. Tickler, on the other hand, was clearly of opinion, that a fair price infers warrandice of every kind, besides steadiness to fur, feather, and flint. The full discussion, however, of this difficult subject was reserved for a future occasion—nor should we have mentioned it now, had it not been that both Tickler and Odoherty are such high authorities, they having written the two best treatises extant on the Game Laws. Our interpreter by this time returned to his countrymen, and succeeded in "smoothing the raven down of their darkness till it smiled." They joined our party in an amicable manner, and we all ratified the treaty of peace over a flowing quech. Indeed, we, whom it is not easy to humbug, could not help having our suspicions, that the whole story of the worried sheep was got up for the occasion, and that these bashful Celts preferred, as it were, storming our intrenchments to get at the grouse and whisky, to that more pacific and more regular approach which they were prevented from adopting by their well-known national modesty.

On returning to the tent, we found that Kempferhausen and Buller of Brazennose had stolen away from the scene of strife, and had been for some time actually playing a pair of formidable knives and forks on the grouse and venison, thus taking the start, in no very handsome manner, of the rest of the party, who had probably as good appetites, and certainly better manners, than themselves. When we were all seated again, "Pretty well, Master Kempferhausen," cried Odoherty, "for a young gentleman with a toothache." Meanwhile, John of Sky kept pacing round the tent, and from his bag-pipes, ornamented with a hundred streamers, blew such soul-ennobling din, that each man felt his stomach growing more capacious within him, and the chairman forthwith ordered a round of mountain-dew. How the dinner came at last to a termination, we never could discover; but the best of friends must part, and so felt we when the last tureen of grouse disappeared. A slight breeze had by this time providentially sprung up among the hills; and as not a wind could blow without our tent standing in its way, and as the lower canvas had been dexterously furled up by Odoherty, a grateful coolness stole over our saloon, and nothing seemed wanting to complete our happiness, but a bowl of good cold rum-punch.*

* Rum punch, made of one part of rum to five of cold sherbet, is the peculiar drink of Glasgow.—M.

We had not been so improvident as to let the baggage-wagon leave Edinburgh without a ten-gallon cask of rum (Potts of Glasgow), and a gross of lemons, individually lodged in paper; and Bailie Jarvie had been busily employed for some time past (though we were all too well occupied to miss him) in manufacturing, not a bowl, but a tub of punch, from the waters of that clear cold spring, which no sun could affect. "I would like to lay my lugs in't," cried the Shepherd, in his most impassioned manner, when the tub appeared; and indeed we all crowded round it with as much eagerness as ever we ourselves have seen parched soldiers in India crowd round an unexpected tank. Dr. Scott, who is constantly armed at all points, requested Peter's man John to bring him his surtout, and slyly asking Mr. Buller of Brazennose if he had ever seen the small dwarf Caribbee lemon, brought to light, from the dark depth of these unfathomable pockets, half a dozen ripe marriageable limes, which we permitted him to squeeze into the tub with all the grace, dignity, and dexterity of a Glasgow Maker.

Of course we again drank the Prince Regent's health, and all the toasts usual at public meetings. The Chairman then rose, and in a speech, of which we regret it is impossible for us at present to give even a sketch, proposed

The Earl of Fife.

When the pealing thunders of applause had in a few minutes ceased, Odoherty rose, and with that charming modesty which so sets off his manifold accomplishments, said, that if not disagreeable to the company, he would recite a few verses which he had that morning composed, as he was drinking a cup of whisky and water at a spring in the mountains behind Mar-Lodge.

POEM.

Recited by Odoherty at a Grand Dinner-Party of the Contributors, in their Tent near Mar-Lodge, on the 12th of August, 1819.

1.

Hail to thy waters! softly-flowing Dee!
Hail to their shaded pure transparency!
Hail to the royal oak and mountain-pine,
With whose reflected pride those waters shine!

2.

And hail, ye central glories of the plain!
All hail, ye towers ancestral of the Thane!
Clear as the Scottish stream whose honor flows,
Broad as the Scottish grove whose bounty grows.

3.

Can he whose eye on many a field of war
Has traced the progress of thy lord, Braemar,
Pass, yet not bless, this grove's majestic sweep,
Where worth can still expand, though valor sleep.

4.

Souls of primeval heroes! nobly won
Is the repose of your heroic son!
Sure in those awful hours of patriot strife,
Macbeth's destroyer nerved the soul of Fife.

5.

A softer influence now your spirits send
Into the bosom of "the poor man's friend"—
Keys, stars, and crosses, are but glittering stuff;
The genuine jewel is THE HEART OF DUFF.

It is impossible to conceive what effect was given to these lines (which are certainly better than any of Mr. W. Fitzgerald's* or Mr. James Thomson's) by the graceful and spirited elocution of the Standard-bearer; and Seward of Christchurch, now above all foolish prejudices, and following the impulses of his own fine classical taste and feeling, vowed that he had never heard more sweetly-pretty verses recited in the Sheldon Theatre, Oxford, at a Commemoration. On Odoherty's health and verses being drunk, that excellent poet again rose, and begged leave to call upon his friend, the Ettrick Shepherd, for a poem or a song. Says the Shepherd, "Ye hae a' eaten a gude dinner I'm thinking—but recollect it was me that killed the sawmon, and I'll now gie you an elegy, or eulogy, on him—deil tak me gin I ken the difference. But I canna stan', I maun recest sitting."

SONG TO A SALMON.

By the Ettrick Shepherd.

I.

Thou bonny fish from the far sea
Whose waves unwearied roll
In primitive immensity
Aye buffeting the pole!
From millions of thy silvery kind
In that wide waste that dwell
Thou only power and path didst find,
To reach this lonely dell.

* This is he of whom Byron wrote—
"Shall hoarse Fitzgerald bawl
His creaking couplets in a tavern hall?"
At the annual dinner of the Literary Fund, in London, he used to mount on one of the tables and recite verses of his own composing, greatly to the amusement of all who heard him. In the "Rejected Addresses," written by Horace and James Smith, there is an excellent parody on one of these compositions.—M.

II.

That wond'rous region was thy own,
That home upon the deep—
To thee were all the secrets known
In that dark breast that sleep—
Thou, while thy form midst heave and toss
Had still the billows play been,
Perhaps knewest more than Captain Ross,
Or yet than Captain Sabine.*

III.

Yea, Fish! nor wise alone wast thou,
But happy—what's far better—
Ne'er did thy fins to Barrow bow,
They feared not Croker's letter—
But far and wide their strokes they plied.
Smooth thro' the ocean smoother,
Nor drab-clad Gifford chilled their pride,
Nor Leslie's buff and blue there.†

IV.

And now, my Beauty! bold and well
Thy pilgrim-course hath been—
For thou, like Wordsworth's Peter Bell,
Hast gazed on Aberdeen!
And all those sweetest banks between,
By Invercauld's broad tree,
The world of beauty hast thou seen
That sleeps upon the Dee.

V.

There oft in silence clear and bright
Thou layest a shadow still,
In some green nook where with delight
Joined in the mountain-rill,
There, 'mid the water's scarce-heard boom,
Didst thou float, rise, and sink,
While o'er the breathing banks of broom
The wild deer came to drink.

VI.

Vain sparry grot and verdant cave
The stranger to detain—
For thou wast wearied of the wave
And loud voice of the main;
And naught thy heart could satisfy
But those clear gravelly rills,
Where once a young and happy fry
Thou danced among the hills!

* Captains Ross and Sabine, engaged at this time in trying to discover the northwest passage.—M.

† Barrow and Croker were then officials in the Admiralty at London. Gifford edited the Quarterly Review, which has a drab-colored cover, and Leslie was contributing to the Edinburgh, which was clothed in the buff and blue of the Whigs.—M.

VII.

The river roaring down the rock,
The fierce and foaming linn,
Essayed to stay thee with the shock,
The dark and dizzy din—
With wilier malice nets did twist
To perfect thy undoing,
But all those dangers hast thou miss'd,
True to thy destined ruin!

VIII.

Sure, no inglorious death is thine!
Death said I? Thou'lt ne'er die,
But swim upon a Poet's line
Down to Eternity,—
While, on our board, we'll all allow,
O! odd Fish bright and sheen!
A prime Contributor art thou
To BLACKWOOD'S MAGAZINE!

It was some hours before we could prevail on any of our friends to favor us with another poem or song, naturally so much awed were they all by the splendid efforts of a Hogg and an Odoherty. At last Tickler, to get rid of unceasing importunities from every side, chanted to the bagpipe the following song, which excited one feeling of regret that its length should have been in an inverse ratio to that of the singer.

TICKLER'S SONG TO A BROTHER SPORTSMAN AT A DISTANCE.

1.

Though I rove through the wilds of majestic Braemar,
'Mid the haunts of the buck and the roe,
O! oft are my thoughts with my dear friends afar,
'Mid the black-cocks of Minnard that go.

2.

O sweet upon bonny Loch-Fyne be your weather,
As is mine on the banks of the Dee!
And light be your steps o'er Kilberry's braw heather,
As on Fife's mine own footsteps can be!

3.

May the scent still lie warm on the heath of Argyle,
Thy pointers stand staunch, and unerring thine aim—
As I bring down the birds right and left—why I smile
To think that my friend may be doing the same.

4.

Nor your trophies alone is my fancy revealing!
Well I picture the scores that have bled
Long—oh! long ere this hour, round the laird's lonely sheiling,
That murderous lair, Caddenhead!

5.

Every shot that we fire, as it peals through the air,
I consider a kind of a greeting—
There is naught of forgetfulness, here, John! nor there—
Taste your flask to our blythe winter-meeting!

Mr. Seward said he had never sung a single stave in his life, and called on Buller of Brazennose, to confirm his statement; but he said, that since the example of simple recitative had been set, he should not hesitate to favor us with a copy of verses which he had written last year for Sir Roger Newdyate's prize—subject, *the Coliseum.* His verses had not indeed gained the prize, but flattering testimony had been borne to their merit by his tutor, Mr. Goodenough,* and many other exquisite judges.

THE COLISEUM.

Ye circling walls, whose melancholy bound,
In lonely echoes, whisper all around!
Ye towers antique, whose shapeless shadows tell
Of Roman glory the forlorn farewell!
Dark o'er the sod with heroes' dust commix'd
Ye frown in monumental silence fix'd!
Ah! could a voice to your faint forms be given
By some supernal sympathy of heaven,
Deep were the descant of departed years,
And marble groans would blend with nature's tears!
The pensive pilgrim bending by the shrine,
Where all is mortal, and yet half divine,
Would mix a sigh as plaintive as your own,
O'er the dim relics of the splendors gone,
Mix with the sobbings of the wind-stirred trees,
Whose roots are in th' imperial palaces!
See!—or does fancy, from her fetters freed,
With airy visions the fond eyeballs feed—
Airy, yet bright, as they which lore sublime
Drew to the enthusiast of the elder time,
In rich redundance of imparted light,
All radiant, rushing on the Augur's sight,
And mocking with their glare the temple's mystic night
Majestic dreams of Rome's primeval day.
Oh list and answer! Oh! &c.

Unfortunately as Mr. Seward warmed in his recitation, he began to speak with such extreme volubility, that to have taken down his words accurately, would have required nothing less than the presence of that PRINCE OF STENOGRAPHERS, MR. JOHN DOW HIMSELF.† So that we hope that Mr. Seward will yield to the solicitations of the Contributors, and give his poem to the world. The next we knocked down was Dr. Scott, who, in compliance with Bailie Jarvie's earnest request, favored us with the following ballad of his own composition, at present the most popular ditty in the west of Scotland!

* Son of Dr. Goodenough, Bishop of Carlisle.—M.

† Dow was the[illegible] for many years after, the best short-hand writer in Edinburgh.—M.

THE MEMORY OF SANDY FERGUSON.

Written, Composed, and Sung, by James Scott, Esq., *of Millar-street, Glasgow.*

1.

If e'er at Peggy Jardine's it was your luck to dwell,
It is odds but ye knew Sandy Ferguson well;
If you opened but *your* window, you could not choose but see
The lemons in *his* window shining one, two, three.

2.

Ochon! for Sandy Ferguson! the lemons still are there—
The jargonelle and pippin and the carvy-seed so fair;
But in spite of figs and oranges, and stalks of sugar candy,
I turn not in—I stagger by—ochon! ochon for Sandy.

3.

A wee wee chap upon the bowl, then I pray you to put in,
And to leave a drop of heeltap I'd hold it for a sin;
For though sad it be and silent—yet a bumper it must be
That ye fill unto the kind ghost of Sandy with me.

4.

There were prouder on the mart—there were gayer on the mall,
There were louder at *the What-you-please*, and wittier at *the Stall*—
But I will give my heart's blood, though every drop were brandy,
If either *Stall* or *What-you-please* knew such a heart as Sandy!

5.

Then fill ye up your bumpers, friends, and join your hands around,
And drink your measure heartily, that sorrow may be drowned;
For what avails our sorrow, friends, the best of beings maun die,
And here's a woeful proof of that—*the Memory of Sandy!*

There is nothing more worthy of observation and praise in the character of that precious fluid, punch, than its power of amalgamation. Under its benign influence the most conflicting qualities become reconciled; and a party of weak, strong, sweet, and sour people, form, like the "charmed drink" which they imbibe, one safe and agreeable whole. This cannot be authorizedly predicted of any other liquid comprehended within the range of our wide experience. We had seen Thracian quarrels around all sorts of "Pocula," except punch-bowls; but there seems to be a divine air breathed from the surface of a circle of china, or even of stone or wood, when a waveless well of punch sleeps within, that soothes every ruder feeling into peace, and awakens in the soul all the finer emotions of sensibility and friendship. We are satisfied, that if punch were the universal tipple of Europe, there would be no more war—especially if all the Continental States were to employ a judicious intermixture of Lime-juice. In our Tent had been assembled for several hours men of different countries, education, and pursuits; and who shall pretend to know all the infinite varieties of principle and opinion that must have been collected within that narrow circumference? Yet all was perfect harmony—the Shepherd sat down with the Dentist—and the Cockney may be said to have played in the Editor's den.

Politics had been drowned in punch; and the following list of toasts, which were all received with boundless acclamations during the evening, will show that we looked only to SPORTING CHARACTERS,

> "And left all meaner things
> To low ambition and the pride of kings."

Mr. H. Mackenzie, ... by Dr. Morris.
Mr. Walter Scott, ... by Ettrick Shepherd.
Mr. Francis Jeffrey, ... by Mr. Wastle.
Duke of Wellington, ... by Mr. Odoherty.
Mr. James Machel, ... by Mr. Mullion.
Mr. Croker, ... by the Editor.
Mr. Canning, ... by Mr. Seward.
Mr. John Hamilton, ... by Mr. Tickler.
Collector M'Nair, ... by Mr. Jarvie.
Mr. Coke of Norfolk, ... by Mr. Buller.
Mr. Wordsworth, ... by Mr. Kempferhausen.
Sir Dan. Donnelly,* .... by Mr. Tims.
Mr. Thomas Belcher, ... by Mr. Price.

We should think very meanly of ourselves were we to attempt to impose on public credulity, by asserting that we have a perfectly distinct recollection of the latter part of the evening. We do, however, clearly remember that Kempferhausen who had most heroically endured a gnawing tooth-ache for many hours, finally submitted his jaw to the algebraical hand of Dr. Scott, who was not long of extracting the square root—and that the ingenious German having soon after incautiously gone into the open air to admire the moon, returned to his seat with one cheek whose magnitude was well entitled to hold the other in derision, and whose colors were, indeed, truly prismatical. Such a face has rarely been seen—and we may say to Dr. Scott of his patient, in the words of his great namesake,

> "Alas! the mother that him bore
> Had scarcely known her child."

Of this subject Dr. Morris made on the spot a most spirited

* "Immediately after his victory over Oliver, Donelly set off in a chariot and four to Brighton, where he was knighted by a Prince Regent. He is therefore, now, Sir Daniel Donelly."—*Irish Paper*. Donelly was a strong, hard-fisted Irishman, a carpenter by trade, who had fought with Oliver, an English pugilist, in July, 1819, and beaten him. On returning to Dublin, Donelly opened a public-house, and used to relate, to gaping and admiring auditors, how the Prince Regent had sent for him, after the fight, and knighted him. A couple of years' hard drinking finished him, and he died in February, 1820,—his immediate cause of illness being thirty-seven tumblers of punch taken in one sitting! Maginn, in Blackwood for May, 1820, gave a "Luctus for the death of Sir Dan. Donelly," in which learning and wit were largely employed and well blended.—M.

sketch, which he intends to finish in oil, and present to us, that when Kempferhausen returns to the Continent, we, his Scottish friends, may still retain the image of one of our most enthusiastic contributors. We have likewise a confused but delightful remembrance of the whole party assembled at the Tent door, (while the domestics were removing the furniture and preparing beds) in solemn contemplation of the starry heavens. Never before did we so feel the genius of Burns as when looking at our old friend the moon and her horns.

" Whether she had three or four,
We could na tell."

The Shepherd most vehemently asserted that he saw the comet—and began spouting some obscure and opaque verses to her as extemporaneous, which were, however, instantly detected by the tenacious memory of Tickler to have been written in 1811, when the pastoral bard was flirting with the long tail of the celestial beauty of that year. It was in vain for him to appeal to a late number of Constable's Magazine, which no mortal had seen, and which the Shepherd himself was forced to acknowledge had a sad trick of trying*

"To mak auld claes
Appear amaist as well as new !"

After this, there surely must have been a match at hop-step-and-jump between Tickler and Dr. Scott—unless, indeed, it were on our part all a dream. Yet we cannot get rid of the impression on our minds, that we saw the latter making most surprising bounds among the heather, and coming down with " a thud" posterior to each essay —while the former cleared the ground like one of those gigantic shadowy figures that are seen stalking across the hills at sunset. There was also a very anxious search among the heather for Peter's man John, and Wastle's man Thomas, who were nowhere to be found—and though the whole party, at one time, agreed that they heard a snore from a jungle of brackens, we tried in vain to start the game. We afterwards discovered that the sound must have proceeded from one of the numerous Highlanders stretched in their plaids in each direction around the Tent; for our two gentlemen had, under the auspices of the Thane's gillies, paid a nocturnal visit to a Still at work no great way off, from which it was not till a decent hour after sunrise that they groped their way back to the encampment. The last thing we recollect before going to bed, was Odoherty's selling to Mr. Tims, for £45, his gun, which we have good reason to know he had purchased at the General Agency Office,

* The letter from Hogg, a copy of which is given in the present edition, will show that even up to the last year of his life, he was addicted to this "sad trick."—M.

Edinburgh, for £4, 4s.; but we must also add, to the credit of the Adjutant, that with his accustomed generosity he returned £5 of the purchase-money. A general anxiety also prevailed among the party, before bundling in, to send presents of birds to some of our chief absent Contributors; but it appeared that we had, "gentle and simple," devoured upwards of sixty brace, and none but the Editor's pack remained, which was judicially retained for the relish at breakfast.

We have no room, now, to describe our feelings on awaking in the morning. For some minutes we could not form even the most distant conjecture where or among whom we were; but as the mist gradually rose up from our brain, and freed our memory from obfuscation, there came upon us a pleasant dawning of the truth; and on beholding the bold nose and piercing eyes of Tickler looking out from below an old worsted stocking tastefully wreathed into a night-cap, with a long tail swaggering behind—and the fine Spanish face of the Standard-bearer enjoying a magnificent yawn under a veteran foraging-cap—we were at once let in to a perfect knowledge of our situation, and we all then sprung from our heather-bed together, just as John of Sky blew up his pipes to

"Hey! Johnnie Coup, are ye waking yet?
Or are your drums a-beating yet?
If ye were waking, I would wait
To gang to the Grouse i' the morning."

Christopher in the Tent.

No. II.—SEPTEMBER, 1819.

We have no wish to inform the public of all the difficulties we had to encounter in bringing out the last Number of our valuable Miscellany.* It was on the evening of the 16th of August that we arrived in Edinburgh from our Tent; and as we had to ship off to London on the 20th, the hurry-skurry and the helter-skelter at the Printing-Office may be more easily imagined than described. Immediately on stepping out of the Aberdeen coach, we came bob against Mr. Blackwood, who exclaimed, "My gracious! Mr. Editor, this is a fine prank you have been playing us all! The cry for copy is most terrible—dog on it . . . . But goodness be praised, here you are—come away up to Ambrose's."

We soon found ourselves sitting before a sirloin of beef and a pot of porter; and Mr. Ambrose, who saw there was something in the wind more than usual, brought in the Steel Pen, our best japan ink, and a quire of wire-wove. Having travelled much in coaches during the early part of our life, we even now ate our dinner as in fear of the horn;† so that in less than quarter of an hour the sirloin was removed with a deep gash on his side, and the empty porter pot rose from the table at a touch. We scarcely took time to wipe our mouths, and fell to, "totis viribus," like a giant refreshed, to the "Twelfth of August," an article which we finished at a sitting, and which we are happy to find has given very great and general satisfaction. Ebony, meanwhile, lost not a moment in running down to the Printing-Office with a packet we had brought from the Tent—and on his return, by way of showing his satisfaction, he whispered mine host to place near our right hand a small bowl of cold punch, which a Glasgow gentleman in the adjacent parlor had been kind enough to manufacture; and we felt it to be no less our duty to ourselves than

* The whole of Blackwood for September, 1819, was devoted to this article relating the sayings and doings of North and his companions in the Tent. There evidently was a number of miscellaneous articles already in type, and, with some ingenuity, these were worked into the narrative,—occasionally, however, without much regard to consistency. The articles so introduced occupied about half of the September number.—M.

† This was in the olden days of mail and stage-coach travelling, before railways were. It may be here incidentally noticed that railway travelling, as we have it now, did not commence in England, until the 15th September, 1830, when the Liverpool and Manchester railway was opened, with great state.—M.

to Messrs. Blackwood and Ambrose, to take a bumper at the close of every paragraph, which may possibly account for their being somewhat shorter than is usual in our full, free, and flowing style of composition.

For three days—and we may almost add nights, there was no occasion to say to us "sæpe vertas stylum," for we boldly dashed at every thing, from Don Juan to Slack, the Pugilist; and flew in a moment from the Cape-of-Good-Hope to the Pyramids of Egypt.* "My gracious, your versatility is most fearsome," murmured our astonished publisher: "It will be one of our best Numbers after all." The truth is, that we felt nettled by the remark of Dr. Morris, in his "Peter's Letters to his Kinsfolk," that we only laid plans for others to execute,† and were determined to show the physician and all the rest of the world,—first, that we are no sinecurists,—and, secondly, that our seat is not at a Board under Government.

We are not personally known at the Printing-Office, so we hobbled down one midnight along with Ebony‡ to witness the operations. What motion of many twinkling hands among compositors! What display of brawny arms among pressmen! What a stir of printer's-devils! "The Editor's MS. is growing worse and worse every month," said a long sallow-faced stripling, with a page of the Twelfth of August close to his eyes, as if he were going to apply a bandage—"What makes the young lads ay sae sair on Hairy Brougham,‖ I wonder," quoth another—"Here's another slap at Macvey," said a third, "that's really too bad." "I would not grudge sitting up all night at another Canto of the Mad Banker of Amsterdam," added a fourth—but not to be tedious, we were pleased to observe, that on the whole a spirit of good humor and alacrity pervaded the Office, and above all, that that vile Jacobinical spirit, unfortunately but too prevalent among persons of their profession, had given way beneath the monthly influence of our principles; and that the inflammatory and seditious lucubrations of the Yellow Dwarf, Examiner,§ Scotsman, and other bawling demagogues, the

* It was even so. Besides the articles already mentioned (page 10), the August number had papers on the opening Cantos of Don Juan, Emigration to the Cape of Good-Hope, the Pyramid of Caphrenes, (opened by Belzoni, in 1818, and found to contain the bones of a cow or bull,) and the conquest, in the prize-ring, of Broughton by Slack, the butcher.—M.

† In Peter's Letters (Vol. ii. p. 225,) we find it thus written :—"It is not known who the Editor is—I do not see how that secret can ever be divulged, as things now stand—but my friend Wastle tells me that he is an obscure man, almost continually confined to his apartments by rheumatism, whose labors extend to little more than correcting proof-sheets, and drawing up plans, which are mostly executed by other people."—M.

‡ "And I looked, and behold a man clothed in plain apparel stood in the door of his house : and I saw his name, and the number of his name ; and his name was as it had been the color of Ebony, and his number was the number of a maiden, when the days of the year of her virginity have expired."—*Chaldee Manuscript*, Chap. I., v. 3. In this Oriental prolixity was mention made of Mr. Blackwood, No. 17 Princes-street, Edinburgh.—M.

‖ A bitter attack, "On a late Attempt to White-wash Mr. Brougham" was one of the articles in Blackwood for August, 1819. There was sarcastic mention, in another paper, on Macvey Napier's dissertation on Lord Bacon.—M.

§ The Yellow Dwarf was a violent weekly journal, published in London by an ultra-Radical, named Wooler. At the same time, The Examiner was conducted by Leigh Hunt.—M.

fruits of whose doctrines are now being reaped by the deluded people of the north of England, were spoken of with indignation and disgust.

We had slyly ordered a few gallons of punch to be brought down to the office, to give a fillup to the worthy workmen at the close of their labors, and an excellent article might be written—indeed shall be—entitled, "The Humors of a Printing-Office;" but for the present, our readers must rest satisfied with the following song, which we understand was written by a devil not exceeding twelve years, an instance of precocious genius unrivalled in the history of Pandemonium.

CARMEN DIABOLICUM.

Sung in Oliver & Boyd's *Printing-Office,* on the Midnight between the* 19*th and* 20*th of August,* 1819.

SOLO, BY BOWZY BEELZEBUB.

1.

When the vessel she is ready, all her rigging right and steady,
  And the fine folks arranged on the shore,
Then they shove her from the dock with a thunder of a shock,
  And the ord'nance salutes with a roar;
But before the hausers slip to give sea-room to the ship,
  To propitiate the winds, there is thrown
A flask of generous red, all along the bowsprit shed—
  Then God bless her, they cry, and she's gone—

Grand Chorus of Devils.

God bless her—God bless her—she's gone—
  With a yo-hee-vo.

2.

SOLO, BY TIPSY THAMMUZ.

Thus when our latest sheet, to make Ebony complete,
  Is revised, and thrown off, and stitched in,
And the Editor so staunch is preparing for his launch,
  Then he plunges his hand in the Bin.
"Now let every jolly soul lay his ears in the punch bowl,
  "And be ready," he cries, with a shout—
"That our enemies may know, when they hear our yo-hee-vo—
  We'll play hell† with them all when we're out."

Grand Chorus of Devils.

"We'll play hell, we'll play hell, when we're out—
  With a yo-hee-vo!"

* At this time Blackwood was printed by Oliver & Boyd. In 1820, it was transferred to James Ballantyne's Office, where it remained for more than thirty years.—M.

† Pope says, of a fashionable preacher.

"And never mentions *Hell* 'fore ears polite."

This, we think, is excellent advice, both to the Clergy and the Laity, even in less refined society: but the reader will bear in mind that this Chorus was written by a devil, and sung by a batch of devils. These local allusions are, therefore, quite in place, and are *sanctioned* also by the authority of Milton.—C. N.

Well, out came the Magazine, as usual, on the 20th, when, according to Hogg's celebrated sonnet,

> "One breathless hush expectant reigns from shore to shore."

But such is the strong inconsistency of all human desires, that no sooner was the load off our shoulders, than we almost wished it on again, and began to wonder what we should do with ourselves for the next fortnight. It was not mere ennui that beset us, for (since the story will out, it is best we ourselves tell it) during our absence we had suffered a domestic affliction which time may alleviate, but never can wholly cure. For home had now no charms for us—that lofty home once so still and pleasant, fourteen flats nearer heaven than the grovelling ground-floors of ordinary men—and commanding a magnificent view, not only of the whole New Town of Edinburgh, but of the kingdom of Fife in front, to the west far as the towers of Snowdon, and to the east the sail-studded expanse of the noble Frith, and the rich corn-fields of Lothian,

> "The empire of Edinburgh, to the farthest Bass."

Our housekeeper* had eloped with an English Bagman, who had met the honest woman as she was coming home from market with a couple of herrings in a kail-blade, and had been but too successful in filling her imagination with those romantic notions of love and happiness which that eloquent and accomplished class of men know so well to instil into the too susceptible heart. The following letter was lying on the little tri-clawed table at which we had so often drunk tea together, and occasionally, perhaps, "sterner stuff,"—and ours, you may be assured, was not a soul to peruse it without tears.

"Best and Kindest of Masters,—Several nights before you read this, my fate will have been indissolubly united with that of Mr. Perkins. I am no love-sick girl, sir, of eighteen—and though I have known Mr. Perkins only a few days, yet I have not entered rashly into this solemn league and covenant. I have observed in him a truly devout and serious spirit, and have no doubt that he will turn out so as to satisfy all my most anxious desires. Our marriage is a marriage of souls—and as our religious principles are to a tittle the same, I trust that, unworthy as we are, some portion of sublunary happiness may be vouchsafed to us. Mr. Perkins, it is true, is some years younger than myself, being about thirty-five, but he looks considerably older than that, and has a sobriety and discretion far beyond his years.† I know well that there will be much evil-speaking throughout Scot-

* Of this very extraordinary woman we shall give a short memoir in an early Number, accompanied with specimens of her compositions, both in prose and verse. Her natural talents were great, and her literary attainments by no means contemptible. She was lost to us in the 57th year of her age, a dangerous time of life to a female of cultivated mind, and rather too strict ideas on the subject of religion.—C. N. [An unfulfilled promise.—M.]

† It is an ascertained fact, that although a young man rarely, with his own free will, marries an old woman, be she spinster or widow: persons of the female sex are never found to have an antipathy to a marriage with men very much their juniors in age. The fortitude and resignation with which an old maid of forty submits to a matrimonial alliance with a bachelor or widower of twenty-five, are very exemplary.—M.

land about this matter,—and that the public, censorious on people far my superiors in all things, will not spare poor Grizzy Turnbull—but my heart knoweth its own purity,—and the idle gossip of an idle world will soon die away.

"And now, my ever dear master, let me confide to you a secret which I have treasured up in my heart these last twenty years—years, alas! of misery and of happiness, never again to return. SINCE THE FIRST NIGHT I SLEPT BENEATH YOUR ROOF I HAVE LOVED, MADLY LOVED YOU! yes, the confession is made on paper at last—written over and over again, crossed and recrossed in every possible way, as it long has been, by the trembling hand of passion on my heart of hearts! O! my sweet master (surely that word may be allowed to me in our parting hour), for twenty years, come the Martinmas term, have I doted upon thee! yes! I have watched the progress of thy rheumatism with feelings which even thine own matchless pen would fail to analyze! Lord Byron himself could not paint the conflict of passions that turmoiled within my bosom, when, under the guidance of that angel of a man, Dr. Balfour, I rubbed that dear rheumatic leg on the sofa! O! our little tea-drinkings! . . . . but in the sweet words of Campbell,

'Be hushed, my dark spirit, for wisdom condemns,
When the faint and the feeble deplore,
Be firm as a rock of the ocean, that stems
A thousand wild waves on the shore!
Through the scowl of mischance, and the smile of disdain,
Let thy front be unaltered, thy courage elate,
YEA, EVEN THE NAME I HAVE WORSHIPPED IN VAIN,
Shall awake not a throb of remembrance again;
To bear is to conquer our fate!!!'

"Mr. Perkins must now be all in all to me—but though I will cherish him in my bosom, no code of laws, either human or divine, passes sentence of oblivion on vanished hours of innocent enjoyment—and be assured, that if I be ever blessed with a family, my second son (for I must call the first after its grandfather) shall bear the christian and surname of my too, too dear master. But away with delightful dreams, never, perhaps, to be realized! and with such feelings as a new-born infant might avow, I subscribe myself, yours as fit only,

"GRACE PERKINS.

"*14th of August,*
"*Written in the dear little blue parlor.*"

Had this unexpected blow fallen upon us during the bustle of winter, we could have borne it. But at this solitary season, there was nothing to lighten that load of grief,—in the words of Michael Angelo,

El importune et grave selma,

that absolutely bowed us down to the earth,—a grief the more acute, from the sad conviction, that our inestimable Housekeeper had been partly driven into Mrs. Perkins, by a hopeless and therefore undivulged passion for the Editor of this Magazine. To kill thought and time, we lay in bed till eleven; then ate some muffins from M'Ewan's, "which did coldly furnish up our breakfast-table," and hobbled down the Mound, witless where to go. All was silence and desolation. Not a soul going into the panorama of Algiers; and the long line of

Prince's Street, from St. John's chapel to the Prince Regent Bridge,* unbroken, save perhaps by some coach wheeling along its pile of dust-covered outsides. At the corner of some cross street sat some hopeless fruiterer, with her basket of gooseberries, "alas! all too ripe;" while perhaps some unlucky school-boy, who was drawling his dull holidays in town, hesitatingly eyed the small red hairy circlets, and had the resolution to pass by with his halfpenny in his hand. The linen-blinds shaded the shop-windows, in winter and spring so gorgeously displayed, and not one gay and buzzing insect was seen to enter or issue from the deserted hive. The Middle Shop itself, two little months ago, before our shoes were old in which we went to the moors,

"So full of laughing faces and bright eyes,"

stood empty and silent, save when some summer-stranger from the South came in to ask for a copy of the last Number of Blackwood's Magazine or of Peter's Letters, or when we ourselves hobbled in, and received an unwitnessed greeting from our publisher, whom the well-known sound of our foot had brought forth with a pen behind his ear, from the Sanctum Sanctorum. Even in Ambrose's the sound of the grinders was low. The ordinary in Barclay's tavern, at which we have seen thirty pair of knives and forks at play, did well if it exhibited half-a-dozen mouths; and the matchless weekly suppers of the Dilettanti at Young's (to which we are sometimes admitted), had, in the heat of the weather, melted quite away. True, the Theatre was open, but it was likewise empty; and O'Neill, Farren, Abbott, and Jones, sighed, wept, doted, laughed, and whisked about in vain. Would you go down to the sea-side? There some solitary bathing machine voided its nudity into the waves, or some parsimonious bachelor sat wiping his hairy length on a stone; while, perchance, one of the London packets sailed briskly from the pier, and seemed soon to carry away into the dim distance the scanty remains of the population of Edinburgh.

In this state of mind, it would have been folly to remain in town; so we resolved once more to join the Tent, which had now taken root in the Highlands; and while trying to take courage to buy a ticket in the Perth Breakneck,† we strolled into our favorite snuff and tobacco shop, and filled our cannister with Princes' mixture and segars. There, while admiring the beautiful arrangements of pipes, boxes, &c., and regarding with a friendly affection the light, airy, and graceful figure of the fair Miss Fanny Forman,‡ we mentally indited the following lines:—

* Localities in Edinburgh.—M. † An appropriate name for a very fast-going stage-coach.—M.

‡ In a previous number of Maga, a sonnet by Mr. Gillies had celebrated the charms of Miss Forman, who kept a tobacconist's shop in Prince's-street, Edinburgh.—M.

LINES TO MISS FANNY FORMAN, ON BIDDING HER FAREWELL.

By the Veiled EDITOR *of Blackwood's Magazine.*

I.

OH! the grass it springs green on the Street of the gay,
And the mall 'tis a desolate sight:
And the beaux and the belles they are all far away,
And the city's a wilderness quite.
And I too will wander—at dawn of the day
I will leave the dull city behind;
I will tread the free hills, and my spirits shall play,
As of old, in the spring of the wind.

II.

Yet, a lowly voice whispers, that, not as of old,
Shall to me the glad spirit be given:
Tho' the lakes beaming broad in their glens I behold,
And the hills soaring blue in the heaven:
That the kind hand of Nature in vain shall unfold
All her banner of innocent glee—
For the depths of my soul in despondence are rolled,
And her mirth has no music for me.

III.

Yes, o'er valley and mountain, where'er I may go,
That voice whispers sadly and true,
I shall bear, lovely Fanny! my burden of woe—
Cruel maid—my remembrance of you!
As some cloud whose dim fleeces of envious snow,
The rays of the evening-star cover,
Thy memory still a soft dimness shall throw,
O'er the languishing breast of thy lover.

While we were casting about in this way whom should we see turning the corner of Hanover-street in an elegant dennet, and at a noble trot, but our excellent friend Mr. John Ballantyne?* We thought he had still been on the Continent, and have seldom been more gratified than by the unexpected apparition. There he was, as usual, arrayed in the very pink of knowingness—grey frock and pebble buttons, Buckskins, top-boots, &c.—the whip—for Old

* John Ballantyne was next brother to James, Scott's printer and confidential friend, and like him, was in the secret of the Waverley Novels. In 1809, he was started by Scott and his brother, in the publishing house of "John Ballantyne & Company," at Edinburgh, in opposition to Constable. One of his first publications was Scott's Lady of the Lake. After the success of Waverley, he published a wretched novel, "The Widow's Lodgings." The publishing business did not succeed, and the firm was dissolved. John Ballantyne then became an auctioneer, a business for which he was well qualified. In 1817, Scott contributed several minor poems to a periodical of his called "The Sale Room." Ballantyne died June, 1821, aged 45. Scott attended his funeral, and said, "I feel as if there would be less sunshine for me from this day forth." Lockhart says, "He was a quick, active, intrepid little fellow; and in society so very lively and amusing, so full of fun and merriment; such a thoroughly light-hearted droll, all over quaintness and humorous mimicry; and moreover, such a keen and skilful devotee to all manner of field-sports, from fox-hunting to badger-bating inclusive, that it was no wonder he should have made a favorable impression on Scott." And again, "Of his style of story-telling it is sufficient to say that the late Charles Mathews's 'Old Scotch Lady,' was but an imperfect copy of the original, which the great imitator first heard in my presence from his lips."—M.

Mortality needs no whip—dangling from the horn behind—and that fine young grew, Dominie Sampson, capering round about him in the madness of his hilarity.* Whenever we met last spring we used to have at least a half-hour's doleful chat on the progress and symptoms of our respective rheumatisms—but Ballantyne now cut that topic short in a twinkling, assuring us he had got rid of the plague entirely—and, indeed, nobody could look in his merry face without seeing that it was so. We never croak to people that are in sound health—and, therefore, not likely to enter into the spirit of our miseries; so, affecting an air of perfect vigor, we began to talk, in the most pompous manner, about our late exploits in the moors, regretting, at the same time, that Ballantyne had not come home in time to make one of our party on the 12th of August. "We are just off again for Braemar," said we. "The devil you are," said John, "I don't much care to go with you if you'll take me." "By all means, you delight us," said we. "Well," cried he, "what signifies bothering, come along, I'll just call at Trinity† for half a dozen clean shirts and neckcloths, and let's be off." "Done," said we, mounting to the lower cushion, "only just drive us over the way and pick up our portmanteau." No sooner said than done. In less than an hour we found ourselves, with all the cargo on board, scudding away at twelve knots an hour on the Queens-ferry road.

During the whole journey to our Tent, we were kept in a state of unflagging enjoyment by the conversation of our companion. Who, indeed, could be dull in immediate juxta-position with so delightful a compound of wit and warm-heartedness? We have heard a thousand story-tellers, but we do not remember among the whole of them more than one single individual, who can sustain the briefest comparison with our exquisite bibliopole. Even were he to be as silent as the tomb of the Capulets, the beaming eloquence of that countenance alone would be enough to diffuse a spirit of gentle jovialty over all who might come into his presence. We do not think Allan has quite done justice to Mr. Ballantyne's face, in his celebrated master-piece, "Hogg's House-heating." He has caught, indeed, the quaint, sly, archness of the grin, and the light, quick, irresistible glance of the eyes; but he has omitted entirely that fine cordial suffusion of glad, kind, honest, manly mirth, which lends the truest charm to the whole physiognomy, because it reveals the essential

* Lockhart says, "His horses were all called after heroes in Scott's poems or novels; and at this time he usually rode up to his auction on a tall milk-white hunter, yclept *Old Mortality*, attended by a leash or two of greyhounds,—Die Vernon, Jenny Dennison, &c., by name.—M.

† In John Ballantyne's latter days, he was fitting up a mansion near Kelso, which he called Walton Hall, but in 1819, he inhabited Harmony Hall, by Trinity, near the Frith of Forth. "Here," says Lockhart, "Braham quavered, and here Liston drolled his best,—here Johnstone, and Murray, and Yates, mixed jest and stave,—here Kean revelled and rioted,—and here did the Roman Kemble often play the Greek from sunset to dawn. Nor did the popular *cantatrice* or *danseuse* of the time disdain to freshen her roses, after a laborious week, amidst these Paphian bowers of Harmony Hall.—M.

elements of the character, whose index that most original physiognomy is. But the voice is the jewel—who shall ever describe its wonders? Passing at will through every note of seriousness and passion, down into the most dry, husky, vibrations of gruffness, or the most sharp feeble chirpings of old woman's querulousness, according to the minutest specialties of the character introduced for the moment upon the stage of that perpetual Aristophanic comedy; his conversation—why, Bannister, Mathews, Liston, Yates, Russel—none of them all is like John Ballantyne, when that eye of his has fairly caught its inspiration from the sparkle of his glass.*

Even here in our gig where we had neither bottle nor glass, a few puffs of one of Miss Forman's segars, as Odoherty describes them,

The true Havana smooth, and moist, and brown,

were enough to kindle and rekindle as much mirth as was consistent with the safety of the vehicle that contained us. Among other things he told us a great many capital stories about his late tour to the Netherlands, expressing, as he went on, in every particular of look, voice, and gesture, the very corporal presence and essence of his friends the Hogan-mogans. Theodore Hook*—Provost Creech—and Joseph Gillon, each had his niche in this Peristrephic Panorama of remembered merriment, and of each he told us innumerable new anecdotes—new to us at least—which we would give not a little to be able to reproduce for the edification of our readers; but alas! it would require a much bolder man than we are to attempt the hazardous experiment of serving up such dainties in a hash. One of Joseph Gillon's good things, however, we shall venture on, because the wit of it is of that kind which disdains to be improved by passing through the lips of any man, even of Ballantyne. Joseph happened to be in a certain pretty numerous party at Edinburgh (would he had never

* High as this eulogy is, contemporary report fully confirms it. Scott used to call John Ballantyne by the name of *Rigdum Funnidos*, while to his brother James, who was pompous and solemn, he gave the familiar title of *Aldiboronte-phoscophornio*.—M.

† Theodore Edward Hook, whose dramas and novels have been very popular, and show lively wit and much knowledge of the world, was born in 1788, and produced his first play before he was 17. The work of fiction called "Sayings and Doings," of which three series were published, rank among his best works—but others were popular also, such as Jack Brag, Gilbert Gurney (in which he sketched some of his own adventures), literally filled with fun. He was editor of the *John Bull*, a London newspaper, commenced in order to aid the Tory party, by keen and humorous attacks upon Queen Caroline, (wife of George IV.) in 1820-21. In that journal appeared the celebrated Letters of Mrs. Ramsbottom, in which, following the example of Smollet's Winifred Jenkins, bad spelling was managed so as to excite the merriment usually elicited by humorous writing. Mr. Thackeray has extended, perhaps not improved, this description of composition. As an *improvisatore*, Hook had no equal in England in his time. He died in August, 1841.—Creech was a bookseller in Edinburgh, who, in the early part of the present century was the Prince of the Trade. Well educated (for he had been intended for the church), he was the life of good society, a capital story-teller, a lively companion, and even a composer of *jeux d'esprit* for the newspapers. He attained the high position of Lord Provost of Edinburgh, but the publication of the *Edinburgh Review*, by Constable, may be said to have virtually dethroned him.—Joseph Gillon was a W. S. (writer of the Signet), and I believe, eventually became one of the door-keepers in the House of Lords, in London.—M.

left us!) at the time when the Northern Whigs were everywhere exerting their lungs in the first of those systematic blasts which have since swelled the inflammable balloon of Brougham to that immoderate bulk. "Joseph," whispered a modest Tory in company, "you have seen this young fellow—what is *your* real opinion of him? *Do you think the man will rise, Joseph?*" "Aye," quoth Joseph, "I'll be bound he will—*at a general rising.*" One day Gillon was very unwell (it was in July), and Mr. Ballantyne went to visit him. He found him on a couch in his writing chamber, surrounded by all his clerks and apprentices; "What, Gillon," said he, "this place is enough to kill ye, man, it is as hot as an oven;" "and what for no, man?" cried Joseph, "it's the place whar I mak my bread, man."* We beg pardon for these stories; but really Joseph was a true wit. Why does he not try his hand at a contribution now and then? But perhaps the worthy "door-keeper in the Lord's house" would have a *text* against us were we to make the application.

A great deal of his talk turned also (*quis dubitaverit?*) on Paris. He seems, in deed and in truth, to have done what Miladi Morgan was said to have done,—he has seen Paris from the garret to the saloon, from the Palais Royal to the Catacombs.† We had great pleasure in hearing his account of all the strange doings and goings on of that remarkable city—a city in which we ourselves have spent many happy—alas! very happy days and nights. While the names of the modern beaux and belles of that Regal City fell glibly from the lips of the bibliopole, faint and shadowy visions of the beaux and belles of her former days rose in dim and fleet succession before our too faithful eye of imagination. Kind, jovial, elegant Duc de la Cirelabouche, friend of our youth—friend and patron!—alas! where be now thy petits soupers! Beautiful, radiant, luxurious Madame la Biche!‡——but wherefore renew yet again these soul-piercing retrospections? While we were in the midst of our melancholy abstraction, our friend began chanting, in his own light, elastic, bounding style, that excellent French song,—

En Angleterre a ce qu'on dit
  C'est une chose des plus rares
Mourir dans son lit—
  Ah! ces Anglais barbares!
Si une dame est cruelle
  Et ne laisse rien d'espoir—
Son adieu a la belle—
  'Est par corde ou razoir, &c. &c.

"By the way, Monsieur Jean," said we, "did you take any lessons

* This is one of the most venerable and notorious of the late Mr. Joseph Miller's Jokes.—M.

† John Ballantyne frequently visited the Continent to purchase, or take consignments of articles of *virtu*, &c., for his very celebrated auctions in Hanover-street, Edinburgh.—M.

‡ These titles appear suspicious. *Cere-la-bouche* might be interpreted wax-mouth, and *La Biche* reminds us of—a dog's sister.—M.

in fencing when you were in Paris?" To be sure," said he, "I spent three or four hours every morning in the Salle des armes, and I believe I could now take my inches even at *contre point* against any swordsman in Scotland." "Not so fast, friend," said we, "not quite so fast, neither. Have you measured foils yet with Francalanza?"* "No, faith," quoth he; "but I have seen his advertisement, and shall certainly call upon him the very day I return to Auld Reekie." "Have your doublet well lined then, Giovanni," we returned, "and see that your mask sits close about your ears, and expect, with all your precautions, to come back with the marks of his button between every pair of your ribs; for we have fenced with the Rolands, the Angelos, and most of the amateurs in the three kingdoms—but Heaven forbid we should ever venture a second trial with this Italian!" "An Italian is he?" cries Ballantyne; "I think I have heard his name mentioned in Paris." "Very probably," said we, "he is well known there—he fenced a great many years ago with Augereau, who said he had the finest turn of a wrist, and, without exception, the most irresistible pair of eyes he had ever met with." "The marshal," quoth John, "must be admitted to be an excellent judge; he is allowed to be the first *homme-d'epeé* in all France, old as he is." "Our own Prince Regent," we continued, "is not a bad judge neither; and we have reason to know that he has seen Francalanza fence, and thinks at least as highly of him as Marshal Augereau.† We ourselves have heard both Leslie and Underwood, the two finest amateur swordsmen in these islands, bear the most unequivocal testimony to his merits; we used to meet with them often at his rooms in Cateaton-street. He is a glorious fellow—and let us tell you, Mr. Ballantyne, his fingers manage the guitar just as well as they do the rapier. He sings and plays much in the same charming style with that prince of good fellows and artists, John Schetky."‡ "Why, he will be quite an acquisition," cried Ballantyne; "we must get him into the Dilettanti with all speed." "We wish to heavens you would get ourselves into the Dilettanti, Mr. John," returned we; "we have spoken of it a thousand times, but you'll never condescend to propose us when a ballot comes about."

* Francalanza and Roland were eminent fencing-masters, in Edinburgh, in 1819.—M.

† Augereau, one of Napoleon's marshals, created Duke of Castiglione, for his bravery at the battles of Castiglione and Arcola, in 1796. He served Napoleon faithfully, yet, on his fall in 1814, was one of the first to join the Bourbons. On the return from Elba, in 1815, he offered to serve his old master, who declined having any-thing to do with him, a double traitor. Augereau. was one of the best swordsmen in the Grand Army.—M.

‡ John Schetky had been a staff-surgeon, under Wellington, in the Peninsular War, and had attained some eminence, as an amateur, before the peace of 1815 ended his professional career. Settling at Edinburgh he earnestly applied himself to painting. Dr. Morris (Lockhart) says, in Peter's Letters, "that his trees—his rocks—his Pyrenees, seem to breathe and be alive with the spirit of their Maker, and he has no superior, but one [Turner ?], in every thing that regards the grand and mysterious eloquence of the cloud and sky." Schetky was one of the Dilettanti Society, of which Wilson was president, which may account for the friendly notice of him as above.—M.

"Wait a little; have patience, my dear Editor," cried John; "there's a braw time coming yet." We shall keep our eye upon Mr. John Ballantyne next winter, and, depend on it, if he neglects to introduce us to this illustrious society, we shall not be easily pacified.* In the mean time, seeing that we had given him a little offence, we proposed to enliven our journey by singing a few duets together, which we did. We think both of us were particularly happy in that exquisite genuine old High Dutch one,—

Persantribat clericus
Durch einem grünem waldt
Videbat ibi stantem, stantem, stantem,
Ein Magdelein wohlgestallt
Salva sis puellula
Godt gruss dich Magdelein fein, &c., &c.

"I hope," said Ballantyne, "that you will return to Edinburgh in time, at least, for the grand Musical Festival. We never could do without you. By the way, I cannot but be rather surprised that you are not one of the directors, Mr. Editor."—We assured our good friend, that the omission of our name in that list was entirely owing to ourselves; that it had been early put down by Lord Gray;† but we hate all kind of notoriety, and therefore requested his Lordship to be so good as to withdraw our name, at the same time promising him, or any other of the directors, every assistance and advice in our power. "You see that we are to have Dragonetti's double bass‡—what a perfect volcano!—a very earthquake it is, Mr. Editor!—but I am extremely anxious that you should hear little Signora Corri."—"Hear little Signora Corri!" we replied: "have we not dandled the little syren on our knee a hundred times, when she was in frock? and were not we ourselves the first to prophecy her future noise in the world, and suggest to her papa the propriety of sending her to Catalani?‖ Those were pleasant nights, John, when we used to sit at the long supper-table of Signor Corri, and sometimes inspirited by noyeau and cherry bounce, venture our own cracked voice in a glee;

* The Dilettanti of Edinburgh professed to be *arbitri elegantiarum* in all matters of art and taste, but really did little more than eat good dinners, and spend social evenings at Young's Tavern.—M.

† A Scottish peer, and not to be confounded with the English Earl Grey, Prime Minister, 1830–'34.—M.

‡ What Bottesini is in 1854 (the best double-bass in the world), Dominico Dragonetti was in 1819, and for more than twenty years after.—M.

‖ Angelica Catalani, who made her *debut* at Rome in 1802; her immediate and immense success obtained her excellent engagements at the principal theatres in Italy. New triumphs awaited her at Lisbon, Madrid, and Paris, which were outshone by her brilliant success in London in 1806. She remained eight years in England, singing at the Italian Opera, and in the provinces. After the Restoration she went to Paris, became manager of the Opera Buffa there, lost her money, returned to England in 1822, and was greeted as an old and deserving favorite. In 1825 she commenced a farewell round of engagements in the chief European cities, and returned in 1830. In her youth she was handsome, and had a good figure; when I saw her, in 1828, she was middle-aged and stout, but her voice had wonderful brilliancy and power. Her husband, a French officer, named Valaberque, used to say, "Doo or dree poupets and mine lady—*voila* the opera." She died of cholera, in 1849, at Paris.—M.

but, in truth, ear is everything—'tutto, tutto, tutto;'—as the Corri used to say, 'I do like vast well for to hear Signor Christophero sing *Il suo gusto e perfetto.*'"

A message from our compositor forces us to cut short, and to reserve for another Number our account of Dunkeld, and other noble Highland scenery which we visited on our way to the Tent. Indeed we have whole volumes in our brain about the Highlands, and can never hope to live long enough to utter all we think, feel, and know of that wonderful country. For the present, gentle reader, imagine yourself sitting between ourselves and Mr. Ballantyne a little forward on the seat for the sake of room, and once more behold our Tent rising before you, almost like a native production—that snow-white graceful pyramid. Who are those figures issuing from the door?—Need you ask?—Tickler and the Standard-bearer. Mr. Ballantyne gently pulled up Old Mortality, when about quarter of a mile from the Tent, and took out of his pocket that seven-league spy-glass of his, presented to him by Adie, that most piercing of opticians; and putting it into our hands, said, "Tak a keek at the callans." We did so—and Tickler and Odoherty seemed standing by the very nose of Old Mortality. The Sage had a prodigious whisky-bottle in his hand, from which the Adjutant was receiving a bumper with a steady hand and determined countenance; and never saw we any mortal man take "his morning" with more relish—we almost thought we heard the smack of his lips, as the warm genial fluid descended into his penetralia. "Give me a keek," said the Bibliopole. He applied the tube to his ogles; but just as he had caught a glimpse of Tickler in the act of having the compliment returned by the Standard-bearer, a fine hare sprung up from a bush on the roadside, and after her away scoured Dominie Sampson. Mr. Ballantyne bounced out of the dennet as if he had been discharged from a catapulta, and lighting upon his feet, he joined the pursuit straight up a steep, stony, heathy hill, shouting aloud, "Halloo! halloo! halloo!" and was out of sight in less than no time. We laid the reins on Old Mortality's back, and told him to jog on quietly to the Tent. "God bless you all, our dear Contributors," was all we could say, for our heart was full to behold them again all looking so well, and so happy to see us. When the first burst of congratulation was over, we were especially delighted to see Tims, whom we again shook cordially by the hand, his little finger being now, he said, quite healed under the care of Drs. Scott and Morris. Tims seemed quite an altered man. He had let his beard grow, that he might have a rural, a pastoral appearance, like the Ettrick Shepherd; and he was ready to leap out of his skin when we remarked the resemblance. This beard of his consisted of perhaps about one hundred hairs, seemingly very soft and silky, and altogether of a different character from the mustachios of the 10th Hussars. "My dear Tims, you are a perfect Aaron."—"I h'ant shove since you went away to Scotland," said the little exulting Cockney—"neither no more has Pricey." The gentleman designated by this endearing diminutive then caught my eye, and beard enough he had with a vengeance. Price is a big lumbering fellow, not so much amiss in the way of good looks; and we do not know how it is, but he always reminds us of that able-bodied barber, who comes lollopping into one's bed-room, of a morning, in the Old Hummums, Covent-Garden, insisting upon the immediate detonsure of you, nolentis volentis. But we had little time to spend upon Mister Price and his whiskers; for we missed Dr. Scott in the throng, and loudly called for the Odontist. Alas! he too soon appeared, mounted upon his white pony—in every respect the same vision that so delighted us some weeks ago.

"But, ohon! the Doctor's departure is near,
Umbrella unfurled, and mounted his gear."

"It's a sad thing, Mr. Editor, for freens to part; but aff I maun gang; I deliver up the Tent and the Contributors all hale and hearty into your ain hauns (the Doctor had been Viceroy during our absence), see you keep them a' as quate as I hae done. O! he's a sair rumpawger, that Odoherty, and gude faith, Tickler's but little better. Mr. Buller,* with the brazen nose, is a fine civil, clever, weel-informed laddie; and I canna say that I dislike that Seward either; but ye ken a' their characters brawly yoursel'—so, fareweel—fareweel. O! Mr. Editor, I'm maist like to greet." We need not say how much affected we ourselves were; and we wanted words to express our concern when the Ettrick Shepherd advanced, and proposed a round of genuine Glasgow punch (from a small bowl which he held in his fist) to the health of the worthy Doctor, a safe journey, and a hearty welcome in No. 7, Millar-street. Just as the Doctor had received his glass, the Shepherd threw his plaid over his shoulder, and fixing his honest light grey eyes, swimming in tears, on the departing Odontist, he thus gave vent to his own and our feelings in immortal song.

L'ENVOY; AN EXCELLENT NEW SONG IN HONOR OF DR. SCOTT.

By the ETTRICK SHEPHERD.

TUNE—"Grammachree."

1.

DRAW water of the coldest—draw ye water from the spring,
And heaps of snow-white sugar into the china fling,
And squeeze the fairest lemon, and pour the richest rum,
That our parting mayn't be dry at least, although it may be dumb.

* John Hughes (son of the Rev. Dr. Hughes, a Canon Residentiary of St. Paul's, London), who is known to the readers of Ebony as "Buller of Brazennose," had his Itinerary of the Rhone kindly and favorably noticed by Scott, in the Introduction to Quentin Durward. In a poem by Mr. Hughes, entitled "Walter Childe," published in Bentley's Miscellany, in 1838, there is an elegant and affectionate tribute to Scott's memory.—M.

2.

We'll consecrate a bumper, and a bumper of the best—
We'll consecrate a bumper to speed our going guest;
And we'll pour the dear libation, with the tear-drops in our een,
For a noble fellow's leaving us, and a nobler ne'er was seen.

3.

With right good will we'd keep him—we would keep him in our Tent;
But since go he must—oh! lightly be his course out owre the bent—
May his pony's feet be steady, through the heather and the whins,
And may ne'er a thorn hae power to jag the hide upon his shins.

4.

May that pony ne'er be startled by brackenbush or post—
May no stravaiging heifer be mistaken for a ghost—
May no reaver bands disturb him, though, in crossing of yon hill,
He'll perhaps have no objection for to stumble on a still.

5.

Oh! may the skies be crystal clear above you as you ride,
And the sun be shining brightly upon the mountains' side,
That the brightness and the beauty may cheer you as ye go,
And your heart may dance within you like a young and happy roe!

6.

May ye ne'er want for good quarters to rest yourself at e'en—
A bonny lass to stir the fire—and a table-cloth fu' clean;
And when ye rise at cock-crow, may that lassie's hand be nigh
To reach the stirrup goblet, and sweetly say—*Good-bye.*

7.

O blythe be a' your journey, and blythe your coming home,
That oft ye may take heart again in the merry hearst to roam;
And whene'er the Doctor's roaming—oh! near him may we be,
For meikle can we do without, but not his canty e'e.

8.

Meantime, if worth and kindness be beauteous in your eyes,
And if genius be a jewel, all with one accord you'll rise;
You'll rise, my lads, as I do, and toss your cups with me,
To—*Blessings on the Doctor's head!* with a hearty three times three!

During the recitation of these noble verses, Dr. Scott occasionally hid his face with his umbrella, and often cast up his eyes to heaven. "Too, too much," he would sometimes exclaim, in a choked, tremulous voice, but when the L'Envoy ceased, he seemed "rapt, inspired;" and rising upon his stirrups, and at the same time elevating his umbrella, till the whole man and his accoutrements seemed something more than mortal, he chanted the following hymn:—

DR. SCOTT'S FAREWELL TO BRAEMAR.

AIR—"Lochaber."

1.

FAREWELL, then, ye mountains in mystery piled,
Where the birth-place and home of the tempest is found;
Farewell, ye red torrents all foaming and wild;
Farewell to your dreamy and desolate sound;
And farewell, ye wide plains, where the heath and the fern
Bloom in beauty forlorn, while above them is skimming,
Far up in the rack, the majestical Earne,
To the lone ear of Nature his orison hymning.

2.

And farewell to thy shadow, thou Queen of Pavillions,
Pitched on turf that is smooth as the eider-bird's wing,
'Neath the dais of his splendor, the monarch of millions
Might envy the bliss that hath hallowed thy ring!
What is purple, that floats in the weight of perfume,
And the gold-circled mirrors that parasites see,
To the rich twilight-breath of the languishing broom,
And the pure native crystal of pastoral Dee?

3.

And farewell to the friends that I leave in thy shade,
Wit, mirth, and affection exalting their cheer!
Oh! ne'er shall their forms from my memory fade:
Still, whate'er may be absent, my *heart* shall be *here;*
Though o'er flood, field, and mountain my wanderings be wide,
Back, still back to Braemar faithful fancy shall flee,
And the beauty of Kelvin—the grandeur of Clyde—
Shall but deepen my sigh for the banks of the Dee.

4.

Yet one cup ere we part, ye dear friends of my bosom!
One sweet-flowing measure—one more—only one!
Life's gay moments are few: then why needlessly lose 'em?
You'll have plenty of time for regrets when I'm gone.
In dulness to meet, and in dryness to part,
Suits the barren of feeling, the narrow of soul—
Be it *ours*, lads, the gladness, the grief of the heart
To improve, to assuage, by the juice of the bowl!

Long did every straining eye follow the Doctor, till the last green gleam of his umbrella faded in the distant woods. "An honester—better—cleverer fallow 's no in a' Scotland than that very same Doctor whom we have lost," said the Shepherd; with which eulogy we all cordially agreed; while Buller, turning toward our own person, repeated sonorously from Aristophanes—

Νυν' σου εργον ἐς', ἐϖειδη
Την ϛολην εἴληφες, ἥνϖερ
Ειχες εξ αρχης—ϖαλιν
'Ανανεαζειν σαυτον αἰει,

Και βλεπειν αὐθις το δεινον.
Ειδε παραληρων ἀλωσει,
Και βαλῃς τι μαλθακον,
Αὐθις αἱρεσθαι σ' αναγκη
Εςι παλιν τα ςρωματα.

We did not, however, come to the Tent to indulge unavailing sorrow; so we issued two regimental orders, one for our breakfast and dinner conjoined, without loss of time; and another for a general muster of Contributors in the Tent after mess, to take into consideration the state of the Magazine. There is no occasion to describe the *déjeunér à la fourchette;* and after it the Editor hung out his well-known signal—"SCOTLAND EXPECTS EVERY MAN TO DO HIS DUTY."

We knew that the eyes of our country were upon us, and felt confident of the result. On the roll being called by the Adjutant, not a man was missing from his post. The *coup d'œil* was most imposing. Wastle took his seat at one corner of the table, almost in the open air, in the same full court-dress which attracted so much notice last May when he walked with the Commissioner; immediately opposite the Laird, Morris sported his black silk stock, and richly-furred surtout;* on the Physician's right hand sat, in earnest confabulation, Buller of Brazennose in his cap and gown, both he and Seward having brought their academical dress down to Scotland to astonish the natives; between ourselves and Buller sat Mr. Price in the cap, or, as Tims called it, the black silk bonnet of the Surrey hunt, and kept his eyes fixed, with unceasing wonder, on Bailie Jarvie, who, in a full suit of black, with his "three cockit" and gold chain, looked up gashly in our face from the right, and obviously contained within himself the germ or elements of future Dean of Guild and my Lord Provost of Glasgow; on the Bailie's right shoulder, that is behind it, for he of the Salt-market absolutely turned his back on him of Ludgate, sat Tims, with a strange mixture of self-importance from feeling himself one of the Tent, and of personal fear from being at such an immense distance from the sound of Bow-Bell, which expression of face was not lessened by the consciousness of the immediate contiguity of Tickler, who had stretched as many feet of his legs beneath the table as possible, to bring his head on a line with the organization of the other in-door Contributors; behind Dr. Morris sat Kempferhausen, who had mounted his Hanseatic Legion cap; and on his right stood uncovered the jocund Bibliopole, with a face incommunicable both to copper and canvas; in front sat Seward, with all the gracefulness of a Christ-church man, on a cask of whisky, from which John of Sky ever and anon let off a quech of the dew, unnoticed from behind; at Seward's

* In Peter's Letters there is a description of this suit (a deputy-lieutenant's uniform of blue and red,) with the little cross of Dannebrog), and the frontispiece (an imaginary portrait) shows Dr. Morris, attired in a coat with a collar of-rich fur.—M.

right hand lay in his plaid the Ettrick Shepherd, his attention wholly absorbed by a large salmon that was floating exhausted to the bank in tow of Wastle's tall valet, who had become quite a prime angler under the tuition of Walter Ritchie; but we refer the world to the Frontispiece, which was sketched on the spot by Odoherty, the only departure from truth of any great moment, being the introduction of Dr. Scott, whom the literary and scientific world will easily recognize in the portly figure smoking a pipe of tobacco on the foreground to the left of the chairman. The affection of the Adjutant could not be satisfied without this tribute to his much-regretted brother bard, and he has introduced his own figure with foraging-cap, &c., reposing close by the side of the Odontist.*

When Kempferhausen sat down, after reading an essay on the character and manners of the Tyrolese, we must say, that the feeling uppermost in our mind was one of regret that he should have brought it so speedily to a termination. In looking round the Tent, however, it is not to be denied that we observed some slight symptoms, as if the whole of our friends had not been quite so uniformly and uninterruptedly delighted as ourselves. In short, Tickler, Odoherty, and the Ettrick Shepherd, manifested pretty plainly, that they thought the Hamburgher was still somewhat subject to his old infirmity of amplification. Wastle and Morris, on the contrary, Jarvie, Mullion, and Buller of Brazennose, were enthusiastic in their applauses of the German's Essay; and, supported by their decision, we could not hesitate to express to the Essayist himself, our conviction that his powers were expanding themselves in a manner most luxuriantly promising, and our hope and confidence that henceforth he would form one of the most efficient and vigorous of all our Contributors. The Shepherd remarked, that "the Essay might be a braw essay for aught he kenned, but he was sure it was an unco lang ane—and luik," quoth he, "gin Hector be not shaking himself frae side to side, and yawning and nuzzling as if he had been listening to ane of Mr. R—— of Y——'s† very weariesomest action-sermons. The lad will not be the worse of a glass to weet his whistle-ony way."—"Gie him a bumper

* This refers to an outline sketch, so indifferent in execution, that we do not think it worth while to have it engraved. In later editions of this number of Maga this sketch was not given.—M.

† Of this excellent gentleman we embrace this opportunity of recording an interesting anecdote. Some years ago, when the Ettrick Shepherd had Dr. Anderson (editor of the British Poets) and Mr. Wordsworth (author of the Excursion) as his guests in Yarrow, he carried them one forenoon to eat some bread and cheese in the manse, and taste the minister's home-brewed, which is proverbial for its good qualities in that part of the country. During this cold collation, a great deal of highly instructive and intellectual conversation occurred, as might have naturally been expected, at a meeting of four such gifted men. As they were going away, the minister called back Hogg, and—"Faith, Jemmy," said he, "he's a fine chiel that Wordsworth—he's very discreet and well-informed. I really never heard of a horse-couper quoting poetry before in all my life." It is almost needless to observe, that the excellent minister had supposed himself to be entertaining the eminent horse-dealer of Leith Walk,—a conjecture which was doubtless sufficiently natural, considering Hogg's well-known love for appearing at the weekly sales at that gentleman's repository. The Shepherd, we suppose, now undeceived him.—C. N.

by all means," quoth Jarvie;—"indeed, if he were to get his right, he would get mair nor ane, for here's twa or three that have not been dry listeners—only look, Mr. Tickler, we've scarcely left enough to *fang** anither bowl."—"You may make the next one yourself, Bailie," says Tickler, "for it's my turn to be spokesman—you know the article goes round the opposite way from the bottle." Then turning to the chair,—"Mr. Editor," continued the Senior, "we've got a new Number of the Edinburgh Review since you left us, and, if you please, I shall read a few remarks I have jotted down concerning it. I would not have taken so much trouble, only I was surprised to see them holding up their heads so briskly on some points, considering what a nailer you gave them so very lately."

"Go on, Mr. Tickler," we interrupted; "you need not hesitate to enter upon any topic from fear of being tedious. As yet *nihil quod tetigisti non ornasti;* and even here we have no doubt, *materiam superabit opus!*"—Encouraged by these words, the Sage drew down his spectacles from his forehead, and after clearing his throat with a few portentous hems, he thrust his left hand in his waistcoat pocket, and stretching forth the dexter with its MSS. to within a few inches of ourself, began to read as follows in a distinct voice. The mysterious music of some of his solemn cadences, seemed at first to alarm and astonish the southern part of his hearers, but the strong sense of the man soon overcame all these lesser emotions, and seldom has even a Tickler been listened to by a more attentive auditory.

[Mr. Tickler's comments on an old number of the *Edinburgh Review* so little suit the humor which prevailed in "the Tent," that they are omitted altogether.]

Here Tickler ceased, and a low breathing of applause from every auditor around hailed him on the conclusion of his labors. The veteran was then invited by Mr. Mullion to refresh himself with a glass of Mrs. Weddel's best cherry brandy from a private bottle, which that worthy produced for the first time on this occasion. Dr. Morris pledged him, and then, with great good humor, made a number of little remarks on the elaborate performance he had just been hearing. We ourselves made only one single observation, and it referred entirely to the last sentence of Mr. Tickler's paper, in which allusion is made to the soft sighs breathed by the Edinburgh Reviewers over some of the supposed inconveniences of the present situation of the Ex-Emperor.† Among other things we remarked, the Reviewers seemed to pity Bonaparte very much, because he is restricted from reading their journal—in spite, as they would insinuate, of his earnest

* We believe, that to *fang a well* signifies to pour into it sufficient liquid to set the pump at work again.—C. N.

† Napoleon. He did not die until May, 1821.—M.

quarterly longings after a participation in that great intellectual banquet—and indeed they show pretty plainly that they consider this a still more grievous kind of restriction than the short commons to which their hero is supposed to be reduced, in regard to bread, cheese, mutton, garlic, and charenton.* Now it so happens, that we have good reason to know this is a point on which Bonaparte himself is very far from soliciting the sympathies of his admirers. Our excellent old friend, Colonel Fehrszen of the 53d, was lately in St. Helena, on his way to India, and he writes to us, that he paid a visit of several hours' length to the Emperor, with whom, on a previous occasion, he had formed a very considerable intimacy. Thinking it might amuse the illustrious captive, the colonel carried a late number of the Edinburgh Review with him to Longwood, and laid it on the table when he was about to take his leave. "*Ha!*" cried Bonaparte —(the Reviewers themselves have remarked with what power this monosyllable expresses the feeling of *contempt*, when uttered by those imperial lips,)—"*Ha! quoi donc! encore plus de ces brochures, à bleu et à jaune? Je croyois que cette Turlupinade là étoit tombée tout-à-fait il-y-a longtemps.*"—Then turning over the leaves, he came upon something about himself,—"Peste!" cried he, "*Ce petit Jeffré pourquoi fait-il toujours de telles sottises sur mon sujet?* Je hais ce Nain envieux—Il n'entend rien sur les grandes choses ni sur les grands hommes, et voilà comme il parle!" A few minutes afterwards, he asked Colonel Fehrszen why he had not rather brought a number or two of Blackwood's Magazine with him? adding, that he had seldom laughed so heartily as when Mr. Baxter† sent him the Number containing the first part of Odoherty's Memoirs. Our modesty prevents us from repeating all that he said in our praise, but we may be pardoned for mentioning the last of the sentences he addressed at this time to the colonel. "Je vous conjure, mon cher colonel, d'écrire à votre ami M. le Conducteur, qu'il m'envoye ce journal aussi régulierement qu'l soit possible. Pour *l'Edinburgh Review*—ma foi!—Ils sont culbutés—renversés—écrasés,—abimés—*Au diable avec ces vieux fripons là! Ils ont perdu la tête!*"

After such a narration as this, we could not do less than propose a bumper to the good health of General Bonaparte‡—a toast which was accepted in high glee by the whole of this assemblage; even the Ettrick Shepherd felt all his old prejudices entirely thawed by the sweet though distant rays of ex-imperial admiration, and chanted an extempore parody on "Tho' he's back be at the wa'," the sentiments of which would not, on reflection, be thoroughly approved by his legitimate understanding. On looking 'round for the next *article*,

* Said to be the favorite beverage of Napoleon Bonaparte and Timothy Tickler, Esq.—C. N.
† The present surgeon to Sir Hudson Lowe.—C. N.
‡ We may add, in excuse of this toast, that Bonaparte hinted to the Colonel his intention of being, at no distant date, a contributor to our Miscellany.—C. N.

Wastle and Odoherty offered themselves at the same moment to our notice, and we had some difficulty in deciding to which of the two the first hearing should be given. The age and aristocratical dignity of the Laird, on the one side, was met, on no unequal terms, by the manly beauty and transcendant genius of the Adjutant, on the other. Odoherty, indeed, conceded the *pas* (when he observed the Laird's anxiety) with his accustomed *Cortesia Castillana;* but this was only a change of difficulties, for nothing could now prevail on that illustrious *Tenant in capite* to accept of the proffered precedence. To put a stop to so much altercation, we were compelled to have recourse once more to our old expedient of skying a copper, the result of which terminated, as usual, in favor of the Standard-bearer. That personage has indeed a wonderful degree of luck in such matters. Never was such an exemplification of the truth of that old text, FORTUNA FAVET FORTIBUS. He made use of the silence with which we now surrounded him, by reading, in his usual fine high Tipperary key, a short continuation of that excellent *series* of his, the Boxiana.*

The face of Kempferhausen, during this sporting article, was most excellent. The practice of pugilism was evidently a mystery which his fine speculative understanding could not penetrate, and though few men have more enthusiasm than our good friend Phillip, he could not go along with the profound disquisition and impassioned feeling of the Adjutant on such a theme. He contented himself, however, with a short quotation out of Emmanuel Kant,† who had, it would

* The No. read referred to the boxing match between Broughton and Slack, in 1759, which ended in the triumph of the latter; who, after being Champion for ten years, was beaten by a worthy rejoicing in the appellation of Bill Stevens, the Nailor.—M.

† Mr. Coleridge has somewhere expressed himself to this effect—That, if Plato were to rise again from the grave and appear in London, any performer of chemical tricks would be looked on as much the greater man; and further, that with respect to any discovery, *he* would have more credit for it who should make it *à posteriori*, (accidentally perhaps, or by benefit of a fine apparatus)—than he who should demonstrate its necessity *à priori*, (i. e. should deduce it from the law which involved it). This remark is well illustrated in the following case: Twenty-six years at least before Dr. Herschel discovered the planet which bears his name (otherwise called the planet Uranus, and in England the Georgian planet), it had been predicted—or, to speak more truly, it had been demonstrated—by Kant, that a planet would be found in that region of the heavens (i. e. a planet superior to Saturn). The difference between the discoveries is this: Herschel's was made empirically, or *à posteriori*, by means of a fine telescope; Kant's scientifically, or *à priori*, as a deduction from certain laws which he had established in his Celestial System (*Himmel's System*). We have unfortunately not brought with us to Braemar the volume which contains Kant's *Himmel's System;* but we will state from memory the course of reasoning which led Kant to this prediction. What is a comet? It is a planet whose orbit is exceedingly eccentric. Are then the planets not eccentric? Yes, but much less so. How much less? Some in one degree—some in another: their eccentricity varies. According to what laws; or does it vary according to any law? In general according to this law: the eccentricity has a tendency to increase, as the distance from the sun increases; that is to say, the planets become more eccentric in their orbits, i. e. more *cometary*—as they approach to that region of the heavens from which the comets descend. Now from this gradual tendency of the planetary motions to become cometary (which tendency, by the way, is itself a necessary consequence from Kant's system, and no accident), Kant suspected, that as nature does not ordinarily proceed *per saltum*, the system of planets must pass *gradatim* into the system of comets—and not so abruptly as it would do if Saturn were the last planet. Therefore, said he, at some future period, there will be found at least one planet superior to Saturn—whose orbit will be much more eccentric than that of Saturn, and will thus supply a link to connect the motions of the planets and the comets into a more continuous chain. The comets will perhaps vary as much in eccentricity as the planets, and according to the same law: so that

appear, considered pugilism as one of those anomalies in the history of the human mind, inexplicable by the transcendental philosophy,—and with hinting, that Randal the Nonpareil could have found no favor in the eyes of the sage of Koningsberg. Odoherty avowed his utter ignorance of all Cant, but was willing to pin his faith on the sleeve of Plato, who, it was well known, was in his day a fighting man of great skill, pluck, and bottom; and who, though desirous of excluding poetry from his republic, recommended an enlightened patronage of pugilism. At the same time, he was very far from thinking, with his quondam friend, Bill Parnell, knight of the shire for Wicklow (whom he now indignantly disowned), that the Irish people, owing to their ignorance of pugilism, "were *base, cowardly, and savage.*"* The man who could utter such a sentiment is unworthy of his potatoes. "*His soul,*" said the Adjutant, with much animation, "has not the true Irish accent—it wants the brogue of his country. I agree with my friend, Lord Norbury,† in thinking 'we are a fine people;' and if I heard Bill Parnell with his own lips say, that '*it is only backed by a mob of his friends that an Irishman will fight,*' I would not tell him, Mr. Editor, to remember the fine lines of my friend, Tom Moore,

> When Malachi wore the collar of gold,
> That he won from the fierce invader—

but I would call upon him, in the words of a pardonable parody, to think,

> How Donelly wore the kerchief of blue,
> That he won from the Deptford gardener.‡

the last planet and first comet will stand pretty much in the same relation to each other as any planet to the next superior planet—or as any comet to the next more eccentric comet.——This was said in the year 1754 at the latest. With respect to the date of Herschel's discovery, having no Astronomy in our Tent later than that of David Gregory, the Savilian Professor, (Astron. Phys. et Geomet. Elementa: Genevæ, 1726.) we cannot assign it precisely; but according to our recollection, it was made in 1781; and certainly not earlier than 1780. Kant then discovered the planet Uranus *à priori*, (that is, he discovered the necessity of such a planet as a consequence of a law previously detected by his own sagacity at least six-and-twenty years before Herschel made the same discovery *à posteriori* by—the excellence of his telescope.——N. B. The reader will perhaps object the case of Mercury and of Mars—the first as contradicting the supposed law, the second as imperfectly obeying it (his eccentricity being indeed less than that of the next superior planet, but yet greater than according to his distance from the sun); these exceptions, however, confirm the system of Kant—being explained out of the same law which accounts for the defect in bulk of these two planets. It might have been supposed that Sir Isaac Newton would have been led to the same anticipation as that here ascribed to Kant, by the very terms in which he defines comets, viz. "*genus planetarum* in orbibus valde eccentricis circa solem revolventibus" (Princip. lib 3. Prop. 41): but he was manifestly led away from any such anticipation by the same reasoning which induced him to conclude that no tenable theory could be devised which should assign a mechanical origin to the heavenly system. Kant has framed such a theory, which we shall lay before our readers in a month or two.—C. N.

* Maurice and Berghetta, or the Priest of Rahery; a tale London, 1819. [Written by Parnell.—M.]

† The Earl of Norbury, commonly called the The Hanging Judge, who jested with criminals, on whom he was pronouncing sentence of death. He was Chief Justice of the Common Pleas in Ireland, from 1800 to 1827, and died in 1831.—In "Sheil's Sketches of the Irish Bar" his career, character, and appearance are very fully described.—M.

* An allusion to the great fight between Sir Dan and Oliver.—C. N. [Daniel Donelly, an

"What, sir! would any Irishman who ever sung 'the sprig of shilelah and shamrock so green,' accuse his countrymen of cowardice? Let me not be misunderstood. I conceive that a duet in a ring at Moulsy-Hurst is pleasanter music than a general chorus at Donnybrook fair. But that is a cultivated, a scientific taste; and let no man rashly assert, that the genius and intellect, and moral worth of a people, may not exhibit themselves as strikingly in the shilelah as in the fist, in a GENERAL ROW, as in a LIMITED SET-TO. Is it the part of a coward, Mr. Editor, for one of the Tipperary lads to step forward and ask the Kerry lads, '*who will snaze?*' and if Roderic Milesius M'Gillicuddy replies, '*I am the boy to snaze in your face*,' is my cousin a coward because the Tipperary shilelahs come twinkling about his nob as thick as grass?* By the staff of St. Patrick, a coward has no business there at all; and what though Mr. M'Gillicuddy *be backed by a mob of friends*, as the county says, has not O'Donnahue his friends too? and where then is the cowardice of knocking down every Pat you can lay your twig upon, till you yourself go the way of all flesh? and if 'twenty men should basely fall upon one,' why, to be sure, their turn will come next, and all odds will be even.

At the close of the day, when the pot-house is full,
And mortals the sweets of forgetfulness prove,
When nought in the tap-room is heard but a bull,
And 'arrah, be easy!' comes soft from the grove.

"No, Mr. Editor, never may Morgan Odoherty live to see that day when the shilelah shall no longer flourish and be flourished in the Green Isle." Here Mr. Tims softly interposed, and after complimenting the Standard-bearer on that liberal philosophy, which discerns and knows how to appreciate the genius of a people in their pastimes, without any invidious preference of one or another, volunteered (if agreeable to the Editor and the Contributors) a song, entitled, "Ye Pugilists of England," which he understood was written

Irishman, who beat Oliver, an English pugilist, in a prize fight, returned to Ireland, declaring that the Prince Regent had knighted him for his prowess, opened a public house in Dublin, was one of his own most bibacious customers, and died soon after this from inflammation, caused by drink.—M.]

* This is a sweet pastoral image, which we ourselves once heard employed by a very delicate-looking and modest young woman, in a cottage near Limerick, when speaking of the cudgels of an affray. A broken head, is in Ireland, always spoken of in terms of endearment, and much of the same tender feeling is naturally transferred to the shilelah that inflicted it. "God bless your honor," said the same gentle creature to us, while casting a look of affectionate admiration on our walking-stick (at that time we had no rheumatism), "you would give a *swate blow with it*." It is in such expressions that we may trace the genius of a people, and they should serve to moderate that indignation with which moralists are wont to speak of the "*brutality*" of Irish quarrels. In the account of the battle between Randal, and Martin the baker, we observed with pleasure, an imitation of this Hibernian amenity. After stating that Randal finished the fight by a knock-down facer, the historian (probably our good friend Mr. Eagan), very prettily remarked, "*Randal is like a bird on the boughs of a tree*." A fine sylvan image!—C. N. Pearce Eagan, at this period, editor of the sporting paper called *Bell's Life in London*, and author of several works on pugilism and its history.—M.

either by Mr. Gregson, Mr. Egan, or Mr. Thomas Campbell. This handsome offer was received with thunders of applause, and nothing could be grander than the trio. We remarked, that during the ode there was not an unclenched fist in the whole Tent.

YE PUGILISTS OF ENGLAND.

As Sung by Messrs. Price, Tims, and Woods (Son of the Fighting Waterman), on the 4th of September 1819, near the Linn of Dee.

1.

Ye Pugilists of England,*
  Who guard your native sod,
Whose pluck has braved a thousand years,
  Cross-buttock, blow, and blood,
Your corky canvas sport again,
  To mill another foe,
As you spring, round the ring,
  While the betters noisy grow;
While the banging rages loud and long,
  And the betters noisy grow.

2.

A Briton needs no poniards
  No bravos 'long his street—
His trust is in a strong-roped ring,
  A square of twenty feet.
With one-twos from his horny fists,
  He floors the coves below,
As they crash, on the grass,
  When the betters noisy grow;
When the banging rages loud and long,
  And the betters noisy grow.

3.

The spirits of prime pugilists
  Shall rise at every round;
For the ring it was their field of fame,
  To them 'tis holy-ground.
Where Slack and mighty Belcher fell,
  Your manly hearts shall glow,
As you peel, true as steel,
  While the betters noisy grow;
While the banging rages loud and long,
  And the betters noisy grow.

4.

The Randal-rag of England
  Must yet terrific burn,
Till Ireland's troublesome knight be beat,
  And the star of Crib return!

* *Vide* Campbell's "Ye Gentlemen of England."—M.

Then, then, ye glutton-pugilists,
The claret red shall flow,
To the fame, of your name,
When the noise of betts is low;
When Sir Dan lies levelled loud and long,
And the noise of betts is low.

Mr. Price, whose voice reminded us of Incledon in his best days, took the tenor; Mr. Tims' sweet and shrill pipe was a most exquisite counter-tenor; and, with the sole exception of Bartleman, we never heard any thing at all comparable to the bass of young Woods.* The accompaniment, too, was exceedingly fine. Wastle blew his bugle affletuoso; Tickler, who fingers with any man in England, though we confess that his bow-hand is not so free, flowing, and unfettered, as that of Yaniewicz, was powerful on his fiddle; and John of Sky, on the bagpipe, at one moment, roused the soul to all the triumph of victory, and at another sunk it into the despondency of defeat. At that line, in particular, which the three voices dwelt upon with mournful emphasis,—

"When Sir Dan lies levelled loud and long,"—

we observed the tear start into Odoherty's eyes, and he veiled them with his foraging-cap, as if wishing to seal his sight from the vision of the conquest of Crib and the downfall of Donelly.

We were apprehensive at one time, that the Standard-bearer and Mr. Tims would have quarrelled; but on the latter assuring Odoherty that he yielded to no man in his admiration of the pluck and prowess of Sir Daniel Donelly, and that he could not be supposed answerable for the prophetic intimations of the poet, the Adjutant extended his hand towards him with his accustomed suavity, and by that pacific overture quieted the incipient alarm of the Cockney. He at the same time offered to back Sir Dan against all Britain, Crib not excepted, for a cool hundred—and against Jack Carter, £100 to £80. The best Irish pugilists, continued the Adjutant, "have been Corcoran, Ryan, Odonnel, Doherty, (filius carnalis, we believe, of Morgan's half-uncle, Father Doherty, an Irish priest, who dropt the O for reasons best known to himself,) and Donelly"—but here we felt it absolutely necessary to interfere, and to request Mr. Wastle to read his article, by way of diverting our thoughts into a different channel. The Laird observed, that he did not feel as if his "Essay on the Study of Physical Science" would sound well after the Boxiana, and therefore would, for the present, content himself with reading a very short paper, on the Scottish Proverbs of Allan Ramsay.

* This entertaining and accomplished young fellow is Mr. Tims' body servant. He is a natural son of the brave Woods, who fought Richmond, the Black, but he is a far better man than his father; and though he has, we believe, never exhibited publicly in the ring, his private turn-ups have been numerous, and he has still been the winner, without a scratch. He is the only man in England a match for Randal. Will the sporting Colonel back the Nonpareil for £200?—C. N.

Just as Mr. Wastle was concluding his acute little article, John Mackay, whom we had dispatched for Braemar to meet the walking postman, returned with a packet of letters—and for half an hour the Contributors were busily employed with their contents—all except Odoherty, who with perfect sangfroid suffered his three to lie unopened on the table, or every now and then gave them, one after another, a chuck into the air with singular dexterity, that showed him to be a perfect adept in legerdemain and slight of hand. On asking our friends if any of their communications were articles for the Magazine, the Adjutant replied, that as far as his letters were concerned it was for ourselves to judge—one being a dun from Scaife and Willis*—another, a short account, he believed, from the keeper of a billiard-table—and the third, he had some reason to think, was a bill for £25 on the Commercial Bank, which he had sent to a friend to whom he was indebted for that sum, but which, he dared to say, was now returned to him with the well-known words "no effects." All this was said with that gay and careless manner that marks the true man of the world, and the Standard-bearer remarked with a smile, that Messrs. Scaife and Willis, though the best natured and most skilful tailors in being, ought not to send accounts to gentlemen whose breeches they had made without pockets capable of holding them, and that therefore he was under the necessity of employing their well-intentioned letter in lighting his pipe. Mordecai Mullion then handed over to us the following letter from his brother Hugh, and, with his permission, we read it aloud.

My Dear Mordecai:—I found all our concerns in a much better way at Glasgow than we could have expected after the late crash; and I verily believe, that our good friend the Skipper will yet beat to windward of the Gazette. Folks don't look the least shy at our bills, and our credit is good. The Skipper requested me not to press him hard, which God knows never was our intention; and he will send us six barrels of the best Bunawe salmon, a hogshead of Jamaica, 500 lbs. of double Gloucester, a choice assortment of best Westphalias, and a ton of dried ling: he lets us have them all very low; and when I have seen them stowed away in our cellars, I shall feel easy about the Skipper. M'Corquindale and M'Clure offered to settle our account at once in cod and craw-fish; but as we suffered much from our cods last year, and craw-fish is a drug, I demanded Loch-fine herring, and kiplings, and got what I believe will cover us. I had most difficulty of all with that wasp M'Huffie, and had to threaten a horning.† My gentleman came to himself when he found me serious; and I saw his reindeers boxed before I left the Gallow-

* Architects of male attire. in Edinburgh.—M.

† *Horning*,—execution, sale under the law.—M.

gate; and finer tongues never pressed a palate. Poor Donald M'Tavish is on his last legs, but I took his debt in branxy, and have no doubt of inflicting it to advantage on our brethren of the Dilettanti. That sumph, Rab Roger, offered me a bill on Cornelius Giffen; I preferred taking him in good Mearns butter; and he sent me ten croaks of thirty lbs. each, as yellow as a dandelion. In short, our books will balance, which is more than some of our acquaintances both here and in the west can say, who hold their heads higher than the Mullions.—So much for business. And now, my dear Mordecai, let me give you an account of a sort of adventure in which I was engaged on my way back from Glasgow. I fear it will lose much in the recital—as I have not the pen of a Tickler or an Odoherty; yet as you requested me to give you the news, I will try to describe the scene just as I saw it acted.

I was jogging along on our "bit powney," with my honest father's wallise behind me as usual, when just where the former road takes up the hill to the auld Kirk o' Shotts,* I met a most extraordinary Cavalcade, which reminded me of Stothard's Picture of the "Procession of Pilgrims to Canterbury," so well engraved by our poor friend Cromek et multis aliis. I really felt as if I had slid back many centuries, and were coeval with Gower and Chaucer. My surprise was not diminished, when the leading pilgrim gravely accosted me with, "How do you do, Mr. Hugh Mullion? When did you hear from your brother Mordecai?" I pulled up old Runciman, and took a leisurely and scrutinizing observation of the pilgrimage. Before I had time to open my mouth, or rather to shut it again, for I believe it was open—the leading pilgrim continued, "I am the Editor of Constable and Company's Magazine, and these are my Contributors.† We are going to pitch our Tent near the Kirk o' Shotts, for you must not think, Mr. Hugh, that we are not allowed a *vacance* as well as Ebony's people. If you are not obliged to be in Edinburgh to-night, will you join us?—I dare say we shall find you useful." I declare to you, my dear Mordecai, that the very thought of this procession so convulses me with laughter, even at this hour, that I can write no better a hand than a member of parliament. For, only imagine, the good worthy editor, in half-clerical, half-lay attire—namely, black breeches, and D. D. boots, black silk waistcoat, pep-

* Between the cities of Edinburgh and Glasgow, about within sixteen miles of the latter place (travelling by the mail-road, before railways were constructed), the country rises up very high. On the summit of the most dreary ridge stands what is called the Kirk of Shotts (whence the ridge is named), and the little dove-cot belfry rises with peculiar expressiveness, amidst a land of so little promise. Descending the hill, with glimpses of the rich, well-wooded, and well-watered valley of the Clyde, the road leads into Glasgow, at once, from its commerce and manufactures, the Liverpool and Manchester of the West.—M.

† Blackwood's Magazine may be said to have fairly laughed Constable's rival Magazine out of existence. Neither publisher, editor, nor contributors could stand the sarcasms perpetually levelled at each and all, from the memorable time when the Chaldee Manuscript attacked them personally.—M.

per and salt coat, and shovel hat most admirably constructed for scooping a draught out of a well, mounted on a remarkably fine jackass, who, on being brought to a stand-still, let down his immense head between his fore legs, like the piston of a steam-engine, and then showing his alligator-like jaws, gave a yawn in which was gaunted* out a whole month's sleeplessness. It requires a very peculiar kind of a seat, to look well on ass-back; long stirrups, and legs nearly if not altogether meeting below; whereas the Editor sat too far forward upon the shoulder, like Don Olivarez, the Spanish minister, in that famous picture of Velasquez, in our last exhibition. Immediately behind him came our excellent friend, the old German doctor, in a full suit of sables, with spurs on his pumps, according to the ancient physical school; and elevated many feet above the editor, on that well-known hack the Paviour, for many years the property of Mr. Campbell, Stabler and Vintner, Canongate. The doctor perspired extremely, and had a Monteith handkerchief hanging over his brows from beneath his hat, which caused him to elevate his chin considerably before he could bring his ogles to bear on any inferior object. As he pulled up, a swarm of flies went off with a loud fuz from his veil, and then all settled again upon it, as if the queen-bummer had been inclosed in a crany of the Monteith. I never saw an elderly gentleman seemingly more uncomfortable; and he could only exclaim, 'Any thing's better than this; I wish I were in the Hartz forest.' Scarcely could I believe mine eyes, when they seemed to behold riding together cheek by jowl, and as like as twins, no less personages than the Editor of the Edinburgh Review, and 'John the brother of Francis." The former marked my astonishment on perceiving him in such company; and to divert my ideas, exclaimed, with his usual vivacity, (there is certainly something very pleasant in Jeffrey's smile.) "Ha! Mullion, my good fellow! these were very tasty hams you sent us out to Craigcrook; as my friend Napier would say, I made an essay on the scope and tendency of Bacon: nothing like repeated experiments—induction is the most satisfactory of all modes of reasoning. I am surprised the ancients never stumbled upon it; though, to tell you the truth, I believe it to be as old as the days of Ham." All this time a very peculiar expression played round the greater Jeffrey's lips, which it would not be fair to call *wicked;* but which certainly had in it a good deal of malice of a small playful kind. As he glanced his hawk eyes towards the Editor, whose back was turned, because his ass insisted it should be so, he said, in an affectionate tone of voice, "En avant, en avant, my dear coz: I hear the wheels of the mail-coach, give little sturdy a

* See Dr. Jamieson once more. There is really no doing without the Doctor's Dictionary; but let no man, on any account whatever, buy the Abridgment.—C. N.

touch of Peter Bell." The ass seemed instinctively afraid of Mr. Jeffrey's voice, and got under weigh,

"With the slow motion of a summer cloud,"

followed by the PAVIOUR, and the more alert nags of the brother-reviewers, which they had obvious difficulty in reining in, so as to prevent them from passing the Editor.

But now a much more formidable Contributor presented himself, in the person of that perfect gentleman, the SCOTSMAN.* He was mounted on that trying animal, a mule, which had planted his fore-feet considerably in advance, strongly backed by his hind ones, brought up as a corps de reserve to support the first line, so that he was intrenched in a very strong position, from which the cudgel of the infuriated Scotsman in vain banged to dislodge him. It was a fair match between wrath and obstinacy; and it was impossible to say which would win the day. There were moments in which the mule seemed to lose heart, under the murderous blows of his rider; while at other times, the stubbornness of the wretched creature he so inhumanly bestrode so irritated the Scotsman, that he would frequently hit his own shins with his own cudgel, and then betray his uneasiness by the most dismal gestures. Beside him rode that thickset, vulgar-looking person, somewhat like a Methodist preacher, a good deal marked with the small-pox, and well known among the town council by the name of the Scotsman's FLUNKY† (there is no need to enrich ye with his name) who told him "to remember his infirmity, and not to allow his passion so to get the better of him as to bring on one of his fits." I thought, my dear Mordecai, that the *Scotsman's* fits had always come on about the same hour on the Saturdays only, but I now found that they are not so regular as to be depended upon, and that he is often overtaken quite unexpectedly, and without any previous intimation. The fit by no means improved his natural beauty and elegance—but caused such unaccountable contortion, both of face and person, that the Flunky himself seemed alarmed—while Dugald Macalpine, the Pimping Caddy of the Laigh Kirk, who accompanied the procession, was heard to exclaim, "Pure fallow, is this him that wishes to mend the constitution? I'm sure nae burrugh's half sae rotten as his ain breast. Gude saf us, hear how he's flitting on the Lord Provost, wha's worth a dizen sic like Gallowa' stots as himsel.—Hush, hush—he's now cursan on Mr. Blackwood.—Wha's he that Dr. Morris he's

* J. R. M'Culloch, afterwards Professor of Political Economy in London University, and now Comptroller of the Government Stationery Office, in London, was editor of the *Scotsman* newspaper, in 1819, and the constant object of Maga's contempt. He contributed largely to the *Edinburgh Review*. Although his salary is £1200 a year, a Whig government was so lavish as to give also him a pension of £300, and, having solicited it, he was so greedy as to accept it.—M.

† The most opprobrious name, in Scotland, for a body-menial.—C. N.

slavering about? I wush him and sum ither Doctor was but here to gie him a dose of Pheesic. O, sirs! luk at the red whites o' his e'en, a' rowan' about in his heed! Hech! how the tae tail o' his mouth gangs up wi' a swurl to his ee-bree! What a lang foul tongue's hanging out o' his jaws! Ach! siccan a girn! I doubt he'el ne'er cum about again. It's shurely an awfu' judgment on him, for swearin, and cursan, and damman on ither folk.—Hech, sers, but he'll mak a grusome corp!"

My attention was luckily diverted from this painful spectacle by one of the most ludicrous exhibitions you can imagine—and one which made me feel the genius of our immortal Shakspeare (I call him ours, Mordecai, for, after our President's famous speech on that great day before the Dilletanti,* Shakspeare belongs exclusively to our society), in bringing together on the same scene the extremes of human wretchedness, and human absurdity.. For I looked, and lo! upon a white horse sat Dr. Search† and the Dominie! I knew the horse well, Mordecai!—a fellow of most rare action—who had run through many a summer's heat and winter's cold in the Dunbar dilly, but who, having become not a little spavined of late, has *degraded* from his wonted diligence, though still it would appear a hack—

"And he now carries who e'er-while but drew."

Dr Search occupied the seat nearest the mane—and the Dominie sat with a grim and dissatisfied face on the haunches, which, being very high, may be likened to the two-shilling gallery in reference to the boxes. He held desperately with one hand by the crupper, while, with the other, he was ever and anon snatching at the reins, which he could not bear to see in Dr. Search's hand, who, to say the truth, is not so good a horseman as Colonel Quintin by 360 degrees.‡ The Doctor had a spur, I observed, on his near heel, which, short and blunt as it was, he contrived, by repeated kicks, to indent into the gushets of the Dominie's black worsted stockings so as to fetch blood. The poor pedagogue implored ride and tie, but to the prayer of this equitable petition, such is the charm of precedence, his ear the practitioner would not seriously incline—and the patient had nothing for it but to submit his leg to the search. They were clothed, "first and last," in black apparel, but the Dunbar hack, who is the oldest horse that ever wore white hairs, seemed to have been rubbed over with

* "Our President" of the Dilettanti Society of Edinburgh, in 1819, was John Wilson,—the Christopher North of the Noctes.—M.

† For farther particulars of this learned Theban, see a pamphlet lately published by him, in reply to the aspersions of Dr. Morris on the University of Edinburgh. By-the-by, Ritson tho antiquary was exceedingly wroth with Dr. Percy for saying "See MSS." when such MSS. were in the sole possession of the Bishop of Dromore himself, and perhaps our readers, on attempting to get a sight of this erudite writer, may feel some surprise at our sending on them a wild-goose chase. Nevertheless, there is such a pamphlet.—C. N.

‡ Colonel Sir George Quintin was considered to be the best cavalry officer in the British army at this time. His daughter, an excellent equestrian, instructed Queen Victoria how to "witch the world with noble horsemanship."—M.

some depilatory preparation, and so freely shed "his longs and his shorts" over the two unfortunate gentlemen, most unjustifiably seated on his back, that they were both in a very hairy condition, and the Dominie indeed was absolutely gray. The spectacle was not lost on two small boys, who were enjoying the summer vacation of the High School in the country, one of whom, like a little Triton, blew a cow's horn in honor of those mounted deities, and the other clapping an immense rush fool's-cap on his head, spouted, as if reciting for a school-medal, that fine line in Gray's Ode,

> "Ruin seize thee, ruthless king,"

while a poor old laborer, who was knapping stones on the road-side, kept his hammer in air, aimed towards the mark at his toe, and seemed to congratulate himself on the appearance of two persons evidently worse off than himself, and in a more hopeless condition. As the "Arcades ambo" ambled by, they were succeeded by a knot of persons evidently attached to the procession, whom I soon perceived to be the "Seven Young Men" of the Chaldee MS.* They wore a sort of uniform, of which lean and shrivelled nankeen pantaloons formed the most distinguishing part. These pantaloons had been so frequently washed, that they had almost shrunk up into breeches, and indeed, I discovered them to be pantaloons chiefly from the want of buttons below the knees. The seven seemed all to be Knights of the Garter—some of them sporting red worsted, but most of them tape. The Editor had obviously distributed to each young man a pair of unbleached thread stockings for the festival, and eke a pair of new shoes, in which, as usual, he showed more genius than judgment, for sorely seemed their feet to be blistered, so that Seven lamer Young Men did not be seen in town or country on a summer's day. Neither did they keep the step properly, but were perpetually treading on each other's kibes, so that they might have been traced along the dry dust of the beaten highway, by the drops of blood that kept oozing from their heels. To keep up their courage, they were all singing pretty much after the fashion of a Dutch concert—and I distinctly heard the voice of one of them quavering a sort of profane parody on a well known English glee,

> "We are Seven poor Contributors,
> From garret just set free," &c.,

while, unless I am much mistaken, another breathed out, in still more Elegiac murmurs, an imitation of Wordsworth's well-known lyrical ballad, "We are Seven," at the pathetic close of which I could not but feel very much affected—

* The unfortunate Seven Young Men, were unnamed contributors to Constable's rival Magazine, and commemorated as such, in the Chaldee Manuscript.—M.

"But still the child would have his will,
Nay, master, 'we are Seven.'"

But I now recollected, that the Editor had requested me to join the party; so, as Runciman was quite fresh, I helped up several of the Seven Young Men upon his back, and cautioning the foremost and hindermost to take a lesson by Dr. Search and Dominie, and hold well by the mane and crupper, at the same time quieting the fears of him in the middle by reiterated assurances of his safety, I turned back pretty sharply on foot, and came up with the Editor and his advanced guard, just as they had fixed upon a spot for their encampment. I was grievously disappointed, however, on missing both the Greater and lesser Jeffrey, who had gone on, as I was told, to pay a visit at Hamilton Palace, to their friend Lord Archibald*—and who had, good-naturedly, lent the party their countenance as far as the Kirk of Shotts, being resolved to play fair by the Editor. In less than half an hour up came the Seven Young Men, who all in one voice returned me thanks for the use of Runciman, without whom they verily believed they could never have reached the camp. Runciman looked at me in a very quisquis sort of a way, as much as to say, "I think nothing of the wallise, but I never bargained for the Contributors." There was some difficulty in getting them all off—but by dropping down one at a time behind, Runciman's decks were at last cleared, and he instantly testified his satisfaction, by throwing his heels up in the air, with an agility scarcely to have been expected from a steed of his standing at the bar. Shortly after, the SCOTSMAN and his FLUNKY, and the PIMPING CADDY, arrived—the first with those dull, heavy, leaden eyes, and that sallow, cadaverous face, so fearful in one just recovered from the epilepsy of passion.† The Caddy had wished to have carried him back to the Infirmary; but this proposal roused every feeling in the Flunky's soul, who, you will remember, made a most eloquent speech last year about foul bandages, and stained sheets, and crowded water-closets, and indeed raved beyond all rational Hope. The Scotsman was, therefore, seated on a stone, where he looked like one of those master-pieces of ancient art—not surely the Apollo Belvidere, nor yet the Antinous—but some solitary Satyr, exhausted by a Morris-dance; and the Editor could only look at him with a true Christian pity, without being able to administer to him the smallest relief.

* Lord Archibald Hamilton, brother of the late Duke of Hamilton, whose principal mansion was in Lanarkshire, in which the Kirk o' Shotts is also situated. When Queen Caroline came to England, a few months after this, Lady Anne Hamilton (the Duke's sister), was her principal—indeed her only companion of rank. The family were then very liberal in politics, which would account for Jeffrey and his brother having sufficient intimacy as to visit at Hamilton Palace.—M.

† The Scotsman's fits are certainly of the nature of epilepsy, a disease thus defined: "a convulsive motion of the whole body, or some of its parts, *with a loss of sense*."—C. N.

I now found that the Tent had been sent by the heavy waggon, and had lain all night on the road-side, so that it was in a sad rumpled condition. An attempt was, however, made to put it into some decent kind of order; but just as we were going to hoist it, a sour Cameronian-looking sort of a farmer came up, and sternly declared, that the Tent should not be pitched there to "fley the stirks," calling us, at the same time, a set of "idle stravaiging fallows," and threatening to send for A Constable,* at which I observed the Seven Young Men faintly smiled. We accordingly shifted our quarters higher up the hill, and were commencing operations a second time, when a band of shearers, Irish and Highland, were attracted by curiosity to the Tent, and their conversation became so extremely indecent, that no respectable set of Contributors could stand it; so we broke ground again, and attempted a lodgment close to the Kirk of Shotts. For some time we were greatly annoyed by numbers of black cattle, who returned wheeling and wheeling around us, in the language of Milton,

"Sharpening their mooned horns,"

probably attracted by the "Galloway Stot;" but they soon grew weary of looking at us, and finally gave up the Magazine.

At last the pole was hoisted, and the canvas displayed, with the words, "CONSTABLE AND COMPANY'S EDINBURGH MAGAZINE," in large letters above the door, surmounted by the whole posse and esse of Beasts.† It was, however, soon but too evident, that not one of the party knew how to pitch a tent of the description; and there was no getting the pole to stand perpendicular, so that the ropes on one side were a great deal too long, and on the other by much too short. There was no deficiency of wooden pegs, but they were blunt and pointless, and could make no impression on the hard ground of the hill of Shotts, parched and baked as it was by two months' drought. The Dominie exerted himself in vain with his great maul, but he missed the mark much oftener than he hit it, and the pegs committed to his charge seemed the bluntest of the whole set. "I think the tent will stand now," said the Editor, with a dubious face and hesitating voice—and the Dominie replied, "It is perfectly glorious." Perfectly glorious! thought I—why it is more like an empty haggis-bag than anything else—and as the old Scotch proverb says, "an empty bag winna stand." The German doctor put his back to the pole, like Sampson carrying the gates of Gaza—but as he had shaved that morning, his strength had departed from him, and he was like other Contributors, so he prudently retired from the championship.

* The Seven Young Men would smile at the feeble joke, inasmuch as A. Constable, was proprietor of the Magazine to which they supplied contributions.—M.

† In the Chaldee Manuscript, the two editors of Constable's Edinburgh Magazine, were spoken of as Beasts, and the same term was applied to the contributors who assisted them.—M.

The pole creaked ominously, and there was a continued starting of wooden pegs—but we sat down nevertheless to a sort of lunch, consisting of kibbuck* bakes* and small beer—with a small allowance of butter to each Contributor, which, I regret to say, was very rancid, melted down into a sort of lamp-oil, and thickly interspersed with flies. There was in a hamper a large store of eggs, which had been previously boiled—but then they had come several months before from the Isle of Arran, and though few of them were chickenny, all of them were a great deal worse—some black as ink, and others of that yellow peculiar to the pus on a long-neglected wound. "I never smelt anything half so noxious," said the Flunky, "but an ulcer last year on an old woman's knee, in the Infirmary, which had not been allowed half its allowance of rag"——but here the Editor mildly stopped the Flunky, reminding him, that the yolk of the Arran eggs was hard enough to bear of itself, without any unnecessary exaggerations. Here I very fortunately went to the door—for, some how or other, small beer never quite agrees with me—and no sooner had I got "*sub dio*" than down came CONSTABLE AND COMPANY'S EDINBURGH MAGAZINE about the ears of the Contributors, while such a noise arose

"As if the whole inhabitation perished,"

Soon as the first wild din ceased, I heard the small plaintive voice of Dr. Search exclaiming, as if he had been under the University of Edinburgh, "The whole edifice is in ruins!" The Scotsman was heard growling like a bear with a sore head—and the Dominie cried loud, "The pole, the pole," though certainly the last man in the world likely to reach it. By-and-by the Flunky rose up with a load of canvas on his back, like a week's sheeting of the Infirmary; and this gave the Contributors an opportunity of escaping from their thraldom, and of making their appearance through the northwest passage. The Editor and senior Doctor were dug out of the ruins with small symptoms of animation—but the Seven Young Men, who had lain down to sleep, escaped with a few inconsiderable bruises. The two Caddies, Pimping Donald and Drunken Dugald, waxed very wroth, and the former burst out, "Tamn her, what ca ye this? The Scots Magazeen? She's na worth a single doit. The bits o' rapes that should haud her up, are a' rotten—ae pluff o' wun 'll coup her. We maunna expec' her to staun by hersel'—faith, hoist her up as you wull, she'll just aye play cloit again."

It was now obvious to all, that the Editor had taken too high ground, and that if the company's Tent was to be pitched at all, it must be in a situation where it would be less exposed to sudden

* See Dr. Jamieson.—C. N.

flaws of wind. It was accordingly carried by the Caddies, Editor, and the Seven Young Men, down a gentle declivity, with slow and cautious steps, till at last they reached a deep hollow, where it was pitched with considerable ease, the soil being bare of all vegetation, except a sort of whitish moss, and so soft and moist that the pole slipt in at once, notwithstanding the awkward interference of the Dominie, who, in spite of the Editor's mild remonstrances, made much needless flustering, and kept running to and fro like a wasp without a sting, very fierce and fudgy. The Magazine was not visible from almost any part of the adjacent country, in this sheltered hollow—and when every thing was properly got up, a glass of small beer was handed round to each Contributor; but, for the reason already assigned, I civilly begged leave

"To kiss the cup, and pass it to the rest."

The scene now became a good deal more cheerful. The little Kirk of Shotts, crowning the hill, made a decent appearance—here and there were small scanty spots of oats and barley, that had, however, got all the ripening they were ever to have—and small insignificant cocks of rushy hay stood pertly enough in various directions. Rather unluckily there was in the Tent a nest of humble bees—of that brown irritable sort called "foggies"—which were far from being agreeable contributors, and some of them took a violent antipathy to the Dominie, entangling themselves in his black sleek hair, and thereby sorely aggravating the natural irritability of his temper. A curlew (Scotticè whawp) uttered its wild cry from a neighboring marsh, and a lapwing (Scotticè pease-weep), afraid that the Editor intended to rob her nest, kept wheeling round and round the tent, and then trundled herself off, with seemingly broken legs and wings, to the strong temptation of Dr. Search, who, getting nettled, made one of his injudicious sallies from the Magazine in chase of her, but came down on his breech in a wet marshy spring, with a squash that was heard in the interior of the Tent, and brought out the Dominie with a copy of Potter's Translation of Æschylus in his dexter hand, to know what had resulted. Dr. Search did not recover his serenity during the whole afternoon, but kept

"Pacing about the moors continually,"—

with his hand on the part that was more sinned against than sinning—extending the wet cloth a few inches from the skin, and with a rueful face watching the progress of the drying, which, from the low situation of the place affected, and of the Tent, was long and tedious.

The Contributors were beginning to bite their nails for want of something to do or think, when the Flunky, who had gone down to the high-road to see the mail-coach pass by, returned with a parcel of letters, all addressed to the Editor, which, being on the public business of Tent or Magazine, were read aloud by him in an agreeable, but somewhat mouthing manner.

I.

DEAR SIR,—I am so busy with my discoveries in Asia, that I cannot come to the Kirk of Shotts. Besides, I think there is going to be a change of weather—and as I have slept in the Tent formerly, when it was in much better repair than now, I really cannot bring my mind to think of risking my health in it, it being said to have so many chinks. Pitch it in a lone place, and be sure you all sleep together to windward. Yours, very sincerely, H. M.*

Excise Office, August 28th.

II.

MY DEAR SIR,—My professional duties will prevent me from joining the Magazine at present. Beside, you know I have all along been against this scheme of the Tent. It is too obvious an imitation of our good friends in Princes'-street, and you really ought not, my worthy sir, to steal from Dr. Morris, and at the same time abuse him, as I was truly sorry to see you doing in your last Number. Depend upon it, that some confounded Chaldee MS. or other will be coming out to put you all into hot water. I am, my dear sir, yours ever.

College Library.

III.

SIR,—It won't pay. Yours, W. H.†

P. S.—Reynolds is off.

Chapter Coffee-House, London, August 24th.

IV.

DEAR SIR,—Gude faith, I maun mind the shop, ma man. Yours, however,

The Corner. D. B., Junior.‡

* H. M. was intended for Henry Mackenzie, author of The Man of Feeling, Man of the World, Julia de Roubigné, &c. Mr. Pitt made him Comptroller of the Taxes in Scotland, which he held until his death in 1831, at the advanced age of 85.—M.

† W. H. indicated William Hazlett, against whom—as a friend of Leigh Hunt's, a contributor to the *Examiner* and *Edinburgh Review*, and an avowed liberal—Maga waged war from 1817 until his death, in 1830. John Hamilton Reynolds was brother-in-law of Thomas Hood. In 1819, he was a sprightly contributor to Taylor and Hessey's *London Magazine*. He wrote a pretty poem, called The Garden of Florence, founded on a story from Boccaccio, and a curious volume entitled Poetical Remains of Peter Corcoran,—the said Peter having been an illiterate prize-fighter. Mr. Reynolds followed the profession of the law, which occupied him so much, that for years before his death, (which took place in 1852), he had not written for any periodical.

‡ D. B., Junior, was a certain David Bridges, who had a clothier's shop in the High-street, Edinburgh, and with great taste for the Fine Arts, and extensive acquaintance with artists, had contrived to make a very curious and valuable collection of paintings, drawings, sketches, engravings, and etchings, together with many fine casts from the antique. As Secretary of the Dilettanti, he was intimate with Wilson, Lockhart, and the rest of the Blackwood writers, (most of whom were in membership), and himself and his collection are duly noticed in Peter's Letters.—M.

V.

Mr. Editor.—*Honored Sir,*—I have got a sore head, having been at a Mason Lodge last night. But I will take care to send you the second canto of the Silliad, when you come back. I return you many thanks for the guinea. I am, honored sir, your grateful Contributor, WILLISON GLASS.*

Please show the following card to the gentlefolks.

Card to the public.

An ordinary every lawful day at 2 o'clock—cow-heel, tripe, liver, and lights, (and a bottle of small beer between every two), for 5½d. Also, on sale a volume of Poems, price 3 shillings; to which is now added, an appendix, containing the Silliad, Canto I., published in the last Number of Constable and Company's Edinburgh Magazine. The succeeding Cantos, which I am fast writing for that celebrated work, will be delivered gratis to the 3 shilling subscribers. Performed by me, WILLISON GLASS.

These apologies threw a considerable damp over the Tent, but, in imitation of Odoherty and his companions, it was now proposed to have a shooting match. I had not previously observed any arms or ammunition about the party, who indeed seemed inoffensive and altogether defenceless—but drunken Dugald now handed out the weapons, and the match was decided as follows. The Scotsman pulled out of a dirty bag (in which he carried his spare shirt) a copy of Peter's Letters—

"Aye me! that e'er green Mona's† skeely childe,
Should draw the breath impure of paynim dungeon vilde!"

and bellowed out, in a voice like that of an ox with a bull-dog hanging by his lips, "Curse him, damn him, blast him;" but here the Flunky stept up, and beseeched the "Mull of Galloway" to remember the state he was in only a few hours ago, and that two fits in one day would infallibly carry him off. The three extended volumes of Dr. Morris were accordingly put up at the distance of 20 yards, forming a line of about 3½ feet long and 1 broad. The Editors and Contributors were drawn up *en potence* by drunken Dugald, who had once served in the sea fencibles, Aberdeen, but a more awkward squad I never clapped eyes upon; and when they came to the "shoulder," some of them threw up their pieces into the right hand, and some into the left, so that there was great confusion, and the Dominie and Dr. Search actually exchanged weapons for a few moments, like Hamlet and Laertes in the play.

* Willison Glass, as may be noticed, kept a small inn, the familiar name of which in Scotland is "a public." He compounded better punch than poetry—the latter being doggerel.—M.

† This quotation from Spenser is very well in Hugh Mullion, for the family of Dr. Morris came, originally, from Anglesea.—C. N.

‡ The *sobriquet* of authorship under which "Peter's Letters to his Kinsfolk" appeared. The name of the work was probably suggested by Paul's Letters to his Kinsfolk, published in 1815, in which Scott described his visit to Belgium and France, immediately after the final downfall of Napoleon.—M.

***Trial on** the 25th, at 20 yards' distance, all shooting with No. 4 (except the Scotsman, who used rusty nails, bits of glass, and broken types), at the expanded three Volumes of Dr. Peter Morris, of Pensharpe Hall, Aberystwith.*

	Wadding.	Shot. Oz.	Grains put in.	Leaves pierced.
Editor......................	Old Sermon.	$\frac{1}{4}$	0	0
1. Trial, found not to be charged				
2. Hung fire.................				
3. Flashed in the pan.........				
4. Went off accidentally.......				
5. Missed....................				
German Doctor..............	Gardener's grass.	$\frac{1}{2}$	Ditto.	Ditto.
Flunky......................	Foul linen.	$2\frac{1}{2}$	Ditto.	Ditto.
Scotsman, gun recalled........	Ditto.	5	Ditto.	Ditto.
Dr. Search..................	Foolscap.	$\frac{1}{2}$	1	Ditto.
Dominie, blunderbuss burst.....	Title-page of the 1st edit. of Cona.	5	Ditto.	Ditto.
Seven Young Men, pop-gun.....	None.	$\frac{1}{2}$ lb. pease.	130	0

It was a hopeless effort—and one of the Seven wise men (I beg his pardon), one of the Seven Young Men proposed a trial at 10 yards; but this was objected to by another of them, as the shot would be like one ball. He then proposed to extend the distance to 30 yards, when their pieces would scatter more widely—and accordingly Peter's Letters were removed by them to a still higher elevation. But just as Dr. Search was going to fire, his eye caught that of the well-pleased, intelligent physician of Aberystwith, and suddenly shutting his eyes very hard, as frightened as a volunteer on a field-day, he let fly, and missed the whole concern by at least twenty yards. Just as the Dominie was going to fire, the honest face of the Ettrick Shepherd guffawed to him from the comely octavo, as if he was laughing to scorn the Tent, and all the helpless creatures about its gates, and the pedagogue's gun, which he had borrowed from the Scotsman, dropped from his hand.

Inutile telum.

The Editor's turn came next, but just as he was taking aim, the calm, thoughtful, philosophical countenance of Mr. Alison beamed from the book,* and at its

Et tu, Brute,

the Editor went to the right about, and walked undischarged into the Tent. The Scotsman then took his station, but the recoil of his piece, on the former trial, had swollen his right cheek to an enormous size and ugliness, so that he was constrained to take aim from the left side, and had nearly committed fratricide on one of the stirks grazing in the minister's glebe. The Flunky and others gave up in

* The Portraits in Peter's Letters.—M.

despair; and Dr. Morris, invulnerable to the banditti into whose hands he had fallen, was recommitted a prisoner to the Scotsman's dirty bag, from which I hope he will escape ultimately, without either infection or vermin.

It was now beginning to get rather chill in this high situation, and the Shott's shower came drifting by, so we sought shelter in our Tent. But never was anything so uncomfortable. A sort of fire had been kindled in it, and drunken Dugald had been at his pipe—so it was filled with smoke, through whose darkness visible frowned at times the uncomely face of the Scotsman. It was also very wet beneath foot; and how, or on what, we were to pass the night, must have been a trying thought to all of us. It soon began to rain in good earnest, a downright plumper, and the water came in as through a sieve. I said nothing, but went out and found Runciman with his haunches pressed close to the leeside of the Tent, imploring shelter. I clapped the saddle and wallise on him, and mounted. Never was a horse happier. He set off at a round trot, and I soon got to Mid-Calder, where I shifted, and made myself comfortable over a jug of toddy with the landlord, who had observed the pilgrimage pass by, and felt much for their helpless condition when the storm should come on. I afterwards understood, that a message had been sent from the Tent to the Manse imploring a night's lodging; but the excellent minister and his lady were from home, and the servant-lasses would not, on any account, admit any but the "Seven Young Men," who looked so cold and innocent that they were taken to the kitchen fireside, and, after a bellyful of buttermilk brose, were shown the door of the barn—but the rest passed a plashy night in the Tent. I am frightened to look back at the length of this enormous letter—crossed and re-crossed like a field in Spring with the harrow. But you are a good decipherer—so, hoping you will pardon all this nonsense, which is at least perfectly good-natured, I am, dear Mordy, your affectionate brother,

HUGH MULLION.

Provision Warehouse, Grass-market, Sept. 1.

Most of us were greatly entertained with this odd letter of Hugh Mullion, though perhaps all its allusions were not understood by more than two or three of the party, of which number we frankly confess that we ourselves were not. To Seward and Buller it seemed wholly unintelligible, though they both continued listening to the broad patois of Mordy with most laudable perseverance; the first occasionally exclaiming, "Cursed witty, 'pon my soul, you Scotch people, if a Christian could comprehend ye;" and the latter as doggedly attentive as a man to a sermon in the incipient stage of drowsiness; while Price and Tims, who seemed quite alarmed at the mystery, took an opportunity of going out of the Tent, with the avowed design of bathing Randal and Flash in the Dee, these two tykes for some time having sorely interrupted the letter-reader by that desperate snuzzling of mouth and nostril which accompanies an unsuccessful flea-hunt. But though the Oxonians were not initiated into these mysteries of the Cabiri, they were highly delighted with the spirited sketch of the pilgrimage—and Buller, who, with all his gravity and taciturnity, is evidently a wag in his way, put himself into an attitude, when sitting behind Seward on the head of the whisky-cask, most ludicrously imitative of the Dominie,

"Alike—but, oh! how different."

"Pray, Mordy," said Dr. Morris, "have you in good faith a brother called Hugh, or is this letter all a quiz?" "It is exceedingly good to hear you talk of quizzing," replied Mordecai—"but do you know, Doctor, that many people in Edinburgh maintain that you—even you yourself—are a fictitious character altogether, and that John Watson's picture is not a *copy* of, but absolutely *the original and only Dr. Morris.* You are a mere man of canvas, Doctor, and that pawky face and skeely skull of yours, so like flesh, blood, and bone, is, I am credibly informed, nothing but a mixture of oil-colors, and that you were begotten, carried forward, born and bred, all in about three sittings." Dr. Morris, who is much given to laugh at others, was somewhat disconcerted by this attack on his very existence, and Tickler recommended him to institute a prosecution against those who absolutely were attempting to deprive him, not of the means of subsistence, for that was a mere trifle, but of a body to be subsisted.—"If," continued Tickler, "you be indeed a fictitious character, you are the most skilful imitation of a human being that I ever met with in daylight. You think nothing of eating a brace of grouse and a pound of branxy to your breakfast—indeed, always saving and excepting our Editor, I will back you to eat against the whole Tent—and as for the mountain dew, ye sip it like a second Ettrick Shepherd. Come, tell us frankly at once, are you, or are you not, a fictitious character?" Hogg chuckled to hear his friend Morris roasted; "for," quoth he, "Pate is aye playing off his tricks on me and my fiznomie; and though I'm as good-natured a chield as maist folks, deil tak me gin I dinna turn about some day on him and some mair o' you daft blades, and try gin I canna write a Chaldee MS. Gray was doing a' he could to put me up to it a gay while syne, but gin I do't at a' I'll do't o' mysell, and no for nane o' his gab—for he's just gaen a' hyte thegither, 'cause Dr. Morris there didna clap him in amang the leeterawti."—Dr. Morris had by this time recovered himself, and he observed, that on a question of this nature he could scarcely be admitted as a witness, still less as a judge. Yet he must be allowed to say, that the charge of nonentity brought against him was far from being handsome in the Whigs of Edinburgh, to whose existence he had not scrupled to bear the most honorable testimony. "Pray," added the Doctor, "is Mr. Jeffrey a fictitious character? Is Professor Leslie a fictitious character? Nay, to come nearer home, is Mr. Wastle here a fictitious character? I am confident that every candid person will at once reply in the negative. Why, therefore, not admit me to the same privilege?

> "Though fame I slight, nor for her favors call,
> I come in person, if I come at all."

The point being at last conceded to the eloquent physician, Mr. Seward rose from the cask with his usual grace, and threw over to us a letter, written in a large gnostic sprawling hand, on massy hot-pressed paper, and enclosed in a franked envelope, with a splash of wax as broad as a china saucer, which he said we were at liberty to read, now that the Cockneys were hunting the Naiads, swearing us at the same time to silence, as from the irascible temper of Tims, who had lately been within an ace of swallowing the Standard-bearer, he could not hope to return to his rooms in Peck-water,* were that illustrious Luddite to discover the nature of his correspondence with old Scribble.

TO HARRY SEWARD, ESQ.

Bedford Coffee-House, Sept. 1, 1819.

I PITY you sincerely, my dear friend, amongst those Scottish savages. You are like Theseus amongst the Centaurs. Buller himself seems to be undergoing a sort of metempsychosis, and his transformation begins at the stomach. He is, probably, by this time, a wolf. As to those two anomalous instances of humanity, those Weaklings of the City, I really expect that they will be devoured in the first dearth of game, and that Tims, being found too meagre even for soup, will be cast as "bones" to those lean and hungry quadrupeds who follow the march of your frightful army. Everything with you seems to wear the same face; from the "imber edax" to the canines themselves.

Well, here I am, the victim of leisure and hot weather. I am waiting my uncle's arrival from Paris, and my only consolation is, that I am at least on duty. I struggle through the day in the most pitiable perplexity, laboring from hour to hour to be amused and amusing in vain. I even suspect that I shall infuse a portion of my languor into this my epistle to you. I don't know how the devil the women contrive to get on, but there is a spirit of perversity about them now and then, which supplies the place of animal strength.

* Mr. Seward has since condescended to inform us that Peck-water is the name of one of the quadrangles (or, as he terms them, *quads*) of Christ-Church, Oxford.—C. N.

The male performers at the Lyceum have evidently been unable to go through three pieces each night; so the women started (all fillies as for the "Oaks"), and ran over the ground alone. This is a piece of impudence on the part of the petticoats which deserves something more than mere remonstrance. Miss Kelly, to be sure, stands out as a fine concentration of the male species (she is the only approximation to the sex), and "serves you out" with a due portion of talk, in order to do justice to her corporate capacity. Mrs. Chatterly, too, is a pleasant evidence of loquacious frailty; and Miss Stevenson, with only one character to support, has a sort of double-tongued attainment, which she puts forth in a way prepossessingly earnest. We feel convinced, at once, that Mr. Ashe is by no means the only person who can perform a duet on one instrument.

I lament, sincerely, that you haven't got your gloves with you; otherwise you might take the conceit out of *Mister* Price, and abolish Tims altogether,—the one for affecting the gentleman, and the other for imitating man at all.

Tims!—there is a monosyllabic thinness in the name that stands in the place of the most elaborate comment. It has no weight upon the tongue, and sounds like the essence of nothing. It scarcely amounts to "thin air;" and when one strives to elevate it to the dignity of a word, one feels a consciousness that the attempt is presumptuous and vain. The letters seem scarcely the legitimate offspring of the alphabet. They have, collectively, none of the softness of the vowel, and none of the strength of the consonant: but seem to be at the half-way house between meaning and absurdity. The name (pronounce it) sounds like the passing buzz of a drone. It is like a small and ill-favored number in the lottery, which seems predestined to be a blank from the beginning. I see Tims "the shadow" before me; and whenever, for the future, I shall quote the saying of the mighty Julius, I will say, "Aut Cæsar, aut Tims!"

And then you tell me of *Mister* Price. I admire your ingenious note about dandies, but the subject is stale, and I cannot revive it. He seems of the same intellectual stature with his friend, but he has more of the leaven of mortality about him. This seems to be the sole distinction between them—one appears to be a vehicle for want of meaning, and the other cannot claim to be even anything. The utterance of the name of "Price" leaves the lips in a state of suspension, and as it were consideration, which alone gives him claim to some attention. One says, almost mechanically, "Price!"—"What Price?"—any Price:—no Price. The fall is like that of the stocks in stormy times, except that the name is scarcely worth a "speculation."

Talking of gloves, as Mr. Aircastle would say, puts me in mind of the real thing, of which gloves are but the representatives.* Cy Davis has retrieved his fame. He has committed a sort of conquest upon a gentleman from the "Emerald Isle," whose genius was anything but pugilistic. They met at Moulsey; the collision was *striking* enough, but altogether in favor of Cy. Your friends are wrong about Donelly. He did not "go immediately to Brighton." I saw him at Riddlesdown about three hours after his *victory*, as it has been pleasantly called (he was within an ace of getting a drubbing), and I heard Shelton invite him very civilly to a renewal of the sport in two or three months' time. "Sir Daniel," however, seemed to have more than enough of conquest, and sported forbearance. He is a heavy, awkward fellow, and beat, by mere accident, Oliver, who is much lighter than himself, and the slowest hitter in the ring. "Mr. Daniel," before the battle, affected to be sorry for poor "Oliver, on account of his family—*becase he should bate him so asily!!*" But what is all this to you, who, it seems, put forth your Oxford fruit in a foreign land, and reduce the Coliseum to couplets.

By-the-by, if Buller should go on blundering at the birds as in the olden time, he will stand a good chance of getting a coup de grace from one or other of your new friends. Perhaps Mr. Odoherty may "do the honors," or the task may be confided to the "shepherd's dog," in one of those snug dells which occur frequently among the mountains. Mr. Odoherty is a pleasant exotic, who would run wild in any soil. Give my compliments to him; and say that, for Dr. Morris, his visage, and his craniology, I profess to entertain the most profound respect.

I have scarcely room to say that I am, as usual, yours very sincerely,

FREEMAN SCRIBBLE.

At the conclusion of this epistle, the Ettrick Shepherd asked Seward, with more asperity than we recollect ever before to have seen him exhibit, "Wha that Scribble ane had in his ee when he tauked o' Scottish savages?" Seward, who had long taken a strong liking to the Shepherd, gave him the most reiterated assurances that there was nothing personal in the remark, but that, on the contrary, it applied to the Editor and all the Contributors indiscriminately—with which satisfactory explanation the Bard seemed quite contented. Nothing could be more delightful than to witness the friendship of those two great men. We had been informed in the morning, by

* A promising plant of the Bristol Garden. He was beat by Turner, and it was thought by some, that he fought shy of the Welshman's left-hand—but t'other day, he smashed Bushnel, the little Irish Ajax, like so much crockery-ware. Cy. is a good hitter—but he is fond of having things his own way, and is thought to pay a compliment better than he receives one. But who is perfect?—C. N. [Cy., or Cyril Davies, was a professional prize-fighter. So was Shelton, and so was Donelly, commonly called "Sir Daniel," on his own report that, after he fought and beat Oliver, in July, 1819, he was invited to meet the Prince Regent, at Brighton, where he received the honor of Knighthood!—M.]

Tickler, that during our absence Hogg and Seward were inseparable. The Shepherd recited to the Oxonian his wild lays of fairy superstition, and his countless traditionary ballads of the olden time —while the Christ-Church man, in return, spouted Eton and Oxford Prize Poems,—some of them in Latin, and, it was suspected, one or two even in Greek,—greatly to the illumination, no doubt, of the Pastoral Bard. Hogg, however, frankly informed his gay young friend, "that he could na thole college poetry, it was a' sae desperate stupid. As for the Latin and Greek poems, he liked them weel enough, for it was na necessary for ony body to understand them; but for his ain part, he aye wished the English anes to hae just some wee bit inkling o' meaning, and, on that account, he hated worse o' a' them that Seward called by the curious name o' Sir Roger Newdigates.* Deel tak me," quoth the Shepherd, "gin the Sir Rogers binna lang supple idiots o' lines, no worthy being set up in teeps." "Similitude in Dissimilitude" is the principle of friendship as well as, according to Mr. Wordsworth, of poetry—and certainly, while Hogg and Seward resembled each other in frankness, joviality, good humor, generosity, and genius, there is no denying that the shades of difference in their appearance, dress, and manners, were very perceptible. Seward was most importunate on the Shepherd to get him to promise a visit to Oxford, where, with his light sky-blue jacket and white hat, he would electrify the Proctors. Nay, the Englishman went so far as to suggest the propriety of the Shepherd's entering himself at one of the Halls, where gentlemen, by many years his senior, sometimes come to revive the studies of their youth—and "who knows," said Seward, "my dear chum, if the Ettrick Shepherd may not one day or other be the Principal of St. Mary's Hall." The Shepherd replied with his usual naivete, that he "preferred remaining the Principal of St. Mary's Loch;" at which piece of pleasantry Buller himself, though a severe critic of jokes, condescended to smile, somewhat after the manner of Dr. Hodgson.†

We took up a little parcel, which had been forwarded to us from Edinburgh, and found it to contain some very beautiful verses by Mrs. Hemans, on a subject that could not but be profoundly interesting to the soul of every Scotsman. Our readers will remember, that about a year ago, a truly patriotic person signified his intention of giving £1,000 towards the erection of a monument to Sir William Wallace. At the same time, he proposed a prize of £50 to the best Poem on the following subject—"The meeting of Wallace and Bruce

* The prize contended for at Oxford, by under-graduates, for the best poem on a given subject, was founded by Sir Roger Newdigate, whose name it bears. Lord Heber, Guenlos, Wilson, and Milman, are about the only true poets who have obtained this prize within the last half century.—M.

† This was the Rev. Dr. Frodsham Hodgson, then Principal of Brazenose College, Oxford.—M.

on the Banks of the Carron." This prize was lately adjudged to Mrs. Hemans, whose poetical genius has been for some years well known to the public, by those very beautiful poems, "Greece," and "The Restoration of the Works of Art to Italy."—Our pages have already been graced with some of her finest verses—witness that most pathetic Elegy on the Death of the Princess Charlotte, which first appeared in our Miscellany. It was with much pleasure that we lately observed, in that respectable journal, the Edinburgh Monthly Review, a very elegant critique on a new volume of Mrs. Hemans, entitled "Tales and Historic Scenes," with copious extracts; and when we mentioned in the Tent, that Mrs. Hemans had authorized the judges, who awarded to her the prize, to send her poem to us, it is needless to say with what enthusiasm the proposal of reading it aloud was received on all sides, and at its conclusion what thunders of applause crowned the genius of the fair poet. Scotland has her Baillie—Ireland her Tighe—England her Hemans.*

We now took up, with great satisfaction, a small packet, the superscription of which was evidently in the hand-writing of our old worthy friend, Dr. Berzelius Pendragon. The Doctor, though now a shining star of the Episcopalian Church, had not been originally destined for holy orders, and for some years bore the commission of surgeon in the 1st regiment of the West-York Militia. On its reduction he naturally enough turned his thoughts to divinity; and having, at the age of fifty, got a curacy worth £80, at least, per annum—he, being a bachelor, may be said to have been in easy, if not affluent circumstances. Just on reaching his grand climacteric he fell into matrimony, and the cares of an infant family ensuing, he very judiciously took boarders and wrote for reviews. The boarders, however, being all north-countrymen, and thence voracious, over-eat the terms; and the reviews paid only £2 2s. per sheet of original matter, where extracts were of no avail. Having heard of our Magazine—as indeed who has not?—he came down into Scot-

* Joanna Baillie, author of Plays on the Passions, and Felicia Hemans, the lyric poet, are too well known to require particular notice here. The name of Mrs. Tighe is less known. She was the lovely and accomplished wife of an Irish gentleman, and was herself a daughter of Erin. She wrote a beautiful poem, in the Spenserian stanza, entitled "Psyche," which did not appear until after her death. The touching lyric on "The Grave of a Poetess," was written by Mrs. Hemans, in view of her last resting-place, and one of Moore's Irish Melodies, ("I saw thy Form in Youthful Prime,") was suggested by her early death. There was as much truth as poetry, if all that is related of Mrs. Tighe be true, in the concluding stanza,

If souls could always dwell above,
  Thou ne'er hadst left that sphere;
Or could we keep the souls we love,
  We ne'er had lost thee here, Mary!
Though many a gifted mind we meet,
  Though fairest forms we see,
To live with them is far less sweet,
  Than to remember thee, Mary!

Moore admits that, in the closing lines, he endeavored to imitate that exquisite inscription of Shenstone's, "Heu! quanto minus est cum reliquis versari quam tui meminesse!"—M.

land in 1818, and took up his abode with Ben Waters.* No man ever so looked the Contributor as the Rev. Berzelius Pendragon (for at that time he had no degree); and we accordingly put him into training in Constable's Magazine, to see as it were what he could do there with the mufflers, before we ventured to back him in a real stand-up fight. His first performances were promising; and his account of a wonderful American animal, twenty feet high, and with soles three yards in circumference (under the fictitious signature of Serjeant Pollock, Blantyre), attracted considerable notice among the naturalists of the united kingdoms. Unfortunately, in the farther prosecution of that animal, he committed himself by some allusion to Sir Joseph Banks, who was then too ill to be taking that active interest in the mastodonton (so the creature of Pendragon's imagination was called) attributed to him; and the suspicions of the sapient Editor having been awakened, he very considerately wrote to Dr. Hodgson of Blantyre for a certificate of Serjeant Pollock's existence. The Serjeant of course turned out to be as completely a fictitious animal as the mastodonton himself, and the soles of his feet precisely of the same dimensions; and of course a very striking anatomical sketch of the latter, which Berzelius had drawn for Constable, was committed to the flames, and the very paper bones of the formidable monster reduced to ashes. Pendragon, however, had acquired reputation by this set-to, and he was matched against the Bagman (See Number for August, 1818),† whom he beat with apparent ease; though we confess, that during the battle he attempted more than one blow of dubious character, which the Bagman, who is a fine spirited lad, agreed to overlook.

His fame getting wind, the Senatus Academicus of the University of Glasgow,. in the handsomest manner, conferred upon him the unsolicited degree of D.D., and rarely has it been by them so judiciously bestowed. From this time, our friend Pendragon, who had been previously noted for a sort of dry humor, that in days of old was wont to set the mess-table of the West-York Militia in a roar, became somewhat grave and formal—nay, even pompous and aphor-

* Ben Waters kept a tavern in Edinburgh, much frequented by "young men about town." Odoherty, who celebrated his praise and that of Bill Young, at whose hostelree the Dilettanti used to meet, speaks of Waters, as

"charming Ben,
Simplest and stupidest of men."

Young and Waters, with their laureate, have passed away and are among the things which have been.—M.

† This was an amusing review of two works simultaneously published in London, in 1817. One was "Letters from the North Highlands," by Elizabeth Isabella Spence; the other, "Letters from Scotland, by an English Commercial Traveller." It is difficult to say which was most amusing—from sheer absurdity. The lady intensely admired every thing Scottish; the gentleman turned up his nose at every thing which was not from "Lun'un." Blackwood seized the tit-bits of each book, and made a "righte merry and delichtful" article from them, concluding with a suggestion, that the Travelling Spinster and the Literary Bagman should marry. The article excited much amusement at the time, (by the way, it sold off two editions of the books! and is often referred to in Blackwood.—M.

istical—so that he reminded us very much of Dr. Sleath, the present head-master of St. Paul's School, London, formerly of Rugby. He is, however, a truly worthy man—"a man of morals and of manners too;" and our readers will be happy to be informed, that what with "the annual comings-in of a small benefice," (such are some words in The Excursion,) and what with our ten guineas per sheet, the Doctor and Mrs. Pendragon contrive to make the ends meet very comfortably, and likewise to support a family which bids fair to emulate in numbers that of the greatest productive laborer of this economical age—the President of the Board of Agriculture! After this slight and imperfect sketch of Berzelius Pendragon, D.D.—for he was not known to the whole conclave—we did not fear to read aloud the following article on

PYNE'S HISTORY OF THE ROYAL RESIDENCES.*

It is quite possible to have too much of a good thing. This may be considered as a somewhat trite and elderly remark, to proceed from the pen of one of our (collectively speaking) original and erratic divan. But fortunately for the existence and well-being of that at present flourishing fraternity, there yet remains amongst them one sober, staid, and quietly disposed gentleman—one true-bred and thoro'-paced Reviewer of the old school—in short, that anomaly in our little museum of natural history at Ambrose's, "a married man between fifty and sixty." By-the-by, that "obscure man," the Editor, seems, during our absence from the shooting party on the twelfth of August, to have entirely forgotten *us*. But we do not wonder at it—for the whole party frequently forget us even in our very presence, when we are sitting in due state over our pint of London porter, after supper at Ambrose's—listening to,—or at least *hearing*, their enormous jokes. And yet there is nothing very strange in this, for, to disclose one of the "secrets of the prison-house," they sometimes, on these occasions, forget themselves.

But observe the effect of "evil communication!" The perpetual example of these flighty fellow-laborers of ours has actually betrayed *us*, Berzelius Pendragon, D.D.† into the unpardonable indecorum of departing from the straight road which we had prescribed to ourselves.

* Printed for A. Dry, London. 1819. 3 vols. 4to. 24 guineas.—C. N. [This was what is called "a skit," in the manner, introduced in Maga, of throwing a great deal of personal allusions into its critical articles. Mr. Pyne, actually *did* produce a work on the Royal Residences in Great Britain.—M.]

† It may be well to state that one of our brethren (the reader will guess *which*), knowing no better, interpreted this D.D. Doctor of Decorum; alluding probably to our increasing, though too frequently ineffectual, efforts to preserve that propriety of conduct at our meetings without which a society of literati are little better than a society of other people. Ever since that time, though there are several other doctors among us, we have been styled THE DOCTOR, par excellence. Perhaps they give us this title as a quiz, but we take it as a compliment.—B. P.

We were about to observe, that if it were not for a Contributor of the kind we have described ourselves to be,—capable and willing to throw in a measure of salutary dulness now and then, by way of ballast,—the vessel would very soon upset, or be blown clean out of the water. With all our sober and constitutional views on politics, properly so-called, yet we are fain to confess, that there is nothing like a republican form of government in societies like ours. Or perhaps it should rather be called an oligarchy. In short, let it be anything rather than a monarchy; for in three months *that* would inevitably degenerate into a flat despotism. Think, for a moment, of our Miscellany being governed or conducted by any *one* among our numerous, and, in their own departments and their own opinions, highly gifted fraternity! why, instead of being, as it is now, a perpetual "Magazin de Nouveautés," a perfect "Theatre de Variétés,"—it would instantly be recast in the mould of the self-love of him into whose hands it might fall, and become, like the walls of Carlisle prison, all of a color, and very hard to get through.

For example:—If the conduct of our work were resigned to Dr. Morris, does any one who knows that worthy Welshman doubt that, notwithstanding his natural acuteness and love of variety, he would be tempted to make it subserve to the aggrandizement of (whatever he may say or swear to the contrary) his favorite study? All its features would be changed. The four sides of the cover, instead of exhibiting the philosophical and philanthropic physiognomy which has been mistaken for that of Mr. Blackwood himself,—and the interesting and instructive advertisements of books published by "John Murray and William Blackwood," or "William Blackwood and John Murray," would be occupied by a front, a back, and two side views of the human skull divine, forming, together, a complete atlas of the geography of the four different quarters of that (in his opinion) celestial globe.* And the internal arrangements would undergo a change no less calculated to "perplex the nations;" for the doctor would certainly convert it into a kind of log-book, to record the discoveries he has made, and intends to make, in his late and future expeditions to examine the regions about the North Pole.

Would the work be better off under the sole guidance of any other among us? Alas! no, Kempferhausen would inflate it into a huge paper-balloon, to go up into the clouds monthly, and carry messages between him and his lady, the moon. Wastle would make it all rhyme—which is bad enough; and Lauerwinkle all reason—which is worse. Nay, we shall candidly confess—(for candor is our foible)—

* The medallion portrait of George Buchanan, the Scottish historian and poet, actually had been taken, in certain dark parts of Scotland, as a representation of Blackwood or Kit North. In "Peter's Letters," the *pseudo*-Dr. Morris affected to be an enthusiastic disciple of Phrenology, a science of recent discovery, in 1819.—M.

that if *we ourselves* had the management of it, it would probably be very little better than Constable's.

Even if Odoherty—the inexhaustible and immortal Odoherty—(I call him "immortal"—for it appears that he has hitherto escaped unhurt from Waterloo, an Irish widow, and whisky punch,) even if *he* were to undertake the care, it would certainly fail—for he would make it anything, which is nothing. That is to say, he would "make nothing of it." Or if he did, it would be only fun:—And if one could conceive an ocean formed all of whisky toddy—(nothing but the antique imagination of the Ettrick Shepherd, or the antic one of Odoherty, *could* conceive such a thing)—it would probably be quite as unpleasant and as unprofitable to be drowned in that as in one of common salt-water.

No. If we regard the welfare of our little community, we must none of us aspire to be Cæsars. Unless, indeed, when a dozen of us are met together at our little library in Gabriel's Road, we can fancy ourselves, for the time-being, THE TWELVE CÆSARS, shut up in a coin-collector's cabinet. The truth is, we form a very strong and handsome bundle as it is; but if any accident should break the string that holds us together, we shall be no better than so many *sticks.*

But we are astonished, and even scandalized, on looking over what we have written! Why, we have been thinking and talking about our flashy and frisky fraternity, till they have actually inveigled us into a fit of momentary mirth! To our contemplation the thing seems as little in keeping, as it would be to see Professor Leslie play at leap-frog,* or Dugald Stewart dance a saraband. A fit of pleasantry!—We would as soon, if not sooner, have had a fit of the gout: For while the former is sure to betray us into some idle and unseemly levity, the latter,—with its concomitants of easy-chair, foot-stool, flannel and Maderia,—gives an air of doctorial dignity to the whole man; and demands a degree of deference and respect oftener—(we grieve to say it)—oftener expected than paid. Truly, we have most strangely departed from the accustomed and required dignity of our department. If we should hereafter learn that we have been so unhappy as to call up a smile to the face of the reader, we shall never forgive ourselves;—and shall never hear the last of it at Ambrose's. But still the reader himself shall not suffer through our misconduct: for, seeing that at the outset of our article we have been more lively than became us, we shall take care, throughout the

* In Peter's Letters there is a description of a day passed with Jeffrey, at Craig-crook, (his country-seat near Edinburgh), in 1818, when Professors Playfair and Leslie were of the party. A trial of strength in leaping was proposed, and, says Dr. Morris, "with the exception of Leslie, they all jumped wonderfully; and Jeffrey was quite miraculous, considering his brevity of stride. But the greatest wonder of the whole was Mr. Playfair. He was, also, a short man, and he cannot be less than seventy, yet he took his stand with the assurance of an athlete, and positively beat every one of us,—the very best of us, at least half a heel's breadth."—M.

remainder of it, to indulge him with more than our usual and stipulated proportion of dullness. But, before proceeding to the immediate subject of our article, it may be well to state, for the satisfaction of all parties, that the foregoing is our very first exhibition of this kind; and is likely to be the very last. We might, to be sure, expunge the objectionable part of what we have written, and re-write the whole article. But,—to say nothing of our being rather behind our time,—we have considered that it will be, upon the whole, better to let it remain; as a salutary warning, both to ourselves and others, not to quit the path which nature, habit, and inclination have marked out for them:—For, if we may judge of ourselves, we cut as strange a figure at a frisk, as the Ettrick Shepherd would at a quadrille party. For be it known to all whom it may concern, (and whom does it *not* concern?)—that we, Berzelius Pendragon, D.D., do hereby disclaim all participation in the merits or demerits of the numerous noisy and nonsensical articles that have from time to time appeared in this Magazine. But as the Public seem to patronize them, well and good. It is their concern, not ours. At the same time, though no one has hitherto thought fit to mention our name—not even the Editor in his account of the late shooting party on the 12th of August—we shall no longer be induced to forego the portion of credit which really does belong to us; and which the Contributors themselves were not very wise in so long withholding from the true claimant, seeing that they would every one of them be sorely averse from taking it upon themselves. All the grave articles, then,—(it is quite needless to particularize them)—which have graced and are to grace these pages—all which by general consent have been stamped with the (in *our* opinion meritorious) character of dullness—were contrived and constructed solely and exclusively by us, Berzelius Pendragon,* D.D. We now return to "the even tenor of our way,"—and proceed to "labor in our vocation."

It has not been our practice to notice works whose chief attractions consist in their pictorial embellishments; but we have been so much pleased in looking over these volumes, that we are induced to make them more extensively known than they are likely to be in this part of the kingdom without our aid.—Among the many richly illustrated works that have of late years evinced the enterprise and liberality of British publishers, perhaps this is at once the most splendid and the most interesting.—Undoubtedly the external character and appearance of the English palaces have long been the theme of vulgar surprise and contemptuous comparison, by foreigners visiting this coun-

* The reader will probably have anticipated, even if we had not informed him, that whenever it is needful for any written communication to pass between *us* and our coadjutors, they invariably place a hyphen between each syllable of our name—Pen-drag-on. Thus transforming a distinguished patronymic into a despicable pun—or rather a trinity of puns. Tria juncta in uno.—B. P.

try; and also by those English *travellers* who visit the *continent* (that is to say, *Paris*), for the notable purpose of discovering and making known in what respects other countries are superior to their own. If you tell these people that London boasts the finest religious temple in the world, they answer, "But look at St. James's Palace, and compare it with that of the Tuileries!" If you point to our Charitable Institutions, unapproached in munificence of endowment and extent of utility by those of any other nation, they exclaim, "But then how miserably inferior are Kew and Hampton Court to St. Cloud and Versailles!" If you prove to them that the Custom House, the East India House, and the Bank, evince more wealth and public spirit than could be found among the same class of persons in all the nations of the continent united, they reply, "But then, what a paltry private residence for a queen is the cottage at Frogmore, compared with the two Trianons!" It is undoubtedly a reasonable subject of surprise, that, during the last two centuries, so little has been added to the external splendor of the English palaces; but, as it regards the people, one should perhaps expect it to form a subject of congratulation rather than regret. Certain it is, however, that the magnificent work to which we now call the reader's attention, fully proves that, in the internal arrangements of the royal residences, there is no lack of splendor which should surround the court and person of the English sovereign; no deficiency of subjects calculated to awaken and renew many of those delightful associations which we are accustomed to connect with times of romance and chivalry; and, above all, no want of evidence of British sovereigns having felt that the walls of a palace can in no other way be so splendidly and appropriately ornamented as by the unfading works of genius and taste: for it is a very interesting feature of the illustrations of this work, that copies are given of all the ancient pictures which enrich the walls of the different apartments—each appearing in the relative situation which it actually occupies. Some of these copies, though necessarily on a very minute scale, are so extremely well executed as immediately to recall to the recollection of those who are acquainted with them, the admirable originals. This is peculiarly the case with respect to the Cartoons, which occupy the walls of one of the apartments at Hampton Court.

Mr. Pyne's work consists of four quarto volumes, containing together one hundred plates, which are all fac-similes of colored drawings made for the purpose by artists of the very first celebrity; each drawing representing, in its present state, some one apartment in one or other of the royal palaces. These drawings were executed by the express permission, and of many we may say, under the actual inspection of the royal inhabitants themselves—who not only patronized, but really took a personal interest in the progress of the work; and it may be not uninteresting to know, that the vignette, repre-

4*

senting the hermitage, in the garden at Frogmore, is copied from a plate etched by the Princess Elizabeth herself.* We have been informed of these particulars by the gentleman to whom we are indebted for a sight of this work; for we confess its price has rendered it quite inaccessible to ourselves. If we were to notice any of the plates in particular, we should point to the exquisite and elaborate workmanship of those representing the splendid architectural decorations of the Royal Chapel and St. George's Chapel in Windsor Castle; and the conservatory and gothic dining-room at Carlton-house. For magnificence of modern embellishment, the golden drawing-room and alcove, and the crimson drawing-room at Carlton-house, are perhaps not surpassed in any palace in Europe.†

We shall not be expected to have much to say with respect to the literary merits of a work like this; and if we admit that the arrangement of the materials appears to be perspicuous, and the style tolerably clear and correct, it is, perhaps, all that the ambition of the author would demand. We shall, however, fairly confess, that we are, for once, reviewing a book that we have not read through. But though it will be easily admitted that this is a work in which pictorial embellishment may not improperly form the principal feature, yet on turning over its pages, and stopping to read here and there, (and this is all we have had time to do,) we find it interspersed with a variety of very amusing anecdotes and circumstances connected with the successive occupiers of the palaces; and also with some interesting historical and critical notices of some of the principal works of art, copies of which pass in review before us; together with biographical sketches of the distinguished persons whose portraits are among the number.

It must not be imagined, by our gentle readers, that during this enunciation we good people in the Tent were under any very severe discipline. We are no Martinet, and are of opinion that, even on actual service, it is better to command by love than by fear. Accordingly, it was understood among the Contributors from the very first, that while no man was to be allowed loud laughter except the Shepherd, in respect to his genius and infirmity, an occasional titter would be overlooked by the Editor; and that even a little whispering in a corner would not excite so much displeasure in his breast as it has been observed to do in that of my Lady Piano F. during the performance of a screeching solo at a musical party in her house. The Contributors kept going out and coming in like bees, so that a low,

* The Princess Elizabeth, third daughter of George III., born 1770, and married to the Langrave of Hesse Homberg, 1818. She was very accomplished, and drew and etched, as well as if she had been an artist.—M.

† Carlton-House, long the favorite residence of George IV., was pulled down in 1827, and the pillars which formed the entrance colonnade, now are to be seen in the front facade of the National Gallery, Trafalgar Square, London.—M.

pleasant, continuous murmur encircled the Tent. There was not even an ordinance against sleep—except with a snore; and it is a singular enough fact in natural history, that those Contributors who performed most powerfully during the night, when such indulgence was freely permitted to us all, took snatches of slumber during an article as silently as so many dormice. This is one of many proofs of the power of the will over the functions of the bodily organs in sleep. We must all remember how, during the course of our travels, we used to awake, to a minute, at an hour fixed mentally with ourselves before going to bed; and, on the present occasion, we could not help smiling, to see with what supernatural accuracy Timothy Tickler would awake at the conclusion of any article at which he had taken an alarm, and avoided by a skilful and well-timed nap. Was it that he first conjectured its probable duration, and then, by an act of the sleeping yet waking will, awoke just as it ceased? Or may the phenomenon be accounted for on a simpler theory, namely, that Tickler awoke as the Editor or Buller, for example, ceased to speak, just as we have heard of naval officers starting up in their hammocks, awakened by the unusual silence, when the morning-gun did *not* fire?

Owing to the relief given to the mind by little interruptions and incidents of this kind, we suspect that the articles of our Contributors seemed much better ones when we read aloud in the tent, than they may do when perused in a brown study, or the Glasgow coffee-room; but this is a disadvantage to which all viva-voce harangues are liable in tent, in church, and in state. Even one of Dr. Chalmers' astronomical discourses, which we heard him preach before the Commissioner, seemed to us more sublime when volleyed by his thunderous voice through those Gothic arches, than when looked at silently in our own little blue parlor, with out feet on the fender, and our worthy housekeeper (but that way madness lies) knitting a worsted stocking for our rheumatic leg, sufficiently long to reach half way up the thigh. In like manner, we remember reading, with scarce any emotion but a slight one of contempt, a speech of Mr. Tierney* in a newspaper, which we were told by Odoherty convulsed with laughter the whole House. In like manner, a joke of Mr. Cockburn's will, in the General Assembly of our Church, well nigh shake the wigs from the heads of hundreds, which, when confidentially communicated afterwards by one of his admirers to some unfortunate gentleman not present at its first delivery, would seem to have been still-born.

* George Tierney entered Parliament in 1796, and became a strong opponent of Mr. Pitt, with whom he fought a duel in 1798. The Addington Cabinet of 1802, made him Treasurer of the Navy, and in 1806, he was President of the Board of Control, but went out the next year, when the Granville ministry resigned. He was one of the leaders of the Opposition until 1827, when he was made Master of the Mint, under Canning, remained in office under Lord Goderich, with whom he retired in 1828, and died in 1830. He was a very heavy debater, and was ridiculed as such, in The New Whig Guide, published 1819, and written by Palmerston, Peel, and J. W. Croker.—M.

The truth is, that as it was necessary to have been in the High Church, the House of Commons, or the General Assembly, fully to feel and admire the eloquence of Chalmers, the wit of Tierney, or the humor of Cockburn—so was it necessary to have been in our Tent, to enjoy, with perfect enjoyment, the eloquence of a Kempferhausen, the wit of a Tickler, or the humor of a Pendragon.

After the last gentleman's article, we were not without hopes that our dear friend Dr. Morris would have favored us with something good; but Peter let us understand that we must not expect any article from him for some months, as he was busy on his "Letters from the Highlands of Scotland," which he hoped to have out early in spring.* Nobody who has not seen the Doctor write, can have the slightest idea of the rapidity of his intellectual and manual operations; and he now lifted up and fluttered before our eyes at least a hundred pages of closely-written MSS., exclaiming,—"Nearly half of the first volume, you dog. When Scotland is finished, then 'for England, ho!'"

It was now wearing pretty far into the afternoon, and the Editor's travelling china punch-bowl, Hogg's jug, and the quechs of the other Contributors, had, as our readers will readily suppose, been plenished and replenished oftener, perhaps, than it is needful to avow. There could have been no getting on without this; for joy is every whit as dry as sorrow, and the tongues of the Contributors would have cloven to the roofs of their mouths without a judicious and well-timed infusion of the true spirit. We were just in the act of proposing a bumper to the health of that most entertaining of all human beings, Mr. John Ballantyne, who had gone out to breathe the fragrance of the heather, and to hear John of Sky

"His Scottish tunes and warlike marches play,"

when that gentleman himself put his facetious face in at the Tent-door; and with an expression of the most profound and solemn respect strangely blended with its natural and invincible archness, he exclaimed, in considerable agitation, "By the author of Waverley, and every other great Known or Unknown, here is Dr. Mansel, the bishop of Bristol. I have been with him for this half-hour—such another famous bishop saw I never at home or abroad. Put in a jaup mair rum into the bit bowlie, for by his talk I warrant him a dreigh sooker. That'll do—rise up, gentlemen, while I fetch in the bishop."

We were all thrown into some consternation by this unexpected visit from so high a dignitary of the Episcopalian Church, and every lidless eye was bent towards the Tent-door, when once more came

* Announced, but never published,—probably never written.—M.

bowing in, hat in hand, our small incomparable Bibliopole, ushering forward, in full sail, and gorgeous array, not Dr. Mansel, bishop of Bristol—but hear it, O Dee, and give ear, thou Clyde—DR. SCOTT, THE CELEBRATED ODONTIST OF GLASGOW. One roar of unextinguished laughter shook the Tent—while that wittiest of doctors looked towards that wittiest of bibliopoles with a countenance of the most solemn assurance, and pompously asked, "What sort of treatment is this for a BISHOP?"

John Ballantyne had never before seen Dr. Scott, and he now kept his small gray piercing eyes suspiciously upon him, as the veil of clerical mystery seemed to be falling off from the shoulders of the self-appointed spiritual peer. "Me a Bishop," cried the exulting Doctor, "I was only *gagging you*, man! Ye nae sooner tald me your name, than I said into myself—hooly, hooly, we hae gotten here the wuttiest and gleggest wee chield in a' Edinburgh, and gin I can but *gagg* Mr. John Ballantyne, what will Carnegie and Provan, and a' the ither clever fallows in Glasgow, think o' me then?" The Doctor's classical and theological imagination had, it seems, suggested to him the idea of personating the Bishop of Bristol; and during half an hour's conversation with Mr. Ballantyne, he had more than half concluded a bargain for the copyright of a volume of Sermons, in which the Socinian controversy was for ever to be laid at rest on both sides of the Tweed.

But how came Dr. Scott to be hereabouts at all? Had he not departed in the morning for Glasgow, or, to call that thriving city by the more rural appellation bestowed on it by its poetical inhabitants, "The West-Country?" No such thing. The Doctor had been the gay deceiver of us all. At the very moment when his soul seemed to be breathing out sighs of scarcely articulate grief at the Parting Hour, and had responded so passionately to the L'Envoy of the inspired Shepherd, even then, had he meditated no farther journey than down to Mar-Lodge to give some medical advice to the Thane,* of whose arrival there he had been confidentially informed by an express the night before; and it was on his return to the Tent that he had fallen in with Mr. Ballantyne, whom curiosity had drawn towards a cottage on the river's side, from the door of which the Doctor said a beautiful Highland girl was "showering her delightful smiles." Such were the ipsissima verba of the Odontist. "Why, Doctor," said the Shepherd, "you are as bad as my freen, Lord Byron, himsel, and it seems ye were just lauching in your sleeve a' the time you were sayin' gude day to me and the ither Contributors, just as he was lauchin' in his, when he said,

* The Earl of Fife claims to be a lineal descendant of the Thane of Fife mentioned in "Macbeth," but his pretensions have been challenged by genealogists and antiquarians.—M.

'Fare thee well, and if for ever,
Still for ever, fare thee well.'

Faith, Doctor, ye great poets, the Scotts and the Byrons, and sic like, are a' thegither past my comprehension." Mr. John Ballantyne frankly confessed that he had, for the first time in his life, been *fairly gagged.* "But," said he, "I shall have my revenge. Henceforth, gentlemen, let you and all the rest of the world combine to call Dr. Scott THE BISHOP OF BRISTOL." This motion was immediately carried by acclamation, and the Bibliopole and the Bishop shook hands, and sat down on the whisky cask, Buller having vacated his seat by accepting the chirper's hamper.

Order having been restored, and the Bishop having bestowed his benediction on us, and a bumper on himself, we took the earliest opportunity of requesting from him a small article; and as he had nothing to offer in opposition to so equitable a request, he asked, "Verse or prose?" "Verse, to be sure." "Long or short metre." "Oh! long, certainly—one would never think of getting short measure from a Bishop." The Peer accordingly cleared his pipes, and chanted, with a tone and manner of gesticulation which at one time strongly reminded us of Wordsworth, and at another of Rowland Hill,* the following very beautiful Poem:

LOVE'S PHANTOMS OF WOE.

1.

DAY's gone down in the west; yet his last tinge of gold
Is not all from the chimneys of Anderstoun rolled—
And already, far eastward, the meek orb of Dian
With a pale struggling lustre the Calton is eyeing;
The Stockwell and the Gallowgate slumber between,
And the brown Molindinar is flowing unseen.

2.

While the hour's holy stillness reigns sad in the soul,
Oh! 'tis sweet with slow steps up the Trongate to stroll,
For the long sleeping shadows of steeple and land
Sink deep in the spirit with harmony bland;
And well does my sensitive heart sympathize
With the hum of the air and the gloom of the skies.

3.

Man may sigh when earth laughs in the rays of the sun
O'er the dreams of ambition whose race hath been run;
Man may weep when the morn in her glory comes forth
O'er the parted memorials of friendship and worth;
But be mine in the dimness of twilight to rove,
When I charm up the long-faded Phantoms of Love.

* The Rev. Rowland Hill, minister of Surrey Chapel, London, for half a century, was in high feather in 1819. He was noted for eccentricities, illustrating the most solemn truths by observations which savored more of the ludicrous than the pathetic,—more of the grotesque than the serious. He was uncle to Lord Hill, Commander-in-chief of the British army from 1828 to 1842. The Rev. Rowland Hill was eighty-eight, at his death, in 1838.—M.

4.

Oh! vainly and wildly the world's eye would seek,
When the forehead is smooth and a smile's on the cheek,
The wide wildering waves of reflection to sound,
Where the soul sleeps beneath in her darkness profound—
Where sorrow, like truth, is contented to dwell
Cold, clear, and unseen, in the spirit's deep well.

5.

Yet not false is the language that floats from my tongue,
When I joke with the joyous, and laugh with the young;
There is naught of deceit in this eye sparkling bright,
All cordial the chorus of festive delight—
All sincere and substantial the raptures I show,
When Wit's rays bid the ether of merriment glow.

6.

Were it wise—were it well—to refuse to mankind
The light of the spirit—the sun of the mind?
Were it wise, wrapt for ever in garments of woe,
Through the world's busy paths like a spectre to go?
Oh, no! life has moments for more things than one,
Man's great soul can find room both for sorrow and fun!

7.

I have left the dim Trongate, and climbed the high stair,
Where the Horns are hung out as the Sign of the Fair;
I have entered the centre and shrine of delight,
Where around Peggy's bowl my friends' faces are bright,
And shall I be in dumps, and a damper? oh, no!
Drown, ye bumpers of friendship, Love's Phantoms of Woe!

8.

Though the mystical musings that feed the lone mind,
Leave a gentle and mellowing softness behind;
Though the eye that with joy should all radiant appear,
Still reveal thy faint trace—Sensibility's tear!
Oh, forget it, my friends, and reproach me not so,
For I'll drown in deep bumpers—Love's Phantoms of Woe!

The lay of the first Bishop was received with high applause, and as the toils of the day were now near a close, the Editor with his Contributors were about to leave the Tent for an evening walk along the Dee and its "bonny banks of blooming heather," to indulge the most delightful of all feelings, such, namely, as arise from the consciousness of having passed our time in a way not only agreeable to ourselves, but useful to the whole of the wide-spread family of man, when John Mackay came bouncing in upon us like a grasshopper, "Gots my life here are twa unco landloupers cumin dirdin down the hill—the tane o' them a heech knock-kneed stravaiger wi' the breeks on, and the tither ane o' the women-folk, as roun's she lang, in a green joseph, and a tappen o' feathers on her pow."

At the word "women-folk," each Contributor

"Sprang upwards like a pyramid of fire;"

and we had some difficulty in preventing a sally from the Tent. "Remember, gentlemen," quoth we, "that you are still under literary law—be seated." We ourselves, as master of the ceremonies, went out, and lo! we beheld two most extraordinary Itinerants.

The gentleman who was dressed in brown-once-black, had a sort of medico-theological exterior—which we afterwards found to be representative of the inward man. He was very tall, and in-kneed*—indeed, somewhat like Richmond the black† about the legs—the squint of his albino eyes was far from prepossessing—and stray tufts of his own white hair, here and there stole lankly down from beneath the up-curled edge of a brown caxon that crowned the apex of his organization. He seemed to have lost the roof of his mouth, and when he said to us, "You see before you Dr. Magnus Oglethorpe, itinerant lecturer on poetry, politics, oratory, and the belles lettres," at each word, his tongue came away from the locum-tenens of his palate, with a bang, like a piece of wet leather from a stone (called, by our Scottish children, "sookers," we forget the English name), each syllable, indeed, standing quite *per se*, and not without difficulty to be drilled into companies or sentences. But we are forgetting the lady. She was a short, fat, "dumpy woman"—quite a bundle of a body, as one may say—with smooth red cheeks, and little twinking roguish eyes;—and when she returned our greeting, we were sensible of a slight accent of Erin, which, we confess, up in life as we are, falls on the drum of our ear

"That's like a melody sweetly played in tune."

She was, as John Mackay had at some distance discovered, in a green riding-habit, not, perhaps, much the worse, but certainly much the smoother for wear,—and while her neat-turned ankles exhibited a pair of yellow laced boots which nearly reached the calf of her leg, on her head waved elegantly a plume of light-blue ostrich feathers. The colors altogether, both those of nature and of art, were splendid and harmonious, and the Shepherd, whose honest face we by chance saw (contrary to orders) peeping through a little chink of the Tent, whispered, "Losh a day, gin there binna the queen o' the Fairies!"‡ We requested the matchless pair to walk in—but Dr. Magnus, who

* It was upon this gentleman that the celebrated punster of the West made that famous pun, "the Battle of the Pyrenees—(the pair o' knees.)"—C. N.

† Richmond, the black, was a pugilist in those days.—M.

‡ Wherever the belief in fairies exists, there also is the belief, that *green* is their favorite color. In some of the country districts of Scotland and Ireland, it is considered unlucky (or *uncannie*) to have even a green lash to your riding-whip.—M.

was rather dusty, first got John Mackay to switch him, behind and before, with a bunch of long heather, and we ourselves performed the same office, with the greatest delicacy to the lady. The improvement on both was most striking and instantaneous. The Doctor looked quite fresh and ready for a lecture,—while the lady reminded us, so sleek, smooth, and beautiful did she appear, of a hen after any little ruffling incident in a barn-yard. We three entered the tent—"Contributors! Dr. Magnus Oglethorpe and Lady on a lecturing tour through the Highlands." In a moment twenty voices entreated the lady to be seated—Dr. Morris offered her a seat on his bed, which, being folded up, he now used as a chair or sofa—Wastle bowed to the antique carved oak arm-chair that had been sent from Mar-Lodge by the Thane—Tickler was lifting up from the ground an empty hamper to reach it across the table for her accommodation—Buller was ready with the top or bottom of the whisky cask, and we ourselves insisted upon getting the honor of the fair burden to the Contributor's box. Seward kept looking at her through his quizzing glass—"Deuced fine wumman, by St. Jericho! demme if she b'nt a fac-simile of Mary Ann Clarke,* only summat deeper in the fore-end —one of old Anacreon's βαθυκολποι." Her curtsey was exceedingly graceful—when, all of a sudden, casting her eyes on the Standard-bearer, who, contrary to his usual amenity towards the sex, stood sour and silent in a corner, she exclaimed, "By the powers, my own swate Morgan Odoherty," and jumping up upon the table, she nimbly picked her steps among jugs, glasses, and quechs (upsetting alone Kempferhausen's ink-horn over an ode to the moon), and in a moment was in the Adjutant's arms.† Mrs. M'Whirter, the fair Irish widow whom the Ensign had loved in Philadelphia, stood confessed. There clung she, like a mole, with her little paws to the Standard-bearer's sides—striving in vain to reach those beguiling lips, which he kept somewhat haughtily elevated about six feet three inches from the ground, leaving an unscalable height of at least a yard between them and the mouth of the much flustered, deeply injured Mrs. M'Whirter. The widow, whose elegant taste is well known to the readers of this Magazine, exclaimed, in the words of Betty‡ (so she called him),

"Ah! who can tell how hard it is to climb
The steep where love's proud temple shines afar!"

* Mrs. Mary Ann Clarke, once the mistress of the Duke of York. From this connexion arose a parliamentary investigation, in 1809, on a charge that he allowed her to dispose of his patronage for money, which showed him guilty of great carelessness, at least. On this he resigned the command of the army, which he subsequently resumed.—M.

† To understand this it must be explained, that a former *Blackwood*, giving a memoir of Odoherty, stated, that when a prisoner of war in Philadelphia, in 1815, he there had married, and soon after deserted, an Irish widow named M'Whirter, who kept the "Goat in Armor" tavern, in that city of brotherly-love.—M.

‡ Dr. James Beattie, author of several philosophical works, and the poem called The Minstrel. He died in 1803.—M.

"Never mind the money—my dearest Morgan—Och! I have never known such another man as your sweet self since we parted at Philadelphia." The Adjutant looked as if he had neither lost nor won—still gently but determinedly repelling the advances of the warm-hearted widow, whose face he thus kept, as it were, at arm's length. At last, with a countenance of imperturbable solemnity, worthy of a native of Ireland and a Contributor to this Magazine, he coolly said, "Why, Mr. Editor, the trick is a devilish good one, very well played, and knowingly kept up—but now that you, gentlemen, have all had your laugh against Odoherty, pray, Mrs. Roundabout Fat-ribs, may I ask when you were last *bateing hemp*, and in what house of correction!" "Och—you vile sadducee."—"I suspect," said Tickler, "that you yourself, my fair Mrs. M'Whirter, were the seducee, and the ensign the seducer." "Why look ye," continued Odoherty, "if you are Molly M'Whirter, formerly of Philadelphia, you have the mark of a murphy (Hibernicé potato) on your right side, just below the fifth rib—and of a shamrock, or, as these English gentlemen would call it, a trefoil, between your shoulders behind, about half way down,".............Here Mrs. M'Whirter lost all temper—and appealed to Dr. Magnus Oglethorpe, if Odoherty was not casting foul aspersions on her character. The doctor commenced an oration, with that extraordinary sort of utterance already hinted at, which quite upset the Adjutant's gravity—and the lady now seizing the "tempora mollia fandi," said, with a bewitching smile, "Come now, my dearest Morgan, confess, confess!" The Standard-bearer was overcome—and, kissing his old friend's cheek in the most respectful manner, he said, "I presume Mrs. M'Whirter is no more, and that I see before me the lady of Dr. Magnus Oglethorpe—in other words, *Mrs. Dr.* Oglethorpe." "Yes, Morgan, he is indeed my husband—come hither, Magnus, and shake hands with the Adjutant—this is the Mr. Odoherty, of whom you have heard me so often spake." Nothing could be more delightful than this reconciliation. We again all took our seats—Dr. Magnus on our own left hand, and Mrs. Dr. Magnus on our right, close to whom sat and smiled, like another Mars, the invincible Standard-bearer. It was a high gratification to us now to find that Odoherty and Mrs. M'Whirter had never been united in matrimony. It was true that in America they had been tenderly attached to each other, but peculiar circumstances, some of which are alluded to in a memoir of the Adjutant's life in a former number of this Magazine,* had prevented their union, and soon after his return

* The article in question somewhat libelled the Hibernian widow, for it distinctly averred that Odoherty had married her, and made her, in her anger at his desertion, perpetrate sundry wrathful verses to him, which end thus :—

> "When you've drunk my gin, and robbed my till, and stolen all my pelf, ye
> Sail away, and think no more on your wife at Philadelphy."

But this belongs rather to the Life of Odoherty, in Dr. Maginn's Works, than to THE TENT, and the sayings and doings therein.—M

to Europe, the M'Whirter had bestowed her hand on a faithful suitor, whom she had formerly rejected, Dr. Magnus Oglethorpe, lecturer on poetry, politics, oratory, &c., a gentleman famous for removing impediments in the organs of speech, and who, after having instructed in public speaking some of the most distinguished orators in the House of Representatives, United States, had lately come over to Britain, to retard, by his precepts and his practice, the decline and fall of eloquence in our Island. As we complimented the doctor on the magnificent object of his pedestrian tour, he volunteered a lecture on the spot, and in an instant—and springing up as nimbly upon the table as Sir Francis Burdett or Mr. John Hobhouse* could have done, the American Demosthenes (who seemed still to have pebbles in his mouth, though far inland), thus opened it,† and spake a

LECTURE ON WHIGGISM.

Ladies and Gentlemen—Fear is "Whiggism"—hatred is "Whiggism"—contempt, jealousy, remorse, wonder, despair, or madness, are all "Whiggism."

The miser when he hugs his gold—the savage who paints his idol with blood—the slave who worships a tyrant, or the tyrant who fancies himself a god—the vain, the ambitious, the proud, the choleric man—the coward, the beggar, all are "Whigs."

> "The 'Whig,' the lover, and the poet,
> Are of imagination all compact.
> One sees more devils than vast hell can hold—
> The madman."

"Whiggism" is strictly the language of *imagination;* and the imagination is that faculty which represents objects, not as they are in themselves, but as they are moulded, by *other* thoughts and feelings, into an infinite variety of shapes and combinations of power. This language is not the less true to nature, because it is false in point of *fact;* but so much the more true and *natural,* if it conveys the impression which the object under the *influence of passion* makes on the mind. Let an object, for instance, be presented in a state of agitation or fear, and the imagination will distort or magnify the object, and convert it into the likeness of whatever is most proper to encourage the fear.

Tragic "Whiggism," which is the most empassioned species of it, strives to carry on the feeling to the utmost point, by all the force of comparison or contrast—loses the sense of present suffering in the imaginary exaggerations of it—exhausts the terror of an unlimited indulgence of it—*grapples with impossibilities in its desperate impatience of restraint.*

When Lear says of Edgar, nothing but the unkind "ministry" could have brought him to this—what a *bewildered* amazement, what a *wrench* of the imagination, that cannot be brought to conceive of any other cause of misery than that which has bowed it down, and absorbs all other sorrow in its own! His sorrow, like a flood, supplies the sources of all other sorrow.

In regard to a certain Whig, of the unicorn species, we may say—How his

* Sir Francis Burdett and Mr. Hobhouse were ultra-liberals in 1819. Burdett lapsed into ultra-toryism in 1836, in which he remained until his death, in 1844. Hobhouse succeeded to a baronetcy on his father's death, successively took office under Grey, Melbourne, and Russell, and was made a Peer in 1851, by the title of Lord Broughton.—M.

† The expression, "*Thus opened his mouth,*" is incorrect, for without a plate it would be impossible to show the manner in which Dr. Magnus opened his mouth.—C. N.

passion lashes itself up, and swells and rages like a tide in its sounding course, when, in answer to the doubts expressed of his returning "temper," he says—

> "Never *Iago*. Like to the Pontic Sea,
> Whose icy current and compulsive course
> Ne'er feels retiring ebb, but keeps due on
> To the Propontic and the Hellespont;
> Even so my 'frantic' thoughts, with violent pace,
> Shall ne'er look back, ne'er ebb to humble 'sense,'
> Till that a capable and wide revenge
> Swallow them up."

The pleasure, however, derived from tragic "Whiggism," is not any thing peculiar to it as Whiggism, as a fictitious and fanciful thing. It is not an anomaly of the imagination. It has its source and ground-work in the common love of "power" and strong excitement. As Mr. Burke observes, people flock to "Whig meetings;" but if there were a public execution in the next street, the "house" would very soon be empty. It is not the difference between fiction and reality that solves the difficulty. Children are satisfied with stories of ghosts and witches. The grave politician drives a thriving trade of abuse and calumnies, poured out against those whom he makes his enemies for no other end than that he may live by them. The popular preacher makes less frequent mention of heaven than of hell. Oaths and nicknames are only a more vulgar sort of "Whiggism." We are as fond of indulging our violent passions as of reading a description of those of others. We are as prone to make a torment of our fears as to luxuriate in our hopes of "mischief." The love of power is as strong a principle in the mind as the love of pleasure. It is as natural to hate as to love, to despise as to admire, to express our hatred or contempt as our love of admiration.

> "Masterless passion sways us to the mood
> Of what it likes or loathes."

Not that we like what we loathe, but we like to indulge our hatred and scorn of it (viz. Toryism)—to dwell upon it—to exasperate our idea of it by every refinement of ingenuity and extravagance of illustration—to make it a bugbear to ourselves—to point it out to others in all the splendor of deformity—to embody it to the senses—to stigmatize it in words—to grapple with it in thought, in action—to sharpen our intellect—to arm our will against it—to know the worst we have to contend with, and to contend with it to the utmost.

Let who will strip nature of the colors and the shapes of "Whiggism," the "Whig" is not bound to do so; the impressions of common sense and strong imagination, that is, of passion and "temperance," cannot be the same, and they must have a separate language to do justice to either. Objects must strike differently upon the mind, independently of what they are in themselves, so long as we have a different *interest* in them—as we see them in a different point of view, nearer or at a greater distance (morally or physically speaking), from novelty—from old acquaintance—from *our ignorance* of them—from our fear of their consequences—from contrast—from unexpected likeness; hence nothing but Whiggism *can* be agreeable to nature and truth.

This lecture gave universal satisfaction—but Dr. Magnus is a man of too much genius not to acknowledge unreservedly his obligations to other great men—and after our plaudits had expired, he informed us, that he claimed little other merit than that of having delivered the lecture according to the best rules and principles of oratory, for that the words were by his friend Mr. Hazlitt. "In the original," said he, "Mr. Hazlitt employs the word 'Poetry,' which I have slightly changed into the word 'Whiggism,' and thus an excellent lecture on politics is procured, without the ingenious essayist having been at all aware of the ultimate meaning of his production.* "As the lecture was but short, will you have another ?"

"No—no—enough is as good as a feast," quoth Odoherty—"perhaps, Mr. Editor, if you request it, Mrs. Magnus will have the goodness to make tea."

There was not only much true politeness in this suggestion of the Adjutant, but a profound knowledge of the female character—and, accordingly, the *tea things* were not long of making their appearance, for in our Tent it was just sufficient to hint a wish, and that wish, whatever it might be, that moment was gratified. Mr. Magnus, we observed, put in upwards of thirty spoonfuls—being at the rate of two and a half for each Contributor—and the lymph came out of the large silver tea-pot "a perfect tincture;" into his third and last cup of which each Contributor emptied a decent glass of whisky; nor did the Lady of the Tent, any more than the Lady of the Lake, show any symptoms of distaste to the mountain dew. The conversation was indeed divine—and it was wonderful with what ease Mrs. Magnus conducted herself in so difficult a situation. She had a word or a smile for every one, and the Shepherd whispered to Tickler, just loud enough to be heard by those near the Contributors' Box, "Sic a nice leddy wad just sute you or me to a hair, Mr. Tickler. Faith, thae blue ostrich plumbs wad astonish Davy Bryden, were he to see them hanging o'er the tea-pat at Eltrive-Lake, wi' a swurl."

Alas! there is always something imperfect in sublunary happiness. Baillie Jarvie seemed very unwell and out of spirits. "What ails you, my dear Baillie," said we, in the most affectionate tone, but still Jarvie sat with a long, dull, dissatisfied aspect, which looked most excessively absurd, close to the small insignificant happy face of Tims, who had some how or other got into an extraordinary high flow of spirits (we suspect he had sipped too much of that stout tea) and was coaxing and cockering up the Baillie with "how now, Mr. Jarvie, I 'ope you are more better now; will you try one of my pills, my good sir, Mamar 'as given me the box; see, it has a picture of Hesculapius on the top. Hopen it, Mr. Bailiff, and take out as many as you choose; but three is a doze."

"I am for none o' your nasty pills, Mr. Tims, swallow them all yourself before you lie down."

"Mr. Bailiff, Mr. Bailiff, three is a doze; was I to do that, Tommy Tims might lie down, but Tommy Tims would never rise hup no more;" and as he ceased speaking, we could not help thinking of that passage in Milton, where it is said of Raphael, that when he came to a house, Adam could not help thinking that the angel had not finished his speech.

* On examination of the commencement of one of Hazlitt's lectures on Poetry, the ingenuity of the alteration will be seen.

"Come, come," said we, "give us a song, Baillie."

"I don't believe you wish me to sing or to do any thing else," was the reply; and in an instant we saw into the very seat of the Baillie's distemper. He manifestly had been offended because we had not asked him for an Article, which, Heaven knows, proceeded from no distrust in his literary talents, but from a notion that he would prefer making his sagacious remarks on the articles of other men, to any exhibition of his own. We were now undeceived, and on reiterating our request, honest Jarvie said, that he would recite a song, not sing it,—but that first of all, he must say a word or two by way of preface:

"Though I was," said he, "in my youth, a little addicted to poetical phantasies, yet have I, for a long while, been justly considered, in the Salt-market, as a mere proser. Some years ago, in my first wife's time, when that good woman was sorely afflicted with an '*income*,'* I was advised by Dr. Ninian Hill of Glasgow, to carry her to the country for a *change of air*, as he called it, or as I have been informed, it is termed by Dr. Gregory, *mutatio cœli*. With this view, I took a lease for a summer, at £27 of rent, from the late Mr. Robert Robison, of the villa and garden of *Leddrie Green*, in the parish of *Strablane*, a sweet spot, and of which parish the present learned and worthy minister of St. Andrew's church in Glasgow, also now professor of Hebrew in our university, was then pastor. I accordingly went thither with my spouse for the time being, and my little niece *Nicky*, that is to say, *Nicolina Jarvie*, at that time a little *skelpy*, but now *Mrs. Mecklehose*, and who paid the most assiduous attention to her aunt in her last illness, reading to her at night Mrs. McIver's Cookery, and the Rev. Ralph Erskine's Sermons. It was on a Saturday evening after tea, as I recollect, and when a little fatigued by my ride from Glasgow in a very warm day, and my wife rather worse, that, in order to recreate myself, I sat down in a little arbor in the garden—the church and manse, and a jug of whisky toddy, full in my view—and composed a trifling ballad, which, with the permission of this company (and if Captain Odoherty would be pleased to give over swearing), I shall now read (though, as I find I have lost my spectacles this morning in the hill in chasing Mr. Constable's bitch, who was worrying a lamb, I wish I may be able), but—"

Here the Baillie was interrupted rather improperly by Mr. Tickler, who briskly offered to read the ballad *without Spectacles*.

"Deil tak me," quoth Mr. Hogg, "if I think you're able."

Instantly *Mr. Wastle*, to put an end to all contention, proposed to read it himself, and this being agreed to by *acclamation*, Buller of

* *Income*—Issue.

Brazennose insisted, with rather an undue vehemence, on a liminary bumper; and this also being instantly agreed to, and instantly swallowed, Mr. Wastle rose, and in his usual graceful and impressive manner, read with much pathos,

LEDDRIE GREEN,

An excellent new Song,

Written by BAILLIE JARVIE, *a good many Years ago.*

"If that be not a bull," cried Odoherty.—"Silence, Mr. Odoherty," and Mr. Wastle proceeded.

1.

YE who, on rural pleasures bent,
  Roam idly round in summer sheen,
From John o'Groat's to southern Kent,
  No spot you'll find like Leddrie Green.

2.

Talk not to me of Brighton's joys,
  Its gay parade and glittering steyne;
I'd leave its crowds and endless noise,
  For the sweet woods of Leddrie Green.

3.

At Tunbridge ye who sip the springs,
  Or at the Sussex Pad' are seen;
Ah! if you heard the rill that rings,
  Perennial close to Leddrie Green,

4.

And ye at Harrowgate impure,
  Who shudder o'er your drafts unclean,
'Twould be a shorter ride, I'm sure,
  And sweeter far, to Leddrie Green.

5.

Saltmarket Muse! now deftly tell
  How rocks basaltic rise and screen
The windings of the upland fell,
  That skirts the strath at Leddrie Green.

6.

Bold crags romantic thence ye view,
  Loch Lomond and its woods I ween;
And Morven's summits tinged with blue,
  Break the far sky at Leddrie Green.

7.

Thy spout, Ballagan, thundering down
  Like Niagara foams between
The darksome pines and shrubs, that own
  The neighborhood of Leddrie Green.

8.

And ye who, vex'd with city noise,
  Retire to breathe the air so keen;
Ah! think of eating Nicky's pies,
  And turkey pouts at Leddrie Green.

9.

Or you who lonely wish to sigh,
  O'er life's short course and winter's e'en,
Go view the mausoleum nigh,
  The parish-kirk at Leddrie Green.

10.

A gentle swain here rests inurn'd,
  The only spot where rest is given;
Between two wives, each duly mourn'd,
  And married still 'tis hoped in heaven.

This poem was applauded to "the very echo" by all but Mrs. Magnus, who was too polite to say anything derogatory to Bailie Jarvie's genius. Indeed, she no doubt admired that genius, but the subject did not seem to interest her. "My dear Mr. Odoherty (for they treated each other with infinite respect), will you give us something amatory?"—"I gives my vice, too, for something hamatory," pertly enough whiffled Mr. Tims;—when the Standard-bearer, after humming a few notes, and taking the altitude from the pitch-key of Tickler (which he carries about with him as certainly as a parson carries a corkscrew), went off in noble style with the following song, his eyes all the while turned towards Mrs. Magnus Oglethorpe, whose twinklers emanated still but eloquent responses not to be misunderstood.

INCONSTANCY; A SONG TO MRS. M'WHIRTER.

By Mr. Odoherty.

1.

"Ye fleeces of gold amidst crimson enroll'd
  That sleep in the calm western sky,
Lovely relics of day float—ah! float not away!
  Are ye gone? then, ye beauties, good bye!"
It was thus the fair maid I had loved would have staid
  The last gleamings of passion in me;
But the orb's fiery glow in the soft wave below
  Had been cooled—and the thing could not be.

2.

While thro' deserts you rove, if you find a green grove
  Where the dark branches overhead meet,
There repose you a while from the heat and the toil,
  And be thankful the shade is so sweet;
But if long you remain, it is odds but the rain
  Or the wind 'mong the leaves may be stirring;
They will strip the boughs bare—you're a fool to stay there—
  Change the scene without further demurring.

3.

If a rich-laden tree in your wanderings you see,
With the ripe fruit all glowing and swelling,
Take your fill as you pass—if you don't you're an ass,
But I daresay you don't need my telling.
'Twould be just as great fooling to come back for more pulling,
When a week or two more shall have gone,
These firm plums very rapidly, they will taste very vapidly,
—By good luck we'll have pears coming on!

4.

All around Nature's range is from changes to changes,
And in change all her charming is centered—
When you step from the stream where you've bathed, 'twere a dream
To suppose 't the same stream that you entered;
Each clear crystal wave just a passing kiss gave,
And kept rolling away to the sea—
So the love-stricken slave for a moment may rave,
But ere long, oh! how distant he'll be?

5.

Why—'tis only in name, you, e'en you, are the same
With the SHE that inspired my devotion,
Every bit of the lip that I lov'd so to sip
Has been changed in the general commotion—
Even these soft gleaming eyes, that awaked my young sighs,
Have been altered a thousand times over;
Why? Oh! why then complain that so short was your reign?
Must all Nature go round but your lover?

The tears flowed in torrents, from the blue eyes of Mrs. Magnus, during the whole of this song; and when Mr. Tims, who was now extremely inebriated (he has since apologized to us for his behavior, and assured us, that when tipsy on tea he is always quite beyond himself), vehemently cried, "Hangcore! hangcore!" the gross impropriety of such unfeeling conduct was felt by Mr. Seward, who offered, if agreeable to us, to turn him out of the Tent; but Tims became more reasonable upon this, and asked permission to go to bed; which being granted, his friend Price assisted the small cit to *lay* down, and in a few minutes, we think, unless we were deceived, that we faintly heard something like his own thin tiny little snore.

Mrs. Magnus soon recovered her cheerfulness; for being, with all her vivacity, subject to frequent but short fits of absence, she every now and then, no doubt without knowing what she was about, filled up her tea-cup, not from the silver tea-pot, but from a magisterial-looking bottle of whisky, which then, and indeed at all times, stood on our table. She now volunteered a song of her own composition; and after fingering away in the most rapid style of manipulation on the edge of the table, as if upon her own spinnet in Philadelphia, she too took the key from Tickler's ready instrument, and chanted in recitativo what follows—an anomalous kind of poetry.

CHAUNT.—BY MRS. M'WHIRTER.

TUNE.—*The Powldoodies of Burran.**

1.

I WONDER what the mischief was in me when a bit of my music I proffered ye!
How could any woman sing a good song when she's just parting with Morgan Odoherty?
A poor body, I think, would have more occasion for a comfortable quiet can,
To keep up her spirits in taking lave of so nate a young man—
Besides, as for me, I'm not an orator like Bushe, Plunket, Grattan, or Curran,†
So I can only hum a few words to the old chaunt of the Powldoodies of Burran.‡

Chorus.—Oh! the Powldoodies of Burran,
The green, green Powldoodies of Burran,
The green Powldoodies, the clean Powldoodies,
The gaping Powldoodies of Burran!

2.

I remember a saying of my Lord Norbury, that excellent Judge,‖
Says he, never believe what a man says to ye, Molly, for believe me 'tis all fudge;
He said it sitting on the Bench before the whole Grand Jury of Tipperary,
If I had minded it, I had been the better on't, as sure as my name's Mary;
I would have paid not the smallest attention, ye good-for-nothing elf ye,
To the fine speeches that took me off my feet in the swate city of Philadelphy.
Oh! the Powldoodies of Burran, &c. &c.

3.

By the same rule, says my dear Mr. Bushe, one night when I was sitting beside Mausey,
"Molly, love," says he, "if you go on at this rate, you've no idea what bad luck it will cause ye;
You may go on very merrily for a while, but you'll see what will come on't,
When to answer for all your misdeeds, at the last you are summoned;
Do you fancy a young woman can proceed in this sad lightheaded way,
And not suffer in the long run, tho' manetime she may merrily say,
Oh! the Powldoodies of Burran, &c. &c.

4.

But I'm sure there's plenty of other people that's very near as bad's me,
Yes, and I will make bould to affirm it in the very tiptopsomest degree;
Only they're rather more cunning concealing on't, tho' they meet with their fops
Every now and then by the mass, about four o'clock in their Milliners' shops;
In our own pretty Dame-street§ I've seen it—the fine Lady comes commonly first,
And then comes her beau on pretence of a watch-ribbon, or the like I purtest.
Oh! the Powldoodies of Burran, &c. &c.

* The POWLDOODIES of BURRAN are oysters, of which more will be said and sung in future Numbers of this Work.—C. N.

† Bushe, afterwards Chief Justice of Ireland; Plunket, Lord Chancellor; Grattan, who truly said of Irish independence, "I sat by its cradle, I followed its hearse;" Curran, the orator and patriot, honest in the worst of times, "over whose ashes," to use his own words, "the most precious tears of Ireland have been shed."—M.

‡ Malahide, near Dublin, supplies the oysters, called the Powldoodies of Burran.—M.

‖ Of "Lord Norbury, that excellent Judge," there is a very particular, though not flattering account, in Sheil's Sketches of the Irish Bar. It could not be said of him that he tempered justice with mercy. In *his* vocabulary neither word could be found.—M.

§ Dublin.—M.

5.

But as for me, I could not withstand him, 'tis the beautiful dear Ensign I mean,
When he came into the Shining Daisy* with his milkwhite smallclothes so clean,
With his epaulette shining on his shoulder, and his golden gorget at his breast,
And his long silken sash so genteelly twisted many times round about his neat waist;
His black gaiters that were so tight, and reached up to a little below his knee,
And showed so well the prettiest calf e'er an Irish lass had the good luck to see.
Oh! the Powldoodies of Burran, &c. &c.

6.

His eyes were like a flaming coal-fire, all so black and yet so bright,
Or like a star shining clearly in the middle of the dark heaven at night,
And the white of them was not white, but a charming sort of hue,
Like a morning sky, or skimmed milk, of a delicate sweet blue;
But when he whispered sweetly, then his eyes were so soft and dim,
That it would have been a heart of brass not to have pity upon him.
Oh! the Powldoodies of Burran, &c. &c.

7.

And yet now you see he's left me like a pair of old boots or shoes,
And makes love to all the handsome ladies, for ne'er a one of them can refuse;
Through America and sweet Ireland, and Bath and London City,
For he must always be running after something that's new and pretty,
Playing the devil's own delights in Holland, Spain, Portugal, and France,
And here too in the cold Scotch mountains, where I've met with him by very chance.
Oh! the Powldoodies of Burran, &c. &c

8.

When he first ran off and deserted me, I thought my heart was plucked away,
Such a tugging in my breast, I did not sleep a wink till peep of day—
May I be a sinner if I ever bowed but for a moment my eye-lid,
Tossing round about from side to side in the middle of my bid.
One minute kicking off all the three blankets, the sheets, and the counterpane,
And then stuffing them up over my head like a body beside myself again.
Oh! the Powldoodies of Burran, &c. &c.

9.

Says I to myself, I'll repeat over the whole of the Pater Noster, Ave-Maria, and creed,
If I don't fall over into a doze e'er I'm done with them 'twill be a very uncommon thing indeed;
But, would you believe it? I was quite lively when I came down to the Amen,
And it was always just as bad tho' I repeated them twenty times over and over again;
I also tried counting of a thousand, but still found myself broad awake,
With a cursed pain in the fore part of my head, all for my dear sweet Ensign Odoherty's sake.
Oh! the Powldoodies of Burran, &c. &c.

10.

But, to cut a long story short, I was in a high fever when I woke in the morning,
Whereby all women in my situation should take profit and warning;

* The *Shining Daisy* was the sign of Mrs. M'Whirter's chop-house at Philadelphia. Sir Daniel Donelly hoisted the same sign over his booth the other day at Donnybrook Fair.—C. N.

And Doctor Oglethorpe he was sent for, and he ordered me on no account to rise,
But to lie still and have the whole of my back covered over with Spanish flies;
He also gave me leeches and salts, castor oil and the balsam capivi,
Till I was brought down to a mare shadow, and so pale that the sight would have grieved ye. Oh! the Powldoodies of Burran, &c. &c.

11.

But in the course of a few days more I began to stump a little about,
And by the blessing of air and exercise, I grew every day more and more stout;
And in a week or two I recovered my twist, and could play a capital knife and fork,
Being not in the least particular whether it was beef, veal, lamb, mutton, or pork,
But of all the things in the world, for I was always my father's own true daughter,
I liked best to dine on fried tripes, and wash it down with a little hot brandy and water. Oh! the Powldoodies of Burran, &c. &c.

12.

If I had the least bit of genius for poems, I could make some very nice songs
On the cruelties of some people's sweethearts, and some people's sufferings and wrongs;
For he was master, I'm sure, of my house, and there was nothing at all at all
In the whole of the Shining Daisy for which he could not just ring the bell and call;
We kept always a good larder of pidgeon pyes, hung beef, ham, and cowheel,
And we would have got any thing to please him that we could either beg, borrow, or steal. Oh! the Powldoodies of Burran, &c. &c.

13.

And at night when we might be taking our noggin in the little back room,
I thought myself as sure of my charmer as if he had gone to church my bridegroom;
But I need not keep harping on that string and ripping up of the same old sore,
He went off in the twinkling of a bed-post, and I never heard tell of him no more,
So I married the great Doctor Oglethorpe, who had been my admirer all along,
And we had some scolloped Powldoodies for supper; and every crature joined in the old song. Oh! the Powldoodies of Burran, &c. &c.

14.

Some people eats their Powldoodies quite neat just as they came out of the sea,
But with a little black pepper and vinegar some other people's stomachs better agree;
Young ladies are very fond of oyster paties, and young gentlemen of oyster broth:
But I think I know a bit of pasture that is far better than them both:
For whenever we want to be comfortable, says I to the Doctor—my dear man,
Let's have a few scolloped Powldoodies, and a bit of tripe fried in the pan.
Chorus.—Oh! the Powldoodies of Burran,
The green, green Powldoodies of Burran,
The green Powldoodies, the clean Powldoodies,
The gaping Powldoodies of Burran.

After Mrs. Magnus had received those plaudits from the Tent due to this exhibition of native genius, the learned Doctor somewhat anxiously asked us what sort of accommodation we had for him and his lady during the night? We told him that the Tent slept twenty easily, and that a few more could be stowed away between the interstices. "But give yourself no uneasiness, Dr. Magnus, on that score; we are aware of the awkwardness of a lady passing the night with so many Contributors, and of the censoriousness of the world, many people in which seem determined, Doctor, to put an unfavorable construction on every thing we do or say. Besides, your excellent lady might find our Tent like the Black Bull Inn of Edinburgh, as it was twenty years ago, when Dr. Morris first visited it, 'crowded, noisy, shabby, and uncomfortable.' Now the inn at Braemar is a most capital one, where the young ladies of the family will pay every attention to Mrs. Magnus. We have already dispatched a special messenger for Dr. Morris' shandrydan, and as it is a fine moonlight night, you can trundle yourselves down to bed in a jiffey."

The sound of the shandrydan confirmed our words, and we all attended Mrs. Magnus and her husband to the road, to see them safely mounted. Our readers have all seen Peter's shandrydan*—a smart, snug, safe, smooth, roomy, easy-going concern, that carries you over the stones as if you were on turf; and where, may we ask, will you see a more compact nimble little horse than Peter's horse Scrub—with feet as steady as clock-work, and a mouth that carries his bit with a singular union of force and tenderness?

"I fear that I cannot guide this vehicle along Highland roads," said Dr. Magnus; "and I suspect that steed is given to starting, from the manner in which he keeps rearing his head about, and pawing the ground like a mad bull. My dear, it would be flying in the face of Providence to ascend the steps of that shandrydan."

While the orator was thus expressing his trepidation, the Standard-bearer handed Mrs. Magnus forward, who, with her nodding plumes, leapt lightly up beneath the giant strength of his warlike arm, and took her seat with an air of perfect composure and dignity; while Odoherty, adjusting the reins with the skill of a Lade or Buxton, and elevating his dexter hand that held them and the whip in its gnostic grasp, caught hold of the rail of the shandrydan with his left, and flung himself, as it were, to the fair side of her who had once been the mistress of his youthful heart, but for whom he now retained only the most respectful affection.

"Mount up behind, Dr. Magnus," cried the Adjutant, somewhat impatiently; "your feet will not be more than six inches from the ground, so that in case of any disaster, you can drop off like a ripe pease-cod—mount, I say, Doctor, mount."

The Doctor did so; and the Standard-bearer, giving a blast on Wastle's bugle, and cutting the thin air with his thong several yards beyond Scrub's nose, away went the shandrydan, while the mountains of the Dee echoed again to the rattling of its wheels.

* In Peter's Letters there was a good deal of quizzing respecting Dr. Morris's *shandrydan*, of which a sketch was given, showing it to be a one-horse gig, on two high wheels, running lightly, and capable of holding two persons.—M.

The Tent had lost its chief charm—so " the dull and dowie " Contributors prepared for repose. In the uncertain light of Luna, we saw the tall, white, ghostlike shirt of Tickler towering over the lower statures; but in a few minutes, the principal Contributors to this Magazine were, like Mr. Constable's authors, sound asleep, all but the Editor. What with the rheumatism, which always gets worse in the warmth of bed; and what with the cares of our profession, our mind was absolutely like a sea full of waves, we will not say running mountains high, far from it, but a vast multitude of active smallish rippling waves, like those that keep chasing each other to the shore, for several hours at a time, till it is high water at Leith. As we lay in this condition, in the midst of the snore of the Tent, a footstep came to our bed-side, and a soft voice whispered, " Maister, Maister! are you wauken?" We sat up and saw the face of our incomparable caddy, John M'Kay. " Here's a letter frae Lord Fife, as braid's a bannock. Black Hamish, that procht it, says there's an awfu' steer doon at the ludge." We went into the moonlight, where, by-the-by, we saw Kempferhausen very absurdly sitting on a stone, staring at the sky, as if he had just then seen it for the first time in his life, and read the Thane's letter. We then returned to bed to revolve its contents in our mind, and to make fitting arrangements for the morning. The letter was short, for his Lordship uses but few words, and these always the very best,—

MY DEAR SIR—TO-MORROW PRINCE LEOPOLD WILL VISIT THE TENT—Yours truly, FIFE.

The Last Day of the Tent.

Having been thus kindly prepared by the letter of our friend the Thane, we ordered a reveillé to be blown about six o'clock in the morning, and hinted to the more active members of our assembly, that it would be proper for them to start in order to replenish our larder with a quantity of game sufficient for the entertainment of these most honored guests. Nor did our suggestion require to be enforced by many words: Morris, Wastle, Tickler, Odoherty, Ballantyne, Hogg, &c., &c., had all started from their couches long before we (fatigued as we had been with our manifold exertions) thought proper to be awake—and when at last we aroused ourselves, the interior of the tabernacle was quite deserted around us. Wrapping ourselves in a blanket, we were stepping forth with the view of bathing (as had been our wont) in the sweet waters of the Dee—but on emerging from the Tent, a very unexpected phenomenon met our eyes.

Within a few yards of our Pavilion, a very remarkable, and certainly a very reverend-looking old gentleman, bearing no resemblance whatever either in outline or habiliments to any of the present members of our fraternity, was seated in a large chair, with a long clay pipe of the genuine Dutch fashion in his mouth. He was arrayed in a full suit of dignified black, with the black silk apron, now worn by few except the Bishops and Deans of the English church, suspended in ample folds from his capacious middle. On his head was a large shovel hat, garnished with a black rose in front, and so low and loosely did this hat sit upon the cranium, that it was evident there was no wig below.

On the right of this surprising personage the Ettrick Shepherd sat squat on the earth—his nether parts protected from the cold soil, yet wet with the morning dew, only by the intervention of his gray maud. He also had a pipe in his mouth—not a long white pipe like the dignitary—but a short little stump of some two inches in length, and all over japanned as darkly and as brightly as if it had been dipt in a pot of Day and Martin's imperial blacking.

Slow, solemn, and voluminous were the puffs that issued from the lengthier tube—quick, vehement and lusty were those of the Shepherd—never did a piece of hogg's flesh seem to be in a fairer way of being cured, in the true Suabian method, than his nose, were the process to be continued much longer. Opposite to these stood Seward and Buller, each with his gun in his hand—the whole group had the appearance of being earnestly occupied in some conversation, and for a moment we almost scrupled to interrupt them.

Seward was the first who observed us, and he immediately beckoned us to join the party. "Here," cried he, "comes the illustrious Editor of the first and last of Magazines; and here, " pointing to the stranger, "is the most illustrious of all the visitors that have yet intruded upon the encampment of Braemar—here, Mr. Editor, is the great Dr. Parr!" But for the want of his wig, we could have been in no need of this information; but it was really with some difficulty that, after the fact was announced to us, we could bring our eyes to recognize in the features before us those of the Facile Princeps of English Scholars; and yet it was wonderful, surely, that it should have been so, for many a pipe had we smoked together in the days of old at Charles Burney's. But nothing, the fact is certain, produces so great a change on a man's aspect as the addition or subtraction of a periwig. Who could recognize in the cropped and whiskered Lord of Session as he jostles his way down the High-street, or in the spencered and gaitered Lord of Session as he ambles on a shelty along Leith Sands, the same being, whose physiognomy had but a few minutes before appeared to him amidst all the imposing amplifications of curl and frizz, lowering in more than marble abstraction over the whole living farrago of the side-bar? A pretty woman also becomes very *dissimilis sibi* when any whiff of the wind, or the dance, or the chandelier, snatches from her the luxurious masterpiece of Urquhart or Gianetti, and exposes to the gaze of her admirers nothing but a pair of red ears projecting from a little tight cap of yellow flannel, or a bare cranium, with here and there a few short ragged hairs, red or gray, in form and disposition resembling the scanty covering of some discarded tooth-brush. These are both sad metamorphoses in their way. But neither of them so complete as those of the Bellendenian Parr.* The change had scarcely been more

* Dr. Samuel Parr, who died in 1825, was one of the last of the truly learned men of the Johnsonian era. He was not the *very* last, because there is now [1854] as President of Magdalen College, Oxford—he was elected in 1791—Dr. M. J. Routh, "a scholar and a ripe one," who is nearly a century old, and whose intellect burns as brightly in the lamp of life now, with a flame as clear and steady as ever it did in youth. Parr, whose highest church dignity was a prebend's stall in St. Paul's Cathedral, London, always considered himself badly used in not having been made a bishop, during the short time (1806–7), that the whig leaders, his personal friends, were in power. No doubt the ultra-liberality of his politics was one barrier. His own assertion was, "Had my friends continued in power one fortnight longer, Dr. Hungerford was to have been translated to Hereford, and I was to have had Gloucester. My family arrangements were made." With all his scholarship, which was large, he did not accomplish any individual literary work of any great merit. He wasted his talents and learning on pamphlets, with the exception of his character of the late Charles James Fox, in two volumes, which fell far short of public expectation, and his Latin preface (in which he sketched the characters of Burke, Lord North, and Fox) to a new edition of the third book of Bellendenus. This has been considered the most successful modern imitation of the style of

appalling, though Circe herself had been there to change the Man into a Hogg.

"All hail!" said we, "and right welcome! This is indeed a most unexpected honor—what can have been the means of bringing Dr. Parr to the valley of the Dee?" "Mr. Editor," returned the Doctor, bowing αρεσκωτατως (for no English word can do justice to the placid courtesy of that classical reverence)—"You do injustice to your own fame when you meet your visitors with such an interrogation as this. Why did I come to the valley of the Dee?

'Ω κλεινοτάτην αἰθέριον οἴκισας πόλιν,
Οὐκ οἷς θ' ὅσην τιμὴν παρ' ἀνθρώποις φέρει,
'Οσους τ' εραςὰς τῆσδ' της χώρας ἔχεις.

Why should you think it so wonderful that one man should have some curiosity in regard to things for which all men have so great admiration? Of a surety, you are the most modest of Editors. And then consider, man," added he, in a light tone, and turning the bowl of his pipe towards the Ettrick Shepherd, "you have many loadstones. Here am I that would not have grudged an inch of my journey although its sole recompense had been this Sicilian vision." The allusion was, no doubt, in chief, at least, to him whom Dr. Morris has called "the Bucolie Jamie"—but surely that vision must have been rendered a thousandfold more interesting to the illustrious Grecian, by finding with what affectionate admiration it was already regarded by the youthful but still kindred spirits of Seward of Christ Church, and Buller of Brazennose. Seldom, we speak for ourselves, have we been more unaffectedly delighted than by the contemplation of this hearty homage paid by these pure and classical spirits of the South to the wild and romantic genius of the Nomadic North. But Hogg was made to unite all men. In him Cam and Isis are found to worship the inspiration of the haunted Yarrow.

We were very happy at this moment; and accepting Seward's offer of a segar, sat down to enjoy more at leisure the society of this interesting group. But sad was the surprise, and sudden the shock, when looking round, we beheld, stiff and gory upon the sod beside us, Hector—even the faithful Hector—the peerless colley of the Shepherd!—"Ah! Editor," sobbed the Bard, "weel may your look be owercast, when ye see that waefu' sight—waes me! that Hector should have deed; and waesomest of a', that he should have deed by mine ain hand." "Truly 'tis a most unfortunate accident that has occurred," said Seward; "our friend here was up with the earliest, and had got so far as those black firs yonder, on his way to the

Cicero. He has been called "the Brummagen Johnson," for his imitation of the Doctor's manner and conversation. He talked a great deal, with a curious lisp, and was pedantic, dictatorial, and egotistical. He wore what was called a buzzwig, because Bentley and Johnson had been so covered, and he was, in his time, the most inveterate smoker in England.—M.

ground; but his piece went off as he was leaping a cut in the heath—and you see the consequences." "You're very good to put that face on't, Maister Sieward," murmured the poet, "but I'm no heedin aboot thae trifles the noo—it was na in lowping a flow, nor naething o' that kind—I ken na hoo it fell out, but I had taen just as good an aim, as I thought, as could be, and a' wheen bonny birds were just whirring afore mine een, but somegait my haund shook—I'll never lippen til't nae mair an' beena with a pen or a keelavine—and I ludgit the hail of my barrel in honest Hector—Puir man! little did ye think when ye stood there, with your tail like a ramrod—puir fallow!—oh! I'll never see the like o' you." Here the Shepherd's agitation increased to such a height, that he ceased to be intelligible. "Cheer up, my dear fellow," quoth Dr. Parr, "cheer up—humanum est errare—Θεων το πανта κατορθȣν. It is of no use to indulge in these regrets, now the unfortunate occurrence has happened; it cannot be undone—ȣ Χρονος ὁ παντων πατηρ. Resign yourself—do not prolong your suffering by keeping your departed favorite in your view; let us bury Hector, and then your feelings may be more gentle, μηδετι παπταινε πορσιον—It is done—it is done—let us dig the grave." "Most willingly," cried Buller and Seward both together; and in a few minutes the corpse of the lamented colley was hid from the eyes of his master, by the replaced sod of the wilderness.

"And now," says Parr, "must Hector lie there without an epitaph? such ingratitude would be abominable, ἀποπτυστον τι—I for one would willingly furnish a modest inscription in Greek—the only language which admits a perfect propriety of epitaphs in verse; but *Juniores ad labores*, I shall leave that to my friend Buller. For vernacular επιταφια, we may certainly trust the muse of Mr. Hogg himself, when he comes a little more to his recollection." "I can mak nae epitaphs the noo," said the Shepherd, in a low trembling key, "I'se leave that to them that has met wi' nae loss—puir Hector!" so saying he resumed his pipe, and retired to some distance from our company. "Let him go," said the doctor, "let him go in silence—as Plato remarks, solitude is ever the best soother of affliction, in its first birth; it is best, says he, to walk apart ποθον καταπεψαι, and so indeed has the poet represented Achilles, after the slaughter of his friend—but to your epitaph."

Having furnished them with tablets and black lead pencils, we left the three Greeks to themselves; and returning in about half an hour, to announce that breakfast would soon be in readiness, we found Mr. Buller putting the last touches to the elegant composition, which we now insert. We wish the reader had been there, to see Dr. Parr's face when the modest Bachelor of Brazennose put the paper into his hands.*

* What follows is a clever parody on Parr's manner of editing a work, or smothering the text beneath an enormous quantity of Latin notes. This travesty, by the way, shows great ability in the manner in which the Latin language is familiarly treated.—M.

Hogg returned just as the doctor was preparing to read, and resuming his old posture, apparently a good deal more composed, listened to the

IN HECTORA,
PASTORIS ETTRICENSIS SIVE CHALDÆI CANEM,
FATO PRÆPROPERO (DUM σκοπῷ τοξον ουκ επεχει* DOMINUS) ABREPTUM,
CARMINA Επιταφια.

'Ως οίγ' αμφιεπον ταφον 'Εκτορος—
Hom. Il. ώ. 804.
——*quantum mutatus ab illo*
Hectore, qui, &c. Virg. Æn. ii. 275.

I.

'Εκτορος† ειμι κονις, τον δη κατεπεφνεν, αηθη
'Οπλα λαβων ὁ Νόμευς, ωφελ' ἁ μηδ' ετ' εην·
Ουδε τι μοι χραισμησεν, ανουτατος‡ ων γε, Νεπηρου
Βακων· ου γαρ εγω στηθεσιν αμφ' εφορουν.

II.

Ω ξειν', αγγειλον Καλεδ-(αι·)-ονιοις,‖ ὁτι τηδε
Κειμαι, τον κτεινεν πηκτονομευς§ ανομως.

NOTÆ.

I.

Cum mos dudum apud omnes hujuscemodi in rebus versatos invaluerit, poematiis —sive suis, sive aliorum—notas versibus plus nimio longiores attexendi, mihi quoque eorum exemplis obsecuto aliquantillum in commentando excurrere visum est. Versus nempe ipsi, utpote minoris pretii, ceu paxilli tantùm deinceps sunt reputandi, quibus annotationes (livoris nonnunquam, sæpius eruditionis ostentandæ gratiâ) *omni scibili* refertæ appendantur.

* Pind. Ol. ii. 160. Accuratius scilicet Pastor ille, et *cantare et respondere paratus,*

—τινα βαλλει
Εκ μαλθακας αυτε φρε—
νος ευκλεας οϊςους
ἱεις.

Sclopporum quippe glande et pulveve nitrato (ut cum lexicographis loquar) oneratorum imperitus sinistram libri, ad quem collineabatur, paginam ne vel unico plumbi grano penetravit. Videsis non semel laudand. Blackw. Magaz. xxix. 600. Dextra ejusdem libri pagina ne ab ullo jaculantium læderetur, in causâ fuit Neperi Dissertatio, de quâ infra copiosius. De Nepero ipso, quicquid contra oblatrent cynici, sermone proverbiali tutò est pronunciandum, "*he has saved his Bacon.*"

† Hæc appellatio quam probè cani Scotico conveniat, documento sit *Swiftii* S. T. P. et S. P. D. apud Hibernos perjucunda illa de Vocabulis Veterum Disquisitio; in quâ Hectoris conjugem Andromachen Caledonii cujusdam nobilis, *Andrew Mackay*, certo certiùs filiam fuisse contendit. Quidni ergo et viri nomen ejusdem quoque patriæ sit? Gaudent quippe Scotigenæ Trojanorum nominibus. Vixit haud ita pridem Hector Monro: vivit hodie, ut ex Actis Diurnis conjicere licet, Leopoldi Principis Illustrissimi hospes, Æneas Mackintosh; synonymique plures

ανιδρωτι in Scotiâ reperiri possunt. Pace vero tanti viri dixerim, nonnihil me in etymo, *hack'd and tore*, ubi copula *and* *ὑπερσυλλαβως* redundet, solitæ ejus subtilitatis desiderare. Meliùs forsan, quia ad linguæ Scoticæ genium accommodatius, "*Heck! tore!*" lacerum quippe herois corpus contemplantis cujusdam exclamatio, rationem nominis redderet. Exemplis item (ut hoc obiter moneam) à *Swiftio* allatis, plurima quivis citò addiderit: e. g. CHARON, qu. *carry-on;* CERBERUS, "*Sir, bear* (i.e. endure) *us*," Æneâ sic monstrum illud *τρικαρηνον* inter transeundum blandiùs compellante, &c. &c.

Συνεκδοχικως quoque, cum Hectora sæpius Mæonides vocaverit *ποιμενα λαων*, pastoris canis præclaro illo nomine ornari posset.

‡ Neperi de Bacone *τῳ ἀνȣτατῳ* dissertationem cum ipse, quæ mea est infelicitas! non perlegerim, valde dubito utrum *non vulneratum* (vulcaniis quippe armis contectum) an *non penetratum* interpretari debeam. Lucem forsan voci affundet quod de eo Christophorus Noster, in *Blackw. Mag.* ib., posteris prodidit; *such* impenetrable *stuff it proved to be.* Quicquid verò de eo sit statuendum, mali propulsatorem Baconem non adfuisse jure miretur aliquis, cum inter ejus Pastorisque Ettricensis nomen (HOGG) necessitudo arctior intercedet; quod tamen clarissimum illud philosophiæ decus pernegâsse, Hoggio quodam per collum mox suspendendo ad miserationem movendam strenuè affirmante, cel. Josephus Millerus lepidâ sane (ut sæpe) narratiunculâ scriptis consignavit: "*A Hog, till it is hung, is not Bacon.*"

Verbosiorem esse de quâ agitur dissertationem, nec tutò vigilare cupientibus sub noctem in manus sumendam queruntur multi; quod profectò vel nominis ejus prænominisque syllabæ primæ fatali quâdam conspiratione prænotare videntur, cum MAC à *μακος* Dor. pro *μηκος* derivetur, et NAP Anglicè *somnum* sonet, ne Mazeppæ quidem ipsius (utpote longioris) auditoribus, si poetæ testi credamus, evitandum. *The king had been an hour asleep.*

Lectorem non fugerit, quibus verbis Hectora ab Ajace percussum Homerus, Il. ξ'. 417, &c., designaverit, quercui illum *ὑπαι ῥιπης πατρος Διος* cadenti assimilans, vernaculâque planè (quod nulli non suboluerit) figurâ addens,——*δεινη δε θεειον γινεται οδμη.*

II.

‖ Olim legebatur,

> Ὠ ξειν', αγϝειλον Λακεδαιμονιοις, ὁτι τηδε
> Κειμεθα, τοις κεινων πειθομενοι νομιμοις.

Hoc, quoad ductum literarum cæteraque in conjecturis criticis observari sueta, quam prope quod in textu dedimus Epigramma contingit!

En artem, quâ ad doloris acriùs urgentis vim plenè exprimendam tmesi factâ, atque plorantis syllabâ AI in medio vocabulo insertâ, poeta tantùm non in fletum secum legentes abripiat! Decantatum istud de Matildâ Pottinger poema, in quo, nullo ad affectum respectu habito, *ὁμοιοτελευτȣ* (Anglicè *Rhyme*) efficiendi causâ verba quædam intercisa sunt: e. g.

> Thou wast the daughter of my Tu-
> tor, Law Professor at the U-
> niversity, &c. (ROVERS.)

quanto hoc nostrum exsuperat! Vehementioris scilicèt est luctûs voculam quàm sententiam discindere; ideoque, me judice, AI istud patheticum omnibus veterum Tragicorum ejulatibus, *ε, ε, ε, οτοτοτοι, οτοτοτοι*, &c. narrationis cursum impedientibus meritò est anteponendum.

Primæ vocum partes, *Λακε* et *Καλε* facillimè inter se permutari posse quis non videt? neu mihi vitio verterit quisquam (Buchanano Junioque auctoribus fretus, quorum hic *Καληδονις ἡ χαριεσσα*, ille *Nympha Caledonias*, &c. scriptum reliquit) me non per *η* secundam syllabam in *Καλεδονιοις* extulisse. Nullus enim dubitat quin id metri necessitati, eodem quo in *αϑανατος* cæterisque ejusdem farinæ verbis modo prima syllaba producitur, acceptum referri debeat. Id si non satis placeat, legat, per me licet, *αγϝειλον συ Καληϝονιοις*, Veneresque omnes in voculá illâ simplice AI delitescentes uno quasi ictu Caligula alter sustulerit.

§ Vocem *πηκτονομευς* non aliàs occurrere si quis objeceit, is velim secum reputet, quot veterum libri in quibus forsan erat reperienda omnino perierint; nec fistulâ canentem pastorem verbo ad sensum aptiori describi potuisse. *Πηκτιδα* quippe musicorum instrumentum pecten esse vel tyronibus notum est.

Cum verò pastoribus septentrionalibus oves non solùm pascere sed etiam tondere moris sit, legant fortassis alii (vulgatæ lectioni, ut mihi quidem videtur, nimis arctè insistentes) *πεικονομευς*.

Hæc dum *αυτοσχεδιαζοντος* more effunderem distichon, quoddam mihi in mentem venit, pace tuâ, lector, leviter emendandum :

Μηδεν αμαρτειν εϛι Θεων, και παντα κατορϑουν
Εν βιοτη. μοιραν δ' ουτι φυγειν επορεν.

Hæc ita correxeris :

Μηδε Μαραττων εστι θεωντων παντα κατορϑουν
Εμбατεων. Μοιραν γ' ουτι φυγειν επορεν.

Quis hic poetam de rebus nuperrimè in India gestis vaticinantem non deprehenderit? nomen ipsum habes Marchionis illius, quem ducem Scotia nostra paucos abhinc annos suspexit, equitatûs jam nunc Mahrattici hàc illàc discurrentis victorem Britannia omnis suaque ipsius Ièrne demiratur.

Aliud item, ne diutiùs te teneam, poetæ è longinquo quid esset futurum prospicientis exemplum accipe ; Drydeni nempe versus binos, in quibus homunculos vulgò dictos Spa-Fields Reformers, ductoremque eorum famosum, quasi nominatim designat:

Better to *hunt* in *fields* for *health unbought,*
Than fee *the doctor* for a nauseous *draught.*

ubi *τῳ corruption* opponitur vox *health*, eodem planè sensu quo *salus* populi suprema lex esse dicitur; *το unbought* venum exposita suffragia tangit; *the doctor* procerem quemdam, ut ita dicam, *with cunning* (Qu? Canning) *finger* indigitat; *το draught* denique (sono quidem atque Metaphorâ juxtâ neglectis) res ærarii forsan subobscure respicit, nisi—quod vix tamen crediderim—Huntii cerevisiam fallacibus olim veneni herbis concoctam vates innuat. Videant Angli annon eundem quem antea potum plebi propinandum *ὁ πανυ* offerat.*

Neque si etymis nonnunquam primo viso tantùm non ridendis usus esse videar, succensebunt mihi qui Bryantii *του μακαριτου*, aliorumque è sectatoribus ejus tomos pervolverint; qualia sunt, e. g., quæ sequuntur.

* If Mr. Buller had passed from the Brewer to the Sportsman, he would have found Henry Hunt, in one of his late letters, complaining of his Lancaster treatment—expressing himself thus, "a week's shooting at Middleton cottage will set all to rights." In the meantime, we find him about to pass through London on his way, prepared, we suppose, in illustration of this expression, like another Xerxes with his myriads—*τηνδε την πολιν θηρασαι* (Æschyl. Pers. 238), not, however, it may be feared, with the view of rendering it *Βασιλει υπηκοος*, (Ibid.) The word *θηρασαι*, besides its obvious allusion, furnishes one of those deep and hidden senses which escape the vulgar eye. We may take its meaning from Herodotus *σαγανευȣσι τȣς ανθρωπȣς τȣτον τον τροπον. ανηρ ανδρος αψαμενος της χειρος* (could there be a more distinct enunciation of what took place on the advent of the Great Known at Manchester?) *δια πασης της νησȣ διελθȣσι εκθηρευοντες τȣς ανθρωπους* (vi. 31.) But we are becoming quite a Buller.—C. N.

Idem valere adagia, *επι των δυσχερεσι και βλαβεροις επιχειρουντων* dicta,

1. *Αιξ την μαχαιραν,*
2. *Κορωνη τον σκορπιον,*
3. *Αναγυρον κινειν,*
4. *Ignes suppositi cineri doloso,*
5. *Τεφρη πυρ ὑποθαλπομενον*) et
6. *Λεοντα νυσσειν,*

apud Parœmiographum quemdam olim legisse me memini. Hoc ita esse, vide, lector, quomodo ipse paucis levitèr immutatis, viâ (ni multūm fallor) haud antè tritâ probatum iverim.

1. Lege itaque, *leni in asperum verso,* 'Αιπ την μαχαιραν (HAY sc. J. P.) et habes nuperum, de in Com. Lancastr. tumultum luce ipsâ clariùs descriptum. Nimis forsan esset verbum premere, si in *τῳ Μαχαιραν Manc. Iron* delitescere me suspicari affirmarem; semi-græcisset licèt lingua anglicana, et vox *επιχειρουντων* sic tandem propriâ suâ significatione gavisura esse videatur—Militum quippe Mancuniensium enses, qui quàm fuerint *δυσχερεις και βλαβεροι* omnibus ferè, à quâcunque demùm parte stent, in ore versatur.

2. *Κορωνη τον σκορπιον* quid sibi velit, jure quis dubitare possit. Addito *ρ* solūm omnis statim difficultas è medio tollitur. *Κορωνηρ* (*Batty, the Coroner*) *τον σκορπιον*, quem noxium quoddam animal esse (Qu? Angl, *a Harmer*) quis non videt?

3. *Αναγυρον κινειν*, quod in Aristophane occurrit, vix ipse, ænigmatum hujusmodi apud recentiores Ædipus, Erasmus expediverit; cūm anagyrum genium quoddam fuisse harioletur, qui propter violatum ejus sacellum vicinos omnes funditùs evertit! apage: non placet. Ego *πανηγυριν* lego, sc. *to disperse a Manchester mob*—utrum *εν κειμενον* (i. e. *well-disposed*) anon, penes alios judicium est futurum.

4. Vice *Cineri* substituas "fineri," pro Finerty (hoc enim, quod aiunt nostrates, *fits to a T;*) et planum fit omne, in quo anteà ob tenebras circumfusas offendebatur.

5. *Τεφρη* interpreteris, penè ad literam, The Free.

6. Denique *Λεοντα νυσσειν* quid propriè sit, non satis liquet: nisi per aphæresin pro *Ναπολεοντα* fuerit dictum, quem inter prospera quidem pupugisse non temerè quivis ausus esset. Hujus ceram quâ, dum fortuna fuit, inimici damnabantur, verè notavit Ovidius; utpote quam

——de longæ collectam flore cicutæ
*Melle sub infami Corsica misit apis.**

Nonne jam vides. ut hæc omnia inter se concinant?

SED MANUM QUOD AIUNT DE TABULA.

* * * * * *

These lucubrations seemed to produce the happiest effect in the wounded spirit of the Shepherd. The grand solemn note in which the Doctor recited the beautiful Greek lines themselves riveted his attention, and delighted (how could it be otherwise?) his ear. But whether it was the physiognomy of the Doctor, or his voice, or his gesture, or all together, we know not. This much is certain, that the Shepherd seemed to be amused, at least, as much as any of us with the *Notae.* The two or three vernacular vocables introduced afforded, perhaps, some little clue of the purport of the annotations—at all events, he laughed considerably every time that Greek proper name Νεϖηρος was repeated in any of its cases. At the end he withdrew

* Anne hic ad Apin, Deum, sc. Ægyptiorum, qualem se Dux iste Gallorum impie professus est, alluditur?—S. P.

arm in arm with Seward, probably in hopes of obtaining from him a more accurate account of what had been said by Mr. Buller about himself—his dog—and the transactions of the Royal Society. We overheard him saying, after a few minutes of colloquy with his oracle, and after three or four portentous cackles of returning merriment, "Od, man, the warst o't is, that the creature would never understand a line o't, even it was put intill the Magazine—Lord safe ye! he kens nae mair about Greek than mysel. There's some o' thae kind o' literary chiels about Edinburgh, that writes themselves esquires, and editors, and a' the lave o't, and yet kens very little mair, to ca' kenning really—than a puir herd like what I was mysel—they're blathering skytes, a wheen o' them; neither genius nor learning—it's nae meikle wonder they mak but a puir hand o't." "Pooh!" said Seward, "he'll get somebody to translate it for him."—"Oo' aye," quoth Hogg, "gie Gray or Dunbar a dictionary, and a day or twa to consider o't, and I daur say they'll be able to gie him some inkling—but I was clean forgetting mysel, he has naething to do, but to gang oureby and speer at Professor Christisin—*that* Professor, they say, is a real scholar;* he'll interpret it as glegg as ye like.—But Losh keep us a', there's Tims coming hame aw by his lain, and what's that he has gotten on the end o' his gun?"

Looking round in the direction indicated by Theocritus, we descried the Cockney at the distance of about 100 yards, advancing in a slow and dignified pace; his piece carried high over his shoulders, and on the summit thereof a something, the genius and species of which were at this distance alike mysterious. "What the deel's that ye've gotten, callan!" cried the Shepherd (who, by-the-way, had all along treated Tims and Price with unsufferable indelicacy). "My man, ye've had a fine morning's sport—Is that a dead cat or a dirty sark ye're bringing haim wi' ye?" "God knows what it is," said the Londoner, "or rather whose it is, for I believe, upon my honor, 'tis a parson's wig—but I thought it was a ptarmigan, sitting on the bough of that there tree by the river side, and I brought it down; but demme if it be'nt a wig."—"You good-for-nothing little pert jackanapes," vociferated Parr—"You believe it to be a wig! and you took it to be a ptarmigan." . . . . "Come, come now, Doctor," interrupted the Shepherd, "ye mauna be owre hard on an inexperienced callant—Preserve us a'! that beats all the wigs that ever I saw! Lord! what a gruzzle!" . . . . Here the burst of laughter was such, that Dr. Parr found himself compelled to join in the roar; and after the first peal was over, he begged pardon of the Cockney for the harsh terms he had employed in the most good-tempered style in the world. He of Ludgate Hill was sorely crest-fallen, but he

* Dr. Christison, one of the Professors in the Faculty of Medicine in Edinburgh University.—M.

harbored no resentment, and all was soon peace and harmony. "This beats old Routh's quite to nothing, Buller," said Seward— "Egad, Seward," cries Buller, "there might be a blackbird's nest in every curl, and a rookery in the top frizzle. Burton's is but a bagatelle to this."—"Enough, enough, my young friends," quoth the Doctor; "my wig was pilloried long ago in the Edinburgh Review by Sidney Smith: it has now been shot through, and that by Mr. Tims, on the banks of the Dee; surely it is high time to give up its persecution.—Leave it, leave it, to repose." "But hoo, in the name of wonder," cried Hogg, "did ye come to leave your wig in the bough o' a fir-tree—what in a daft like doing was that?"—"Why, Mr. Hogg," answered the Bellendenian, with wonderful suavity, "when you're as old a man as I am, your faculties will not perhaps be quite so alert on all occasions; you will perhaps learn to make blunders then as well as your neighbors. Be merciful, most illustrious Shepherd; I stripped myself, about two hours ago, to bathe in this beautiful river of yours, and hung my wig on the tree that was nearest me; I forgot to take it down when my bath was over, and you see the consequence. Let's say no more about the matter, κακον εὑ κειμενον Mr. Seward."—"Yes, yes," cried Buller, "μη κινει—μη κινει." Dr. Morris's servant was at hand; at our suggestion the periwig was intrusted to his care, and in a few minutes it made its appearance on the sinister hand of that accomplished valet, in full puff and fuzz, apparently blooming only the more vigorously from the loppings it had sustained.

Fifteen years ago, when James Hogg was tending sheep on the hills of Ettrick, what would a judicious person have thought of the man, who should have predicted, that the Shepherd was destined, in the book of fate, or some future day, to replace "the μεγα θαυμα of the literary world" on the head of the eulogist of the "Tria lumina Anglorum?"* Yet, with our own eyes have we beheld this thing. Dr. Parr "stooped his anointed head" to the author of the Queen's Wake, and that genuine bucolic, taking the wig from the hand of Tims, placed it with all the native dexterity of a man of genius, on the brows of Philopatris Varvicensis.† "Μα Δια," cries the Prebendary, "the old reproach, πολυθρυλλητον illud; the Βοιωτιος ὑς has been nobly wiped away by this unlearned Theban. To speak with the immortal Casaubon, "Talia quis non amisisse vellet, per te denique, vir egregi recuperaturus." This weighty matter having been

* So Burke, Lord North, and Charles James Fox were designated, in Parr's Preface to Bellendenus, who—and this is mentioned for the special benefit of "the country gentleman," was William Bellenden, a native of Scotland, who was educated at Paris, where he was Professor of Belles-Lettres in 1602. He wrote a work called *Cicero Princeps*, which was published in 1608, and afterwards included in his *Bellendenus de Statu*, which Parr partly edited in 1787.—M.

† Parr's residence, at Hatton, in Warwickshire, was about eighteen miles from Birmingham, and he published his Character of Fox under the *nom-de-plume* of Philopatris Varvicensis.—M.

adjusted, we bowed the illustrious scholar into our Tent, and sat down at the head of the breakfast-table, with Dr. Parr on our right, and James Hogg on our left hand. Buller supported the preacher of the Spittal sermon,* and Seward was still the "fidus Achates" of the bard of Yarrow. At some distance sat Tims eyeing the reinstated wig, and mentally calculating the number of grains of shot which it now contained; for, unlike a certain paper in the transactions of the Royal Society of Edinburgh, it was not made of impenetrable stuff. We are rusty in our Greek now-a-days, and could not help wishing that Dr. Search, that truly attic wit, had been present to whisper into our willing ear a little of his profound erudition. But we soon found, that at breakfast a great scholar, like ὁ ϖαρρος, rightly deemed that he had something else before him than Greek roots, and that the pleasantest of all tongues is that of the rein-deer. The Doctor is evidently not a man to pick a quarrel with his bread and butter; and though we, Buller, and Hogg, ran him hard, he at last gained the plate. A Highland breakfast is sometimes too heavy a meal; and the board is inelegantly crowded. But on the present occasion, we took for our guidance the old adage,

Est modus in rebus, sunt certi denique fines,

and ordered John Mackay on no account whatever to put on the table anything more than a couple of dozen of eggs, a mutton ham, a tongue, a cut of cold salmon, a small venison pasty, some fresh herrings, a few Finnan haddies, a quartern loaf, oatmeal cakes, pease scones, barley bannocks, honey, jelly, jam, and marmalade; so that one's attention was not likely to be distracted by a multiplicity of objects, and we all knew at once where to lay our hand on something comfortable. "Hah! Buller, you dog," said the Doctor, between two enormous mouthfuls of broiled herring, superbly seasoned, under the guidance of our master Celt, with Harvey sauce and Cayenne, "*jentaculum mehercule ipsi Montano, ipsi Cripso invidendum.*" "What say you, you dog?

'Such food is fit for disembodied spirits.'

Good eating is not confined, as of old, *intra centesimum lapidem!*" A long and animated discussion ensued concerning the comparative merits of Rutupian and Kentish, or Gauran Mullets—a favorite breakfast dish it seems with the Emperor Vitellius. When this was beginning to wax a little less vehement, and Parr had at last put his

* There has long existed an endowment for having a sermon annually preached in Christ-Church, Newgate-street, London. This, which is called the Spittal Sermon, from the name of the person who bequeathed the amount, from which payment is made to the preacher, was delivered by Dr. Parr in 1800, and published by him soon after, with voluminous notes. Parr, who was desultory in his writings, contrived to drag in Godwin's Political Justice. which then had recently been published; and having attacked it, brought down upon himself a pamphlet, by Mr. Godwin, in which the divine was treated with less ceremony than he conceived himself entitled to.—M.

tea-spoon into his seventh cup, to show that he had given in; a loud noise was heard of shouting voices, and echoing bugles; so, running hastily into the open air, we beheld a sight worthy of the mountains. The Thane, with his usual fine taste, had, by sunrise, escorted PRINCE LEOPOLD* to the forest, that he might partake of the

> Wild mirth of the desert, fit pastime for kings.

And now many a hill-side was gleaming with his Celtic tenantry

> "All plaided and plumed in their tartan array,"

when a magnificent stag came bounding along, close by the Tent, pressed hard by those enormous hounds whose race is not yet extinct in the Highlands, and whose fierce and savage career in the chase carries back the mind to remote ages,

> "When the hunter of deer and the warrior trod
> O'er his hills that encircle the sea."

As the "desert-boon" went by,

> "Wafting up his own mountains that far-beaming head,"

the heather was stained with his blood, for had he not been wounded he would soon have distanced his pursuers. It was delightful to observe the enthusiasm of the fine old man, when all the wild pomp of this mountain-chase hurried tumultuously by—and to hear with what energy he repeated some of those majestic lines of Virgil, descriptive of that hunt where Dido and Æneas shone.

The feelings of Seward found quite a different form of expression. A fine animal by Diana—"demme, Buller, if the scoundrel has not the horns of an Alderman." Tims startled at this simile, but said nothing, and probably relapsed into a dream of the Epping-Hunt, at which the stag is very conveniently made to jump out of the hinder parts of a wagon. Price joined the rout in his Surrey cap, and gave the whoop-holla with the lungs of a stentor, while Seward continued: "The Duke of Beaufort's hounds used to run down old Reynard,

* Prince Leopold, of Saxe-Coburg, now King of the Belgians, really was in Scotland in September, 1819. He visited Sir Walter Scott, at Abbotsford. There is an amusing account, in one of Scott's letters to Lord Montagu, of the domestic anxiety which this visit caused at Abbotsford. The Prince, it seems, had come from Edinburgh to see "fair Melrose," which is close by the town of Selkirk. Scott, who was Sheriff of the county, attended at Selkirk to do the honors. "The Prince very civilly told me," said he, "that, though he could not see Melrose on this occasion, he wished to come to Abbotsford for an hour." There was no declining the visit, but "a domiciliary search for cold meat, through the whole city of Selkirk, produced one shoulder of cold lamb." However, with broiled salmon, and black cock, and partridges, a lunch was made out, and Scott adds: "I chanced to have some very fine old hock, which was mighty germane to the matter." In 1819 much sympathy was felt for Prince Leopold. In May, 1816, he had married the Princess Charlotte, daughter of George IV., who had fallen in love with him at a time when his worldly property was only £300 a year. They lived most happily until November, 1817, when the Princess Charlotte unexpectedly died, after her accouchement. The national grief for her loss was deep beyond parallel, and great was the sympathy for Leopold in his bereavement. The marriage of the late Duke of Kent with Prince Leopold's sister (of which Queen Victoria is the sole surviving issue) would probably not have taken place (in 1818), if there had not been the previous family connexion created, by the Princess Charlotte's union with Leopold.—M.

breast-high all the time, in twenty minutes—and Parson Simmons' pack were not so much amiss, though the field indeed was rather raffish—but the Grand Signor yonder would leave them all behind —poor devil, he is never again to revisit his seraglio."

All the world has read the Lady of the Lake, and he who has forgotten the description of the Stag-chase in that poem, may be assured, that had he been born when mankind were in the hunter-state, he must have died of hunger. It may be just as well not to do over again any thing that it has pleased Walter Scott to do; and therefore, should any of our readers be tired of us, let them turn to Fitz-James and his gallant Grey. Now, as of old, A PRINCE was on the mountain-side, and while the wild cries of the Highlanders echoed far and wide, from rock to rock over that sublime solitude, as every glen sent pouring down its torrents of shouting hunters, LEOPOLD must have felt the free spirit of ancient days brooding over the desert, and what true glory it is to be loved and honored by the unconquered people of the mountains of Caledonia.

The tumult at length faded away far up among the blue mists that hung over the solitary glen of the Linn of Dee. We found ourselves deserted in our Tent. Even Dr. Parr had strayed away among the rocks in search of some watch-tower, from which he might yet catch a glimpse of the skirts of the vanished array. But the noble Thane had not been neglectful of us. A strong band of the finest Highlanders that could be selected from the population of his immense estates, with many too of the Grants and Gordons, came, bonnets waving, plaids flying, and pipes sounding, to the Tent, to form a guard of honor to receive THE PRINCE, not unworthy the flower of the House of Saxony. They immediately disposed themselves in the most picturesque positions among the wild scenery round the Tent—one band cresting a rocky eminence with a gorgeous diadem of scarf and plume—another seen indistinctly lying as in ambush among the high bloom of the heather—and a third, drawn up as in order of battle, to salute LEOPOLD on his arrival with a discharge of musketry. Meanwhile pipes challenged pipes, and pibrochs and gatherings resounded like subterraneous music from a hundred echoing hills.

By the munificence of the THANE our table had been furnished up with a splendor fit for the reception of a PRINCE—and just as all the arrangements were finished, we saw the noble party descending a steep, and advancing straightway to the Tent. To our delight and astonishment a bevy of fair ladies joined the train ere it reached the banks of the Dee; and, as if suddenly built by magic, a little pleasure-boat, beautifully painted, rose floating on that transparent river, into which Prince, Lord, and Lady, lightly stepped, and in a few minutes they stood on the greensward before our Tent.

John of Sky—Lord Fife's own piper—and several others, blew up that well-known pibroahd (Phailt Phrase), or Prince's welcome, that made the welkin ring, while two hundred Highlanders, in the garb of old Gaul, with bonnets waving in the air, gave

> "That thrice-repeated cry,
> In which old Alpin's heart and tongue unite,
> Whene'er her soul is up, and pulse beats high,
> Whether it hail the wine-cup or the fight,
> And bid each arm be strong, or bid each heart be light."

A discharge of musketry from the guard of honor followed well those proud huzzas, and when the din ceased, nothing was heard but the wild cry of the eagle wheeling in disturbed circles far up in the sky.

The Standard-bearer* advanced to receive PRINCE LEOPOLD, who, in the most gracious manner declared what "high satisfaction it gave him thus to visit our Tent, and that he would have the pleasure of staying dinner." Nothing could exceed the graceful affability of the Marchioness of Huntly† and her fair friends, who, after expressing their delight with our characteristic reception of the Prince, and their admiration of our Tent and all its arrangements, withdrew under the protection of the Thane, who soon, however, returned again to the scene of festivity. Every moment stragglers kept coming in, till the whole party was complete, and we sat down in the Tent to a feast which it would be endless to describe, consisting of every delicacy from air, flood and field, and enriched with all generous and mighty wines in cup and goblet, from the ancient catacombs of Mar-Lodge.‡

The presence of our ILLUSTRIOUS GUEST, so justly dear to the "soul of this wide land," shed a calm and dignified tranquillity throughout the Tent—and the feelings then awakened in the hearts of us all will cease only when those hearts shall beat no more. During dinner PRINCE LEOPOLD sat on our right hand, and Lord Huntly on our left, while Wastle, who acted as croupier, had the honor of being supported by Baron Addenbroke and the Thane. The Prince, the moment he recognized Dr. Parr, requested him, with the most affectionate respect, to sit by him; and Lord Huntly,‖ remarking that the highest of all rank was that conferred by genius, took the

* Odoherty.—M. † Now Duchess of Gordon, residing at Huntly Lodge, Aberdeenshire.—M.

‡ The Earl of Fife's Shooting Lodge. It is close to Balmoral, the Scottish residence of Queen Victoria.—M.

‖ Afterwards Duke of Gordon. On his death, in 1837, without legitimate male issue, the Dukedom and most of the estates went to his next-of-kin, the present Duke of Richmond, and the Earl of Aboyne, another relative, succeeding to his second title, became Marquis of Huntly. This last was a character, and died in June 1853, at the advanced age of ninety-two, actually continuing to the last, to act as aide-de-camp to the Queen. His affectation of youth, almost to his dying day, was curious. The faded beau, described in Gil Blas, who daily rose an old man, and was *made up*, after a three hours' toilette, into the semblance of a young Lothario, was somewhat like the Marquis of Huntly,—who, however, even went to the extremity of wearing cork *plumpers* in his mouth, to swell out his cheeks, which had fallen in from age! At the age of 87, I saw him dance a polka, and his affectation of juvenility would have been amusing, if, by contrast, it were not almost painful.—M.

Ettrick Shepherd by the hand, and kindly seated him between himself and Mr. Seward. Every one, in short, being proud and happy, was placed to his mind—and time flew so swiftly by, that the cloth was removed before we had found leisure to revolve in our mind a few words of address on rising to propose the

Health of the Prince Regent.*

"Little would it coincide with our ideas of propriety to enlarge at any considerable length upon topics not immediately suggested by the proper object of our meeting, far less upon any, concerning which it might be possible that any difference of opinion, or of sentiment, should be found among those who have this day the honor of being assembled in this distinguished presence. It is not possible, however, that we should proceed, in these circumstances, to propose the health of the actual sovereign of these islands—the Prince Regent of England—without prefacing a few words concerning those rumors of disturbance and disaffection,† of mad and rancorous outrage against the peace of this great empire, and of elaborate insult against all those institutions by which the prosperity of that empire has hitherto been maintained and balanced—rumors which reach our ears with an effect of so much strange and portentous mystery here among these regions of lonely magnificence, where the primitive loyalty of the Scottish mountaineer is still as pure as the air which he inhales. Throughout by far the greater part of these rich and mighty realms we nothing question the loyal affection and reverence of our fellow-subjects are as deep and as secure—but the tidings of these things cannot fail to be heard with emotions of new wonder and new disgust, amidst scenes, where the happiness and repose of a virtuous, high-

* In 1811, when insanity had disqualified George III. from governing Great Britain, his eldest son, the Prince of Wales, was appointed Regent, in which capacity he continued until January, 1820, when he succeeded to the throne, as George IV.—M.

† Something more than simple "rumor of disturbance" existed in the autumn of 1819. Public discontent largely existed, in consequence of the popular desire of Parliamentary Reform. Public meetings, largely attended, took place in various parts of England and Scotland. One, held at St. Peter's Place, Manchester, on the 16th August, 1819, had a tragical termination. Henry Hunt, one of the popular leaders, attended, to harangue the multitude, which included men, women, and even children. The magistrates determined to arrest Hunt and his fellow-leaders, and called in a body of armed Yeomanry cavalry to aid the police. An affray took place. The Yeomanry attacked the unarmed and peaceable multitude, killing and wounding many with their sabres. Hunt and his friends were made prisoners, on a charge of high-treason, which was abandoned; but they were tried and convicted of sedition. Angry debates on what has since been called The Manchester Massacre, and The Peterloo Butchery, took place in Parliament, in which ministers (who had sent a formal letter of thanks to the magistrates and Yeomanry of Manchester, for their "prompt and spirited conduct,") defended what was done, and the result was that Parliament finally passed an Act of Indemnity, to protect the doers of this massacre, and also placed on the statute-book six restrictive acts,—to prevent seditious meetings, to prohibit training and arming, to check blasphemous and seditious writings, and to tax cheap periodical publications. Cobbett, at that time, was selling his celebrated and influential Political Register at two-pence,—the new act imposed a stamp-duty of four-pence upon each number. At the time that this article was written, not later than the middle of August, 1819, the fatal affray at Manchester could scarcely have been known in Edinburgh. If it had, no doubt Christopher North would have been delighted to praise the Manchester Yeomanry.—M.

spirited, and noble race, have never yet been disturbed, even by the thought or the suspicion of any of those wild and vicious theories, which, in most of the other districts of the empire, have now, we fear, some profligate advocates and some miserable dupes. My Lords and Gentlemen,—It is indeed high time that these things should cease to be spoken of, with any difference of language, by any conscientious adherents of either of those great political parties, whose existence as such is perhaps a necessary consequence of the nature of our constitution, and a necessary mean of its preservation. It is high time that they whose education enables them to look at the troubles of the present, through the clear, steady, and impartial medium of the past, should see the necessity of combining, with head, heart, and hands, to repress, with a decision in which there must be at least as much of compassion as of justice, the encroachments of this frenzied spirit, which has its only existence and support in the desperate depravity of a few pestilent demagogues—men alike bankrupts in fortune, principle, and character—and in the rashness with which the ignorant and the weak listen to the audacious brutality of their treason and their blasphemy.

"Ours, gentlemen, is not the only country wherein ages of happiness and loyalty have been suddenly disturbed by the plebeian preachers of anarchy and confusion. The Woolers, the Watsons, the Harrisons, the Wolseleys, the Burdetts, the Hobhouses*—all have had their prototypes, both in ancient and in modern times—and the characters of all of them have been described, even to their minutest shadings, by writers, with whom some of themselves must be not imperfectly acquainted. Of all these, however, the importance seems now to be on the wane—and the shout of vulgar acclamation waits only, in its utmost violence, upon one, whom, but a few short months ago, the greater part even of these would have regarded with any feelings rather than those of serious jealousy and anxious emulation. Yet it is well that the choice of the rabble has at last fallen upon one for whom even the rabble cannot long remain without contempt. In their present demi-god these misnamed patriots have found a leader, who answers, in all things, to the prophetic minuteness of the Roman historian's description,—*Summæ audaciæ—egens—factiosus :*

* Radical leaders in 1819. Wooler was editor and publisher of a weekly paper called the Yellow Dwarf, one peculiarity of which was, that, being himself a compositor, he set it up without "copy," his mind and his *composing-stick* being at work together. Watson had been tried for high-treason, and acquitted; but, on a subsequent charge being made, found safety in flight to the United States. About Harrison I know nothing. Sir Charles Wolseley was a baronet, with large landed estates in Staffordshire, who so strongly advocated Parliamentary Reform, that he allowed himself to be returned, by a radical meeting at Birmingham (which was not directly represented until 1832), as Legislative Attorney for that town, but actually attempting to take his seat in Parliament in that capacity, was arrested, indicted, tried, convicted, fined, and imprisoned—all of which moderated his future political conduct. Sir Francis Burdett closed his liberal career by joining the Tory party. Hobhouse, who came into Parliament from Westminster as an extreme radical, settled down into a placeman, and is now a peer.—M.

quem ad perturbandam Rempublicam Inopia simul atque Mali Mores stimulaverunt. There wants not one iota to complete the resemblance, except only some tincture of that noble blood which was never so debased and degraded as in the person of the *Roman Cataline*—the total absence of which, however, and of all that it implies, lends even a more odious air of abomination to the rough and unvarnished ferocity of his English rival.*

"When the poor are in distress, God forbid that they should not share the pity, and feel the helping hand of their superiors. When the poor and the ignorant are led astray, God forbid that compassion should not be the first and last feeling on the minds of men who have enjoyed opportunities for reflection very different from those which can be afforded to their weak and untrained spirits, amidst their only leisure, the idleness of calamity. But God forbid, also, and the prayer we would fear is more a necessary than a frequent one—that we should suffer ourselves, from any mistaken or misdirected sympathies, to learn the lesson of regarding, without a just and unswerving feeling of abhorrence, the characters of those who make their sport of the poverty, and their prey of the ignorance of the vulgar. The worst of all the bad symptoms which meet our eyes, in the narratives of the late melancholy transactions, is the daily increasing urbanity of the terms in which the authors of all this evil are spoken of by the compilers of these narratives. It is a sad thing indeed, when the souls of those that are or ought to be enlightened, betray, on such momentous crises as these, any stains of that darkness which it is of right their vocation to dispel, and of which, above all things, it behoved them to have rejected and scorned the contamination. Let there be no foolish gentleness toward those who fight against all that is good—no mad courtesy for those who would destroy all that is noble. Let all that have any claim to the name of gentleman be anxious to keep their spirits pure from the very vestige of this degradation. In this hour of darkness let all stand together. In this hour of battle—for the word is not too strong in itself, nor the less applicable, because the contest to which it refers is more one

* Henry Hunt, the person here alluded to, was a very popular demagogue for several years; but having sat in parliament in 1830–'31, was such a mere nobody in that assembly, that his constituents did not re-elect him. It is recorded that he made one hit in the House of Commons. He was a man of considerable landed property, inherited from his ancestors, when he entered public life, but "the broad acres" had gradually slipped through his fingers, and he entered into business for a livelihood, first as a brewer, and afterwards as a vender of burnt corn (or an untaxed substitute for coffee, and called "Hunt's Breakfast Powder,) and then as a manufacturer of Blacking. William Peel brother-in-law to Sir Robert, was in Parliament when Hunt sat there. The Peel family, although possessing immense wealth, made as manufacturers, had sprung from nothing—as far as "birth" was concerned. Peel alluded, somewhat rudely, to Hunt's blacking, insinuating that Hunt was not a gentleman. The reply was brief and sufficient. Hunt rose, and fixing his eyes on Peel, said, "The honorable member has alluded to my business, and spoke of the difference of our respective stations. Let me tell him what that difference is. I am the first of my family who ever was engaged in trade. He is one of the first of his who could afford to lay claim, from wealth only, to the rank of gentleman." Hunt sat down, applauded on all sides, and William Peel did not again provoke him.—M.

of principles than of men—in this hour of battle let us all rally around those old banners, which have for so many ages been our guides to victory, and our ornaments in repose.

THE PRINCE REGENT."

We ought perhaps to beg our readers' pardon for the seeming vanity of recording this little address; but we feel assured that no such apology will be necessary for inserting the words of a song, with which our friend Mr. Wastle was good enough to preface the next toast on our list. It is needless to add, that this was the health and prosperity of our Royal Guest.

SONG, BY MR. WASTLE,

On Proposing the Health of H. R. H. PRINCE LEOPOLD.

I.

LOOK, oh! look from the Bower—'tis the beautiful hour
When the sunbeams are broad ere they sink in the sea;
Look, oh! look from the Bower—for an amethyst shower
Of grandeur and glory is gemming the Dee;
While the mountains arise more sublime in the skies,
'Mid that lustre of mildness, majestic and clear,
And the face of the land seems in smiles to expand—
Surely Nature proclaims that a Festival's here.

II.

Let your goblets be crowned like the sky and the ground,
With a light that is bright as their purple may be;
Let your goblets be crowned, like all Nature around,
To welcome our Prince in the vale of the Dee.
Fill, fill ye with wine, fill your goblets like mine,
Till the rich foam be ready to gush o'er the brim,
And let thoughts, sad and high, 'mid your raptures be by,
While the stream of devotion flows radiant for Him.

III.

What though rarely the sod of Green Albyn be trod
By the feet of a Prince—Nay, though ages have sped
Since the eye of a King has adventured to fling
One beam on these hills where his fathers were bred;*
Like the flower of the North, which, when winter comes forth,
Blooms secure and unseen, 'neath her garment of snow—
So our Faith, undefiled, is still fresh in the wild,
Amidst chillness to bud, and in darkness to blow.

IV.

Oh! glad was the day when her snow fell away,
And the softness of spring again mantled her sky;
And her beauty shone out with the old Scottish shout,
That proclaimed to our mountains the Saxon was nigh.

* In August, 1822, Scotland was visited by George IV., who had gone to Ireland and Hanover in the preceding autumn.—M.

Not the less we adore the Red Lion of yore,
That alone on the Scutcheon of Albyn was seen,
Because England and Erin are mixed in the bearing,
And the shield where the dark bend is wreathed with the green.

V.

With our loyalty's gladness, some breathings of sadness
Have been heard—and our smiles have been mixed with a tear;
But perhaps the warm heart but ennobles its part,
When in Sympathy's guise it bids Homage appear.
Take our hearts as they are 'mid the heaths of Braemar,
And remember, when deep flows the dark purple wine,
That the Hill and the Glen would be proud once again,
To pour for their Princes the blood of their line.

We must not repeat the handsome terms in which thanks were returned for our own speech and the song of our friend—suffice it to say, that, after a most animated conversation of a political cast had been sustained for some time by several ingenious and ardent interlocutors, the Thane of Fife rose (the occasion was on his own health being proposed from the chair), and hinted, in his usual elegance of style and manner, that the illustrious Prince who had condescended to become our visitor, would be fully more gratified should we thenceforth dismiss these topics—which, however treated, could not fail to have something of a formal air and effect—and resume in full and entire freedom our own usual strain of amusement. In short, his Lordship as well as the Prince wished to see the doings of the Tent in their own simple and unsophisticated essence.

We lost no time in obeying this hint—and by way of breaking the ice for a descent into the regions of perfect mirth and jollity, we called on the Ettrick Shepherd to sing, with the accompaniment of the bag-pipe, one of those wild and pathetic ballads of which his genius has been so creative. Those who have had the pleasure of being in company with the Shepherd, know full well what deep and gentle pathos, and, at the same time, what light and playful gracefulness, are to be found in the notes of his unrivalled voice, and will not need to be told what effect he produced upon the whole company, by the following exquisite strain!

I PITY YOU, YE STARS SO BRIGHT, &c.

I pity you, ye stars so bright
That shine so sweetly all the night,
Beaming ever coldly down
On rock and river, tower and town,
Shining so lonely.

I pity you, ye stars so bright,
That shine so sweetly all the night,
With your rays of endless glee,
On the wide and silent sea,
Shining so lonely.

I pity you, ye stars so bright—
While I'm with Anna all the night,
Thro' the cold blue sky ye rove,
Strangers to repose and love,
Shining so lonely.

I pity you, ye stars so bright,
And Anna pities you to-night,
What a weary way you've been
Since yon first balmy kiss yestreen,
Shining so lonely!

This song was succeeded by a round of toasts, of which our memory has preserved only the following, viz:—

1. The Author of Waverley—by Prince Leopold.
2. Mr. Alison—by Mr. Wastle.
3. The Bishop of St. Davids, the unwearied and enlightened friend of Wales—by Dr. Morris.
4. Professor John Young, of Glasgow, the great Grecian of Scotland—by Dr. Parr.
5. The Right Hon. Robert Peel, the Member for Oxford—by Mr. Seward.
6. Charley Bushe, the most admirable Judge, the most eloquent speaker—and the most delightful companion in Ireland—by Mr. Odoherty.
7. Mr. Davison, of Oriel, the star of Isis—by Mr. Buller.
8. The Rev. Francis Wrangham, the star of Cam.—by the Editor.
9. The young Duke of Buccleugh—and may he live to be as great a blessing to Ettrick as his father—by the Shepherd.
10. Counsellor Ellis—by Mr. Tickler.
11. Lord Byron—by Dr. Scott.
12. Dr. Chalmers—by Baillie Jarvie.
13. Mr. John Kemble—by Mr. John Ballantyne.
14. The Earl of Fife (to whose turn the toast, by some accident, was long of coming round) paid us the elegant and classical compliment of proposing the health of our excellent Publishers, Messrs. Blackwood, Cadell, and Davies*—three times three—to which (need we add?) the whole of the company gladly assented.

Dr. Parr was the first to hint his wish for another song—and called loudly upon Buller of Brazennose, who, after a little hesitation, took courage, and told the Doctor if he had no objection he would give him an old Oxford strain. "By all means, you dog," quoth the Bellendenian—"I remember the day when I could sing half the Sausage† myself."

THE FRIAR'S FAREWELL TO OXFORD.

To the Tune of "Green Sleeves."

1.

T' OTHER night, as I passed by old Anthony-wood,
I saw Father Green in a sorrowful mood—
Astride on a stone, beside Magdalene gate,
He lamented o'er Oxford's degenerate state;

* Cadell and Davies were the London agents for the sale of *Blackwood*.—M.

† A collection of songs, chants, and other college versicles, entitled "The Oxford Sausage. A like collection, elsewhere, is "The Cambridge Tart."—M.

The beer he had swallowed had opened his heart,
And 'twas thus to the winds he his woes did impart.
With a heigh ho! &c.

2.

"Oh, Oxford! I leave thee—and can it be true?
I accept of a living? I bid thee adieu?
Thou scene of my rapture, in life's early morn,
Ere one pile of soft lambskin my back did adorn—
When sorrows came rarely, and pleasures came thick,
And my utmost distress was a long-standing tick.
With a heigh ho! &c.

3.

"Oh! the joys of the moderns are empty and vain,
When compared with our mornings in Logical-lane;
There seated securely, no Dun did we fear,
Tommy Horseman hopped round with his flagons of beer:
With cow-heel and tripe we our bellies did cram,
And for Proctors and Beadles we cared not a damn.
With a heigh ho! &c.

4.

"In the alehouse at evening these joys we renewed—
When our pockets were empty our credit was good;
Tho' scrawlings of chalk spread each smokified wall,
Not a fear for the future our souls could appal.
What tho' Sanctified Hall at our doctrines may scoff?
Yet enough for the day is the evil thereof.
With a heigh ho! &c.

5.

"All encircled with fumes of the mild curling shag,
We derided the toils of the book-plodding fag:
For careless was then every puff we did suck in,
And unknown in the schools were the terrors of plucking.
No Examiners, then, thought of working us harm,
A beef-steak and a bottle their wrath could disarm.
With a heigh ho! &c.

6.

"Good beer is discarded for claret and port,
Logic-lane is no longer the Muse's resort—
The cold hand of Chronos has reft Dinah's bloom,
And tobacco is banished from each common-room,
And the days I have seen they shall ne'er come again—
So adieu to old Oxford"—I answered, amen!
With a heigh ho! &c.

The pleasure we all testified on hearing this genuine academical strain, which, as Dr. Parr observed, was "enough to transport one to the very pinnacle of Maudlin" (we suppose he meant one of the Oxford Colleges which goes by the name of Magdalen College, orally corrupted as above), encouraged Mr. Seward to comply with Buller's request, who tossed the ball to his friend on this occasion with a plain insinuation, that the former story of his not being able to sing was all mere fudge. The Christ-Church man, whose proper designation we understand (for he has not yet taken his bachelor's degree), is that of a *sophista generalis*, said, that he was the more inclined to sing a particular set of verses, because the present company would be able at once to appreciate their merit, they being a parody on one of the songs in the Lady of the Lake, composed by an eminent university wit, in honor of a late occurrence, which he declined explaining at greater length.

SONG—*Sung by* GENERAL SOPHIST SEWARD *of Christ-Church.*

To the Tune of " Rhoderick Dhu."

HAIL to the maiden that graceful advances!
'Tis the Helen of Isis if right I divine.
Eros! thou classical god of soft glances,
Teach me to ogle and make the nymph mine.
Look on a tutor true,
Ellen! for love of you
Just metamorphosed from blacksmith to beau.
Hair combed, and breeches new,
Grace your trim Roderick Dhu—
While every gownsman cries, wondering, " Ho! ho!"

In Greek I believe I must utter my passion,
For Greek's more familiar than English to me;
Besides, Byron of late has brought Greek into fashion—
There's some in his " *Fair Maid of Athens*,"—Let's see—
Psha! this vile modern Greek
Won't do for me to speak——
Let me try—*Ζωη, μȣσας αγαϖω*!
Zooks! I don't like its tone:
Now let me try my own—
ΚΑΥΘΙ ΜΕΥ, ΕΛΕΝΗ, ΣΟΥ ΓΑΡ ΕΡΩ!

But, ha! there's a young Christ-church prig that I plucked once!
I fear he'll make love to her out of mere spite;
Ha! twirl thy cap, and look proud of thy luck, dunce,
But *Greek* will prevail over *grins*, if I'm right.
By Dis! the infernal God!
See, see! they grin! they nod!
Ω μοι δυϛηνω! Ω ταλας εγω!
Zounds! should my faithless flame
Love this young Malcom Græme,
'Οτατοι! τοτατοι! φευ! ϖοϖοι! Ω!

But come! there's one rival I don't see about her,
I mean the spruce tutor, her townsman Fitzjames;
For though of the two I believe I'm the stouter,
His legs are much neater, much older his claims.
Yet every Christ-church blade
Swears I have won the maid;
Every one, Dean and Don, swears it is so.
Honest Lloyd blunt and bluff,
Levett, and Goodenough—
All clap my back and cry, " Rhoderick's her beau!"

Come, then, your influence propitious be shedding,
 Gnomes of Greek metre! since crowned are my hopes;
Waltz in Trochaic time, waltz at my wedding,
 Nymphs who preside over accents and tropes!
  Scourge of false quantities,
  Ghost of Hephæstion rise,
Haply to thee my success I may owe.
  Sound then the Doric string,
  All, all in chorus sing,
Joy to Hephæstion, black Rhoderick & Co.

By this time the Shepherd began to get very weary of the claret, and insisted upon being allowed to make a little whisky toddy in a noggin for himself. We always humor, as far as prudence will permit, the whims of our Contributors, however they may be at variance with our own private taste and judgment, so we at once granted our permission to Mr. Hogg, and a proud man was he, when, after his toddy was fairly made, the Prince and the Thane both requested a tasting of it. "Od," cried he, "I wad gie your Royal Highness and Lordship every drap o't, an' it were melted diamonds—but I'm sure you'll no like it—we maun hae a sang frae the Captain, and that will gar ony thing gang down." Odoherty could not withstand this flattery, and at once favored us with the following, of which both words and music are his own.

SONG—"*That I love thee, charming Maid,*" *to its own Tune.*

By MORGAN ODOHERTY, ESQ.

THAT I love thee, charming maid, I a thousand times have said,
 And a thousand times more I have sworn it,
But 'tis easy to be seen in the coldness of your mien
 That you doubt my affection—or scorn it.
  Ah me!

Not a single pile of sense is in the whole of these pretenses
 For rejecting your lover's petitions;
Had I windows in my bosom, Oh! how gladly I'd expose 'em
 To undo your phantastic suspicions.
  Ah me!

You repeat I've known you long, and you hint I do you wrong
 In beginning *so late* to pursue ye,
But 'tis folly to look glum because people did not come
 Up the stairs of your nursery to woo ye.
  Ah me!

In a grapery one walks without looking at the stalks,
 While the bunches are green that they're bearing—
All the pretty little leaves that are dangling at the eaves
 Scarce attract even a moment of staring.
  Ah me!

But when time has swell'd the grapes to a richer style of shapes,
And the sun has lent warmth to their blushes,
Then to cheer us and to gladden, to enchant us and to madden,
Is the ripe ruddy glory that rushes.
Ah me!

Oh 'tis then that mortals pant, while they gaze on Bacchus' plant—
Oh! 'tis then—will my simile serve ye?
Should a damsel fair repine, tho' neglected like a vine?
Both ere long shall turn heads topsy-turvy.
Ah me!

We had scarcely finished the speech, in which we proposed the health of the Standard-bearer, when our eye dropt upon the physiognomy of the Bishop of Bristol, evidently in a fit of deep abstraction. His broad forehead was drawn down into his face with a complexity of deep indented furrows; his under lip was lifted close to his nostrils; and his eyes were dilated like those of Parasina in the Judgment Hall, resting with the gaze of a Newton upon some invisible point in the vacant air around him. From what delightful or dreadful dream our laugh (for we could not repress it), withdrew the wondering phantasy of the illustrious Bishop, we cannot pretend to offer any conjecture. "I'm not absent, nae mair nor yoursel, Mr. Chairman," were the first words he uttered. "I was only just casting about for a verse or two that I cannot remember, of a sang that I was thinking to offer you—I canno bring them up, however—but no matter, there's a gay twa-three as it is." The Bishop's volunteer was greeted with tremendous acclamation; and—having hummed the air for about a minute, and ordered us all to join the chorus—in a low plaintive voice, broken, without doubt, by the intensity of many painful recollections, he thus began,

CAPTAIN PATON'S LAMENT.*

By JAMES SCOTT, *Esq.*

1.

TOUCH once more a sober measure, | and let punch and tears be shed,
For a prince of good old fellows, | that, alack a-day! is dead;
For a prince of worthy fellows, | and a pretty man also,
That has left the Saltmarket | in sorrow, grief, and woe.
Oh! we ne'er shall see the like of Captain Paton no mo!

2.

His waistcoat, coat, and breeches, | were all cut off the same web,
Of a beautiful snuff-color, | or a modest genty drab;
The blue stripe in his stocking | round his neat slim leg did go,
And his ruffles of the Cambric fine | they were whiter than the snow.
Oh! we ne'er shall see the like of Captain Paton no mo!

* Captain Paton's Lament, which has been a popular song in Scotland since it first was chanted in the Tent, was written by Mr. Lockhart.—M.

3.

His hair was curled in order, | at the rising of the sun,
In comely rows and buckles smart | that about his ears did run;
And before there was a toupeé | that some inches up did grow,
And behind there was a long queue | that did o'er his shoulders flow.
Oh! we ne'er shall see the like of Captain Paton no mo!

4.

And whenever we foregathered, he took off his wee three-cockit,
And he proffered you his snuff-box, which he drew from his side pocket,
And on Burdett or Bonaparte, he would make a remark or so,
And then along the plainstones like a provost he would go.
Oh! we ne'er shall see the like of Captain Paton no mo!

5.

In dirty days he picked well | his footsteps with his rattan,
Oh! you ne'er could see the least speck | on the shoes of Captain Paton;
And on entering the Coffee-room | about *two*, all men did know,
They would see him with his Courier | in the middle of the row.
Oh! we ne'er shall see the like of Captain Paton no mo!

6.

Now and then upon a Sunday | he invited me to dine,
On a herring and a mutton-chop | which his maid dressed very fine:
There was also a little Malmsey, and a bottle of Bourdeaux,
Which between me and the Captain passed nimbly to and fro.
Oh! I ne'er shall take pot-luck with Captain Paton no mo!

7.

Or if a bowl was mentioned, the Captain he would ring,
And bid Nelly run to the West-port, and a stoup of water bring;
Then would he mix the genuine stuff, as they made it long ago,
With limes that on his property in Trinidad did grow.
Oh! we ne'er shall taste the like of Captain Paton's punch no mo!

8.

And then all the time he would discourse | so sensible and courteous,
Perhaps talking of the last sermon | he had heard from Dr. Porteous,
Or some little bit of scandal | about Mrs so and so,
Which he scarce could credit, having heard | the *con* but not the *pro*.
Oh! we ne'er shall hear the like of Captain Paton no mo!

9.

Or when the candles were brought forth, and the night was fairly setting in,
He would tell some fine old stories about Minden-field or Dettingen—
How he fought with a French major, and despatched him at a blow,
While his blood ran out like water on the soft grass below.
Oh! we ne'er shall hear the like of Captain Paton no mo!

10.

But at last the Captain sickened | and grew worse from day to day,
And all missed him in the Coffee-room | from which now he stayed away;
On Sabbaths, too, the Wee Kirk | made a melancholy show,
All for wanting of the presence | of our venerable beau.
Oh! we ne'er shall see the like of Captain Paton no mo!

11.

And in spite of all that Cleghorn | and Corkindale could do,
It was plain, from twenty symptoms | that death was in his view;
So the Captain made his test'ment, and submitted to his foe,
And we layed him by the Rams-horn-kirk—'tis the way we all must go.
Oh! we ne'er shall see the like of Captain Paton no mo!

12.

Join all in chorus, jolly boys, and let punch and tears be shed,
For this prince of good old fellows, that alack a-day! is dead;
For this prince of worthy fellows, and a pretty man also,
That has left the Saltmarket in sorrow, grief, and woe!
For it ne'er shall see the like of Captain Paton no mo!

At the conclusion of this song, which, to those who know the voice, taste, and execution of the gentleman who sung it, we need not say gave general delight, Prince Leopold, who had attentively listened to it with the most gracious smile, arose, and saying, "that it was wise for friends to part in a mirthful moment," with the utmost benignity bade us all farewell. At this very moment, Mr. Tims (who was long ere now as bowsy as a fly in a plate of "quassia,") jumped upon his chair in order to attract our notice, and insisted upon singing "SCOTS WHA HAE WI' WALLACE BLED;" but the Shepherd frowned with such a deadly darkness at the suggestion, that the Cockney lost not a moment in resuming his former posture. "Aye, aye, that's richt," said the Shepherd, "saufus only to think o' ROBERT THE BRUCE acted by —— TIMS!"

As our Illustrious Visitor and his Noble Friends withdrew, the pipes slowly and solemnly played "Farewell to Lochaber;" and our Tent seemed, at their departure, quite melancholy and forlorn. We soon retired to repose, but not to sleep; for all night long the Highland host kept playing their martial or mournful tunes, and the voices of distant ages seemed, in the solitary silence of the midnight desert, restored to the world of life. We felt, that with such a glorious day our reign in the Highlands nobly terminated, and we gave orders by sunrise to strike the Tent, exclaiming, in the words of Milton,—

"TO-MORROW FOR FRESH FIELDS AND PASTURES NEW."

Noctes Ambrosianae.

NO. I.—MARCH, 1822.

CHRISTOPHER NORTH, Esquire, *solus*.

Enter Ensign MORGAN ODOHERTY.

Editor. I am glad to see you, Odoherty. I am heartily glad of the interruption. I won't write any more to-night.—I'll be shot if I write a word more. Ebony may jaw as he pleases. The Number will do well enough as it is. If there is not enough, let him send his devil into the Balaam-box.*

Odoherty. I have just arrived from London.

Editor. From *London?*—The Fleet, I suppose. How long have you lain there?

Odoherty. I have been out these three weeks. I suppose, for any thing you would have advanced, I might have lain there till Kingdom-come.

Editor. I can't advance money for ever, Adjutant. You have not sent me one article these four months.

Odoherty. What sort of an article do you want?—A poem?

Editor. Poems! There's poetry enough without paying you for it. Have you seen Milman's new tragedy?†

Odoherty. No; but I saw the proofs of a puff upon it for the next

* The Balaam-box, which is repeatedly referred to in The Noctes, was supposed to contain a variety of articles, from voluntary contributors, as well as from the usual writers in the Magazine. Mr. Blackwood received the *sobriquet* of Ebony from a pun upon his name, which originated in the "Chaldee Manuscript," where he was spoken of a man whose "name was as it had been the color of ebony."—M.

† "The Martyr of Antioch, a dramatic poem, by the Rev. H. H. Milman," was published by John Murray, of London, in March, 1822. At that time Milman was Professor of Poetry in the University of Oxford. He had written a prize poem when he was an under-graduate. In 1817 he produced the tragedy of "Fazio," in which Miss O'Neill sustained the part of the heroine. This play retains its place in the Acted Drama. "Samor, Lord of the Bright City," a heroic poem in twelve books, appeared in 1818. "The Fall of Jerusalem," and "Anna Boleyne." were followed by "The Martyr of Antioch" and "Belshazzar." Milman has contributed largely to the *Quarterly Review*, edited Gibbon's Decline and Fall, and written a History of the Jews, and other serious works. He entered the Church in 1817, had a good vicarage at Reading, whence he removed to the rectory at St. Margaret's (the church which adjoins Westminster Abbey, partly concealing that stately structure from view), and was appointed Dean of St. Paul's in 1849. As a poet, Dr. Milman's reputation is even now almost traditionary. Of his dramatic works, 'Fazio" alone is known to the bulk of the present generation, and that from its frequent representation on the stage. Dr. Milman is now [1854] aged sixty-three.—M.

Quarterly. He's a clever fellow, but they cry him too high. The report goes, that he is to step into Gifford's shoes one of these days.*

Editor. That accounts for the puffing; but it will do a really clever fellow, like Milman, no good.

Odoherty. It will, Mr. North. I know nobody that puffs more lustily than yourself now and then. What made you puff Procter† so much at first?

Editor. It was you that puffed him. It was an article of your own, Ensign.

Odoherty. By Mahomet's mustard-pot, I've written so much, I don't remember half the things I've done in your own lubberly Magazine, and elsewhere. At one time I wrote all Day and Martin's poetry. They were grateful. They kept the whole mess of the 44th in blacking.

Editor. Then you wrote the *World*, did not you?

Odoherty. I never heard of such a thing. They've been quizzing you, old boy. Impostors are abroad.

Editor. Then somebody has been sporting false colors about town.

Odoherty. Like enough. Set a thief to catch a thief.

Editor. You've been writing in Colburn, they say, Master Morgan?

Odoherty. Not one line. The pretty boys have applied to me a dozen times, but I never sent them any answer except once, and then it was an epigram on themselves.

Editor. Let's hear it.

Odoherty. Now, by Jupiter! I have forgotten the beginning of it. I think it was something like this:—

> Colburn, Campbell, and Co. write rather so so,
> But atone for 't by puff and profession—
> Every month gives us scope for the *Pleasures of Hope*,
> But all ends in the *Pains of Possession*.

Editor. How do they get on? Heavily, Ensign?

Odoherty. D— heavily! They lay out a cool hundred on advertisements every month; but Campbell does very little—at least so it is to be hoped—and the Subs are no great shakes.‡ They have a

* Milman would never have done justice to the *Quarterly Review*;—his prose is deficient in force and terseness. The present Sir John T. Coleridge, now one of the Judges of the Queen's Bench in England, edited the *Quarterly* in the brief interval between Gifford's retirement and Lockhart's accession.—M.

† Procter, who was Byron's schoolfellow at Harrow, assumed the *nom de plume* of Barry Cornwall, when he published his first volume of Dramatic Sketches, in 1815. He wrote a tragedy called Mirandola, played in 1821, at Covent Garden Theatre. Marcian Colonna, The Flood of Thessaly, a Life of Edmund Kean (which was severely criticised in Blackwood), and a variety of songs, many of which are admirable, complete the list of his writings—except his magazine articles, which have been collected in this country (but not yet in England), and published as his "Essays and Tales in Prose." As a song-writer, vigorous, yet delicate, in thought and expression, Procter has won a name "the world will not willingly let die."—M.

‡ Campbell, the poet, edited Colburn's *New Monthly Magazine*, from 1821 to 1831, at £500 per annum, with separate payment, as a contributor, for all articles by himself. This im-

miserable set of bullaboos about them—broken-winded *dominies*, from the manufacturing districts, and so forth. Even Hazlitt does the drama better.

Editor. O, Hazlitt's a real fellow in his small way. He has more sense in his little finger, than many who laugh at him have in their heads, but he is bothering too long at that *table-talk.*

Odoherty. Proper humbug!

Editor. Did you see any of the Cockneys? What's the gossip about Murray's, Ridgeway's,* and so forth? Did you make a tour of the shops?

Odoherty. Of course—I went round them all with a bundle of discarded articles you gave me to line my trunk with, when I went to the moors last year. I passed myself off for a country clergyman, wanting to publish a series of essays. I said I had a wife and seven small children.

Editor. You have some tolerably big ones, I believe.

Odoherty. Which you never will have, old boy. The booksellers are a very civil set of fellows: Murray took me into a room by myself, and told me of the row between him and the Divan.

Editor. What row? and with whom?

Odoherty. Why, they call Murray Emperor of the West, and Longman and Company the Divan. They've fallen out about Mother Rundell's book upon cookery. I told Kitchener the next day, that I thought his own book as good a one.†

Editor. Shameless fellow! Don't you remember how you cut it up? I wonder you could look the doctor in the face.

Odoherty. By jing! he thought I was a doctor myself. I had a black rose in my hat, and talked very wisely about the famous mistake touching *a Mr. Winton of Chelsea.* I'll tell you about that, too, some other time.‡

mense payment, in fact, was for his *name*. The Magazine was actually edited by Cyrus Redding (whose later Recollections of Campbell and Beckford are full of interest and truth), and the dramatic criticism was supplied, for many years, by T. N. Talfourd (afterwards one of the Judges of the Court of Common Pleas in England), so well known, subsequently, as the author of "Ion."—M.

* What Murray's, in Albemarle-street, was for Tory literati and politicians in London—a pleasant lounging place, where public affairs, books, and personal gossip, supplied the conversation—Ridgeway's, in Piccadilly, was for the Whigs. To this hour, both places retain this distinctive character.—M.

† In Dr. Kitchener's "Cook's Oracle" there was a boast, that every receipt in it had been tried by the author—and his friends, might have been added, for he was right hospitable, in his snug house close to Fitzroy-Square, and was pleasantly addicted to giving charming dinner-parties at which the number of the guests was regulated on the classic rule, "Not less than the Graces, nor more than the Muses." At these entertainments, which Theodore Hook frequently attended, judgment was solemnly passed upon the Doctor's gastronomic inventions or improvements since the last repast. Sometimes, it is true, opinions would be balanced (particularly if the dinner was very good, and the party very agreeable), and the Doctor would then invite the same party for that day week, in order to give the culinary treasure another trial. *All* his receipts were treasures—if his own report were to be credited. He was a clever, well-informed man, who gracefully rode his hobbies—all but one. He had invented a digestive pill, 'yclept the Perisaltic Persuader, and sometimes would insist on coaxing his guests into swallowing one or two before dinner!—M.

‡ The story never was told in *Blackwood*, and is too good to be lost;—Dr. Tomline had

Editor. The Bishop's first two volumes are not quite *the potato.* I hope the others are better.

Odoherty. Who cares? I shall never read them. Have you seen Horace Walpole's Memoirs?

Editor. I have. A most charming book. A most malicious, prying, lying old fox.* What a prime contributor he would have made!—but, to be sure, he was a Whig.

Odoherty. So am I. For that matter, half your best contributors are Whigs, I take it.

Editor. Mum, for that, Ensign. But, at least, I have nothing to do with the Scotch Kangaroo Canaille.

Odoherty. They have nothing to do with you, you mean to say.

Editor. They're a dirty, dull, detestable set. I hate them all—I despise them all—except little Jeffrey.

Odoherty. He's a clever chap, certainly,—I have not given him a dressing these two years; I shall give you a song upon him one of these days.

Editor. Do. What's afoot among the Tumbledowns?

Odoherty. The Holland House gentry are chuckling very much over a little tit-bit of blasphemy, sent over by a certain learned Lord from Italy,—'tis call'd the "Irish Advent,"—'tis a base parody on the Advent of our Saviour,—'tis circulated widely among the same Thebans who blarneyed about Hogg's Chaldee.†

been College tutor, at Cambridge, to William Pitt, was made Bishop of Lincoln by him, and in 1820, was translated to the wealthy See of Winchester. He had long been preparing a Life of Pitt, and in 1821, wrote briefly to Murray, to ask whether he would publish it, and on what terms. English Bishops sign with the Latin names of their respective sees instead of their own surnames. The letter to Murray was dated "Chelsea," where the Bishop had a suburban dwelling, and was signed *Geo. Winton*—in contraction of Georgius Wintonensis, which would have been his full Latinized signature, as Bishop of Winchester. It happened that Murray was ignorant of this, and considering it a great liberty for an utter stranger to write a three-line letter to him, sent a sharp reply to the effect, that "Mr. Murray had received Mr. George Winton's note, and declined the proposed publication." Presently, Mr. Croker, (of the Admiralty), came in, and Murray, whose dignity continued to be slightly ruffled, threw the unfortunate "Winton," epistle across the table to him. "The very book," said Croker, "and the very man to write it." Murray, in amaze, demanded an explanation, and Croker answered, "The Bishop of Winchester was Pitt's tutor, private secretary, correspondent, friend, and literary executor." "My dear fellow," said Murray, "what has the Bishop of Winchester to do with that letter?" Croker explained the matter of the Episcopal signature. "Bless me," said Murray, "I thought it was some Grub-street compiler, and wrote him a stiff and saucy answer. I hope it has not been posted." On inquiry, it was found that the letter had already been taken, with others, to the Two-penny Post-office. With some difficulty, Freeling, the Secretary of the General Post-office, allowed Murray to get back the letter, in place of which he sent a very courtly epistle, offering to wait on the Bishop, and so on. The result was the publication of the first part, in two volumes, of Tomline's Life of William Pitt. A third volume did not complete the work, which it was understood that the Bishop was busy on up to his death, in 1827. The biography was large and dull. The best of the "Winton" joke was that Croker, who knew the Bishop, and spared no one, told it to his Lordship, who let Murray know, once or twice, that he was in the secret.—M.

* Horace Walpole's Memoirs and Correspondence, to say nothing of his other writings, show extraordinary industry, lively wit, close observation, and sly satire. They give on the whole, more of political, literary, fashionable, artistical, and scandalous gossip during the last sixty years of the Eighteenth Century, than we have yet received. Walpole became Earl of Orford, by succession, in 1791, but never took his seat in the House of Lords. He died in 1797, in his eightieth year.—M.

† The poem alluded to, was "The Irish Avater," written in September, 1821, on the visit which George IV. had paid to Ireland, in the preceding August. Byron, who was shocked at

Editor. Hogg's Chaldee !—good.

Odoherty. You would notice the puffs about another thing, called "the Royal Progress;"—they say 'tis writ by Mrs. Morgan's ex-chevalier; and I can believe it, for it is equally dull and disloyal.

Editor. Are these all the news you have picked up? How do the minor periodicals sell?

Odoherty. Worse and worse. Taylor and Hessey are going down like the devil.* Colburn pays like a hero, for what you would fling into the fire. The copyright of the European was disposed of t'other day for about 1600*l.*, back numbers, plates, and all included. 'Twas about the best of them.

Editor. I hope old Sir Richard is thriving.

Odoherty. Capitally. He circulates between three and four thousand; and his advertisements are very profitable.† Why don't you sport a little extra matter of cover?

Editor. At present mine are mostly *preserves.* I'll enlarge them, if you won't poach.

Odoherty. Depend on't, 'twill pay.

Editor. I hope Nicholas gets on.

Odoherty. Very fair. 'Tis the only Gentleman's Magazine besides your own.‡

Editor. What is that thing called the Gazette of Fashion?

Odoherty. 'Tis a poor imitation of the Literary Gazette. Mr. ——————,‖ they say, patronizes it; but this can't be true, for it attacks, very shamefully, *the man who did* HIM *more good than any body else ever will be able to do him, here or hereafter.*

Editor. Hercles' vein with a vengeance! You've been studying the Eclectic, one would think.

the enthusiasm with which the Irish Catholics received a monarch who had the power, but lacked the will, to give them Emancipation, headed his stanzas, which are strong and stinging, with this motto, from Curran, "And Ireland, like a bastinadoed elephant, kneeling to receive the paltry rider." The poem, which gracefully closes with complimentary notices of Grattan, Curran, and Moore, was so personal on George IV., that it was not published in his life-time. But Byron sent it to Moore, at Paris, and allowed him to have a dozen copies printed, for private circulation. Some of these found their way to London, and were handed about, in literary society, until the poem became pretty generally known. It was first *published*, in England, in 1831.—M.

* After John Scott, the original editor of the *London Magazine*, was shot in a duel by Mr. Christie, the periodical fell into the hands of Taylor and Hessey, of Fleet-street, very intelligent publishers. The duel (as will be more particularly stated in the Memoirs of Lockhart, in the present edition of The Noctes), arose from a quarrel which sprung out of some articles in Blackwood.—M.

† Phillips was a bookseller, who had been one of the sheriffs of London, and was knighted, on presenting some city address to George III. He was proprietor, publisher, and editor of the *Monthly Magazine*, at one time a thriving periodical. The *European Magazine* gave a variety of good engravings, (landscapes and public buildings, with very good portraits of living characters), and was long the property of Mr. Aspern, who published the letters of the famous John Wilkes.—M.

‡ The *Gentleman's Magazine*, commenced by Edmund Cave, early in the reign of George II., flourishes in that of Victoria, under the editorship of the Rev. John Mitford. For nearly half a century, it was conducted by John Nichols, an able writer on literary and antiquarian subjects. He died in 1828.—M.

‖ I am unable to say what person is here alluded to.—M.

Odoherty. The Eclectic is not so poor an affair as you insinuate, Mr. Christopher. The principal writers tip us a little of the *Snuffle* and *Whine*,—but you are up to that yourself, when it serves your turn. Montgomery's articles are such as you would like very well to lay your own fist upon, I fancy.

Editor. If Foster still writes in it, they have one of the first thinkers in England beneath their banner.* I wish you would read him, before you begin to write the auto-biography you've been talking about these three years.

Odoherty. Coleridge's did not pay.†

Editor. But yours may,—nay, will,—must pay. I'll insure you of 3000*l*. if you go to "the proper man." I intend to give him the first offer of my own great work,—my Armenian Grammar, which is now nearly ready for press.

Odoherty. Your name will sell anything. Is there much personality in the notes?

Editor. I have cut up the commentators here and there. I have fixed an indelible stigma on old Scioppius.‡

Odoherty. I'll defy you to write a sermon without being personal.

Editor. I'll defy Dr. Chalmers to do that. He is deuced severe on the Glasgow Baillies and Professors! I am told.

Odoherty. Do many clergymen contribute?

Editor. Droves.

Odoherty. What do the lads chiefly affect?

Editor. Jocular topics. 'Twas an arch-deacon sent me the Irish Melodies, which I know you have been owning everywhere for your own.‖

Odoherty. I follow one great rule,—never to own anything that is my own, nor deny anything that is not my own.

Editor. 'Tis the age of owning and disowning. It was a long while ere I believed Hope to be Anastasius.§

* John Foster, author of the "Essays" which have procured for him the reputation of being one of the most original thinkers of his age, was a frequent contributor to the *Eclectic Review*, then more decidedly religious in its tone than at present. He died in 1843. James Montgomery, the poet, was a casual contributor to the same periodical, and died in 1854. *The Eclectic*, which occasionally contains very able articles, is now edited by Dr. Thomas Pryse, of London, who is its proprietor.—M.

† Coleridge's "Biographia Literaria," was only a fragment, and not a very satisfactory one. It went through several editions in his life-time, and will always command a certain degree of attention.

‡ Gaspar Scioppius, a learned German, who wrote in the seventeenth century, was called "the grammatical cur," on account of his spiteful and injurious way of calumniating all who were eminent for their erudition. He was one of the class who, themselves not meriting nor obtaining success, consider it unpardonable in others to be more deserving and fortunate.—M.

‖ A series of Irish Melodies, purporting to be sent by "Morty Macnamara Mulligan," of Dublin, but really written by Maginn, and published, with music and words, in Blackwood, for December, 1821. They were to have commenced a series, but only No. 1 appeared, containing six melodies.—M.

§ When "Anastasius" first appeared, in 1819, it was reviwed, in *Blackwood*, as written by Lord Byron. The late Thomas Hope, whose previous literary publications, had been "The Costumes of the Ancients," and "Designs of Modern Costumes," avowed himself the author, in a brief letter which was printed in Blackwood.—M.

Odoherty. It will be a long while ere I believe that Anastasius wrote those quartos about mahogany. I believe he might furnish the wood, but, by Jericho, did he carve it at all?

Editor. You are an incorrigible Irishman. Have you any news from your country? It seems to me to be in a fine state.

Odoherty. Why, for that matter, I think we are very commonplace in our national diversions. Sir William Chambers complained of nature being monotonous, for furnishing *only* earth, air, and water. Blood and whisky may sum up all the amusements of the Irish Whigs.—Burning, throat-cutting, shooting an old proctor or policeman—that's all. They fight in a cowardly fashion. There's my cousin, Tom Magrath, writes me he saw 500 of them run away from about forty gentlemen. One of the chief stimulants the poor devils have, is a prophecy of the papist Bishop Walmesley, (the same that goes under the name of Pastorini,) that the Protestant church is to be destroyed in 1825.*

Editor. Why, some few years ago, a godly squire in Ayrshire here, published a thumping book, to prove that Bonaparte would die *in* 1825, *at the siege of Jerusalem.* The year 1825 will be a rare one when it comes.

Odoherty. These events will furnish fine materials for a new hour's *Tête-à-tête with the public.*†

Editor. What a world of things will have happened ere 1825!

Odoherty. You will be knocked up ere then. You talk about your stomach—only see how little remains in the bottle!

Editor. I had finished two ere you came in. I can never write without a bottle beside me. Judge Blackstone followed the same plan, he had always a bottle of port by him while he was at his commentaries. When Addison was composing his Essay on the Evidences, he used to walk up and down the long room in Holland House—there was a table with the black strap at each end, and he always turned up his little finger twice ere he had polished a sentence to his mind.‡—I believe he took brandy while he was doing the last act of Cato. There is no good writing without one glass.

"Nemo bene potest scribere jejunus."

Odoherty. I prefer smoking, on the whole. But I have no objection to a glass of punch along with it. It clears our mouth.

* The prophecy was:

"In the year eighteen hundred twenty-five,
There will not be a Protestant alive."

I was in the south of Ireland, on New Year's Day, 1825, and recollect seeing several Protestants, who were going to attend divine service, stealthily take loaded pistols with them, fearing that a general massacre was in contemplation, and resolving to sell their lives dearly.—M.

† The name of an amusing, chatty article which had appeared in *Blackwood,* some time before (evidently written by Wilson,) and had gained great approbation from the patient public.—M.

‡ This is the tradition at Holland House.—M.

Editor. "Experto crede. Roberto."

Odoherty. I am glad to see you have dropt your cursed humbug articles on German Plays. I hate all that trash. Is Kempferhausen defunct?

Editor. I had a present of two *aums* of Johannisberg from him not a week ago.

Odoherty. The piperly fellow once promised me a few dozens; but he took it amiss that I peppered him so at the *Tent.*

Editor. I am sure you would have sold it to Ambrose if you had got it.—Will you have some supper?

Odoherty. Excuse me, I never eat supper.

Editor, (*Rings.*) Waiter, Welsh rabbits for five, scolloped oysters for ten, six quarts of porter, and covers for two.

Waiter. It is all ready, sir; Mr. Ambrose knew what you would want the moment the Captain came in.

Odoherty. I am thinking seriously of writing some book. What shape do you recommend? I was thinking of a quarto.

Editor. A duodecimo you mean; will a quarto go into a sabretache, or a work-basket, or a reticule? Are you the bishop of Winchester?*

Odoherty. What bookseller do you recommend? (These are prime powldoodies!)

Editor. Ebony to be sure, if he will give the best price. But be sure you don't abuse his temper. There was a worthy young man done up only a few months ago by the cockney poets. He gave £100 to one for a bundle of verses, (I forget the title,) of which just thirty copies were sold. They were all at him like leeches, and he was soon sucked to the bone. You must not tip Ebony any shabby trash—you must be upon honor, Mr. Odoherty. You have a great name, and you must support it. If you mind your hits, you may rise as high as any body I know in any of the slang lines.

Odoherty. You flatter me! Butter!

Editor. Not one lick! Egan is not worthy of holding a candle to your Boxiana; and yet Egan is a prime swell. You should get little Cruikshank to draw the vignettes; your life would sell as well as Hogg's, or Haggart's, or any body else, that I remember.†

Odoherty. You'll cut a great figure in it yourself.

Editor. A good one, you mean?

Odoherty. No, d——, I scorn to flatter you, or any man. I shall tell the truth, all the truth, and nothing but the truth. Do you

* The Bishop's Life of William Pitt had appeared in quarto.—M.

† The articles called "Boxiana,"—which have been generally attributed to Maginn—ran through several volumes of *Blackwood.* They gave the history of the English prize-ring. Pierce Egan wrote the work on which they were based, and was additionally notorious as Editor of Bell's Life, a sporting paper, and author of "Life in London," which, when dramatized, had more success than any performance which the London play-goers had seen for years. "Life in London" was illustrated by George Cruikshank and his brother Robert.—M.

expect me to say that you are a handsome man? Or that you have slim ankles? Or that you don't squint? Or that you understand the whole doctrine of quadrille? Or that you are the author of Waverley? Or the author of Anastasius? Are these the bams you expect?

Editor. Say that I am the author of the Chaldee, and I am satisfied.

Odoherty. No, I'll stick to my own rule. I'll claim it myself. I'll challenge Hogg if he disputes the point.

Editor. I hope you'll shoot potatoes; for I could not afford to lose either of you! you are both of you rum ones to look at, but devils to go.

Odoherty. I intend to be modest as to my amours.

Editor. You had better not. The ladies won't buy if you do so. Your amour with Mrs. Macwhirter* raised my sale considerably.

Odoherty. This is a very delicate age. I fear nothing at all high would go down with it.

Editor. Why there's a vast deal of cant afloat as to this matter; people don't know what they are speaking about. Show me any production of genius, written in our time, which does not contain what they pretend to abhor.

Odoherty. Why, there's the Edinburgh Review—you must at least allow 'tis a decent work.

Editor. Have you forgotten Sidney Smith's article about missionaries?—I won't repeat the *names* of some of them.

Odoherty. The Quarterly?

Editor. Why, Gifford and I are old boys, and past our dancing days; but I believe you will find some very sly touches here and there.

Odoherty. Byron?

Editor. Poh! you're wild now. We may despise the cant about him, but you must confess that there's always a little of *what's wrong* in the best of his works. Even the Corsair seems to have flirted a bit now and then. And Juan, you know, is a perfect Richelieu.†

Odoherty. Have you anything to say against the Waverley novels?

Editor. Not much. Yet even the old Dame Norna in the Pirate seems to have danced in her youth. I strongly suspect her son was a mere *filius carnalis.*

Odoherty. What of Kenilworth, then?

Editor. 'Tis all full of going about the bush. One always sees what Elizabeth is thinking about. She has never some handsome

* This amour is related, rather particularly, in the Memoirs of Odoherty, and the lady's last appearance was, in The Tent.—M.

† Not the Cardinal, but the Duc de Richelieu, of the Orleans Regency, equally distinguished for his profligacy and valor.—M.

fellow or other out of her mind. And then the scene where Leicester and Amy get up is certainly rather richly colored. There is nothing a whit worse in the Sorrows of Werter, or Julia de Roubigné, or any of that sentimental set.

Odoherty. Milman is a very well-behaved boy. You can say nothing of that sort against him.

Editor. He is a very respectable man, and a clergyman to boot; but the bridal songs in his Fall of Jerusalem are not much behind what a layman might have done. There are some very luxurious hits in *that* part of the performance. Did you attend old P——'s sale when you were in town?

Odoherty. No, I can't say I did; but I hear there was a fine collection of the Facetiæ, and other forbidden fruits. A friend of mine got the editio princeps of Poggio,* but he sweated for it. The Whigs bid high. They worked to keep all those tit-bits for themselves.

Editor. Does this affair of Lord Byron's Mystery† create any sensation in London?

Odoherty. Very little. The parsons about Murray's shop are not the most untractable people in the world, otherwise they would never have abstained so long from attacking Juan, Beppo, and the rest of Byron's improprieties—they that are so foul-mouthed against Shelley, and such insignificant blasphemers as that Cockney crew.

Editor. I have often wondered at the *face* they show in that omission.

Odoherty. Really?

Editor. No doubt a bookseller must have something to say as to his own Review. But the thing should not be pushed too far, else a noodle can see through it.

Odoherty. Meaning me?

Editor. Not at all. But as to Cain, I entirely differ from the Chancellor. I think, if Cain be prosecuted, it will be a great shame. The humbug of the age will then have achieved its most visible triumph.

Odoherty. I never saw it, but I thought it had been blasphemous.

Editor. No, sir, I can't see that. The Society might have had some pretence had they fallen on Don Juan; but I suppose those well-fed Archdeacons, and so forth, have their own ways of observing certain matters.

* Poggio Bracciolini, Apostolical Secretary to eight Popes, but a profligate in his conduct and writings. He lived in the fifteenth century.—M.

† "Cain, a Mystery," dedicated to Scott, was written at Ravenna in the autumn of 1821, and published in December of that year. It was pirated. Murray applied for an injunction against the pirates, and the Chancellor (Eldon,) declared that an immoral or irreligious book was not entitled to protection.—M.

Odoherty. Have you seen Lord Byron's letter on the subject to Mr. Murray?

Editor. Yes; 'tis in the papers.

Odoherty. A bite! that's the prose edition. It was written originally in verse, but Murray's friends thought it would have more effect if translated into prose; and a young clergyman, who writes in the Quarterly, turned the thing very neatly, considering; I believe I have a copy of Lord Byron's own letter in my pocket.

Editor. Let's see it.

Odoherty. You shall have it.

BYRON TO MURRAY.*

Attacks on me were what I look'd for, Murray,
  But why the devil do they badger you?
These godly newspapers seem hot as curry,
  But don't, dear Publisher, be in a stew.
They'll be so glad to see you in a flurry—
  I mean those canting Quacks of your Review—
They fain would have you all to their own Set;
  But never mind them—we're not parted yet.
They surely don't suspect you, Mr. John,
  Of being more than *accoucheur* to Cain;
What mortal ever said you wrote the Don?
  I dig the mine—you only fire the train!
But here—why, really, no great lengths I've gone—
  Big wigs and buzz were always my disdain—
But my poor shoulders why throw *all* the guilt on?
  There's as much blasphemy, or more, in Milton.

* *Letter from Lord Byron to Mr. Murray.*

PISA, Feb. 8, 1822.

DEAR SIR—Attacks upon me were to be expected; but I perceive one upon *you* in the papers, which, I confess, that I did not expect. How, or in what manner *you* can be considered responsible for what *I* publish, I am at a loss to conceive. If "Cain," be "blasphemous," Paradise Lost is blasphemous; and the very words of the Oxford Gentleman, "Evil be thou, my good," are from that very poem, from the mouth of Satan; and is there any thing more in that of Lucifer in the Mystery? Cain is nothing more than a drama, not a piece of argument. If Lucifer and Cain speak as the first murderer and the first rebel may be supposed to speak, surely all the rest of the personages talk also according to their characters; and the stronger passions have ever been permitted to the drama. I have even avoided introducing the Deity, as in Scripture (though Milton does, and not very wisely either;) but have adopted his angel, as sent to Cain, instead, on purpose to avoid shocking any feelings on the subject, by falling short of, what all uninspired men must fall short in, viz. giving an adequate notion of the effect of the presence of Jehovah. The old mysteries introduced him liberally enough, and all this is avoided in the new one.

The attempt to *bully you*, because they think it will not succeed with me, seems to me as atrocious an attempt as ever disgraced the times. What! when Gibbon's, Hume's, Priestley's, and Drummond's publishers have been allowed to rest in peace for seventy years, are *you* to be singled out for a work of *fiction*, not of history or argument? There must be something at the bottom of this—some private enemy of your own—it is otherwise incredible.

I can only say. "*Me—me adsum qui feci*," that any proceedings directed against you, I beg may be transferred to me, who am willing and *ought* to endure them all; that if you have lost money by the publication, I will refund any, or all of the copyright; that I desire you will say, that both *you* and Mr. Gifford remonstrated against the publication, as also Mr. Hobhouse; that I alone occasioned it, and I alone am the person who either legally or otherwise should bear the burthen. If they prosecute, I will come to England; that is, if by meeting it in my own person, I can save yours. Let me know—you sha'n't suffer for me, if I can help it. Make any use of this letter which you please. Yours ever, BYRON.

The thing 's a drama, not a sermon-book;
  Here stands the murderer—that 's *the old one* there;
In gown and cassock how would Satan look?
  Should Fratricides discourse like Doctor Blair?
The puritanic Milton freedom took,
  Which now-a-days would make a bishop stare;
But not to shock the feelings of the age,
I only bring you angels on the stage.
To bully You—yet shrink from battling Me,
  Is baseness. Nothing baser stains "The Times."
While Jeffrey in each catalogue I see,
  While no one talks of priestly Playfair's crimes,
While Drummond, at Marseilles, blasphemes with glee,
  Why all this row about my harmless rhymes?
Depend on 't, Piso, 't is some private pique
'Mong those that cram your Quarterly with Greek.

If this goes on, I wish you'd plainly tell 'em,
  'T were quite a treat *to me* to be indicted;
Is it less sin to write such books than sell 'em?
  There's muscle!—I 'm resolved I 'll see you righted.
In me, great Sharpe, *in me converte telum!*
  Come, Doctor Sewell, show you *have* been knighted.
—On my account you never shall be dunn'd,
  The copyright, in part, I will refund.
You may tell all who come into your shop,
  You and your Bull-dog both remonstrated;
My Jackall did the same, you hints may drop,
  (All which, perhaps, you have already said.)
Just speak the word, I 'll fly to be your prop,
  They shall not touch a hair, man, in your head.
You 're free to print this letter; you 're a fool
If you do n't send it first to the JOHN BULL.*

Editor. Come, this is a good letter. If I had been Murray I would not have thought of the prose. I'll be hanged if I would.

Odoherty. Is there any thing new in the literary world here?

Editor. Not much that I hear of. There's Colonel Stewart's History of the Highland Regiments, one of the most entertaining books that have been published this long time. You're a soldier, you must review it for me in my next number.†

Odoherty. I think I'll tip you a series of articles on the history of the Irish regiments. I'm sure I know as many queer stories about them as any colonel of them all. Is the book well written?

Editor. Plainly, but sensibly, and elegantly too, I think. Not much of the flash that's in vogue, but a great deal of feeling and truth. Some of the anecdotes are quite beautiful, and the Colonel's view of the Highland character is admirably drawn.

* The poetical version was by Maginn.—M.
† In the April number of *Blackwood*, the opening article was a review of Colonel David Stewart's Sketches of the Highland Regiments—not written, however, by Odoherty.—M.

Odoherty. I'm glad to hear it. Few officers write well except Julius Cæsar, the Heavy Horseman,* and myself.

Editor. You forget General Burgoyne.

Odoherty. Aye, true enough. The General was a sweet fellow.†

Editor. So are you all. Have you done nothing to your Campaigns? I'm sure they would sell better than Southey's.

Odoherty. That's no great matter, perhaps. I don't think the Laureate has much of a military eye.‡

Editor. How does the John Bull get on?

Odoherty. Famously, they say. I'm told they divided £6000 at the end of the first year. I intend contributing myself if you do not pay me better.

Editor. Why, how much would you have? Are you not always sure of your twenty guineas a-sheet? I'm sure that's enough for such articles as yours. You never take any pains.

Odoherty. If I did, they would not be worth five.—Have you seen John Home's Life?

Editor. To be sure.—'Tis very amusing. The old gentleman writes as well as ever.‖ I wish he would try his hand at a novel once more.

Odoherty. Why, no novels sell now except the Author of Waverley's.

Editor. Write a good one, and I warrant you 'twill sell. There's Adam Blair has taken like a shot; and Sir Andrew Wylie is almost out of print already.§

Odoherty. I don't think Sir Andrew near so good as the Annals of the Parish.—What say you?

* Poems by Edward Quillinan (who was successively the son-in-law of Sir Egerton Brydges and Wordsworth,) were reviewed, in *Blackwood*, by Captain Hamilton, who, because their author was or had been in the army, treated them as if written by a Heavy Dragoon. The critique was so personal as to be offensive, and Captain Quillinan went to Edinburgh to challenge the reviewer, whoever he might be. Accidentally sitting next Hamilton at dinner, Quillinan was so much pleased with him as to accept his invitation to have a cigar and walk home together. In the course of their conversation Quillinan mentioned how difficult he found it to ascertain the authorship of an article in *Blackwood*, and mentioned his own particular grievance of the critique. Hamilton smiled, and said, "My dear fellow, there was no private spleen in the matter. I, who wrote the article, knew nothing of the author I was quizzing, and am sorry that, by accident, I annoyed you." There was no more enmity nor anger, and they remained warm friends through life.—M.

† This is the General Burgoyne who had a British command here, in the Revolutionary war, and issued an address to the native Indians, in such an inflated and turgid style as to fix on him the *sobriquet* of Chrononhotonthologos. His surrender at Saratoga, with all his army, caused much dissatisfaction in England, and one of the epigrams of the day, which also embodied the name of the successful American general, ran thus:

> Burgoyne, unconscious of impending fates,
> Could cut his way through woods—but not through *Gates*.

He was dismissed the British service for having refused to return to America, (his visit to England being on his parole) pursuant to the terms of the convention, but was restored three years after. He was a successful dramatic writer.—M.

‡ Southey's History of the Peninsular War.—M.

‖ Life of John Home, author of "Douglas," by Henry Mackenzie.—M.

§ "Adam Blair," a tale of intense passion, suffering, and expiation, by Lockhart. "Sir Andrew Wylie," one of Galt's novels of familiar life, improbable in incidents, and exaggerated in character, but clever, amusing, and full of natural interest.—M.

Editor. I agree with you. The story is d— improbable; the hero a borish fellow, an abominable bore! but there is so much cleverness in the writing, and many of the scenes are so capitally managed, that one can never lay down the book after beginning it. On the whole, 'tis a very strange performance. I hear the Provost is likely to be better, however.

Odoherty. The Author has a vast deal of humor, but he should stick to what he has seen. The first part of Wylie is far the best.

Editor. The scene with old George is as good as possible.

Odoherty. It is. Why did he not produce the present King too?

Editor. He will probably have him some other time. If he could but write stories as well as the King tells them,* he would be the first author of his time.

Odoherty. Were you ever in company with the King, North?

Editor. Three or four times,—long ago now, when he used to come a-hunting in the New Forest.

Odoherty. Will he come to Scotland this summer?

Editor. One can never be sure of a King's movements; but 'tis said he is quite resolved upon the trip.†

Odoherty. What will the Whigs do?

Editor. Poh! the Whigs here are nobody. Even Lord Moira could not endure them. He lived altogether among the Tories when he was in Scotland.‡ The Whigs would be queer pigs at a drawing-room.

Odoherty. Sir Ronald Ferguson seems to be a great spoon.

Editor. He is what he seems. At the Fox dinner, t'other day, he came prepared with two speeches; one to preface the memory of old Charlie; the other returning thanks for his own health being drunk. He forgot himself, and transposed them. He introduced Fox with twenty minutes' harangue about his own merits, and then, discovering his mistake, sat down in such a quandary!

Odoherty. Good! they're a pretty set. What sort of a thing is the Thane of Fife—Tennant's poem?

Editor. Mere humbug—quite defunct.

Odoherty. What are they saying about Hogg's new romance, "The Three Perils of Man; or, War, Women, and Witchcraft,"—Is not that the name?

Editor. I think so. I dare say 'twill be like all his things,—a mixture of the admirable, the execrable, and the tolerable. It is to be published by some London house.

* Scott repeatedly said that George IV. was an admirable story-teller.—M.

† George IV. visited Scotland in the autumn of 1822.—M.

‡ Lord Moira, in the peerage of Ireland, and afterwards, Marquis of Hastings, in that of England, bore the name of Lord Rawdon, when he served in the British army, during the Revolutionary war. He died in 1825, after having been Governor-General of India and Governor of Malta. One of his daughters was Lady Flora Hastings, "done to death by evil tongues," in the Court of Queen Victoria, in 1839.—M.

Odoherty. Does he never come to Edinburgh now?

Editor. Oh yes, now and then he is to be seen about five in the morning, selling sheep in the Grassmarket. I am told he is a capital manager about his farm, and getting rich apace.

Odoherty. I am glad to hear it. I'm sorry I wrote that article on his life.* It was too severe, perhaps.

Editor. Never mind; 'tis quite forgotten. He is now giving out that he wrote it himself.

Odoherty. It was a devilish good article. He could not have written three lines of it.

Editor. No, no, but neither could you have written three lines of Kilmeny, no, nor one line of his dedication to Lady Anne Scott. Hogg's a true genius in his own style. Just compare him with any of the others of the same sort; compare him with Clare for a moment.† Upon my word, Hogg appears to me to be one of the most wonderful creatures in the world, taking all things together. I wish he would send me more articles than he does, and take more pains with them.

Odoherty. Is Dr. Scott in town?

Editor. No—he's busy writing the Odontist.‡ They say it will be the oddest jumble. All his life—every thing he has seen, or might have seen, from a boy—and some strange anecdotes of the French Revolution.

Odoherty. Was he ever in the Bastile?

Editor. Oh yes, and in the Temple too. He has been everywhere but at Timbuctoo.

Odoherty. Where is Timbuctoo?

Editor. Somewhere in Egypt, I am told. I never was there.

Odoherty. What is your serious opinion about the present state of literature?

Editor. Why, we live in an age that will be much discussed when 'tis over—a very stirring, productive, active age—a generation of commentators will probably succeed—and I, for one, look to furnish them with some tough work. There is a great deal of genius astir, but, after all, not many first-rate works produced. If I were asked to say how many will survive, I could answer in a few syllables. Wordsworth's Ballads will be much talked of a hundred years hence; so will the Waverley Novels; so will Don Juan, I think, and Manfred; so will Thalaba, and Childe Harold's Pilgrimage, and the Pilgrimage to the Kirk of Shotts, and Christabel —

Odoherty. And the Essay on the Scope and Tendency of Bacon.‖

* A "slashing" review in *Blackwood*, of the life of Hogg, which had appeared in Constable's Magazine.—M.

† John Clare, the Northamptonshire Peasant (as he was called), wrote pretty verses. Some of Hogg's poetry will perish only with the language in which they are writ.—M.

‡ He was not Doctor, and "The Odontist" never was written.—M.

‖ This unfortunate Essay, the constant *butt* of the wits of Ebony, was written by Professor Macvey Napier, who succeeded Jeffrey in the editorship of the *Edinburgh Review*.—M.

Editor. You wag, I suppose you expect to float yourself.

Odoherty. Do you?

Editor. None of your quizzing here, Mr. Odoherty. I'll get Hogg to review your next book, sir, if you don't mend your manners.

Odoherty. Do—I would fain have a row, as I say in *my* song,—

"O, no matter with whom—no, nor what it was for."

Editor. Aye, you are always in that mood.

Odoherty. Sometimes only. Do you disapprove of personality?

Editor. No, no. I am not quite fool enough to sport that; least of all to you. In reviewing, in particular, what can be done without personality? Nothing, nothing. What are books that don't express the personal characters of their authors; and who can review books, without reviewing those that wrote them?

Odoherty. You get warm, Christopher; out with it.

Editor. Can a man read La Fontaine, Mr. Odoherty, without perceiving his personal good nature? Swift's personal ill-nature is quite as visible. Can a man read Burns without having the idea of a great and a bold man—or Barry Cornwall, without the very uncomfortable feeling of a little man and a timid one? The whole of the talk about personality is, as Fogarty* says, cant.

Odoherty. Get on.

Editor. I have done. Did you pick me up any good new hands when you were in town?

Odoherty. Several—two or three, that is. But I think the less you have to do with the Cockney underscrubs, the better.

Editor. You're right there.

Odoherty. Oh yes, I have no love of the "Young Geniuses about town." The glorious army of Parliamentary reporters has no magnificence in my eyes. I detest news-writers—paragraphers—spouting-club speechifiers—all equally. You have them writing on different *lays*, but they are at *bottom*, with very few exceptions, the same dirty radicals,—meanly born,—meanly bred,—uneducated adventurers, who have been thrown upon literature only by having failed as attorneys, apothecaries, painters, schoolmasters, preachers, grocers ——

Editor. Or Adjutants.—Ha! ha!——This Barry Cornwall, do they still puff him as much as ever?

Odoherty. Yes, they do; but the best joke is, that in one of his own prefaces he takes the trouble to tell us that Mirandola, (a character in one of his playthings,) is not the same man with Othello.

Editor. One might as well say that Tom Thumb is not the same man as Richard the Third.

* Fogarty O'Fogarty was the *nom de plume* of Mr. Gosnell, son of an apothecary in Cork, who wrote a poem in *Blackwood*, in six Cantos, edited by Maginn, and called "Daniel O'Rourke."—M.

Odoherty. Or that Joseph Hume is not Edmund Burke.

Editor. Or that the friend of Gerald* is not the exemplar of Sir Philip Sidney.

Odoherty. Or that a painted broomstick is not an oak.

Editor. Or that Baby Cornwall is not Giant Shakspeare. To be serious, do you think Campbell is gaining reputation by his editorship?

Odoherty. No; nor do I think Byron will by his.†

Editor. How are you sure of that, Ensign?

Odoherty. The Duke of Wellington would not raise himself by the best of all possible corn-bills. Hannibal did not raise himself by his excellent conduct at the head of the Carthaginian Police. Even if Tom Campbell had turned out the prince of Editors, I should still have preferred him thinking of

> On Linden when the sun was low,
> All bloodless lay the untrodden snow,
> And dark as winter was the flow
> Of Iser rolling rapidly.

Editor. You are getting sentimental now, I think. Will you have another tumbler?

Odoherty. Hand me the lemons. This holy alliance of Pisa will be a queer affair.‡ The Examiner has let down its price from a tenpenny to a sevenpenny. They say the editor here is to be one of that faction, for they must publish in London of course.

Editor. Of course; but I doubt if they will be able to sell many. Byron is a prince; but these dabbling dogglerers destroy every dish they dip in.

Odoherty. Apt alliteration's artful aid.

Editor. Imagine Shelley, with his spavin, and Hunt, with his stringhalt, going in the same harness with such a caperer as Byron, three-a-breast! He'll knock the wind out of them both the first canter.

Odoherty. 'Tis pity Keats is dead.‖—I suppose you could not venture to publish a sonnet in which he is mentioned now? The Quarterly (who killed him, as Shelley says) would blame you.

Editor. Let's hear it. Is it your own?

Odoherty. No; 'twas written many months ago by a certain great Italian genius, who cuts a figure about the London routs—one Fudgiolo.§

* "The friend of Gerald" was Sir James Mackintosh.—M.

† Of "The Liberal."—M.

‡ The alliance between Byron, Shelley, and Leigh Hunt, in the production of the Liberal.—M.

‖ John Keats, author of "Endymion," and other poems. He died at Rome, in December 1820, aged twenty-four. With some mannerisms, he had wonderful imagination, delicate taste, deep sensibilities, and musical expression of no common order.—M.

§ Ugo Foscolo, an Italian poet and exile, established his fame by his "Letters of Ortis." He contributed largely to the higher periodicals, and died in London, in 1827.—M.

Editor. Try to recollect it.

Odoherty. It began

Signor Le Hunto, gloria di Cocagna
  Chi scrive il poema della Rimini
Che tutta apparenza ha, per Gemini,
  D'esser cantato sopra la montagna
Di bel Ludgato, o nella campagna
D'Amsted, o sulle marge Serpentimini
Com' esta Don Giovanni d'Endymini
  Il gran poeta d'Ipecacuanha?
Tu sei il Re del Cocknio Parnasso
  Ed egli il herede apparente,
Tu sei un gran Giacasso ciertamente,
  Ed egli ciertamente gran Giacasso!
Tu sei il Signor del Examinero
Ed egli soave Signor del Glystero.

Editor. I don't see why *Examinero* and *Glystero* should be so coupled together.

Odoherty. Both vehicles of dirt, you know.

Editor. You have me there. Who is Regent at present during his Majesty's absence?

Odoherty. Of course Prince John.* I don't think Hazlitt is in the Council of Regency. From the moment King George went to Hanover, King Leigh was in the fidgets to be off.

Editor. What a cursed number of sonnets he'll write about the Venus de Medicis and the Hermaphrodite! The pictures and statues will drive him clean out of his wits. He'll fall in love with some of them.

Odoherty. If he sees Niobe and her Nine Daughters, he's a lost man.

Editor. Quite done for.

Odoherty. Will the ladies admire his sonnets when they come over?

Editor. According to Dr. Colquhoun,† there is one parish in London, Mary-le-bone, which contains 50,000 *ladies* capable of appreciating his poetry.

Odoherty. Is the new novel nearly ready—The Fortunes of Nigel—is not that it?

Editor. I hear it will soon be out,‡ and that it is better than the Pirate.

Odoherty. I can believe that.

* John Hunt.—M.

† Dr. Patrick Colquhoun was a Police Magistrate in London, of much ability and shrewdness. He published several works, chiefly connected with statistics and jurisprudence. Of these his "Treatise on the Police of the Metropolis," attracted general attention, from its anatomy of the lower grades of society in London. He died in 1820, aged seventy-five.—M

‡ "The Fortunes of Nigel," was published in May, 1822. It was reviewed, very briefly, in *Blackwood*, for June.—M.

Editor. The subject is better. The time a very picturesque one. I am informed, that we may expect to have the most high and mighty Prince, King Jamie, and old Geordie Heriot, introduced in high style.

Odoherty. In London, I hope.

Editor. I hope so, too. I think he shows most in a bustle.

Odoherty. I don't know. I like the glen in the Monastery.

Editor. Your affectation is consummate. You that never breathed at ease out of a tavern, to be sporting romance.

Odoherty. I have written as many sentimental verses as any *Sempstress* alive. I once tried an epic in dead earnest.

Editor. How did you get on?

Odoherty. My heroine was with child at the end of the first canto, but I never had patience to deliver her.

Editor. Have you still got the MS.?

Odoherty. Yes; I think of sending it to Tom Campbell, or Taylor and Hessey, or the Aberdeen Review, if there be such a book still.

Editor. I never heard of it; but steamboats and magazines are all the go at present. They've got a magazine at Brighton—another at Newcastle, for the colliers—another at Dundee—and, I believe, five or six about Paisley and Glasgow. You may choose which you like best—they're all works of genius—Hogg writes in them all.

Odoherty. I'll sing you a song. (*Sings.*)

Thus speaks out Christopher,
To his gallant crew—
Up with the Olive flag,
Down with the Blue;

Fire upon Jeffrey,
Fire on Sir James,
Fire on the Benthams,
Fire on the Grahams.

Fire upon Bennet,
Fire on Joe Hume
Fire upon Lambton,
Fire upon Brougham.

Fire upon Hallam,
Fire upon Moore,
Spit upon Hazlitt,
* * * * * *.

I've forgot the last line. 'Tis my call. Your stave, Christopher!

Editor. (*Rings.*) Waiter! if Willison Glass be in the house, desire him to come up stairs, and he shall have a bottle of porter.

Enter WILLISON GLASS.*

Willison. What's your will?

Editor. Sing the dialogue between yourself and Jeremy Bentham.

Willison. I have it in my pocket, sir—I will sing directly, sir—there's a running commentary, sir—would you be pleased to hear it too, sir?

Editor. Tip us the affair as it stands, Willison.

DIALOGUE BETWEEN WILLISON GLASS, ESQ., OF EDINBURGH, AND JEREMY BENTHAM, ESQ., OF LONDON.

1.

Willison inviteth Jeremy to the sign of the Jolly Bacchus, whereof he speaketh in commendation.

JEREMY, throw your pen aside,
And come get drunk with me;
We'll go where Bacchus sits astride,
Perch'd high upon barrels three;
'Tis there the ale is frothing up,
And genuine is the gin;
So we shall take a liberal sup,
To comfort our souls within.

2.

Jeremy refuseth the invitation, blandly alleging that he had much rather destroy the young man of the west, and other persons.

O cheerier than the nappy ale,
Or the Hollands smacking fine,
Is sitting by the taper pale,
And piling line on line;
Smashing with many a heavy word
Anti-usurers† in a row,
Or pointing arguments absurd‡
To level the Boroughs low.

3.

Whereupon Willison remindeth him of the Quarterly, and extolleth the good liquor.

Jeremy, trust me, 'tis but stuff
To scribble the livelong night,
While the Quarterly bloodhounds howl so rough,
And so gruesome is their bite.
But down at the sign of the Triple Tun,
There's nothing like them to fear,
But sweet is its brandy's genial run,
And barmy is its beer.

4.

Jeremy disvalueth beer, brandy, and the Quarterly, declares that he chooseth rather to eat lawyers than drink brandy.

Brandy, I know, is liquor good,
And barmy the beer may be;
But common law is my favorite food,||
And it must be crunch'd my me:
And I'm writing a word three pages long,
The Quarterly dogs to rout,
A word which never will human tongue
Be able to wind about.§

* Willison Glass, vender of strong liquors and maker of weak verses, has been already noticed and annotated in The Tent.—M.

† See Essay on the Usury Laws. ‡ Reform Catechism. || Theorie de Legislation.—C. N.

§ Jeremy Bentham, in *his* day, like Thomas Carlyle in *ours*, invented a new phraseology which had the advantage of being particularly obscure.—M.

5.

Jeremy, never shall tongue of mine
 Be put to such silly use;
I'll keep it to smack the brandy-wine,
 Or barleycorn's gallant juice.
Then mount your mitre on your skull,
 And waddle with me, my lad,
To take a long and hearty pull,
 At the brimmer bumpering glad.

Willison preferreth long draughts to long words.

6.

Though ale be comforting to the maw,
 Yet here I still shall dwell,
Until I prove that judge-made law
 Is uncognoscible,—
That the schools at Canterbury's beck*
 Exist but in the mind,——
And that T. T. Walmsey, Esquire, *Sec.*
 Is no more than a spirit of wind.†

Jeremy bringeth up his nine-pounders, and declareth that he is a Berkleian philosopher.

7.

Jeremy, never mind such trash,
 And of better spirits think,
And out of your throat the cobwebs wash
 With a foaming flagon of drink;
For 'tis sweet the pewter pots to spy,
 Imprisoning the liquor stout,
As jail-bird rogues are ring'd in by
 Your Panopticon roundabout.

Willison compareth Jeremy's Panopticon to a porter-pot in a pretty simile.

8.

Sweeter it is to see the sheet
 With paradox scribbled fair,
Where jawbreaking words every line you meet,
 To make poor people stare.
And Sir Richard of Bridge-street my books shall puff,
 And Ensor will swear them fine,‡
And Jeffrey will say, though my style is tough,
 Yet my arguments are divine.

Jeremy calleth on three great men,

Sir Pythagoras, Geo. Ensor, and Master Francis Jeffrey.

9.

Jeremy, trust me, the puff of the three,
 (I tell you the truth indeed,)
Is not worth the puff you'd get from me,
 Of the pure Virginian weed.
And beneath its fume, while we gaily quaff
 The beer or the ruin blue,
You at the world may merrily laugh,
 Instead of its laughing at you.

Willison disparaging the three; recommendeth to blow a cloud.

* Church of Englandism.—C. N.

† Mr. Walmsley was Secretary to the then Archbishop of Canterbury.—M.

‡ Mr. Richard Phillips, (of Bridge-street, Blackfriars), publisher and editor, was very likely to "puff" Bentham. Mr. Ensor was an Irish writer on Population, Political Economy, &c.—M.

10.

Jeremy proposeth pleasant reading to his friend Mr. Glass,

The world may lay what it likes to my charge,
May laugh, or may say I'm crack'd.
If it do, I shall swear that the world at large
Is no more than a jury pack'd;
Such a jury as those on which I penn'd*
A Treatise genteel and clear;
And I'll read it now to you, my friend,
For 'twill give you joy to hear.

11.

who thereupon recoileth horror-struck and departeth to the sign of the Jolly Bacchus, there to sing about Prince Charlie, and other goodly ballads. And Jeremy abideth in his place.

Jeremy, not for a gallon of ale
Would I stay that book to hear;
Why, even at its sight my cheek turns pale,
And my heart leaps up like a deer.
So I must off without more delay,
My courage to raise with a glass;
And as you prefer o'er such stuff to stay,
I'll toast you, my lad, for an ass.
(*Exit Willison Glass.*)

Editor. Well, but say candidly, what have you been doing for us? Your active mind must have been after something. I heard lately, (perhaps it was said in allusion to your late detention in London,) that you were engaged with a novel, to be entitled "Fleeting Impressions."

Odoherty. You are quite mistaken. I have not patience for a novel. I must go off like a cracker, or an ode of Horace.

Editor. Then why don't you give us an essay for our periodical?

Odoherty. To prove what? or nothing. When I last saw Coleridge, he said he considered an essay, in a periodical publication, as merely "a say" for the time—an ingenious string of sentences, driving apparently, with great vehemence, towards some object, but never meant to lead to anything, or to arrive at any conclusion, (for in what conclusion are the public interested but the abuse of individuals). Fortunately, there is one subject for critical disquisition, which can never be exhausted.

Editor. What is this treasure?

Odoherty. The question, whether is Pope a poet?

Editor. True! But confess, Odoherty, what have you been after?

Odoherty. The truth is, I have some thoughts of finishing my tragedy of the Black Revenge.

Editor. Ye gods! what a scheme!

Odoherty. The truth is, I must either do this, or go on with my great quarto disquisition, on "The Decline and Fall of Genius."

Editor. I would advise to let alone the drama. I do not think it at present a good field for the exertion of genius.

Odoherty. For what reason, Honey?

* Elements of Packing.—C. N.

Editor. I think the good novels, which are published, come in place of new dramas. Besides, they are better fitted for the present state of public taste. The public are merely capable of strong sensations, but of nothing which requires knowledge, taste, or judgment. A certain ideal dignity of style, and regularity of arrangement, must be required for a drama, before it can deserve the name of a composition. But what sense have the common herd of barbarians of composition, or order, or any thing else of that kind?

Odoherty. But there is also the more loose and popular drama, which is only a novel without the narrative parts.

Editor. Yes, the acting is the chief difference. But I think the novel has the advantage in being without the acting, for its power over the feelings is more undisturbed and entire, and the imagination of the reader blends the whole into a harmony which is not found on the stage. I think those who read novels need not go to the theatre, for they are in general beforehand with the whole progress of the story.

Odoherty. This is true to a certain extent. But novels can never carry away from the theatre those things which are peculiarly its own; that is to say, the powers of expression in the acting, the eloquence of declamation, music, buffoonery, the splendor of painted decorations, &c.

Editor. You are perfectly right. Novels may carry away sympathy, plot, invention, distress, catastrophe, and everything—(Vide Blair.)

Odoherty. Do you mean Dr. Blair, or Adam Blair?

Editor. The latter. I say the novels may carry away all these things, but the theatre must still be strong in its power of affecting the senses. This is its peculiar dominion. Yet our populace do not much seek after what strikes and pleases the senses; for the elegances of sight and hearing require a sort of abstract taste which they do not seem to have. Any thing which is not an appeal through sympathy to some of their vulgar personal feelings, appears to them uninteresting and unmeaning.

Odoherty. They think it has no reference to *meum* and *tuum.*

Editor. It probably would not be easy to find a people more lamentably deficient in all those liberal and general feelings which partake of the quality of taste.

Odoherty. You sink me into despair. I think I must betake myself to my old and favorite study of theological controversy, and furnish a reply to Coplestone. I perceive that Lord Byron, in his Mystery of Cain, tends very much to go off into the same disputes.

Editor. A skeptically disputatious turn of mind, appears a good deal here and there in his poetry.

Odoherty. I suppose you think Sardanapalus the best Tragedy he has written.*

* One scene in Sardanapalus is worth nearly all, (from its intensity of regretful tenderness,

Editor. Yes. The Foscari is interesting to read, but rather painful and disagreeable in the subject. Besides, the dialogue is too much in the short and pointed manner of Alfieri. When a play is not meant to be acted, there is no necessity for its having that hurry in the action and speeches, which excludes wandering strains of poetical beauty, or reflection and thought, nor should it want the advantages of rhyme. The Faustus of Goethe seems to be the best specimen of the kind of plan fit for a poem of this kind not meant to be acted.

Odoherty. Pindarum quisquis.

Editor. Byron's Manfred is certainly but an Icarian flutter in comparison; his Sardanapalus is better composed, and more original.

Odoherty. How do you like Nimrod and Semiramis?

Editor. That dream is a very frightful one, and I admire the conception of Nimrod.*

Odoherty. You know that I am not subject to nocturnal terrors, even after the heaviest supper; but I acknowledge that the ancestors of Sardanapalus almost made my hair stand on end; and I have some intention of introducing the ghost of Fingal in my "Black Revenge." The superstitious vein has not lately been waked with much success. I slight the conception of Norna in relation to fear. The scorpion lash, which Mr. David Lindsay applied to the tyrant Firaoun, is not at all formidable to the reader, but there is solemnity and sentiment in the conception of the people being called away one by one from the festival, till he is left alone. That same piece of the Deluge would be very good, if it were not sometimes like music, which aims rather at loudness than harmony or expression. The most elegant and well composed piece in Lindsay's book is the Destiny of Cain.

Editor. How do you like the Nereid's love?

Odoherty. It is vastly pretty, but too profuse in images drawn from mythology. However, there are many fables of the ancients on which poems might be successfully made even in modern times, and according to modern feeling, if the meaning of the fables were deeply enough studied. It does not necessarily follow that all mythological poems should be written in imitation of the manner of the ancients, and much less in the pretty style of Ovid, and those moderns who have adopted the same taste.

Odoherty. You do not think Mr. Lindsay's Nereid French?

Editor. By no means. It is free from any fault of that kind. In

"the late remorse of love,") that modern playwrights have written. This is the hero's parting with his "gentle, wronged Zarina."—M.

* The description of Nimrod is a picture:

"The features were a giant's, and the eye
Was still, yet lighted; his long locks curl'd down
On his vast bust, whence a huge quiver rose,
With shaft-heads feather'd from the eagle's wing,
That peep'd up bristling thro' his serpent hair.—M.

some of Wordsworth's later poems, there appears something like a reviving imagination for those fine old conceptions, which have been and always will be.

An age hath been, when earth was proud,
  Of lustre too intense
To be sustain'd: and mortals bow'd
  The front in self-defence.
Who, then, if Dian's crescent gleam'd,
Or Cupid's sparkling arrow stream'd,
While on the wing the urchin play'd,
Could fearlessly approach the shade?
Enough for one soft vernal day,
If I, a bard of ebbing time,
And nurtur'd in a fickle clime,
May haunt this horned bay;
Whose am'rous water multiplies
The flitting halcyon's vivid dyes,
And smooths its liquid breast to show
These swan-like specks of mountain snow,
White, as the pair that slid along the plains
Of heaven, while Venus held the reins.

Odoherty. Beautifully recited; and now touch the bell again, for we're getting prosy.

Editor. Positively Ensign, we must rise.

Odoherty. Having now relinquished the army, I rise by sitting still, and applying either to study, or——will you ring?

Editor. 'Tis time to be going, I believe. I see the daylight peeping down the chimney. But sing one good song more, Odoherty, and so wind up the evening.

Odoherty. (*Sings.*)

ARIA—*With boisterous expression.*

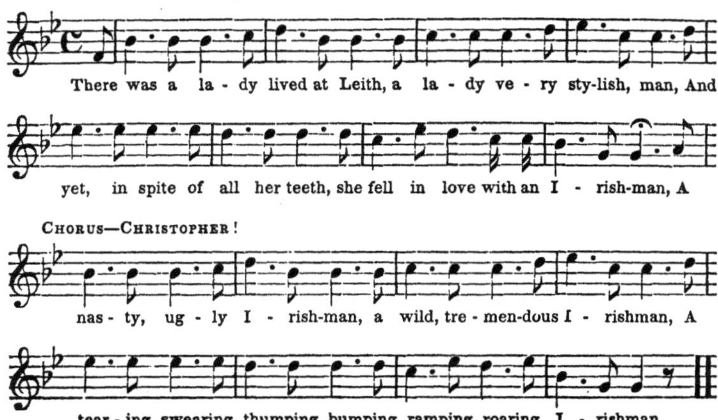

2.

His face was no ways beautiful,
For with small-pox 'twas scarr'd across;
And the shoulders of the ugly dog
Were almost doubled a yard across.
O, the lump of an Irishman,
The whisky-devouring Irishman—
The great he-rogue, with his wonderful brogue, the fighting, rioting, Irishman.

3.

One of his eyes was bottle-green,
And the other eye was out, my dear;
And the calves of his wicked-looking legs
Where more than two feet about, my dear,
O, the great big Irishman,
The rattling, battling Irishman—
The stamping, ramping, swaggering, staggering, leathering swash of an Irishman.

4.

He took so much of Lundy-Foot,
That he used to snort and snuffle—O;
And in shape and size, the fellow's neck,
Was as bad as the neck of a buffalo.
O, the horrible Irishman,
The thundering, blundering Irishman—
The slashing, dashing, smashing, lashing, thrashing, hashing Irishman.

5.

His name was a terrible name, indeed,
Being Timothy Thady Mulligan;
And whenever he emptied his tumbler of punch,
He'd not rest till he filled it full again.
The boozing, bruising Irishman,
The 'toxicated Irishman—
The whisky, frisky, rummy, gummy, brandy, no dandy Irishman.

6.

This was the lad the lady loved,
Like all the girls of quality;
And he broke the skulls of the men of Leith,
Just by the way of jollity.
O, the leathering Irishman,
The barbarous, savage Irishman—
The hearts of the maids, and the gentlemen's heads, were bother'd,
I'm sure, by this Irishman.*

I think I hear the rattles, Christopher. By Saint Patrick, there's a row in the street! Come along, old one! Up with your crutch!

(*Exeunt* AMBO.)

* This song was written by Dr. Maginn.—M.

NO. II.—APRIL, 1822.

Scene.—*The little wainscotted room behind—a good fire—a table covered with books and papers, decanters and glasses.* Time—*Nine o'clock in the evening:—a high wind without.*

Present—Mr. Christopher North, *and* Mr. Buller *of Brasennose (seated in arm-chairs at the opposite sides of the fire-place.)*

Mr. North. So—Mr. Buller, you've been reading Henry Mackenzie's Life of John Home.* What say you to the book? I am sure your chief objection is, that it is too short by half.

Mr. Buller. It is; for, to tell you the truth, I know very little about the characters with whom Mr. Mackenzie seems to take it for granted that every body is as familiar as himself. Do you remember John Home?

North. Perfectly. I remember going out to his farm-house, in East Lothian, and spending two delightful days with him there, so far back as the year seventy-seven. I was then a very stripling, but I can recall a great deal of what he said quite distinctly. After he came to live in Edinburgh, I was not much in Scotland; but I once called upon him, and drank tea with him here, I think about 1807 or 1808—very shortly before his death. He was, indeed, a fine highly-finished gentleman—and bright to the last.

Buller. What sort of looking man was he?

North. A fine, thinking face—extremely handsome he had been in his youth—a dark-gray eye, full of thought, and, at the same time, full of fire—his hair highly curled and powdered—a rich robe-de-chambre—pale green, if I recollect, like one John Kemble used to wear—a scarlet waistcoat—a very striking figure, I assure you.

Buller. He had been a clergyman in his early life!

North. Yes, and, you know, left the kirk in consequence of a foolish outcry they were making about his Douglas. I remember him sitting in their General Assembly, however, as an elder—and once dressed in scarlet; for he had a commission in a fencible regiment.

* In 1822, when his Life of John Home was published, Henry Mackenzie was seventy-five years old. But his reminiscences of the illustrious men whom he had long survived, were vivid to the last, and extremely graphic. When he died, in 1831, he was eighty-five years old.—M.

Buller. Dr. Adam Fergusson,* too, was in the church at first, I think?

North. He was—and he went out chaplain to the forty-second, in the Seven Years' War. Colonel David Stewart tells a fine story of his heroism at the battle of Fontenoy. He could not be kept back from the front line.

Buller. 'Ιερευς μεν αλλα Μαχητης, like somebody in Homer. The Scotch literati of that time seem to have been a noble set of fellows. Good God! how you are fallen off!

North. We may thank the Whigs for that—*transeat cum cęteris.*

Buller. I don't exactly understand your meaning. Do you allude to the Edinburgh Review?

North. Certainly, Mr. Buller. They introduced a lower tone in every thing. In the first place, few of them were gentlemen either by birth or breeding—and some of the cleverest of them have always preserved a sort of plebeian snappishness which is mighty disgusting. What would David Hume, for example, have thought of such a set of superficial chattering bodies?

Buller. David Hume appears in a very amiable light in this volume. He was, after all, a most worthy man, though an infidel.

North. He was a man of the truest genius—the truest learning—and the truest excellence. His nature was so mild that *he* could do without restraints, the want of which would have ruined the character of almost any other man. I love the memory of David Hume—the first historian the modern world has produced—*primus absque secundo*, to my mind! His account of the different sects and parties in the time of Charles I. is worth all the English prose that has been written since. At least, 'tis well worth half of it.

Buller. Why are not his letters published? The few that have been printed are exquisite,—one or two very fine specimens in this very volume—and what a beautiful thing is that notice of his last journey to Bath by the poet†—a few such pages are worth an Encyclopædia.

North. What a sensation was produced in England when that fine constellation of Scotch genius first began to blaze out upon the world! You thought us little better than Hottentots before.

Buller. And yet Dr. Johnson always somehow or other kept the first place himself.

North. He could not, or would not, make so good books as other

* The Historian. He was chaplain of the 42d Highlanders, in Flanders, until the peace of Aix la Chapelle, and actually joined in the charge of his regiment at Fontenoy. Returning to Edinburgh, he was chosen Professor of Natural Philosophy, but afterwards took the chair of moral philosophy. His chief work is a "History of the Roman Republic." He died in 1816, aged ninety-two.—M.

† David Hume's interesting correspondence has since been collected and published, under the editorship of J. Hill Burton, of Edinburgh. He stands at the head of the modern philosophical skeptics, and his History of England is the most permanent proof of his ability and researches.—M.

people, but God knows there was a pith about old Samuel which nothing could stand up against. His influence was not so much that of an author as of a thinker. He was the most powerful intellect in the world of books. He was the Jackson of the literary ring—the judge—the emperor—a giant—acknowledged to be a Saul amongst the people. Even David Hume would have been like a woman in his grasp; but, odd enough, the two never met.

Buller. Your Magazine once had a good Essay on Johnson and Warburton.

North. Yes; I wrote it myself. But, after all, Warburton was not Johnson's match.* He had more flame but less heat. Johnson's mind was a furnace—it reduced everything to its elements. We have no truly great critical intellect since his time.

Buller. What would he have thought of our modern reviewers?

North. Why, not one of the tribe would have dared to cry *mew* had he been alive. The terror of him would have kept them as mum as mice when there's a cat in the room. If he had detected such a thing as Jeffrey astir, he would have cracked every bone in his body with one worry.

Buller. I can believe it all. Even Gifford would have been annihilated.

North. Like an ill-natured pug-dog flung into a lion's cage.

Buller. He did not like your old Scots literati.

North. He hated the name of Scotland, and would not condescend to know what they were. Yet he must have admired such a play as Douglas. The chief element of John Home's inspiration seems to have been a sort of stately elevation of sentiment, which must have struck some congenial chords in his own great mind.

Buller. What is your opinion of John Home as a poet?

North. I think nobody can bestow too much praise on Douglas. There has been no English tragedy worthy of the name since it appeared.† 'Tis a noble piece—beautifully and loftily written; but, after all, the principal merit is in the charming old story itself. Douglas is the only true forerunner of the Scotch imaginative literature of our own age. Home's other tragedies are all very indifferent —most of them quite bad. Mr. Mackenzie should not have disturbed their slumbers.

Buller. The natural partiality of friendship and affection—

North. Surely; and it is most delightful to read his Memoir, simply for its overflowing with that fine strain of sentiments. He is like Ossian, "the last of all his race," and talks of his peers as they

* Dr. Warburton, Bishop of Gloucester, was more highly praised by Johnson, (in his Life of Pope), than he really deserved. He knew a great deal, but knew few things so as to master them. As an author he was diffuse, coarse, and dogmatical.—M.

† This is one of the instances where North's judgment was clouded by his nationality. The tragedy of Douglas by no means merits the high praise here given to it.—M.

should be talked of. One may differ from his opinions here and there, but there is a *halo* over the whole surface of his language. 'Tis to me a very pathetic work.

Buller. Mackenzie is himself a very great author.

North. A discovery indeed, Mr. Buller! Henry Mackenzie, sir, is one of the most original in thought, and splendid in fancy, and chaste in expression, that can be found in the whole line of our worthies. He will live as long as our tongue, or longer.

Buller. Which of his works do you like best?

North. Julia de Roubigné and the story of La Roche. I thought that vein had been extinct, till Adam Blair came out. But Nature in none of her domains can ever be exhausted.

Buller. But an author's invention may be exhausted, I suppose.

North. Not easily. You might as well talk of exhausting the Nile as a true genius. People talk of wearing out a man's intellectual power, as if it were a certain determinate sum of cash in a strong box. 'Tis more like the income of a princely estate—which, with good management, must always be improving, not falling off. A great author's power of acquisition is in the same ratio with his power of displaying. He who can write well might be able to see well—and his eyes will feed his fancy as long as his fingers can hold the pen.

Buller. At that rate we shall have three or four more new Waverley romances every year?

North. I hope so. There's old Goethe has written one of the best romances he ever did, within the last twelve months—a most splendid continuation of his Wilhelm Meister—and Goethe was born, I think, in the year 1742. I wish Mackenzie, who is a good ten years his junior, would follow the example.*

Buller. Voltaire held on wonderfully to the last, too.

North. Ay, there was another true creature! Heavens! what a genius was Voltaire's! So grave, so gay, so profound, so brilliant—his name is worth all the rest in the French literature.

Buller. Always excepting my dear Rabelais.

North. A glorious old fellow, to be sure! Once get into his stream, and try if you can land again! He is the only man whose mirth exerts the sway of uncontrollable vehemence. His comic is as strong as the tragic of Æschylus himself.

Buller. We are Pygmies!

North. More's the pity. Yet we have our demi-gods too. In manners and in dignity we are behind the last age—but in genius, properly so called, we are a thousand miles above it. They had little or no poetry then. Such a play even as Douglas would, if published now-a-days, appear rather feeble. It would be better as a

* Instead of Mackenzie's being ten years younger than Goethe, he was four years' older. Mackenzie was born in 1745, Goethe in 1749.—M.

play certainly—but the *poetry* of Byron, Scott, and Wordsworth, would be in men's minds, and they would not take that for poetry, fine though it be.

Buller. What would people say to one of Shakspeare's plays, were it to be written now?

North. The Edinburgh Reviewers would say it was a Lakish Rant. The Quarterly would tear it to bits, growling like a mastiff. The fact is, that our theatre is at an end, I fear. A new play, to be received triumphantly, would require to have all the fire and passion of the old drama, and all the chasteness and order of the new. I doubt to reconcile these two will pass the power of any body now living.

Buller. Try yourself, man.

North. I never will—but if I did, I should make something altogether unlike anything that has ever been done in our language. Unless I could hit upon some new—really new—key, I should not think the attempt worth making. Even our dramatic verse is quite worn out. It would pall on one's ear were it written never so well.

Buller. Why? Sophocles wrote the same metre with Æschylus.

North. No more than Shakspeare wrote the same blank verse with Milton—or Byron, in the Corsair, the same measure with the Rape of the Lock. Counting the longs and shorts is not enough, Mr. Bachelor of Arts.

Buller. You despise our English study of the classics. You think it carried too far. I understand your meaning, Mr. North.

North. I doubt that. I suspect that I myself have read as much Greek in my day as most of your crack-men. In my younger days, sir, the glory of our Buchanans and Barclays* was not forgotten in Scotland. In this matter again, we have to thank the blue and yellow† gentry for a good deal of our national deterioration.

Buller. They are not scholars.

North. *They* scholars! witlings can't be scholars, Buller. Knowledge is a great calmer of people's minds. Milton would have been a compassionate critic.

Buller. Are you a compassionate one?

North. Sir, I am ever compassionate, when I see anything like nature and originality. I do not demand the strength of a Hercules from every man. Let me have an humble love of, and a sincere aspiration after what is great, and I am satisfied. I am intolerant to nobody but Quacks and Cockneys.

* There are *five* Barclays, whose names are recorded:—Alexander Barclay, translator of the "Navis Stultifera," or Ship of Fools, died 1532; Robert Barclay, author of "An Apology for the Quakers," died 1690; William Barclay, Professor of Law at Angers, in France, and a great civilian, died 1605; John Barclay, his son, author of "Euphoronium," a Latin Satire, and "Aryenis," a romance, died 1621; and John Barclay, of Cruden, who wrote a rare and curious work in verse, now very scarce, called "A Description of the Roman Catholic Church.—M.

† "The blue and yellow" was the *Edinburgh Review*, published with a cover of blue and yellow paper.—M.

Buller. Whom you crucify, like a very Czar of Muscovy!

North. No, sir, I only hang them up to air, like so many pieces of old theatrical finery on the poles of Monmouth-street.

Buller. But to return to John Home and Henry Mackenzie—I confess, I think the History of the Rebellion in 1745 is a far better work than it is generally held to be.

North. Why any account of that brilliant episode in our history must needs be full of interest, and Hume being concerned so far himself, has preserved a number of picturesque enough anecdotes; but on the whole, the book wants vigor, and it is full of quizzibles; what can be more absurd than his giving us more pages about the escape of two or three Whig students of Divinity from the Castle of Doune than he spends upon all the wild wandering of the unfortunate Chevalier?

Buller. The young Pretender.

North. The Chevalier—the Prince, sir. My father would have knocked any man down that said *the Pretender* in his presence.

Buller. Ask your pardon, Christopher. I did not know you were a Jacobite.

North. Had I lived in those days I should certainly have been one. Look at Horace Walpole's Memoirs, if you wish to see what a paltry set of fellows steered the vessel of the State in the early Hanover reigns. It is refreshing to turn from your Bedfords, and Newcastles, and Cavendishes, to the Statesmen of our own times.

Buller. Wait for fifty years till some such legacy of spleen be opened by the heirs of some disappointed statesman now living.

North. There is something in that, sir; but yet not much. Sir, nobody will ever be able to bring any disgraceful accusations against the personal honor and probity of the leading Tory statesmen who now rule in England. They are all men of worth and principle. They have their faults, I believe, but no shameful ones.

Buller. Whom do you place highest?

North. Lord Londonderry without question. He wants some of the lesser ornaments which set off a public man—I mean in his style of speaking*—but sense, sir, and knowledge, and thorough skill in affairs, are worth all the rest a million times over; and he has something besides all these, that distinguishes him from every body with whom he can at present be compared—a true active dignity and pith of mind—the chief element of a ruling character, and worth all the eloquence even of a Burke.

Buller. His fine person is an advantage to him.

* He was so deficient as a speaker, confused in ideas, and unable to put them, properly, into sentences, that Byron said he was an orator framed in the fashion of Mrs. Malaprop. In action he was bold and decisive, in manners gentle and courtly. He committed suicide in August, 1822, while George IV. was in Scotland.—M.

North. The grace of the Seymours would be an advantage to any man. But just look at the two sets of people the next time you are in the House of Commons, and observe what a raffish-looking crew the modern Whigs are. I'm sure their benches must have a great loss in the absence of George Tierney's bluff face and buff waistcoat.*

Buller. What manner of man is Joseph Hume?

North. Did you never see him? He is a shrewd-looking fellow enough: but most decidedly vulgar. Nobody that sees him could ever for a moment suspect him of being a gentleman born.† He has the air of a Montrose dandy, at this moment, and there is an intolerable affectation about the creature. I suppose he must have sunk quite into the dirt since Croker curried him.

Buller. I don't believe anything can make an impression on him. A gentleman's whip would not be felt through the beaver of a coal-heaver. Depend on't, Joseph will go on just as he has been doing.

North. Why, a small matter will make a man who has once ratted, rat again. We all remember what Joe Hume was a few years ago.

Buller. A Tory?

North. I would not prostitute the name so far; but he always voted with them.‡ As a clever poet of last year said—

> "I grant you he never behaved, anno 12, ill—
> He always used then to chime in with Lord Melville.
> There were words, I remember, he used to pronounce ill;
> But he always supported the Orders in Council.
> At the Whigs it was then his chief pleasure to rail—
> He opposed all the Catholic claims, tooth and nail;
> Nay, he carried his zeal to so great an excess,
> That he voted against Stewart Wortley's address;
> And while others were anxious for bringing in Canning—
> His principal point seemed to be to keep Van in."*

Buller. What a memory you have! Joseph has not so good a one, I'll swear, or he would not look the Tories in the face after such a ratting!

North. Why, no wonder then he hates the Tories. They never

* Tierney, who had been a sort of Parliamentary leader of the Whigs, was not in Parliament in 1822. In 1827, Canning made him Master of the Mint, which he resigned, early in 1828, (when Lord Goderich retired from the Premiership), and died in 1830. In the bluff face, and buff waistcoat, and I might add the bluff manner in which he spoke, an imitation of Fox was palpable.—M.

† Nor was he. Hume's mother kept a small stand, on market-days, in Montrose, and Fox Maule (afterwards Lord Panmure), was seized with a whim of apprenticing him to a druggist, which led to his becoming a surgeon in the East Indies, where he made a fortune.—M.

‡ Hume, originally entered Parliament, from January to November, 1812, as a *Tory* member, for the Borough Weymouth. In 1818, when he returned to the House of Commons, it was as a Radical member for Montrose.—M.

‖ See Letter to a Friend in the Country. London, Triphook. 1821.—C. N. ["Van" meant Mr. Vansittart, Chancellor of the Exchequer, afterwards Lord Bexley.]—M.

thought of him while he was with them—and now the Whigs do talk of Joe as if he were somebody. But as John Bull says—

" A very small man with the Tories
Is a very great man 'mong the Whigs!"

Buller. If you were to rat, North, what a rumpus they would make about you! Why, they would lift you on their shoulders, and huzza till you were tired.

North. That would not be long. Away with stinking breath, say I.

Buller. At first they pretended to say you were dull. But that was soon over. Jeffrey persuaded them that would never pass, I am told.

North. I can believe it. Jeffrey is a king among the blind.

Buller. I suppose he hates you cordially, however.

North. No doubt, in a small toothy way: just as a rat hates a terrier. But what makes you always speak about him? I'm sure you don't mind such folks.

Buller. Not much; but, next to abusing one's friends, what, after all, is so pleasant as abusing one's enemies?

North. Try praising them, my friend: You'll find that embitters them far more fiercely. There's an air of superiority about commendation which makes a man wince to his backbone. The Whigs can't endure to be lauded.

Buller. That's the reason you always lash them, I presume.

North. *Me* lash them! I would as soon get on horseback to spear a tailor. I just tickle their noses with the tip of my thong. Put me into a passion, and I'll show you what lashing is.

Buller. I have no curiosity, Christopher. I'll take it all upon trust. When you cock your wig awry, you look as if you could eat a Turk.

North. I would rather eat any thing than a Whig. When you cut them up, 'tis all stuffing, and skin and gall.

Buller. They cry each other up at a fine rate.

North. Why, I believe there is but one animal who may, in a certain sense, commit *all* crimes with impunity, and its name is WHIG. To have been detected in the basest embezzlement of money would not hinder one of them from being talked of as the light of the age. I suppose the next thing will be to have some habit and repute thief or housebreaker proposing a reformation of the criminal code. A Whig is never cut by the Whigs. Fox and Tom Erskine stuck by Arthur O'Connor to the last, and *swore* that they believed him to have the same political principles as themselves.* I suppose, in spite of his behavior to Mackerrel, Brougham could get a certificate! Even Bennet is something with them still!

* O'Connor was tried for high treason.—M.

Buller. Not much. 'Tis a fine thing to be Whig, however. How the Chaldee would have been praised had it been written against the Tories!

North. Why the English Tories would have laughed at it, and the Scotch Tories would have joined trembling with their mirth—and Jamie Hogg would have been dinnered to his death, poor fellow.

Buller. I have a sort of lurking hereditary respect for the name of Whig. I can't bear its having come to designate such people.

North. What stuff is this? You might as well wax wroth because *a cicerone* is not the same thing with *a Cicero*, nor *a bravo* the same thing with *a brave man.*

Buller. Why is it that the Whigs attack you so much more bitterly than they do Gifford?

North. Why, Mr. Buller, the crow always darts first at THE EYE.

Buller. Their attacks on you are as zealous as their laudations of themselves.

North. And as ineffectual.

> " Talk and spare not for speech, and at last you will reach,
> And the proverb hold good, I opine, sirs,
> *In spite of ablution, scent and perfume, pollution*
> *Show'd still that the sow was a swine, sirs.*"

Buller. What is that you are quoting now?

North. Aristophanes—Mitchell, I mean.* I think the verses are in his version of The Wasps.

Buller. I have not seen his new volume yet. Is it as good as the first?

North. I don't know. The dissertations on the first volume were the most popular things in it, and there are no dissertations in this; but, 'tis full of capital notes, and the translation is quite in the same spirited style. Nothing can be more true, I imagine. I am quite sure nothing can be more spirited or more graceful.

Buller. That's high praise from a Cynic like you, Mr. Christopher. I suppose 'tis the first thing of the sort in our language, however.

North. Oh! most certainly it is so. None of the ancient dramatists have ever had anything like justice done them before. There is so much *poetry* in some of the passages in this last volume, that I can't but wish Mitchell would take some of the tragedians in hand next. What a name might he not make if he could master Æschylus as well as he has done Aristophanes? or perhaps some of Euripides' plays would fall more easily into his management. I wish he would try the Bacchæ or the Cyclops.

* Thomas Mitchell's chief title to fame rests upon his admirable translation into English verse, of the Plays of Aristophanes. He was a good philologist; wrote several papers in the *Quarterly Review*, on subjects connected with Greek manners and literature; and edited a few of the classical works printed at the Clarendon press, Oxford. He died in 1845, aged sixty-two. —M.

Buller. Spout a little piece more of him, if you can.

North. I will give you part of a passage that I consider nobody has so good a right to quote as myself; for *I* am the true representative of the *Vetus Comœdia*—

" When the swell of private rage foam'd indignant, that The Stage
  Dared upbraid lawless love and affection,
And will'd our poet's speech, (guilty pleasures not to reach)
  Should assume a more lowly direction:—
Did he heed the loud reproof? No—he wisely kept aloof,
  And spurn'd at corruption's base duress;
For never could he choose, to behold his dearest Muse,
  In the dress of a wanton procuress."

Buller. Why, this certainly looks as if it had been written since Rimini and Juan.

North. Listen, man—

" When first the scenic trade of instruction he essay'd,
  Monsters, not *men*, were his game, sirs;
Strange Leviathans, that ask'd strength and mettle, and had task'd
  Alcides, their fury to tame, sirs!"

Buller. The Shepherd of Chaldea may hold up his head now, I think.

North. Hush—

" In peril and alarms was his 'prenticeship of arms,
  With a SHARK fight and battle essaying,
From whose eyes stream'd baleful light, like the blazing balls of sight
  Which in CYNNA'S (*query, Jeffrey's?*) fierce face are seen playing.
Swathed and banded round his head, five-score sycophants were fed—
  Ever slav'ring, and licking, and glueing, (*young Whigs to be sure,*)
While his voice scream'd loud and hoarse, like the torrent's angry course,
  When death and destruction are brewing.
Rude the portent, fierce and fell, did its sight the poet quell,
  Was he seen to a *truce* basely stooping?
No; his blows still fell unsparing that and next year, when came warring
  With foes of a different trooping."

Buller. No! nobody can say that of you, Christopher.

North. There's another passage—a semi-chorus of *Wasps*, which I must give you. It seems as if I heard a certain "CLEVER OLD BODY" singing in the midst of all his *disjecta membra.*

" O the days that are gone by, O the days so blithe and bland,
When my foot was strong in dance, and the spear was in my hand,
Then my limbs and years were green, I could toil and yet to spare,
And the foeman, to his cost, knew what strength and mettle are.
  O the days that are gone by, &c.

Enter MR. AMBROSE.

Mr. Ambrose. Mr. Tickler! [*Enter* MR. TICKLER.

Tickler. Ha! Buller, my dear boy—may you live a thousand years.

Buller. Allow me to congratulate you on your marriage. I trust Mrs. Tickler is tolerably well—not complaining very much?

Tickler. No bantering, you dog—I might marry without losing any good fellowship, which is more than you can say, Mr. Brazen-nose. Why the devil don't you all marry at Oxford? What could be more interesting than to see Christ Church Walk swarming with the wives, children, and nurses of senior fellows?

Buller. Spare us, Tickler, spare us. What are you about? Not a single article of yours has gladdened England for a twelvemonth.

Tickler. I am engaged on the Pope Controversy.* My work will embrace three quarto volumes. I begin with pointing out the difference between nature and art, which has been often written about, but never understood. Do you know the difference?

Buller. No!—confound me if I do.

Tickler. Take an illustration. Mr. Bowles walking to church in a suit of black—with a gown, bands, and shovel hat—is an artificial object, though he may not think so; and therefore, according to his own principles, an unfit theme for the highest species of poetical composition. So is Mr. Bowles in his night-shirt and night-cap—but Mr. Bowles going in to bathe in *puris naturalibus*, is artificial no more—he is a natural—and, as such, a fit subject for the loftiest song.

North. Very well, Tickler—but I love and respect Bowles.

Tickler. Very well, North—but I love and respect Pope. And of all the abject and despicable drivelling, ever drivelled by clerk or layman, is all that late drivelling about the eternal principles of poetry, and the genius of the Bard of Twickenham. Why, there is more passion in that one single line of Eloisa to Abelard, "Give all thou can'st, and let me dream the rest," than in all the verses Mr. Bowles ever wrote in his life, or Mr. Campbell either.

Buller. Wordsworth says Dryden's Ode is low, and vulgar, and stupid.

Tickler. Wordsworth is an ass—that is, as great an ass as Dryden. Pray, is his poem of Alice Fell worth a bad farthing? Only think of the author of the Lyrical Ballads sitting by himself in a post-chaise, driving like the very devil into Durham. No poet ought to have made such a confession. Besides, it is well-known that it was a *return*-chaise, and I question if the post-boy "who drove in fierce career," (such are the Bard's absurd words) gave his master the coin. I shrewdly suspect he fobbed it.

North. Stop, Tickler—you are becoming personal. I discountenance all personalities, either here or elsewhere.

Tickler. I beg your and Mr. Wordsworth's pardon. I mean no

* The Pope Controversy, (as it was called) was carried on by Bowles, Campbell, Byron, Dr. Gilchrist, Roscoe, and three or four minor writers. The dispute ramified into a variety of subjects, but the main question was—*Was Pope a Poet?*—M.

disrespect to that gentleman—but as long as my name is Tickler, he shall not abuse Dryden without getting abused himself.

North. Why, Tickler—many of the poets of our days are, with all their genius, a set of enormous Spoons. Wordsworth walks about the woods like a great satyr, or rather like the god Pan; and piping away upon his reed, sometimes most infernally out of tune, he thinks he is listening, at the very least, to music equal to that of the spheres, and that nobody can blow a note but himself.

Buller. Ay, ay, Mr. North—there is Satan reproving sin, as you presbyters are wont to say. Believe me, you have never yet done Southey justice in your work. He is a splendid genius. His mind has a high tone. Southey, sir, is one of the giants.

Tickler. Why, the Whigs, and Radicals, and Reformers, abuse Mr. Southey, I observe, because, when an enthusiastic youth, soon after the French Revolution, he spoke and wrote a quantity of clever nonsense; and twenty years afterwards, when a wise man, he spoke and wrote a far greater quantity of saving knowledge.

Buller. Just so: you could not state the fact better, were you to talk an hour.

Tickler. Pray, North, are you for pulling down Lord Nelson's Monument?

North. It is no great shakes of an erection; but I would let it stand.

Tickler. If Lord Nelson's Monument is to be pulled down,* because a better one might be built up, then I have a small proposal to make, namely that the whole New Town of Edinburgh shall be pulled down. Does there exist in Europe—in the world—a more absurd, stupid, and unmeaning street than George's-street? Why, this very tavern of Mr. Ambrose,† admirable as it is beyond all earthly taverns, ought on the same principle to be pulled down. But may I never live see that time! [*Much affected.*

Buller. You will pardon me, my beloved and honored friends, but do you not think that the "Modern Athens," as applied to the good town of Edinburgh, is pure humbug?

[TICKLER *and* NORTH *rising from their chairs at once.*

Both. Humbug! aye, humbug, indeed, Buller!

Buller. I wish to hear Mr. Tickler. He is the elder.

Tickler. No, sir, I am no Elder. I never stood at the plate; but young as I am, I am old enough to recollect the day when such an

* On the rocky apex of the Calton Hill, in Edinburgh, (an elevation of 350 feet above the level of the sea), stands a monument to Lord Nelson, in the form of a tall shaft springing from an octagonal base. As a work of art, nothing can be meaner. But the panoramic view from its summit is magnificent, embracing views on land and water, with the city lying far beneath, but full in sight. The lodge in the base of the Monument is rented to a vendor of nuts, cakes, "sweeties," (as comfits are called in Scotland), and an effervescing fluid apparently composed of bottled soap-suds, sweetened with molasses, and dignified with the name of ginger beer.—M.

† This was Ambrose's *old* hostelrie, back of Princes'-street.—M.

impertinence would not have been tolerated in Auld Reekie. In the days of Smith, and Hume, and Robertson, we were satisfied with our national name, and so were we during a later dynasty of genius, of which old Mackenzie still survives; but now-a-days, when with the exception of Scott, yourself North, and myself, and a few others, there is not a single man of power or genius in Edinburgh, the prigs call themselves *Athenians!* Why, you may just as appropriately call the first Parallelogram, that shall be erected on Mr. Owen's plan, the Modern Athens, as the New Town of Edinburgh.

Buller. Excellent, excellent, go on.

Tickler. Where are our sculptors, painters, musicians, orators, poets, and philosophers?—But give me my tumbler of gin-twist, for I am sick.—(*Drinks and recovers.*)—The ninnies have not even the sense to know that our Calton Hill is no more like the Acropolis than Lord Buchan* is like Pericles, or Jeffrey like Demosthenes. It is the Castle Rock that is like the Acropolis, or may be said to be so; and if the Parthenon is to be built at all, it *must* be built on the Castle Rock. This is the first egregious blunder of our Modern Athenians.

Buller. Take another tift—now for blunder second.

Tickler. It is all one great, big, blown, blustering blunder together. We are Scotsmen, not Greeks. We want no Parthenon—we are entitled to none. There are not ten persons in Edinburgh—not one Whig I am sure, who could read three lines of Homer "*ad aperturam libri.*" There are pretty Athenians for you! Think of shoals of Scotch artisans, with long lank greasy hair, and corduroy breeches, walking in the Parthenon!

Buller. Spare me, spare me—not a word more.

Tickler. Nay, we are to have the Kirk of Scotland in the naked simplicity of her worship, put under the tutelary power of the Virgin Goddess. Will the Scottish nation submit to this?

North. How fares the subscription for this Parthenon?

Tickler. One parish has subscribed, I understand, about nine guineas—Aberdour, I think. One old farmer there, has come forward with a sixpence for the Grand National Monument;† but perhaps he has not yet advanced the sum: it is only on paper.

North. It seems to me, that if the people of Scotland really desire a National Monument, they will build one. They are not building one—*ergo*, they do not desire one.

* The Earl of Buchan, who affected to be the patron of Art and Letters in Edinburgh, was a silly nobleman, whose two brothers were eminently gifted. One, Thomas Erskine, went to the English Bar and rose to the Chancellorship, with a peerage. The other, Henry Erskine, was a member of the Scottish Bar, eminently shrewd, witty, and learned.—M.

† The National Monument, which was an unfortunate attempt to imitate the Parthenon of Athens, was erected between 1824 and 1830, on one of the summits of the Calton Hill. It never was, and never will be completed, and its thirteen columns simply record the expenditure of £20,000.—M.

Tickler. Michael Linning goes incessantly about poking the public on the posteriors, and pointing to a subscription paper, but the public won't stir. Such conduct is very teasing in Michael Linning, and should not be permitted.

Buller. Well, let Michael Linning go to the devil.—But I wish to know what all the young Whigs are about. I see none of them!

Tickler. Look into a ditch in dry droughty weather, and you will behold a sad mortality among the tadpoles. The poor Powheads, (see Dr. Jamieson) are all baked up together in a mud-pie, and not a wriggle is in the ditch.

North. Why, Buller, in other times these tadpoles shot out legs and arms, and became small bouncing frogs. Their activity was surprising, and their croak loud. But the race is nearly extinct, and in a few years must be entirely so; for the old frogs don't spawn now—very seldom at least; and when they do, the spawn is either not prolific, or immediately destroyed. Now and then a young Whig or two comes forth, nobody can conjecture whence; but we either take him and throw him aside, or he leaps off himself into some crevice or cranny, and is no more seen.

Buller. I cannot agree with you, Tickler, in thinking Jeffrey a poor creature.

Tickler. I don't think him a poor creature—I never said so. But I think he is a small-minded man. His ambition is low. He talks about it—and about it—and about it. He is contented to be a critic—that is, a palaverer. His politics are enough to damn him for ever, as no Scotchman. But he is not worth talking about. He is just like a small black-faced mountain sheep, who, spying a gap in a fence, bolts through it with his hinder clooties jerked up pertly and yet timidly in the air, and is immediately followed by all the wethers and ewes, who ask no questions at their Leader, but wheel round about upon you with spiral horns, and large gray glowering eyes, as much as to say, "What think you o' that?" We think merely, that they are a set of silly sheep, whose wool is not worth the clipping,—but that do very well *when cut up.*

Buller. I observed t'other day an article in the Edinburgh Review, in which Oriel College is described as a sink, into which ran every thing vile and loathsome, and Coplestone sneered at as a pompous ninny. In the next number, Oriel College was said to be the most distinguished in Europe, I believe, and Coplestone one of the most illustrious writers of the age. Must not Jeffrey, if a gentleman and a scholar, or a gentleman and no scholar, which I believe is the case, feel ashamed of such childish and beggarly contradiction as this? What right has he to make a fool of himself to that extent? Is not Jeffrey an Oxonian?

North. Upwards of thirty years ago, he remained for a few weeks in a small garret in Queen's—does that make him an Oxonian?—But enough of this little personage. Tickler, start a new subject.

Tickler. I hate novelties. Is the prosecution mania about to subside, think you? Now-a-days, every word is said to be actionable. You cannot open your mouth, or put pen to paper, without feeing a libel-lawyer. An Edinburgh Whig, and really some of the London ones seem no better, is an animal without a skin. True, he is often covered with long shaggy hair, and he roars like an absolute lion; but the instant you give him a kick, or stir him up with a long pole, he begins to yell out in the most piteous strain, and you tremble lest you have killed him. You then perceive that under this formidable-looking hair, the creature's body is quite raw, and that a prick with the point of the pen gives him intolerable anguish. Nay, if you but turn the round nose of a quill towards him, he bellows; and more than once have I put him to flight with my keelie-vine.*

Buller. What is the Prosecution-mania?

Tickler. The Whigs here have, as you know, been laughing at every body for twenty years—indulging in every species of stupid personalities and slanders—nay, they are doing so still hourly—in all the envenomed bitterness of impotent and mauled malice—and yet they have entered into a cowardly compact to *prosecute* every syllable that shall ever be written against any one of their degraded and slanderous selves. Is not this base and cravenlike? These are the Slaves of Freedom—the dolts of wit—these are *our modern Athenians.*

North. I am a prejudiced person—what think you of the London periodicals lately, Tickler?

Tickler. Campbell's Magazine is a respectable work, on the whole. It is seldom very personal, although sometimes. That, in my opinion, is a great point, whether gained or lost, it is hard to decide. It is often unaccountably dull. It cannot be read after dinner, at the fireside, with your feet on the fender, and your back on an easy chair, without immediate sleep. But that is a severe test to try any periodical by. It has no plan, aim, object, or drift. You are swimming in fresh water; there is no buoyancy, one number is precisely like another—sometimes a little more, sometimes a little less dull—that is all, and it is a distinction without a difference.

Buller. What think you of its politics?

Tickler. Very badly. Its politics consist in concealed, suppressed, discontented, yawmering (see the Dr.) whiggism. There is nothing manly in them—be a Tory—be a Whig—but don't go mumbling your political opinions, and stuttering out sentiments of liberty, and whispering reform below your breath. If you have got any thing to say, out with it; if not, shut your mouth, or open it and go to bed.

* *Keelie-vine;*—a pen, a pencil of black or red lead.—M.

Buller. I intend to take Campbell's Magazine, for I wish to know his opinion of his contemporaries.

Tickler. Do you? Put him on the rack then, or threaten to break his bones on the wheel; for without some prompt and vigorous measure of that sort, he will utter nothing satisfactory. He gets Cockneys to criticise his contemporaries.

North. Who are the poor creatures?

Tickler. What! you pretend you don't know. But let them rest. It is a sad sight to see a true poet and gentleman like Tom Campbell with such paltry associates, to hear the Attic bee murmuring among a set of blue-bottle-flies, moths, and midges. Wasps are better than great fat stingless bummers... But notwithstanding, Campbell's Magazine is a very respectable one, and I will not suffer you, North, out of pure jealousy, to run it down. You ought rather to give it a lift—if it does not deserve, it at least requires one.

North. Tickler, if you saw Tom Campbell falling out of a window four stories high would you try, at the risk of your bones, to break his fall? Would it make any difference whether he had flung himself over, or Mr. Colburn had insidiously opened the sash and enticed him over? Not a whit. You would stand out of the way. There can be no successful interference with the great laws of nature, especially gravitation.

Buller. Taylor and Hessey's Magazine—is it better?

Tickler. Sometimes much better, and often much worse. Elia in his happiest moods delights me; he is a fine soul; but when he is dull, his dulness sets human stupidity at defiance. He is like a well-bred, ill-trained pointer. He has a fine nose, but he won't or can't range. He keeps always close to your foot, and then he points larks and titmice. You see him snuffing and snoking and brandishing his tail with the most impassioned enthusiasm, and then drawn round into a semicircle he stands beautifully—dead set. You expect a burst of partridges, or a towering cock-pheasant, when lo, and behold, away flits a lark, or you discover a mouse's nest, or there is absolutely nothing at all. Perhaps a shrew has been there the day before. Yet if Elia were mine, I would not part with him, for all his faults.*

Buller. Who, in the name of St. Luke's, Bedlam, and the Retreat at York, is the English Opium-Eater? He ought to go to Smyrna.

Tickler. The English Opium-Eater would be an invaluable contributor to any periodical, especially if it were published once in the four years.† He threatened to make the London Magazine the

* In later years, Lamb did write for *Blackwood.*—M.

† De Quincey, speaking of the *London Magazine*, says, "Meantime, the following writers were, in 1821–33, among my own *Collaborateurs*;—Charles Lamb; Hazlitt: Allan Cunningham; Hood; Hamilton Reynolds; Cary, the unrivalled translator of Dante; Crowe, the Public Orator of Oxford. And so well were all departments provided for, that even the monthly abstract of politics, brief as it necessarily was, had been confided to the care of Phillips, the celebrated Irish barrister."—There were others, among whom were John Clare, the peasant poet

receptacle of all the philosophy and literature of Germany. "Os magna sonaturum!" "Vox et nihil præterea."

North. When he writes again in the London Magazine, it will be well worth half-a-crown. By the way, Tickler, what do you think of the Continuation of Dr. Johnson's Lives of the Poets in that periodical?

Tickler. Mere quackery.* Why, the compiler manufactures a life of this and that poet from materials in every body's hands, and then boldly calls it "A Continuation of Dr. Johnson's Lives," &c. There seems no attempt to imitate his style at all. According to this notion, every thing that comes after another is a continuation of it. Is this quackery, or is it not, North?

North. I see no harm in a little quackery; all we editors are quacks. I acknowledge myself to be a quack.

Tickler. Ay, here carousing over Ambrosia and Nectar. But would you, publicly?

North. Yes; on the top of St. Paul's—or in my own Magazine, that is, before the whole universe.—Buller, what are you about?

Buller. Mr. North, have you seen a new periodical called the Album?

North. I have; it promises well.† The editor is manifestly a gentleman. The work is on beautiful paper, admirably printed, and the articles are well written, elegant and judicious. I think that in all probability the next number will be better. The editor has not attempted to make a splash-dash-flash all at once; but he has stuff in him, I know that, and so have some of his coadjutors. I know him and them extremely well; I pat them on the back, bid them be good boys, and always speak truth, and they will have nothing to fear.

Tickler. Nothing amuses me more than to see Magazines—which, after all, are not living beings, but just so many stitched sheets of letter-press, *going to loggerheads and becoming personal.* Up jumps Ebony's Magazine, and plants a left-handed lounge on the bread-basket of Taylor and Hessey's. That periodical strips *instanter*, a ring is formed, and the numbers are piping hot as mutton-pies. Can

of Northamptonshire; Talfourd, then the undistinguished, but future author of "Ion;" Wainwright, whose *nom de plume* was "Janus Weathercock," whose crimes subsequently supplied real tragic incidents, on which Bulwer founded his domestic romance—full of tragic interest—called "Lucretia; or the Children of Night!" I think, too, that Haydon sometimes wrote for *The London*, which gave etchings from his pictures of Christ's Agony in the Garden, and the Entry into Jerusalem. With such an array of contributors, the *London Magazine* should have flourished. In the words of the Irish Keeners, when they apostrophize the departed whose remains lie cold before them, we might ask, "Ah, why *did* you die?"—M.

* To continue Johnson's Lives of the Poets might have been "mere quackery," in North's opinion, but the Continuator was the Rev. Henry Francis Cary, the Translator of Dante, of the Odes of Pindar, and of the "Birds of Aristophanes."—In the last London edition of Johnson's Lives of the Poets, beautifully illustrated, the continuation by Cary has been incorporated, and gives additional value to a work, which, with many faults (for Johnson had numerous literary and personal prejudices), is one of the most remarkable books in the English language, not having been commenced until the author was seventy years old!—Cary died in 1844.—M.

† It was edited by Charles Knight (assisted, I believe, by Charles Ollier, author of "Inesella") and was short-lived.—M.

any thing be more ridiculous? Colburn's Magazine, on the other hand, is a Corinthian, and won't show fight. All I mean is, that Magazines ought not to quarrel; there are snuff-dealers and pastry-cooks enow for us all; and a sale will be found for us all at last.

North. Who the devil is more pugnacious than yourself, Tickler? Why, you lay about you like a bull in a china shop.

Tickler. Not at all. I have serious intentions of turning Quaker. If not—certainly a clergyman. Quakers and parsons may be as personal as they choose. The same man might then either give or take the lie direct, who would, as a layman, have boggled at the retort courteous.

North. What is the world saying now about me, do you think, my Tickler?

Tickler. They flatter you so in all directions, that you must become a spoiled child. A few weeks ago I met an elderly young woman in a coach going to Glasgow, who could not speak of you without tears. She said you were the most pathetic man she had ever read. The coach was crowded—there were seven of us inside, for we had kindly taken in a grazier during a hail-storm near Westcraigs, and there was not a single dissentient voice.

North. Did the grazier entertain the same sentiments as the lady?

Tickler. He said, with a smile that would have graced a slaughter-house, that it was not the first Stot you had knocked down. The lady seemed to understand the allusion, and blushed.

North. Did you proceed to Glasgow?

Tickler. Yes; I had been elected an honorary member of the "Oriental Club of the West." I went to take my seat. They are a set of most admirable despots. We all sat cross-legged like Turks or tailors, as if Glasgow had been Constantinople. I will give you a description of us for your next Number.

North. Do so. But then the London people will say it is *local.* And why not? London itself is the most provincial spot alive. Let our Magazine be read in the interior of Africa, along with either, or both of the two Monthlies, and which will seem most of a cosmopolite to the impartial black population? Ebony. The London people, with their theatres, operas, Cockneys, &c., &c., are wholly unintelligible out of their own small town. The truth must be told them—*London is a very small insignificant place.** Our ambition is, that our wit shall be local all over the world.

Tickler. It is so. It is naturalized in all the kingdoms of the earth. What can *John Bull* mean by saying he does not understand many of your allusions? He is mistaken. John Bull understands every thing worth understanding—and therefore, his knowledge of Ebony is complete. But even if he did not, is it not pleasant some-

* Yes!—particularly in 1854, with a population of 2,500,000.—M.

times to see things under a tender, obscure, and hazy light? John Bull's notices to correspondents I do not always thoroughly understand; but I read them with delight: and I never lay down a No. of his paper without repeating that wise saw of Hamlet, "There are more things in heaven and earth than are dreamt of in my philosophy."

North. It is not at all like *John Bull* to accuse us of laughing occasionally at the Quarterly Review, "because there has been a quarrel between Blackwood and Murray." What do we care about Blackwood or Murray? Not one sous. But when, how, why, or where did these mighty personages quarrel? I never heard of it before last Wednesday.

Tickler. Don't you recollect, North, some years ago, that Murray's name was on our title-page; and that, being alarmed for Subscription Jamie, and Harry Twitcher,* he took up his pen and scratched his name out, as if he had been Emperor of the West, signing an order for our execution? The death-warrant came down, but we are still alive.

North. I do indistinctly remember reading something to that effect in a Whig newspaper, but of course I supposed it to be a lie; but, if true, what then? Are we angry now with a gentlemanly person like Mr. Murray, for attempting to cut his own throat some years ago? Too absurd a great deal.

Tickler. Certainly. John Bull himself knows that we laugh at the Quarterly Review, only when it is laughable. He knows we admire it, and say so, when it is admirable. Of all the periodicals now flourishing or fading, BLACKWOOD'S MAGAZINE IS THE MOST IMPARTIAL. Yes, its illustrious editor despises all the chicanery of the trade. Trojan or Tyrian, that is, Murray or Constable,—Longman and Rees, or Taylor and Hessey,—Richardson of Cornhill, or Ollier of Bond-street,—with you they are held in no distinction. Their good books you toss up to the stars, and their bad you trample down to Tartarus.

North. John Bull also says, that the Edinburgh and Quarterly Reviews are works of a *higher class* than Blackwood's Magazine. I am truly vexed to differ from him here. They are works of an older, thicker, and heavier, but not of a higher class. A review is not necessarily a higher work than a magazine—any more than a magazine is necessarily a higher work than a weekly newspaper—or a weekly newspaper than a daily one. Genius, learning, and virtue, constitute the only essential difference between work and work; and in these, we never heard it whispered, that this Magazine is inferior to any work, living or dead.

* Sir James Mackintosh and Henry Brougham.—M.

Tickler. John Bull may be right after all. He is an incomprehensible mortal.*

North. The John Bull newspaper is a chariot armed with scythes —the Morning Chronicle is a market cart, out of which a big empty turnip or cabbage keeps trundling ever and anon against honest people's legs; but a dexterous turn of the ankle shys it into the kennel, and no harm done.

Tickler. However, in sober seriousness, you are an almost universal favorite. You burn like a gas-light among oil-lamps. The affection felt for you is a mixture of love, fear, and astonishment,—three emotions that play into each other's hands. The sex regard you with a mixed passion, of which the fundamental feature is love. Fear is the chief ingredient in the ruling passion towards you of literary gentlemen under fifty—and with Grey Bennet,† and old women in general—astonishment.

Buller. (*Yawning.*) Would you like to marry an actress?

Tickler and North. Whom are you speaking to?

Buller. To any body.

Tickler. Not for my first wife. After a private spouse or two, I should not care for marrying a pretty young actress to rub my bald pate in my old age; at the same time, a man should consider his posthumous fame. Now, if your relict, before you are well warm in your grave, marry an Irishman forty years younger, and three feet broader across the back than you her late dearly beloved husband, your posthumous fame receives a blow that demolishes it at once irretrievably—that should be considered.

Buller. Why, I begin to get drowsy—was I snoring?

Tickler. Like a trooper. Ring the bell, my buck.

Enter MR. AMBROSE.

North. What's to pay?

Mr. Ambrose. I beg you won't mention it. I am so happy to see Mr. Buller in Scotland again, that I cannot think of making any charge for a few hundred oysters, and a mere gallon of gin.

North. Assist me on with my great-coat—there—there—easy—easy. Now, my cane. Give me your arm, Ambrose—am I quite steady?

Mr. Ambrose. As steady as York Minster, sir.

[*They vanish into thin air.*

* In those days Theodore Hook was the presiding genius of the *John Bull* newspaper,—and made it overflow with wit, satire, scandal, humor, Toryism, and dashing personalities.—M.

† Henry Grey Bennett, an active liberal, represented Shrewsbury in Parliament for many years, but on the discovery of certain criminal practices, fled to Paris, where he died.—M.

No. III.—MAY, 1822.

SCENE I.—TIME—*Six o'clock, P. M.* SCENE—*The Blue Parlor.*

To MR. NORTH, *standing in the centre of the room, in full fig,*
Enter MR. TIMOTHY TICKLER.

North. Good day, sir; I'm glad I'm not to dine quite alone. I began to think nobody was coming.

Tickler. I beg your pardon, Mr. North, but I really had no notion it was so far in the day. I took my chocolate as usual about two, and then went out into the Meadows* and wandered about.

North. About what, you old rogue, you? But no apologies. I'm glad you've made your appearance at least.

Tickler. I hope you'll excuse my gaiters, North; I had not the least idea you were to sport a regular blow-out to-day. I looked into the other room, and saw such a smash of covers—and you in your silk stockings too!—I suppose you've been sporting your ankles with the Commissioner.

North. Not I; but I expect several strangers to dinner, and an editor is nothing without black breeches, you know—but you need not say a word about your dress. Upon my honor, that's a most natty surtout—and your spatterdashes, why they are quite the potato. For a contributor you are well enough—and, after all, there's no ladies in the party.

Tickler. What! not even Mrs. M'Whirter!† I'll do well enough as I am for your Kempferhausens and Mullions, *et hoc genus*, if that's all the party.

North. That's not it quite either, Mr. Timothy. I expect two or three gentlemen you have never been in company with, and I believe the meeting will give pleasure on all sides—There's Sir Andrew Wylie for one.‡

Tickler. What! he of that Ilk? Old Wheelie?

* The Meadows lie south of Heriot's and George Watson's Hospital's, in Edinburgh, and, with Bruntsfield Links, extend to about 200 acres, which are open for the recreation of the inhabitants, by virtue of royal grants to the city. The national game of Golf is played on the fine open downs of Bruntsfield Links.—M.

† Mrs. M'Whirter, Odoherty's ancient Philadelphia flame, never honored The Noctes with her presence. Her last appearance was—in The Tent.—M.

‡ Galt, in the novel of "Sir Andrew Wylie, of that Ilk," (equivalent to "of Wylie") had narrated the adventures of a poor Scottish lad who went to London to seek his fortune, and returned home with riches and rank.—M.

North. The same—he's an Elder in this General Assembly, and his chum, Dr. Scott,* who is also a member of the venerable court, introduced him to me a few mornings ago at the Moderator's breakfast. I declare the western worthies eclipsed even the ministers! I never saw two such twists—I beg your pardon—I hope Mrs. Tickler is well.

Tickler. So, so, North:—Of course Sir Andrew wrote his own Life?

North. Why, you know every body writes books in our days, and nobody owns them. But I suppose he and the Odontist patched up the Life between them. They're a couple of queer comical old devils. The Baronet, a deuced rum fellow, to be sure; but Countesses and Duchesses adore him, and we must all confess he is one of the cleverest, and at the same time best-tempered creatures alive.

Tickler. Whom else have ye?

North. Mr. Pendarves Owen—a very pretty-behaved young gentleman.

Tickler. By Jove, if he leaps out of a window here, there will be a pretty end of the pretty-behaved gentleman. Imagine a fellow clearing the Cowgate, or Hopping over the Horse Wynd, fourteen stories deep, from a skylight to a chimney top.† Of course the lad has a bee in his bonnet.

North. Perhaps you'll find it a wasp if you go too near. He's a cursed hot fellow—but so are all the Taffy breed. But what was I thinking of? There's Feldborg behind.‡

Tickler. Feldborg the Dane?—really?

North. Feldborg—ipsissimus ipse! I hear his cough on the stair this moment. He arrived in the Roads last night at a quarter after eleven.

Enter MR. AMBROSE.

Mr. Ambrose. Professor Feldborg! [*Exit.*

Enter FELDBORG, THE DANE.

Feldborg. With joy and ravishment, O illustrious man, do I once more contemplate thee. From the very first instant of the time I

* Dr. Scott, "the Odontist," as shown in Maga, was nearly as imaginary as Sir Andrew Wylie.—M.

† In the summer of 1822 was published, by Blackwood. of Edinburgh, a novel called Pen Owen, in three volumes It was written by the Rev. Mr. Hook, who was cousin to the facetious Theodore. Another novel, called "Percy Mallory," was all that the same pen contributed to public amusement, in the way of prose fiction. Pen Owen was reviewed in *Blackwood* for June. 1822, by which its merits were widely made known. The reviewer said that it was an eminently successful "attempt to revive the old style of the time of George II. and apply it to the time of George IV."—The work took its hero into all sorts of plays: now in the House of Commons, listening to a debate; in Newgate, in company with Cobbett; in Albemarle-street, dining at John Murray's, next to Tom Sheridan; in a sort of Cato-street Conspiracy, with an examination at the Home Office as a wind-up; at Smithfield, amid the drovers, (how capitally Noah Tup robs simple Tom Crossthwaite!); in a political debating society; in fact, in all places and with all people in London, in the year of grace 1822. Pen Owen, the hero, was the most impulsive of beings, and this is the gentleman brought into the Third of the Noctes.—M.

‡ The Dane was imaginary—as far as the Noctes were concerned.—M.

re-landed on the Albionean coast, did my mind—my soul—my spirituous part thirst after thee. And to thee, also most admired and honorable Mr. Tickler, I offer my heartfelt salutations. Heaven surely, what I hope, has favored you both, *me absente*, dum in Daniâ meâ moratus sum.

North. All hail, Prince of Denmark! And how is the little Prince that you told so many pretty stories to, and how are Oehlenschlaeger, and Baggesen, and Bombardius, and all the rest of the Danes?

Feldborg. All quite hearty, quite the charming agreeable spirits, and all in louf with you. Baggesen is writing a very big book all about you. Its title is *De Amore Northi apud Danos.* The book will make a sensation—it is dedicated what you call to Oehlenschlaeger.

North. What?—so they have made up matters!

Feldborg. Quite reconciled—I saw with mine own eyes Baggesen smoking one, two, three long, very long puffs out of Oehlenschlaeger's pipe. I wrote a very pretty poem on that subject in the Copenhagen Chronicle. It has already been translated into Swedish and Lapp.

North. It must now be well known if that's the case—but here comes the rest of our friends. Sir Andrew, your most obedient humble servant.

Enter Sir Andrew Wylie, Dr. Scott, Mr. Pendarves Owen, Ensign O'Doherty, and the Rev. Donald Wodrow, D.D.

—— I'm exceedingly proud of having the honor to see you all here, gentlemen—Dr. Scott, don't pull my wrist out of joint, man—Mr. Owen, I'm delighted—Dr. Wodrow, how-do-you-*do*, my good sir? Has the overture come on yet? [*Aside.*] Order dinner, Odoherty.

Rev. Dr. Wodrow. Why, Mr. North, you see that business from the Ayr brethren has occupied the committee so long, that our overture ——

North. Gentlemen, allow me to make you all acquainted. Sir Andrew Wylie, Mr. Tickler—Mr. Tickler, Sir Andrew Wylie. Professor Feldborg, Captain Odoherty—Captain Odoherty, Professor Feldborg. Captain Odoherty, allow me the pleasure of introducing you to my friend Dr. Wodrow—I'm sure you're no strangers to each other's names at all events. Well, now, are all the salaams over? Do any of you choose a whet before dinner?

Rev. Dr. Wodrow. It is not my custom to take any thing before dinner; but really, you folk in the town, you dine so late—and I took, thoughtlessly, some very salt ham this morning at the Moderator's.

North. There's a variety of liquors on the side-table—Odoherty, give Dr. Wodrow a little Seltzer-water, or something cooling.

While **Odoherty** *is handing round a salver, covered with small glasses, &c., enter* **Ambrose,** *with a towel under his arm.*)

Ambrose. Gentlemen—dinner.

North. Gentlemen, I'll show the way. Sir Andrew, your arm.

[*Exeunt* C. N. *and* Sir A. W.

Odoherty. Seniores sint priores! Cedant arma togæ.

[*Exit* Professor Feldborg.

Tickler. I can't walk before so many Doctors. Walk away, Dr. Scott.

Rev. Dr. Wodrow, (*brushing hastily out of the room.*) Come away, Dr. Scott.

Dr. Scott. Mr. Tickler, if *you* please, sir.

Tickler. O fie, Doctor—after you, Doctor.

[*Exit* Dr. Scott—*exit* Tickler.

Odoherty. Come along, Mr. Owen. What a hubbub these old Puts make, with their hanged precedence! Did you notice how the D.D. hopped off? As brisk as a beetle, by St. Patrick!

SCENE II.

C. North, Esq.

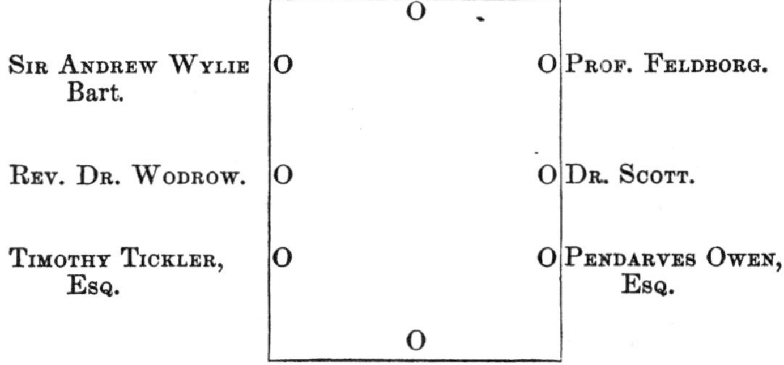

Ensign Odoherty.

North. A bumper! The King! God bless him!

Omnes. The King!!! [*Three times three. Trumpets without. Air—God save the King.*]

Tickler. A bumper—the Kirk of Scotland!

Omnes. The Kirk of Scotland! [*Air—The Bush aboon Traquair.*]

Rev. Dr. Wodrow. Gentlemen, all your very good healths! I am extremely sensible of the honor you have done —

North. —A bumper! "The general joy of the whole table!"

Odoherty. (*Aside.*) Vide Shakspeare! hem!

Omnes. The General joy, &c. (*Three times three.*)

(*Air, we are the Lads, &c.*

North. Now, gentlemen, these three bumpers being discussed, I leave the filling of your glasses to your own discretion.

Odoherty. Let each man fill his neighbor's glass, and push the port and sherry into the middle of the table. Mr. Chairman, give Sir Andrew a little drop; I'm sure he'll do as much for the Reverend Doctor on his right.

Sir. A. Wylie. Na, wha ever heard o' sic like doings as this! and me a ruling Elder too! Oh dear, you literary men are the most unconscionable chields I ever foregathered wi'—but to be sure it's ill to make a silk purse out of a sow's lug.

Dr. Scott Hear till him! Would any body think the Baronet had lived sa mony years out of his ain country, and been in high life too, Lord preserve us,—(I beg your pardon, Dr. Wodrow, it just slipped frae the tongue, man)—and kittled ladies of quality in his time—and crackit a bottle with Mr. Pitt himself—an' a' the lave o't? Ane that did not ken the history, would, saving his presence, just take him for some Paisley baillie, that had never had the stink of the Sneddon out of his nostrils!

North. Mr. Odontist, I disapprove of personalities.

Dr. Scott. Hout! Like the Duke of Bedford, I meant nothing personal, upon my honor.

Sir A. Wylie. Dr. Scott having in the handsomest manner declared that he meant no allusion to me personally, I am now perfectly satisfied. Fill your glass, Dr. Scott.

Rev. Dr. Wodrow. That puts me in mind of a story of Mr. Tham of Govan—a queer fellow—but sound, very sound in his doctrine. He had been rebuking a young lad and lassie one day in his kirk, and he had in his rough way, (for Tham was a very rough brother, sirs,) gone a great length in miscalling the lad; and as they were a' coming out of the kirk, the lad he came down from the cutty-stool and runs up to the minister, and says he, "I dinna ken what you meant by yon blackguard language about me. I think you're exceedingly impertinent, Mr. Tham." And wi' that Mr. Tham up with his stick, (he had aye a good bit sapling in his hand,) and comes a clink o'er the chield's head, and gar'd him reel away back, and he fell on the braid o' his back among the dirt,—hee! hee! hee!

Dr. Scott. A bonny parallel, my certy!

Feldborg. When Baggesen and Oehlenschlaeger first began to write pamphlets concerning each other—Ay, what pamphlets Baggesen does make!—there was some talk of their fighting with the sword,—and to be sure they went one day into Hamlet's Garden what we call, and they drew their swords so bright, so clear, and up comes I by accident, and says I, "What fools you are, let us go dine all together at the White Feather." This is a great inn, what you call, in Elsinore.

North. And did you go, accordingly?

Feldborg. Oh, what for a dinner we did eat that day! At the head of the table was a sausage-pie.—O, what for a pie! and at the foot there was a boiled goose with mustard pudding; and there was one dozen big black bottles of the best beer, and how we did rejoice!—Oh, me!

Pen Owen. (*Aside to* ODOHERTY.)—Noctes Cœnæque Deûm.

Odoherty. (*Aside to* PEN OWEN.)—Noctes Cœnæque de *hum.*

Pen Owen. Pray, Dr. Scott, what is that book called the Percy Anecdotes?—I saw it in a window at York as I came through, and bought it to divert us in the chaise, and I can make very little meaning of it, although it is an amusing production enough in its way.*

Dr. Scott. I only possess two or three numbers of the work; there's one of them called "Anecdotes of Instinct, with a portrait of the Ettrick Shepherd;" I was much amused with it.

Pen Owen. Yes; but why *Anecdotes of Instinct with a Portrait of Hogg?*—Do they mean to represent Hogg as being *totally* devoid of *Reason?*—A mere new edition of *the Learned Pig?*

Dr. Scott. It did not strike me before; but now you point it out, 'tis absurd. Then there's one, "Anecdotes of *Genius*, with a portrait of *Mr. Southey;*" and, immediately after, comes another, "Anecdotes of *Crime and Punishment*, with a portrait of Sir James Mackintosh." Now, I for one, can make neither head nor tail of this.

Pen Owen. Do you suppose they mean to insinuate that Sir James stands in the same relation to Crime and Punishment in which Southey stands to Genius? If so, what has been the learned knight's crime? What has been his punishment?

Tickler. What say you, Sir Andrew?

Sir A. Wylie. I suppose they mean to let us to wit, that Sir James Mackintosh is *above* Crime and Punishment, just as the Poet Hogg is *above* Instinct?†

Rev. Dr. Wodrow. Good, very good, I'm clear for Sir Andrew's way of expounding the dubiety, 'tis like *Lucus a non lucendo*—ehem!

Odoherty. (*Sings.*)

This is the wine
That in former time
Each wise one of the Magi
Was wont to carouse
In a frolicsome bowse.
Recubans sub tegmine fagi

* It was published in London. It was neatly illustrated. It formed a series of 40 numbers, or 20 duodecimo volumes. It professed to consist of "Anecdotes, original and select, by Sholto and Reuben Percy, brothers of the Benedictine Monastery, Mont Benger."—Sholto, being a Mr. Robertson, for many years editor of the *Mechanics' Magazine* and the *Railway Record* newspaper.—M.

† The actual reason why a portrait of Sir James Mackintosh illustrated the volume on Crime and Punishment, may be traced to the fact, that Sir James had been a Judge in India, and, as a member of Parliament, had endeavored to mitigate the severity of the English penal code.—M.

Mr. North, you're keeping the bottle rather long by you.

North. Well, Odoherty, since your pipe is so clear, suppose you do sing us another song—and if it be one of your own, so much the better for Dr. Wodrow.

Odoherty. Well,—since you will have it, I shall tip you what I wrote last month, on the interesting occasion of the marriage of Mr. Timothy Tickler, if you know any such person.

North. You're quizzing, Odoherty—Sing, but remember, that I depend upon your good feelings, to introduce nothing that could call up a blush on the delicate cheek of Mrs. Tickler, if she were present.

Tickler. Delicate cheek! hem,—

"O call it fair, not pale!"

Odoherty. (*Sings.*)

SONG.

ON THE WEDDING-DAY OF TIMOTHY TICKLER, ESQ., AND MISS AMARANTHA ALOESBUD.

1.

Fill, fill to the brim, fill a bumper to him,
 Who is call'd to a happier duty away,
Who, seated beside his own loved one—his bride—
 Drinks large draughts of joy from her eyes' sunny ray;
And let not the toast to the man we love most,
 Be silently pass'd round the board as we sit;
But rising about, with a heart-stirring shout,
 Let us hail the dear union of Beauty and Wit.

2.

Though, perhaps, now no more, shall our friend, as before,
 Join his bachelor mates in their frolicsome knot;
Nor pour forth his soul over bottle and bowl,
 That soul free from taint of dishonoring thought;
Though that eloquent tongue upon which we have hung
 So oft with delight, may no more glad us here;
Yet still his loved name a full bumper shall claim,
 And it still shall be hail'd with a thrice given cheer.

3.

O, blest be this day, by the smile of the gay,
 By the bright eyes of beauty, by music and dance!
O, blest be this day—and as life wears away,
 May he joy on its moments his thoughts back to glance!
May the maid, whose bright charms are resign'd to his arms,
 Still be loved with the love that he feels for her now!
And may her dear lord be by her still adored,
 As when first she lisp'd forth the unchangeable vow.

4.

Then fill to the brim, fill a bumper to him,
  Who is called to a happier duty away,
Who, seated beside his own loved one—his bride—
  Drinks large draughts of joy from her eyes' sunny ray:
And let not the toast to the man we love most
  Be silently pass'd round the board as we sit;
But rising about, with a heart-stirring shout,
  Let us hail the dear union of Beauty and Wit!

D. Scott. (*Singing.*)

"Let us hail the dear union of Beauty and Wit."

Devilish good song, upon my honor, Mr. North, I crave a bumper—Mrs. Tickler, with three times three.

Rev. Dr. Wodrow. Cheers or children, Dr. Scott? ha! ha! ha! the like o' that! (*Trumpets without.*)

Omnes. Mrs. Tickler! [Air—*Green grow the rashes, O.*]

Mr. Pen Owen. (*Aside to* ODOHERTY.) They're getting dull at that end of the table. May I tip them a touch of the long pole?

Odoherty. (*Aside to* PEN OWEN.) To be sure, honey! Where's Liberty-hall, think ye? Plant the prong!

Pen Owen. Mr. North, with your permission, and with the permission of the distinguished company, whom I have now the honor of seeing assembled around this festive board, there is a name which I would earnestly but respectfully entreat permission to join with the smack of a bumper.

North. Contributors, a bumper, Mr. Pendarves Owen's toast.

Pen Owen. I beg leave to propose the health of THE SMALL KNOWN.

North. Gentlemen, this is an appeal to your liberality, and I am sure your conduct will justify it. Take the time from me.

Omnes. THE SMALL KNOWN!!! !!! !!!

(*Trumpets without—Air—Saw ye my wee thing?*)

Sir A. Wylie, (*aside to Dr. Wodrow.*) We've all heard enough of the *Great Unknown*, but wha is this we've been drinking, Doctor?

Rev. Dr. Wodrow. Dr. Cook, I take it.

North. Pooh, pooh, 'tis our friend, the Prince of Reviewers, Sir Andrew.

Dr. Wodrow. The like o' that—ha! ha! *The Small Known!* well, I never heard sic like toasts! I'se propose it myself at the Moderate Club, the morn's night,—may I?

North. By all means. A toast is nothing until it comes into general vogue, like *The Cause for which Sidney bled on the Scaffold, and Hampden on the field, &c.*

Pen Owen. Which is pretty much the same thing with "the

Cause for which Sandt died by the axe, and Thistlewood by the drop."

Odoherty. I beg leave to propose a bumper, Mr. Chairman,—To the memory of Thistlewood ! ! !

Professor Feldborg, (*aside to Dr. Scott.*) What man was Thistlewood ? Was he a Tory Reviewer ?

Dr. Scott. Ask your friend Mr. Owen. I think he's like to give you the best notion.*

Pen Owen. Come, come ! you should not make such allusions, Mr. Odoherty. I'm sure you will admit that I was most innocently present on that unfortunate occasion, when Thistlewood —

Odoherty. I could have forgiven any thing but that humbugging note, in which you, or whoever *did* your history, says the chapter about that affair was writ before the affair happened.

Pen Owen. 'Pon honor it was.

Odoherty. Nay, nay, man ; a joke's a joke—but do you mean to say, that you thought of that quotation about " Cato's little senate," before the night you made your famous leap over the little back court behind Cato-street.

Pen Owen. What *do* you believe, Mr. Odoherty ?

Odoherty. I believe that any man may with impunity, (so far as a certain concern goes,) touch the King,—abuse the Lords,—blackguard the Commons,—and ruffianize the prime writers of the age and country ; but that vengeance will fall on his head if he dares but to lay his little finger on the smallest of Critics.

Feldborg. What ? call Baggesen the smallest of critics ? What for a joke ! Baggesen ? He that did compose *the glorious garland ?* Oh, what ignorance !

Odoherty. I meant not Baggesen—I talked of Jeffrey. Clap not thy wings so fiercely, Cock of the North.

Sir A. Wylie. What ? aye at the Sma' Known ? Will you never be done with your personalities about that gentleman ?

Tickler. Fie, Odoherty ! And after that beautiful rebuke of his, in his last number, which, I am sure, will shut Lord Byron's mouth for ever and a day.

Odoherty. As effectually as a prime pouldoodie of Burran† would shut my potato-trap for three seconds.

* Arthur Thistlewood, who had previously been acquitted on a charge of treason, and was discontented with the British Government, threw himself into what was called the Cato-street Conspiracy, and conspired to murder the Ministry, at a Cabinet-dinner at Lord Harrowby's, and thereon raise an insurrection in London. This was early in 1820, immediately on the accession of George IV., and a spy having revealed all that was done and intended, a party of police and soldiers went to arrest the conspirators. Thistlewood resisted, killed one of the police with a sword, escaped, was captured, tried, and condemned. Thistlewood and four others were executed, as traitors, on May 1, 1820.—One of the scenes in " Pen Owen" was marvellously like the actual scene in Cato-street.

† The Pouldoodies of Burran were a description of Irish oysters, anent which, Mrs. M'Whirter chanted a laudatory song, in presence of Christopher in the Tent, which see, *ante.*—M.

Dr. Wodrow. Well, now, I must say that I read that passage with delight; there is no doubt that Lord Byron is very much to blame, if it really be so, which I am no judge of, that he was the first who wrote in a personal manner. It was introducing a dangerous—a deadly trick. There's no saying where it may end yet. Christian folk should dwell together like brethren in unity. Oh! sirs, there's a deal of needless heart-burning and hot water among you literary folk of this time, take ye my word for that.

Dr. Scott. Ay, and so is there among the *illiterary folk* of this time, Dr. Wodrow—what say ye to your bickers in the aisle, oure bye yonder? My faith! you ministers and elders, ye're the most tinkler-tongued pack of illiterati, when ye begin your collieshangie.

Sir A. Wylie. Come, come, Odondist, you need not be so bitter, though you could not manage to get yourself returned for the University of St. Andrews this Assembly—but what is all this that you're saying? Does Mr. Jeffrey really charge Lord Byron with being the author and institutor of the sin of personality?

Tickler. "'Tis true, 'tis pity; and pity 'tis, 'tis true."

Dr. Scott, (*closely imitating Tickler in enunciation.*) 'Tis trash, 'tis certain; and certain 'tis, 'tis trash.

Pen Owen. I have not yet seen the last Number of the Edinburgh burgh Review—but if the Small Known has said so, he has certainly not a large memory.

Tickler. Alas, he will never have such a memory as Smithers!

Pen Owen. But I'm speaking in earnest. What, sir? Has Jeffrey forgot that he could once read without spectacles? Has he forgot that he was not always a dandy of sixty? Has he forgot how, from the beginning of his career, he abused SOUTHEY? Has he forgot how he lashed his friend, TOMMY MOORE? Was it not *personality* that pointed the path to Chalk Farm? Has he forgot *Thelwall?* Was there no personality in calling Thelwall *a Tailor?* Was there no personality in his attacks on COPPLESTON? Was there no personality in comparing Mr. DAVISON TO A RAT IN A GUTTER? Was there no personality in the lucubrations, concerning that patriotic, that most enlightened Peer, my Lord ELGIN? Was there no personality in that most flagitious insinuation concerning the birth of our late venerable venerated Sovereign?* Bah!—

North. Take your breath, young sir, and fill a bumper. The bottle is with you, and we would rather be excused waiting till you have done with such a catalogue as this.

Sir A. Wylie. I would be very sorry to interrupt Mr. Owen, but I would fain ask one question, for really and truly, sir, I'm to seek

* One of the scandals of the last century was, that George III. was son—not of Frederic Prince of Wales, but of the Earl of Bute. It was the influence of the Princess of Wales (Frederic's widow) that placed Lord Bute in the high office of Premier, (for which he was by no means adequate) shortly after George III. became king.—M.

in sic matters. Did Lord Byron ever write any thing personal about Mr. Jeffrey himSELF?

Tickler. Bravo! bravissimo! Rem acu tetigisti!

Odoherty. (*Sings.*)

" Vain is every fond endeavor
  To resist the gentle dart;
For examples move us never,
  We must feel to know the smart."
When the bard, in verse undying,
  Pays the Prose of the Review,
Vanity, her aid supplying,
  Bids them think it not their due.
CHORUS—Vanity, her sting supplying,
  Pokes the Yellow and the Blue.

North. Thank ye, Adjutant! But now there's been so much fighting about the bush, let's to the scratch with it at once. Mr. Pendarves Owen, what do you understand by the word *Personality?*

Pen Owen. I don't know—I can't well say. I suppose Jeffrey means, when he accuses Lord Byron of it, to allude to his cuts at Coleridge, and Southey, and Sotheby, and Wordsworth, and Bowles, and Sam Rogers, and the King, and so forth.

North. Sir, did you ever read a poem called "English Bards, and Scotch Reviewers?"

Pen Owen. I remember seeing such a thing in Mr. Mapletoft's library long ago, and glancing over it; but at that time I was young and ignorant, and took no interest in it. I understood very little about what was meant or insinuated.

North. Very likely; but still you can't have forgot the two great and general facts, that this poem was written by Lord Byron, and that it contains many most bitter pungent lines of personal satire against Hallam, Pillans, &c., and least not last, against Mr. Francis Jeffrey himself, whose birth is ridiculed, whose person is derided, whose genius is scorned, whose personal honor and courage even held up to utter and open contempt, and all this in a manner equally unmerited—unparalleled —

Tickler. (*Interrupts him.*) And unpardoned.

North. Ay, there's the rub! Look ye, it would take a bat not to see through the whole of this mighty millstone. The Edinburgh Reviewers (Jeffrey himself, 'tis generally supposed,*) began the row with a violent attack on Lord Byron's juvenile poems, in a review, in the conclusion of which there is certainly not a little *personality.* This is done in utter ignorance of Lord Byron's talents, in utter contempt of him, and all that pertains to him. Very well, Lord Byron writes and publishes the poetical satire of which we have been speak-

* Brougham is generally supposed to have written the article.—M.

ing, and the Edinburgh Reviewers are laughed at for several weeks all over England, Ireland, Scotland, and the town of Berwick-upon-Tweed, to say nothing of Yankeeland and Botany Bay. So far so well. But in a few years, out comes CHILDE HAROLD, and Lord Byron is at once placed *nem. con.* by the side of the first poets of our age. What a moment of mortification must that have been, when Mr. Francis Jeffrey first discovered whom he had to do with! Why, did you ever see a little slim greyhound, half the Surrey breed perhaps, attack a strong Yorkshire fox who had jumped up from the cover, when they were whipping for hares? Jeffrey was just in such a quandary. Down he goes on his knees, and worships the rising star. Puff! puff! puff!—nothing but puffing!—nothing but who shall puff the highest.

Sir A. Wylie. Under favor, ye're forgetting to mention that Lord Byron had been putting himself forrit as a Whig also.

North. True—but I don't make much of that in this particular instance. Lord Byron, however, does not intimate any particular sensibility in his olfactory nerves, to the stimulus of the Blue and Yellow incense.

Tickler. Censer and censure, sir, came alike to him;—he was incensed by their very incense.

Dr. Scott. He became quite the rage with them; yet his rage waxeth not cool, neither was his anger appeased.

Dr. Wodrow. O, that Chaldee! it has spoiled even the Odontist.

North. On proceeds "Byron my Baron," meantime, in his glorious, but not stainless, any more than gainless career. The critics of the English press in general applaud, as they ought to do, his rising and resplendent genius; but many, very many of them, at least, have the candor and the justice to complain of the immoral, irreligious, and unpatriotic tendency of too many of his productions. Two only, and these the two highest authorities, are silent as to the faults of the splendid sinner. The Quarterly Cerberus had got a sop—and as for the Edinburgh, what think ye kept its mouth mum?

Odoherty. Could it be our old acquaintance, "Corporal Fear?"

Tickler. I am inspired. *Anch'io improvisatore.* I shall tip you an *extempore* Parody on one of Mrs. Pilkington's old favorites. (*Aside*) —You all remember "Stella, darling of the Muses."

Jeffrey, darling of the Muses,
   Strong probation now we bring;
Knowingly, the poet chooses,
   Who of thee essays to sing.
While his keen derision traces
   Every fault of form or mind,
He gets on in thy good graces—
   Stings, but leaves no wound behind.

(*Plaudite Omnes.*)

Omnes (sing.)

"Very good song,
Very well sung,
Jolly companions every one," &c. &c. &c.

Rev. Dr. Wodrow. Well, I never was in such a company as this since I was ordained. Why it beats Presbytery dinners, Moderator's breakfasts, and even settlement-occasions, a' to nothing. The mist's just clearing away from my eyes every moment! How I'll enlighten the Baillies when I win back to the Manse.

Dr. Scott. Haud your tongues! Haud your tongues! Do ye no see how the chairman's drinking three bumpers all by himsel? (*Aside*)—He's clearing his pipes, I'se warrant. Od, how he's glowering on yon decanter!

North. Revenons a nos moutons! Childe Harold raved with impunity against Talavera, Wellington, and the Bible. Lord Byron insulted with impunity the most complete gentleman that has sat on the English throne since the time of Charles I., and this too in the most offensive way. He insulted his Prince by meddling with his domestic affairs—Lord Byron insulted all England in Beppo—Beppo was lauded—He flung the insults with tenfold vigor from the luscious lip of Don Juan—Don Juan was never alluded to, except once or twice, in the way of commending its *style*—and even so it goes on, until at length, after five or six years of silence, and utter forbearance, the Edinburgh Review does pluck up courage—and to do what?

Omnes. What?

North. To say feebly what had been said strongly by fifty other people—to say late what should have been said early, or never said at all—to creep out under the shadow, and in the rear of Universal-Indignation—and, making a big mouth, stammer out a single, silly, senile, insignificant sarcasm!—(*Hear! hear!*)

Odoherty. It puts me in mind of a thing I once saw at Doncaster.—I was sitting in the inn there with the landlady—a pretty, comely body, I assure ye—and through came Reynard, and all Lord Darlington's hounds in full cry at his tail. A little puppy dog—a queer, odd, grim-looking thing belonging to the landlady, was sitting close beside us, on the end of the sofa. It stared like a stuck pig, till the last red-coat was passing, and then out with a small frightened snarl—I thought at first it had smelt a mouse behind the wainscot.

Dr. Scott. Mr. North, this is very good claret—I make no objections to the claret—but really I cannot thole it, it is so very cold.

(*Sings*)—Fill me a bowl—a mighty bowl,
Large as my capacious soul,
Vast as my thirst is; let it have
Depth enough to be my grave—

I mean the grave of all my care,
For I intend to bury't there.
Let it a bowl of China be,
Worthy of punch composed by me,
To drown pale cant and fat humbug,
And stretch a Tory on the rug.
Fill me a bowl, &c. [*Enter* PUNCH.]

North. Tip us a blast of the trombone, or the Gaelic sermon, or any thing you like—Do make yourself agreeable.

Odoherty. The Instrumentality or the Parsonality ?—Both are at your service.

Omnes. The Parsonality! the Parsonality!

[*Odoherty gives a fac simile of a Gaelic sermon. While he is performing, exit, unobserved, the* REV. DR. WODROW.]

North. What! bless me the minister's off, I think.

Sir A. Wylie. Ay, ay, just gang round the company. Rub every one's shins, and ye'll have a toom table belyve. I'se warrant the Doctor will be concocting an overture against personality, ere lang be.

Pen Owen. What! the reverend divine could not stand that little shadow of a shade of personality? Bah! if he had been an Edinburgh Reviewer, he would have been as tender in the skin as any Small Known among them all.

North. Heaven preserve us! I believe nothing will put down this accursed cant but a thumping folio disquisition. I shall certainly, when I die, bequeath to the world a regular treatise *de re personali.*

Tickler. Proving that every person had been personal, as well as Byron and Jeffrey?

North. To be sure—To begin with the blind old Mæonian—Does any body doubt his Thersites is a lump of personality? Without question, Polyphemus was a sore wipe against some purblind, bloody-minded reviewer of his day. But why talk of Homer? Has not the Stagyrite told us that his last poem, the MARGITES, stood to the old Greek Comedy in the same relation in which the Iliad and Odyssey did to the old Greek Tragedy?—And what was the old Greek Comedy?

Pen Owen. —— "Comœdia prisca VIRORUM est!"

North. True! 'tis a manly comedy; but what is it but a string of personalities? There is not one line in all Aristophanes that is not personal.

Pen Owen. Aristophanes was, I suppose, just what Jeffrey says SWIFT was, "nothing but a great libeller."

North. Yes, and yet you see this same critic, who, four years ago, said "Swift was nothing but a great libeller," has now thought proper to say that personality was a thing unknown until Lord Byron set the example.

Pen Owen. It looks like a contradiction—but go on with your sketch of the great treatise *in posse*, however.

North. Is Horace not personal in his satires? He is so in every line of *them*, and in half his odes to boot. Was not Virgil abominably personal about the old soldier that got his bonnet-lairdship? Is there no personality in Cicero's Philippics, or in his master, Demosthenes? or in Sallust? or in Tacitus? By Jupiter Tonans, you might as well say that Jeffrey had began the sin of charlatanism as that any man now living began that of personality.

Sir A. Wylie. Weel, weel, but I would like to hear ye on some authors that we hae heard mair about than thae auld heathen Greeks and Romans.

North. Swift we have already heard of. You know Shakspeare owed his rise in life and letters to a song which he wrote against a Warwickshire Justice of the Peace. And *Justice Shallow* is altogether a personal attack on the same worthy body. Ben Jonson was a perfect Turk for personality—his whole life was past in hot water.—*Vide* D'Israeli!—Why should I allude to the Greens and the Nashes?

Tickler. These fellows were always at cat and dog—quite *more recentiorum.*

North. Nay, nay, forbid that we should be quite so bad as that *ætas avorum!* I would rather die upon a pile of blazing Magazines, like Sardanapalus on his throne, than write one word within one million of miles of the personalities of Milton—the divine Milton—against Salmasius!

Dr. Scott. Keep us a'! Is that the same great gospel-gun that wrote the Paradise Lost, that the Spectautor speaks sae muckle about?

Pen Owen. The same, the same. Bah! 'tis all fudge, and fudge fusty—as fusty as Benthamism.

North. Come down to the polite era of Charles II. Is there no personality in Dryden? or rather, is there any thing else in half his most eternal master-pieces? Is there no personality in Butler's Hudibras, nor in Cowley's Cutter of Coleman-street? Or take the glorious days of Queen Anne. There's Swift for one, and there's Pope. I suppose we've all heard of such a thing as the Dunciad. There's one Arbuthnot too—he wrote a work called the History of *John Bull*—that is commonly supposed to be something personal, I believe.

Dr. Scott. As bad as the present John Bull?

North. Yes, very truly, nearly as bad, and indeed rather worse, I take it; inasmuch as John Duke of Marlborough was rather a greater man than the present John Duke of Bedford; and inasmuch likewise, as to be a WHIG was not quite so bad a thing a hundred years ago, thank God! as it is now.

Pen Owen. But in those days there were no reviews nor magazines.

North. True, but they came not long after, and personality, which no literature ever was without, blended itself with them *ab ovo.* Is it possible that you have need for ME to tell you all the old stories about Samuel Johnson and Ossian Macpherson and the oak cudgel? or about Dr. Smollett and the Critical? and Fielding? How he kept the Thames on fire with his farces and novels, and roasted all his brother justices to cinders?

Tickler. Why, you know, all the old novelists dealt in nothing but personalities; about *that* there was *no* manner of dispute. The only question was, not whether there were a real Morgan or a real Trunnion, but *which* of the author's competing friends had sat for the *portrait.*

North. Just so; and to tell you the truth, I'm really sick of such hackneyed truths—you may just trace personality as distinctly as stupidity, down the whole line of our Whig literature in particular. Turn over D'Israeli's nice little books, if you have doubts—The Quarrels of Authors above all—

Nocturnâ versate manu, versate diurnâ.

Tickler. Once landed in our own times, we can be at no great loss to find our way. Plenty of fine staring finger-posts as one moves along. The Fudge Family, a production of one of the most charming Whigs that ever breathed—and a more disloyal piece of Whiggery was never written, even by that charming Whig,—stands pretty visible yonder against the sky.

Pen Owen. Yes, the black and lowering sky of disgustful remembrance.

Tickler. The Twopenny Post-bag! 'Tis sufficient to mention the name of such a bag of poison—base brutal poison. Hone's nice little books, (worthy man! the Whigs subscribed for *him*, you know, as well as for Gerald—I hope the money did *him* much good!) The Morning Chronicle, with so many of Tom Moore's songs against kings and ladies introduced into it by good Mr. Perry, whom Sir James Mackintosh so disinterestedly lauded in the House of Commons. The Old Times, stinking of Cockney radicalism and Cockney personality in every column—there's no want of landmarks to guide one along the *mare magnum* of Whiggish ruffianism.

Sir A. Wylie. And after a' this poor Lord Byron must be charged, forsooth, with beginning the vice o' personality. Oh dear! what a thumper!

North. The fact is, that Lord Byron, instead of being the sole personal libeller, is only a unit in the Whig array, whereof Mr. Jeffrey himself is another unit—and if the question were, which of these two is the more deserving of the title of *leader* in such work, I protest I think I should have no difficulty in giving my vote to the commoner. I beg leave to propose the memory of Dr. Jonathan Swift, Dean of St. Patrick.

Omnes. Dean Swift!!! (*Music without.—Air, Diogenes, surly and proud.*)

Odoherty (*sings.*)*

'Tis not when on turtle and venison dining,
And sipping Tokay at the cost of his Grace;
Like the plate on his sideboard, I'm set to be shining—
(So nearly a mug may resemble a face.)
This is not the dinner for me—a poor sinner;
Where I'm bound to show off, and throw pearls before swine.
Give me turnips and mutton,—(I ne'er was a glutton)—
Good friends and good liquor—and *here* let me dine.

Your critic shows off, with his snatches and tastes
Of odd trash from Reviews, and odd sorts of odd wine;
Half a glass—half a joke—from the Publisher's stock
Of Balaam and Hock, are but trash, I opine.
Convérsazioni—are not for my money,
Where Blue Stockings prate about Wylie and Pen;
I'd rather get tipsy with *ipsissimi ipsi*—
Plain women must yield to plain sense and plain men.

Your dowager gives you good dinners, 'tis true;
She shines in liqueurs, and her Sherry's antique;
But then you must swear by her eye's lovely blue,
And adore the bright bloom that is *laid* on her cheek.
Blue eyes in young faces are quite in their places;
One praises and gazes with boundless delight
And juvenile roses ne'er trespass on noses,
As the custom of those is, I've cut for to-night.

Your colonels talk but of a siege or a battle—
Your merchants of naught but the course of exchange—
Your squires, of their hounds, of the corn-bill or cattle—
Your doctors their cases and cures will arrange-
Your lawyer's confounding, on multiple poinding—
Your artists are great on expression and tone—
Parsons sport *Moderators* and *Church-procurators*,
Each set is the devil when feeding alone.

But *here*, where all sets and all topics are mingled—
The hero—the dentist—the parson—the squire—
No *one* branch of blarney's selected or singled,—
But our wine and our wit each discussion inspire;
Where the pun and the glass simultaneously pass;
Where each song seems quite heavenly, each bumper divine;
Where there's drinking and smoking, and quizzing and joking,
But nothing provoking—HERE! HERE! let me dine.

(*Here! here!*)

* This song was written by Dr. Maginn.—M.

Pen Owen. Talking of Dean Swift,—what is Mr. Maturin about?

Odoherty. Grinding, grinding! Isn't it a shame for people to run him down at such a rate? and the man a Tory—an Aristocrat—a well-dressed gentleman-like author! 'Tis abominable. 'Tis too bad to think of such a man being poor, and you know he complained of it himself in his preface.*

Pen Owen. Mr. Odoherty, I don't mean to defend the Quarterly—but did you never take a wipe at Mother Morgan yourself?

Odoherty. I believe I may have done such a thing—But how different the case: why that little *çidevant Miladi* absolutely brags of her cash,† and sets off public reprobation with a balance of pounds, shillings, and pence.

Tickler. Her motto is, no doubt—

> "Populus me sibilat: at mihi plaudo,
> Ipsa domi, simul ac nummos contemplor in arcâ."

But did not Maturin write something called the Universe?

Odoherty. *That* has reached long ago the uttermost ends of the earth—but why allude to such things? when are we to have the Southside Papers?

Tickler. Why, I am kept back by a late decision. I fear the judge who refuses his protection to Byron's *Cain*, would scarcely take my *rattan* under his wing.

Sir A. Wylie. Gentlemen, I've sat here a long while, and been greatly diverted with many things I've heard, and edified with some —but the Chancellor, I have the honor to say, is my friend, and I must quit the company, if I hear any thing further in a similar strain. Besides, he was perfectly right in that decision.

Pen Owen. Multum dubito.

Odoherty (*aside to Pen Owen.*) You had better not enter into any dispute with Sir Andrew. Not much flash, but the longest Scotch head I am acquainted with. And his humor,—why even you might find him ill to deal with.

* The Rev. Robert Charles Maturin lived and died a curate in the richest Church Establishment in the world—that of Ireland. He was a native of Dublin, and was curate of St. Peter's Church, in that city. A limited income, which always kept him in difficulties, led him to proffer his tragedy of "Bertram," to the management of Drury Lane Theatre. It was accepted, acted, (Kean playing the hero), and brought Maturin £500. Another of his plays, called "Montorio," was offered to John Kemble, by Scott, (who took a strong and kind interest in Maturin). but nothing advantageous came from it. He also wrote the tragedies of "Manuel" and "Fredolpho," the wild romance—as interesting as any of Mrs. Radcliffe's—called "Melmoth, the Wanderer," a novel, entitled "Woman, or Pour et Contre," and a poem called "The Universe." He published three other novels, very popular in their day: "The Fatal Revenge," "The Wild Irish Boy," and "The Milesian Chief;"—these three appeared with the name of Dennis Jasper Murphy on the title-page. In 1824, the year before he died, Maturin published six "Controversial Sermons," which exhibit him as a well-read scholar and an acute reasoner. Poverty was ever at the heels of this gifted man, whose private character was excellent.—M.

† Lady Morgan's receipts from literature cannot have been less than £25,000. Besides this, for many years past, she had a pension of £300 a-year from the British Government.—M.

Pen Owen. You are right. He is indeed a canny clever Scotchman. *Entre nous* THE KING was delighted with his book. You may depend upon this. I heard him say so myself.

Tickler. I have been much interested by your delightful description of a certain beautiful creature, Mr. Owen? Have you and Mrs. O. any family, by-the-by?

Pen Owen. Three —

Odoherty. You mean *volumes*—and if so, I can tell you very seriously, the third is the best of the batch.

Pen Owen. To be candid, what is your opinion of my book?

Odoherty. Your book is a jewel; but if you had happened to be a Scotsman, and writ such a book about Scotland, and Scots people, you might just as well have leaped from the top of the Monument as published it.

Pen Owen. Why? I assure you, I wrote the book in the greatest possible good nature.

Odoherty. Devil doubts you. I dare say Hogg was never in half such a benign disposition, as he was when he wrote THE CHALDEE.

Pen Owen. Satire is upon the whole a good-humored vice, in my opinion.

Odoherty. 'Tis in my estimation the most placid of virtues. Pick me up some day with a face like a lemon rind—hazy—dumpish—sulky—bitter—perhaps just escaped from a detestable dun of a tailor, or a dozen of prating whiglings or the like—and take me into the nearest tavern. Order a hot beef-steak, a rummer of brandy and water—bring out a good pen and a few sheets of hot-pressed paper, and a bundle of segars, and say, "At it, Odoherty! Up with your back, Adjutant!"

Pen Owen. What follows?

Odoherty. A calm! a perfect Claude, the most beautiful, serene, delightful, dewy atmosphere, spreads its wide embracing canopy over all the troubled surface of my soul. My spirit, enshrined as it were in the divine depths of contemplation, exerts her energies sweetly, nobly, sublimely! It is then that I comprehend how true to nature and to virtue is the exquisite apostrophe of the Epicurean bard—

> "Suave mari magno, turbantibus æquora ventis,
> Ex tuto alterius longum spectare laborem."

On the whole, I consider Tom Cribb and myself as the two best-natured men in Britain!

Pen Owen. Well, now, I confess 'twas not in that high-placed vein I composed my most cutting chapters. I have sometimes wakened of a morning, God knows how or why, in a strange mixed state of feeling—ready to go any lengths, in short—up to any thing—utterly reckless—that's all I can say about the matter—deuced good fun!

Odoherty. Ay, but how inferior that is to the chosen "moods of MY mind?" On such occasions, it may almost be said I would not harm a fly.

Pen Owen. The scope and tendency of some of your observations perplex me.

North. I hate this sort of committee business. We're all getting into knots and corners. Owen and the Adjutant upon satire and segars—Feldborg and the Odontist on the Czar of Muscovy's tooth-powder—Tickler dozing—and Sir Andrew Wylie and myself left quite alone to the great topic of things in general! Why, this will never do.

Dr. Scott, (*tapping his spoon against the side of the bowl, sings.*)

Jolly Tories, fill your glasses,
Odoherty (*sings.*) Hear the tinkle on the rim.
Tickler (*sings.*) All the Whigs are geese and asses.
North (*sings.*) Hollow heart and vision dim!
Chorus.—Fa! la! la! la! la! la! la! la! &c.

Feldborg, the Dane. Allow me to give you a little Scandinavian solo.

North. (*Knocking with his hammer.*) Silence! Feldborg's solo.

Feldborg (*sings.*)

Hvern morgin ser horna,
Hlock a tems—àr backa,
Skala hanga ma hungra,
Hrae—shod litud blodi
Hre sigr—fickin saekir,
Snarla borgar karla
Dynr a Brezkar bryniur
Blod is Dana visi!!!
Dynr a Brezkar, &c.

North. Come, it suits you very well, after what happened not quite fifty years ago, to sing such a ditty as this.

Dr. Scott. Keep us a'! Do you ken what he was singing? I thought it was Danish or Dutch at the lowest penny.

North. The last two lines, being interpreted, signify,

"The King of Denmark's bloody hail
Resounds against the British mail."

Is it not so, Professor?

Feldborg. I suffer this no longer! Golt und Teufel! I quit the Nomber. [*Exit* FELDBORG.

North. Why, this is beyond all bearing! Tickler, you are a new-married man,—you are or ought to be nimble,—run after the Dane, and recall him.

Tickler. Sir, do you suppose that because I'm a contributor, an editor has a right to cast personal reflections upon me? to rend away the veil of my domestic concerns?—Sir, I scorn your sneers!—Sir, your servant!—Good night, gentlemen.

[*Exit* TICKLER, *furiosus.*

Odoherty. Ye gods! How infernally drunk Tickler has been these two hours! Honest Tickler! he too, to be up!

> Timotheus placed on high,
> Amid the sounding quire!!!

I suppose the next thing will be Sir Andrew Wylie bolting upon some absurd allusion to his autobiography.

Sir A. Wylie. Mr. Odoherty,—I beg your pardon, *Captain* Odoherty! I crave leave to say, ance for a', that, although my life fill three volumes, and yours but seven pages, mine does not contain any narrative, either of seeking after a snuff-box in the midst of a battle, or of marrying the mistress of a chop-house, and escaping as soon as the till was sucked*—do you take me?

Dr. Scott. Life in a mussel! Weel said, Sir Andrew—stick it into him. A foul-mouthed creature! Clink down with sic clanjamphray!

Odoherty. (*Showing a lemon cut into a caricature of* SIR ANDREW.) Do you know that phiz, Mr. Baronet?

Sir A. Wylie, (*Throwing down his card.*) Mr. Ensign, there's my address. Good night, gentlemen. [*Exit* SIR A. WYLIE.

Dr. Scott, (*Aside to North.*) Od sauf us! How Sir Andrew's staggering! Your last bowl has clean done him! I maun just see him as far as Maclean's; for if he were to be ta'en up to the Police Office, it would never answer—him an Elder, too, ye ken.

[*Exit* DR. SCOTT.

North. So, Odoherty, we're left almost to ourselves. I think the nature and effects of personality have been decently discussed this evening, however. I hope nothing of what has happened will ever transpire. Pen Owen, I think, is asleep.

Odoherty. Snoring. But, Lord love ye, I've a short-hand writer behind that screen yonder. Every word is down. 'Twill make a prime article; and you knew it would, else we should not have dined here to-day; but as LUTTRELL says,

> " O, that there might in England be
> A duty on Hypocrisy,

* In the brief account of the Life and Writings of Odoherty, in *Blackwood's Magazine,* which first introduced the Standard-bearer to the reading public, these two incidents *were* mentioned, I confess. Odoherty, who was in the 44th infantry, in the battle of New Orleans, unfortunately was prevented from participating in that contest, having been delayed in search of a much valued snuff-box, which he had mislaid. What of that?—Colonel Mullins, commanding the 44th, was brought to a court-martial for like absence, (like Colonel, like Ensign) and broke. The other little accident referred to by Sir Andrew, in which Mrs. M'Whirter, late of Philadelphia, was a fair participant, was fully explained—as the reader of " Christopher in The Tent," in this volume, may have seen, and if the explanation satisfied the lady, why should Sir Andrew Wylie cast a reproach in Odoherty's face?—M.

A tax on Humbug, an excise
On solemn plausibilities,
A stamp on every man that canted!
No millions more, if these were granted,
Henceforward would be raised or wanted;
But Van, with an o'erflowing chest,
Might soon forgive us all the rest."*

North. Well, I think the reporter must be dry enough by this time. Come forth, thou rat i' the arras! You shall have your share of one bowl at the least;—and thou, heir of Cym Owen, rouse thee! rouse thee for the field! [*Curtain falls.*

Epilogue.

Spoken by CHRISTOPHER NORTH, *Esquire, and* SIR A. WYLIE, *Baronet.*

Mr. North. "Something too much of this!" I hear you cry—
Ye canting creeping vermin! What care I?
If Whigs there be (methinks there *must* be some)
Not in their secret souls the slaves of Hum,
Let them for once speak truly!
Sir A. Wylie. ———or be dumb.
Mr. North. Confess it, Jeffrey, (for you needs must know)
That Jest and Earnest hand in hand may go,
That sober truth may be inweaved with fun,
Philosophy be pointed in a pun,
Candor be calm beneath a forehead knit—
Keenly, yet kindly, flash the shafts of wit—
Sir A. Wylie. ———And Tories round a harmless table sit.
Mr. North. Confess; speak out, man!
Sir A. Wylie. ——Once upon a time
You loved a joke yourself, if not a rhyme!
Mr. North. Confess quaint Quizzery, though it makes one wince
Sir A. Wylie. —I bar what wounds a LADY or a PRINCE.—
Mr. North. —Is, after all, not quite a hanging matter!
—What, Jeffrey? Not one word for poor dear Satire?
Sir A. Wylie. Well, well, I wish ye wiser, man, and fatter!
Mr. North. I find I can make nothing of these Whigs.
Sir A. Wylie. We'll try to do without them, please the Pigs!
Mr. North. To you, to you, ye Tories of the land!
To you we turn, with you we take our stand!
Not you, ye "PLUCKLESS," who, when things look blue,
Distrust a cause sublime in spite of you,
Abandon those who bear the blazing brunt,
And fight, ye fools, your battle in your front—
No—ne'er to court your favor shall we stoop,
Nor fawn for shelter where your crestless eagles droop,

* See Letters to Julia, second edition, p. 104. By-the-by, these elegant letters are much improved in the second edition. The book is now quite a bijou.—C. N. [Luttrell, one of the most sparkling wits of his time, who may be reproached with not having written enough.—M.]

To shun the conflict but hold fast the spoil—
Clutch at the trophy, having shirk'd the toil—

Sir A. Wylie. —And gloat, while others sweat, on your snug roast and boil!

Mr. North. These are your maxims! Venal vapid crew!
Low we may come, but ne'er so low as YOU!
"Low we may come!" forgive the hasty phrase,
YE Tories true! whose patronage IS praise!
High the good eminence we now possess,
Nor shall we e'er be lower down—

Sir A. Wylie, (*loosening a fifth button.*) ——Or less—

Mr. North. While YOU our trumpet hear, and round our banner press.

Both. Though gourdish scions of the "*Servum Pecus,*"
Rise as if glare should dim or weight should break us,
Like some tough tree these pithless boughs between,
Knotted and gnarled, appears THE Magazine!
Some last one summer; some, with much ado,
Spin out a speechless Life-in-Death through two;
But wanting depth of soil, and length of root,
Though buds a few and blossoms they may shoot,
One looks in vain to them for genuine juicy fruit,
Squeeze hard! One painful mouthful they supply,
But thirsty wits must turn to US, or die!

No. IV.—JULY, 1822.

SCENE—*Transferred* (*by poetic license*) *to Pisa.**

Odoherty, (*solus.*) Jupiter strike me! but that cabbage soup and roasted raisins is an infernal mixture—Blow all Italian cookery, say I. Every thing is over-done here—how inferior to the Carlingford!† The dishes done to rags.

Enter WAITER.

Waiter. Milordo, here is questo grand Lord is come, for to have the onore of kissing the manos for sua eccellenza.

Odoherty. Kissing my what? Show in the shaver—hand him in upon a clean plate. [*Exit Waiter.*

Enter LORD BYRON.

Byron. Mr. Doherty,—I trust I—

Odoherty. Odoherty, if you please, sir.

Byron. Mr. Odoherty, I have to beg pardon for this intrusion—but really, hearing you were to remain but this evening in Pisa, I could not deny myself the pleasure of at least seeing a gentleman of whom I have heard and read so much—I need scarcely add, that I believe myself to be in the presence of THE Odoherty.

Odoherty. You may say that; but, may I take the liberty of asking, who you are yourself?

* A large portion of the preceding Noctes were written by Maginn, but that which followeth (to wit, No. IV.) is entirely from his pen. It has so many actual points of *vraisemblance*, that even Byron himself is said to have exclaimed, after reading it, "By Jupiter! the fellow has me down regularly, in black and white." The scene was laid in Pisa, whither Byron had removed in the autumn of 1821, and remained until September, 1822, when he went to Genoa, and thence, in 1823, to Greece.—The mention of this reminds me, by the way, of what the Guiccioli said, in her visit to London; when she was so lionized as having been the lady-love of Byron. She was rather fond of speaking on the subject, designating herself by some Venetian pet phrase which certainly was not to be found in any dictionary, but which she interpreted as meaning "Love-wife." At Pisa, he had been sounded on the subject of going to Greece, where it was believed he had immense wealth, where it was known that he loved the country, and had written warmly in its favor. He was undecided. Again and again he was solicited, each time more strongly. At last, he sportively said to the Guiccioli, "Let fourteen captains come and ask me to go, and go I will." "Ah," said the dama, "there are not fourteen Greek captains in Italy; now I know that you will remain." She mentioned, to show how slight the chance was of his leaving Italy, what he said. As it was known that he strictly adhered to his word, on all occasions, a letter was written to Greece, and fourteen captains actually were sent out. They waited on him, pressed him to go, backing their request with letters from Prince Mavrocardato, (who offered to resign his leadership in favor of Byron,) and the result was that, what he had playfully said, being taken for earnest, he believed he could not honorably get out of it. The result was—his departure for Greece in August, 1823.—M.

† A hotel in Dublin.—M.

Byron. My name's Byron.

Odoherty. Byron! Lord Byron! God bless you, my dear fellow. Sure I was a blockhead not to know you at first sight. Waiter! waiter! waiter! I say. They don't understand even plain English in this house!

Enter WAITER.

Waiter. Milordo!

Odoherty. Instantaneously a clean glass—if you have any thing clean in this filthy country—and, my lord, what will you drink? I drink every thing bating water.

Byron. Why, Mr. Odoherty, to be plain with you—you will find but poor accommodation in these Italian inns—and I should, therefore, recommend you to come with me to my villa.* You will meet fellows there—asses of the first water—native, and stranger, whom you can cut-up, quiz, and humbug without end.

Odoherty. With deference, my lord, I shall stay where I am—I never knew any place where a man was so much at home as in a tavern, no matter how shy. Ho! waiter.

Waiter. Milordo!

Odoherty. What-a have-a you-a to drink-a, in this damned house-a of yours? (*Aside*.)—I suppose to make the fellow understand, I must speak broken English.

[*Lord Byron whispers waiter, who exit; and after a moment returns with two flasks of Montifiascone.*†

Byron. Fill, Mr. Odoherty. Your health, sir; and welcome to Italy.

Odoherty. Your health, my lord; and I wish we both were out of it. But this stuff is by no means so bad as I expected. What do you call it?

Byron. Lacryma Christi.‡

Odoherty. Lacryma Christi! A pretty name to go to church with! Very passable stingo—though Inishowen is, after all, rather stiffer drinking.

Byron. Inishowen! What's that?

Odoherty. Whisky, made in the hills about Inishowen, in the north.‖

* In July, 1822, Byron and Shelley had their town-residences at Pisa. Byron had a *villeggiatara* (or country house) at Mont Nero, near Leghorn—Shelley's was at Lerici. Byron's Pisan dwelling was the Casa Lanfranchi, (on the river Arno, which runs through the city,) and is said to have been built by Michael Angelo. It was in this palace that Byron gave rooms to Leigh Hunt and his family, and here the first number of The Liberal was prepared.—M.

† This I take to be a mistake. They were in the region of Montepulciano, which Rêdi, (in his "Bacco in Toscano") has pronounced to be The King of Wines.—It is a pleasant tipple, smelling like a fresh nosegay, but, unfortunately, does not bear transportation. It must be drunk, not only in Italy, but in the very district where it is made.—M.

‡ There are *two* wines bearing this name. One is light-colored, like Hock, with a flavor something like aërated lemonade and sherry,—weak and sweet. The other (chiefly made in Sicily) has a ruby tint, is rough to the taste, being nothing more nor less than an Italian port-wine. This red Lacryma Christi is much used in England to adulterate the Portuguese port-wine. The sweet, pale Lacryma, mixed with an equal portion of good brandy, used to make a passable libation.—M.

‖ Of Ireland.—M.

General Hart patronizes it much. Indeed the Lord Chancellor, old Manners, is a great hand at it.

Byron. I cannot exactly say I recognize whom you speak of; nor did I ever hear of the liquor.

Odoherty. Why, then, I wrote rather a neat song about it once on a time, which I shall just twist off for the edification of your lordship.

Odoherty (*sings.*)

1.

I care not a fig for a flagon of flip.
  Or a whistling can of rumbo;
But my tongue through whisky punch will slip
  As nimble as Hurlothrumbo.
So put the spirits on the board,
  And give the lemons a squeezer,
And we'll mix a jorum, by the Lord!
  That will make your worship sneeze, sir.

2.

The French, no doubt, are famous souls,
  I love them for their brandy;
In rum and sweet tobacco rolls,
  Jamaica men are handy.
The big-breech'd Dutch in juniper gin,
  I own, are very knowing;
But are rum, gin, brandy, worth a pin,
  Compared with Inishowen?

Extempore verse additional.

Though here with a Lord, 'tis jolly and fine,
  To tumble down Lacryma Christi,
And over a skin of Italy's wine
  To get a little misty;
Yet not the blood of the Bourdeaux grape,
  The finest grape-juice going,
Nor clammy Constantia, the pride of the Cape,
  Prefer I to Inishowen.

Byron. Thank ye, Mr. Odoherty. Oh! by Jupiter, you have not been flattered; you are a prince of good-fellows; ay, and of good-looking fellows.

Odoherty. The same compliment I may pay you, my Lord. I never saw you before. By-the-by, you look much older than the print which Murray gave me when I was up at the Coronation.

Byron. Ah! then you know Murray? Murray is an excellent fellow. Not such a bookseller between the Apennine and the Grampian.

Odoherty. Always excepting Ebony, my Lord?

Byron. How is Ebony? I'm told he's been getting fat since I saw him.

Odoherty. A porpoise. No wonder, my lord; let them fatten who win. As for laughing, that you know, we may all screw a mouth to.

Byron. On the same principle, my old friend Jeffrey must be thinning apace.

Odoherty. A perfect whipping-post. But I have not seen the little man this some time. I don't think he goes much into public—his book I know does not.

Byron. Have you been in London lately, Mr. Odoherty?

Odoherty. O yes, past through about a fortnight ago. But let me request your Lordship to sink the *mister* entirely, and call me by my name quite plain—Odoherty, as it is.

Byron. Certainly, Odoherty, as you wish it—but you in return must sink the Lord, and let me be plain Byron.

Odoherty. To be sure, Byron. Hunt, you know, called you "Dear Byron" some years ago in a dedication;* and if you would allow the familiarity of a poor devil of a Cockney editor of a sneaking Sunday paper, you would be squeamish indeed, if you wanted to be Lorded by me. And yet, after all, Le Hunto is a cleverer fellow than most of the Cockneys.

Byron. He's worth fifty Hoggs. These *plebs* occasionally write good verses.

Odoherty. I shan't give up Hogg. Have you seen his last work?

Byron. His *last* work! I am glad to hear it has come at length.

Odoherty. It is quite a Chaldee.

Byron. Oh! that's his *first* work. Seriously, however, I have heard nothing of him since your good-humored notice of his Life in Blackwood.†

Odoherty. Thank you, Baron! I take you. By-the-by, what a right good poem that was of yours, on old Bam Rogers.‡ You and I may leave off quizzing one another. We at least are too much up to trap. But the old banker was as mad as blazes about it.

* The poem of "Rimini" was dedicated to Byron, by Leigh Hunt, who commenced what he had to say in prose with the words "My dear Byron." Many years after, when Byron's books came to be examined, after his death, it was found that the words "My dear Byron" had been marked out, with ink, and "Impudent Varlet," in his Lordship's own hand-writing, written opposite!—M.

† In the summer of 1821, there appeared in Edinburgh, a third edition of Hogg's "Mountain Bard," with an auto-biography. In *Blackwood*, for August, 1821, appeared a critique upon this Memoir, in which the Shepherd's adventures were greatly ridiculed—particularly one sentence, on which he positively asserted that he had written The Chaldee Manuscript, and another in which he affirmed that *Blackwood's Magazine* was an original suggestion of his own. It was a savage, slaughtering article, but Christopher North insisted (in Maga), that Hogg himself had written it, to gain notoriety!—M.

‡ A set of dogrel rhymes, in which Rogers was complimented as possessing, among other personal advantages,

"Features that would shame a knocker."

The story goes, that when Rogers visited Byron in Italy, the noble bard placed the satire, as aforesaid, under the sofa-cushion on which the banker-bard reposed, and chuckled at the idea of his sitting, as it were, on a sort of literary volcano!—M.

Byron. Non mi ricordo. I was in a state of civilation* when I wrote it—if indeed I did ever write such a thing.

Odoherty. 'Twas Wordsworth told me of it, and I doubt he's given to humbugging much.

Byron. Oh! the old Ponder! The great god Pan! is he extant still?

Odoherty. Alive and sulky. He has been delivered of two octavos this spring.

Byron. So have I, for that matter. Are his as heavy as mine?

Odoherty. The Giants' Causeway to a two-year old paving-stone—thundering fellows, about Roman Catholic Emancipation, which he has dished into little sonnets. Yours, however, were lumpish enough, in the name of Nicholas.

Byron. The sale, at least, was *heavy.*

Odoherty. Your tributary, his Majesty, the Emperor of the West, grumbled like a pig in the fits, I suppose.

Byron. Come, come, no personalities on this side of the Alps.

Odoherty. Satan reproving sin. That's pretty from you—the bottle's out—after what Jeffrey has said of you—call for another—in the last number of the Edinburgh—fill your glass—of the Edinburgh Review. No bad bottle this.

Byron. Why, Odoherty, you and I may joke, but such fellows as these to be preaching about Cain, and canting about Don Juan is too bad. I once thought Jeffrey had a little brains, but now I see he is quite an old woman.

Odoherty. Nay, by the eternal frost, and that's as great an oath as if I swore by the holy bottle, I agree with Jeff on this point. I don't care a cracked jews-harp about him in general; but here, faith, I must say I think him quite right. Consider, my lord—consider, I say, what a very immortal work Don Juan is—how you therein sport with the holiest ties—the most sacred feelings—the purest sentiments. In a word, with every thing—the bottle is with you—with every thing which raises a man above a mere sensual being. I say, consider this, and you will not wonder so much that all England is in an outcry against it, as that Murray, surrounded with the rums and buzzes of parsons as he is, should have the audacity to publish it—or Sir Mungo Malagrowther —

Byron. Who?

Odoherty. His editor—now-a-days commonly called Sir Mungo

* Maginn made a mistake in putting such a word as *civilation* into Byron's mouth, as it was one which he (Maginn), had invented, and solely used for a long time. De Quincey records Maginn's opinion "that no man, however much he might *tend* to civilization, was to be regarded as having absolutely reached its apex until he was drunk;" also the fact, that, after 10 P. M., civilization being an odiously long word to utter, it might be abridged to *civilation.* Therefore, in De Quincey's neological dictionary of English, he entered it thus:—"*Civilation* by ellipsis, or more properly by syncope, or vigorously speaking, by hic-cup, from *civilization.*"—M.

Malagrowther. I say it is really astonishing that Murray should print, or Sir Mungo have the face not to cut up, a book so destructive of every feeling which we have been taught to cherish.

Byron. Are you serious, Ensign?

Odoherty. Serious as the rock of Cashel.

Byron. I did not expect it. I thought this silly outcry about Don Juan and Cain was confined to the underlings of literature; so much so, that I was astonished to find even Jeffrey joining in it—but that you, one of the first and most enlightened men of the age, should adopt it—that Ensign and Adjutant Morgan Odoherty should be found swelling in the war-whoop of my antagonist Dr. Southey, is indeed more than I expected.

Odoherty. I am not an old quiz, like Malagrowther and the Laureate: yet, my Lord Byron, I am a man and an Englishman, (I mean an Irishman,) and disapprove of Don Juan.

Byron. The devil ye do! Why, most illustrious rival of Dr. Magnus Oglethorpe, why?

Odoherty. I have already sufficiently explained myself.

Byron. You have uttered nothing, sir, but the common old humbug. In Don Juan I meant to give a flowing, free satire on things as they are. I meant to call people's attention to the realities of things. I could make nothing of England or France. There every thing is convention—surface—cant. I had recourse to the regions where nature acts more vividly, more in the open light of day. I meant no harm, upon my honor. I meant but to do what any other man might have done with a more serious face, and had all the Hannah Mores in Europe to answer his Plaudite.

Odoherty. I don't follow your lordship.

Byron. Not follow me, sir? Why, what can be more plain than my intention? I drew a lively lad, neglected in his education, strong in his passions, active in his body, and lively in his brains; would you have had me make him look as wise as a Quarterly Reviewer? Every boy must sow his wild oats; wait till Don Juan be turned of fifty, and if I don't represent him as one of the gravest and most devout Tories in the world, may I be hanged. As yet he has only been what Dr. Southey once was, "a clever boy, thinking upon politics (and other subjects) as those who are boys in mind, whatever their age may be, do think." Have patience. The Don may be Lord Chancellor ere he dies.

Odoherty. The serious charge is your warmth of coloring.

Byron. Look at Homer, remember the cloud scene. Look at Virgil, remember the cave-scene. Look at Milton, remember the bower-scene, the scene of "nothing loth." Why, sir, poets are like their heroes, and poets represent such matters (which all poets do and must represent) more or less warmly, just as they are more or less men.

Odoherty. Well, but what do you say for Cain? 'Tis blasphemous.

Byron. Not intentionally, at least—but I cannot see that it is so at all. You know—for I suppose you know theology as well as you know everything else.

Odoherty. Like Dr. Magee—an old friend of mine, who has lately been made an Archbishop.*

Byron. You know then that there is no question so puzzling in all divinity—no matter under what light you view it—as the origin of evil. There is no theory whatever—I say not one—and you may take your countryman, Archbishop King's, among them,† which is not liable to great objection, if the objectors be determined to cavil. Now I assert, and that fearlessly, that it is quite possible to reconcile my scheme, bating a few poetical flights of no moment, with views and feelings perfectly religious. I engage to write a commentary on Cain, proving it beyond question a religious poem.

Odoherty. Warburton did the same for the Essay on Man—but convinced nobody.‡

Byron. And yet Warburton was a Bishop—yea, more than a bishop—one of your brightest, deepest, profoundest, most brilliant theologians. I only ask you to extend to me the same indulgence you extend to Milton—ay, even to Cumberland—if his Calvary be still extant.

Odoherty. Nay, my lord, there is this difference. The *intention* of Milton and Cumberland makes a vast distinction. They wrote poems to promote religion—your lordship wrote ——

Byron. Mr. Odoherty, I presume—nay, I know—I am talking to a gentleman. I have disclaimed irreligious intention, and I *demand*, as a gentleman, to be believed. Cain is like all poems in which spiritual matters are introduced. The antagonist of Heaven—of whom the Prometheus of Æschylus is the prototype—cannot be made to speak in such terms, as may not be perverted by those who wish to pervert. I defy any man—I repeat it—I defy any man to show me a speech—a line in Cain, which is not defensible on the

* Dr. William Magee, author of "Discourses on the Scriptural Doctrines of the Atonement and Sacrifice," (directed against the tenets of the Unitarians,) after having been Dean of Cork and Bishop of Raphoe, was made Archbishop of Dublin, in 1822. He died in 1831.—M.

† Dr. William King, Archbishop of Dublin, born in 1650, died in 1729. In his treatise "De Origine Mali," or the origin of evil, he undertook to show how all the several kinds of evil with which the world abounds are consistent with the goodness of God, and may be accounted for without the supposition of an evil principle.—M.

‡ Dr. William Warburton, Bishop of Glocester, (author of the Divine Legation of Moses,) published, in a periodical entitled The Works of the Learned, a vindication of Pope. who had been charged with having evinced a tendency to Spinocism and naturalism, in his Essay on Man. When this poem was translated into French, it had been skilfully attacked, on the above grounds, by Professor Crousaz, of Switzerland. Pope eventually declared that he never had any intention of propagating the principles of Bolingbroke, and that Warburton had made his (Pope's) views clearer even to himself!—M.

same principle as the haughty speech of Satan, in the fifth book of Milton—or the proud defiance of Moloch in the second. In both poets—I beg pardon—in the poet, and in Cain, speeches torn from the context, and misinterpreted by the malevolent or the weak-minded, may be made to prove what was directly contrary to the intention of the writer.

Odoherty. To be sure, as Chief Baron O'Grady says, in his Letter to Mr. Gregory, remove the words "the fool has said in his heart;" and you can prove by Scripture that "there is no God."

Byron. I know nothing of your Chief Baron, but what he says is true—and it is *so*, that I have been criticised. I don't complain of Lord Eldon. Perhaps it became his high station to deliver the judgment he did—perhaps it was right he should bend to public opinion—which opinion, however, I shall for ever assert, was stimulated by a party of more noise than number. But I do confess—for I was born an aristocrat—that I was a good deal pained when I saw my books, in consequence of his decree, degraded to be published in sixpenny numbers by Benbow, with Lawrence's* Lectures—Southey's Wat Tyler—Paine's Age of Reason—and the Chevalier de Faublas.

Odoherty. I am sorry I introduced the subject. If I thought I should have in the slightest degree annoyed your lordship —

Byron. I am not annoyed, bless your soul; there is nothing I like better than free discussion. *That*, you know, can never be, except between men of sense. As for all your humbug of Reviews, Magazines, &c., why, you are, at least, as much as any man alive, up to their nothingness.

Odoherty. 'Tis the proudest of my reflections, that I have somewhat contributed to make people see what complete stuff all that affair is.

Byron. I admire your genius, Mr. Odoherty: but why do you claim this particular merit?

Odoherty. Merely as a great contributor to Blackwood. That work has done the business.

Byron. As how, friend Morgan?

Odoherty. Call another flask, and I'll tell you—Ay, now fill a bumper to old Christopher.

Byron. With three times three with all my heart. The immortal Kit North! !! !!! !!! (*Bibunt ambo.*)

Odoherty. Why, you see, what with utterly squabashing Jeffrey, and what with giving Malagrowther an odd squeeze or so,—but most

* Lawrence, a celebrated anatomist in London, whose published Lectures were so tinged with materialism that, becoming so popular as to be printed, the law declined protecting him, on the score of their irreligion. So, Wat Tyler, an early poem of Southey's, which he had never published, having got into print, the law did not allow an injunction on its sale, inasmuch as it was a republican poem. In 1836 Southey included Wat Tyler in his collected works, without altering a line of it, and it certainly does not appear so republican as was originally represented.—M.

of all, by doing all that ever these folks could do in one Number, and then undoing it in the next,—puffing, deriding, sneering, jeering, prosing, piping, and so forth, he has really taken the thing into his own hands, and convinced the Brutum Pecus that 'tis all quackery and humbug.

Byron. Himself included?

Odoherty. No—not quite that neither. As to two or three principles—I mean religion, loyalty, and the like, he is always as stiff as a poker; and although he now and then puts in puffs on mediocre fellows, every body sees they're put in merely to fill the pages; and the moment he or any of his true men set pen to paper, the effect is instantaneous. His book is just like the best book in the world—it contains a certain portion of *Balaam.*

Byron. And this sort of course, you think, has enlightened the public?

Odoherty. Certain and sure it has. People have learnt the great lesson, that Reviews, and indeed all periodicals, merely *quâ* such, are nothing. They take in his book not as a Review, to pick up opinions of new books from it, nor as a periodical, to read themselves asleep upon, but as a classical work which happens to be continued from month to month;—a real Magazine of mirth, misanthropy, wit, wisdom, folly, fiction, fun, festivity, theology, bruising, and thingumbob. He unites all the best materials of the Edinburgh, the Quarterly, and the Sporting Magazine—the literature and good writing of the first—the information and orthodoxy of the second, and the flash and trap of the third.

Byron. You speak *con amore,* sir: Why the devil am I cut up and parodied in Ebony?

Odoherty. Come, come, pop such questions to the marines! Have you ever been half so much cut up there as I have been? Fill your glass! Here's to *Humbug.* Three times three, my lord! No two men alive should fill higher to that toast than we that are here present, thank God; and I'm very glad to be here, with my legs under the same board with the author of Cain and Don Juan.

Byron. What, after abusing them both so savagely just this moment.

Odoherty. So I do still;—but I had rather have written a page of Juan than a ton of Childe Harold—that was too great a bore entirely.

Byron. Well,—waive my works in toto. How is Sir Walter Scott?

Odoherty. I have not seen him for nearly six months; but he is quite well, and writing Peveril of the Peak; that is, if he be the Author of Waverley.

Byron. Which he is.

Odoherty. I won't swear to that, knowing what I do about Anastasius. Did you see how Hope bristled up in the back in Blackwood, when somebody, I forget who, perhaps myself, said that you were guilty of that most admirable book?

Byron. Yes,—but no matter. Could you give me any more information *de re periodicali*, as the Baron of Bradwardine would have said?

Odoherty. I shall sing a stave touchant that point—

1.

O! gone are the days, when the censure or praise,
  Of the Monthly was heard with devotion;
When the sight of the blue of old Griffith's Review,*
  Set each heart in a pit-a-pat motion;
We care not a curse, now, for better or worse,
  For the prate of the maundering old mumper;
And, since it is dead,—why, no more can be said,—
  Than " Destruction to Cant" in a bumper.

2.

When the sense of the town had the Monthly put down,
  Mr. Jeffrey a new caper started:
Every fourth of a year he swore to appear,
  To terrify all the faint-hearted.
Then with vigor and pith, Brougham, Jeffrey, and Smith,
  Began to belabor the natives;
Who, bother'd at first by their bravo and burst,
  Sunk under the scribblers like caitiffs.

3.

Quite vex'd at their blows, Johnny Murray arose,
  Assisted by mild Billy Gifford—
The Edinburgh work he squabash'd like a Turk,
  So that folks do not now care a whiff for't.
But soon such a gang, there grew up slap-bang,
  Of scribblers and nibblers reviewing,
That people got sick of the horrible trick,
  And it almost had set them a-sp——g.

4.

But a figure of light soon burst on their sight,
  In Bill Ebony's beautiful pages—
The immortal Kit North in his glory came forth,
  With his cycle of satellite sages.
He can cant, it is true—he can sport a review,
  Now and then, when it suits his devices;
But who trusts to his prog is a bothersome dog,
  If he says he is stingy of spices.

Byron. Not a bad song! Cazzo. I have quite lost the knack of song-writing. Tom Moore is the best at it now alive.

* Dr. Griffith was Editor of *The Monthly Review* for many years.—The *Monthly* was conducted by Sir Richard Phillips.—M.

Odoherty. The present company excepted, you mean; but truly, my lord, I don't care a tester for that piperly poet of Green Erin. I don't think he ever wrote one real good song in his days. He wants pith, by Jericho! and simplicity, and straight-forward meaning. He's always twining and whining. Give me your old stave.

Byron. You prefer Burns, perhaps, now you've been so long a Scotchman, and heard all their eternal puffing of one another.

Odoherty. Poh! poh! I was too old a cat for that straw. Burns wrote five or six good things; Tam o'Shanter, M'Pherson's Lament, Farewell, thou fair Earth, Mary's Dream, the Holy Fair, the Stanzas to a Louse on a Lady's Bonnet, and perhaps a few more; but the most of his verses are mere manufacture—the most perfect common-place about love and bowers, and poverty, and so forth. And as for his prose, why, Gad-a-mercy! 'tis execrable. 'Tis worse than Hogg's worst, or Allan Cunningham's best. His letters are enough to make a dog sick.

Byron. Come, you are too severe; Burns was a noble fellow, although Jeffrey abused him. But indeed that was nothing. After praising the Cockneys, who cares what he reviles?

Odoherty. Not I.

Byron. No, no; I don't suspect you of any such folly. Pray, have you seen any of our Italian Improvisatores as yet? What do you think of their art?

Odoherty. That I can beat it.

Byron. In English or Irish?

Odoherty. In any language I know—Latin or Greek, if you like them.

Byron. Try Latin, then.

Odoherty. Here's Ritson. Turn him over; I'll translate any song you like off-hand.

Byron. Here, take this one—"Back and side go bare." 'Tis not the worse for having a bishop for its father.*

Odoherty. Old Still must have been a hearty cock,—here goes. Read you the English, and I'll chaunt it in Latin.†

Byron reads.	Cantat Dohertiades.
1.	1.
Backe and side go bare, go bare, Both foot and hande go colde: But, bellye, God sende thee good ale yenough, Whether it be newe or olde.	Sint nuda dorsum, latera— Pes, manus, algens sit; Dum ventri veteris copia Zythi novive fit.

* John Still, Bishop of Bath and Wells, flourished in the reign of Elizabeth, and died in 1607. He is the reputed author of "Gammer Gurton's Needle," a dramatic piece of low humor, very characteristic of the manners of the English in that day. The fine old chant, "Back and side go bare," is introduced into this drama.—M.

† This Latin version has been considered one of Maginn's best translations. It gives not only the actual meaning, but the measure, with rhymes and double rhymes.—M.

I cannot eat but lytle meate.
  My stomacke is not good;
But sure I thinke that I can drynke
  With him that weares a hood.
Though I go bare, take ye no care,
  I am nothing a colde;
I stuff my skyn so full within,
  Of jolly good ale and olde.
Backe and side go bare, go bare,
  Both foote and hande go colde;
But, bellye, God sende thee good ale enoughe,
  Whether it be newe or olde.

2.

I love no rost, but a nut-browne toste,
  And a crab laid in the fyre;
A little breade shall do me stead,
  Much breade I not desyre.
No frost nor snow, nor winde, I trowe,
  Can hurt me if I wolde;
I am so wrapt, and throwly lapt,
  Of jolly good ale and olde,
    Backe and side go bare, &c.

3.

And Tyb, my wyfe, that, as her lyfe,
  Loveth well good ale to seeke;
Full oft drynkes shee, tyll ye may see
  The teares run down her cheeke:
Then dowth she trowle to mee the boule,
  Even as a mault-worme shuld;
And sayth, "Sweete hart, I took my parte
  Of this jolly good ale and olde."
    Back and side go bare, &c.

4.

Now let them drynke, till they nod and wynke,
  Even as good felowes should doe:
They shall not mysse to have the blysse
  Good ale doth bringe men to.
And all poore soules that have scowr'd boules,
  Or have them lustely trolde,
God save the lyves of them and their wyves,
  Whether they be yonge or old.
    Backe and syde go bare, &c.

Non possum multum edere,
  Quia stomachus est nullus;
Sed volo vel monacho bibere
  Quanquam sit huic cucullus.
Et quamvis nudus ambulo,
  De frigore non est metus;
Quia semper Zytho vetulo
  Ventriculus est impletus.
Sint nuda dorsum, latera—
  Pes, manus, algens sit;
Dum ventri veteris copia
  Zythi novive fit.

2.

Assatum nolo—tostum volo—
  Vel pomum igni situm;
Nil pane careo—parvum habeo
  Pro pane appetitum.
Me gelu, nix, vel ventus vix
  Afficerent injuriâ;
Hæc sperno, ni adesset mî
  Zythi veteris penuria.
    Sint nuda, &c.

3.

Et uxor Tybie, qui semper sibi
  Vult quærere Zythum bene,
Ebibit hæc persæpe, nec
  Sistit, dum madeant genæ.
Et mihi tum dat cantharum,
  Sic mores sunt bibosi;
Et dicit "Cor, en! impleor
  Zythi dulcis et annosi."
    Sint nuda, &c.

4.

Nunc ebibant, donec nictant
  Ut decet virum bonum;
Felicitatis habebunt satis,
  Nam Zythi hoc est donum.
Et omnes hi, qui canthari
  Sunt haustibus lætati,
Atque uxores vel juniores
  Vel senes, Diis sint grati.
    Sint nuda, &c.

Byron. Bravo—bravissimo!—why, you would beat old Camillo Querno if you would only learn Italian.*

Odoherty. I intend to learn it between this and the end of the

* Camillo Querno was a Neapolitan poet of the 15th century, who acquired great fame by his faculty for extempore versification, and obtained the name (first given him by some of his convivial friends, while at Rome, in 1514) of Arch-Poet. Leo X. was much pleased with his buffoonery, and often admitted him to his table. He died in 1528.—M.

week. There is no language on the face of the earth I could not learn in three days,—except Sanscrit, which took me a week.* It took Marsham of Serampore seven years. Would your lordship wish to hear a Sanscrit ode I wrote to A. W. Schlegel?

Byron. No, thank you, not just now. You are not doing the Lacryma justice.

Odoherty. Curse it,—it is getting cold on my stomach. Is there no more stout potation in the house?

Byron. Brandy, I presume,—but the sugar is execrable.

Odoherty. No matter, it makes superb grog,—almost as good as rum—far better than whisky. Have you any objection, Byron?

Byron. Not the least; whatever is agreeable to you. Hola!—

Enter waiter—exits—and returns with a skin of brandy.

Odoherty. Ay, this skin is a pretty thing. It puts a man instinctively in mind of a skinful. Gargle it most delicately. Flow, thou regal amber stream. Talk of the Falls of the Rhone in comparison with such a cascade as this! Here—water—aqua pura. Ay, that will do. You are putting too much water, my lord—it will rise on your stomach, as old Doctor Rumsnout often told me.

Byron. Nay, mix as you please, and let me settle my own tipple.

Odoherty. Oh! of course, freedom of will. But this is far superior to the rascally quaff we have been drinking. By all accounts your lordship leads a gay life here.

Byron. Not more gay than you have led elsewhere. But if you allude to what you see in the papers, and the travels of impertinent and underbred tourists;—underbred they must be, else they would not publish anecdotes of the private life of any gentleman, to satisfy the multitude, even if they were true—nothing can be more false or ridiculous. I sedulously cut the English here, on purpose to avoid being made food for journals, and Balaam to swell the pages of gabbling tourists. Indeed, I have not been in general treated well by these people. Then there are my Memoirs, published by Colburn ——

Odoherty. A most audacious imposture! He had heard the report of your having given your Life to Moore, and, accordingly, thinking he might make a good thing of it, he hires at once Dictionary Watkins to set about Memoirs,† which, to give old Gropius credit for industry, he touched up in a fortnight; and advertised it was, as *the* Memoirs of Lord B., particularly in the country papers.

Byron. Industry! it was only the industry of the scissors, for half the book is merely cut out of the Peerage, giving an account of my

* Maginn scarcely exaggerated his wondrous faculty in acquiring a knowledge of languages. He was acquainted with nearly all the dead, and most of the living tongues.—M.

† Dr. Watkins was a sort of general life-writer. He compiled Memoirs of Byron, which sold very well, and wrote a Life of Sheridan, composed from newspaper paragraphs, play-books, and Parliamentary reports.—M.

old grim ancestors—and newspapers, magazines, and other authentic vehicles of intelligence supply the rest.

Odoherty. I can assure you, my lord, it imposed on many simple, chuckleheaded, open-mouthed people, as your Autobiography.

Byron. Impossible. An idiot must have known that I had not any thing to do with it, even from its style.

Odoherty. Style—as to style, that is all fudge. I myself have written in all kind of styles from Burke to Jeremy Bentham. But I assure your lordship the mob charge you with these Memoirs.

Byron. Why, really some people believe me capable of any kind of stuff. You remember I was accused of writing puffs for Day and Martin.

Odoherty. A calumny, I *know*, my dear Byron, for *I* am myself author of them. By the way, have you heard the epigram on your disclaimer?

Byron. No—tell it me—I hope it is good.

Odoherty. You shall judge.

ON READING THE APPENDIX TO LORD BYRON'S TRAGEDY OF THE TWO FOSCARI.

Is Byron surprised that his enemies say
He makes puffing verses for Martin and Day?
Why, what other task could his lordship take part in
More fit than the service of Day, and of Martin?
So shining, so dark—all his writing displays
A type of this liquid of Martin and Day's—
Gouvernantes—Kings—laurel-crown'd Poets attacking—
Oh! he's master complete of the science of Blacking!

Byron. No great affair. But there are "many more too long" to trouble you with, which the public give me credit for.

Odoherty. As for instance, the attack on Ebony. Give me a specimen of that—or give me the thing itself, and I shall make him print it.

Byron. It is too stale now; besides, I have quite forgotten it. Murray has the only copy I know of—and I shall write to him to give it to you on your return.*

Odoherty. Thank you—and a copy of the Irish Advent, too?

Byron. Hush! Hush!

Odoherty. You need not be afraid of me, my lord, I *have* seen it; there are a dozen copies in existence.

Byron. Let's change the subject. Giving my Memoirs was not the first trick Colburn served me. You remember the Vampire affair.

* The Letter to the Editor of *Blackwood's Magazine* was first printed in 1830, in Moore's Byron.—M.

Odoherty. Ah! poor Jack Polidori! Lord rest him. Polidori was bribed on the occasion.*

Byron. I am sorry for it. I once thought him a fair fellow. But you see in this catchpenny Life how Colburn's hack pretends to censure the forgery, though his employer was the *sole* planner and manager of the affair—and it was he who got some people in the Row to father the published pamphlet—the separate one, you know.

Odoherty. Ay—and I heard, on authority which I believe, that Colburn cancelled a disavowal of your being the author, which some person had written and prefixed to the notice of the Vampire in the New Monthly.

Byron. Hand me the brandy, that I may wash my mouth after mentioning such things. How is the New Monthly?

Odoherty. Dying hard. Nobody of talent about it except Campbell himself, who is too lazy. As for ******* ***** ***** and other mere asses —

Byron. I have never heard of the worthies you mention.

Odoherty. By jingo, I am sure of that. **** is a great officer. He sits in the theatre taking notes, as magisterially as a judge does on a trial, and with as much dignity.

Byron. Transeat. Murray sends me shoals of periodicals. There appears to be a swarm of them lately, and I find I am a popular subject for all. Not a fellow takes pen in hand without criticising me.

Odoherty. Oxoniensis gave you, or rather Murray, a good rib-roasting. I trouble you for the bottle.

Byron. I think too harshly—but the Oxonians are great big-wigs.

Odoherty. Oh! thundering tearers, in their own opinion. I remember ****, who, n'importe—going into Covent Garden a few years ago, simultaneously with the Prince Regent. The audience, of course, rose out of respect to his Royal Highness, and remained for some time standing; on which the delighted Tyro—hot from Rhedycina, exclaimed—God bless my soul—these good people, who mean well, I dare say, have been informed that I am in the first class, and about to stand for Oriel.†

Byron. Ha! ha! ha! I shall, however, look back always with pleasure to the days,

> When smitten first with sacred love of song,
> I roamed old Oxford's hoary piles among;‡

* When Byron was in Switzerland, in 1816, the Shelleys and himself agreed that each should write a prose story. Mrs. Shelley produced "Frankenstein," Byron wrote a fragment, and Dr. Polidori, (his physician.) wrote a tale called "The Vampire," which has repeatedly been dramatized, although very deficient in literary merit. When Polidori came to England, he published this story as Byron's, which drew a disclaimer from the noble poet. Polidori finally perished by his own hand.—M.

† For a Fellowship?—M.

‡ Maginn has a *lapsus pennæ* here. It was not "old Oxford's hoary piles among" which Byron roamed. He was a member of Trinity College, Cambridge.—M.

and forgive Oxoniensis, whom I know. But let us return. I do not want information about the great magnates of your English literature —or those reputed such—but I should wish to hear something of the minors—the insect tribes. Who are your magazine, &c., scribblers?

Odoherty. Innumerable as the snipes in the bog of Allen. There is Clare poetizing for the London.

Byron. An over-puffed youth, that plough-boy appears to be.

Odoherty. He may have written some pretty things, but he is taken now to slum, scissoring, namby-pamby, and is quite spoiled. But it is a good thing to have a good conceit of one's self, and that's the boy who has it. He has pitted himself against Hogg, whom he considers as his inferior.

Byron. Quelle gloire! they should have an amabean contention, like the clowns in Virgil. Suggest this to North, with my compliments.

Odoherty. Surely—it is a good hint. But Clare never will write any thing like the "Dedication to Mr. Grieve," or "The Flying Tailor of Ettrick," until he is boiled again.

Byron. I am told he is a delicate retiring young man. And that's more than can be said of you, Ensign and Adjutant. You have been always too much a lady's man.

Odoherty. Ay,—and so has somebody else who shall be nameless. I have had, I take it, somewhere about 144 pretty little bantlings—God bless them—of all colors in various quarters of the globe.

Byron. You would be a useful man in a new colony. Why don't you take the Quarterly hint, and settle in Shoulder of Mutton Bay, Van Diemen's Land?

Odoherty. Thank you for the hint—as much as to say, I ought to be sent across the water to Botany. But to the insects. Taylor, also, its publisher, is a writer for the London. He continues Johnson's Lives of the Poets!

Byron. Surely you joke.* It is as good a jest as if Hazlitt were to take it into his head to continue Chesterfield.

Odoherty. Yet such is the fact. But don't mention it; for Taylor, who really is a decent fellow, wishes it to be kept secret, being heartily sick of the concern. There are fifty other "Gentlemen of the Press," but really they are too obscure to bother your lordship with. Some new periodical—name unknown—is supported by Procter, the great tragedian.

Byron. Nay, I am jealous of Cornwall, as of a superior poet. His Mirandola floated proudly through the theatre. My Faliero was damned.

* The continuation was written, not by John Taylor, but by Cary, the translator of Dante.—M.

Odoherty. I know it was d——d ungenteel in Elliston to put it in the way of being so.* But there is no making a silk purse out of a sow's ear.

Byron. How is my old friend, "My Grandmamma's Review, the British?"

Odoherty. Just as merry and jocular as ever—but the British Critic is dying. Rivington has started the Monthly Literary Censor, it is said, to supersede it.

Byron. And my old foe, the Literary Gazette?

Odoherty. Doing well. But what need you be so thin-skinned as to mind such little flea-bites?

Byron. *Flebit* et insignis tota cantabitur urbe. Faith, I don't like to be pestered with impunity. Has it any rivals?

Odoherty. Lots. Valpy set up the Museum, a weekly paper,† the other day, against it. When I tell you that black-letter Tom Fogrum Dibdin‡ is the chief hand, I need not add that it is dull and harmless.

Byron. No—that's pretty evident. But truce with periodical chit-chat.

Odoherty. Shall I give you news from Parnassus?

Byron. No—no—no—I am sick of that. Did you see my Werner and my New Mystery?

Odoherty. Yes—Murray showed them to me in sheets.

Byron. Well, what did you think of them?

Odoherty. Like every thing that comes from your lordship's pen, they are tinged with the ethereal hues of genius,—and perfumed with fragrance of the flowers that grow upon the brink of Helicon.

Byron. Ho! I see, my friend, you have joined the Irish school of oratory. But as that goes for nothing, what do you, without trope or figure, think of them?

Odoherty. Seriously, my lord, I admire them when they are good, and dislike them when they are bad. (*Aside.*)—That is, I like five pages, and dislike fifty. (*To Lord B.*)—But, my lord, why do you not try your hand at your own old style—the tale—the occasional poetry; you know what I mean?

* As the law then stood, once that a play was printed, a manager might put it on the stage, without payment to the author, or even asking his permission. Elliston, when manager of Drury Lane, in 1821, produced "Marino Faliero," though Byron, in the preface, had said that it was neither intended nor written for the stage. It did not succeed in representation.—M.

† The *British Review, British Critic, Monthly Literary Censor,* and *Museum,* have long been of the past.—M.

‡ Thomas Frognall Dibdin, nephew of the song-writer, was a zealous bibliographer. Originally intended for the law, he entered the church in 1804. His "Bibliomania," which at once established his character as a writer, was published in 1809, and was followed by a variety of books, on a great many subjects. Of these, the most remarkable is a "Biographical, Antiquarian, and Picturesque Tour," (on the Continent, in 1818), and his "Reminiscences of a Literary Life," in 1836. He was one of the founders of the Roxburghe Club, in 1812, and died in 1847, aged seventy-two. I knew him in his later years, and found him full of literary information, and as eager to communicate as I was to receive it. He was small in stature, with a countenance expressive of much firmness, and a profusion of gray hair.—M.

Byron. Because I am sick of being imitated. I revolt at the idea of the lower orders making desperate attempts to climb the arduous mount. I have been publicly accused of seducing, by my example, youths

Doom'd their fathers' hopes to cross,
To pen a stanza when they should engross.

And I shall not,—at least just now I think I shall not—lead the way for sentimental and poetical hard-handed and hard-headed good people to follow. There is no danger of their following me into the lofty region of tragedy.

Odoherty. Whew! Why, you are playing the aristocrat with a vengeance. There is, however, one lowly poet whom I would recommend to your attention.

Byron. Whom?

Odoherty. He is so modest, that he does not wish his name to be mentioned, and writes his "lays" under the title of Ismail Fitz-Adam.*

Byron. I never heard of him.

Odoherty. I did not imagine you did: and yet he has written some things which would not have disgraced the pen of a Byron. I could not say more of any man, (*Lord B. bows and smiles.*) Nay, my lord, I am quite in earnest; and though very poor, and only a common sailor, he has that spirit of independence which I hope will always animate our navy, and refuses all direct pecuniary assistance.

Byron. What, in heroics again! But he is quite right. Do his books sell?

Odoherty. Not as they ought—very slowly.

Byron. I am sorry for it. On your return, bid Murray put my name down for fifty copies.

Odoherty. You were always a gentleman, my lord: but the bottle is out, and I am some hundred yards distant from civilation yet.

Byron. Pardon me—do as you like; but I shall not drink any more.

Odoherty. Not till the next time, you mean. Could I get a song out of your lordship?

Byron. On what subject?

Odoherty. On any. Parody one of your own serious humbugs. Suppose—"There's not a joy that life can give."

Byron. Very well—here goes—accompany me on the pipes, which I see you have brought with you to alarm the Italians.†

* In 1820, Ismail Fitz-Adam published a spirited poem called "The Harp of the Desert," descriptive of the battle of Algiers. In 1821, he brought out "Lays on Land," which attracted considerable notice. In June, 1823, he died. This author's real name was John Macken, and he was a native of Ireland. Although of respectable family and classically educated, he served as a common sailor in the Battle of Algiers, in 1816.—M.

† The bag-pipes are nearly as well known, and as much played on, in the North of Italy, as in Scotland.—M

SONG.

THERE'S NOT A JOY THAT LIFE CAN GIVE,* &c.

Tune—Grand March in Scipio.

1.

There's not a joy that WINE *can give like that it takes away,*
When slight intoxication yields to drunkenness the sway,
'Tis not that *youth's smooth cheek* its *blush* surrenders to the nose,
But the stomach turns, the forehead burns, and all our pleasure goes.

2.

Then the few, who still can keep their chairs amid the smash'd decanters,
Who wanton still in witless jokes, and laugh at pointless banters—
The magnet of their course is gone—for, let them try to walk,
Their legs, they speedily will find as jointless as their talk.

3.

Then the mortal hotness of the brain, like hell itself, is burning,
It cannot feel, nor dream, nor think—'tis whizzing, blazing, turning—
The heavy wet, or port, or rum, has mingled with *our tears,*
And if by chance we're weeping drunk, each drop our cheek-bone sears.

4.

Though fun still flow from fluent lips,† and jokes confuse our noddles
Through midnight hours, while punch our powers insidiously enfuddles,
'Tis but as ivy leaves were worn by Bacchanals of yore,
To make them still look fresh and gay while rolling on the floor.

5.

Oh! could I walk *as I have* walk'd, *or* see *as I have* seen;
Or even roll as I have done on many a carpet green—
As port at Highland inn seems sound, all corkish though it be,
So would I the Borachio kiss, and get blind drunk with thee.

Odoherty. Excellent—most excellent.

Byron. Nay, I don't shine in parody—Apropos, de bottes—Do you know any thing of Bowles?

Odoherty. Your antagonist?

Byron. Yes.

Odoherty. I know he's a most excellent and elegant gentleman, who gave your lordship some rubbers.‡

Byron. I flatter myself he had not the game altogether in his own

* The actual title of these "Stanzas for Music," (as they are called in Byron's Poems,) is not correctly given here. The first stanza runs thus:

"There's not a joy the world can give like that it takes away,
When the glow of early thought declines in feeling's dull decay;
'Tis not on youth's smooth cheek the blush alone, which fades so fast,
But the tender bloom of heart is gone, ere youth itself be past."

These lines bear date March, 1815.—M.

† The *ipsisima verba* are "Though wit may flash from fluent lips."—M.

‡ One of Bowles's pamphlets, during the controversy with Byron, on the merits of Pope, as a poet, had the motto "He who plays at *Bowles* must expect *rubbers*."—This was about the best thing in the work.—M.

hands. He, indeed, is a gentlemanlike man, and so was Ali Pacha—but a heretic with respect to Pope. By-the-by, is not Murray going to give a new edition of the great Ethic, the Bard of Twickenham?

Odoherty. No, not now. He was, but in the mean time Roscoe, the gillyflower of Liverpool, announced his intention of coming forth—and Murray's editor declined. His Western Majesty, however, took the merit of declining it himself, and made a great matter of his condescension to Roscoe, who swallowed it. In the meantime, one of Murray's huff-caps cut Roscoe to pieces, in the review of Washington Irving's Sketch Book, in the Quarterly.

Byron. Ha! ha! Well done, Joannes de Moravia. But is Bowles as thin-skinned as ever with respect to criticism?

Odoherty. No—I should think not. Tickler, at Ambrose's, drew rather a droll description of him the other night, painting him in a shovel-hat, &c., which somehow or other got into print, and Bowles was quite tickled by it.

Byron. The devil he was!

Odoherty. Ay, and accepted the office of bottle-holder to North, in the expected turn-up between Christopher and Tom Moore,* in the most handsome manner possible, chanting *à la Pistol,*

> Thou hast produced me in a gown and band,
> And shovel, oh! sublimest Christopher,
> And I shall now thy bottle holder be,
> Betting my shovel to a 'prentice cap,
> That neither Tom nor Byron [*meaning you, my lord,*] will stand up
> A single moment 'gainst your powerful facers,
> When you set to in fistic combat fairly.

But now that I have told you so much about British literature, give me something of the literature of this, I am sorry to say it, your adopted country.

Byron. I might perhaps shock your political principles.

Odoherty. I have not any. So push on.

Byron. This poor country is so misgoverned—

Odoherty. Ay, so your man Hobhouse says—

Byron. What, Hobbio—mobbio—Psha! But really the Austrian domination is so abom— (*Left speaking.*)

* *Blackwood*, for January 1822, opened with a truculent Preface, in very large type, in which Christopher North stated that he happened to know that Moore had written a satirical poem on the Magazine and its contributors, and recommended him not to publish it; adding that, if he did, North would republish it, so as to fill the right-hand columns of about a dozen pages of the Magazine, and to fill the left-hand column with original verses, on the same measure, (whatever that might be) upon Moore. To have fair play in this *set-to*, Christopher suggested that umpires be appointed from among the friends of the distinguished combatants,—"We appoint for ourselves Neat [the pugilist] and the Rev. William Lisle Bowles—and we suggest to Moore, in the true spirit of British courage, Gas [also a bozer] and Mr. Montgomery, the "author of the World before the Flood." In the words of the Ring, I have to state that Moore *did not come to the scratch!*—M.

Metricum Symposium Ambrosianum.

SEU PROPINATIO POETICA NORTHI.*

COME, Morgan, fill up my boy, handle the ladle,
The brat in old Ireland is sent to the cradle—
Get out of those dumps, man, they hurt soul and body—
Put a *stick* in the bowl, my boy, push round the toddy.

That's right, my brave Ensign, what spirit now lightens
From out your two eyes—how your brow it up-brightens—
You now look yourself, man, and not *a la Werter*,
When you near blew your brains out for Mrs. M'Whirter.

And now since we're merry, come fill up the glasses—
We'll drink to our Poets, (we've toasted our lasses,)
To all the high bards of our beautiful Islands,
From famed Connemara, all round to the Highlands.

A bumper, my boys, here's the profligate Baron [1]
Who his Pegasus broke to a Tragedy Garron [2]
In carrying logs to the temple of Belus,
To burn that half man they call Sardanapalus.

His Lordship, who, in the dull play, the Foscàri,
Wrote worse than e'er Cockneyland's regent, mild Barry,
And whose fame and whose genius came down to their Zero
In the robberies and wretchedness of Faliero.

He with folly inflated, with vanity reeling,
And mocking at nature, at morals, and feeling,
At the pride of the brave, at the tears of the tender,
And who cares for them all and their ties not a *bender*. [3]

Who spouts out more venom than an Amphisboena
On the land of his birth; and, like laughing Hyena,
Mocks at the brave country, he scarce should dare dream on—
At whose blood and whose glory he sneer'd like a demon.

Who in Italy lives, and who babbles of slavery,
And who lately displayed his high mettle and bravery,
In hotly pursuing an old drunken sergeant— [4]
On his arms he should quarter a halbert in argent.

* This chant, too full of personalities not to be given, appeared in *Blackwood*, July, 1822, and was originally intended (as a brief foot-note indicated,) to be introduced in The Noctes, No. III., of the preceding number. "This," quoth North, "was before the Adjutant went on his Italian tour." The Noctes, No. IV., had its locality transferred to Pisa, and the dialogue was solely between Odoherty and Byron.—M.

1 George Gordon Byron, born 22d January, 1788, in London, died in Greece, April 19, 1824.—M.

2 A Poney—Hibern.—C. N.

3 Alias, a tester—alias, a sixpence.—C. N.

4 Byron, who had previously resided at Ravenna, removed to Pisa with the Gambas (father and brother of the Countess Guiccioli, who accompanied them) in the autumn of 1821. Here, as in other parts of Italy, he was suspected, and not without cause, of having secretly joined the Carbonari. The result was, that the military attempted to arrest him, a *fracas* ensued, which ended in the removal of Byron and his friends, first to Leghorn, and finally to Genoa.—M.

But, his health !—like ourselves, he is fond of a frolic,
May he ne'er die in child-bed, or faint with the colic !
May he die an old man, good, religious, and hoary,
And win and wear long the *true* wreath of his glory !

But would he were here—He could have wine and laughter,
And when wakened to-morrow—maybe the day after—
With head like sick lily—a lily of Hermon's,
We'd give him some soda, and Maturin's sermons.

Here, fill up for Sir Walter !—but stop, he's no poet,
When the Cockneys think meet, they will easily show it.[5]
Sir Walter a poet ! Faith, that's a misnomer,
But still, here's success to our Northern Homer.

Come, fill high for Tom Moore ! would this bumper could gain us
A truce with the sweet *little* Pander of Venus ![6]
'Tis diamond cut diamond when he and we quarrel,
But we value his wrath as the dregs of that barrel.

Then Tommy, agra ![8] if you fall out with Blackwood,
For dying luxuriously, purchase a Packwood—
Frank Jeffrey, *and all that*, was nothing for certain,
To us; but that's all in my eye, Betty Martin.

Then, here's to poor Tom, and his verses so sunny,
That made all our maids and young widows so funny;
Which sent half the *spalpeens* of Munster dragooning,
And sent all the punks in the kingdom *salooning*.

Now, the Minstrel of Gertrude[9]—Compiler of Colburn—
Once the bard of high Scotland—now that of High Holborn;
Whose jinglings the Cockney-lambs lead like a ram-bell,
And, after the toast, strike up "Ranting Tom Campbell."

Now, here's to Will Wordsworth, so wise and so wordy,[10]
And the sweet simple hymns of his own hurdy-gurdy—
Who in vain blows the bellows of Milton's old organ,
While he thinks he could lull all the snakes on the Gorgon.

Now drain for mad Coleridge[11]—the mystical Lacon,
Who *out-cants* Wild Kant, and out-Bacons old Bacon—
The vain, self-tormenting, and eloquent railer,
Who out of his tropes *jerries* Jeremy Taylor.

[5] It was laid down, in the Cockney canons of criticism, that Sir Walter Scott was—no poet !—M.

[6] To be pronounced Hibernically, Va-nus, *rhythmi gratia*.—C. N.

[7] *Blackwood*, before and after this day, was not only kind, but forbearing towards Thomas Moore, whose genius was duly appreciated in its pages. but it had been stated that "the poet of all circles and idol of his own," had written a saucy pasquinade upon Wilson, and his friends; hence, the tone of truculent defiance in the song.—M.

[8] Anglice, my darling.—C. N.

[9] Thomas Campbell, at this time, and for some years later, was editor of Colburn's *New Monthly Magazine*.—M.

[10] William Wordsworth, born in April, 1770, died in 1850. His Descriptive Sketches appeared in 1793; Lyrical Ballads, in 1798; Poems in 1807; The Excursion, in 1814; White Doe of Rylstone, in 1815; Peter Bell. in 1819; Sonnets, in 1820; Memorials of a Tour on the Continent, in 1822, and Poems of Early Years, in 1842.—M.

[11] Samuel Taylor Coleridge, born in 1770, died in 1834.—M.

Success to the Bard of the Bay!—may he wear it
Till we see from his temples one worthy to tear it—
And, though his hexameters are somewhat mouthy,
This glass will make greener the laurel of Southey.[12]

And, after the Minstrel of Roderic and Madoc,
We'll be pardon'd to give our poetical Sadoc,
Mad Shelly,[13] the wild atheist Coryphœus,
Whose Poems and Thoughts are a "Curse and a Chaos."

Now, here's Billy Bowles,[14] both for epic and sonnet,
Who Lord Byron has bother'd, I lay my life on it—
And here's our best wish to the long-sodden'd flummery,
So thick and so slab, of mild Jemmy Montgomery.[15]

And here's the Poetical Bank of Sam Rogers—
Firm still by the aid of old England's old Codgers,
Whose notes are as good as those given by Lord Fanny,[16]
Or Lord Byron, who puffs them—a critical zany.[17]

Here's Milman, the Idol of Square-caps at Oxford,
Though his verses will scarce ever travel to Foxford;[18]
His Pegasus broken, no longer is skittish,
Though he's puff'd in the Quarterly, puff'd in the British.

Though his verse stately be as the dance call'd the Pyrrhic,
And his high harp be tuned to the epic and lyric,
Yet we fear that his glory but stubble is built on,
And his hymns we scarce fancy quite equal to Milton

For of late we remember of nothing grown tamer,
Than the steed that bore "Fazio," and paced under "Samor;"
And the "Martyr," "Belshazzar," and "Fall of Jerusalem,"
We think will scarce live to the age of Methusalem.[19]

Here's to splendid John Wilson,[20] and John Wilson Croker,[21]
Whose satire's as dreadful as Jarvie's red poker,

12 Robert Southey, born 1774, died 1843. He was appointed Poet Laureate in 1813. A mere recapitulation of his writings would fill a page.—M.

13 Percy Bysshe Shelley, born in 1792, drowned in the Gulf of Lerici, on the Italian coast, July 8, 1823. No man, in his life, more thoroughly opposed the conventionalities of society. Few have exhibited higher poetic genius.—M.

14 William Lisle Bowles, (born in 1762, died in 1850), whose sonnets, published in 1789, first drew Coleridge's attention to poetry.—M.

15 James Montgomery, born in 1771, died in 1854. He belonged to what has been called the Evangelical School of Poetry, and such of his compositions as are not religious, are serious and moral. His "World before the Flood," "The Pelican Island," and some sacred songs and lyrics will preserve his reputation, as a second-rate poet.—M.

16 This can surely require no explanation.—C. N.

17 Samuel Rogers, born in 1760, published an Ode to Superstition, in 1787; Pleasures of Memory, in 1792; Epistle to a Friend, in 1798; Vision of Columbus, and Jacqueline, in 1814; Human Life, in 1819; and Italy, in 1822. It is by his Pleasures of Memory, that Rogers will best be remembered as a poet of great taste and skill,—the workmanship being better than the materials, as in Ovid's Palace of the Sun.—M.

18 West of Ireland, *ni fallor*—or elsewhere, *inter barbaros*.—C. N.

19 Henry Hart Milman, now Dean of St. Paul's Cathedral. London, author of many dramatic poems, (of which "Fazio" alone is acted or actable,) a variety of prose histories, and many critical articles in the *Quarterly Review*.—M.

20 A full memoir of "Splendid John Wilson," is given in the second volume of this edition of The Noctes: "For particulars, inquire within."—M.

21 John Wilson Croker, born in Ireland, in 1780, Secretary of the Admiralty from 1809 to

Who cut up poor Joe, and that booby—the other—[22]
As Joe for economy cut up his brother.

Now fill up a bumper for Catiline Croly,[23]
The compeer of Massinger, Fletcher, and Rowley,
And confusion to Elliston, Kemble, and Harris,
Who were blind to the beams of the author of "Paris."

Now, the bards of the drama—from Ireland—all tragic—
Here's first Nosy Maturin, the mild and the magic,
Who into a ball-room as gracefully twitches,
As Bertram—fourth act—enters buttoning his breeches.

May his stays never crack while quadrilling[24] or preaching;
May his wig ne'er grow grey, nor his cravat want bleaching·
May his muse of her quinzy be cured by a gargle;
May he faint at Miss Wilson, and dream in the Dargle.[25]

May he send out a dozen more heroes from Trinity,
And for that be made Provost, its prop of divinity—
We wish Melmoth well, for he is a true Tory,
Whate'er Coleridge may say, and let that be his glory[26]

Here's to poor Skinny Sheil, whose entire occupation
Is gone, since O'Neil ceased delighting the nation;
Whose head's much more empty than Maturin's wig, sirs,
But, nevertheless, we'll give *Sheelahnagig*,[27] sirs.[28]

1830,—author of some satirical verse, editor of Boswell's Johnson, and other works, and, from its commencement to the present time, [July, 1854], one of the most frequent, powerful, and sarcastic contributors to the *Quarterly Review*. The individual familiarly mentioned as "Joe, that booby," was Joseph Hume, now oldest member, or Father of the House of Commons, who by no means merited the title, being a shrewd Scotchman with much common sense and a good deal of perseverance.—M.

22 See note 6.

23 The Rev. George Croly, now rector of a Metropolitan parish, in London, author of Paris, in 1815; The Angel of the World; Life of Burke; the prose romances of Salathiel and Marston; the comedy of Pride Shall have a Fall, and a variety of political, theological, and controversial works, is a native of Ireland, born about 1788. His Catiline, a tragedy in five acts, appeared in 1822. It is founded on what Horace Walpole has called "the most brilliant episode in the History of Rome." It was offered to Elliston, Kemble, and Harris, then managers of Drury Lane and Covent Garden Theatres. In reviewing it (*Blackwood*, June, 1822), Wilson said, "We never read any first tragedy, by any dramatist whatever, abounding so much in happy dramatic situations." The character of Catiline is one which, perhaps, at this moment could be properly personated by only one great actor—Edwin Forrest.—M.

24 The Reverend Mr. Maturin is one of the first quadrillers now extant. He also is a great grinder—and a true Tory.—C. N.

25 A beautiful pass in the Co. Wicklow. You ought to go and see it. *Ans.* We are too old to go touring.—C. N.

26 Coleridge, who was an unsuccessful dramatist, devoted a portion of Biographia Literaria to the ridicule of Robert Charles Maturin, whose play of Bertram had succeeded. [This last word reminds me, *en passant*, of a play-wright who produced a play, in which the acknowledged humorist of the company had not even the ghost of fun to bring before the audience. The curtain fell "in solemn silence." It was again played, with like result, and then withdrawn. A friendly critic, wishing to break the play-wright's fall, went out of his way to show why "it had failed,"—which he ingeniously attributed to every cause, except the true one, of want of dramatic ability. The play-wright's gratitude was expressed in one sentence, in which he stated himself aggrieved at its being said that the trifle had failed. The critic, who rather expected thanks, said that it certainly had not succeeded. "Sir," responded the sensitive author, "*it does not follow that a play has failed, because it did not succeed!*"] Maturin, who was much of a dandy in his attire, added to the narrow income derived from a poor curacy in Dublin, by reading with (or *grinding*), young men who wished to pass creditably through Trinity College. He died in 1825.—M.

27 A nickname bestowed on Sheil, by the late Right Honorable John Philpot Curran, Master of the Rolls in Ireland, much to the satisfaction of the poet. Sheelahnagig, is the name of a popular tune in the Sister Island, but, we are sorry to say, to words of rather an immoral tendency.—C. N.

28 Sheil's three plays, (of which Evadne was the most successful), were written for the

And, now, Mr. Knowles—who with feelings once vented,[29]
While our living bards HE *so well* represented;[30]
And with him we'll couple a man they call Banim,[31]
Though a bard, we scarce think him—a bard we scarce feign him.[32]

Here's Haynes' "Bridal Night"—in five acts—'tis no wonder
He kill'd the poor maiden—yet, faith, 'twas a blunder
To christen that "conscience"—'twas very ironical;[33]
But he floats down to fame through the sink of the "Chronicle."

And here's the last bard of the buskin, poor Bertridge,
Whom Miss Wilson was near blowing up like a cartridge—
Simple Clarke! in the tragic you're yet but a tyro,
Though, faith, there was something not bad in "Ramiro."[34]

Here's Charley from Sligo,[35] whose finical verses,
Each bog-trotter on black Benbulben rehearses,
As flimzy and sloppish as waiting-maid's washes,
Or a speech of his own, or Sir James M'Intosh's.[36]

And while we pass over the Cockneyish dastards,
We must drink to the poet of beggary and bastards;
For there's something so strong in his old-fashioned gab, sirs,
We'll empty a glass to the Veteran Crabbe,[37] sirs.

Here's to Mitchell, restorer of dear Aristophanes,
Who has made all his fun, and his fire, and his scoffing his.

purpose of giving new characters for embodiment by Miss O'Neil, the Irish *Tragedienne*, born in 1793. Sheil died in 1851.—M.

29 This is a great undervaluation of James Sheridan Knowles, whose Caius Gracchus and Virginius had been successfully performed in London. William Tell followed, and, a few years later, The Hunchback, The Wife, and other dramas which have placed him high among the dramatists of England. Knowles was born at Cork, in Ireland, in August, 1784.—M.

30 A Poet mentioned by Cornelius Webb, under the title of "Green Knowles." Rather personal this of Corney. At a public dinner of the Literary Fund, Mr. Knowles, we read in the papers, on the health of the Poets of England being proposed, returned thanks! Air, "How prettily *we* apples swim." On the same occasion an Alderman, (we never mention names,) Captain of Trainbands, returned thanks on the health of the Duke of Wellington and the British Army being given. We have an obscure remembrance of Sir Ronald Ferguson doing the same thing on a similar occasion. Air, "See the conquering hero."—C. N.

31 John Banim, an Irishman, author of "Damon and Pythias," a drama, and of a considerable portion of the prose fictions which appeared as if written "By the O'Hara Family."—M.

32 Banim? Quære. Is it possible there is such a name?—C. N.

33 Mr. Haines, an Irishman, was a writer on the London press, and published a play called "Conscience, or The Bridal Night," which never was performed.—M.

34 J. Bertridge Clerk, Esq. Sch. T. C. D., wrote a play called Ramiro—a perfect tragedy, all being killed in it except the servants, who were judiciously employed to carry off the dead. Harris, the manager of the Dublin theatre, and he, had some rumpus about it;—so had Miss Wilson—the Miss Stephens of Dublin, a very pretty woman, and a very pretty actress. The house was nearly demolished by his brother students—a peaceful body of ingenuous youth.

35 Charles Phillips, had not only come out, as a "celebrated Irish Orator," but published a prose romance, and a great many verses.—M.

36 Late recorder of Bombay—and father of *the* pretty bantling of which Mrs. Divan is not yet delivered. [Mrs. Divan was the *sobriquet* of the London publishing firm of Longman, Hart, Rees, Orme, & Brown.]—M.

37 Crabbe—Mr. North, why do I not ever see an article in your Magazine doing justice to the powerful talents of this powerful poet? *Ans.* There's a braw time coming.—C. N. [A pretty close examination of *Blackwood* enables me to say, that any notice of the Rev. George Crabbe,

"Nature's sternest painter, but her best."

was not made until after his death. *Then*, the merits of the author of The Library, The Village, The Borough, Tales of the Hall, &c., were mentioned and acknowledged. Crabbe was born in 1754, and died in 1832.—M.

Here's to Frere, who some time since wrote Dan Whistlecraft,
And to Rose, who is busy with Roland the Daft.[38]

And here's to the lady-like, lisping, sweet fellow
Who thinks he can write in the vein of Othello,
Without plot or passion—Alas! Peter Proctor—
But it scandals the muse that makes him need a Doctor.[39]

But still he has written some stanzas of merit,
And caught a fine spark of the delicate spirit
Of the rich Bards of old—and might be an apology
For a Minstrel—wer't not for Cockaigne and Mythology.[40]

And now to the dames of the sky-color'd stocking,
Who side-saddle Pegasus, his long switch-tail docking,
Who tatter fine cambrics in rythmical labors,
And dream to the lullings of hautboys and tabors.

Here's first Mother Morgan, akin to morality
As near as she is to a woman of quality—
And the sweet sapphic verses of Maidenly Sydney,
That so tickle the fancy and touch up the kidney.

Those verses so mawkish, so fat, and so gawdy,
A girlish first fire of the bold and the ———
Which give a fair promise all wisely and wittily
Of the Jacobin cant of her "France" and her "Italy."

But in spite of Canidia and her doubty càvalier,
At her follies full often we purpose to have a leer—
Unless to Algiers she fly off, as we task her,
Or become the she-Solon[41] of mad Madagascar.[42]

Here's Lucy,[43] in whom wit and wisdom are blended,
By whom everything's seen, felt, and comprehended—

[38] Thomas Mitchell, translator of the plays of Aristophanes into English verse, was born in 1783, and died in 1845. John Hookham Frere, the friend of Scott and Southey, will principally be recollected by his facetious poem written under the *nom de plume* of Whistlecraft (and called The Monks and the Giants), which suggested to Lord Byron the stanza, in which he afterwards wrote Beppo and Don Juan. Frere, born in 1769, died in 1846. William Steward Rose, the translator of Ariosto, Letters from the North of Italy, and other works, was intimate with Byron, Davy, Scott, Southey, and, in short, with all eminent literary men during the whole period of his life. He survived Scott.—M.

[39] Alias Barry Cornwall. A young gentleman most unjustifiably treated by Blackwood. What a shame it is, that a rising young man cannot be allowed to kill his people in fine tragedies, without the sneer of envy, and the murmuring of malice! Take that, Christopher! See how differently he is appreciated in London—where he, author of Mirandola, is made one of a committee to erect a monument to his congenial spirit, William Shakspeare, author of Hamlet, and other agreeable dramas. *Ans.* We defy any one to point out a passage in which we have not extolled Mr. Cornwall. In fact, he is one of our own pets; and if we *do* sometimes give him a little gentle and benignant correction, it is only because we remember the precept of Solomon, "He that spareth the rod, spoileth the *child*."—C. N.

[40] Bryan William Procter, author of the tragedy of Mirandola; concerning which, he published a solemn statement that one of the characters was *not* the double of Othello! Under the name of Barry Cornwall, he has won high repute as a writer of short Dramatic Scenes, and a variety of popular songs.—M.

[41] Observe, not a *Solan* goose.—C. N.

[42] Sydney Owenson, afterwards Lady Morgan—by marriage. It is somewhat impertinent to allude to a lady's age, but she was born not later than 1770.—M.

[43] Lucy Aiken, author of Biographies of Queen Elizabeth and James I.—M.

And here's to the genius of Helen Maria,
Of all that is frothy the *Entelecheia.*[44]

Here's to Opie the sweet—Here's to high-minded Hannah—
Here's to Shakspeare in Petticoats, noble Joanna—
Here's to all from soft Hemans as rich as a ruby,[45]
To the brogue and the blarney of pretty Miss Lubè.[46]

Now here are four bards, to whom genius is pater,
Who never suck'd poetry from Alma Mater—
Who just knew so much of the great Aristotle,
As they got from the fields, from their feelings, and bottle.

Fill first for the Chaldee—the shepherd of Ettrick,
Who stole from the Hills' hums his musical rhet'rick—
For Hogg's rhyme is no gruntiug—and here's a libation
To Bloomfield, the simplest sweet Bard of the nation.[47]

Here's to Clare and his verses, so simple and pleasant,
The *London one's Bard*—The Northamptonshire peasant:
And here's to the Galloway boy and his lyrics,
That have put all the Bards of Cockaigne in hysterics.[48]

Here's to Luttrell and Dale, and the Dante of Carey;
Here's to Lloyd, the preserver of great Alfieri;
And this bumper to Lamb we send gratefully greeting,
For we love his deep baaing and beautiful bleating.[49]

Here's Thurlow half-witted, and Spencer half-attic,
Yet not lame in the light and the epigrammatic;

44 Helen Maria Williams, certainly one of the English "strong-minded women," born in 1762, died in 1827; author of Letters of France, during the first Revolution, in which she assisted and recommended the principles of the Girondists. On their fall she was arrested, and narrowly escaped the guillotine. She also published a Narrative of Events in France in 1815.—M.

45 Amelia Opie, widow of the painter, and an authoress of some note. She died in 1853. Hannah More, (born in 1744, died in 1833,) an eminent writer.—Joanna Baillie, author of Plays on the Passions, and other dramas and poems. She died in 1851. Felicia Hemans, the best of the female lyrists of England, born in 1794, died in 1835.—Of Miss Luby I only know that she published, but was unable to sell a volume of poems.—M.

46 Pretty, indeed, and very pretty—but no brogue, or no blarney, Mr. Paddy.—C. N.

47 Full particulars about James Hogg,(born 1772, died 1835). are to be found in my Memoir of him, in this edition. Robert Bloomfield, author of The Farmer's Boy, and other poems of great merit; born 1766, died 1823.—M.

48 John Clare, the Northampton Peasant and Poet, now [1854], in a lunatic asylum. Allan Cunningham, a Scottish poet, novelist, critic, and biographer, born in 1785, died in 1842.—M.

49 Luttrell, author of Advice to Julia, an epistle in verse, will long be traditionally remembered as one of the wits of the regency and reign of George IV.—The Rev. Doctor Dale, author of The Widow of Nain, Irad and Adah, and other poems, is now prebendary of St. Paul's and Rector of St. Pancras, the largest parish in London.—Charles Lloyd, translator of Alfieri, and an early friend of Southey and Coleridge.—Charles Lamb, the gentle Elia, was born in 1775, and died in 1834. Few authors have won more sincere and genial regard from "hosts of friends." His Essays form one of the most popular works in the language. A great deal of good pity has been expended on the fact that Lamb was "doomed to the cruel desk in daily toil." He was a clerk in the accountant's office in the East India House, commencing on a respectable and rising salary, his sole labors being to copy papers into books of record. When he retired, after thirty-five years' service, his income had increased to £700 a-year, and he was then allowed a retiring life-allowance of £450 a year. Great consideration was shown him by his superiors. On one occasion, however, (the usual office-hours being nominally from 10 to 4), he entered his office at noon. The principal said, "Mr. Lamb, you really *do* come so late." Lamb paused, and said, with the arch simplicity which distinguished him, "True, sir, but then—I go away so early!"—M.

Herbert, tasteless and black, as a glass of bad negus;[50]
And Strangford, who gather'd some gold from the Tagus.[51]

And now to the bards of the famed silent sister;[52]
We own, for some seasons or so, we have miss'd her.
And the prize-winning poets of Isis and Cam,
Very fine—very learned—and scarce worth a d——.

And now into dozens the poets we'll trundle:
We must drink to them now at least twelve in the bundle.
Here's Williams and Darley, Bartòn and Fitzgerald,
Who might shine in a page of the "Times" or the "Herald."[53]

Here's to all the rest, both esquired and anonymous,
May they all in their times find their own Hieronymus;
Thòugh their verses may live until Saturday se'nnight,
Or as long as the speeches of Brougham or of Bennett.

We can give no more names—faith, we ne'er could be able;
If we did, we would soon be laid under the table.
Then one glass to them all, male and female together,
Who recite in the dog-days, in spite of the weather.

This last three times three, boys.—Hip, hip, hurra!
The Poets of England—by jingo! 'tis day.
Can Alaric[54] save them?—No; our *personality*
And Maga alone can give them immortality.

50 Hibernice Nagus. See note 4.—C. N.

51 This is the Lord Thurlow, whose volume of middling rhymes, in 1813, so much excited the ridicule of Byron, that he perpetrated some satires on them, which are to be found in his poems, and place some of Thurlow's lines, therein quoted, in a situation akin to that of flies in amber.—William Robert Spencer, a lively poet of the Regency, born in 1770, died in 1834.—Dr. Herbert, son of the Earl of Carnaervon, dean of Manchester, author of Attila, and other poems of marked merit, and also of Mr. Henry William Herbert, the best sporting writer in America, ("Frank Forrester"), distinguished as poet, novelist, critic, historian, and artist.—The translator of Camoens was addressed in Byron's English Bards and Scotch Reviewers, as

> Hibernian Strangford! with thine eyes of blue
> And boasted locks of red or auburn hue.

with a declaration, by way of annotation, that "The things given to the public as the poem of Camoens, are no more to be found in the original Portuguese, than in the Song of Solomon."—M.

52 By "Silent Sister," is meant Trinity College, Dublin—A most unfounded and ridiculous calumny, as we shall have the pleasure of proving ere long.—C. N. [Which was never done.—M.]

53 Darley eventually became critical preface-writer to Cumberland's British Drama.—Bernard Barton, the Quaker poet, died in 1849.—Fitzgerald, called "The Small-beer Poet," by Cobbett, used annually to deliver a poetical address at the Literary Fund Dinner.—M.

54 Alaric A. Watts, Esq., who is employed about what we doubt not will be a most interesting work, Specimens of the British Poets. Of course, he must exhibit us in full fig.—C. N. [The work appeared, in two volumes, but was not a good collection of poems.—M.]

No. V.—SEPTEMBER, 1822.

ACT I.—Scene—*Back Parlor—Cold Supper just set.*

Manet Mr. Ambrose *solus.*

Mr. Ambrose. I think it will do. That plate of lobsters is a little too near the edge. Softly, softly, the round of beef casts too deep a shadow over these pickles. There—that's right. Old Kit will be unable to criticise —

Enter Mr. North.

Mr. North. Old Kit! will be unable to criticise!!—Why, upon my honor, Mr. Ambrose, you are rather irreverent in your lingo.

Mr. Ambrose, (much confused.) I really, sir, had not the least idea you were at hand. You know, sir, with what profound respect —

Mr. North. Come, Ambrose, put down the pots of porter. The King has left the Theatre, and we shall be all here in a few seconds. I made my escape from the manager's box, just before the row and the rush began. Hark! that is the clank of the Adjutant.

Enter Odoherty, Tickler, Seward, Buller, Highland Chieftain, *and* Mr. Blackwood.

Odoherty. Allow me, my dear North, to introduce to you my friend, the Chief of the Clan —

Mr. North. No need of a name. I know him by his father's face. Sir, I will love you for the sake of as noble a Gael as ever slaughtered a Sassenach. Sit down, sir, if you please.

(Highland Chieftain sits down at Mr. North's right hand.)

Mr. Seward. Well, did he not look every inch a King,* this evening? A King of Great Britain, France, and Ireland, ought, if possible, be a man worth looking at. His subjects expect it, and it is but reasonable they should.

Mr. North. Fame does no more than justice to his bow. It is most princely—so—or rather so. Is that like him?

* In August, 1822, George IV. visited Scotland. He had visited Ireland and Hanover in the preceding year. He remained in the vicinity of Edinburgh (the guest of the Duke of Buccleugh, at Dalkeith Palace, within six miles of the capital,) for fifteen days, and his return was hastened by the intelligence that the Marquis of Londonderry, Foreign Secretary, had committed suicide in London. When he was proceeding, amid tens of thousands, to the Palace of Holyrood, the ancient abode of the Scottish Kings, the demeanor of the multitude was so quiet and respectful (very unlike the wild enthusiasm which greeted him at Dublin) that he said "This is a nation of gentlemen." This compliment is referred to, over and over again, in the following Noctes.—M.

Odoherty. No more than a hop-pole is like a palm-tree, or the Editor of the Edinburgh Review like him of Blackwood's Magazine. The King's bow shows him to be a man of genius; for, mark me, he has no model to go by.* He must not bow like the Duke of Argyll, or Lord Fife, well as they bow, but like a King. And he does so. The King is a man of genius.

Mr. Blackwood. Do you think, sirs, that the King would become a contributor to the Magazine? I have sent his Majesty a set splendidly bound by ——

Mr. North. Hush, Ebony, leave that to me. You must not interfere with the Editorial department.

Mr. Buller. What do you Scotch mean by calling yourselves a grave people; and by saying that you are not, like the Irish, absurd in the expression of your loyalty? I never heard such thunder in a Theatre before.

Odoherty. I would have given twenty ten-pennies that some of the young ladies in the pit had remembered that a pocket handkerchief should not be used longer than a couple of days. Some of the literary gentlemen too, showed snuffy signals. But the *coup d'œil* was imposing.

Buller. I hate all invidious national distinctions. Let every people hail their King in their own way.

Odoherty. To be sure they should. But then the Scotch are "a nation of Gentlemen;" and the Irish "a nation of ragamuffins;" and the English "a nation of shopkeepers." How then?

Mr. North. His Majesty knows better than to satirize us. We are not a nation of gentlemen—thank God;—but the greater part of our population is vulgar, intelligent, high-cheeked, raw-boned, and religious.

Mr. Seward. I could not help smiling, when I looked across the pit and along the boxes this evening, at the compliment towards yourselves as a nation, which some self-sufficient soul put into his Majesty's mouth. I never saw a more vulgar pit in my life. The women looked as if ——

Odoherty. One and all of them could have kissed the King. But, Seward, my boy, you are mistaken in calling the pit vulgar. Your taste has been vitiated, Seward, by Oxford Milliners, and ——

Mr. North. The conversation is wandering. (*Turning to the Chief-*

* Byron admits the fascination of this bow. In Don Juan we have

"There, too, he saw (whate'er he may be now)
A Prince, the prince of princes at the time,
With fascination in his very bow,
And full of promise, as the spring of prime.
Though royalty was written on his brow,
He had *then* the grace, too rare in every clime,
Of being, without alloy of fop or beau,
A finished gentleman from top to toe."—M.

tain.) I saw you talking to the Thane in the Theatre.* Would to heaven you had brought him here!

Chieftain. He is gone to Dalkeith or he would have come.

Mr. North. How popular the Thane is all over Scotland. Depend upon it, gentlemen, that the best man is, in general, the most popular. Nothing but generosity and goodness will make peasants love peers.

Mr. Blackwood. His Lordship never comes to town without calling at the shop.

Enter MR. AMBROSE *and Waiters with rizzard haddocks, cut of warm salmon, muirfowl, and haggis.*

Mr. Tickler. Adjutant, I will drink a pot of porter with you—THE KING,—(three times three—*surgunt omnes*)—Hurra, hurra, hurra—Hurra, hurra, hurra—Hurra, hurra, hurra! (*Conticuere omnes.*)

Mr. North. Odoherty, be pleased to act as croupier.

Odoherty. More porter.

Mr. Tickler. Did you see how the whole pit fixed its face on the King's—till the play began? It was grand, North. His eye met that loyal "glower" with mild and dignified composure. The King, North, was happy. I'll swear he was. He saw that he had our hearts. Every note of "God save the King" went dirling though my very soul-strings. I'm as hoarse as a howlet.

Mr. North. I think the people feel proud of their King. As he past the platform where I stood, on his entrance into Edinburgh, I heard a countryman say to his neighbor,—"Look, Jock; look, Jock,—isna he an honest-looking chiel? Gude faith, Jock, he's just like my ain father."

Mr. Seward. Curse the Radicals! A king must abhor even a single hiss from the vilest of his subjects. The King, Mr. North, is with us as popular a King as ever reigned in England. He has only to show himself oftener, and —

Mr. Buller. I have seen the king in public often; but I never saw him insulted except in the newspapers. The "Scotsman in London" is a common character.

Odoherty. Mr. Seward, a little haggis. See "its hurdies like twa distant hills."

Mr. Seward. What are hurdies?

Mr. Tickler. See Dr. Jamieson.

Chieftain. Mr. North, I am delighted. I hope I may say so without flattery. I never drank better Glenlivet.—Why, gentlemen, not come and pay me a visit this autumn? No occasion for a tent. I am a bachelor, and have few children.

Odoherty. Settled.—Name your day.

* The Earl of Fife;—he has already been introduced to the reader in "The Tent."—M.

Chieftain. 14th of September. I cannot be home sooner. Is it a promise?

Omnes. 14th of September. WE SWEAR!!

Odoherty. Well done, old Mole, in the cellarage.—Hamlet—see Shakspeare.

Enter MR. AMBROSE.

Mr. Ambrose. Mr. North, a communication.

Tickler. Read—read.

Mr. North. I cannot say I am quite able to do so. My eyes are a little hazy or so. But there is the letter, Tickler.—Up with it.

Tickler, (*reads.*)

De'il tak the kilts! For fifty year, nae honest soon of Reikie's
Wad ever think to walk the streets, denuded o' his breekies.
And ony kilted drover lad, wi' kyloes or a letter,
Was pitied, or was glower'd at, "Puir chiel, he kens nae better;"
And apple-wives look'd sidelins, and thocht he came to steal or beg,
Whene'er they saw a callant wi' his hurdies in a philabeg.*
And even chiefs o' clans themselves, whene'er they ran to towns, man,
Were fain to clothe their hairy knees in breeks, or pantaloons, man.
But now! Lord bless your soul! there's no a Lawland writer laddie
Can wheedle a pund note or twa frae his auld cankered daddie,
But aff he sets, (though born betwixt St. Leonard's an Drumsheugh) an
He fits himsel' wi' bannet, plaid, and hose, and kilt, and spleuchan.†
Ye'se ken the cause o' a' the steer;—the Heeland Dhuine Wassals‡
Began to tire o' wearin' breeks whene'er they left their castles;
So they coaxed the honest citizens to join in a convention
To tak' the corduroy from off the pairt I daurna mention;
That, like the tod‖ that tint his tail, they mightna cause derision,
And find their faces in a flame, while elsewhere they were freezin.
The town's-lads snappit at the plan, and thus began the Celtic,
A medley strange frae every land, frae off the shores o' Baltic;
Frae England, Ireland, Scotland; Border lairds and ancient British,
There were Dutchmen, Danes, and Portuguese, and French and Otaheitish;
And a' professions, frae the lad that's only just apprenticed,
To the great hero of the west—e'en Doctor Scott the Dentist—
And they wad dine, and drink, and strut, as big's Macallum More, sir,
And skraigh attempts at Gaelic words, until their throats were sore, sir.
An' a' was canty for a while, for these were still their gay days,
An' a' could lend a hand to pay for balls gi'en to the ladies;
And there they danc'd the Highland fling, and kick'd their kilts and toes up,
Tho' whiles their ruler-shapit legs refused to keep their hose up.
But when the pawky Highland lairds had fairly set the fashion,
Up gets an angry Chief o' Chiefs in a prodigious passion:
"Fat Teil hae you to do wi' kilts, gae wa' and get your claes on,
Get out, ye nasty Lowland poys, and put your preeks and stays on;

* *Hurdies in a philabeg*,—his buttocks in a kilt.—M.
† *Spleuchan*;—tobacco-pouch.—M.
‡ *Dunnie-wassal.*—A Highland gentleman, generally the cadet of a family of rank, who received his title from the land he occupied, though held at the will of his chieftain.—M.
‖ *Tod.*—A Fox.—M.

Ye shanna wear your claes like me, I look on you as fermin,
Ye hae nae mair o' Highland pluid than if you were a Cherman."*
This sets them up, "Chairman indeed! Ye never shall be ours, sir!
Except it be to carry us when we go out of doors, sir!
Like ithers o' your kintra men." And thus they flyte thegither,
And haud the hail town in a steer, expellin' ane anither.
And how the bus'ness is to end, is mair than I can tell, sir,
Indeed it seems to fickle and perplex the Sheriff's sell, sir;
But this I ken, that folk that's wise think they maun be nae witches,
Wha ever let a Highland Kern† entice them out o' breeches.

Highland Chief. Come, gentlemen, if you please, I will propose a toast,—"Glengarry!" His Majesty would not have sent the message he did to the chiefs, if he had not been pleased with them and their highlanders.‡

Omnes. Glengarry. Hurra, hurra, hurra!

Odoherty. What does Glengarry mean by saying that few members of the Celtic Society could shoot an eagle? It is easier, a damned deal easier, to shoot an eagle than a peacock. But the easiest way of any is to knock an eagle down with a shillelah.

Mr. Seward. Do you shy the shillelah at his head from a distance?

Odoherty. No. I refer to the Chieftain. You must walk slowly up to him at the rate of about four miles an hour, (Townsend, the pedestrian, would do it half backwards and half forwards,) and hit him over the periwig with your sapling.

Chieftain. Perfectly true. When an eagle has eat a sheep or a roe, he sits as heavy as a Dutchman—cannot take wing—and you may bag him alive if you choose. The shepherds often fling their plaids over him. But let him take wing, and he darkens the sundisk like an eclipse.

Mr. Blackwood. I beg your pardon, sir, but I should wish much to have a sound, sensible Article on the State of the Highlands of Scotland. I suspect there is much misrepresentation as to the alleged cruelty and impolicy of large farms. Dog on it, will any man tell me, sir, that —

* German.—C. N. † *Kerne.*—A freebooter.—M.

‡ Every one seemed to have gone mad on the subject of Highland costume, the use of which had been prohibited by the 19th, George II. The late Sir John Sinclair, in the early part of the present century, had this act repealed; and although this took place in mid-winter, all the Highlanders north of Stirling threw off the hated breeches, and adopted the cooler and more ventilatory kilt! Even at his first levee, George IV. appeared in full Highland garb—which no royal Stuart, Prince Charles excepted, had ever worn in Holyrood. General Stewart of Garth, assisted at this Celtic toilet, and saw that the king was correctly attired. There, too, in the same costume, appeared the bulky frame of the London alderman and banker, Sir William Curtis, (immortalized in Don Juan, as

"The witless Falstaff to a hoary Hal,")

whose appearance, in such a garb, was very ludicrous. When the King was about leaving Scotland, an official letter was addressed by the late Sir Robert Peel, then Home Secretary, in which, after thanking Scott, for his own immense and successful efforts to make the royal visit a pleasant one, he added, "The king wishes to make you the channel of conveying to the Highland Chiefs and their followers, who have given to the varied scene, which we have witnessed, so peculiar and romantic a character, his particular thanks for their attendance, and his warm approbation of their uniform deportment."—M.

Chieftain. Mr. Blackwood, I wish I could write an article of the kind you mention. You are a gentleman of liberal sentiments. In twenty years the Highlands will be happier than they ever have been since the days of Ossian. Lowland lairds have no right to abuse us for departing from the savage state.

Blackwood. Could you let us have it for next Number, sir? We stand in need of such articles prodigiously—sound, sensible, statistical articles, full of useful information. We have wit, fun, fancy, and feeling, and all that sort of thing in abundance, but we are short of useful information. We want facts—a Number now and then, with less fun and more facts, would take, and promote the sale with dull people. Yes, it is a fact, that we want facts.

Odoherty. Damn your Magazine, Ebony! You gave Napoleon no rest at St. Helena till he became a contributor. You are beginning to send sly hints to the King. And here we have you smelling as strong of the shop as a bale of brown paper, dunning the Chieftain the very first time he has come among us.

Mr. Seward. Chieftain, you mentioned Ossian—may I ask if his Poems are authentic?

Chieftain. As authentic as the heather and the hail on our misty mountains.*

Mr. Seward. Wordsworth the poet says, that in Ossian's Poems, every thing is looked at as if it were one, but that nothing in nature is so looked at by a great poet. Therefore, Ossian's poetry is bad, and written by Macpherson.

Chieftain. I have not the pleasure of being familiar with Mr. Wordsworth's name or writings. Neither do I understand one syllable of what you have now said. Ossian's poetry is not bad.† Did the gentleman you speak of ever see a lake or a mountain?

Buller. He lives on the banks of a tarn about a mile round about.

Chieftain. I am sorry for him.

Mr. North. He also says, if I recollect rightly, that Ossian speaks of car-borne chiefs in Morven—but that Morven is inaccessible to cars.

Odoherty. So it is to jaunting cars. Wordsworth was in a sort of mongrel shandrydan, a cross between a gig and a tax-cart; and

* Sir Walter Scott's opinion on the authenticity of Ossian's Poems ought to be conclusive. Scott was a man so thoroughly national, that he would almost strain a point rather than part with any belief likely to do credit to Scotland. His deliberate opinion was this:—"After making every allowance for the disadvantages of a literal translation, and the possible debasement which those now collected may have suffered, on the great and violent change which the Highlands have undergone, since the researches of Macpherson, I am compelled to admit that, incalculably the greater part of the English Ossian must be ascribed to Macpherson himself, and that his whole introductions, notes, &c. &c., are an absolute tissue of forgeries."—M.

† So thought Napoleon, who was quite Ossian-struck at one period of his life, before he wore the imperial purple. It was by way of compliment to this fancy, and with the tact of a courtier, (rough soldier as he affected to be,) that Bernadotte gave his eldest son the name of one of Ossian's heroes. Since 1844, ho has been Oscar, king of Sweden.—M.

no wonder he was shy of Morven. But unless he had been a most ignorant person indeed, (all poets are ignorant,) he would have known that there are cars in Morven to this day.

Chieftain. There are—and scientifically constructed, though of old date. I have seen the Highlanders coming down the steep and rocky hills with them, full of peats, with a rapidity that would have pleased Fingal himself. Besides there are many straths and level places in Morven.

Mr. North. Pray, were not all the Highlands once called "Morven?"

Chieftain. They were, not unfrequently, nor by a few.

Odoherty. So goes the flummery of the water-drinking laker about Ossian,—the bard who brewèd his own whisky, and drank like a whale.

Mr. Tickler. Tell Wordsworth to let other people's poetry alone, from Ossian to Pope, and make his own a little better. Who prefers Alice Fell to Malvina? or Peter Bell to Abelard? Oh! that the English lakes were all connected by canals! A few steamboats from Glasgow would soon blow up their poetry. Wishy-washy stuff indeed!

Mr. North. Our conversation, gentlemen, is degenerating into literature. I will fine the first of you that tattles in a bumper.

Odoherty. The Paradise Lost of Milton has ever ap——

Mr. Tickler. He blabs for a bumper. But in with the salt.

Mr. Blackwood. One of the great merits of *The Magazine* is that it has less literature ——

Odoherty. Than libels.

Mr. Blackwood, (*rising.*) Mr. Odoherty, I have lately seen you walking on all occasions with the enemy? Did you review O'Meara in the Edinburgh?

Odoherty. No, no, my good fellow; they throw out their bait, but I won't nibble.

Mr. Blackwood. All I know is, that it is at once more honorable and more lucrative to write in our Maga, than in any other existing work.

Mr. Tickler, (*ringing the bell.*) What cackling, as of geese, is that we hear through the partition?—Mr. Ambrose, remove that sideboard, and throw open these folding-doors.

Mr. Ambrose. There is a small party in the next room, Mr. Tickler.

Mr. Tickler. I want to count them.

(*Sideboard is removed, and doors flung open.*)

SCENE II.

Odoherty. Whigs—Whigs—a nest of Whigs. A conspiracy against our lord the King. How do you, Mr. Bunting?

Mr. Bunting. I scarcely understand this, Mr. Odoherty. But, during the King's Visit, all party distinctions should be forgotten. I hope you did not cry, Whigs, Whigs, Whigs, offensively.

Mr. North. Young gentleman, we have been all Whigs in our day. It is a disease of the constitution. Will you and your friends join our table? Help Mr. Bunting to some haggis.

Buller. This is a formidable coalition. It is as bad as Mr. Fox joining Lord North.*

Mr. Blackwood. Mr. Bunting, I seldom see you or any of your friends about the shop now-a-days. I hope, now that the King comes to see us, you will step up the front-steps. (*Aside to Mr. Bunting.*)—Are not these three of the Seven Young Men?

Mr. Bunting. I was glad to see the King, and I trust he will not be misinformed of our sentiments towards him. I respect him as the chief magistrate.

Mr. Tickler. That is infernal nonsense, Master Bunting, begging your pardon. Have you no feeling, no fancy, no imagination, Master Bunting. Your heart ought to leap at the word King, as at the sound of a trumpet. Chief magistrate!—humbug. Do you love your own father, because he was once Provost of Crail? No, no, Master Bunting, that won't pass at Ambrose's.

Young Man. I hope that the King's Visit will be productive of some substantial and lasting benefit to this portion of the united empire.

Mr. North. What do you mean? Mention what ought to be done, and I will give a hint to Mr. Peel.

Young Man. In my opinion the question of borough reform ——

Odoherty. Sheep's head or trotters, sir?

Mr. Bunting. Unless his majesty's ministers assist the Greeks, and ransom the young women ravished from their native Scio into Turkish harems, the inhabitants of modern Athens will ——

Odoherty. What will they do?—But I agree with you, Mr. Bunting, in thinking the Greek girls deucedly handsome. Were you ever in Scio?

Mr. Bunting. No. But I attended a meeting t'other day, at which

* Fox and Lord North had been in the habit of grossly abusing each other, in public and in private. In April, 1782, they formed a Coalition, and entered the Cabinet together,—much against the King's will. In the following December, Fox's India Bill was rejected by the House of Lords. The same evening, Fox and Lord North were literally turned out of office by the King. Lord North never again entered it, and it was nearly 23 years, before—for the last few months of his life—Fox again was in place.—M.

the affairs in general of Greece were admirably discussed. And are we to countenance rape, robbery, and murder?

Odoherty. Why, I don't know. As an Irishman, I am scarcely entitled to answer in the negative. But what has all this blarney to do with King George the Fourth's Visit to Scotland?

Mr. Blackwood. I will be very happy to give Mr. Bunting, or any of his Whig friends, five guineas for an article of moderate size, containing a few facts about the Greeks. Pray, Mr. Bunting, what may be the population of the isle of Scio?

Mr. Bunting, (*after a pause.*) Well—well—I shall not push the conversation any farther in that direction. The haggis is most excellent. Mr. North, may I have the honor to pledge you in a pot of porter?

Odoherty, (*ringing the bell.*) Pipes. (*They are brought in.*)

Mr. Tickler. No spitting-boxes. They are filthy.

Mr. North. Where art thou, Odoherty? I discern thee not through this dense cloud of smoke.

Odoherty. We may all come and go without being missed. I have an appointment at one o'clock.

Voice, as of one of the Young Men. I have just been perusing the fresh number of the Edinburgh Review. I scarcely think that the Duke of Wellington will go to the Congress—after it.

Mr. Tickler. Has Frank Jeffrey stultified the Duke of Wellington?

Voice, as of one of the Young Men. Bonaparte, Benjamin Constant, Madame de Stael, John Allen, Esq., Sir James Mackintosh, and Jeffrey himself, all think him *un homme borné.*

Mr. Seward. Pray, sir—I beg your pardon, but I do not see you very distinctly; what do you mean by *un homme borné*? How do you translate the words?

Voice, as of one of the Young Men. I am no French scholar; but it sounds like French. It is an epithet of opprobrium. The precise meaning is of no consequence to our argument.

Odoherty. O! the Duke of Wellington is an ass! what a pity!—Who is that sick in that corner?—Waiter, waiter. Throw open the window—down pipes, till it clears off a little. Soho! it is my eloquent young Man of the Mist?—Carry him out, Ambrose—there he is *un homme borné.*

Mr. Bunting. We, all of us, hate smoking. But, Mr. North—gentlemen—good night.

(*Exeunt* Mr. Bunting *and the Young Men.*)

Mr. Buller. Are these a fair specimen of your young Edinburgh Whigs?

Mr. North. I fear they are. Their feebleness quite distresses us. Jeffrey himself, I am told, is unhappy about it. What am I doing?

lighting my pipe with an article that I have not read. There, (*flinging it over to Buller*) read it aloud for the general edification and delight.

Buller reads.

TO CHRISTOPHER NORTH, ESQ.,

From an occasional Contributor, living at Cape Clear, who was applied to for an article about the King in Edinburgh.

1.

Chief of scribblers! Wondrous Editor!
Why d'ye seek assistance here?
Little you'd gain of praise, or credit, or
Any thing else by me, my dear.
Those who, like Boreas,
Greeted uproarious,
Visit so glorious, loudly should sing,
How Miss Edina,
Looking so fine-a,
Smart and divine-a, welcomed the King,

2.

One would think it only rational,
That you had poets there on the spot:
Stir up your own Bard truly national,
First of all Minstrels, Sir Walter Scott:
High o'er Fahrenheit,
Our hearts are in heat,
When that Baronet thrums the string.
Can he refuse us
Aid from his muses?
No, no, he chooses to welcome the King.

3.

Have you not there, too, Crabbe, the veteran?
Ask that old poet to do the job.
For describing, show me a better one,
Bailies or beggarmen, flunkies or mob:
Hubbub, bobbery,
Crowd and mobbery,
For all such jobbery he's the thing.
So then for a bard,
List the Borough Bard,
Being a thorough bard to welcome the King.*

* In 1821. at John Murray's, in London, Sir Walter Scott was introduced to Crabbe, the poet, who promised to visit him. He arrived in August, 1822, when Scott was immersed in what has truly been called "the tumultuous preparations" for the King's visit. Scott could give little of his time to Crabbe, who was astonished (as it were), at the fulness and freshness of Scottish loyalty. Lockhart had just cause for lamenting (in his Life of Scott), that the English bard had not seen the Scottish, "at Abbotsford among his books, his trees, and his own good simple peasants." In fact, Scott had little time for private matters. Scott's family, says his son-in-law. were more fortunate than himself in this respect. They had from infancy been taught to reverence Crabbe's genius, and they now saw enough of him to make them think of him ever afterwards with tender affection. At this time, Crabbe was 68 years old, and Scott 51. Crabbe died in 1834, aged eighty; Scott in 1832, aged sixty-one.—M.

4.

Mr. Croly, my brother Irishman,
  Was there with you, as I am told;
He, I think, could give you a flourish, man,
  In verses bright of gems and gold.
        Soho, Cataline!
        Prime hand at a line!
Haste, and rattle in your verse to bring;
        Singing so gorgeous,
        How knight and burgess,
Throng'd round Great Georgius, welcomed the King.

5.

Then, there's another to do it cleverly,
  He the great poet who writes in prose;
Sure I mean the Author of Waverley,
  Whoe'er he be, if any one knows.
        Truce to Peveril!
        There are several
People who never will miss the thing,
        If he will vapor
        On hot-press'd paper,
And cut a caper to welcome the King.

6.

Or ask Wilson, the grave and serious
  Poet, who sung of the Palmy Isle;
Or the sweet fellow who wrote Valerius
  (Pray, what's his name?) would do it in style.
        Could you get once
        Some of these great ones,
Tender or sweet ones for you to sing,
        We'd think the lasses
        Had left Parnassus,
To sing trebles and basses, to welcome the King.

Mr. Seward. I have had enough of "tobacco reek." O, for a gulp of fresh air!

Chieftain. The barge of the Duke of Atholl is now lying near the Chain Pier? It is under my orders. Might I propose a water-party? I can have her manned with ten oars in ten minutes.

Mr. North. With all my heart. I am fond of aquatics.

Omnes, (*crowding around the Editor.*) Take my box-coat—No, no, my cloak—here is my wrap-rascal. Tie my Barcelona round your neat neck.* Ring for a coach and six.

(*Exeunt Mr.* NORTH, *leaning on the arm of the Highland Chief—and* MR. AMBROSE *with a flaming branch of wax-lights in each hand.*)

END OF ACT FIRST.

* The line occurs in the song of "The Sprig of Shillelah," in which an Irishman, at Donnybrook Fair, is described as wearing "a new Barcelona tied round his nate neck." The Barcelona was a thick silk handkerchief, boasting of many bright hues, among which mustard-color was predominant. It was "neat but not gaudy."—M.

ACT II.

SCENE I.—*Duke of Atholl's Barge off the Chain Pier, Newhaven.*

Chieftain. She pulls ten oars. Mr. North, will you take the helm? I ask no better Palinurus.

Mr. North. I am but a fresh-water sailor; yet in my day I have sailed a few thousand leagues. Byron says he has swam more leagues than all the living poets of Great Britain have sailed, with one or two exceptions. Had he said the living critics, he had grossly erred.

Odoherty. Coxswain, give North the tiller. Now, lads, down with your oars—splash—splash. Are we all on board?

Omnes. All—all—all—pull away.

Mr. North. For the King's yacht. Beautifully feathered! Remember whom you have on board!

Buller. Seward! this beats Brazen-nose. Yet I wish one of old Davis's wherries were here, to show how an arrow whizzes from a bow.

Mr. North. Seward—Buller, behold the Queen of the North! What think you of the Castle, with the crescent moon hung over her for a banner? The city lights are not afraid to confront the stars. I hope Arthur's Ghost is on his mountain-throne to-night. Yonder goes a fire-balloon. See how the stationary stars mock that transient flight of rockets. Yonder crown of gas-light burns brightly to-night,—now it is half veiled in cloud-drapery,—now it is gone. Hurra! Again it blazes forth, and tinges Nelson's Pillar with its ruddy splendor.

Odoherty. By the powers, North, you are poetical!

Mr. Tickler. Nelson's Pillar—ay—may it stand there for ever! Did they not talk of pulling it down for the Parthenon? *We* held it up. Pull down a Monument to the greatest of British admirals! Fie—fie.

Mr. Buller. We Englishmen thought the proposal an odd one. But the Pillar, it was said, was in bad taste, and disfigured the modern Athens.

Mr. North. It is in bad taste. What then? Are Monuments to the illustrious dead to lie at the mercy of Dilletanti? But, as Mr. Tickler said, *we* preserved that Monument.

Mr. Seward. I admire the Parthenon. Most of you will recollect my poem on that subject. I am glad the foundation-stone has been laid.

Mr. North. So am I. Let Scotland show now that she has liberality as well as taste, and not suffer the walls to be dilapidated by time before they have been raised to their perfect height.

Odoherty. The Parthenon will be an elegant testimonial. Is it not, too, a national testimonial? Why then should not the Scottish nation pay the masons? Why sue for Parliamentary grants? Are you not "a nation of Gentlemen?" Put your hands then into your breeches-pockets, (I beg your pardon, Chieftain), and pay for what you build.

Mr. Tickler. The Standard-Bearer speaks nobly. We admire the Parthenon. We resolve to build it. We call ourselves Athenians, and then implore Parliament to pay the piper. Poor devils! we ought to be ashamed of ourselves.

Mr. Buller. Mr. Odoherty, I agree with you. A rich nation does well to be magnificent. Up with towers, temples, baths, porticos, and what not; but for one nation to build splendid structures, and then call on another for their praises and their purses, is, in my opinion, not exactly after the fashion of the Athenians.

Mr. Blackwood. I have no objection to publish an additional Number any month in behoof of the Parthenon. I think Mr. Linning deserves the highest praise for his zeal and perseverance.

Odoherty. And I hope you will also publish an additional Number the month following for behoof of the Foundling Hospital, Dublin, which is generally overstocked. There is not milk for half the brats.

Mr. North. Shall I steer under her stern, or across her bows?

Coxswain. Under her great clumsy stern, and be damned to her —Jung-frau! Dung-cart! She can't keep her backside out of the water.

Mr. Seward. Whom are you speaking of? Not a female, I hope.

Odoherty. Sir William Curtis's yacht—a female, to be sure. Look, you may read her name on her bottom by moonlight.

Mr. Blackwood. How many guns does she carry?

Coxswain. Twenty stew-pans.

Chieftain. Lord bless the worthy Baronet, however; he wins the hearts of us Highlanders by mounting a kilt. I hope he will wear it occasionally in Guildhall. I believe he is an honorary member of the Celtic Society.

Mr. Seward. Are turtles ever caught on the coast of Scotland?

Chieftain. Occasionally—but they are found in greatest numbers in the inland lochs. They were originally fresh-water fish.

Mr. Seward. You surprise me. Have these inland lochs no communication with the sea?

Chieftain. Many of them only by means of torrents precipitous, several miles high, and inaccessible, I suspect, to turtles.

Coxswain. Old gentleman, helm a-lee, or we run foul of that hawser. Helm a-lee, old gentleman, helm a-lee, or we all take our grog in Davy's locker.

Mr. Blackwood. Dog on it, Mr. North, you would steer, and you would steer, and a pretty kettle of fish you are making of it—I wish I were safe at Newington!* These boating expeditions never answer. My brother Thomas told me not to —

Coxswain. All's well. Unship oars.

SCENE II.—*State-cabin Royal Yacht.*

Mr. North. Admirable simplicity! nothing gorgeous and gaudy,—one feels at sea in such a cabin as this. The King, who designed it, knows the spirit of the British navy.

Mr. Tickler. No broad glittering gilding; there is no smell of gingerbread; one can think of grog and sea-biscuit. A man might be sick in squally weather here, without fear of the furniture.

Odoherty. Would it not be a pretty pastime to spend a honey-moon now and then in such a floating heaven as this? Calm weather and a clear conscience, soft sofa, liberty and love.

Buller. Nay, confound it, the prettiest girl looks forbidding when she is squeamish. The dim orange hue of sea-sickness is an antidote to all foolish fondness. Terra firma for me.

Tickler. Unquestionably. I gave Mrs. Tickler, a few days after our union, a voyage on the New Canal. The track-boat of this Cut was appropriately called The Lady of the Lake. We were hauled along, at the rate of three miles an hour, by a couple of horses, "lean, and lank, and brown, as is the ribbed sea-sand." Yet, even then, Mrs. Tickler felt queer, and we had to disembarge before changing cattle.

The Adjutant. One may travel now for twenty pounds all over Great Britain. Go it toe and heel in cool weather—take a lift occasionally in cart, buggy, or shandrydan, by the side of a fat farmer—tip the guard of Heavies a sly wink, and get up behind in the basket, thirty miles for a couple of shillings; now for a cheap circuitous cut by a canal, when you live cheap with the chaw-bacons, and, see a fine flat country—into a steamboat before the mast, and smoke it away fifty leagues for six and eight pence—*da capo*—and in about six weeks you return to your wife and family, with a perfect geographical and hydrographical knowledge of this Island, and with a five pound note, out of the twenty, for a nest-egg.

Mr. Blackwood. That looks all very well upon paper.

Odoherty. On paper, Mr. Blackwood!

Mr. Blackwood. I say it is a mere theory, and cannot be reduced to practice. I cannot go to London, to stay a fortnight, see my friends, and return under fifty guineas.

Odoherty. But then you indulge in luxuries, extraneous expenses—works of supererogation.

* Blackwood's country residence was at Newington, near Edinburgh.—M.

Mr. Blackwood. Not at all, Adjutant. To be sure hunting costs a good deal.

Buller. Hunting! Are you a sportsman? Do you join the Surrey? and conspire with your friend, Leigh Hunt, to worry hares in the dog-days?

Mr. Blackwood. No, no. It is hunting contributors. For example, I hear of a clever young man having been at a tea-and-turn-out in the city. I lay on a few idle dogs to scent him out—I trace him to Temple Bar—there he is lost, and the chase may be repeated for several days before we secure him. Then I have to dinner him divers times, and, before leaving town, to advance money on his articles. Perhaps I never hear more of him, till I read the identical article, promised and paid for, in the London or New Monthly.

Odoherty. There is a melancholy want of principle, indeed, among literary men. Nobody will accuse me of being straight-laced; but while the love-fit lasts, I am true as steel to one mistress and to one Magazine. I look upon an attachment to either, quite as an affair of the heart. When mutually tired of each other, then part with a kiss, a squeeze of the hand, a courtesy, and a bow. But no infidelity during the attachment. What sort of a heart can that man have, while he is openly living with the New Monthly, insidiously pays his addresses to the modest and too unsuspecting Maga? It is a shocking system of promiscuous Cockney concubinage, that must at no distant period vitiate, the taste, harden the sensibility, vulgarize the manners, and deprave the morals of the people of Great Britain. It ought to be put down.

Buller. Do you seriously opine, Mr. North, that much money is made by periodical literature in London?

Mr. North. Assuredly not. There is little available talent there. The really good men are all over head and ears in wigs and work. There do not seem to be above a dozen idlers in all London who can get up a decent article; these are all known, and their intellects are measured as exactly as their bodies by a tailor;—each man has his measure lying at Colburn's, &c., and is paid accordingly. When a spare young man quarrels with one employer, he attempts another; but his wares are known in the market, and "he drags at each remove a heavier chain."

Odoherty. The contributors are all as well known as the pugilists—height, weight, length, bottom, and science. Mr. F. can hit hard, but is a cur, like Jack the butcher. Mr. R. can spar prettily, like Williams the swell, with the gloves, but can neither give nor take with the naked mauleys. Mr. T. is like the Birmingham Youth, and "falls off unaccountably." And Mr. —— is a palpaple cross—fights booty, and it ends in a wrangle or a draw.

Mr. Blackwood. Dog on it, Adjutant, why don't you give us some more Boxiana articles?

Odoherty. I do not wish to interfere with old —— in the "Fancy Gazette." He is a rum one to go—a most pawky and prophetic pugilist. He knows the whole business of the ring better than any man alive, and writes scholastically and like a gemman; but he was rather out there about Barlow and Josh. Hudson. Ebony, you should exchange Magazines. The prime object of the "Fancy Gazette" is to kick curs and crosses out of the ring.* It is full of the true English spirit. Why, I gave a few numbers of it to my friend the Rev. Dr. Wodrow, who was once, as you know, Moderator of the General Assembly of the Kirk of Scotland, and nothing would satisfy the old divine but a couple of pairs of gloves. I sent them out from Christie's; and on my next visit, there were he and Saunders Howie, one of the elders, ruffianing it away like old Tom Owens and Mendoza. "That's a chatterer," quoth the elder, as I entered the study, he having hit Wodrow on his box of ivories. "There's a floorer," responded the ex-Moderator, and straightway the Covenanter was on the carpet.

Chieftain. Is not this a somewhat singular conversation for the state-cabin of our most gracious Sovereign's yacht?

Odoherty. Not at all. I saw Randal welt Macarthy in a room about this size, and Jack Scroggins serve out Holt —

Mr. Seward. Where is North? I hope he has not leapt out of the cabin window.

Omnes, (*rising from the King's sofa.*) North—North—Editor—Christopher—Kit,—where the devil are you?

Mr. North, (*from within his Majesty's bed-room.*) Come hither, my dear boys, and behold your father reposing on the bed of royalty! (*They all rush in.*)

Buller. Behold him lying alive in state! Let us kneel down by the bed-side. (*They all kneel down.*)

Omnes. Hail, King of Editors! Long mayest thou reign over us, thy faithful subjects. *Salve, Pater!*

Mr. North. Oh! my children, little do you know what a weary weight is in a crown! Alas, for us Monarchs! Oh! that I could fall asleep, and never more awake! Posterity will do me justice.

Mr. Blackwood, (*in tears.*) Oh! my good sir—my good sir—it is quite a mistake, I assure you—every living soul loves and admires you. You must not talk of dying, sir—(*handing over the gem*† to

* At this time, Mr. George Kent was editor of *The Fancy Gazette.* I mention (for the information of the ladies,) that "The Fancy" included not only sporting men, but was understood sometimes to take in the members of the swell mob.—M.

† *The Gem.* The Chaldee manuscript (chap. 1, v. 34) had thus described Blackwood's snuff-box;—"And he took from under his girdle a gem of curious workmanship of silver, made by the hand of a cunning artificer, and overlaid within with pure gold; and he took from thence something in color like unto the dust of the earth, or the ashes that remain of a furnace and he snuffed it up like the east wind, and returned the gem again into its place."—M.

Mr. North)—The world can ill spare you at this crisis. Here is Canning, Secretary of State for Foreign Affairs.* With yourself, in the Home Department, things will go on gloriously; and I calculate on 1000 additional subscribers to our next Number.

Odoherty. Let me smooth this pillow.

Mr. North. How many of my poorest subjects are now asleep.

Chieftain, (*aside to Mr. Tickler.*) Is he subject to moody fits of this kind? Is he liable to the blue devils?

Mr. Tickler. Only to printers' devils, Chieftain; but let him alone for a few minutes. Strong imagination is working within him, as he lies on the King's couch. See, he is recovering—what a gray piercing eye the old cock turns up! He is game to the back-bone.

Mr. North. Would I had a bowl of punch-royal!

Young Midshipman. That you shall have, Mr. North, in the twinkling of a bed-post. We drink nothing else on board, on a trip of this kind. Hollo, Jenkins, bring the crater. (*Enter Jenkins with punch royal.*) We call this the crater.

Mr. North (*drinks.*) Punch-royal indeed!

Odoherty. Fair play is a jewel, North. Leave a cheerer to the Chieftain.

Mr. North, (*rising.*) Gentlemen, let us re-embark. My soul is full.—Adjutant, lend me your arm up the gangway. Kings lie on down—but, oh, oh, oh! (*Striking his forehead.*)

Mr. Blackwood. This will end in an article.

SCENE III.—*The Deck of Mr. Smith's Cutter, the Orion.*

Chieftain. Bargemen, there are five guineas for you to drink the King's health, from Mr. North and his friends.

Bargemen. Kit and the King! Huzza—North for ever!

Mr. Seward. Let us beat up the Frith; the breeze is freshening. I only wish the worthy Commander had been on board. He can lay a bowsprit in the wind's eye with any man that ever touched a tiller.

Odoherty. Where the devil is the moon? Well tumbled porpus. A sea-mew—lend me a musket. There, madam, some pepper for your tail—roundabouts like a whirligig—up like an arrow—and then off "right slick away," and down upon the billow, safe and sound, as dapper as a daisy. I always miss, except with single ball. I recollect killing Corney Maguire at the first fire, like winking, and hardly ever an aim at all at all.

Mr. Buller. She will lie nearer the wind, Seward,—thereabouts—thereabouts—her mainsail has the true Ramsey cut. She looks quite snakish.

Odoherty. Put her about. The breeze is snoring from the king-

* Canning, on the eve of embarking to fill the office of Governor-General of India, was appointed to succeed Lord Londonderry, as Foreign Secretary.—M.

dom of Fife. See now, Seward, that you don't let her miss stays. She goes round within her own length as on a pivot. Well done, Orion!

Mr. Tickler. I vote we set off for the Western Isles.

Odoherty. I have too much regard for Mrs. Tickler to allow her husband to leave her in her present interesting situation. Besides, it would not be civil to the absent commander of the cutter, to overpower the crew, and carry her off, like pirates.

Mr. Seward. Demme—there's a schooner, about our own tonnage, beating up in ballast to Alloa for table beer—let us race her. I will lay the Orion on her quarter. There, lads—all tight—now she feels it—gunwale in—grand bearings—I could steer her with my little finger. We are eating him out of the wind.

Odoherty, (*through his hands as a speaking trumpet.*) Whither bound?—What cargo?—Timber and fruit, staves and potatoes? Son of a sea-cow, you are drifting to leeward.

Mr. North. I have been glancing over O'Meara. Bonaparte's tone, when speaking of the intended invasion of this country, did not a little amuse me. He laid his account with conquering Great Britain.*

Mr. Buller. Great insolence. Did his troops conquer divided and degenerate Spain? The British nation would have trampled him under foot. O'Meara records his ravings, as if he went along with them. I hate the French for snivelling so through their noses. No nasal nation could conquer a great guttural people.

Mr. North. Good. It is quite laughable to hear him telling the surgeon what he intended to have done with the Bank of England, and what sort of a constitution he had cut and dried for us.†

Odoherty. Bonaparte says sneeringly, that Wellington *could not* have left the field of battle, if he had been defeated at Waterloo. Does he mean, that his position was a bad one, in case of retreat? I ask, was his own a good one? Was not his army cut to pieces as it fled?

Mr. Tickler. Odoherty, did you read t'other day, in the newspapers, of a Liverpool barber, shaving eighty chins, in a workmanlike style, within the hour?

Odoherty. I did; but a Manchester shaver has since done a hundred.

Mr. Tickler. It must have been a serious affair for the last score of shavées. When the betting became loud, 6 to 4 on time, I am surprised the barber got his patients to sit.

* Napoleon's own statements on this head (they are too lengthy to be quoted here,) will be found in volume I., p. 215, and volume II., p. 223, of O'Meara's "Voice from St. Helena."—M.

† He intended proclaiming a republic, abolishing the peerage, setting Burdett to re-model the constitution, and dividing the property of the nobility among the partisans of this new revolution.—M.

Mr. North. Was he allowed to draw blood?

Odoherty. Only from pimples. I like these sort of bets. They encourage the useful arts. I won a cool hundred last winter, as you may have heard, by eating a thousand eggs in a thousand hours.

Mr. Tickler. Hard or soft?

Odoherty. Both—raw, roasted, and poached. It was a sickening business. I ate a few rotten ones, for the sake of variety.

Chieftain. One of my Tail drank a thousand glasses of whisky in a thousand hours; and we had great difficulty in keeping him to a single glass an hour. He did it without turning a hair.

Mr. North. Suppose we take a look at the Dollar Academy?

Mr. Tickler. Tennant's in town; he dined with me last week. I have a copy of Anster Fair in my pocket. I took it to Holland with me on my last trip, and read it in the Zuyder Zee. It is a fine thing, North, full of life, and glee, and glamour.* So is Don Juan.

Mr. North. I shall not permit any more poetry to be published before the year 1830, except by fresh ones. The known hands are all stale. Poetry is the language of passion. But no strong deep passion is in the mind of the age. If it be, where? Henceforth I patronize prose.

Mr. Tickler. So does Mr. Blackwood. Confound him, he is inundating the public. I wish to God Galt was dead!

Mr. Blackwood. You are so fond of saying strong things. Gracious me! before he has finished the Lairds of Grippy?†

Mr. Tickler. Well, well, let him live till then, and then die. Yet better is a soil, like that of Scotland, that produces a good, strong, rough, coarse crop, than the meagre and mangy barrenness of England.

Mr. Seward. Buller, take the helm. The meagre and mangy barrenness of England! Do you speak, sir, of the soil or soul of England? You Scotch do wonders both in agriculture and education; but you cannot contend against climate.

Mr. North. Come, come—you don't thoroughly understand Tickler yet. But the moon is sunk, the stars are paling their ineffectual fires,—and what is worse, the tide is ebbing. So let us put about, and back to the Chain Pier. Or shall we make a descent on the coast? See, we are off Hopetoun House.‡

Odoherty. Hark! the sound of the fiddle from that snug farm-

* In 1810, William Tennant, author of "Anster Fair," and other poems, was elected classical teacher of the academy at Dollar, in Fifeshire. In 1837, he was made Professor of Oriental Languages in the University of St. Andrews. He died in 1843.—M.

† The Entail, or the Lairds of Grippy, one of John Galt's best novels, was in the press at this time.—M.

‡ Hopetoun House, in Linlithgow-shire, was the seat of the gallant Earl of Hopetoun, with whom George IV. breakfasted on the morning of his leaving Scotland.

house amidst a grove of trees! Pity they should be Scotch firs,—a damnable tree, and a grove of them is too bad. Let us land.

Boatswain. The water is deep close to the water's edge. Down helm, master. There, her gunwale is on the granite!

(MR. NORTH *leaps out, followed by the Standard Bearer, Chieftain, &c.; and the Orion, her sails soon filling, wears, and goes down the Frith, goose-winged, before the wind.*

END OF ACT SECOND.

ACT III.

SCENE I.—*Kitchen of the Farm-house of Girnaway. Gudeman in his arm-chair, by the ingle*—MR. NORTH *on his right hand—Gudewife in her arm-chair, opposite*—ODOHERTY *on her right—Lads and lasses all around.*

Reel of Tullochgorum.

Gudeman. Ma faith, but the Highlander handles his heels well. You were saying he is a Chieftain—Has he his tail in the town wi' him?

Mr. North. He has a tail twenty gentlemen long.*

Gudeman. I'm thinkin' it wad be nae jeest to cast saut on his tail. He's a proud, fierce-lookin' fallow. He's bringing the red into Meg's face yonner, with his kilt flaff flaffing afore her, wi' that great rough pouch. Hear till him, hoo he's snappin' his fingers, and crying out, just wi' perfect wudness. The fiver o' his young Hieland bluid wunna let him rest. Safe us! look at him whirling Meg about like a tee-totum.

Gudewife. Gudeman, this gentleman here, he is an Irisher, is priggin on me to tak the floor. I fin' as gin I couldna refuse.

Gudeman. Do as thou likes, Tibbie, thou'rt auld enough to take care o' thyself.

Mr. Blackwood, (to a pretty young Girl in a white gown and pink ribbons.) My dear, it's to be a foursome reel. May I have the pleasure of standing before you? Fiddlers, play " I'll gang nae mair to yon town,"—it's the King's favorite.

Chieftain, (to his Partner, after a kiss.) Let me hand you to the dresser.

Meg. I'm a' in a drench o' sweat, see it's just. pooran down. My sark's as wat's muck.

Chieftain. You had better step out to the door for a few minutes, and take the benefit of the fresh air.

Meg. Wi' a' my heart, sir. (*Exeunt Chieftain and Meg.*)

Odoherty. Madam, you cannot go wrong, it is just the eight figure—so—8. Jig, or common time?

* The personal importance of a Scottish Chieftain was estimated by his Tail, or number of immediate followers.—M.

Gudewife. Oh! Jig—jig.

A Foursome Reel by the Standard-bearer, the Gudewife, Mr. Blackwood, and Maiden.)

Gudeman. Mr. North, you hae brocht a band o' rare swankies wi' you. I'm thinking you're no sae auld's you look like.

Mr. North. I'm quite a young man, just the age of the King,* God bless him. I hope we'll both live thirty years yet.

Mr. Tickler, (*to Mr. North.*) Look how busy Buller is yonder in the corner, at the end of the kitchen dresser.

Mr. North. Laird, the gudewife foots it away with admirable agility. I never saw a reel better danced in my life.

Gudeman. She's a gay, canny body; see hoo the jade puts her twa neives to the sides o'her, and hauds up her chin wi' a prie-my-mou sort o' a cock. Tibby, ye jade, the ee o' your auld gudeman's on you. What ca' ye that lang land-louper that's wallopping afore her? said you, the Stawner-bearer? Is he a Flag-Staff Lieutenant on half pay?

Mr. Tickler. Fiddler, my boy, you with that infernal squint, I beg your pardon, with the slight cast of your eye, will you lend me your fiddle for a few seconds?

(*Takes the fiddle and plays with prodigious birr.*)

Gudewife. Stap him—stap him, that's no the same tune. I canna keep the step. That's Maggy Lauder he's strumming at; they're playing different tunes. (*Dance is stopped.*)

Mr. Blackwood. I beg your pardon, Mr. Tickler; but you have put us all out; I was just beginning to get into the way of it.

Mr. Tickler. Come, I volunteer a solo. The Bush aboon Traquair. (*Plays.*)

Odoherty. The Hen's March, by jingo.

One Fiddler, (*to another.*) He fingers bonny, bonny, but he has a cramp bow-hand. He's shouther-bun'. I like to see the bow gaun like a flail back and forward.

Gudewife. Mr. Odoherty, sit down aside me again, and let's hear something about the King.

Odoherty. Mrs. Girnaway, you are quite a woman to please the King—fat, fair, and forty. And I assure you that the King is quite a man to please any woman. The expression of the under part of his face is particularly pleasing; his mouth, madam, is not unlike your own, especially when you both smile.

Gudewife. Do you hear that, gudeman? Mr. Odocterme says, that I am like the King about the mouth, when I smile.

Gudeman. When you smile, gudewife? Whan's that? Your mouth, ony time I see't, is either wide open, wi' a' its buck-teeth in a guffaw, or as fast as a vice, in a dour fit of the sourocks.

* Rather an error. According to North's own showing, subsequently, he was many years older than George IV., who was sixty in August, 1822.—M.

Mr. North. May I ask, sir, who is that maiden with the silken snood, whose conversation is now enjoyed by my young Friend, Mr. Buller of Brazen-nose?

Gudeman. That's our auldest dochter, Girzzy Girnaway; she'll be out o' her teens by Halloween; and she's as gude's she's bonny, sir,—she never gied her parents an ill word, nor a sair heart.

Mr. North. The dancing is kept up with wonderful spirit, and you and I now have all the conversation to ourselves. A country-dance, I declare! See, the gudewife, sir, is coming over to join us. We shall just have a three-handed crack.

Gudewife. Ae reel's eneugh for me. My daft days are ower; but I couldna thole his fleeching—that ane you ca' the Adjutant. Look at yon lang deevil how he is gaun down the middle wi' Mysie below his oxter. Ca' ye him Tickler? Hech, sirs, but he's well named. He's kittlin her a' the way down.

Mr. North. There is much happiness, Laird, now before us. My heart enjoys their homely hilarity. We must take human life as we find it.

Gudeman. What for did ye say that Mr. Buller had a brazen nose? I think him a very douce, quate, blate callan, an' less o' the brass nose than ony single ane o' your forbears.

Mr. North. He belongs to an English college called Brazen-nose.

Gudeman. Na, na, Mr. North, that'll no gang down with Gibby Girnaway. An English college called Brazen-nose! Na, na.

Gudewife. He's gane fain on our Girzzy. But he can mean nae ill. He wadna be a man, to come down frae England and say aught amiss to our bairn. Oh! Gibby, but he's a neat dancer, and has sma' sma' ankles, but gude strong calves. I thocht the English had been a' wee bit fat bodies. Aiblins his mither may hae been frae Scotland.

Mr. North. Laird Girnaway, I fear the times are extremely bad.

Gudeman. They are so. But if the landlords will let down their rents, and indeed they must, and if the crops are as good next year as they are this, and if, and if, and if—then, Mr. North, I say the times will not be bad. They will be better for poor people than I ever remember them. And let rich people take care of themselves.

Mr. North. Can the landlords afford to do so? Will it not ruin them?

Gudeman. I cannot tell what they can afford, or wha may be ruined. But what I say must happen; and the warld will not be warse off than before. They must draw less, and spend less. That's the hail affair.

Gudewife. I'm a wee dull o' hearing, and thae fiddles mak sic a din—and there is sic a hirdum dirdum on the floor, I canna hear either my gudeman or you, sir. But I'm awa' into the spence to mak some plotty, and baste the guse. [*Exit.*

Mr. North. It does my heart good to see such a scene as this. I hope our dancers are all loyal subjects. Or do they care nothing about their King?

Gudeman. I daresay, sir, not ane o' them is thinking o' his Majesty at this minute. But why should they? a time for a' things. But they've been maist o' them in to Embro' to hae a keek o' him. There's no chiel on the floor that wadna fecht for the King till his heart's blood flooded the grass aneath his tottering feet.

Mr. North. Have you any sons, Mr. Girnaway?

Gudeman. Twa—that's ane o' them, the big chiel wi' the curly pow clapping his hauns, and the ither is a schoolmaster in Ayrshire —a douce laddie, that may ae day be a minister. Davie there is a yeoman, and a fearfu' fallow with the sword. And then he wad ride the Deevil himsel'.

Mr. North. Have you yourself seen his Majesty, Mr. Girnaway?

Gudeman. Not yet: but I will see him, God willing, when he takes his leave o' his ain Scotland, frae Hopetoun House. The auld royal bluid o' Scotland, I ken, is in his veins; and there is something, sir, in the thocht o' far-back times that's grand and fearsome, and suits the head o' a crowned Monarch. The folk in this parish dinna respeck me the less, that I am ane o' the Girnaways, whose family has lived here for generations and generations; and it maun be just the same wi' a King, whose ancestors hae lang ruled the land. If we hae a feeling o' sic a thing, sae maun he: and Davie said, "O, father, but he was a proud man when he looked up to the Calton, and doun on auld Holyrood. I couldna help greeting."

Mr. North. I trust, Mr. Girnaway, that your enlightened sentiments are general.

Gudeman. Wha doubts 't? Now and then, ye hear a dauner'd body telling ye that the King is just like ither men; and that Kings care naething for puir people; and that the twa Houses o' Parliament should haud him in wi' baith snaffle and curb; but that doctrine doesna gang doun just the now; and the very women-folk, who, in a general way are rather sillyish, you ken, laugh at it, and praise the King up to the very ee-brees.*

Mr. North. Never beheld I so much mirth, happiness, and innocence. I have often thought, Mr. Girnaway, of becoming a farmer in the evening of life.

Gudeman. There's mirth eneugh and happiness eneugh, and, as the world goes, innocence eneugh, too, on the floor, Mr. North. But you maunna deceive yoursel' wi' fine words. Mirth isna for every day in the year; and we are often a' sulky and dour, and at times raging like tigers. Happiness is a kittle verb to conjugate, as our dominie says; and as to innocence, while lads and lasses are lads and lasses,

* *Ee-brees*,—eyebrows.—M.

there'll be baith sin and sorrow. But there's ae thing, sir, keepit sacred amang us, and that is religion, Mr. North. We attend the kirk and read the Bible.

Mr. North. I hope, Mr. Girnaway, that when you come to Edinburgh, you will take potluck with me.

Gudeman. Dinna Mr. me ony mair, sir; call me just Girnaway. I'll do't. Now, sir, may I ask, cannily, what trade ye may be when you are at hame?

Mr. North. I am Editor of Blackwood's Magazine, of which you may have heard.

Gudeman. Gude safe us! are you a loupin', livin', flesh and bluid man, with real rudiments and a wooden crutch, just as gien out in that ance-a-month peerioddical? Whan will wonders cease? Gies your haun. Come awa' into the spence; the wife maun hae made the plotty by this time. Come into the spence. Come awa—come away. This is maist as gude's a visit frae the King himsel.

[*Exeunt* NORTH *and* GIRNAWAY *into the Spence.*

SCENE II.—*The Spence.*

Gudewife (*sola.*) It's no every ane can set down a bit supper like Tibbie Girnaway. Had that guse been langer on the stubble, he might hae been a hantle fatter about the doup. But he'll do as he is, wi' the apple sauce.

Enter GIRNAWAY *and* NORTH.

Girnaway. Gudewife, you ken that buik our son sends us every month, wi' the face of Geordie Buchanan on't. Would ye believe that we hae under our roof tree the very lads that write it. Here's the cock o' the company, Mr. North himself.

Gudewife. I jaloused something wonderfu', whene'er I saw the face of him, and that Adjutant ane. Siccan a buik I never read afore. It gars ane laugh they canna tell how; and a' the time ye ken what ye'r reading, is serious, too—Naething ill in't, but a' gude—supporting the kintra, and the King, and the kirk.

Girnaway. Mr. North, I hae not much time to read, but I like fine to put my specs on to a sensible or droll buik, and your Magazine is baith. I'm a friend to general education.

Mr. North. Girnaway, do you think that there are many profane or seditious books hawked about the country? It seems to be the opinion of the General Assembly.

Girnaway. 'Deed, sir, I can only speak o' my ain experience. Doubtless, there are some, but no great feck; and I hae seen my ain weans and servants, after glowring at them a while on the dresser or the bunker, fling them frae them, like rowans, and neist time I see them it's on the midden. Hawkers come mair speed wi' ribbons, and shears, and knives, and bits o' funny ballads, than profanity and sedition. But the General Assembly should ken best.

Gudewife. Now, ma man, Gibbie, the guse is getting cauld. I maun inveet the lave o' them in. The fiddles and the skirling is baith quate.

(*Exit the Gudewife, and enters with the* STANDARD BEARER, CHIEFTAIN, BULLER, SEWARD, TICKLER, *and* MR. BLACKWOOD.)

Mr. North. Might I take the liberty of requesting the pleasure of your daughter's company, maäm. Mr. Buller will go for his partner. (BULLER *darts off.*)

Gudewife. I like to see my bairns respecket, sir, and Grace can show her face ony where,—sae can her cousin Mysie. (TICKLER *darts off.*) And her friend, Miss Susy, the only dochter o' the Antiburgher minister, wha was dancing wi' Mr. Blackwood. (MR. BLACKWOOD *darts off.*) And Meg herself, though she hasna ta'en on muckle o' a polish, sin' she came from about Glasgow, is a decent hizzie. (*Chieftain darts off.*) Yon bit white-faced lassie, wi' the jimp waist, and genteel carriage, is the butcher's only bairn, and a great heiress. (SEWARD *darts off.*) Preserve us, are they a' coming to soop? Weel, weel, we maun sit close. Where's Mr. Odocterme?

Adjutant. Here, maäm.

(*Gudeman says grace, and the Company fall to.*)

Gudewife. I fear, Mr. Adjutant, that you fin' that spawl o' the gusy rather teuch?

Odoherty. As tender as a chicken, I assure you, ma'am. If it were as tough as timber I care not. I never made a better supper in all my life, than I did one night in Spain, on the tail of an old French artillery horse. It was short, but sweet.

Gudewife. Let me lay some more rumble-te-thumps on your plate, Colonel Odocterme. The tail o' a horse! What some brave sodgers hae gone through in foreign parts, for our sakes at hame! I could greet to think on't.

Mr. North. Mrs. Girnaway, I propose to drink the health of your absent son, Mr. Gilbert Girnaway, student of divinity, and teacher at Torbolton.

Gudeman. He couldna leave his scholars, or he would hae been to Embro' to see the King, like the lave. I'se drink the callan's health wi' richt good will. "Here's our Gilbert." Hoots, Tibbie, you silly thing, what for are you greeting?

Odoherty. "Oh! Beauty's tear is lovelier than her smile." But gentlemen, Miss Grace Girnaway will give us a song. Mr. Buller, will you prevail upon Miss Girnaway for a song—something plaintive and pathetic, if you please.

Miss Grace (sings)

Oh! white is thy bosom, and blue is thine eye,
The light is a tear, and the sound is a sigh!
Thy love is like friendship, thy friendship like love,
And that is the reason I call thee—my Dove.

Oh! sweet to my soul is the balm of thy breath,
As a dew-laden gale from the rich-blossom'd heath;
Can it be that all beauty doth fade in an hour?
Then let that be the reason I call thee—my Flower.

On the wide sea of life shines one unclouded light,
And still it burns softest and clearest by night;
But its lustre, though lovely, alas, is afar,
And that is the reason I call thee—my Star.

But the dove seeks her nest in the forest so green,
And the flower in its fragrance is fading unseen;
The star in its brightness the sea-mist will hide,
So come to my heart, while I call thee—my Bride.

Gudeman. She's no a taucht singer, our Grace; but neither is a lintwhite nor a laverock. Her father, Mr. North, likes to hear her singing by the ingle—and he likes to hear her singing in the kirk. Mr. Buller, you English winna like the hamely lilt o' a Scottish farmer's dochter?

Mr. Buller. Liveliness, modesty, cheerfulness, innocence, and beauty, I hope can be felt by an English heart, loved and respected, wherever they smile before his eye, or melt upon his ear. "Your fair and good daughter's health and song—and may she long live to be a blessing and a pride to her parents."

Gudewife. Ay, ay, a blessing, but no a pride. Pride's no for human creatures, but gratitude is; and we thank God, Gilbert and I, for naething mair than for gieing us weel-liked and dutiful bairns.

Mr. Tickler. If ever I saw a singing face in my life, it is that of my sweet Mysie's. My dear, will you sing, now that your fair cousin has broken the ice?

Gudewife. Will she sing? We'll gar her sing. We maun a' contribute.

Mr. Blackwood, (starting.) We maun a' contribute! Whose voice was that promising an article?

Gudewife. I say, sir, we maun a' contribute. Mysie's gaun to gie you a sang. Aiblins it may get into print. Come, Mysie, clear your pipes.

Miss Mysie. Grace, let us sing THE SHEPHERDESS AND THE SAILOR. I shall be the Sailor this time.

Sailor. When lightning parts the thunder-cloud
That blackens all the sea,
And tempests sough through sail and shroud,
Even then I think on thee, Mary.

Shepherdess. I wrap me in that keepsake plaid,
And lie doun 'mang the snaw;
While frozen are the tears I shed
For him that's far awa', Willy!

Sailor. We sail past mony a bonny isle,
Wi' maids the shores are thrang;
Before my ee there's but ae smile,
Within my ear ae sang, Mary.

Shepherdess. In kirk, on every Sabbath day,
For ane on the great deep
Unto my God I humbly pray—
And as I pray, I weep, Willy.

Sailor. The sands are bright wi' golden shells.
The groves wi' blossoms fair:
And I think upon the heather-bells
That deck thy glossy hair, Mary.

Shepherdess. I read thy letters sent from far,
And aft I kiss thy name,
And ask my Maker, frae the war
If ever thou'lt come hame, Willy.

Sailor. What though your father's hut be lown
Aneath the green-hill side?
The ship that Willy sails in, blown
Like chaff by wind and tide, Mary?

Shepherdess. Oh! weel I ken the raging sea,
And a' the steadfast land,
Are held, wi' specks like thee and me,
In the hollow of his hand, Willy.

Sailor. He sees thee sitting on the brae,
Me hanging on the mast;
And o'er us baith, in dew or spray,
His saving shield is cast, Mary.

(*Song interrupted by loud cries of murder heard from the Kitchen, and a crash of chairs, and tumbling of tables. Omnes rush out.*)

SCENE III.—*The Kitchen.*

Saunders M'Murdo—Smith. I'll no tak a blow frae the haun o' ony leevin' man.—Kate Craigie, I say, ma woman, tak away your grips. He may be the miller, but I awe him nae thirlage; and mak room, and I'll gie him the floor, like a sack o' his ain meal.

Pate Muter. He wud rug Kate aff my knee, so I gied him a clour on his harn-pan. I'm no for fechtin'. I haena fochten since Falkirk Tryst, when I brak the ribs o' that Hieland drover. Peace is best. But stan' back, Burniwin', or you may as weel rin into the fanners or the mill-wheel at ance.

Davie Girnaway. I'll hae nae fechtin' in my father's house.—Mysie, bring my sword.—Saunders M'Murdo, you're an unhappy man when you get a drap-drink—Lowsen his neckcloth, he's getting black i' the face.

Mr. North. Saunders M'Murdo, Pate Muter,—I speak to you both as a peace-maker. Why this outrage in the family of the Girnaways? Has party instigated this unbecoming, this shameful brawl? Party! and the King in Scotland? Smith, Miller, you are both honorable men. Your professions are indispensable. Without you, what is this agricultural parish? Will you shake hands, and be friends? I see you will. Advance towards each other like men. There, there. Go where I will I am a peace-maker.

(*Smith and Miller shake hands, and quiet is restored.*)

Gudewife. Weel, weel; little dune's soonest mended. But I never saw a kirn yet without a fecht, sometimes half-a-dozen. After a storm comes a calm; ye may say that. There ye a' sit, every lad beside his lass, as douce as gin the Gudeman were gaun to tak the Book. It's a curious world.

Gudeman. Haud your tongue, Tibbie. Bring ben the plotty and a' the spirits into the Kitchen; and a' bad bluid shall be at an end, when ilka ane, lad and lass, wife and widow, drinks a glass to the KING.

Davie Girnaway. Here's the plotty; put out the tables.—Thank ye, Mr. Odoherty.—Tak tent ye dinna lame yourself, Mr. North, Hooly and fairly—hooly and fairly.

(*The tables are set out, and quaichs and coups laid.*)

Gudeman. Now, Mr. North, we're a' looking to you. Ye maun gie us twa or three words to the king's health. I canna speechify, but I can roar. And I'se do that wi' a vengeance at the hip, hip.—Fill a' your quaichs till they're sooming ower.

Mr. North. MR. AND MRS. GIRNAWAY, LADIES AND GENTLEMEN, We are now assembled round the table of a Scottish yeoman, to drink to the health of his Most Gracious Majesty King George the Fourth. He is within about twelve miles, as the crow flies, of where we now stand. Is it not almost the same thing as if he were actually here, in this very room, standing there beside the Laird himself, and with the light of that very fire shining upon his royal visage? I speak now to you, who have, most of you, seen the King. You saw him surrounded with hundreds of thousands of his shouting subjects, who had then but one great heart, whose looks were lightning, and whose voice was thunder. You had all heard, read, thought of your King. But he was to you but the image of a dream—a shadowy phanthom on a far-off throne. Even then you were leal and loyal, as Scotsmen have ever been, who in peace prove their faith by the sweat of their brows, and in war by the blood of their hearts. Now, do not the elder among you feel like the brethren, and the younger like the children, of your King? He has breathed our free northern air—he has felt one of our easterly haars upon his brows—he has heard our dialect—he has trodden our soil—he has eaten our bread, and drunk our water—he has hailed, and been hailed, by countless multitudes, on the ramparts of our unconquered citadel—and he has prayed to the God of his, and our fathers, in our ancient and holy temple. Therefore, by our pride, by our glory, and by our faith, do we now love great George our King. What if he had not known the character of the people over whom he reigned? Their patience, their fortitude—their courage—their unquaking confidence in their own right arms—and their sacred trust in God? What if he had trembled on his throne, and imagined in that terror that its foundations were shaken by that great earthquake that shook to pieces the powers on the Continent? We had then been lost. England, Scotland, would, at this hour, have been peopled by slaves.—Our harvests would not have been reaped, as they now are, by the hands of freemen—the stack-yard would not have belonged to him who built it—we should not have been assembled round this ingle—nor would there have been on the earth these faces, fair and bright with beauty, intelligence and virtue. The British monarchy would have been destroyed—equal liberties and equal laws abrogated, effaced, and obliterated, for ever—our parish schools and our kirks levelled with the dust, religion scorned, and education proscribed—the light of knowledge and of love equally extinguished, and darkness on the hearth, and on the altar. It was he, George the Fourth, who, under God, saved us and our country from such evils, and who has preserved to us, unscathed by the fire through which they have passed, our liberties and our laws. He saw into our hearts, and knew of what stuff they were made. He saw that to us death was nothing—but that disgrace and degradation was more than we could—more than we *would* bear. Toil, taxes, tears and blood, were demanded of us, not by the voice of our own King, but by the voice of all our kings and heroes speaking through him—by the voices of our own Wallace and our own Bruce. We fought, and we conquered—and we are free. Therefore, now let each maiden smile upon her friend or lover—fill your cups to the brim—join hands—take a kiss, my lads, if you will—THE KING.

Hip, hip, hip—hurra, hurra, hurra—Hip, hip, hip—hurra, hurra, hurra—Hip, hip, hip—hurra, hurra, hurra—Hip, hip, hip—hurra, hurra, hurra!

The Smith. I was in the wrang, I was in the wrang—I acknowledge't. Gies your haun again, Miller. If ever need be, we'll fecht thegither, baith on ae side, for the King.

The Miller. There's flour of speech for you. Gif he were but in

Parliament, he would lay his flail about him till the chaff flew into the een o' the Opposition frae the threshing-floor. Will ye stan' for the borough, Mr. North? I'll secure you the brewer's vote o'er bye yonder; or would you prefer the county? Ye'se hae either for the asking.

Mr. North. My highest ambition, Mr. Muter, is to retire into the rural shades, and become a farmer.

The Miller. Come out, then, near the Ferry. Take a lease frae Lord Hopetoun. I'll grin' a' your meal, wheat, aits, and barley for naething. A' the time you were speaking, I felt as if I could hae made a speech mysel. When you stopt, it was like the stopping of a band o' music on the street, when the sodgers are marching by. It was like the stopping o' the happer o' the mill.

Gudewife. Mysie, Girzzy, Meg, or some o' you, open the wunnock-shutters. (*They do so.*)

Mr. North. A burst of day! The sun has been up for hours. What a bright and beautiful harvest morning! The sea is rolling in gold. See, there is the Orion beating up—close hauled. The best of friends must part.

(*The whole party breaks up, and accompany* NORTH, *&c. to the beach.*

END OF ACT THIRD.

No. VI.—DECEMBER, 1822.

DIE VENERIS, *Nocte* 15*ta Mensis Decemb.*

PRESENT—THE EDITOR'S MOST EXCELLENT MAGAZINITY IN COUNCIL.

North, (*proloquitur.*) Mr. Odoherty, it is to be hoped you have not come to such an affair as this, to eat the flesh of the wild boar of the forest, and the red deer of the hills, at the expense of our noble friend, without preparing a small canticle in honor of his gifts—something in the occasional way, as it were?

Odoherty. If the Hogg will take the Boar, I will venture on the Deer.

Hogg. Done for a saxpence—here's my thumb: sing ye awa, Captain, and I'll be casting for an *edèea* in the meantime.

Odoherty. Look sharp, if you get a nibble, Shepherd—*I nunc et versus*,—here goes then.

Odoherty (*sings.*)

1.

There's a Spanish grandee on the banks of the Dee,*
  A fine fellow is he—a finer is none;
For though he is so great, and high in estate,
  He is also first-rate in the peerage of fun.
Then fill to Lord Fife, in condiments rife
  To the end of this life his career may he run;
And his tree that hath stood, at the least since the Flood,
  Oh! may't flourish and bud till our Planet's undone!

2,

When our Monarch was here, this munificent peer
  Did in glory, 'tis clear, make the famousest show,
With his swapping gray fillies, and "naked-feet" gillies;
  Their Set-Outs look'd like Dillies—but his was the go.
Even the King took delight, in that equipage bright,
  Through Auld Reekie, by night, for to ride to and fro;
When I look'd through the pane, I saw Him and the Thane:
  Ere I die, once again let me look on them so.

3.

How genteel were his looks—not at all like some dukes,
  Who stood shivering like rooks in a pluvious day—

* The Earl of Fife holds a Spanish title of nobility, and is also a General officer in the Spanish army. He obtained these honors during the Peninsular War.—M.

Sure his graceship of Brandon has but little to stand on,*
 When he doth abandon the Gothic array.
If a man of that rank must sport such a shank,
 My Maker I thank for my humble degree ;
But I'd rather by half, have the Thane's rousing calf,
 And enjoy a good laugh, with fine trews to my knee.

4.

Fill a glass to the brim, and down pour it to Him
 Who our grave Sanhedrim doth so love and revere;
Who hath given his command, that the fat of his land
 Be bestowed on the band of philosophers here.
The Boar of the wood hath to-day been our food,
 And some slices we've chewed of a very fine Deer;
Till expires life's last ember, I'm sure we'll remember
 The fifteenth of December—the chiefest of cheer.

5.

Let us hope he'll produce such affairs for the use
 Of our gastric juice, merry years not a few ;
Our bountiful friend may on one thing depend—
 Such a feast shall not end sans disturbing the screw ;
No ! by jingo, each throttle shall imbibe the sum-*tottle*†
 Of a tappit-hen bottle of Chateau-margaux,—
Excepting old Hogg, who must stick to his grog,
 Or else speedily jog to give Satan his due.

North. Very well, Adjutant. You are all filled; take the time from me—The Thane !—(*Here the roof is nearly brought down with a three-times-three.*)

Hogg. But wha ever heard o' wild boars in Scotland at this time o' day ?

North. Why, I believe the Thane has introduced the breed among the remains of the old Caledonian forest on his Mar estate.

Hogg. What a grand country that is o' the Thane's ! Did you never see it, Mr. North ?

North. Only a slight view when I was at Deeside, for our famous 12th of August—but I'm sure 'tis not for want of invitations I don't see more of it. Here is a letter I had from the Thane this morning, in answer to my acknowledgment of the hamper which has just been contributing to your comforts.

Kempferhausen. I believe it is acknowledged, that the Thane has as fine estates as any nobleman in Scotland, and has done a vast deal for them.

Hogg. Oh ! nothing like that magnificent country—nothing in all the North ; and anybody may see it, for there are most noble roads through woods extremely valuable and important to the country, being now almost the only remains of the Caledonian Forests ;

* The Hereditary Keeper of Holyrood Palace, head of the Douglas family, is the Duke of Hamilton in Scotland, and Brandon on the peerage of England.—M.

† Vide Hume *passim.*—C. N.

and if you will look at Barlow on the Strength of Timber and his Experiments, you will see that the timber there beats the Riga red pine. The Thane is careful to preserve it for the use of the country, whenever it may be wanted. The roads extend over mountains, the sides of some are defended by great dykes, and all planted to join the old wood, and to preserve the young natural plants. I assure you, Mr. North, that the place is well worth your attention whenever you can find time to see it.

North. I shall go next year, I think.

Tickler. What is best of all is, that the comfort of the people is attended to, and I do not believe there is a Highland district where the poor are so well provided. There is one side of the country kept for sheep, and the other for deer. Some of the highest mountains in the kingdom are to be seen. One of them is considered to be as high or higher than Ben Nevis—the Dee also rises in the Forest. All through Lord Fife's country great improvements are taking place. The Abbey of Pluscardine, near Elgin, has been restored.

Odoherty. Hogg, you've been "glowring frae you," and preaching long enough; *incipe nunc, musa!*

Hogg. I canna sing yet, Captain: just bear wi' me till I've had another tumbler or twa—that's a good fellow, now—I'll gie ye sangs anew or the morn's morning.

North. No compulsion here; this is Liberty Hall: but you must tell a story, Shepherd, or drink the forfeit.

Hogg. Ae braw simmer day I was sitting wi' my corbie-craw piking at my taes: and auld Hector, puir chield, him that's awa—and wha should step in to tak his morning wi' me but Tammy Braidshaw, ye ken—

Tickler. Come, come, Chaldean sage; we've all heard that a hundred times.

Hogg. Weel, try your haund yoursell. I'm to tell a' my new stories here forsooth, and what would come of my new Winter Evening Tales, think ye.

Tickler. To be sure mutton's a drug at present. What news from Germany, Meinheer Kempferhausen?

Kempferhausen. The celebrated professor of Ingolstadt, Doctor Blumensucker, is about to put forth his long-expected work "*De Re Chaldea*,"—full notes, capital portraits of every body.

North. Bravo! Vir Clariss.—I wonder no London bookseller gets up an illustrated edition of the Chaldee—Barker for Editor.*

Tickler. The Constitutional would be at it.†

* Edmund Henry Barker (born 1788, died 1839.) was one of the most eminent of modern scholars. He edited Stephens' "Thesaurus Linguæ Græcæ," a gigantic performance. Besides this, he edited Prolegomena to Homer, Lempriere, and other school books. He contributed largely to the Classical Journals, the British Critic, and other periodicals.—M.

† The Constitutional Society, in London, prosecuted small vendors of sedition and irreligion, but were too well bred to trouble offenders of rank or wealth.—M.

Odoherty. A fig for the Constitutional—you see they don't dare to meddle with Lord Byron!

Hogg. What has Byron been doing in their line?

Odoherty. The Liberal, you know.

Tickler. Poo, poo, Odoherty, you know as well as I that he had very little to do with that humbug.

Odoherty. To be sure I do—There's nothing of his in it but the Vision of Judgment, and the Letter to Granny Roberts.

North. What do you think of those compositions, Timotheus?

Tickler. I have never thought much about them. But it strikes me that the VISION is vastly inferior to BEPPO, to say nothing of the exquisite DON JUAN. It contains a dozen capital stanzas or so, but on the whole 'tis washy.

Odoherty. What a shame it is to banter such a respectable man as Dr. Southey at this rate—so uncalled for—so out of taste—so indefensible—so scurrilous!

Hogg. Hear till him! He has face for ony thing.

Tickler. I think Dr. Southey is the fairest of all subjects, for my part. The man's arrogance and dogmatical airs are worthy of much severer castigation than they have ever yet met with. Just open one of his articles in the Quarterly—what slow, solemn, pompous, self-conceit runs through all he writes. Do you remember the conclusion of his Brazil Balaam?

North. I am ashamed to say I never saw the work.

Tickler. Who ever did? but at the end of those two thumping leaden quartos about Caziques, hieroglyphical pictures, and so forth, thus saith the Doctor—"Thus have I finished one of those great and lasting works, to which, in the full vigor of manhood, I looked forward as the objects of a life of literature."—'Tis something like that, however—did you ever hear such like stuff?

Odoherty. Often from the Lakers. They're a high speaking set of boys.

Kempferhausen. Oh, Mr. North, Mr. North! that I should live to hear such words spoken at your table. I'm sure *you* respect Southey, and adore Wordsworth in your heart. Mein gott! mein gott!

North. I respect Southey as one of the most accomplished scholars of the age; but I no more dream of mentioning him in the same day with the god Pan, than I should of classing a Jeffrey with a Hogg.

Tickler. Allow me to utter a few mouthfuls of common sense.

Omnes. Out with them, Timothy.

Tickler. The fact of the matter is this—Lord Byron overdoes his satire. People won't suffer a Dunciad now-a-days with but one Dunce in it. And the world were not thinking of Mouthy Southey or his hexameters.

North. There's some truth there. Nothing should be parodied but what is well known.

Tickler. Is the old song of *An Hundred Years Hence* well known ?

North. Come, away with your parody then, if you have it in your pocket.

(TICKLER *sings, accompanying himself on the fiddle.*)

2.

In this year eighteen hundred
  And twenty and two,
There are plenty of false ones
  And plenty of true.
There are brave men and cowards;
  And bright men and asses;
There are lemon-faced prudes;
  There are kind-hearted lasses.
He who quarrels with this
  Is a man of no sense,
For so 'twill continue
  An hundred years hence.

3.

There are people who rave
  Of the national debt,
Let them pay off their own,
  And the nation's forget;
Others bawl for reform,
  Which were easily done,
If each would resolve
  To reform Number One:
For *my* part to wisdom
  I make no pretence,
I'll be as wise as my neighbors
  An hundred years hence.

4.

I only rejoice, that
  My life has been cast
On the gallant and glorious
  Bright days which we've past;
When the flag of Old England
  Waved lordly in pride,
Wherever green Ocean
  Spreads his murmuring tide:
And I pray that unbroken
  Her watery fence
May still keep off invaders,
  An hundred years hence.

5.

I rejoice that I saw her
  Triumphant in war,
At sublime Waterloo,
  At dear-bought Trafalgar;
On sea and on land,
  Wheresoever she fought,
Trampling Jacobin tyrants
  And slaves as she ought:
Of CHURCH and of KING
  Still the firmest defence:—
So may she continue
  An hundred years hence.

6.

Whey then need I grieve, if
Some people there be,
Who, foes to their country,
Rejoice not with me;
Sure I know in my heart,
That Whigs ever have been
Tyrannic, or turnspit,
Malignant, or mean:
THEY WERE AND ARE SCOUNDRELS
IN EVERY SENSE,
AND SCOUNDRELS THEY WILL BE
AN HUNDRED YEARS HENCE.

7.

So let us be jolly,
Why need we repine?
If grief is a folly,
Let's drown it in wine!
As they scared away fiends
By the ring of a bell,
So the ring of the glass
Shall blue devils expel:
With a bumper before us
The night we'll commence
By toasting true Tories
An hundred years hence.

Hogg. It is glorious! it is perfectly glorious, as Gray would say.

Kempferhausen (*sings.*)

Stille, hersch', andacht, und der seel'erhebung,
Rings umber! Fern sei was befleckt von sundist,
Was dem Staub anhaftet zu klein der mencheit
Hoperen aufschwung!
Tilly leeri, oiko, hi oiko, hi oiko!
Tillee oiko, oiko. Tilli oi-i-oi-i-oiko!

North. Your voice is much improved. You really begin to sing now, Meinheer.

Kempferhausen. Give me a flash of the Rudelsheimer—(i-oiko! i-oko—)

Hogg. Wheesht, wheesht, callant—you're deafening Mr. Tickler.

Tickler. Let me tip ye another bit of sense, will ye, lads?

Odoherty. Indulge the quizz.

Tickler. That song of Privy Counsellor Kempferhausen is as bad as "Naked feet, naked feet."

Omnes. No, no, no, Tickler—don't dish the Privy Counsellor.

Tickler. Well, then, I won't for this once. But, after all, what do you think, General Christophe, of this production of Pisa?

North. I think, Colonel Timothy, that it is naught. Not that I am in any danger of joining in the vulgar cries that ring in one's ears, but really Lord Byron should remember that he is now a man towards forty*—and that if he passes that era without taking up, the whole world will pronounce him an incurable.

Hogg. Lord keep us! whatfor an incurable?—he's just ane of the finest, cleverest chiels of the age, and if he was here just now, he would be a delight to us all.

Odoherty. Experto crede. The odd fish is only just trying how far he may go; give him line, he'll soon come in.

Tickler. He must cut the Cockney.

Odoherty. I lay a tester he has cut him already. Did you look at that rascally specimen of the Cockneyfied Orlando Furioso?

* In December, 1822, he was within a month of being 35.—M.

North. I did. But what was *there* to surprise you? He had already done Theocritus into the psalm measure (long metre)—was there any farther march in the kingdom of absurdity?

Tickler. No, no; but one really cannot suffer such a fellow to be choppifying and patchifying at the Orlando Furioso, without bringing a whip across his withers. Why, the whole concern is abominably, nauseous, filthy, base, gingerbread, Cockney stuff. One might read him for a mile without knowing it was Ariosto he was after, if he did not clap old Ludovico's name and surname at the top of his pages! What impudence!

Odoherty. Do you see me now, I think you are hard on King Leigh. His description of Pisa affected me.

Tickler. What affectation!—

Odoherty. Well, I was seriously pleased with him. There is a merit in such candor. The man tells you plainly, without going round about the bush, that he had never seen a hill or a clear stream before, and that both of them are fine things in their way. The Cockney is candid. I love the King. *Viva Le Hunto Signior di Cocagna!*

North. What an abortion is that tale of the Florentine Lovers!* How unavoidably the Bel Ludgato peeps out! Suffer any given Cockney to write three sentences on end in any book in the world, and if I don't pick them out *ad aperturam*, dethrone me.

Hogg. That's a stretcher, my man.

North. No; for example, just the other day, my friend little Frank Jeffrey, in one of those good-humored moments of utter silliness that now and then obscure his general respectability, permitted Lecturer Hazlitt to assist him in doing a review of Byron's tragedies for the Edinburgh. If any one here has brought the blue and yellow with him for the lighting of his tube, I engage, under pain of drinking double tides till noon, to mark every paragraph that Billy dipped his ugly paw in.

Odoherty. By Jove, here's a libel for you! Jeffrey and Hazlitt working at the same identical article, like two girls both sewing of one flower, upon one sampler! Tell that to the marines.

Kempferhausen. You will at least admit that Mr. Shelley's version of the Mayday-night scene has its merits. I assure you 'tis goot, very goot.

North. Yes, yes, I had forgot it. 'Tis indeed an admirable *morçeau*,—full of life, truth, and splendor. I think it must be very like Goethe's affair.

Kempferhausen. Oh, very like,—only the Cockney Editors did not know a word of the original, and they've blundered awfully now and then, in their printing,—for example, there is a wizard call of " Come

* A prose tale in The Liberal, by Leigh Hunt, severely reviewed in Maga.—M.

to me from *the Sea of rocks*," which is in my father-tongue *felsensee*. The Her Shelley, I suppose, had noted the German word on his paper, not having an English one just ready. But the Hunts print in English "Come to me from *felumee*,"—which is no meaning at all, any more than if they had said, "Come to me from *philabeg*."

Hogg. Oh, what ignoramuses—But, I dare say, yon German chiels sometimes make as braw blunders themsels, when they're yerking awa at the Queen's Wake, or the Three Perils of Man, ower bye yonder——

Odoherty. 'Tis like they may,—I don't doubt many of your little exquisite touches of elegance evaporate under the hands of your translators. Kempferhausen, himself, has mauled you at a time, if he would but own it.

Kempferhausen. *Confiteor. Miserere Domine!* I wrote a translation of Kenilworth, you know, when I was at Hamburgh. Well, I had forgot that you English spell the beast with an *a*, and the tipple with an *e*, so I made mine host of Cumnor sport *the Beer and the broken ladle*, instead of *the Bear and the Ragged Staff*, for his sign-post. All Germany, at this moment, believes that that was the real sign. Indeed, it is now a favorite one among our Teutonic Tintos.

Hogg. Dinna lose a night's rest for that, my man: ae thing's just a good as anither. It's nae matter what ane pits in a book; my warst things aye sell best, I think. I'm resolved, I'll try and write some awfu' ill thing this winter.

Odoherty. Do, the Agriculturists really must exert themselves in these hard times.

Tickler. You were always a diligent fellow, Hogg; of course The Three Perils have a fine run.

Hogg. That's civil——

Odoherty. One of your principal objects appears to have been The Vindication of the Chaldee of Hogg, (ut cum Glengarry loquar)—for I see one of your characters is yourself, always sporting that venerable lingo.

Hogg. Hoot! It was just the ither five chapters of the Chaldee; them that Ebony would not print: they were lying moulding in my drawers, and I thought I would put them into the Novel for Balaam; naebody fand me out,—I kent that would be the way o't.

Odoherty. After all, Hogg, what devil possessed you to own the Chaldee?

Hogg. I wish ye would let me eat my victuals, and drink my liquor in peace; I've been up since four in the morning among the drovers, and I'm no able to warstle wi' you the night.

North. Don't mind these scamps, Hogg. Why, there's not one of 'em but would give his ears to write any thing half so fine as the opening chapters of the second volume of your PERILS.

Tickler. Has Hogg heard or seen the Epigrams by Mr. Webb, and Mr. Hazlitt, on General North's arms?

Hogg. Deil a bit o' me. Od! there's nae wale o' Epigrams on Yarrow water.

Tickler. Then listen. William Hazlitt, in the first place, being asked by Leigh Hunt, why North's crest is a Rose, a Thistle, and a Shamrock, made these lines by way of answer. At least they are attributed to him by the Whigs here. But, to be sure, he must have been in a sweet humor:

"You ask me, kind Hunt, why does Christopher North
For his crest, Thistle, Shamrock, and Rose blazen forth?
The answer is easy: his pages disclose
The splendor, the fragrance, the grace of the Rose;
Yet so humble, that he, though of writers the chief,
In modesty vies with the Shamrock's sweet leaf;
Like the Thistle!——Ah! Leigh, you and I must confess it,
NEMO ME (is his motto) IMPUNE LACESSET."

Hogg. Very weel, very weel, indeed; the lad's on the mending hand I think, sirs.

Tickler. Yet I think Corny Webb's verses are neater:

"Each leaf which we see over Christopher's helm
Is an emblem of part of our insular realm:
The well-fought-for Rose, is of England the bearing,
The Thistle of Scotland, the Shamrock of Erin:
And they therefore are borne by the Star of the Forth,
FOR KIT NORTH LOVES ALL THREE, AND ALL THREE LOVE KIT NORTH."

Odoherty. Rather jaw-breaking that last line, like Cornelius's sonnets; but truth may well compensate for want of melody.*

Hogg. It often surprises me when I think on't. But, after a', there's but few of the First-raters, except Christopher himself here, that really excels in periodical writing; I confess I never thought I myself for ane was ony great dab in that department.

Tickler. Let me see—this is an ingenious start of the Shepherd's. But, after all, is there truth in what he says? Is not he himself a goodish periodicaller?

Kempferhausen. Donner and blitzen! do you talk so of the author of the Chaldee?

Tickler. Aye, that, to be sure, is one *chef-d'œuvre;* but on the whole, I, though I love and admire Hogg as much as any one, must honestly and fairly say, that I consider him as inferior to Jeffrey *in re periodicali*.

North. No doubt he is. In fact, Hogg has always had his eyes on other affairs—perhaps on higher.

Hogg. Na, na—nane o' youa jeers, auld man!

* Cornelius Webbe, a London writer, author of Glancesat Life, Sonnets, &c.—M.

North. I don't so much wonder at Hogg; but what do you say to Tom Campbell?

Tickler. Why, I don't know that we have any proper *data* yet to judge of Tommy. His magazine is a very queer book. It is almost all (I mean the large print) very decently written. There is a certain sort of elegance in many papers, and a certain sort of very neatish information in others; but the chief, and indeed the damnifying defect, is a total want of *gist.* Is there any one can tell me at this moment of any one purpose that work appears to keep in view?

Kempferhausen. Mr. North, did *you* not like the letters of Don Leucadio Doblado?*

North. To be sure I did, and did I not like the Confessions of the Opium Eater, too?—but I do no more think of judging of the two London Magazines by these things, than I would think of estimating the Edinburgh Review, as a book, by the few occasional pages of the old Arch-libeller's own penmanship, which now and then adorn it in these its degenerate days.

Tickler. The real defect is in my friend Tom. He is lazy, and he is timorous,—are not these qualities enough for your problem?

Odoherty. Let them pass. Lord Byron is neither lazy nor timorous,—and yet, you see, he is also a failure in this line.

North. Not at all—he is a man made for that sort of fun. But what would the Duke of Wellington himself do, if he were obliged to consult Jeremy Bentham about his movements? Knock off his handcuffs—I mean the Cockneys—and you'll see Byron is a sweet fellow yet.

Tickler. I was distressed to see John Bull abusing The Liberal as he did. John should be above such palaver; but I see he, with all his wit, makes a few sacrifices to humbug. What now can be more exquisitely ludicrous than the anti-Catholic zeal of such a chap as Bull?

Odoherty, (*laying finger on nose, and eyeing Mr. Editor.*) Poo! poo! we could match that elsewhere.

North, with an agreeable knitting of brows. Silence, Standard-bearer!

Hogg. I'll no hear Lord Byron abused, for he has ay been a kind friend to me. But, oh, sirs! what could gar him put in yon awfu' words about the gude auld King; and now that the worthy sant's in heaven, too? or whare did ever ony body see ony thing like yon epigrams† on Lord Castlereagh's death?

* By Rev. J. Blanco White, a Spaniard.—M.

† The "Vision of Judgment," (a burlesque on a very pretentious poem of the same name, by Southey,) appeared in The Liberal, edited by Byron and Leigh Hunt. The three epigrams on Castlereagh's death appeared in the same periodical. They were worth little. The best rnn thus

"So, He has cut his throat at last!—He! Who?
The man who cut his country's long ago."—M.

Tickler. Shocking trash! shocking, shocking!

Odoherty. I suppose Byron thought, since The Courier abused dead Shelley, The Liberal had a right to abuse dead Castlereagh.

North. Sir, Lord Byron thought no such thing. Lord Byron could never have thought that he had a right to insult all England, merely because one poor drivelling hypocrite had insulted his friend's memory in a newspaper. No, no, there is no defending these things.

Odoherty. Particularly as they happen to be utterly dull and helpless, and as devoid of point as the Ettrick Shepherd's own *gaucy* under-quarter, which, by the way, I wish he would give over scratching.

North. Once more, Hogg, never mind them. Your affection for Lord Byron, and concern to see him acting amiss, do you much honor. Whatever examples other people may set or follow, I hope you will always continue to be of opinion, that the few men of genius in the world ought to respect each other, rejoice in each other's triumphs, and be cast down by each other's misfortunes. Such a way of thinking is generous, and worthy of your kind heart, my good worthy friend.

Odoherty. Sir Richard Phillips is another great genius, and yet he does not write a good Magazine.

Tickler. Why, Pythagoras, my dear fellow, is one of the most contemptible Magaziners in the world. He is a dirty little jacobin, that thinks there is more merit in making some dirty little improvement on a threshing machine, than in composing an Iliad. He is a mere plodding, thick-skulled, prosing dunderpate; and every thing he puts forth seems as if it had been written by the stink of gas in the fifth story of a cotton-mill—a filthy jacobinical dog, sir.

North. Poor idiot! he is hammering at Napoleon still; now, indeed, he has taken to exhibiting a two-penny-half-penny bust of him, in his house in Bridge-street. Gentlemen and ladies one shilling—children and servants sixpence only!

Hogg. Speaking about Bonaparte, I wad like if ye wad lend me that lad Barry O'Meara's book out wi' me for a week. I'll return it by the next carrier.

North. Don't read it, Hogg. It's a piece of mere trash.

Hogg. Od! I thought I saw some commendation o't in the Magazine.

North. Yes—but Mr. Croker's letter of 1818 had not been published then—at least I had not seen it, else I would have scored out the paragraph.*

* Copy of the official Letter which notified to Mr. O'Meara his removal from the situation of a Surgeon in the Navy:

"ADMIRALTY OFFICE, Nov. 2, 1818.

"SIR—I have received and laid before my Lords Commisioners of the Admiralty your letter

Hogg. What does Crocker say about him? 'Tis like he might ken something about him in Erland.

North. Why, you see, Mr. Hogg, the story was just this:—Mr. O'Meara——

Odoherty. O'Mára, if you please, North.

North. Well, Mr. O'Marra writes to the Admiralty in 1818, saying that Sir Hudson Lowe had asked him to poison Bonaparte for him in 1816. Stop there, my friend, says Mr. Croker, either you are telling a bit of a bouncer, and Sir Hudson never made any such proposals to you at all; or you are a pretty behaved lad, (are you not?) to keep the thing in your pocket for two years, and bring it out now, not for the sake of justice, but for the sake of gratifying your own spleen. In short, "Le Docteur O'Meara" was dismissed his Majesty's service for this affair, and that's all.

Kempferhausen. Has he never made any answer to all this?

Tickler. Answer!—Poo! poo!—The dilemma is inevitable—he can only make his choice on which horn he is to ride.

Odoherty. We shall see what he says for himself in due time. He is a cleverish kind of fellow, is O'Meara, and we must, at least, admit that he has dish'd old Walter of the Times.

(and its enclosure) of the 28th ult., in which you state several particulars of your conduct in the situation you lately held at St. Helena. and request 'that their Lordships would, as soon as their important duties should allow, communicate to you their judgment thereupon.'

"Their Lordships have lost no time in considering your statement; and they command me to inform you, that (even without reference to the complaints made against you by Lieut. General Sir H. Lowe) they find in your own admissions ample grounds for marking your proceedings with their severest displeasure.

"But there is one passage in your said letter of such a nature as to supersede the necessity of animadverting upon any other part of it.

"This passage is as follows:—'In the third interview which Sir Hudson Lowe had with Napoleon Bonaparte in the month of May, 1816, he proposed to the latter to send me away, and to replace me by Mr. Baxter, who had been several years surgeon in the Corsican Rangers. This proposition was rejected with indignation by Napoleon Bonaparte, upon the grounds of the indelicacy of a proposal to substitute an army surgeon for the private surgeon of his own choice. Failing in this attempt, Sir Hudson Lowe adopted the resolution of manifesting great confidence in me by loading me with civilities, inviting me constantly to dinner with him, conversing for hours together with me alone, both in his own house and grounds and at Longwood, either in my own room, or under the trees and elsewhere. On some of these occasions he made to me observations upon the benefit which would result to Europe from the death of Napoleon Bonaparte, of which event he spoke in a manner which, considering his situation and mine, was peculiarly distressing to me.'

"It is impossible to doubt the meaning which this passage was intended to convey, and my Lords can as little doubt that the insinuation is a calumnious falsehood; but, if it were true, and if so horrible a suggestion were made to you, directly or indirectly, it was your bounden duty not to have lost a moment in communicating it to the Admiral on the spot, or to the Secretary of State, or to their Lordships.

"An overture so monstrous in itself, and so deeply involving not merely the personal character of the Governor, but the honor of the nation, and to the important interests committed to his charge, should not have been reserved in your own breast for two years, to be produced at last, not (as it would appear) from a sense of public duty, but in furtherance of your personal hostility against the Governor.

"Either the charge is in the last degree false and calumnious, or you can have no possible excuse for having hitherto suppressed it.

"In either case, and without adverting to the general tenor of your conduct, as stated in your letter, my Lords consider you to be an improper person to continue in his Majesty's service, and they have directed your name to be erased from the list of Naval Surgeons accordingly. I have, &c., (Signed) J. W. CROKER.

"MR. O'MEARA, 28 Chester Place, Kensington."

Tickler. Not much to brag of, that, if he had done it,—but I doubt the fact.

Odoherty. Well, well, as Samuel Johnson said, "Tis no great object to arrange the precedence between a louse and a flea."

Blackwood. All I say is, that the more the book is abused, the better it sells. I think there is never an hour but I hear it called for. It has had as great a run as the Cook's Oracle ever had.

North. I'll lend you the book, however, old Hogg.

Hogg. Thank ye, sir; after a' you're the discreetest of your divan, and I'll sing ye a sang for you're civility.

Kempferhausen. Bravo! Colonel, sing, sing—hurra! hurra! hurra!

Hogg (*sings.*)

I've thought, an' thought, but darna tell;
I've studied them wi' a' my skill;

I've loe'd them better than mysel';
  I've tried again to like them ill.
Wha sairest strives, will sairest rue,
  To comprehend what nae man can:
When he has done what man can do,
  He'll end at last where he began.
O, the women folk, &c.

That they hae gentle forms, and meet,
  A man wi' half a look may see,
An' gracefu' airs, and faces sweet,
  An' wavin curls aboon the bree—
An' smiles as saft as the young rosebud,
  An' een sae pawky bright and rare,
Wad lure the lavrock frae the clud;
  But, laddie, seek to ken nae mair.
O, the women folk, &c.

Even but this night, nae farther gane,
  The date is nouther lost nor lang,
I tak' ye witness ilka ane,
  How fell they fought, an' fairly dang;
Their point they've carried right or wrang,
  Without a reason, rhyme, or law,
An' forced a man to sing a sang,
  That ne'er could sing a verse ava.
O, the women folk, &c.

Tickler. Well done, kind Shepherd; I do love to hear your voice once more. Oh! Hogg, those were charming times when you used to pop in upon me of an evening after the chain was on the door, and practise the fiddle till the cattle danced upon the meadow.

Hogg. Hoh! sirs, we're a' turnin' auld noo: we've seen our best days, my dear Mr. Tickler.

Odoherty. Come, come, none of your humdrum sentiment here, my hearties. I will sing you a song I heard last year on board a 74—it was sung by its author, the surgeon of the vessel—a choice lad.

North. What is it about?

Odoherty. I don't recollect the words exactly, but I's give you something to the same tune, and similar in its scope and tendency, (ut cum Macveio loquar.) But you must be all ready with a chorus, mind that—

Odoherty (*sings.*)

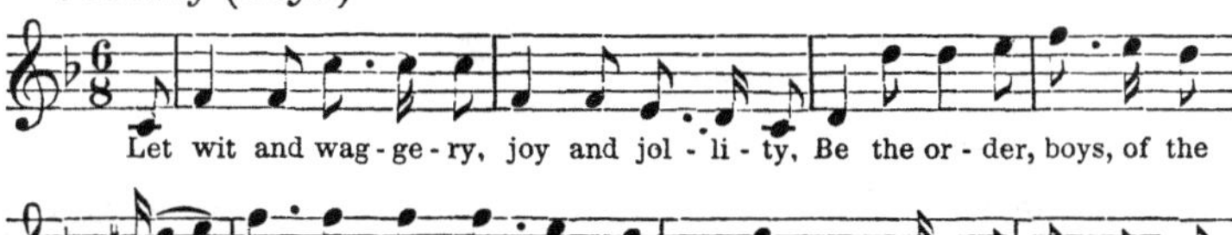

2.

He who of tax or tythe is gabbling—
  Mark him down for a Jeremy Ben;—*
Or account him a blockhead babbling,
  As great a blockhead as Council Ten.

Tickler. Council Ten! Who is that, in the name of Grub-street?

Odoherty. An ass.—(*Sings.*)—Chorus my——

Hogg. I never heard of him.

Odoherty. Of course not; but don't interrupt the song. *Tchorus*, a Mulligan has it. (*Sings.*) Chorus my song then, &c.

3

He who prates of Reform in Parliament,
  Send him adrift to the right or left,—
Why need we care what the big whig Charley† meant—
  Whether 'twas TREASON, or only THEFT?—
        Chorus my song, &c.

4.

He who'd bore us with jabber critical,
  On your curst scribes of verse or prose;—
Turn him loose with the ass political;—
  I never would wish to get drunk with those.
        Chorus my song, &c.

5.

Better it is to toast our pretty ones—
  To chaunt—or chorus while others sing;—
To laugh *at* dull men—and laugh *with* witty ones;
  Or drink the health of our own dear King.
    Chorus my song then, joyously chorus it;
      Why should *we* look dull or blue?
    There are some moments of pleasure before us yet.
      Folderol, tolderol, lolderol, loo!

Hogg, (*coughing.*) Hoh! hoh!—I'll be as hoarse as as a cuddie for

* Bentham.—M.

† Charles James Fox.—M.

a week after this wark. And div ye no find that sangs maks a body fou as soon as whisky ?

Odoherty. Yes—when they act kindly together, like Wellington and Blucher, I confess these affairs have an exhilarating scope and tendency.

Hogg. I wush Mr. Canning wad let down the tax on the sma' stells. A man like him should be aboon garrin' sae mony folk sip poishon night and morn.

North. I believe the Highlands have not yet been included in the Foreign Department; but Mr. Peel was here with the King, you know, and he must have tasted good Glenlivet himself, I should suppose.

Tickler. I beg leave to crave a bumper—Mr. Canning!

Omnes. Mr. Canning!!! !!! !!!

North. Yes, indeed, Canning is the man to carry the country with him.

Hogg. Is it not a very grand thing to be set as he has been at the head of things, just as it were by a kind of an acclamation?—no doubting, nor donnering;—every body just agreeing that he's the grandest statesman, and the maist glorious orator of the time.

North. I hope he will give himself the trouble to spend about three minutes apiece this Session upon little Grey Bennet, Lord Archibald Hamilton, and Jamie Abercrombie; for I'm really getting sick of these prosers.

Tickler. How despicable is Bennet's persecution of Theodore Hook. Lord! had Hook been a Whig, like Tom Moore, how little we should have heard of all this.

North. Why, to be sure, Hook and Moore stand precisely in the same situation—both of them clever men,—both of them wits,—both of them sent out to manage Colonial matters,—both of them meeting with queerish underlings,—both of their underlings cutting their throats on detection—and then both of them deprived of their offices, and in arrear to the public, not through any purloining of their own, but through circumstances which every one must regret as much as themselves.

Tickler. Aye, but here stops the parallel. Mr. Moore is pitied by every body, and no Tory ever alluded, or will allude, to his misfortunes in the House; while Mr. Hook is, week after week, and year after year, made the subject of attack by all that contemptible fry of the Bennets, Humes, and so forth.

North. And you think he would have been in smoother water if he had been a Whig?

Tickler. I do.—Only look at their protection and *proné*-ing of such a fellow as Borthwick,* a person who, according to his own story,

* One of the persons connected with the *Beacon* and *Glasgow Sentinel* newspapers, just then in very bad odor, in the law courts, from the number of libel suits against them.—M.

betrayed all manner of confidence, which he himself had solicited with all manner of solemnity, for the sake of a few paltry pounds, or rather for the sake of avoiding a day's work in THE JURY COURT —where, after all, he might probably have been let off for a shilling. Just think of a gentlemen like James Abercrombie taking up with such a creature—

North. And all in the silly and absurd hope of giving a little annoyance to the very people who ennobled his own family but (for which he would have been Nobody) about twenty years ago—no more.

Tickler. Have you seen Alexander's pamphlet?

North. Not yet—Is there any thing new in it?

Tickler. Why, after all, it turns out that the Lord Advocate's signature, which they make such a work about, was a FORGERY.

North. Very likely; I think that's not by any means the most heinous of all the tricks they've been guilty of. But who forged it?

Tickler. Alexander does not say *who*, but he states the fact broadly.*

Odoherty. John Bull, who has eyes everywhere, ought to take it up.

North. Why, Bull seldom meddles with Scotch affairs; and, after all, the scent of that humbug has got cold as charity.

Tickler. By-the-by, what an absurd thing it is that there should not be something better here in Edinburgh in the shape of a Newspaper—Ballantyne's Journal is nothing.

North. Oh! 'tis very well for the theatricals, very well indeed; and now and then it contains good sensible business articles too; but whenever there comes any thing like a political question of importance, nobody can say, *a priori*, whether James Ballantyne is like to take the best possible view of the matter, or the worst possible one. He behaved like a very goose about the Manchester affair; and, upon the whole, 'tis an inconsistent concern—hot and cold is not the thing for me.

Odoherty. Stick it into the hero;—but after all, he's the best.

Tickler Bad's the best; but, perhaps, Edinburgh is not a good place for a smart paper—too narrow and limited—people all egg-shells—damned stupid people too—all taken up with their own little jokes, that are unintelligible when you pass Cramond Bridge.

Odoherty. THE BEACON, for example, what a lump of dulness it was! It seemed to me to be got up just for the private amusement of three or four spalpeens.

* The pamphlet as entitled. "Letters to Sir J. Mackintosh, Knt. M. P. Explanatory of the whole circumstances which led to the robbery of the Glasgow Sentinel Office, to the Death of Sir Alexander Boswell, Bart; and the Trial [June 10, 1822] of Mr. James Stuart, younger, of Dunearn; and ultimately to the Animadversions of the Hon. James Abercromby, in the House of Commons, upon the conduct of the Right Hon. the Lord Advocate, and various individuals. By Robert Alexander, Editor of the Glasgow Sentinel."—M.

Hogg. Puir callants, nae doubt they boud to hae their ain bit cackle in a corner—let them abee.

Odoherty. Now what a proper name *Beacon* was. By the holy poker, a mangy mongrel could not have lifted his leg, in passing, without putting it out.

Tickler. A fine thing for the lawyers, however.

Odoherty (*sings.*)

"Ye lawyers so just,
Be the cause what it will, who so famously plead—
How worthy of trust!
You know black from white—
You prefer wrong to right,
As you chance to be feed.
Leave musty reports,
And forsake the King's courts,
Where Dulness and Discord have set up their thrones;
Burn Salkeld and Ventris,
With all your damn'd entries.
Hark, away to the claret! a bumper, 'Squire Jones."

[*An accident in the gas-pipes.*

No. VII.—MARCH, 1823.

SEDERUNT—CHRISTOPHER NORTH, Esq., Chairman; TIMOTHY TICKLER, Esq., Croupier; MORGAN ODOHERTY, Esq., JAMES HOGG, Esq., &c., &c.

SCENE—*The Blue Room—the Table crowded with Bottles, Pitchers, Devils, Books, Pamphlets, &c.*

TIME—*One in the Morning.*

Hogg (*proloquitur.*) It's just needless for you to deny 't, mon; it was a real bad number. An binna my ain bit paper on Captain Napier,* there was naething worth speaking o'? What were ye a' about?

Odoherty. I was in quod—hang it, they say John Bunyan and Sir Walter Raleigh wrote books there, but my spirits always sink.

Hogg. And wha brought ye out?

Tickler. Poo! poo! he took the benefit of the *cessio* as usual.

North. I'm sure if he would but exert himself, he need never be in any such scrapes; but I'm weary of speaking. Confound——

Hogg (*aside to the Adjutant.*) Never heed, he'll mind you in his wull for a' that—his bark was aye waur than his bite.

Odoherty. N'importe! Here I am once more. I'll be cursed if I don't marry a dowager ere the next month is over. How well it will look—"At her Ladyship's house, by special license, Morgan Odoherty, Esq., to Lady ——!"

Tickler. "Do or die," is the word with you, it would appear. Well, you had better get a Highland garb without delay. Nothing to be done *sans* kilt now, sir. Even "legs and impudence" won't go down unless *in puris.*

Odoherty. Did you see Hogg the day of the Celtic cattle-show? I am told he looked nobly.

Tickler. Yes, indeed. Hogg makes a very fine savage. He was all over in a bristle with dirk, claymore, eagle's feather, tooth, whisker, pistol and powder-horn. His ears were erect, his eyebrow indignant, his hands were hairy, his hurdies were horrible, his tread

* This was entitled "The Honorable Captain Napier and Ettrick Forest," and was a notice of "Napier's Treatise on Practical Store-Farming, as applicable to the Mountainous Region of Ettrick Forest," &c. Truth to say, it was a strong puff of the Captain—the same who, when Lord Napier, died in China, in 1834.—M.

was terrific. I met him even where our merchants most do congregate, at the Cross, and truly he had the crown of the causeway all to himself.

Odoherty. Had you your tail on, Clanhogg?

Hogg. Ye ill-tongued dyvour.* But what's the use o' argufying wi' the like o' you?—(*Sings.*)

Knees an' elbows, and a',
Elbows and knees, and a';
Here's to Donald Macdonald,
Stanes an' bullets, an' a'!

North. Ay, ay, Jemmy, that's the way to take it; but I'm sorry you thought it a bad Number. I should have supposed that its containing a touch of your own would have been enough to save it with you, at least, and the rest of the Ettrick lads.

Tickler. You deceive yourself, editor.

North. Nay, Tickler, I know what you mean. Upon my word, I shall insert that thing of yours very soon; don't be so very impatient.

Tickler. What, you old quiz! do you suppose I was angry at your omitting my little production? You may kick it behind the fire for what I care, I assure you of that, sir.

North. Not so fast, Timotheus; but what was your chief objection?

Tickler. That shocking, that atrocious lie, about Brodie—or rather, I should say, that bundle of lies.†

Odoherty. I wrote it. 'Ware candlesticks.

Hogg. Haud your haund there. Hoot, hoot, sirs; the present company are always excepted, ye ken.

Omnes. Agreed! Agreed!

Tickler. I disdain all personality, but that paragraph was full of shocking mis-statements. The fact is, I saw Brodie hanged, and he had no silver tube in his windpipe, and no flowered waistcoat on. It is true that he sent for a doctor to ask if there was any probability of escaping with life, but Degravers told him at once, sir, that he would be "as dead as Julius Cæsar;" these were the words. But Brodie would hold his own opinion; and nobody e'er threw down the pocket handkerchief more assured of resuscitation. Poor devil! he just spun round a few times, and then hung as quiet as you please, with his pigtail looking up to heaven.

* *Dyvour*—a debtor who cannot pay.—M.

† In *Blackwood*, for February, 1823, was a review of D'Israeli's Curiosities of Literature, in which, noticing the fact that the Earl of Morton died by the Maiden, which he introduced into Scotland, the critic affirmed that Deacon Brodie, who had been hanged (off a drop of his own invention) for robbing the Excise Office at Edinburgh, thirty years before, actually was executed with a silver tube in his windpipe,—but that all attempts to re-animate his body were fruitless. The reviewer said, "We have reason to say we *know* this, for we are old enough to have often talked with the surgeon who was present when the experiment was made."—M.

Odoherty. Alas! p r Brodie!—To tell you the truth, I wished to hum D'Israeli a little.

North. Pleasant, but wrong! For shame upon all humming!

Odoherty. Farewell!—a long farewell to all our Noctes.

Hogg. Ye mak mair trumpeting about a collector chiel, like D'Israeli, than mony a man of original genius and invention. Ye've never reviewed my "Three Perils of Man" yet.

North. The more shame to me, I confess; but wait till the "Three Perils of Woman" appear, and then we'll marry them together in one immortal article.

Odoherty. What, then, are "The Three Perils of Woman?" I think, "The Three Perils of Man" were, according to our kilted classic, "Women, War, and Witchcraft."

Hogg. Aye ware they—but faith, guess for yoursell, my cock. I ance told ane of you the name of a book I was on, and ye had ane wi' the same name out or I had won to my second volume.

North. Horrid usage for a man of original genius and invention. But, let's see, I think you should make them, "Man, Malmsey, and Methodism."

Mr. Tickler. Or, what say ye to "Ribbons, Rakes, and Ratafie?"

North. "Flattery, Flirting, and Philabegs?" Three F's, Hogg.

Hogg. Weel, I thought of some o' thae very anes. I thought of "Kirns, Kirkings, and Christenings," too; and then I thought of "Dreams, Drams, and Dragoons"—but I fixed at last on three L's.

Odoherty. "Legs, Lace, and Lies?"

Hogg. Na, na, you're a' out. "Love, Learning, and Laziness."

Odoherty. O, most lame and impotent conclusion! But no doubt, you'll make it rich enough in the details. Your "Love" will no doubt end in the cutty stool; your "Learning," in Constable's Magazine; and your "Laziness," in Black Stockings. Thus we shall have an imposing and instructive view of life and society.

Hogg. If ye say another word, I'll dedicate the buik to you, Captain.

Odoherty. Do. I always repay a dedication with a puff.

Hogg. Yon D'Israeli chap dedicated to you, I'se warrant?

Odoherty. In writing the tale of "Learning," (for, if I understand you rightly, there are to be three separate tales,) I beg of you to imitate, above all other novel writers, my illustrious friend, the Viscount D'Arlincourt.*

Hogg. Arlincoor, say ye? Wait till I get out my kielevine pen. Od! I never heard tell of *him* afore.

Odoherty. For shame! "Not to know him." (*Shakspeare.*) In a word, however, my worthy friend, he is the greatest genius of the age. If you doubt what I say, I refer you to Sir Richard Phillips. I think I see him lying there beside the head of North's crutch.

* A modern French novelist.—M.

North. (*Handing the Old Monthly to the Ensign.*) There is the production.

Odoherty. Ay, and here's the puff. "This is the work of a man of genius, and the translation has fallen into very competent hands." Need I read any more of Sir Pythagoras?

Hogg. Oh, no. But what is't ye wad have me particularly to keep an ee upon? Troth, I wad be nane the waur of a hint or twa to help me on with the sklate.

Odoherty. 'Tis more especially in the tale "Learning," that I venture to solicit your attention to my noble friend's works. He is the most learned novelist of our era. Follow him, and you will please Macvey himself.

Hogg. Weel, let's hear a wee bit skreed o' him. I daresay Mr. North will hae him yonder amang the lave, beside his stult. Sauf us! the very table's groaning wi' sae mony new authors.

North. You may say so, truly; and I groan as well as my table. Here's "The Renegade," however. Will that do, Odoherty?

Odoherty. Yes, yes—any of them will do. You see, Hogg, the noble author plunges us at once into the deepest interest of his tale. An invading army of Saracens carries ruin and horror into the hills of the Cevennes. A Princess, the heroine of the book, is driven from her paternal halls—she flies with her vassals—the black flag of Agobar floats awful on the breeze—all alarm, terror, dismay, desolation—

Hogg. That's real good. I'll begin my "Laziness," wi' an invasion too.

Odoherty. Certainly—and now attend to this illustrious author's style, for it is that I wish you to copy, my dear Hogg. Hear this passage, and thirst for geology. You understand that the description refers to a moment of the deepest and the most overwhelming emotion—our Princess is in full flight, the hall of her ancestors blazing behind her—

"While the Princess, borne on her gentle palfrey, abandoned herself to these sad thoughts, Lutevia, at a turn of the rock, again presented itself to her view. Lighted torches were seen to glance here and there upon the platforms of the castle. These moving lights, the signal of some new event, announced a tumultuous agitation among the soldiery. The fatal bell again was heard. Ezilda could doubt no longer that the Saracens had attacked the fortress. She immediately struck into the depths of the mountains. The bright stars directed her march, as she pursued an unfrequented road across untrod rocks, and by the edges of precipices. At every step Nature presented inexplicable horrors, *produced by the various revolutions which had acted upon this region.* In one place were seen streams of *basaltic lava*, thick beds of *red pozzolanum*, *calcareous spars*, and gilded *pyrites*, thrown out by the numerous *volcanoes*. In another, strange contrast! the ravages of *water* had succeeded to those of *fire*; transparent *petrifactions*, marine shells, *sonorous congelations*, *sparkling scoriæ*, and *crystallized prisms*, were mixed accidentally with the confused *works of different regions*. A *crater* had become a lake; an ancient bed of flames, a cascade; the waves of the ocean had driven back the blazing volcanoes, had placed the peaks of mountains where their bases had been, and had rolled *pêle mêle, zeolites and silices, cinders and crystals, stalactites and tripoli!!!* From a reversed cone covered with snow, and which contained freezing springs, boiling waters spouted. In the dark ages, it would have seemed that the two terrific genii of devastation, fire and flood, had contended; and as the mysteries of Providence put to fault the reason of the philosopher, these mysteries of nature embarrassed all the systems of the learned.

"The heavens were covered with clouds, a small rain had begun to fall, and each step had become more perilous; the narrow road cut in the rock seemed to offer only a succession of precipices.

"After some hours' journey, the Princess approached a torrent, whose waters thundered between a *double colonnade of basaltic pillars.* At the bottom of a glen, which seemed almost inaccessible, the road enlarged. Upon a barren flat, surrounded by pointed rocks and enormous *calcareous* stones, the virgin of Lutevia perceived a sort of wild camp, lighted by scattered fires. Terror was a stranger to her soul, and believing that she was covered by the buckler of the Lord, and that her path through life was to be marked by frightful events, Ezilda was resigned to her stormy destiny!!!"

Hogg. Oh man, that's awfu' grand; thae lang words gie siccan an air to the delineation. I dare say some o' the bonny words would suit very well in my "Learning." Will you lend me the buik, Mr. North?

North. Say no more. The volumes are thine own.

Hogg. Thank ye kindly, sir. Od, I'll gut this chiel or lang be. I wonder what Gray will think of me? But I'll easily bam him, noo he's ower the water.*

Odoherty. Ay, here's another prime morceau. 'Tis a description, you are to suppose, of a grotto where a love adventure goes on.

"This celebrated grotto was sunk in the base of a misshapen and rugged rock. Its peak had been a volcano; its arid summit, scorched by its eruptions, covered with *black lava, green schorl, metallic molliculi,* with *calcined and vitrified* substances, bore in every part the destructive marks of *fire;* while the sunken earth, the *schistous* stones, the beds of *mud,* the irregular mixture of volcanic with marine productions, and the regular piles of *basaltic prisms,* were evidences of the operation of *contending elements.*"

Hogg. "Evidences of the operations of contending elements!" It's perfectly sublime. It dings Kilmeny—na, it clean dings her!

North. Nil desperandum! Spout us a bit more, Odoherty.

Hogg. Speak weel out, Captain—gie yoursel breath.

Odoherty. Read yourself, Hogg; there's a fine place.

Hogg. Na, wha ever saw the like o't—Ze-ze-ze-oleet—Montlos—Girand—Salaberry—berry. Ay, it's just Salaberry. Od, this is worse than the Eleventh of Nehemiah.

Odoherty. Poo! You're at the notes. Let me see the book again. Did you ever describe a handsome fellow, Hogg? Well, hear how

* In Canada.—M.

this virgin Princess here describes one she saw sleeping in his own bed-room, to which she had penetrated. "His chest," said she, "his chest half-bared, white as the marble of Paros, was like that of the athletic Crotona. As *vigorous* as the Conqueror of the Minotaur, as *colossal* as the Grecian Ajax, as beautiful as the Antinous of the Romans——.

North. Stop, stop; fold up the bedclothes again, if you please. Upon my word, this is worse than Sophy Western and Mrs. Honour about Tom Jones's broken arm.

Hogg. My gudeness! This is just the book I wanted. Od, I'll come braw speed noo.

Odoherty. To be sure you will. But a man of your stamp should not follow with any servile imitation. No—Admire D'Arlincourt, but cease not to be Hogg.

Hogg. De'il a fears o' me!

Odoherty. If your heroine is to be woo'd about St. Leonards, be sure you turn up Pinkerton, or Jameson, and tip us the Latin or German names of all the different strata in that quarter. It will have a fine, and, in Scotland at least, a novel effect. If she climb Arthur's Seat, tell us how the thermometer stood when she was kissed at the top. If there is a shower on her wedding night, take a note of the cubic inches that fell. If her petticoat be stained with green, tip us the Linnæan description of the grass. And if you are afraid of going wrong in your science, Mr. Leslie will perhaps look over the MS. for you.

Hogg. I'll send him a copy of the second edition; but I'll let nae Professors look at my manuscripts. Od! I mind ower weel what cam o' my *Waterloo.*

North. *Your* Waterloo! God bless me. Did you help Mr. Simpson,* then?

Hogg. Ye're a' to seek. It wasna Jamie Simpson's book I had aught to do wi', (although it was a very bonny bit bookie, too.) It was a Waterloo o' mine ain, a poem I had written, and I sent it in to Grieve; and awheen o' them had a denner at Bill Young's, to read it over, forsooth. And od! heard you ever the like o' sic tinkler loons? they brunt it bodily, and sent me a round-robin that it was havers—mere havers.

Odoherty. Paltry, envious souls! Insensate jealousy! Despicable spleen!

North.

Κωρακες ὡς
Ακραντα γαρυεμεν
Διος ϖρος ορνιθα θειον.

* James Simpson, an Edinburgh lawyer, published an interesting account of his visit to Waterloo, in 1815. In the late editions he gives some delightful recollections of Sir Walter Scott.—M.

Hogg. Eh!

North. Græcum est.

Odoherty. (*Sings, accompanying himself on the trombone.*)

1.

Greek and Latin
Will come pat in
Our Chaldean Shepherd's page.
With geology,
And petrology,
Sans apology,
He, he alone is born to cram our age. (*bis.*)

2.

'Tis he will tickle ye
With Molliculi,
Pouzzolanum, Schorl, and Schist;
'Tis he will bristle,
With cone and crystal,
His shepherd's whistle
Is now, in loathing and high scorn, dismist. (*bis.*)

3.

Show your glory
In shells and scoriæ!
Pour your lava, drop your spar!
With Stalactites,
And Pyrites,
And Zeolites,
Hogg now will make thee stare, prodigious Parr! (*bis.*)

4.

When he prints it out,
The French Institute
Will enrol one Scotchman more;
How we'll caper,
When Supplement Napier,*
For a physical paper,
Bows low, nor bows in vain, by Altrive's shore! (*bis.*)

5.

Grasp your slate, sir,
Scratch your pate, sir,
You must speak—the world is dumb!
Logic, Rhet'ric,
Chemic, Metric,
Fresh from Ettrick,
With glorious roar, and deaf'ning deluge come! (*bis.*)

Hogg (*much affected*). Gie me your hand, Captain. Oh, dear! Oh, dear me!

North. Enough of this, boys.—What new book have you been reading, Tickler?

* Macvey Napier edited the Supplement to the Encyclopædia Britannica.—M.

Tickler. From Hogg to Foscolo the transition is easy. I have been much gratified with Essays on Petrarch.

Odoherty. Fudgiolo's new affair?

Tickler. He must now drop that title. 'Tis really a very elegant volume, full of facts, full of fancy, full of feeling,—a very delightful book, certainly.

North. I glanced over it. There seemed to be a cursed deal of Balaam, in the shape of Appendixes, and so forth.

Tickler. True enough. But there's sail enough to do even with that quantity of ballast.

North. Have you seen a little volume about the Spanish affair, by one Pecchio, a Carbonaro Count from Italy?

Tickler. Not I, faith; nor never will.

North. No, no, 'tis not worth your seeing. It is full of Blaquiere. Edward Blaquiere, Esq. writes the preface, and puffs his excellency Count Pecchio, and Count Pecchio repays Edward Blaquiere, Esq. in the body of the book. It contains, however, and that's what brought it to my recollection just now, some most eulogistic pages about Ugo Foscolo. Here is the book, however.—Read for yourself.—(*Handing Pecchio.*)

Tickler (*as musing.*) Ay, my Jacopo Ortis! and so this is the way you go on, (*reads*) "His cottage is isolated, but well furnished. A canal is near it, that looks like the troubled Lethe. One might take our friend's abode for a hermitage, were it not for the TWO PRETTY CHAMBERMAIDS that one observes moving about the precincts." Two!—Yes, by Jupiter, 'tis so in the bond. Two! O, ye Gods!

Hogg. TWA hizzies!—Less might serve him, I fancy.

Odoherty. Two! Pretty well for the latitude of the Regent's Park.*

Tickler. Well done, Mr. Last Words! But these are your Zante tricks.—"The isles of Greece! the isles of Greece!"

North. Pooh, pooh! Timothy, you're daft. I confess I regret that he should have been called Fudgiolo—for a man never finds it easy to lose a nickname.

Odoherty. Of my making.

North. Sorrow on your impudence!—You have cost many a worthy body a sore heart, in your time, with your nicknames.

Odoherty. True, O King!—O King, live for ever!

Hogg. That's just what I ay thocht. If Mr. North could get his ain gait, there would not be a better-natured book in a' the world—it's just that lang-legged Adjutant that pits the deeviltries intill't.

Odoherty. Hioicks! hioicks?—but, after all, isn't it odd that

* Ugo Foscolo occupied what he called Di-Gamma Cottage, St. John's Wood, London. Instead of *two* pretty attendants, he had three sisters, all of them very handsome!—M.

Reviews, &c., and all their wit, and all their malice, and all their hypocritical puffing, are not able to produce the smallest effect, good or bad, upon the permanent reputation of any writer. I confess I wonder that this should be the case.

North. I confess I should wonder if it were the case.

Odoherty. Aha! by this craft he hath his living!—but be honest for once, Kit North, and tell me the name of that author that has been permanently raised, or permanently depressed, beyond his merits by our periodicals?

North. *Permanently* is a queer word. You think to get out by that loophole.

Odoherty. Why, do but think of things as they are. Does Wordsworth stand a whit the lower, for having been a general laughing-stock during twenty long years?—Or does Jeffrey stand a whit the higher, for having been puffed during a period of about equal extent.

North. It was I that brought up the one, and put down the other of them.

Odoherty. Huzza! A trumpeter wanted here! Why, big fellow as you think yourself, they would just have been where they are by this time, although you had stayed in Barbadoes till this moment.

Hogg. Barbaudoes! Was North in Barbaudoes?

Odoherty. Yes, this man who now rules, and with no light rod, the empire of European literature, consumed many years of his life among the sugar plantations of the other hemisphere. He has been a jack of all trades in his day.

North. Wait, man, he'll see it all in my autobiography—which, if so please the fates, shall see the light

"Ere twelve times more yon star hath filled her horn."

Hogg. Meaning me?—Od, I'll no be lang about twal tumblers, if that's a' the matter.

Odoherty. Ha! ha! honest Jemmy!—But, to be serious, old boy, who then is the man that hath been elevated?—who is he that hath in this sort been depressed?

North. Why, as I said before, you will creep out upon your "*permanently.*"

Odoherty. And you may say that. The fact of the matter, or *ut cum Josepho loquar*, "the tottle of the whole," is, that all the criticism that has been written since the Flood, might just as well have remained in non-existence. For example, does any one really dream that there slumbers at this moment, on the shelves of the British Museum, any real fellow whose works are not known, and deserve to be known? Has my friend D'Israeli, or any of that tribe, ever been able to ferret out a long-concealed author of *genius?*—No, no.

Depend on't, my dear, there's no Swift, nor Pope, nor Gibbon, nor Smollet, nor Milton, nor Warburton, nor Dryden, nor any body really worth being up to, but what all the world *is* up to. The critical bowstring has been justly applied, or baffled—there is no third to these two ways of it.

Tickler. I side with the Adjutant. And the longer things go on, there will be but the more need for plying the cord tightly. No age ever possessed, nor does ours for what I see, more than a very few great ones; and to smother the small ones is but doing justice to these and to the public.

Odoherty. Well said, Timothy.—If one looks round among our periodicals, there is scarcely one of them that is not laboring away to hoist up some heavy bottom. The Quarterly and the British Critic tell us that Milman is a mighty poet. The New Monthly Magazine, and five or six inferior books, keep up a perpetual blast about Barry Cornwall—Waugh winds his sultry horn for the glory of Mrs. Hemans—Taylor and Hessey pound the public with Barton and Allan Cunningham.

North. Well, and what do ye make of all this? Is it not true, that Mr. Milman *is* a very elegant and accomplished man, and that he deserves to be lauded for his fine verses? Is it not true, that Barry Cornwall's dramatic scenes formed a delightful little book? and ought they to be quite forgotten, merely because he has written three or four confounded trashy ones since? Is it not true that Mrs. Hemans is a woman of pretty feeling and writes sweetly?—Is it not true that Bernard Barton and Allan Cunningham are both of them deserving of commendation?

Hogg. Hear! hear!

Odoherty. The question is not whether these people deserve some praise, but whether they deserve the highest praise—for that is what they get in the quarters I have indicated. And just to bring you up with the curb, my dear, do you really suppose that any of these names will exist *anno* eighteen hundred and forty-three?

Hogg. The Forty-Three's a long look—heh, me! we may a' be aneath the moulds by that time.*

Tickler, (*dejectedly.*) The wicked shall cease from troubling —

Hogg, (*ditto.*) And all their works shall follow them —

Odoherty. Come, come; what's the fun of all this? (*Sings.*)

1.

Time and we should swiftly pass;
He the hour-glass, we the glass.—
Drink! yon beam which shines so bright
Soon will sink in starless night:

Tchorus, now, Tchorus —

* All were, except Wilson, who died in 1854.—M.

Ere it sink, boys, ere it sink —
Drink it dim, boys! drink, drink, drink!

2.

Drink, before it be too late—
Snatch the hour you may from fate;
Here alone true wisdom lies,
To be merry's to be wise.—
Ere ye sink, boys—ere ye sink—
Drink ye blind, boys! drink, drink, drink!

(*Much applause.*)

North. Odoherty, Odoherty! I say you are an absolute bar to business. Which of you will give me an article on the last Number of the Quarterly Review?

Hogg. I write in The Quarterly myself now and then, sae, if you please, I would rather it fell to the Captain's hand.

Odoherty. Well, I like that notion—as if I had not written in every periodical under the sun, and would not do so if I pleased to-morrow again. Why, open your gray gleamers, you Pig—you should not be quite so obtuse at this time of day, I think —

Hogg. Whatna warks do you really contribute till, Captain?

Odoherty. I write politics in the Quarterly—Belles Lettres sometimes for the Edinburgh; ditto, for the Monthly Review, (particularly the Supplemental Numbers about foreign books.) Divinitv for the British Critic—these are pretty regular jobs—but I also favor now and then Colburn, Constable, Waugh, &c., in their Magazines. In point of fact, I write for this or that periodical, according to the state of my stomach or spirits, (which is the same thing,) when I sit down. Am I flat—I tip my Grandmother a bit of prose. Am I dunned into sourness—I cut up some deistical fellow for the Quarterly. Am I yellow about the chops—do I sport what Crabbe calls

"The cool contemptuous smile
Of clever persons overcharged with bile;"

Why, then, there's nothing for it but stirring up the fire, drawing a cork, and Ebonizing—*ainsi va le monde!*

North. So, Principle, Mr. Odoherty, is entirely laid out of view?

Odoherty. Not at all, not for the Bank of England, my dear fellow. But what has Principle to do here? no more than Principal Baird, I assure ye. Why, don't we all know that little Cruikshank did the caricatures of the King for Hone, and those of the Queen for the other party,* and who thought the less either of him or his caricatures? Are a man's five fingers not his own property?

North. *Dans sa peau mourra le Reynard.* So you seriously think yourself entitled to play Whig the one day and Tory the next.

* He did not.—M.

Odoherty. "Tros Tyriusque mihi nullo discrimine agetur"—

North. You talk *en Suisse.*

Odoherty. Ay, and as you know to your cost, old boy, *d'argent, point de Suisse!*

Hogg. I dinna follow you vera weel, but I'm feared you're r a very shameful story of yourself, Captain Odoherty.

North (*aside to Hogg.*) My dear Corydon—he's only bammi I believe.

Hogg. Oh! the neerdoweel! to bam Mr. North! this beats

Odoherty. "This beats York races, Doncaster fair, and Judges come down to hang folks."

North. Enough! enough!—but once more to business, my friends! what say you as to the Quarterly?

Tickler. 'Tis certainly a first-rate Number, the best they have had these three or four years; but I don't see why *you* should have an article upon it.

North. I do see it, though. Sir, the Quarterly has done itself immortal honor by that paper "On the Opposition." I should willingly give something to know who wrote it.

Tickler. Why, 'tis well argued and well written; but after all, your own work had said the same things before, and perhaps as well.

North. No, indeed, sir. We had uttered the same sentiments and opinions; but neither so wisely nor so well: the clear, quiet, masterly exposure in that paper has not often been rivalled. We have had few things so good since Burke's pamphlets. Once more, I would like to know the author's name.*

Hogg. Can it be Mr. Canning?

North. No, no; it has neither his rhetoric nor his oratory: nor has it the air of being written by so old or so high a statesman as Canning.

Tickler. Croker?

North. Out again. It wants his rapidity and his *vivadi vis.* Compare it with the *Thoughts on Ireland.* They, to be sure, were written when he was very young, and the style has the faults of youth, inexperience, and over imitation of Tacitus; but still one may see the pace of the man's mind there; and a very fiery pace it is.

Odoherty. I do not think it can be Gifford's own handiwork.

North. I would not swear that. It has much of the masculine determined energy of Gifford's mind; and if it has none of the bad jokes that used to figure in his diatribes, for bitter bad some of them were, why, such a man may very well be supposed to have discovered his own weak points by this time. Of late, more's the pity, his pen has not been very familiar to us even in the Review.†

* Dr. Maginn.—M.

† Gifford retired from the Quarterly in 1824, and died in 1826.—M.

Tickler. It will be a great loss to literature when he retires from his Review. I wonder who is to succeed him.

North. I wish, with all my heart, he had a successor worthy of himself: a man inspired, like him, in spite of all his defects, with a true and deep reverence for the old spirit of English loyalty and English religion; and, what will be even more difficult to match, imbued with a thorough knowledge of the old and genuine classics of our literature. I fear no young man will do; and I know of no old one likely to buckle to such a labor. Murray should look twice ere he leap; but perhaps Gifford himself may stand it out longer than seems to be generally expected.

Tickler. I hope so. After all, the Tories might find it almost as difficult to replace him, as the Whigs would find it to replace our friend Jeffrey.

North. Just so. The truth is, that both Gifford and Jeffrey have done many wrong things—the latter many hundreds, perhaps; but take them all in all, they are scholars and gentlemen, and literature must number them among the *bene meriti* of *her* republic. Compare them with the fry they have so long kept in the shade.

Hogg (*testily.*) Neither the tane nor the tither has said a word about "The Three Perils."

Odoherty. Come, that's shabby, however. But cheer up; I will do you in both, ere three months be over, or my name's not Morgan.

North. Lord keep us! Does an old stager like the Shepherd feel sore upon such points as these? I profess I had no notion of it, or I should have buttered you with the thumb long ago myself.

Hogg. Praise is praise, an it be but frae a butcher's calland.

North. Elegant, Hogg! How you would squeal if I put the knife in your hide! No jokes on me, my *formose puer.*

Hogg. Dinna gloom that gait. Od! I was na meaning ony offence —

Tickler. Kiss and be friends. But, North, don't you wonder at the Quarterly's taking no notice of the Spanish affairs? I confess I expected a paper on that subject, full of real information; which, indeed, we need not look for in any other quarter.

North. Wait a little. I suppose it will keep cool for a little, like that dishing of O'Meara.

Odoherty. I give up my brother bog-trotter. He is indeed dished.

Tickler. Ay, and yet I am not sure whether it be not Cobbett that has given him the *coup-de-grace.* Did you see the Statesman's article? No?—Well, then Cobbett just says the truth smack out.* O'Meara may bother away with paragraphs till Doomsday.—He is a gone man, until he denies the letters printed in the Quarterly.

* Cobbett wrote leading articles, at that time, in *The Statesman*, which soon went down.—M.

North. "Elegant O'Meara," indeed!—but if it be true that he's turned out of the menagerie, I suppose no more need be said of him. I'll tell you what is my opinion—the puff on that fellow in the last Edinburgh Review must now be making my friend Jeffrey feel as sore as Dr. Phillpotts' letter itself. Oh! sir, these are the sort of rubs that make a man bite the blood out of his nails.—Phillpotts' calm, dignified, unanswerable smashing has done them more harm than any thing they had met with these many days, and then on the back of that comes this vile *exposée.*

Odoherty. My private opinion is, that O'Meara's book was got up in a great measure as a puff on the Edinburgh Review. The art of puffing has made great progress of late. Devil a book comes out without some dirty buttering in it, either of you, North, or the Edinburgh, or the Quarterly, or some other periodical the author wants to conciliate. Witness D'Israeli buttering Gifford—Lord John Russell buttering Tom Campbell—O'Meara buttering John Allen;*—and last not least, Billy Hazlitt buttering you in the Liberal.

North. Call you that buttering your friends? A shame on such butter!

Odoherty. What would you have?—The boys can't write three pages without mentioning you. If that is not butter enough for you, you must be ill to please.

Hogg. The captain's in the right. An author's aye commended when he's kept before the public. That's what gars me pit up with the jokes of some of you chields.

Odoherty. Ditto. But the fact is, that the Cockneys are mad—they can tell a hawk from a handsaw on other occasions; but whenever the wind is *North*, due *North*, 'tis all up with them—out it comes, the absolute slaver of insanity. You have much to answer for. We shall hear of some tragedy among them one of these days.

North. Any thing but another Mirandola—say I.

Hogg. Hoot, hoot, ye're ower severe now, Mr. North. The poor lads had eneugh to do to gar the twa ends meet, and now ye've rooked them clean out. If they were stout, braid-backed chields like the Captain and me, it wad be less matter, they could yoke to some other thing; but the puir whitefaced tea-drinking billies, what's to come o'them?—I'm wae when I think o't.

Tickler. The parishes of Wapping and Clerkenwell have good actions against North—he must have raised their poor-rates confoundedly.

* John Allen travelled on the Continent, in 1802, as medical attendant and companion, and continued a hanger-on, a literary toad-eater at Holland House for many years. In 1811 he was elected Warden, and in 1820, Master of Dulwich College. He contributed largely to the *Edinburgh Review*, and died in 1843.---M.

Odoherty. Oh, dear!—Slops won't come to so much.—I would contract to corn and water them at sixpence a head *per diem.*

Hogg. Wull ye put me in the schedule?—Here's my thumb!

Odoherty. You, you monster, you Cyclops, you Polyphemus! why, you would swallow porridge enough to ruin me in a fortnight: but if you'll part with three grinders to the Odontist's museum, I may give you, as Mrs. Walkinshaw says, another interlocutor of the Lord Ordinary.

North. Come, come, Hogg, take your revenge in your novel. I have seen some of the proof sheets, and I assure you I think it will take to a hair. Indeed, my dear fellow, you cannot, if you would, launch any thing that will not have talent enough to swim it out. For my part, I liked the Perils of Man extremely well—rough, coarse pieces, no doubt—but, on the whole, a free rapid narrative, some eminently picturesque descriptions, a great deal of good blunt humor, and one or two scenes, which I wonder the play-wrights have not laid paw upon long ere now. Indeed, I think the Devil, the eating Ploughman, the two Princesses, &c. &c., would all do capitally on the stage. You should send a copy to Terry* or Murray. Murray, by the way, deserves much credit for his dramatization of Nigel.

Hogg. He's a clever lad, Murray. I like him better than ony play-actor they have.—He never gangs beyond Nature, and he never buckles to ought but what he's up to.

Odoherty. Would all actors and all authors had wit to follow that example!—There is really an immensity of quiet comic humor about Murray—how good is his Jerry Hawthorn! but he did wrong to leave out Almacks in the East, and the Tread-mill—these were absurd sacrifices to the squeamishness of the modern Athens—they were, in fact, the best things in the original piece.†

North. I hobbled out one night to see the thing, but although the acting was excellent, with the single exception of the row, the affair struck me as a confoundedly dull one—no incident, no story, no character,—a precious heap of trash assuredly.

Tickler. Well, good acting is a jewel—Murray, with his bluff humor, Calcraft, with his true gentlemanlike lightness, and Jones with his inimitable knowing grin, made it go down with me sweetly.—What do you think of Mr. Vandenhoff?

Odoherty. No Vandal—but Young has been here!

North. Come, come, nobody starts with being a Young. Rome was not built in a day—link by link the mail is made—we must all creep before we walk.

* Terry was then manager of the Haymarket Theatre in London, and Murray of the Edinburgh Theatre.—M.

† Pierce Egan's "Tom and Jerry."—M.

Odoherty. You're as great in proverbs as Sancho himself, I swear. Why don't you write a rational book on them? Nothing worth twopence in that way, since Erasmus's Adagia—all our English books contemptible—poor—imperfect—dull—stupid—and devoid of all arrangement. As for D'Israeli, he, as I said in my review of him, knows nothing whatever of the subject; for he quotes, for great rarities, a few of the most hackneyed ones in existence—old Plutarchs, Joe Millers, and the like.

North. I admire no proverbs more than those Dean Swift used to *make* (not to repeat.)

Odoherty. It would be a good thing to revive the manufacture, and apply it to literary topics.

North. We shall see—what would you think of reviving Cowper's rhyming prose* in the mean time? I think you might do that easily, Hogg, or you, Odoherty; either of you have rhymes, God knows, *quantum suff.*

Hogg. I fear 'twill be stuff—but let's try our hand——

Odoherty. On Peveril of the Peak——

Hogg. The story's ill plann'd, and the foundation very weak; yet, begin where you please, I rather think you'll not stop—Great authors like these may jump or hop, they may leap over years, in one chapter a score or more, yet no gap appears, one reads on as before; but if I or any other should follow after that great brother, skipping and hipping, notching and botching, I rather apprehend my very best friend would vote me a Bore.

Odoherty. You need not feel sore although that should be the case, I make bold, my dear Jamie, to tell ye the truth to your face, there's something so sweet, and so mellow, and so little of the air of being got up, about the style of that right fellow, that whatever he touches pleases everybody, male and female, from Grizzy to the Duchess, from the porter to the peer; and, this is what's so queer, all's one whether he describe King Charles or King Charles's little pet pup, or beer foaming in a night cellar's barrels, or muscat wine sparkling in a jewell'd cap—high or low, with him we go; no affectation, no botheration, sound sense, a high feeling for honor and arms, a heart

* A few years later, this rhyming prose was actually revived, and by no less an author than D'Israeli, in his "Wondrous Tale of Alroy." However, he did not make very much use of it. In May, 1833, Maginn, who wrote nearly all the letter-press to the "Gallery of Literary Characters" in *Fraser's Magazine*, (the etched portraits were by Daniel Maclise, then a young Irish artist rising into celebrity, and now one of the first painters in Europe,) hit off this rhyming prose very neatly. The sketch thus commenced: "O Reader dear! do pray look here, and you will spy the curly hair, and forehead bare, and nose so high, and gleaming eye, of Benjamin D'is-ra-e-li, the wondrous boy who wrote *Alroy* in rhyme and prose, only to show how long ago victorious Judah's lion-banner rose." It is as easy to write this as to write prose, as any one can ascertain who will make the experiment. Maginn could *talk* in this rhymed prose for half an hour at a time, without ever pausing for a word or rhyme. I have no doubt that the next few pages, in which continuous examples are given, are written by Maginn.—M.

that the black eye of a pretty girl warms, gently and gaily, but never ungentaly, a pawky glance into everything mean, yet somehow or other a loftiness of spirit that never ceases to be felt and seen; these are the qualities, by which he contrives to make all the rest of your tribe look like nullities, and by which—no offence, for you must not be disappointed of your rhyme, though it comes a little disjointed—he contrives, thanks to his long nob, to draw into his own fob such a noble shower of pounds, shillings and pence.

Hogg. I wish out of his next book, for which I suppose we may soon begin to look, he would be so kind as to pay down what I owe to the Duke, and also to the Crown, for rents and taxes and so forth; or you, why won't you do the same good turn for me, Mr. North?

North. If I were you, Dear Jem, when money became due to them, I would instantly take my pen and compose an ode; they never would dun you again, if your verses flowed, as I think they would, easy and good, and sweet and pleasant, as your prose does at present; but as for me, my dear honey—as for me paying down money, for you or any other pastoral poet, I must have ye to know it, the idea's quite absurd—I won't do it, upon my word—I am not so green.—In point of fact, I have entered into a compact, (with myself, I mean) to keep all my cash, making no sort of dash, buying neither pictures nor plate, nor a Poyais estate; eating nothing better than plain veals and muttons, and drinking nothing better than simple claret and champagne; dressing up my old coats with new collars and buttons; and, in a word, cutting all expenses that are foolish and vain, and driving on with the old phaeton, the old horses, and the old postilion; in short, maintaining the most rigid economy, until it be universally known o' me, that I am fairly worth my cool million. When that is done, there will be something new seen under the sun; for I'll let nobody then call me a niggard, but mount everything in the grandest style, that was ever seen in this part of the isle, showing off, whoever may scoff, like a second Sir Gregor Macgregor.*

Hogg. I suppose you speak of his highness the Cazique: but, after all, what could he have expected, if he had but recollected, that ever since the reign of Canmore was ended, the clan of might and main from which that potentate is descended, have condescended to patronize as their favorite air, that fine old pibroch, "Pacckhundsaidh gu bair."

* This was a Scotchman, who declared, during the South American contest for independence, that he had received the grant of a Province called Poyais, with the title of Cacique. He created himself baronet, by the title of Sir Gregor MacGregor—proclaimed that he had a right to confer titles of nobility in Poyais—instituted an Order of Knighthood, of which he was Grand Master—invited adventurers to fight under his banner—wore the dress of a General officer, green, with gold embroidery—succeeded in making up "the Poyais Legion," promising grants of land to all who joined him—took his dupes over to Poyais, where most of them perished, most miserably, of want and other discomforts—and, in a word, made many dupes.—He was an impudent and successful charlatan.—M.

(*Sings.*)

O ne'er such a race was, as there in that place was
And there ne'er such a chase was at a', man;
From ilk other they run, all without tuck o' drum—
Deil a body made use of a paw, man;
And we ran, and they ran,
And they ran, and we ran,
But wha was't run fastest of a', man?

Whether they ran, or we ran, or we wan, or they wan,
Or if there was winning at a' man,
There's no man can tell, save our brave general,
Wha first began running of a', man;
And we ran, &c.

North. When I am a king, which, after all, is a sort of a thing, (to speak with civility,) that in these days of pudding and praise, nobody will call a mere impossibility—Well, when I am a King, like his Majesty Gregor, lesser or bigger, the very first thing that I will do, will be to send home a ship, inviting you, I mean James Hogg, you comical dog, to make a trip, and you also, Sir Ensign, you rip—all the way out to my realms, you shall sip, you two schlems, grog and flip; and whenever you arrive, as sure as I'm alive, I'll come down to the shore, with my princes and peers, and the cannon shall roar, and we'll give you three cheers. But as for you, Morgan, ere you're well in the bay, you will hear the church organ sounding away, and we'll lead you at once, all rigged out for the nonce, to the highest altar, to be noosed in Hymen's halter; for so great is my regard, my richest prettiest little ward, whether Duchess or Caziquess, you need look for nothing less, as sure as my name's King Christopher, it is you shall have the fist of her. But for you, Jamie Hogg, don't think to come *incog*—you shall have a butt of sherry, to make your heart merry—a grand golden chain, to wear over your maud—and the Lords of my train shall shout and applaud, crying Christopher *floreat, et* sus *suus Laureate!*—With Odoherty for my field-marshal, and Tickler for my premier, I think, but I may be partial, things will go on airer and jemmier—and Blackwood will come out to be my bookseller, no doubt; he shall have the completest of monopolies in my metropolis, for we'll suffer nobody to squint at any thing that's in print, unless it drop from his transatlantic shop; and the Magazine will in lieu of a Queen amuse the leisure hours of me and my powers; and with all these alliances, aids and appliances, I don't think I need speak either modester or meeker, why, if Macgregor 's Cazique, I shall rank as Caziquer.

Hogg. Will you be a despot, though?

North. Let me see—no—no—no—too much trouble—but no sedition within the bounds of *my* bubble. Instant perdition shall fall on Joseph Hume, if he dares to come out Disaffection to illume, to move for any papers, or stir up any rows about tithe-pigs or sealing-wax or my magazinish spouse, whom, though she be spotless as unsunned snow, I would have you, and all the Bubblish Nation to know, I will discard whenever I please, sirs, cutting your heads off if you sneeze, sirs.

Odoherty. I envy not your pomp, I envy Hogg! (*Sings.*)

How happy a state will two poets possess,
When Hogg has his wreath, I my rich Caziquess;
On the wife and the Muse we'll depend for support,
And cringe, without shame, at great Christopher's court.
What though Hogg in a maud and gray breeches does go,
He will soon be bepowdered and strut like a beau;
On a laureate like him, 'twon't be going too far,
To bestow, mighty monarch, St. Christopher's Star.

North. On the wings of imagination, I now overfly time and space; behold me exercising the kingly vocation among the mighty Bubblish race—in my mind's eye, here am I, this is my court, and you the potent nobles that resort to do me *honneur* and *hommage* in the hopes of *fricassee* and *frommage*, wherein if I disappoint you *grande dommage*:—Great Shepherd, kneel—thy shoulder-blade shall feel, ere long, the weight of my cold steel, in reward for thy song!

Odoherty. Come, Hogg,—mind your eye, tip us something *à là* Pye.*

North. I forgot to observe, that from customary modesty not to swerve, and preferring to imitate your old Bourbon or Guelf, to any Macgregor or Iturbide that may be laid ere a week's over on the shelf, I shall christen the chief of knightly orders established within my borders, by the name of a worthy that is now dead, whose good looking old-fashioned head has served me in good stead, being always displayed on my Magazines' backs, to the horror of all Whiggish clamjamphrey, Jeremybenthamites, and Cockney hacks.

(*Odoherty whispers for some time to Hogg, and then rising, picks out a volume of the Right Hon. the Lord Byron.*)

Tickler. What's all this mummery? Let your proceedings be more summary—I'm tired of such flummery.

* Henry James Pye was the Poet Laureate, who immediately preceded Southey, and was born in 1745, appointed Laureate in 1790, made London police Magistrate in 1792, and died in 1813. He wrote a great many bad verses:—the best known being an epic, called "Alfred."—M.

Odoherty (*reads.*)

ON THE STAR OF "THE LEGION OF HONOR."

(*From the French.*)

Star of the brave!—whose beam hath shed
Such glory o'er the quick and dead—
Thou radiant and adored deceit,
Which millions rush'd in arms to greet!
Wild meteor of immortal birth,
Why rise in Heaven to set on earth!

Souls of slain heroes form'd thy rays;
Eternity flashed through thy blaze!
The music of thy martial sphere
Was fame on high and honor here;
And thy light broke on human eyes,
Like a volcano of the skies.

Like lava roll'd thy stream of flood,
And swept down empires with its blood;
Earth rocked beneath thee to her base,
As thou didst lighten through all space;
And the shorn sun grew dim in air,
And set while thou wert dwelling there.

Before thee rose, and with thee grew,
A Rainbow of the loveliest hue,
Of three bright colors,‡ each divine,
And fit for that celestial sign;
For Freedom's hand had blended them
Like tints in an immortal gem.

One tint was of the sunbeam's dyes,
One, the blue depth of Seraph's eyes,
One, the pure Spirit's veil of white
Had robed in radiance of its light;
The three so mingled, did beseem
The texture of a heavenly dream.

Star of the brave! thy ray is pale,
And darkness must again prevail!
But oh! thou Rainbow of the free!
Our tears and blood must flow for thee.

Hogg (*extemporizes.*)

ON THE HEAD OF GEORGE BUCHANAN.

(*From the Chaldee.*)

HEAD OF THE SAGE! whose mug has shed
Such jollity o'er quick and dead—
O'er that bright tome presiding high,
Which MILLIONS rush each month to buy,
That meteor of immortal birth!
Read rather more than "Heaven and Earth."*

Limbs of torn authors form its rays;
Eternity attends its praise;
The music of its partial puff
Gives fame and honor *quantum suff.*
And its fist darkens hostile eyes,
Like Randal† hammering for a prize.

Like lava, it in wrathful mood
Swept down Hunt's kingdoms with its flood!
Leigh bow'd before it, looking base,
And wiped the spittle from his face;
And Hazlitt's nose burnt dim for care,
Spite of the purple dwelling there.

Behind thee rose, behind thee grew
A Rainbow of the loveliest hue.
Of three bright fellows, each divine,
And fit at Ambrose's to dine:
For HUMBUG's hand had blended them
Much like three posies on a stem.

One loves to sport the rose of red,§
One, the rough thistle's burly head,
One—he of Ireland's modest mien—
Is deck'd out with the shamrock green;
The three so mingled, do beseem
The texture of a heavenly dream.

Head of the Sage! thy own old bones‖
Lie snug beneath Greyfriars stones.
But, oh! thou Rainbow of the three!
North—Tickler—and Odoherty!

* A poem by the Right Hon. the Lord Byron.—C. N.

† Randal, a prize-fighter.—M.

‡ The tri-color.—C. N.

§ It is not, perhaps, generally known, that Tickler's family was originally English. It is supposed that they lived at the Southside in the days of Edward I., who was himself a Tickler.—C. N.

‖ To the disgrace of the city of Edinburgh, and indeed of all Scotland, no stone marks where the mortal remains of her greatest scholar—the wit, the poet, the historian; the son, of whom she, perhaps, has most reason to be proud, are deposited. Should not this be corrected? It certainly should.—C. N. [It has not yet been corrected.—M.]

When thy bright promise fades away, Our life is but a load of clay.	Were thy bright look to fade away, Our life were but a load of hay.
And Freedom hallows with her tread The silent cities of the dead; For beautiful in death are they Who proudly fall in her array— And soon, oh, Goddess! may we be For evermore with them or thee!	Scorn hallows with a hearty kick, The dumb posteriors of Sir Dick;* And beautiful, but dead, we deem Tom Campbell's mess of curds and cream; And soon, O, Taylor! will it be A match in Balaam ev'n for THEE!

(Hogg kneels, a solemn air is heard from Odoherty's trombone, Tickler, with dignity, hands the poker to Mr. North; while it is descending slowly towards the Shepherd's shoulder, the curtain is dropt down very gradually upon the dramatis personæ, who form a perfect picture.)

* Sir Richard Phillips, editor of the *Monthly Magazine*.—M.

No. VIII.—MAY, 1823.

Present—Ettrick Shepherd, Chairman; Kempferhausen, Croupier; Tickler, Odoherty, Dr. Mullion, &c.

SCENE—*The Chaldee Chamber—Table as it should be.*

Time—*Ten P. M.*

Kempferhausen. Ah, mein Gott! what for a barbarian! And you came to town on purpose?

Hogg. Deed did I, lad. And what for no? I aye come in when there's ony thing o' the kind gaun forrit.

Kempferhausen. O shocking! you really horrify me! You like to see such things? You really find a pleasure in them?

Hogg. Pleasure here, pleasure there, I cannot bide away from a hangin'—I tell you plainly that I think it's worth a' the Tragedy Plays that ever were acted—I like to be garred to grue.

Odoherty. And of course a female exit is the more piquant—how did the old lady go off then?

Hogg. Were *you* no there, Ensign? Odd, I thought I heard your cough in the cro'wd. You *were* there, you deceiver—you were—you were not the length of a cart-tram ahint mysel.

Kempferhausen. O, Mr. Odoherty, you too!

Tickler. Pooh, pooh! Odoherty went to get materials for an article—he has promised Ebony a series of Horæ Patibulanæ, and they will be taking papers I believe, after all.

Hogg. I think I could contribute to that series mysel. Odd! I've seen a matter of fifty hangings in my time.

Odoherty. Fifty! why, Hogg, you're old enough to be my grandfather—and yet I've seen *three* times that number myself—besides plenty of shootings, and all manner of outlandish doings—guillotine—sword—axe——

Hogg. I wad gang a lang gait to see a beheading. A beheading for my siller—it's clear afore ony other way.

Odoherty. Genteeler, I confess—but otherwise so so; and as for the matter of cleanliness, your cord is certainly the very jewel of them all for that. Why, Hogg, I've seen half the breadth of a street smeared over with one fellow's claret; and then the assistants trundling in a wheelbarrow of saw-dust, and all that sort of thing—is disgusting, and apt to spoil one's breakfast.

Hogg. Weel, I never saw onybody gang aff easier than Lucky M'Kinnon—I keepit my ee upon her, and she never made ae single steer either wi' foot or hand. She was very easy, poor woman.

Dr. Mullion. Just a stroke of apoplexy—nothing more.

Odoherty. You are right, I believe, and that after all is the best way it can operate.

Dr. Mullion. In former times, when the poor devil had to leap from a ladder, he might go up two or three steps higher and make such a spring that he was sure of breaking his spine; but now-a-days the fall is so short and so perpendicular, that they all die of apoplexy or strangulation—which last is bad.

Odoherty. What did your friend Brodie die of,* Mr. Tickler?

Tickler. Apoplexy, I suppose. His face was as black as my hat.

Hogg. Lucky M'Kinnon's bonny face was black too, they were saying.

Dr. Mullion. Yes, "black, but comely." I saw her a day or two afterwards—very like the print.

Tickler. Those infernal idiots, the Phrenologists, have been kicking up a dust about her skull, too, it appears. Will those fellows take no hint?

Odoherty. *They* take a hint! Why, you might as well preach to the Jumpers, or the Harmonists, or any other set of stupid fanatics. Don't let me hear them mentioned again.

Dr. Mullion. They have survived the turnip. What more can be said?

Hogg. The turnip, Doctor?

Dr. Mullion. You haven't heard of it then? I thought all the world had. You must know, however, that a certain ingenious person of this town lately met with a turnip of more than common foziness in his field—he made a cast of it, clapped it to the cast of somebody's face, and sent the composition to the Phrenological, with his compliments, as a *fac-simile* of the head of a celebrated *Swede*, by name Professor Tornhippson. They bit—a committee was appointed—a report was drawn up—and the whole character of the professor was soon made out as completely *secundem artem*, as Haggart's had been under the same happy auspices a little before. In a word, they found out that the illustrious Dr. Tornhippson had been distinguished for his Inhabitiveness, Constructiveness, Philoprogenitiveness, &c.—nay, even for "Tune," "Ideality," and "Veneration."

* Brodie, who was a Deacon, invented the *drop*, (for execution,) and was the first who perished by it. So with the Earl of Morton, who constructed the instrument of decapitation called The Maiden. Dr. Guillotin, who improved on this, did not fall a victim of his ingenuity, as has been reported, but survived until 1814.—M.

Odoherty. I fear they have heard of the hoax, and cancelled that sheet of their Transactions. What a pity!

Hogg. Hoh! hoh! hoh! The organization of a fozy turnip! Hoh! hoh! hoh! hoh! the like o' that! The Swedish turnip—the celebrated Swede!

Odoherty. Le Glorieux himself never carried through a better quizz. The whole thing is perfect—*Fuit Ilium!*—The worst of the whole was, that a couple of the leading members had been disputing rather keenly, which of their own two organizations bore the greater resemblance to that of the enlightened defunct.

Tickler. Name, name.

Hogg. Wha *were* the twa saps? Name them, name them.

Odoherty. No, I shall spare their names; for I hear your New Novel is to be a deuced personal thing, and you would perhaps introduce them.

Hogg. Here's my hand.

Odoherty. Tush, tush. I'll tell you no more, but that the one of them belongs to the Stot's establishment, and the other jobs occasionally in the balaam line for the Crany Review.* Really, they're not worth your libelling them, kind Shepherd.

Hogg. We'll see—we'll see.

Tickler. And is it really to be a personal work, Hogg?

Hogg. It sets you weel, hinney—but ha' done, ha' done. Ye'll a' read and judge for yourselves in the course of a week or twa; for, now that Quentin Durward's out o' his hands, Ballantyne will surely skelp on wi' me. His presses have been a' sae thrang this while, that I havena gotten aboon half the third volume set up. But I'll spur up the lad, noo. De'il mean him, I think he's no blate to keep me taiglin for ony Quentin Durward that ever came out o' Glenhoulakin.

Tickler. Come now, Hogg, confess that Quentin Durward is a fine, a noble, a glorious thing.

Hogg. Wait a wee.

Odoherty. As your work is still *in secretis*, of course we can't institute any comparisons—but I, for one, shall say honestly, that I look upon Quentin Durward as the very best thing that has come out since Old Mortality.

Hogg. Ay, man——? and div ye really think sae in earnest? Weel, I cannot but confess it, I'm muckle of the same opinion mysell, between friends. It's clean afore Peveril—ay, and Needgill too—clean afore them.

Tickler. It has all the novelty of another Ivanhoe—and yet all the ease and lightness of another Guy Mannering—and by the way, Hogg, the author seems to be as fond of hanging-matches as yourself—what

* The *Scotsman* newspaper and the *Phrenological Review*.—M.

capital characters those two ladder boys are—and then their never stirring without rope and pulley, any more than a parson without a corkscrew!

Hogg. Gleg chields, faith. Ad! my flesh creepit whenever they cam on the boards—I just thought I saw the rape dangling in the wind before my very een. Yon tinkler Moograbbin—what a devil of a spurling yon daur-the-mischief would mak! I think I see him flung aff.

Odoherty. Your imagination is lively, good Shepherd. Have you introduced any similar scenes in your work?

Hogg. Ha! lad—wait a wee, again—pumping, pumping!

Odoherty. You seem to think every body is on the *qui vive* for your bundle of balaam.

Hogg. Balaam? Gude have mercy on us! he's ca'in't balaam or e'er its out!

Mullion. Well, that's not so bad after all, as calling it balaam after it *is* out; which, however, I am sure nobody will do; at least, nobody but the Standard-bearer.

Hogg. And *his* tongue's nae scandal, Doctor—Od! every thing's balaam wi' him, amaist. He ca'd the Brownie of Bodsbeck balaam, and yet it gaed through three editions.

Odoherty. Three editions? Are you serious?

Hogg. Dead serious—Od! does a new title not make a new edition?—If ye deny that, I'll hae ye afore The Three, and see how you'll like shoolin out your gowd, but to be sure your brass is mair plenty, my man.

Odoherty. Mr. Hogg, you and the Author of Waverley are beginning to give yourselves a confounded deal of airs upon your cash. I don't see what he had to do with blowing such a trumpet about his beeves, and muttons, and so forth, in that introduction of his. As for his sneers about garreteers, and chops, and Grub Street, I hope the gentlemen of the press will take the illiberality as it deserves. Upon honor, I don't think it was worthy of the Great Unknown to take such a fling at the innocent misfortunes of a set of gentlemen, who have all of them done their best to please the public—which is more than I opine any body will venture to say for him.

Hogg. Come, come, Captain Odoherty, what's your drift?—Do you mean to say that I am a gentleman of the press, sir?

Odoherty. Much may be said on both sides—but, however, you have beeves and muttons enough, I suppose, as well as Peveril; and you don't live in Grub Street.

Hogg. I live in as decent a place as yoursell, Captain. I put up at Mackay's* noo, when I'm in town'—tis a very comfortable house, and I can gang into the traveller's room, and get pleasant company when-

* Mackay's Hotel, Prince's Street, Edinburgh.—M.

ever my fingers are dinnled wi' driving the pen. And I'm a' in the heart o' business too—Mr. Constable's grand new shop's just fornent my window—Mr. Blackwood's no a hap-stap-and-lowp amaist farrer west—and Ballantyne's deevils, they can come jinking back and forrit in no time by the playhouse stairs—and Ambrose's here, I can skelp ower, if it were a perfect steep, without weeting my shoon.

Odoherty. Your top-boots you mean—but I beg your pardon, you are as sore about the boots as old Philip of Argenton himself. I beg your pardon, good Monsieur Bête-bottée.

Hogg. You needna be moushying me. I ken naething ava about your parleyvouzing system—that's my apothegm.

Odoherty. Hogg, I think I have heard you say, that you sometimes find things take in the ratio of their unintelligibility.

Hogg. What's that now ?——

Odoherty. I mean to say, that you think people are at times best pleased with what they can't make neither head nor tail of.

Hogg. 'Tis as true a word as ever came out of a fause loon's cheese-trap. I aye thocht weel of the non-comprehensible system—and there's a lang-nebbit word for you too, my braw Captain.

Odoherty. Well then, just to please Hogg, Gentlemen of the Press, I shall tip the company a French chanson—new—original—unpublished—fresh from the pen of my good friend Béranger—the very last thing Béranger has done.

Tickler. Ha! I've seen very little of his works,—they say he's the Tommy Moore of France.*

Odoherty. Why, he wants Tommy's delicacy and bright fancy; but then he perhaps has more spirit with him than Tommy. He has written some abominable things in the licentious way; but so, to be sure, has Tom Moore.

Tickler. Ah! but has he repented, or at least refrained, like your amiable countryman ?

Odoherty. I don't wish to chatter about humbugs just now. I shall give you the chanson I spoke of, and you will see, that it at least is as pure as if Hogg himself had indited the goodly matter.

Tickler. The Edinburgh Reviewers, I think, say, that Béranger is "the Poet of the People." Is he so very popular then ?

Odoherty. Popular he is; but not with *the People*, nor is he the least in their line. So far from that indeed, that he is far too deep in

* Béranger, the greatest song-writer France ever had, was born in 1780. The brilliant successes of France, under young Bonaparte, excited him into composition, and no man did more for the nationality of Frenchmen. He did not flatter Napoleon even in the fulness of his power. When the Bourbons returned—forgetting nothing and having learned nothing—he sang the strains of Freedom. For this he was prosecuted, fined, and confined. Under Louis Philippe he did not fare much better. The Revolution of 1848 brought the old poet into public life, and he was elected a member of the National Assembly—but Age and the Song had stronger claims than Politics, and he gladly returned to private life. He lives at Passy, near Paris, in honorable and happy retirement.—M.

his allusions for the worshipful Reviewers themselves, seeing that they quoted as a specimen of a "Poet of the People," a verse with a most *indecent* allusion, touching the Jesuits—the which, it is right manifest, neither the critic himself, nor the editor, could have understood.

Hogg. You may be sure, the lads just acted upon my principle.

Odoherty. Well, I wish they would act upon *your principle* only concerning our own books, and not make us a laughing-stock among the outlandish—but now for the chanson. (*Sings.*)

L'OMBRE D'ANACREON.

Air: de la Sentinelle.

Un jeune Grec s'écrit à des tombeaux:
Victoire! il dit; l'écho redit: Victoire!
O demi-dieux, vous nos premiers flambeaux,
Trompez le Styx et voyez notre gloire.
Soudain sous un ciel enchanté
Une ombre apparait et s'écrie:
Doux enfant de liberté, (*bis.*)
Le plaisir veut une patrie,
Une patrie.

O peuple Grec, c'est moi dont les destins
Furent si doux chez tes ayeux si braves;
Quand il chantait l'amour dans les festins,
Anacreon en chassait les esclaves.
Jamais la tendre volupté
N'approcha d'une âme flétrie.
Doux enfant de la liberté, (*bis.*)
Le plaisir veut une patrie,
Une patrie.

De l'aigle encore l'aile rase les cieux,
Du rossignol les chants sont toujours tendres;
Toi, peuple Grec, tes arts, tes lois, tes dieux,
Qu'en as tu fait, qu'as-tu fait de nos cendres?
Tes fêtes passent sans gaieté,
Sur une rive encore fleurie.
Doux enfant de la libertè, (*bis.*)
Le plaisir veut une patrie,
Une patrie.

Déjà vainqueur, chante et vole au danger,
Brise tes fers, tu le peux si tu l'oses:
Sur nos débris, quoi! le vil étranger
Dort enivré du parfum de tes roses!
Quoi! payer avee la beauté
Un tribut à la barbarie!
Doux enfant de la liberté, (*bis.*)
Le plaisir veut une patrie,
Une patrie.

C'est trop rougir aux yeux du voyageur,
Qui d'Olympie évoque la memoire.
Frappe, et ces bords, au gré d'un ciel vengeur,
Reverdiront d'abondance et de gloire.
Des tyrans le sang detesté
Réchauffe une terre appauvrie ;
Doux enfant de la liberté, (*bis.*)
Le plaisir veut une patrie,
Une patrie.

A tes voisins n'emprunte que du fer,
Tout peuple esclave est allié perfide.
Mars va t'armer des feux de Jupiter,
Cher à Venus son étoile te guide.
Bacchus, dieu toujours, indompté,
Remplira la coupe tarie.
Doux enfant de la liberté, (*bis.*)
Le plaisir veut une patrie,
Une patrie.

Il se rendort, le sage de Theos . . . . . .
La Grèce enfin suspend ses funerailles,
Thébes, Corinthe, Athène, Sparte, Argos,
Ivres d'espoir, exhumez vos murailles ;
Vos vierges même ont répété
Ces mots d'une voix attendrie,
Doux enfant de la liberté, (*bis.*)
Le plaisir veut une patrie,
Une patrie.

Hogg. A bonny tune, and, I daursay, a bonny sang too. What was't a' aboot, sirs ?

Tickler. Love and country, and so forth. The shade of——

Hogg. I daursay it's just plunder't out o' my *Perils.** Does it mention ony thing aboot a bonny lassie, and the flowers and the gloaming ?

Tickler. These are all alluded to, Mr. Hogg.

Hogg. And the birds singing ?

Tickler. Yes, that too, I think.

Odoherty (*singing*).

"Du Rossignol les chants sont toujours tendres,
Toi, peuple Grec !——"

Hogg. Na, na—time about's fair play, Captain. Ye've gien us the copy—I think I may be allood to gie you the original ; for I'm sure the French thief has just been takin' every idea I had frae me—I mean——

* Hogg's "Three Perils of Man."—M.

Odoherty. Ha! a new light!—Béranger, too, robbing Hogg!—But begin, begin, dear James.

Hogg. Ae mair round of the bottles ere I begin—(*Drinks a bumper of toddy*).—Ay, now—my whistle will do now.—(*Sings.*)

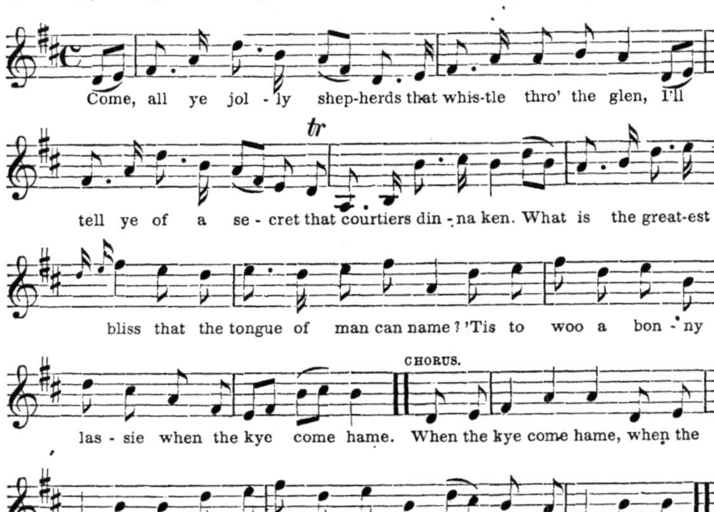

'Tis not beneath the burgonet, nor yet beneath the crown,
'Tis not on couch of velvet, nor yet in bed of down—
'Tis beneath the spreading birch, in the dell without the name,
Wi' a bonny, bonny lassie, when the kye come hame.

(*Chorus, lads.*)

When the kye come hame, when the kye come hame,
'Tween the gloaming an' the mirk, when the kye come hame.

There the blackbird bigs his nest for the mate he lo'es to see,
And up upon the topmost bough, oh, a happy bird is he!

* The song, by Hogg, was very popular, not only in Ettrick Forest, but in all the rural districts of Scotland. The *refrain* originally was, "When the kye comes hame," but some of the Shepherd's critical friends pointed out to him that, as the nominative and the verb should agree, the singular *comes* was not in accordance with the plural *kye*. Hogg accordingly removed the superfluous and peccant *s*. When next the song was printed it had the correction, and the words were, "When the kye come hame,"—but his rural admirers refused to adopt the alteration, which they said was "dreadfu' affeckit," and, to this hour, the words are sung as originally written. Hogg used to relate this anecdote with great glee, in justification of his unmitigated and undisguised contempt of verbal criticism.—M.

There he pours his melting ditty, and love 'tis a' the theme,
And he'll woo his bonny lassie when the kye come hame.
When the kye come hame, &c.

When the bluart bears a pearl, and the daisy turns a pea,
And the bonny lucken gowan has fouldit up his ee,
Then the lavrock frae the bluelift drops down, and thinks nae shame
To woo his bonny lassie when the kye come hame.
When the kye come hame, &c.

Then the eye shines sae bright, the hail soul to beguile,
There's love in every whisper, and joy in every smile:
O wha wad choose a crown, wi' a' its perils and its fame,
And miss a bonny lassie when the kye come hame?
When the kye come hame, &c.

See yonder pawky shepherd that lingers on the hill,
His ewes are in the fauld, and his lambs are lying still;
Yet he downa gang to bed, for his heart is in a flame,
To meet his bonny lassie when the kye come hame.
When the kye come hame, &c.

Away wi' fame and fortune, what comfort can they gie?
And a' the arts that prey on man's life and liberty:
Gie me the highest joy that the heart of man can frame,
My bonny, bonny lassie, when the kye come hame.
When the kye come hame, &c. (*Much applause.*)

Odoherty. Upon my honor, 'tis admirable. Why, when did you make this, Hogg? You have done nothing so sweet these three years.

Hogg. An' ye never saw nor heard it afore?

Odoherty. Not I—how should I?

Hogg. Ye invincible ne'er-do-weel! and yet you reviewed my Three Perils o' Man for two reviews, and three newspapers forbye.

Odoherty. Well, and what is that to the purpose?

Hogg. Not much, I confess—only the next time ye're for reviewing an author, ye might maybe come as braw speed if ye began wi' reading his book.—Tak' ye that hint, my noble Captain?

Odoherty (*a little confused*). Why, is it possible? I really can scarce swallow you, Hogg.—Is *that* song in "The Three Perils of Man?"—You are thinking of "The Three Perils of Woman," an't ye?

Hogg. Fient a bit o' me. In the book of "The Three Perils of Man"—the third volume thereof, and the 19th page, you will find it written as I have sung unto you.

Odoherty (*aside to Tickler*). I never saw the book—hang it!

Tickler (*tipping the Adjutant the wink*). Come, Hogg, don't be too severe upon Odoherty. The song is a good deal altered since then, and much for the better. As it stands in the novel, if I recollect right, it begins with some trash about "Tarry woo'," and "whistling at the plow." The Standard-bearer might easily think the song a new one.

Hogg. I'se no deny that—for to tell you the plain fact, Christopher, I had clean forgotten't mysel'. When the book was sent out a' printed to Yarrowside, od! I just read the maist feck on't as if I had never seen't afore; and as for that sang in particular, I'll gang before the Baillies the morn, and tak' my affidavy that I had no more mind o' *when* I wrote it, or *how* I wrote it, or ony thing whatever concerning it —no more than if it had been a screed o' heathen Greek. I behoved to have written't sometime, and someway, since it was there—but that's a' I kent. I maun surely hae flung't aff some night when I was a thought dazed, and just sent it in to the printer without looking at it in the morning. I declare I just had to learn the words or I could sing the sang, as if they had been Soothey's, Tam Muir's, or some other body's, and no my ain.

Odoherty. Coleridge over again, for all the world, and the Black-stone of Blarney—"a psychological curiosity," Hogg! Take one hint, however, and henceforth always write your songs when you are *dazed*, as you call it—*Hibernice*, when you are in a state of civilation.*

Hogg (testily). Thank ye, Captain. I need scarcely be after bidding you *read* the songs I write, when you find yourself in that same honorable and praiseworthy condition.

Odoherty (rings). Hallo—Champagne there! Cool this fellow with something that has been in the ice-pail. This eternal hot toddy is setting his bristles on edge. (*Enter Ambrose.*) Champagne there, Ambrose!

Kempferhausen. Champagner! champagner for Hogg. Ha! that's your sort! what for a cork!

Hogg. Eh! siccan a clunk as that chiel's loupit awa wi'! There—haud yer hand, Mr. Ambrose—eh! siccan a ream! (*Drinks.*)

Odoherty (drinking). I pledge you, my Chaldean Shepherd. Well, the wine is prime. Ferguson for ever, say I!

Hogg. Oh dear! I never faund ony thing sae gude since ever I was born—heh, there's anither glassfu' there yet, Mr. Ambrose. This way, bring't this way, man! Oh, dear! what a wagang! What may it come to the dozen now, Mr. Ambrose? (*Ambrose whispers the Shepherd.*)—Losh keep us a'!—Losh keep us a'!—heh me!

Kempferhausen. O, what for a groaning and sighing!—what is the wish to you, Herr Hogg?

Hogg. Just that a body could get that same at three bawbees the bottle.

Tickler. I suppose you would never think of small beer with your porridge again?

* *Anglice*—Half-seas over.—M.

Hogg. Na, faith I—nor tryacle neither—no, nor porter and sugar, which is better than tryacle ony day in the year.

Odoherty. This fellow Champagne!—Come now, Hogg, tell me honestly what is your idea of a really luxurious dinner? Describe—describe.

Hogg. Come ye out our way i' the har'st, and I'll spare myself the fash of descriptions, Captain. Let's see—let's see—what suppose I set you down to a gaucy tureenfu' o' hotch-potch, or hare-soup—remove that wi' a sawmon, just out o' Yarrow—a whacken fellow wi' his tail in his mouth—his flesh perfect curds—and then a thumpin' leg of blackface,* maybe with gravy-juice enough in him to drown a peck o' mealy potatoes—or what wad ye say to a tup's head and trotters?—That's the way we live in Yarrow.—Match us in Cork or Kilkenny, if ye can.

Odoherty (*solemnly*).

> "And is this Yarrow? this the stream
> Of which my fancy cherished
> So beautiful a waking dream,
> A vision which hath perished."

Hogg. What says the lad?

Odoherty. Well, then, I say with Mr. Wordsworth—

> "Whate'er betide, we'll turn aside,
> And see the braes of Yarrow."

Hogg. That's a man.—I thought I could busk a fly that would please your e'e, you saucy ane—but come, come, wha's ready wi' a stave?—Mr. Kemperhausen, the call is for you.

Kempferhausen (*sings*).

> Der wind geht durch die Baüme;
> Aus grunen Schatten schwebt
> Die milde schaar der traüme
> Aus Luft und Lust gewebt.
> "Was bringt ihr aus der ferne
> Und locket mich zur Ruh?
> Sprücht ihr von Leibgen, gerne
> Drückt ich die Augen zu!"

Hogg. Awfu' toothbreakers! wheesht, wheesht.

Kempferhausen. Well, very well, mein Herr Hogg. Ich sange nichts mehr—Potztausend!

Odoherty. D—— German!—Dr. Mullion, what are you ruminating?—And you, Tickler, what book is that you are fumbling with?

* The Black-faced sheep are found to thrive so extremely well on the Scottish hills, that the breed has become very general.—M.

Tickler. Only the last Edinburgh. I was thinking we should come the cat-o'-nine-tails across some of these scamps.

Odoherty. With pleasure, Mr. Tickler—hand me the pamphlet if you are agreeable. Ay, here it is! what a deuced piece of humbug is this opening article.

Tickler. Of course it is—but why are *you* so particularly moved, Adjutant?

Odoherty. Hibernicus sum; nihil Hibernici a me alienum puto.

Tickler. O, you expected something about your dear countrymen, and the Marquis of Wellesley—did you?

Odoherty. Your ears for a moment, Mr. Croupier—and you, good Gentlemen of the Press, your ears.

Hogg. The Captain's going to make a speech—fill a' your glasses.

Tickler. Hush!—hush!—out with it, then, Odoherty.

Odoherty. We are told that there are tricks in all trades, so well understood by the public, as to take off all moral imputation of falsehood. We are told, for instance, that it is intolerable to accuse of low mendacity a man of letters, even though no tradesman, for palming off, as a second edition, the heavy remainder of a first impression garnished by an additional half sheet of superfluous stuff. Be it so; but of all the tricks of trade with which I happen to be acquainted, the trickery of the announcement of this leading article of No. 75 of the Edinburgh Review, is the most barefaced. For weeks before its appearance, the newspapers were filled with interesting paragraphs, headed with "We are able to announce the contents of the forthcoming Number," &c.—Such, gentlemen, such are the Day-and-Martin manœuvres to which this once famed Journal is reduced; and, in due course of time, this demi-official information was ratified by the more regular announcement by advertisement, penned, of course, by the same hand that gave the important intelligence in the former shape. In all these, this first article was placarded as "Art. I.—Reflections on the State of Ireland in the Nineteenth Century."

Tickler. I remember well, that all this was as you have been saying. Such were the advertisements.

Odoherty. And what title could just now be more taking? I speak for myself.—Vast visions of bottles and rattles floated before my mental optics*—my mind yearned to hear the Whig Oracle's opinion of *ex-officio* informations, after the Grand Inquest of the country had

* The Marquis Wellesley, elder brother of "the Duke," was sent to Ireland, in 1821, as Viceroy. It was known that he had a strong desire to see the Roman Catholics relieved, by the removal of certain disabilities of which they long and loudly had complained. This political leaning made Lord Wellesley unpopular with the Orangemen, and the Dublin Corporation, then exclusively composed of ultra-Protestants. At the theatre, one night, some ruffians of this party threw a bottle at him, from the gallery, and very nearly struck him. Arrests were made, and bills of indictment preferred; the Grand Jury issued the bills. Mr. Plunket, then Attorney General, presided *ex-officio*, but the Government, alarmed at the prospect of defeat, never brought the accused to trial, and thus gave a triumph to the Orangemen.—M.

ignored the bills—I longed to hear how the staunch advocates of the Revolution of 1688 would treat the memory of William III.—I expected savory remarks on the Beef-steaks—and, in general, looked for somewhat ingenious and piquant on Forbes, Standwich, Graham, Daniel O'Connell, Mr. Plunket, Major-General Sir John Rock, K.C.B. —*cum multis aliis.*

Tickler. So did the public.

Odoherty. And what did the purchaser, who sported his six shillings, or, to speak Hibernically, his six and sixpence,* on the strength of being "pleased with a rattle, tickled with a bottle," as Pope remarks, get for his money?

Hogg. I wonder what it could be?

Odoherty. You need not waste your time in guessing, for you would not hit it in a thousand years. In fact, nothing more or less than the "History and Settlement of Tithes in Scotland!" which is the running title at the head of the pages in the Review; but which, if announced beforehand, would have most effectually damaged the sale.

Hogg. I'm no that sure—I wad like to see the article for ane.

Odoherty. You would like—pooh! pooh! Who, beyond the parties concerned—the poorly paid minister, the financial elder, the griping heritor, and the blethering advocate—cares the end of a fig about the history or the details of such an affair? The Kirk of Scotland is a most excellent church beyond doubt, but it is also beyond doubt, that all this prate about rescissory statutes, teind records, Lords of Erections, laicke patrons, &c. &c., is altogether balaam, of most unquestioned description. To be sure, the scribe endeavors to connect the lumber, by a kind of *apropos des bottes*, with the fraudulent title advertised in the newspapers, by means of a head and tail-piece; which have, however, all the appearance of coming from another hand. It appears, by his account, that the people who have a design upon the revenues of the English and Irish churches, wish for as much information as possible, on the most approved practical method of doing the business. "Their expectation," quoth the Balaamite, "is reasonable, and we hope the information may not be altogether without advantage!!!" Was there ever a more stupid piece of *make-believe* attempted to be played off? These worthy characters care little about the arrangements of the kirk, having a very pretty sweeping plan of their own already. Andrew Fairservice remarked long ago, that the Kirk of Scotland would not be the worse for it, if the dwellings of its clergy were made something more nearly equal to the dog-kennels of the fox-hunting squires of England. But the present radical church-

* Until the year 1825, every English shilling, of *twelve* pence sterling, passed for *thirteen* pence in Ireland. The gain was exactly forty cents, or one shilling and eight pence sterling, upon each pound. An act was passed to assimilate the currency, and the British coinage, then first introduced at no more than its real value, was familiarly spoken of as "Breeches Money."—M.

reformers would take care to leave the parson no dwelling at all, which is a simplification of the system. In truth, as has been long ago observed by a better authority than mine, there are so many points of dissimilitude between the circumstances of the two countries, that analogies drawn between their Church establishments stand on very insecure ground.

Tickler. The *true* history of the article is this—Jeffrey had picked up a dull paper on Scotch tithes from some hum-drum contributor——

Odoherty. Whom he should immediately present a *5l.* note, a good character for sobriety, and his discharge.

Tickler. ——And Jeffrey thought he could make the young idiot go down by giving his effusion a catching name. That's all, Odoherty.

Odoherty. Even so, Timotheus—nor is the trick a new one. We are often baulked the same way in the newspapers, where you are seduced into reading a paragraph by the attractive heading of "A Great Personage not long ago remarked," or "It is strange that when Mr. Canning so pointedly told Mr. Brougham that his assertion was FALSE," or "SIR JAMES MACKINTOSH and MR. GERALD," &c., and find, after all, that its scope and tendency is to recommend Prince's Russian Oil, or Tom Bish's tickets and shares.

Tickler. What think you of the article on the two poems about the angels?

Odoherty. This I beg leave to skip altogether. Jeffrey has certain reasons to be civil to both Moore and Byron; and here we have a little small criticism, puffing their last poems. It is the production of a fourth-rater. I have read critiques as deep in Ackerman's Repository.*

Tickler. You won't say that of Brougham's article on Grattan?

Odoherty. No, no—the article is full of talent—of such talent as Mr. Brougham possesses—and, to say truth, I loved old Grattan, and I like very well to see him puffed, even by such a man as Brougham; for Brougham, though a Whig, is not a goose.

Tickler. How shabby is the notice of Croly!

Odoherty. Right shabby certainly, and right shallow at the same time, as I shall show you. Brougham, if you observe, sets out with abusing my good friend young Grattan for publishing panegyrics on his father, written by men of various abilities, but particularly for giving to the world that by "*a certain Rev. Mr. Croly, whoever he be.*" This little impertinence is in the same taste as the "Ricardus quidam Bentleius" of Alsop, a forgotten prig; but in his day, just as conceited as the pertest reviewer in the pack. It is with no pride I say it, but it is undeniable that such will be the fate of the reviewing tribe in

* A magazine exclusively devoted to fashions and mantua-makers' literature.—M.

general; and in particular, when it will be altogether forgotten that such an article as this review of Grattan's speeches had ever existence, the genius and talents of this "certain Rev. Mr. Croly, whoever he be," will have secured him an honorable place among the great names of English literature.* But, look ye, the mock ignorance of the reviewer is rendered quite comical by the naiveté of the avowal in the next page. He was induced, he says, to cut up Mr. Croly, not because he is an obscure and unknown scribbler, but because "*there has been shown such a disposition to* PUFF *him in certain quarters.*" As it so happens that these "certain quarters" have ten times more circulation, and twenty times more weight among the literary world than the vehicle which contains the opinions of this sage critic, there is something irresistibly droll in his pretending not to know who the object of their panegyric, or puff—no matter about a word—can possibly be. As to his abuse of Croly's splendid character of Grattan, as it merely consists in tearing a brilliant sentence or two from their context, and, after garbling them, then venting some little absurdities at their expense—there is no more to be said on the occasion.

Hogg. Croly need never fash his thumb about what the like o' them says. Will ony of them ever write a "Paris in 1815," or a "Catiline?"

Odoherty. Some of them might be more likely to *act* a Paris in 1792, or to *act* a Catiline.† But to proceed—"Even-handed justice returns the poisoned chalice to our own lips." According to Brougham, one of the chief excellencies of Grattan is, his tremendous power of invective. He is not less enraptured with the unsparing use he made of this foul-mouthed faculty. Now I shall confess, that I, for one, rank fish-wife oratory somewhat low, but yet I do not object to other people's criticising according to their propensities. He quotes with delight Mr. Grattan's celebrated reply to Mr. Corry in 1800, and in truth, it must be allowed to be most classical and well-turned Billingsgate. Corry, on the authority of a sworn evidence, before the Irish House of Lords, had stigmatized Grattan as being in some degree connected with the bloody rebellion of 1798, to which Grattan replied in a torrent of abuse, in which this sentence occurs:

"HE HAS CHARGED ME WITH BEING CONNECTED WITH THE REBELS—THE CHARGE IS UTTERLY, TOTALLY, AND MEANLY FALSE."

For saying this Mr. Grattan is praised by Mr. Brougham—I suppose so—but at least by one of Mr. Brougham's coadjutors in preaching Whiggery through this Review. Well, the book was scarcely in

* The Tories allowed Croly to continue a Curate, though his pen was ever employed to assert and defend their principles and conduct. It was Brougham, when Lord Chancellor, with Church-patronage in his hands, who—looking on Croly as a man of genius, and laying aside party considerations—gave him the Rectory of St. Stephen's, Walbrook, London.—M.

† Croly's tragedy of Catiline, chiefly based on one of Sallust's brilliant fragments of Roman history, is one of the noblest specimens of the unacted drama ever produced in England.—M.

London, before Mr. Brougham made an attack on Mr. Canning, for *truckling*, as he elegantly termed it, to the Lord Chancellor, from so mean a motive as desire of place; to which Mr. Canning, in reply, did not foam or rant like Grattan, but simply and quietly uttered the following brief sentence:

"I SAY THAT THAT IS FALSE!"*

For my part, looking at the mere taste of the thing, I cannot help saying, that I think Canning's reply far superior. It goes straight forward to the point at once, and as a contradiction was all that either had to give, so every word that did not convey one was waste.

Tickler. I can't help thinking that both retorts were highly unparliamentary—shockingly so—quite wrong. But perhaps the reporters are alone to blame.

Odoherty. It may be so—it may be that this last affair is newspaper fudge. But grant Grattan and Canning to have, both of them, really made these retorts—and grant both of them to have been highly unparliamentary retorts, still there is this marked and characteristic difference between the cases. No tumult was made about the circumstance in the Irish Parliament; the speech is reported in a regular edition of the orator's works; the Whig reviewer extols the eloquence of the retort coolly three-and-twenty years after it was given. There is, in short, no Tory angry, and no Whig undelighted. In the other case, there is a row, the Whigs are indignant, their newspapers uproarious, and nothing can be more horrible in their eyes than Mr. Canning's indecorum, quite forgetting the panegyric pronounced on Grattan, for doing precisely the same thing, by their principal organ.

Tickler. You may just reverse your second last sentence—there is no Whig void of wrath, and no Tory—we mean of that base set among us, who are our greatest disgrace, the Pluckless—not in mourning.

Hogg. Hoch! hoch! hoch! heegh! heegh! hoch! hoch! hoch!

Odoherty. One word more—I, of course, know nothing of the facts of the case, nor pretend to pronounce an opinion which party was right. I am merely criticising the oratorical power displayed by Grattan and Canning. I know not whether Corry or Brougham was justifiable in the charge originally made.

Tickler. Perhaps the whole is an invention of the Gentlemen of the Press.

* In 1822, Canning—who was on the eve of going into splendid exile, as Viceroy of India—was appointed Foreign Secretary, on the suicide of Lord Londonderry. The Whig party were annoyed at his joining Lord Liverpool's ultra-Tory administration, and, in the course of the following Session, (in 1823,) Brougham stigmatized him as having exhibited the most incredible specimen of monstrous trickery, for the purpose of obtaining office, that the whole history of political tergiversation could afford. Canning turned white as a sheet, (as a looker-on informed me,) and, pointing his finger at Brougham, exclaimed, "I rise to say that that is false!" Eventually, it appeared that the retort and rejoinder had been made only in a Pickwickian sense.—M.

Odoherty. Hogg, have you had any thing to do with this?

Hogg. I'll tell you what it is, Hogg kens naething about the Edinburgh Review, nor Mr. Brougham neither—I have not seen a paper this month—and as for the Review, that Number's the first I've seen of the blue and yellow these twa years, I believe.

Odoherty. No great loss. But choose your subject, Chairman; what have you seen of late?

Hogg. There's for ae thing The Sextuple Alliance. Deevil o' siccan poem ever I saw; but the dedication is capital.

Odoherty. What is it?

Hogg. See there, man.

TO
A MAN OF LETTERS,
A MERCHANT, POLITICIAN, AND ECONOMIST;
A GENTLEMAN
WHO MIGHT BE NAMED TO FOREIGNERS, AS A MODEL OF AN ENLIGHTENED
AND LIBERAL
BRITISH TRADER;
A JUST AND ZEALOUS MAGISTRATE,
AN ESTIMABLE PRIVATE CITIZEN,
AN ABLE WRITER,
AND ORIGINAL THINKER;
TO THE ROSCOE AND RICARDO OF GLASGOW,
JAMES EWING, Esq.,
THESE VERSES ARE RESPECTFULLY DEDICATED,
BY
THEIR AUTHORS.

Odoherty. Very elegant, and most appropriate. Have you any thing else new?

Hogg. Let me think—ay, there's for ae thing, Miss Joanna Baillie's Collection of Poems.

Tickler. Ha! I had not heard of her being in the press. Tragic, I hope.

Kempferhausen. You will find the book on the side-table, I believe, Tickler. Yes—that's it—that octavo in greenish—you will see that 'tis only edited by Miss Baillie, although there are several pieces of hers included.

Hogg. And some very bonny pieces amang them—rax me the volume, Mr. Tickler.

Tickler. With your leave, Mr. Hogg—just let me look over the index—ha! "Macduff's Cross, a drama, by Sir Walter Scott." What's this, Hogg?

Hogg. Oo, just a bit hasty sketch—but some grand bits in't, man.*

* Early in 1823, Joanna Baillie published a collection of Poetical Miscellanies, in which appeared a dramatic sketch by Sir W. Scott, entitled "Macduff's Cross"—so called from an erection (of which the bottom-stone or socket alone remains now) on which was recorded the bounty of King Malcolm Conmore to the unborn Thane of Fife.—M.

Od! ony body else could have keepit the story for a three volume job at the least. Rax me the book—thank ye, Tickler—now, listen to this, —the twa priests are watching at the sanctuary of the Macduff's Cross, when twa horsemen are seen advancing—listen.

> "See how they strain adown the opposing hill!
> Yon gray steed bounding on the headlong path
> As on the level meadow—and the black,
> Urged by the rider with his naked sword,
> Stoops on his prey, as I have seen the falcon
> Dashing upon the heron.—Thou dost frown,
> And clench thy hand as if it grasped a weapon.
> * * * * *
> 'Tis but for shame to see one man fly thus,
> While only one pursues him! Coward! turn."

Odoherty. Well spouted, Shepherd—and admirable lines indeed—but I'll read it for myself; what more is there?

Hogg. Whoay, there's almost every name that's a name ava here, an be not mine ain and Byron's. There's Wordsworth—twa sair teugh sonnets o' his—and Soothey, Lord keep us a'! they're the maist daft-like havers I ever met wi', the lines of his about a Linn.

Odoherty. Pass the Laureate—does Coleridge figure?

Hogg. No—no wi' his name at ony rate, (I had clean forgotten Coleridge.)—But there's Crabbe and Milman, and Mrs. Grant, and General Dirom, and Miss Holford, and John Richardson.

Tickler. Ah! "Otho?"

Hogg. And ane Sir George Beaumont, that Wordsworth dedicates ane of his poems to—the White Doe if I mind right—and Rogers, and Hook.

Odoherty. What!—Theodore? Let's hear his chant.*

Hogg. This Hook's a minister—the Reverend——

Odoherty. Ah! then pass him over, for I'm sure Theodore is not in orders.

Hogg. And Bowles, and Lady Dacre, and Miss Anna Maria Porter, and Mrs. Barbauld, and Mr. Merivale.†

Tickler. Let's hear Merivale's contribution.

Hogg. It's ane o' the very best in the book—'tis really a most elegant poem, but rather ower lang may be for receetin just now. Take this

* It was Theodore Hook's cousin, and the author of the lively romances or novels (for they are of a mixed character) called "Pen Owen," and "Percy Mallory."—M.

† To this volume, Miss Catharine Fanshawe (described by Lockhart as "a woman of rare wit and genius, in whose society Scott greatly delighted") contributed some *jeux d'esprit*, and William Howison's ballad of Polydore, which introduced him to Scott, when a mere lad, was also among the contents. The John Richardson, in the above list of writers, was Scott's most intimate friend and a London lawyer, "with a pretty taste for poetry." Miss Holford also wrote verses. General Dirom had a call in the same line. Lady Dacre (whose play of "Ina," performed when she was Mrs. Wilmot, was a failure) afterwards won reputation not only as a translator of Petrarch and a novelist, but as an amateur sculptor. She died in May, 1854. The others are too well known to need more particular attention.—M.

for a specimen, now. You are to know that the poem's all about the scenery on a water called the Axe, somewhere in England. Are not these equal to Smollett's Leven Water itself?

"Hail, modest streamlet, on whose bank
No willows grow, nor osiers dank;
Whose waters form no stagnant pool,
But ever sparkling, pure and cool,
Their snaky channel keep between
Soft swelling hills of tender green,
That freshens still as they descend,
In gradual slope of graceful bend,
And in the living emerald end.
On whose soft turf, supinely laid,
Beneath the spreading beechen shade,
I trace, in Fancy's waking dream,
The current of thine infant stream."

And wi' that he's awa wi't at ance—celebrating a' the auld monasteries and castles. Od! it maun be a bonny classical water. I could just have thought I was reading about Yarrow, and Newark, and Bowhill, and a' the lave o't.

Odoherty. They seem to be graceful verses—I, however, should rather have likened them to the flow of Dyer, or Milton's Penseroso, than to Smollett's charming ode.

Hogg. Na, I'm nae critic. I only *feel* that Merivale has the soul of a poet, and that his verse is delicious music to my ear.* I meant nae close comparisons.

Odoherty. You read so nobly when the passage suits your taste, that you would make any thing appear beautiful.

Hogg. Nane o' your quizzes, Captain,—but I'll tell ye what, I'm no gaun to read ony mair o't; but if ye like, I'se try to sing you a famous good song that's in this book—a real good song of Mr. Marriott's—and though it's about a Devonshire lane, it would just do as weel for an Ettrick Forest "Green Loaning."

Omnes. Do—do—sing away.

Hogg (*sings to the tune of Derry down*).

THE DEVONSHIRE LANE.

In a Devonshire lane, as I trotted along,
T'other day, much in want of a subject for song;
Thinks I to myself, I have hit on a strain,—
Sure marriage is much like a Devonshire lane.

In the first place, 'tis long, and when once you are in it,
It holds you as fast as the cage holds a linnet;

* Merivale subsequently translated Schiller and Dante, with marked success.—M.

For howe'er rough and dirty the road may be found,
Drive forward you must, since there's no turning round.

But though 'tis so long, it is not very wide,
For two are the most that together can ride;
And even there 'tis a chance but they get in a pother,
And jostle and cross, and run foul of each other.

Oft Poverty greets them with mendicant looks,
And Care pushes by them o'erladen with crooks,
And Strife's grating wheels try between them to pass,
Or Stubbornness blocks up the way on her ass.

Then the banks are so high, both to left hand and right,
That they shut up the beauties around from the sight;
And hence you'll allow, 'tis an inference plain,
That Marriage is just like a Devonshire lane.

But thinks I too, these banks within which we are pent,
With bud, blossom, and berry, are richly besprent;
And the conjugal fence which forbids us to roam,
Looks lovely, when deck'd with the comforts of home.

In the rock's gloomy crevice the bright holly grows,
The ivy waves fresh o'er the withering rose,
And the ever-green love of a virtuous wife
Smooths the roughness of care—cheers the winter of life.

Then long be the journey, and narrow the way;
I'll rejoice that I've seldom a turnpike to pay;
And whate'er others think, be the last to complain,
Though Marriage is just like a Devonshire lane.

Odoherty. Upon my word, Devonshire is up just now.—Is there much humor in the collection?

Hogg. Some capital jeesting bits—particularly some riddles and the like. What think you of this on a PILLION?

A RIDDLE.

Inscribed on many a learned page,
In mystic characters and sage,
  Long time my *first* has stood:
And though its golden age be past,
In wooden wall it yet may last
  Till clothed with flesh and blood.

My *second* is a glorious prize
For all who love their wandering eyes
  With curious sights to pamper;
But 'tis a sight, which should they meet
All improviso in the street,
  Ye gods! how they would scamper!

My *tout's* a sort of wandering throne,
To woman limited alone,
 The Salique law reversing;
But while th' imaginary queen
Prepares to act this novel scene,
 Her royal part rehearsing,
O'erturning her presumptuous plan,
Up climbs the old usurper—man,
And she jogs after as she can.

Odoherty. "PILLION!" Well, that's truly excellent.—Well, we're all much obliged to Mrs. Baillie. Toss back old Kit's octavo, dear. I shall buy one of them for myself, to-morrow.

Hogg. There, it's just lighted on the bunker!

Odoherty. Not among the Liberals, I hope.—Ah! 'tis safe. Have you seen the last Pisan,* Hogg?

Hogg. Peezan!—Pushion, say rather—it's a' dirt now. Lord Byron, I aye said, wadna put up wi' sic company lang—and ye laughed at me; but you see I'm right after a'.

Odoherty. Me laugh at you? I only wonder what the deuce it can have been, that made him countenance them even for the little time he did. His articles were libellous sometimes, (these fellows, by the way, can no more libel than a tailor can ride,) but they had no connection with, or resemblance to the sort of trash the Cockneys stuffed them in the heart of——The last number contains *not one line* of Byron's.—Thank God! he has seen his error, and kicked them out.

Hogg. I canna gie him up. I canna thole't. I aye think he'll turn ower a new leaf, and be himself ere lang.

Odoherty. Quod felix faustumque!—But as to these drivellers, they are all in their old mire again.—Just Rimini Hunt, and three or four more——

Hogg. "Lewd fellows of the baser sort,"—to use scriptural language, touching a most unscriptural crew.

Tickler. And whether you take "lewd" in the old or the new sense, you could not have hit on a fitter epithet for the authors of some of these disgusting farragos. The fellow that reviews Apuleius would look at home upon the treadmill. Filthy, dirty creature! Latin, forsooth!—and what think ye of King Leigh comparing Pope's face to a FAWN'S?

Hogg. Which rhymes of course to THORNS or SCORNS.

Tickler. Of course.—Have you seen the LIBER AMORIS?

Odoherty. Not I,—what is it?—a Cockneyism?

* "The Liberal," a quarterly magazine and review, published at Pisa, and edited by Lord Byron and Leigh Hunt, with assistance from Hazlitt. In the earlier numbers, several of Shelley's poems had appeared. His death, in July, 1822, sealed the fate of this periodical, which had very few redeeming features.—M.

Tickler. Ay, and a most profligate Cockneyism too.* But wait a little, wait a little. I can a tale unfold. You shall hear the whole story in due time,—"the whole truth, and nothing but the truth;" and well know I at least ONE COCKNEY that would shake in his shoes if he heard what I am saying.

Hogg. Ye gar me shake mysel' when ye speak with that groaning key, and lay out your leg that way. O, Mr. Tickler, ye're an awfu' auld carle when your birr's up. Sic an ee too! ye put me in mind, no offence, sir, of Galt's Archbishop.†

Tickler. Hah! hah! the Archbishop of St. Andrews? Old Hamilton?

Hogg. Ay, just him. I have Ringan in my maud here.‡ I coft him for our bit Yarrow Subscription Leebrary.

Odoherty. Read the description of Timotheus.

Hogg (*reading from Ringan Gilhaize*). "He used to depict him as a hale black-a-vised carl, of an o'ersea look, with a long dark beard inclining to gray: his abundant hair flowing down from his cowl, was also clouded and streaked with the kithings of the cranreuch of age—there was, however," (here's for you, Timothy!)—"there was, however, a youthy and luscious twinkling in his eyes, that showed how little the passage of three and sixty winters had cooled the rampant"——

Tickler. Stop, you old Boar.

Hogg. A devilish weel-sketched portrait in its style—very picturesque, 'faith—and I dare say, very like.

Tickler. Why, I profess to be tolerably read in the history of that period, and much as I detest the Covenanters, I must allow that Galt has authority for every fact he introduces.

Hogg. There wad nane o' you believe me, when I said I had authority for the misusage of that priest o' mine, in the Brownie.§

Tickler. It did not signify, whether you had or not—but here the case is altered, quoth Plowden. This book is really something of a history.

Odoherty. Faith, I read it as a novel, and, though not quite so laughable as the Entail, I thought it a devilish good novel.

Tickler. And so it is—but mark my words, the Book will live when most Novels we see just now are forgotten, *as a history.*‖ 'Tis really a very skilful, natural, easy, and amusing History of the Establish-

* "Liber Amoris, or the New Pygmalion," a strange production of William Hazlitt's, written with great earnestness—as if, in truth, the man must pour out his confessions or have his heart burst—but open to ridicule and hostile criticism, for many causes.—M.

† One of the characters in "Ringan Gilhaize, or, The Covenanters," by John Galt, which was

‡ *Maud.*—A Scottish peasant's plaid.—M.

published in May, 1823.—M.

§ "The Brownie of Bodsbeck," one of Hogg's first prose stories.—M.

‖ On the contrary, like the rest of Galt's historical novels, "Ringan Gilhaize" was never of much mark or note, and was soon forgotten.—M.

ment of the Reformed and Presbyterian Religion in this kingdom—very great art in the management, I assure you.

Hogg. Oh, it's a braw book—it's a real book—I aye liked Galt, and I like him better than ever now. He has completely entered into the spirit of the Covenanters—far better than The Unknown—clean aboon him, head and showthers. The real truth of the character——

Odoherty. Who the devil cares about the Covenanters? Confound the old bigoted idiot, say I! Have you seen Murray* in Claverhouse?

Tickler. I have, and he plays it and looks it nobly. The drama is one of the best from those novels. Mackay's Cuddie Headrigg, Mrs. Nichol's Mause, and Mason's old Milnwood, are particularly excellent.

Hogg. What for have they no had the sense to keep the one table with the saltfoot, as in the novel? They've clean missed a fine point by that silly alteration.

Tickler. They have. Tell them of it, and they'll mend it.

Hogg. I had a letter from an Ettrick lad that's settled in America, the other day, and he says they've made a play there out of my THREE PERILS already, and it takes prodigiously. They've mair sense owerby there than here at hame, in some particulars. They turn a' my novels into plays. Od! I cannot but say it makes me prood to think that I'm acting just now, at this very moment, in New York, maybe, and Boston, and half a dozen mair of their towns intill the bargain; and then, how they translate me in Germany; but Kempferhausen can tell you better aboot those things.

Kempferhausen. Pooh! they translate every thing in Germany; you need not take that as any very great compliment. And in France too, faith I believe they translate any thing in Paris that's written in England.

Hogg. I wad like to see mysell moushified. If ye have the French Brownie of Bodsbeek, let me hae a lend o't;—od! I would not wonder if it garred me tak to learning their lingo.

Odoherty. And then, perhaps, we shall have you writing a book in French yourself, like a second Sir William Jones, or Mr. Beckford. By the way, was there ever such a failure as this new imitation of Beckford's Vathek, ADA REIS?

Tickler. I could not get through with it for one; wild and dull together won't do. Lady Caroline† is a very clever person certainly, but she should really take a little time and thought. Graham Hamil-

* W. H. Murray, manager of the Edinburgh Theatre, of which his sister, Mrs. Henry Siddons, was lessee. He was an excellent actor.—Charles Mackay, whose Baillie Nicol Jarvie, in "Rob Roy," was never equalled, was one of the main supports of this theatre.—M.

† Lady Caroline Lamb (whose husband became Lord Melbourne, after her death in 1828, at the age of forty-two) possessed some literary talents, and made herself not a little notorious by the zeal with which, as a canvasser among the electors, she assisted her brother-in-law (the Hon. George Lamb) when he was a candidate for the representation of Westminster. Her wild passion for Lord Byron was fatal to her domestic felicity, ruined her character, and alienated her friends. She wrote three novels,—"Glenarvon," (of which she is supposed to have made Byron the hero,) "Graham Hamilton," and "Ada Reis."—M.

ton was bad, and this is worse. I wonder Murray took the trouble to publish it.

Odoherty. Nevertheless, Tickler, there are some fine passages, some noble things, after all. But to imitate VATHEK and to fail were very nearly the same thing. Vathek, sir, is one of the most original works that our age has seen.* It will live when Fonthill is in ruins—*ære perennius.*

Hogg. I wish you would tell me your notion of some more of the *new* books, sirs; for I've gotten some of the Ettrick lads' siller yet, and I'm resolved to carry them out every thing that I can coff. Blackwood says, "The Monks of Leadenhall" is a good novel.

Tickler. It is very fair; the author has spirit and imagination, and knowledge too,—he will be a rising man yet, you will see—if he takes a little more time and consideration. By all means, export The Monks of Leadenhall to St Mary's. 'Tis a very promising work.

Hogg. Thank ye,—I'll e'en buy't then,—and "The Pioneers," that's a book of Murray's—I suppose it will be worth its price, since it comes out of his shop,—for John's no that keen o' novels now-a-days.

Tickler. Why, the author has very considerable talents—but "The Spy" was far better. This is rather a heavy book;—but, however, it will go down on Yarrow and elsewhere;—any thing is valuable in so far that paints new manners—and, American manners are a rich mine—and this writer bids fair to dig to purpose in it.†

Kempferhausen. Washington Irving is, I hear, busy with German manners now. He has taken up his residence there,—and is determined to give us a German Sketchbook in the first place‡—(what a present this will be!)—and then a series of works, all founded on German stories, and illustrative of the characters and customs of German life.

Odoherty. Come, this is good news, Kempferhausen—I am truly happy to hear Geoffrey Crayon has got hold of so fine a field. In the meantime, do you stick to your tackle, and devil-a-fear but there's enough for you both.

Hogg. I've bought D'Israeli's book, and Butler's Reminiscences.§

Tickler. Right in both. Butler is a delightful writer—so calm, so

* William Beckford's singular tale of "Vathek," was originally written by him in French. It is so splendid in description, so true in eastern costume, and so wild and vivid in imagination, that Lord Byron considered it difficult to believe that it was written by an European, and said, "Even Rasselas must bow before it; the Happy Valley will not bear a comparison with the Hall of Eblis."—Fonthill Abbey, which was sold in 1822, has long been shorn of its architectural beauties, and the last I heard of it was that it had been converted into a factory!—M.

† Fenimore Cooper's sea and Indian novels obtained very large prices in England, where (to secure the copyright) most of them were first published.—M.

‡ Washington Irving (says "*The Men of the Time*") passed the winter of 1822 in Dresden, returned to Paris in 1823, and moved to London in May, 1824, to publish his Tales of a Traveller, which appeared in August of that year.—M.

§ Isaac D'Israeli, best known by his "Curiosities of Literature," was father of the brilliant English statesman and writer, and died in 1848, at the age of eighty-one.—Charles Butler, a well known Roman Catholic lawyer, published his agreeable and instructive "Reminiscences" in 1823. He also was eighty-one when he died, in 1832.—M.

sensible, so judicious, so thoroughly the scholar and gentleman. I love Butler, and wish his Reminiscences had been five times as large. I read the book through at a sitting—and delightful reading it was.

Odoherty. There's another new book has just come out, something between D'Israeli's manner and Butler's; but I don't know whether it will be in Hogg's way—the "Heraldic Anomalies."

Tickler. O, a very clever book—I mean to give North a review of it one of these days, and then Hogg will judge for himself. It is really quite full of information and amusement too.*

Odoherty. Who wrote it?

Tickler. God knows! some old pawky Barrister—some venerable quizzer among the benchers, I should guess. There's a vast bunch of good legal jokes; and a sort of learning that nobody but a lawyer could have acquired. He is a good-natured, polite and genuinely aristocratic writer—I wish we had more such. Mayn't it be Butler himself?

Kempferhausen. I should have thought it possible, but he quotes and praises Butler's books, and of course Butler is above all that sort of trick. Somebody mentioned Dr. Nares.†

Tickler. Ah! a good guess too. Why, the man that can write both that Glossary of the Old English Tongue, and that admirable novel of "Thinks I to Myself," may do any thing he pleases. The Archdeacon is a first-rate man, or at least might be so if he chose to give himself the trouble.

Odoherty. Well, I hope we shall have more both of him and of Butler. I shall be happy to see the review, Timothy; but you know you promised to do Allan's picture, and yet where is it? The article, I mean.

Tickler. Upon my soul, I had quite forgot. I hope the picture is sold ere now.

Odoherty. I see it is considerably lauded in the Literary Gazette and elsewhere. Raeburn and he always keep up our art at the exhibition.

Tickler. And Wilkie—but I shall say nothing of him, for I observe Hazlitt abuses us for being so proud of him.

Odoherty. I think he might take to abuse of you for being so proud of Allan too—really Allan rises every day.‡

Tickler. Yes, sir—that figure of John Knox is the finest effect his

* By Miss Hawkins, I believe. She was daughter of Sir John Hawkins, the friend and executor of Dr. Samuel Johnson, of whom he wrote a biography, severely handled by the critics—but with peculiar acerbity by "Peter Pindar."—M.

† Dr. Robert Nares, whose novel "Thinks I to Myself" was very popular, about half a century ago, was co-editor for many years (with Mr. Beloe) of the British Critic, a high-church literary review. He wrote several recondite philological works, and when he died in 1829, held four or five rich preferments in the Church.—M.

‡ It is scarcely necessary to go into details respecting painters so well known as Raeburn, Wilkie, and Allan.—The first, who was the best portrait-painter of his time in Scotland, died

pencil has made. Heavens! to think of these rich people buying Tenierses and Gerard Dows at such prices, when they could get something so infinitely better—with all *their* merit, and something fifty times beyond them into the bargain—for, comparatively speaking, a mere trifle.

Odoherty. Come, I don't know what you mean by *trifles*—and as for Allan, he can't complain, for devil a piece of his own handiwork has he upon his hands.

Tickler. That's right—so much genius united with so much industry always must command success. I am glad to hear he gets on so well, however.

Odoherty. You'll see him in his chariot ere he is three years older.

Hogg. Set him up wi' chariots! Deil mean him! I think if yon auld clattering rickerty of a gig does for a poet like me, a shelty may serve ony brushman amang them. Chariots!

Odoherty. Pooh! I mean to sport a coach and six myself one of these days. What do you think I have been offered for my new work?

Tickler. "THE WEST COUNTRY, A NOVEL?"

Odoherty. The same.* Guess, Timothy.

Hogg. Five hundred?

Tickler. A cool thousand?

Odoherty. Fifteen hundred guineas, by the holy poker! What think ye of that, Jamie Hogg?

Hogg. Fifteen hundred guineas! hoh, sirs! What will this warld come to! Thae booksellers are turned princes. It will be an awfu' book for selling though, Captain. It is all about Glasgow.

Odoherty. Glasgow, Paisley, and Greenock—these clasical haunts are all included under this most rural title. It is to be my *chef d'œuvre.* I intend to take Galt and annihilate him—I mean *his* "West Country," the old "West Country," the "Entail."

Hogg. Do that, and you'll do something.

Tickler. Depict a living idiot equal to Wattie,† and *eris mihi Magnus Apollo!*

Odoherty. No want of idiots; but, as Hogg says, "wait a wee." Have any of you seen the concluding cantos of Don Juan?

Tickler. Oh! we have all seen them. North has had a copy of them these six weeks. I wonder if they're ever to get a publisher.‡

in 1823,—in subjects of domestic life, none surpassed the second, whose death took place in Gibraltar Bay, in 1841,—the last, who had mastered the difficulties and reproduced the spirit of Eastern life, died in 1850. All three were successively presidents of the Royal Scottish Academy, and had been knighted.—M.

* Which never was written.

† The half-witted hero of "The Entail."—M.

‡ Cantos I. and II. of Don Juan were published in July, 1819, without the name of author or publisher. Cantos III., IV. and V. appeared together, in August, 1821, still without the name of either author or bookseller. Cantos VI., VII., and VIII., written at Pisa, in July, 1822, were published in London in July, 1823.—M.

Hogg. They're extraordinary clever—they're better even than the twa first; but that mischievous Constitutional Association will not let ony body daur to print them.* And, after all, it's maybe as weel sae, for they're gey wicked, I must alloo; and yet, it's amaist a pity

Odoherty. I have a great mind to turn bookseller myself, just on purpose to put an end to all this nonsense. A pretty story, truly that two cantos of Byron's best poetry should be going a begging for a midwife! Horrible barbarism!

Tickler. Just retribution——! How are the mighty fallen! "Crede Byron! !"‡

Odoherty. Crede humbug! (*Left speaking.*)

* A Society which was organized in London, to prevent and punish the publication of immoral and seditious works. It raised large funds by subscription, but did little more than spend them, chiefly in heavy salaries and good dinners.—M.

† "Crede Byron,"—the heraldic motto of the house of Byron.—M.

No. IX.—JUNE, 1823.

Odoherty. Make your mind easy, my old poet, about it. They stand no more in need of your assistance, than a seventy-four wants to be towed through the Bay of Biscay by a six-oared yawl.

North. There would be no harm, however, in saying, that Quentin Durward is a splendid book?

Odoherty. And as little good. Why need you hold your farthing candle to the sun? Hang it, man, never deal in axioms. I was truly sorry to see you in your last Number so anxious to show up the Vicomte Soligny as an ass, when every body saw his measureless ears, pricked up in proud defiance, affronting the daylight.*

Buller. We punsters of Rhedycina are indignant with the Great Magician for missing a capital pun, and making a poor one. You remember what Louis says to Tristan L'Hermite when he is confined, and wishes to have the astrologer hanged—that pun about *finis.*

Tickler. Yes; here's the passage. "Tristan, thou hast done many an act of brave justice—*finis*—I should have said *funus* coronat opus."

Buller. Read it, meo periculo, *funis* coronat opus. "We must crown the business by a rope." Isn't it more professional?

North. Decidedly, a much better pun. Is it yours?

Mullion. Has Durward been dramatized yet?

North. I don't know; but I suppose it has. Terry would have but little labor on his hands, for many of the scenes are dramatic enough for the stage even as they are.†

Mullion. The defiance of Crevecœur, for instance. There need not be a word added or diminished there.

Tickler. That certainly is a magnificent scene—a model for all defiances.

Odoherty. Could not we get up a thing of the kind here, in our own way?

North. How! What the deuce have we to do with such things?

Odoherty. Why, then, I'll tell you, my ancient biscuit-biter. As soon as Constable's new shop is finally settled—painters, glaziers, ma-

* A review, in the May number of *Blackwood*, of "Letters on England, by Victoire, Count de Soligny," published by Colburn, of London, and affiliated, by Maga, upon little Tims, the Cockney, who was one of the guests in the Tent, in August, 1819, as heretofore related.—M.

† Quentin Durward, published in June, 1823, was the first of Scott's fictions which obtained reputation on the Continent. Terry, who adapted several of the novels for the stage, did not take this in hand, but it *was* dramatized, and made a splendid spectacle.—M.

sons, tilers, slaters, carpenters, joiners, upholsterers, paperers, and all that fry, bowled out clean, there is to be a high dinner given to all the men of blue and yellow. Jeffrey *in persona* in the chair.

North. Well, what then?

Mullion. I suppose that when the Reviewers are mustered, Odoherty wishes them to be peppered.

North. Knit him up to the stanchions for that pun. It is beyond question the worst I have heard since the days of Harry Erskine. *Perge, Signifer.*

Odoherty. Would not it be a good thing for you to defy him then and there, when surrounded by the host of the ungodly?

Tickler. Who would be the ambassador?

Odoherty. My own mother's son; and you should be herald, being a man of inches. I should not dress exactly à la Crevecœur; but hand me the first volume of Quentin, and I shall follow it as close as possible.

North. Here, most worthy legate.

Odoherty (*reading Quentin Durward*, vol. i. p. 205, *with a slight deviation from the words of the text*). Would not this read grandly in future ages, "Ensign and Adjutant Morgan Odoherty, a renowned and undaunted warrior——"

Mullion (*aside*). Over a tumbler of punch.

Odoherty. "Entered the apartment, dressed in a military frock-coat, thickly frogged, black stock, Cossack trowsers, Wellington boots, and steel spurs. Around his neck, and over his close-buttoned coat, hung a broad black ribbon, at the end of which dangled a quizzing-glass. A handsome page——"

Hogg. Wha the deil will he be?

Odoherty. Don't interrupt me. "A handsome page, James Hogg, Esq., Shepherd of Ettrick——"

Hogg. Hear till him! Me a page to a stickit Ensign?*

Odoherty. "Bore his hat behind him. A herald preceded him, bearing his card, which he held under the nose of Francis; while the ambassador himself paused in the middle of the hall, as if to give present time——"

Tickler. What, by the way, did the Great Unknown mean by such a phrase as "*present time?*"

Mullion. Perhaps, because the business was no *past time.*

North (*springs up in a rage*). By Jupiter Ammon, Mullion, another such pun, and I will fine you a bumper of magnesia water!

Odoherty. "As if to give present time to admire his lofty look, commanding stature, and the modest assurance which marked the country of his birth."

* When a licentiate of the Scottish church, whose devotion or ambition has led him into the pulpit, happens to fail as a preacher, he is usually spoken of as "a stickit Dominie." In like manner, no doubt, Hogg thus alluded to Odoherty as a mere carpet-knight.—M.

Omnes. Hear, hear, hear!

Odoherty. Well, I'll skip on to the defiance at once. Turn to page 213. (*A rustling of leaves is heard.*) "Hearken, Francis Jeffrey, King of Blue and Yellow—Hearken, scribes, and balaamites, who may be present—Hearken, all shy and shabby men—and thou, Timothy Tickler, make proclamation after me—I, Morgan Odoherty, of the barony of Iffa and Offa west, and the parish of Knockmandowny, late Ensign and Adjutant of the 99th, or his Majesty's Tipperary regiment of infantry, and Fellow of the Royal, Phrenological, Antiquarian, Auxiliary Bible, and Celtic Societies of Edinburgh; in the name of the most puissant chief, Christopher, by the grace of Brass, Editor of Blackwood's and the Methodist Magazines; Duke of Humbug, of Quiz, Puffery, Cutup, and Slashandhackaway; Prince Paramount of the Gentlemen of the Press, Lord of the Magaziners, and Regent of the Reviewers; Mallet of Whiggery, and Castigator of Cockaigne; Count Palatin of the Periodicals; Marquis of the Holy Poker; Baron of Balaam and Blarney, and Knight of the most stinging Order of the Nettle, do give you, King of Blue and Yellow, openly to know, that you having refused to remedy the various griefs, wrongs, and offences, done and wrought by you, or by and through your aid, suggestion, and instigation, against the said Chief, and his loving subjects, the authors in particular, and the Tory people in general, of this realm, he, by my mouth, renounces all belief in your assery, pronounces you absurd and trashy, and bets you sixpence, that he beats you as a critic and as a man. There, my tester is posted in evidence of what I have said."

Omnes (*with enthusiasm*). Hear him! hear him! hear him!

Odoherty. Let me go on, for I think the remainder would be applicable. "So saying, he plucked the sixpence from the bottom of his breeches pocket, and flung it down on the floor of the hall.

"Until this last climax of the bet, there had been a deep silence in the Whig apartment during this extraordinary scene; but no sooner had the jingle of the tester, when cast down, been echoed by the deep voice of Timotheus, the Blackwoodian herald, with the ejaculation 'Vive Tête de Buchanan!' than there was a general tumult; while Brougham, Sydney Smith, Leslie, and one or two others, whose coats, whole at the elbows, authorized the suspicion that they could sport the coin, fumbled in their pockets for wherewithal to cover the sixpence; the Seven Young Men exclaimed, 'No bet with you, Butcher! Bubble, bubble! Comes he here to insult the King of the Libellers in his own hall?'

"But the King appeased the tumult, by exclaiming, in a voice agreeably composed of the music of an English coachee grafted upon a genuine Embro' brogue, 'Silence, my lieges! Cover not the bet, for you would lose your blunt; Christopher is too rum a customer for me.'"

Hogg. Od, man, that's the verra way Advocate Jeffrey speaks.

Tickler. It would be a fine subject for a picture. I shall suggest it to Allan, when I see him next.

Mullion. It could be called the "Defiance of Doherty."

Odoherty. I trouble you for the vowel, my friend—Odoherty, if you please—I have no notion of any body's being alliterative at my expense.

Tickler. Yes, it would be a grand historical painting. The stuck-pig stare of the great man himself—the scowling fury of Brougham—the puckered-up nose of the Mercurial Parson—the jobbernowl gape of "our fat friend"*—the sentimental visage of the "Modern Pygmalion"—the epileptical frenzy of the half-human countenance of the ——, and the helpless innocence of the Seven Young Men, would be truly awful and sublime, while the magnificence of the Odoherty——

Odoherty. The stateliness of the Tickler——

Tickler. And the beauty of the Hogg, would afford a fine foreground.

Buller. Allan should lose no time. If he does not do it at once, as I am off for London to-morrow, I shall speak to that other great master of the sublime, George Cruikshank.

North. There is another defiance in the third volume, where De la Marck sends Maugrabbin to the Duke of Burgundy.

Mullion. If you copy that defiance, send Hogg as ambassador, for he has the best title to be Rouge Sanglier.

Hogg. I wish, doctor, ye would let Hogg alane. What for are ye aye harling me intill your havers, by the lug and the horn?—I dinna like it.

Odoherty. What! surly?

Hogg. It's no decent to be aye meddling wi' folks' personalities. I'm sure by this time the whole set o' you might ha' mair sense. Ye ken what ye hae gotten by your personalities.

North. A decreet o' Court, Jamie, as Leddy Grippy† would have said.

Tickler. Softly on that score.

North. What do you mean?

Tickler. Have you not heard the news? Why, the old woman is still alive.

Hogg. Godsake! is she till the fore yet?

Odoherty. Yes; all alive and kicking—and in town too. Galt was taken in by the *jeu d'esprit* in the respectable elderly paper, announcing that she died much and justly regretted.

* Sir John Leslie, described by Scott as "a great philosopher, and as abominble an animal as ever I saw."—M.

† The heroine of Galt's novel of "The Entail."—M.

Tickler. I see by the twinkle of North's eye that he was at the bottom of the story?

Mullion. What story?

Tickler. Of her death. The notice of her decease was a hoax, they say, got up in the back shop.

Hogg. That naebody need misdout; mony a hoax and ither black jobs hae been clecket there.

Odoherty. The Chaldee, Jamie.

Tickler. The leddy means to raise an action. She lays the damages at five thousand pounds sterling.

Hogg. And I'll lay the wad o' a crown, that she'll no fake a farthing; but, Captain, tell us a' about it—Man, this is capital. I'll obligate Ebony to pay us for an extra number—an extra number clears his scores for Christopher's pranks.

Buller. Do, Captain, let's have it. Sure we are all alike implicated in whatever affects the general concern?

Odoherty. The fact is, that Galt did not well know how to wind up the Entail; and I advised him to kill the old hen off.

Buller. And you cleared the way by the premature notice of her death, did you?

Odoherty. Just so—but had the facetious paragraph which I prepared to contradict the melancholy intelligence been inserted in Ballantyne's Classical Journal, it would have dried all eyes in the happiest style imaginable.

Mullion. And why did it not appear?

Odoherty. I took it myself to the office, but with all the taste and discrimination which distinguishes the management of that weekly obituary of taste and fine writing, the communication was declined, unless the editor might be permitted to announce that it was "from a correspondent." I should, however, add, that the refusal was couched in the politest manner possible.

Buller. Suaviter in modo, fortiter in re.

Mullion. O yes—the newspaper editors have of late grown so cursedly conscientious, that no ordinary consideration will induce them to insert the most indirect puff possible, upon their own responsibility, save to serve an unknown friend.*

(*Enter a Devil with a proof-sheet, which is handed to Odoherty —Hogg looks over the Ensign's shoulder.*)

* A newspaper announced the suicide of a much respected gentleman. The same day, he came to complain of the statement as wholly unfounded, and likely to injure him. "You must insert a contradiction in to-morrow's paper," said he to the editor. "I will do what I consistently can to satisfy you," was the reply, "but as to admitting that I was misinformed, or *could* be, it is out of the question." The other exclaimed, "But I am here, in excellent health!" After a pause, in which he seriously thought upon the point, the editor closed the matter by saying, "I'll tell you what I can do—I shall say that the rope broke, before life was quite extinct, and that immediate and skilful medical assistance restored the vital spark. Beyond *that*, you cannot expect me to go." There is nothing, in a newspaper, so systematic as proclaiming your own infallibility and questioning that of all others.—M.

Hogg. Eh! Captain—are ye sae far forrit already wi' your novel?

Tickler. How! Odoherty! are you really then at press with "THE WEST COUNTRY?"

Hogg (*taking hold of the proof-sheet and looking at it*). 'Deed is he—and—na, as I'm a soul to be saved, he has a' Galt's folks. There's Doctor and Mrs. Pringle at the very head o' the chapter—the seventeenth chapter.

Omnes. Read, read, Hogg!

Odoherty. There—take it.

Hogg (*reads*). "The General Assembly,"—that's the name o' this chapter.

Odoherty. No sneers at the institutions of the country. I revere the General Assembly—I respect the King's Commissioner—I admire the table and triumphant arches thereof—I laud the procession—I love the Moderator's cocked-hat and breakfast. But, proceed, Jamie.

Hogg (*reads*). "Doctor Pringle and the Mistress took up their first abode at Leith, in the Exchange Hotel, one of the quietest houses for persons and families of sedate and clerical habits, in the whole country—for having brought in their own carriage, the distance from Edinburgh was of no consequence, though Mrs. Pringle daily grudged the high shilling toll on Leith Walk, and thought the Baillies of Edinbro' great extortioners for exacting so much." Odd, Captain, ye wagered that ye would write a book about the West in Galt's style—noo, this is no ae bit like it.

Omnes. Proceed! proceed!

Hogg (*reads*). "Sir Andrew Wylie had promised to take tea with them—and Andrew Pringle had also engaged himself, at his mother's earnest entreaties, to be present, in order to help his worthy father and her to entertain the little Baronet. The Count and Countess Milani, alias Mr. and Mrs. Goldenball, had returned from their matrimonial excursion to the North, and the Doctor——" This, Captain, will never do.

Odoherty. Turn over to the tea-making—there you will find, I flatter myself, some smack of the original.

Hogg (*turns over a leaf or two and reads*). "I ne'er," said Doctor Pringle, "could hae thought it within a possibility, that after the sore trials Mrs. Oswald had come through——"

Tickler. Mrs. Oswald! Who the deuce is she? I remember no such person in any of Galt's works.

Odoherty. "Margaret Lyndsay!" The Doctor was speaking of her.*

Tickler. What has she to do in your work, Odoherty?

Odoherty. Read on, Hogg.

* Wilson's "Trials of Margaret Lyndsay."—M.

Hogg (*reads*). "I ne'er," said Doctor Pringle, "could hae thought it within a possibility, that after the sore trials Mrs. Oswald had come through, she would have been so soon persuaded by Mr. MacTaggart to change her life."

"She took him in her advanced years for a bein down-seat," said Sir Andrew Wylie.

"Ay, ay," replied Mrs. Pringle, "nane o' your overly peeous, sweet-lippit madams for me—Mrs. MacTaggart—Mrs. Oswald that was—I'll ne'er deny she didna meet wi' an affliction, but we hae a' had our calamities."

"It's a very just observe," said the Doctor; "and though me and Mrs. Pringle there have lived long together in a state o' very pleasant felicity for mony a day and year, yet, if it be the Lord's will to take me to himself first, I would think it no sin in her to marry again;" and he added, looking tenderly to the Mistress, "but, deed, Jenny, my dear, I wouldna like to see't."

Omnes. Bravo, Captain!

Odoherty. Yes—I think you must allow that pathetic touch to be Galt to the backbone.

Hogg. Ye may brag as ye like, Captain; but it's nae mair like his way, than the baukie bird's like the peacock. What say ye till't, Christopher?

North. I have my suspicions. Confess at once, Captain. Throw yourself on our mercy. Acknowledge that Galt assisted you with the General Assembly chapter.

Buller. Veniat manus auxilio, quæ sit mihi——

Tickler. But joking apart. Is Galt really the author of these books?

Buller. I have heard——

Omnes (*in amazement*). What have you heard?

Enter AMBROSE.

Ambrose. Mr. North, a lady would speak with you.

North. Me! 'Tis too early in the night. What like is she?

Ambrose. "Rather oldish."

Odoherty. What, Kit—does the taste of your loyalty go that length? —But show the gentlewoman in. (*Exit* AMBROSE.)

Mullion. A lady inquiring for a gentleman at Ambrose's between eleven and twelve!

Tickler. You never told us, North, of your marriage? But murder will out, you see. Enter MRS. NORTH!

Enter AMBROSE *showing in* LEDDY GRIPPY.

Omnes (*all rising*). Mrs. Walkinshaw!

The Leddy. That's my name for want of a better.

North. A glass for Mrs. Walkinshaw.

The Leddy. Whilk's Mr. North?

Hogg. Yon's him—ye might hae kent him by the powdered wig and the green specks, and the stult at the chair back.

The Leddy. Hae ye sare een, Mr. North, that ye canna thole the light, or is't only because ye ken that ye darena look me in the face? —but if ye'll no face me, ye'll maybe hae to face far waur—for I'll be as plain as I'm pleasant wi' you, Mr. North. This night I will hae justice done, or the morn's morning I'll maybe gar you claw whare it's no yeuky. Gentlemen—for nobody should be bird-mouthed in a case of extremity—I'll pannel you for a jury atween me and Mr. North, there sitting, and ye sall be, in the words of law and gospel, a covenant and jurisdiction in the great thing between us.

North. I know nothing about it—I know nothing about it—if you have any business with me, call again, this is neither a fit time nor place.

The Leddy. Warna ye art and part guilty of a *fama clamosa*, in the Hebrew tongue, and on the language of Scripture?

North. I don't understand you, madam. Whatever I am responsible for, these gentlemen are equally responsible.

The Leddy. Then ye're a' conjoint and colleague for a *cessio bonorum*, to help one another.

Omnes. All!

Odoherty. May I be so bold as to ask in what way does a gentlewoman of your years of discretion desire our help?

The Leddy. Touts! Nane o' your animal eagerness, as Mr. Peveril the author ca's 't. I camna here for pastime—but on a salacious case and question; in short, I'm an injured woman—a damaged person, seeking redress in consequence of Mr. Jamphrey——

Odoherty. The devil! What has Jeffrey done to you?

The Leddy. Done!—what hae ye done to him, that he has in a manner washed his hands clean o' Mr. North, and a' his connections—the whilk decision and verdict on his part obligates me to come here myself—*in propria persona*—and form of pauper.

North. Well, and what is it that you want?

The Leddy. Heh, Mr. North! but ye're a pepper-box. I rede you to keep ony sma' share of temper that ye enjoy—ye'll hae need for't a'. Ye see, gentlemen, as I was saying, having had a comfable wi' Mr. Jamphrey, and hearing, as I was telling, how he's under the greater and lesser excommunication, and put to the horn with you and by you—and is thereby terrified out of his senses at the thought of having any thing to say to you, I thought, thinks I, before the outlay o' feeing ither counsel, I would try my hand at an amicable arrangement. Mr. North, there where he sits, hiding his face like an ill-doer, as he well knows he is to me and mine—But no to summer and winter—in short, gentlemen, I hae come for a *solacium*—being informed that Mr. North has been art and part in causing it to be set forth and published to the world, that I was dead, though the malice prepense was softened, as Mr. Jamphrey said, by the much and justly regretted. Now, is it not a most injurious and damageous thing, to put forth a calamity of that kind against a living and life-like woman? For, supposing I had a friend in the jaws o' death—thinking o' making his last will and testament, wherein he was mindit to leave and bequeath unto me a handsome legacy in free gratis gift, as a testimony of his great regard, and the love he bare—and supposing the doctor at his bedside were to tell him I was dead, or ony sympathizing relation then and there present were to give him a newspaper to read, containing that interesting intelligence—and supposing that he was thereby moved to score me out of his will, and to depart this life—would not I have sustained a great damage—and could not I thereupon constitute a ground of action, and raise a salacious plea, to damnify me for the loss, detriment, and disappointment?

North. Madam!—you cannot expect us to deliver an opinion upon a case, to which it would appear we are likely to be parties.

The Leddy. No—but I'll be content if ye'll just compound with me for the felony.

North. We can never, gentlemen, after such an appeal, be so ungallant as to allow a lady to go into court.

Omnes. Certainly not; we shall agree to her terms at once.

The Leddy. Then, Mr. North, are ye willing to confess a fault towards me?

North. I throw myself at your merciful feet.

The Leddy. Ye hear that, gentlemen; he confesses that he has been guilty of raising a *fama clamosa* against me.

Omnes. He has: he has confessed.

The Leddy. And he said ye were ilk and a' alike concernt and guilty, art and part, delinquent and culprit in the case.

Omnes. We did, we freely own it; we are all responsible for this matter, and, like him, cast ourselves at your merciful feet.

Odoherty. And we hope your leddyship will spare us in the kicking.

The Leddy. I will do that; ye'll find me very gentle.

Tickler (*aside to North*). Agree to any thing, Kit, to get rid of her.

The Leddy. And, Captain Odoherty, ye hae acknowledged yoursel as guilty as Mr. North.

Odoherty (*astonished*). What is she after now?

The Leddy. I take ye a' to witness, for I will produce the ane against the other in court, that ye have acknowledged yourselves guilty, with Mr. North, in the damage and detriment of a *fama clamosa* on me. Noo, though I'm content with a *solacium* of a hundred pounds, and a hundred pounds for cost frae Mr. North, yet I hereby give you notice, in due form of law, that I intend forthwith, unless satisfied in the interim, to bring an action against you all severally, saving and excepting Mr. North, whose offer I have accepted; and having estimated my damage at five thousand pounds, I will have that paid down to the uttermost farthing.

(*Exeunt Omnes, in the greatest panic and consternation.*)

No. X.—JULY, 1823

A FRAGMENT.

* * * * * * *

Odoherty. Chorus then. Buller, awake, man. Chorus, all of you, I say.

Chorus of Contributors.

So triumph to the Tories, and woe to the Whigs,
And to all other foes of the nation;
Let us be through thick and thin caring nothing for the prigs
Who prate about conciliation.

Dr. Mullion. Bravo, Odoherty, bravissimo!—that is decidedly one of your very best effusions.

Odoherty. No blarney to me, *mon ami.* I have taken my degrees in that celebrated university. In candor, however, and equity, I am bound to say, that I do think it a pretty fairish song, as songs go now-a-days.

North. Why, it must be admitted, that there is an awful quantity of bad songs vented just now.

Tickler. It must be the case as long as they issue in such shoals; the bad must bear a huge proportion to the good at all times; for they are just the off-throwings of the ephemeral buoyancy of spirit of the day; and as actual buoyancy of spirit generally breeds nonsense, and affectation of it is always stupidity, you must e'en be content with your three grains of wheat in a bushel of chaff.

North. Yes, yes—they must be from their very nature ephemeral. Which of all our songs—I don't mean particularly those of the present company—but of all the songs now written and composed by all the song-writers now extant—will be alive a hundred years hence?

Odoherty. Just as many as are now alive of those written and composed, as you most technically phrase it, a hundred years since.

Tickler. And that is but poor harvest indeed. Look over any of the song-books that contain the ditties of our grandmothers or great-grandmothers, and you will scarcely ever turn up a song familiar to any body but professed readers.

Odoherty. More's the pity. By all that's laughable, the reflection saddens me. "Pills to purge Melancholy," has become a melancholious book in itself. . You read page after page, puzzling yourself to make out the possibility—how any human mouth could by any device have got through the melodies—the uncouth melodies——

Buller. You know Tom D'Urféy's plan? He used to take a country dance, the more intricate the better—for as you see by his dedication, he prided himself on that kind of legerdemain—and then put words to it as well as he could.

Odoherty. I know—I know—but I was saying that it is an unpleasant sort of feeling you have about you, when you peruse, like a groping student, songs that you are sure made palace and pot-houses ring with jollity and fun in the days of merry King Charles, and warmed the gallantry of the grenadiers of Britain at the siege of Namur, under hooked-nose Old-glorious,* or of

Our countrymen in Flanders
A hundred years ago,
When they fought like Alexanders
Beneath the great Marlboro'.

North. Ay, "the odor's fled." They are like uncorked soda-water. Honest Tom D'Urféy, I think I see him now in my mind's eye, Horatio. Holding his song-book with a tipsy gravity, and trolling forth——

Joy to great Cæsar,
Long life and pleasure,

with old Rowley leaning on his shoulder, partly out of that jocular familiarity which endeared him to the people in spite of all his rascalities, and partly to keep himself steady, humming the bass.

Buller. Have you seen Dr. Kitchener's book?

North. I have, and a good, jovial, loyal book it is. The Doctor is, by all accounts, a famous fellow—great in cookery, medicine, music, poetry, and optics, on which he has published a treatise.†

Odoherty. I esteem the Doctor.

North. The devil you do!—after cutting him up so abominably in my Magazine, in an article, you know, inserted while I was in Glasgow, without my knowledge.

Odoherty. Why are you always reminding a man of his evil-doings?

* William III., whose "pious, glorious, and immortal memory" used to be the Orange charter toast in Ireland.—M.

† Dr. William Kitchener, more distinguished by gastronomic than medical knowledge, wrote a book called "The Cook's Oracle," invented new and improved old dishes, had his friends, as a "committee of taste," to pass judgment upon them at dinner, had very pleasant *conversaziones* for the male and female literati, and enjoyed life much. He insisted on punctuality, and had a placard over his chimney-piece, inscribed, "Come at seven, go at eleven." George Colman slily interpolated a monosyllable, making the line run, "go it at eleven." Optics and music, as well as gastronomy, supplied subjects for Kitchener's pen. He died in 1827.—M.

Consider that I have been white-washed by the Insolvent Court since, and let all my sins go with that white-washing. To cut the matter short, I had a most excellent cookery-book written, founded on the principles practised in the 99th mess, and was going to treat with Longman's folks about it, when Kitchener came out, and pre-occupied the market. You need not wonder, therefore, at my tickling up the worthy Doctor, who himself enjoyed the fun, being a loyal fellow to the backbone; a Tory tough and true. We are now the best friends in the world.

Mullion. Well, let that pass—what song-writer of our days, think you, will live?—Moore?

North. Moore! No, he has not the stamina in him at all. His verses are elegant, pretty, glittering, any thing you please in that line; but they have defects which will not allow them to get down to posterity. For instance, the querulous politics, on your local affairs, Odoherty, which make them now so popular with a very large class of your countrymen, are mere matters of the day, which will die with the day; for I hope you do not intend to be always fighting in Ireland?

Odoherty. I do not know how that will be—better fighting than stagnating; but, at all events, I hope we will change the grounds somewhat—I hate monotony; I trust that my worthy countrymen will get some new matter of tumult for the next generation.

North. It is probable that they will—and then, you know, Moore's —"Oh! breathe not his name," "Erin, the tear," &c., &c., will be just as forgotten as any of the things in Hogg's Jacobite relics.

Tickler. Which will ever stand, or rather fall, as a memento of the utter perishableness of all party song-writing.

North. And then there's Moore's accursed fancy for showing off learning, and his botany, and zoology, and meteorology, and mythology.

Odoherty. O ay, and the mixed metaphor, and the downright nonsense—the song you quoted just now could be finely amended.

North. What song?

Odoherty. "Erin, the smile, and the tear in thine eyes, blend like the rainbow," &c. Now, that is a washy, watery comparison for my hard-drinking country. I lay £5 that a jug of punch would be a more accurate and truly philosophical emblem; as thus. There's the Protestant part of the population inferior in quantity, superior in strength, apt to get at the head, evidently the whisky of the compound. The Roman Catholics, greater in physical proportions, but infinitely weaker, and usually very hot, are shadowed forth by the water. The Orangemen, as their name implies, are the fruit, which some palates think too sour, and therefore reject, while others think that it alone gives grateful flavor to the whole.

Mullion. And what's the sugar?

Odoherty. Why, the conciliators dropped in among us to sweeten our acidity—and you know some think that they have supplied with too liberal a hand—very much at the risk of turning the stomachs of the company.

North. A hopeful illustration—but in truth, Odoherty, your whole conversation is redolent of nothing but drink.

Odoherty. I am like Tom Moore's First Angel—the gentleman without a name, and admire compotation, not exactly "the juice of Earth," however, as Tom calls it, that being, I take it, ditch-water.

Mullion. You never saw the song Tom intended for this drunken angel of his after his fall?

Odoherty. Not I—parade it—is it not in the poem?

Mullion. No; Denman, who is Moore's doer of late, cut it out, just as he cut up the Fables.* I have a copy, however, which I shall sing.

SONG OF A FALLEN ANGEL OVER A BOWL OF RUM-PUNCH.

By T. M., Esq.

Heap on more coal there,
  And keep the glass moving,
The frost nips my nose,
  Though my heart glows with loving.
Here's the dear creature,
  No skylights—a bumper;
He who leaves heeltaps
  I vote him a mumper.
          With hey cow rumble O,
            Whack! populorum,
          Merrily, merry men,
            Push round the jorum.

What are Heaven's pleasures
  That so very sweet are?
Singing from psalters,
  In long or short metre.
Planked on a wet cloud
  Without any breeches,
Just like the Celtic,†
  Met to make speeches.
          With hey cow rumble, &c.

Wide is the difference,
  My own boozing bullies,
Here the round punch-bowl
  Heap'd to the full is.

* It was believed that Moore's "Fables for the Holy Alliance" were submitted to Lord Denman, then Common Sergeant (one of the local judges) of London, previous to publication, that he might decide on the question how libellous they were.—M.

† The Celtic Society, at their annual dinner, always wore the kilt.—M.

Then if some wise one
  Thinks that up "yonder"
Is pleasant as we are,
  Why—he's in a blunder.
    With hey cow rumble, &c.

North. A very hopeful and well-behaved angel, by my word.

Mullion. Enough of Moore. Campbell——

North. Has written one song which I hope will live long as "the flag of Old England waves lordly in pride,"—that is, I hope for ever. I mean the Mariners of England.

Tickler. A glorious song indeed! But Campbell has disgraced himself by a shabby song, in the New Monthly, about the Spaniards. It is not fit for a gentleman like Campbell to fall into the filthy slang of the blackguards of the press, and write low stuff about Prince Hilt,* or to call the grand old stainless flag of France (which *he* knows—the blackguards do not—is linked with so many splendid recollections) the "White emblem of white liver."

Dr. Mullion. Some of Sir Walter's songs will certainly live.

North. Perhaps—those in his Poems and his Novels, if they are his; but I do not recollect any thing particular of any other; and, in point of fact, you never do hear them sung by any body. Bishop, by the way, has very poorly set County Guy, very poorly indeed.

Odoherty. I like Bishop, a worthy pleasant fellow; but, somehow or other, I think his music generally but compilation,—a bar from this body and a bar from that body—curiously indented and dovetailed, I admit, but still only joinery and cabinet-making.†

North. Nobody has said a word about Byron.‡

Tickler. Dead as Harry the Eighth, and it is a pity. Heavens! who can think that the author of Childe Harold, and Manfred, and Don Juan, should have sunk to what he is now, a scribbler in a dirty magazine, and a patron of the Hunts! It, however, speaks volumes in favor of the morality of the country, after all, when we find that even genius, such as his, must sink, if it dares oppose what we are still determined to call religion and loyalty.

Odoherty (*handing The Island to North*). I have brought down Christian.§ Would you wish to look at it?

Buller. Does it sell?

Odoherty. Not at all, though the third edition is advertised. I was told at Longman's that they had not disposed of a hundred. It would have a better chance with Murray; but he and his lordship have bro-

* So the Duc d'Angoulême was called.—M.

† Mr. Bishop, who has composed several operas, and the music for hundreds of songs, was elected Professor of Music in the University of Oxford, and has been knighted.—M.

‡ In August, 1823, Byron embarked at Genoa, on his last, and glorious visit to Greece.—M.

§ "The Island," which contains some passages as fine as Byron ever produced, was written in Genoa, and published in June, 1823.

ken, after a furious quarrel. The correspondence between them is said to be curious.

Buller. Of course we shall have an awful libel on Joannes de Moravia in due time.

Odoherty. I hope so, from the bottom of my soul; for then Murray will take vengeance in turn. I had rather than a tenpenny, and that cash, we *could* print Byron's Critique on the Pot of Basil.

Tickler. Faugh, don't mention it.

North. Christian, I see, is a poor thing, with a good bit here and there in it, but not the least originality. He is the old hero—the Lara, the Conrad, the fellow of whom his lordship found the germ in Miss Lee's Kruitzner, transported to Botany Bay, or thereabouts, where, instead of mosques, and kiosks, and tambourgis, and phingaris, we are entertained with Toobonai, and Boolootoo, Mooa, Figi, Hooni, Licoo, Guatoo, Goostrumfoo, *et omne quod* endeth in oo. And the womankind are the old womankind, not a bit the worse for the wear.

Tickler. Yes, and you have the same amazing industry in transferring Bligh's Narrative, that he has shown so often before. But the introduction, and indeed some other passages, remind us of the better days of Byron. Listen!

"The morning watch was come; the vessel lay
Her course, and gently made her liquid way;
The cloven billow flashed from off her prow,
In furrows formed by that majestic plough;
The waters with their worlds were all before;
Behind, the South Sea's many an islet shore.
The quiet night, now dappling, 'gan to wane,
Dividing darkness from the dawning main;
The dolphins, not unconscious of the day,
Swam high, as eager of the coming ray;
The stars from broader beams began to creep,
And lift their shining eyelids from the deep;
The sail resumed its lately shadow'd white,
And the wind fluttered with a fresh'ning flight;
The purple ocean owns the coming sun,
But ere he break—a deed is to be done."

Odoherty. Very toploftical, to be sure. Commend me to the panegyric on what our friend Fogarty (from whom his lordship seems to have taken the idea) calls "Tobacco, lord of plants."

But here the herald of the self-same mouth
Came breathing o'er the aromatic south,
Not like a "bed of violets" on the gale,
But such as wafts its cloud o'er grog or ale,
Borne from a short frail pipe, which yet had blown
Its gentle odors over either zone,
And puff'd where'er winds rise or waters roll,
Had wafted smoke from Portsmouth to the Pole,

Opposed its vapor as the lightning flashed,
And reek'd, 'midst mountain-billows unabash'd,
To Æolus a constant sacrifice,
Through every change of all the varying skies.
And what was he who bore it? I may err,
But deem him sailor or philosopher.

Sublime tobacco! which from east to west
Cheers the tar's labor or the Turkman's rest;
Which on the Moslem's ottoman divides
His hours, and rivals opium and his brides;
Magnificent in Stamboul, but less grand,
Though not less loved, in Wapping or the Strand;
Divine in hookas, glorious in a pipe,
When tipp'd with amber, mellow, rich, and ripe,
Like other charmers wooing the caress
More dazzlingly when daring in full dress;
Yet thy true lovers more admire by far
Thy naked beauties—Give me a cigar!

And as we are talking of it, do hand us over that paper of Cotton's best, until I blow a cloud.

North. Why, Odoherty, you have scarcely brought us any news from London.

Odoherty. How could you expect blood from a turnip? There's no news there. Parliament was just spinning down, when I quitted the city, as drowsily as a tetotum—nothing doing in the *monde littéraire*—the Haymarket gay, to be sure, and our friend Terry,* drollest of actors, as he is among the worthiest of men, making the populace laugh—but I brought you down a special article on London, from a friend of mine, which will tell you every thing tellable,† so you need not pump me.

Dr. Mullion. Did you see any of the gentlemen of the press

Odoherty. Saw the whole goodly army of martyrs in full array; just as stupendously dull as ever, and, unless I mistake, more *vicious*, to speak as a jockey among the lower orders, than varmint. When I knew the body first, they were a fine hard-drinking, pudding-headed race, who just got through their balaam as fast as their fingers would let them—spouted at the Eccentrics—regaled themselves with cheese and porter, and occasionally, when the funds were good, with Hollands and water, not caring a single sixpence for politics, or thinking themselves at all primed up with the opinions they were advocating—and there are still some of that good old school surviving, with two or

* Terry, who was very intimate with Scott and his friends, made his reputation at Edinburgh Theatre. In 1819, he became manager of the Haymarket Theatre, London, and joint lessee and manager with Yates of the Adelphi in 1825. He died in 1828.

† This special article was the leader in *Blackwood*, for July, 1823, and was written by Dr. Maginn, who had removed, a short time before, from Cork to London. The article bears the name of "London Oddities and Outlines," and is smart, lively, and satirical.—M.

three of whom I got misty one night at Offley's*—but, sir, the Cockney portion of them have been horribly altered for the worse.

North. How?

Odoherty. The poor creatures have actually set up to have opinions of their own—the idiots—and to have personal quarrels, and animosities, and principles, and fiddle-de-dee.

Tickler. Mighty audacious. Can't they eat their victuals when they get them in peace?

North. The newspaper press is unquestionably becoming very base. What a hideous, a detestable attack, some of the Whig and Radical papers made on John Bull!

Odoherty. Well, do the press-gang itself justice! There was almost a universal outcry at that brutal business even among themselves. It was abominable. John, however, put it down like a man.

North. Well now, had the unfortunate Beaconites, which we still have thrown in our faces, though heaven knows their worst crime was stupidity, done any thing approaching that in atrocity, what an uproar would have been raised by the whole Whig party!

Tickler. And deservedly, for they would have been base assassins; but the Whigs may do any thing—the basest as well as the most malignant of people.

Odoherty (*sings*).

1.

Rail no more, Tories, rail no more;
Whigs are but asses ever,
On land, on wave, on sea, on shore,
All rascals of white liver.
Then rail not so,
But let them go,
And be you blithe and bonny,
Converting sounds of wrath and woe
Into hey ninny! nonny.

2.

Sing merry ditties, and no mo
Of lumps so dull and heavy;
The heads of Whigs were ever so,
Since summer first was leavy.
Then rail not so, &c.

There's a touch Shakspearian for you, in the twinkling of a bedpost.

North. You are not drinking any thing, Tickler.

Tickler. I cannot say I like your wine. It is souring on my stomach.

North. Cannot you get spirits then? I'll concoct a jug.

* Near Covent Garden—now Evans's.—M.

Tickler. So be it. (*Sings.*)

Drink to me only from a jug,
  And I will pledge in mine;
So fill my glass with whisky punch,
  And I'll not look for wine.
The thirst that in my throat doth rise
  Doth ask a drink divine;
But might I of Jove's nectar sip,
  That honor I'd resign.

The second verse is not worth parodying. Ay, this is something like. Your health, Mr. Editor.

North. Mr. Tickler, I have the pleasure of drinking your very good health. Apropos, has not Boone published a poem* on things in general?

Odoherty. I saw one in a certain place sadly mutilated, and have read only two pages. It is a puff on Mr. Canning.

Tickler. Very superfluous, therefore. It is, moreover, a good joke to see the great man of the Council of Ten, the essence of gravity, thinking to flatter the witty Antijacobin by his balaam.

North. Canning must have laughed at the idea, in his sleeve, I mean—for a minister can never laugh otherwise.

Buller. I suppose he addressed the book,

——O Boone, ne te
Frustrere.

* * * * * * *

* This was entitled "Men and Things in 1823, a Political Sketch, in Three Epistles, to the Right Hon. Geo. Canning, with copious Notes. By James Shergold Boone, M. A."—Of poem and poet, I am free to confess utter ignorance.—M.

No. XI.—AUGUST, 1823.

North. Nay, do not blush, Ensign. I thought you had dipped in the Shannon. I believe you sing extempore?

Mullion. Ay, and ex-trumpery.

North. Curse your punning. Quaver away this.

(*Throwing M. a paper.*)

Mullion (*hums a preludio*). Then, therefore, give due audience and attend. Milton, hem!

1.

The birds have sung themselves to rest,
  That sang around our bower;
The weight of the night-dew has bow'd
  The head of every flower.

2

The ringing of the hunter's horn
  Has ceased upon the hill,
The cottage windows gleam with light,
  The harvest song is still.

3

And safe and silent in the bay
  Is moor'd each fisher's prow,
Each wearied one has sought his home,
  But where, my love, art thou?

4

I pick'd a rose, a red blush rose,
  Just as the dews begun,
I kiss'd its leaves, but thought one kiss
  Would be a sweeter one.

5

I kept the rose and kiss, I thought
  How dear they both would be!
But now I fear the rose and kiss
  Are kept in vain for thee!

Really a very pretty song. It was spoony in you to drop it out of your pocket, Odoherty!

Odoherty. And amazingly genteel in you to sing it under the circumstances. It was about as bad as Brougham's reading in Parliament Mr. Saurin's letter, picked out of Lord Norbury's pocket.*

North. Is the author a secret?

Odoherty. Not the least. Rest her soul! she died of love. Her name was Quashie Maboo—quite a sentimental negress, who kept a canteen in the Bowery Way, New York. Poetry and peach-brandy were the death of her. I got her a great wake in 1816, for she was tenderly attached to me.

North. Wilberforce ought to quote this song as a proof of negro capacity. Was she pretty?

Odohorty. Yes, black but comely—she squinted furiously, but it passed for ogling; and I can assure you her pine-apple rum was superb.

Mullion. You were then a rum customer, I take it. Apropos of love, Tom Moore is in Ireland, I understand.

North. So I am informed by letter from Killarney. He travels in the train of the Marquis of Lansdowne,† who is visiting his Irish estates.

Tickler. Tom goes as joculator, I suppose. Lansdowne, when in office, was distinguished as a dancing-master, and gave Thomas, if I mistake not, the place in the West Indies for his piping.‡

North. I do not blame him for that. I rejoice to see literary merit patronized, but there was something base and grovelling—in a word, something truly Whig—in the ruffian treatment Dibdin§ experienced from the gang which got into power in 1806.

Tickler. Dirty revengeful—and beggarly to the last degree. They could not forgive him for having, in his glorious songs, stirred the

* Mr. Sheil, in his "Sketches of the Irish Bar," (Article, Lord Norbury, vol. ii., p. 83,) gives a different and uncontradicted version. Norbury "was in the habit of stuffing papers into the old chairs in his study, in order to supply the deficiency of horse-hair which the incumbency of eighty years had produced in their bottoms. At last, however, they became, even with the aid of this occasional supplement, unfit for use, and were sent by his Lordship to a shop in which old furniture was advertised to be bought and sold. An individual of the name of Monaghan got one of these chairs into his possession, and, finding it stuffed with papers, drew them out. He had been a clerk in an attorney's office, and knew Mr. Saurin's handwriting."—It was a letter from Saurin, the first law-officer of the Crown in Ireland, to Lord Norbury, Chief Justice, recommending him, when on circuit in the King's County, to talk to Protestant gentlemen about and against the Catholics and their claims! The authenticity of the letter was undoubted, the affair was discussed in Parliament, and the then Tory Ministry effectually screened Norbury and Saurin!—M.

† Mrs. Gilpin, we are told by Cowper, was economical, and had a frugal mind, even when

"She to pleasure was inclined."

Moore might have been her blood-relation, adroitly managing, on most occasions, to "travel in the train" of somebody who paid all the expenses. In his Diary are numerous records of this.—M.

‡ No.—Moore was appointed Registrar to the Admiralty Court, at Bermuda, in 1803, and Lord Lansdowne did not enter office until 1806!—M.

§ Dibdin, who wrote a great number of patriotic sea-songs, during the naval contests which terminated at Trafalgar, received a Government pension, in acknowledgment of the service they had done by inspiring and exciting the British tars. When the Whigs came into office in 1806, they struck Dibdin's name out of the pension-list! As a party, they had opposed the war, and were determined to punish the poet for doing any thing to encourage it.—M.

spirit of Britain against their friends the Jacobins; and accordingly, in his old age, the filthy fellows deprived him of a pension which he had earned by services to his country, more solid than the nine-tenths of those which have been the foundation of many a Whig property.

North. Well, well—they stick to one another, however; which is more than can be said of other people who shall be nameless. You know we have often contrasted the different treatment experienced by this very Tommy Moore and Theodore Hook, under the very same circumstances.*

Odoherty. Theodore, however, is winding up after all, and must eventually be cleared of all slur. If the details of his case were published, it would be the exposé of all the most rascally piece of pitiful persecution ever heard of; and I hope it *will* be published some fine day or other.

Mullion. You have heard Theodore's joke on his misfortune?

Buller. No, never. (*Aside.*) Plus millies jam audivi.

Mullion. Poh, man, you *must* have heard it; it is in print. When he came from the Isle of France, he touched at the Cape of Good Hope, where he met Lord Charles Somerset. "Bless me," said his lordship, "what sends you home so soon, Hook—a complaint in your liver?"—"No," replied Theodore; "a disorder in my *chest.*" You certainly heard it?

North. Why, yes; it's almost as venerable as any thing in Joe Miller.

Mullion. I was aware of that, and only told it as a preface to the Duke of Sussex's admirable version of the story. The Duke, you know, is very bright.

Odoherty. Yes, as one of Lambton's coal-scuttles.

Mullion. And hates Theodore, whom he suspects—with what reason I cannot say—of having demolished him in Bull.†

Tickler. Why, certainly, his highness has no great reason to be obliged to the tribe of Bull; for he was only suspected to be a block head formerly, but now is written down as an ass regular.

Mullion. Well, sir, an ultra fit of candor every now and then seizes on him, and he panegyrizes Hook's wit. "I don't like the man, sir," he says—"I don't like the man; but to do him justice; let us be fair; he's a droll fellow, sir—a droll fellow; he tells you a good thing —a devilish good thing now—ha, ha, ha!—a most excellent thing. You know he was at the Isle of France; ay, and he came back from

* Both had held colonial appointments of trust. Each had suffered by his deputy's misconduct. Hook was sent home in chains, and not even his own friends, the Tories, wiped away the claim, but even seized his property while he was dead and unburied. Moore fluttered about in society, spent a season or two at Paris, (with occasional flights to London,) and finally compromised for a few hundreds.—M.

† Theodore Hook, as Editor of John Bull, spared no leader of the antagonist Whig party. The Duke of Sussex, pompous and proud, was frequently a victim.—M.

the Isle of France too—ha, ha, ha! and we all know why—ha, ha, ha! Well, then, coming home, he stopped at the Cape of Good Hope—some place in India, you know—where he met Charles Somerset. Says Charles to him, 'Why, Hook,' says he, 'what the devil,' says he, 'brings you home? I hope,' says he, 'it is nothing ails your liver?' Well, now, just mind what Hook said—devilish good—very good, faith—I don't like the man, sir—I don't like the man; but let us be fair; he *is* a droll fellow, sir—a droll fellow. 'No,' says Hook, 'nothing ails my liver—never was better in my life,' says he; 'but there is a deficiency in my accounts, which I must go over to answer.' Ha, ha, ha! Devilish good, was it not? When I heard it first, every body laughed. Ha, ha, ha!"

Tickler. You are a capital mimic, Mullion. I wish Mathews had that story.

North. No, no; it would be scandalous to bring a prince of the blood on the stage. Remember that he is a son of George III., and brother of George IV.

Tickler. Pooh! Mathews could tell it of Signor —— ———, or any other of the Duke's select circle.

Mullion. Who, by the way, regularly laugh at the joke, whenever it pleases the Duke to tell it. It is his highness's best story, and is always told on great occasions, state days, holidays, and the like.

North. Come, gentlemen, change the subject, if you please. I do not like to hear any thing disparaging to any son of HIM, who, no matter what king may reign, shall be king of *my* heart to the end of the chapter.

Come fill up your wine,
Look, fill it like mine;
Here, boys, I begin,
A good health to the KING!
Tims, see it go round,
Whilst with mirth we abound.

Chorus.

For we will be dull and heavy no more,
Since wine does increase, and there's claret good store.

Nay, don't us deceive——

Odoherty. Upon honor, I filled a bumper from the foundation.

North. I did not address *you*, my good fellow. I spoke to Mullion, who is fighting shy; but do not interrupt me.

Nay, don't us deceive,
Why this will you leave?
The glass is not big,
What the deuce, you're no Whig.
Come, drink up the rest,
Or be merry at least.

Chorus.

For we will be dull and heavy no more,
Since wine does increase, and there's claret good store.

Tickler. Out of Pills to Purge Melancholy, if I mistake not?

North. Yes, from the aforesaid. It was a favorite chant of worthy Dr. Webster, some forty years ago, when we used to meet in the Gude Auld Town, at the White Horse in the Canongate. Many a scene I have got through since the Aughty-Three. "And I said, the days of my youth, where are they? And Echo answered, Where are they?"

Odoherty. Pr'ythee, no more of your antediluvian recollections—your dramas of the ancient world.

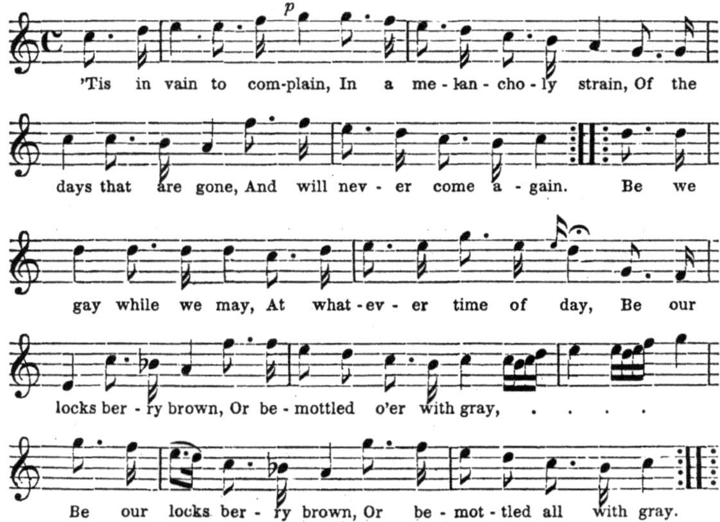

2

We have laughed,
We have quaffed,
We have raked it fore and aft,
But out of pleasure's bowl have not emptied all the draught.
Never mind
Days behind,
But still before the wind,
Float after jolly souls, full flasks, and lasses kind.

Buller. Extempore? Stans pede in uno?

Odohety. Yes, on honor. I was seized with a fit of poetical fury.

Buller. You are almost as great as Pistrucci himself.

Odoherty. I knock under to Coleridge only; for he makes verses asleep. I make music sometimes in that state, but never poetry.

North. Have you heard Coleridge's late epitaph on himself, which he composed in that way?

Tickler. No. Repeat it.

North.

Here lies poor Cole, at length and without screaming,
Who died as he was always wont, a-dreaming;
Shot, as with pistol, by the gout within,
Alone, and all unknown, at Embro' in an inn.

Tickler. "Alone, and all unknown, at Embro' in an inn." How mournful and musical! I hope, before the day comes when my epitaph will be required for him, he will have the firmness to put forth his strength, and take his place among our great men.

Mullion. What are you thinking of, Ensign?—You don't hear what any body says to you. You did not hear the Epitaph.

Odoherty. Beg your pardon—beg your pardon a thousand times over—I was looking at these prints—they're new ones surely.—What the devil are they?

North. Pooh! they're some new affairs—materials that Dr. Mullion has got together for his Lectures on the Fine Arts.

Odoherty. Oh! is that the case? What are the subjects, pray?

Mullion. Don't you see well enough what they are?—Why, they're the new set of prints come out by way of illustrations to Leigh Hunt's poem of "The Choice," in the last Liberal. I shall lecture on them one of these days.

Odoherty. The artist?

Mullion. Nay, as to that I can't say. There's no name to the articles; but 'tis whispered that they are Haydon's.

Odoherty. Haydon's?—Impossible!—impossible—not the least like his style.* Why, they seem to be mere caricatures.

Mullion. Not a bit—I assure you 'tis all dead earnest. There is much gusto about them—a fine free sweep of pencil—a delicate sense of the grace of things. They're very pretty sweet prints. I intend to make Ambrose a present of them after my lecture is fairly done and delivered.

Odoherty. By jingo, I can't make either head or tail of these things.

* Haydon mistook his vocation, when he became a Historical Painter,—although he was as good, in that line, as most of his contemporaries. As a teacher he was never surpassed. Landseer, Lance, Harvey, Eastlake, and a score more, are living examples of this. They were his pupils. As a public lecturer on the principles and practice of painting, no one ever approached him. He was written down, talked down, sneered down by the Royal Academy, which should have invited him to accept its highest honors. His mind was overthrown, and he perished by his own hand, on June 22, 1846.—M.

There should have been a motto, or something, at the bottom, to let one into the artist's meaning. What, now, is this here one, Mullion?

Mullion. There are mottoes to each of them, taken from the poem itself; but the frame-maker has, by some mistake, covered them with his pasteboard and gilding. Here, however, is the Liberal, No. IV. I believe I can easily point out the appropriate passages for your benefit.

Odoherty. That's a good fellow. Well, then, what is the *bit* alluded to here?—(I haven't seen the last Liberal myself yet.)

Mullion. This print, sir, represents his Majesty of Cockaigne in the attitude of doing what he says in his poem he is very fond of—admiring Nature.

Odoherty. NATURE?—Why, he's at the tea-table.

Mullion. No matter—he's admiring the "Goal of life."

Odoherty. The Bowl of life, you mean—he has the Slop-basin in his dexter paw.

Mullion. Well—and what should he have? He is talking in the poem about bowers and showers, and treeses and breezes, and so forth; and he breaks out into this fine apostrophe, which is the motto to your print:

"Come then, ye scenes of quiet and content,
Ye Goals of life, on which our hearts are spent,
Meet my worn eyes—I LOVE YOU EVEN IN VALES
OF CUPS AND SAUCERS, AND SUCH Delfic DALES——"

Are not they sweet natural lines?

Odoherty. Why, Wales is a pretty country—and I dare say, even on delft-ware, such as he seems to have on his table, the representation yet may be charming. Seriously, this print gives us an amicable idea of his Majesty.

Kempferhausen. Dear divine enthusiast! Well, only to think of people making a laughing-stock of this innocent-hearted, good, worthy, gentle soul, that is quite happy, quite upon the air, with having a rural peep of a few blue trees and cottages on a piece of crockery ware!—For shame! for shame!

Odoherty. What the deuce is this grand roll, North?

North. You talk of Dr. Mullion's lectures—I would have you know, I mean to cut in upon that series of his myself. In a word, here goes my lecture on these prints, and on the poem from which they sprung. I shall read it to you. Listen, boys!

MR. NORTH'S LECTURE ON "THE CHOICE,"

A Poem recently written by Leigh Hunt, a Convert and Vice-Poet-Laureate to Blackwood's Magazine.

Our innumerable delightful qualities of head and heart, and, above all, our invincible good nature, have at last made a complete convert of Leigh Hunt, and he is never happy except when lauding Black wood's Magazine to the seventh heaven. No sooner does he put on his yellow breeches,* in the morning early, than he trips crisply down from his attic story into the breakfast-parlor, and seasons every mouthful of muffin with the mustard of Ebony. He cannot write a note to Mr. Pygmalion the painter, or Mistress Molly the charwoman, without trumpeting our praises; and will sit up for hours together in his bed, with his perked-up mouth, and swaling night-cap,† gazing himself away through an opening in the dimity, on a striking likeness of us, sketched by our common friend Haydon, during his last visit to Scotland. He is absolutely possessed—haunted—waylaid—bedridden —not by an Incubus, God forbid, but by a most affable and benign spirit, hight Christopher North, who purifies, by gentle ministrations, the corruptions of his Cockney blood, and so fills his brain with "fancies chaste and noble," that he is henceforth appointed our Vice-Poet-Laureate, with a salary of four gallons of gin-twist, and a keg of best Dunbar red-herrings, to be paid at Hampstead at "ten of April morn, by the chime." Let no envious railer scoff at Leigh Hunt as a placeman and pensioner. No doubt, the situation is a lucrative one, and with judicious economy, our laureate, if he may not live upon it and lay by money, cannot fail to become a richer man every year. He must not, however, buy any more busts of those "down-looking" Greeks, and we recommend him (if he has not done so already) to sell his piano-forte. He has but an indifferent ear for instrumental music, and tuning is expensive. The position, too, either of a man or a Cockney, at the ivories, is below the dignity of our laureate, and unworthy an eater of red-herrings. The barrel-organ is a preferable instrument; and we have heard that Mr. Hunt's execution upon it is to be equalled only by his command over the hurdy-gurdy. But we are intruding into the sacred privacy of domestic life, and therefore shall not again panegyrize Mr. Hunt's musical powers, our Laureate although he be, till we have the pleasure of meeting him in the street with a salt-box, or in a lane with a Highland bagpipe. Meanwhile, let him be to us our MAGNUS APOLLAR.

We refer such of our readers as may not have heard of Mr. Leigh Hunt, to various papers in this miscellany with the signature Z. These will tell what he was; but we have his own words for what he wishes to be;—and the following morceaux are from the intended life of our Vice-Laureate, adumbrated or shadowed forth in his beautiful poem, "The Choice."‡

* Leigh Hunt was educated at Christ's Hospital, London. The dress of the school-boys there consists of no cap, (the head is always uncovered, and a small woollen covering, such as would be too small for a four-hours-old baby, is worn on the girdle,) a long blue frock, festooned round the waist by a leathern belt, a girdle, *yellow breeches* and stockings, and thick shoes,—M.

† "With a perked feather swaling in his bonnet." The line *was* to be found in Hunt's "Rimini." He has cut it out of the later editions.—M.

‡ See Liberal, No. IV.—C. N.

The poem opens with a panegyric upon Pomfret, the author of that great original poem The Choice, on which Mr. Hunt's is modelled.

"I have been reading Pomfret's *Choice* this spring,
A pretty kind of-sort-of-kind of thing,
Not much a verse, and poem none at all,
Yet, as they say, extremely natural.
And yet I know not. There's a skill in pies,
In raising crusts as well as galleries;
And he's the poet, more or less, who knows
The charm that hallows the least thing from prose,
And dresses it in its mild singing clothes.
Poetry's that which sets a thought apart,
To worship Nature with a choral heart:
And may be seen where rarely she intrudes,
As birds in cages make us think of woods.
Beaux have it in them, when they love the faces
Of country damsels, and their worsted graces."

"Mild singing clothes." What are they? Not surely your yellow breeches, Mister Hunt. Perhaps caps and bells. Are kilts mild singing clothes? Petticoats are liker the thing when they rustle. The two last lines are not original, but filched from the Filcher. They were shown publicly in prose by the new Pygmalion some time ago, that is, without their mild singing clothes. And pray, our good Vice-Laureate, what may they mean?—When a Cockney chucks a country wench under the chin, and gloats upon her linsey-woolsey petticoat, call you that "poetry?" The author of Rimini ought to know better; but we hope that he is merely shamming innocence to please us; in which hope we are strengthened by the subsequent strapping Alexandrine—

"The ladies rise in *heaps,* and give them *sweet admissions!*"

A little further on, our Vice shows he is no such simpleton about such affairs as he would pretend to be; but, on the contrary, somewhat peevishly complains, that, in the present day, a man cannot write lusciously and liquorishly without being shook by the ears, or nose-pulled by some Z. or other.

"Else I would print my fancy by itself,
And be 'a love' on every lady's shelf;
Perhaps I shall be so some day or other," &c.

Promiscuous concubinage not yet being the order of the day, the publication of the "loves" alluded to is deferred till a fitter opportunity; and meanwhile the Vice writes, he tells us, such verses as "smile on tables in the parson's nose." For smile, *nostro periculo,* read smell. How elegant the use of the word parson! And, altogether, what dignified and gentlemany ease does Mr. Hunt exhibit in these his "mild singing clothes!" Instead of one, he shall have two kegs of Dunbar reds.

But now for him. Hear—hear—hear!

"First, on a green I'd have a low, broad house,
Just seen by travellers through the garden boughs;
And that my luck might not seem ill bestowed,
A bench and spring should greet them on the road.
My grounds should not be large; I like to go
To Nature for a range, and prospect too,
And cannot fancy she'll comprise for me,
Even in a park, her all-sufficiency:
Besides, my thoughts fly far; and when at rest,
Love, not a watch-tower, but a lulling nest.
But all the ground I had should keep a look
Of Nature still, have birds'-nests and a brook;
One spot for flowers, the rest all turf and trees:
For I'd not grow my own bad lettuces.
And above all, no house should be so near,
That strangers should discern me here and there;
Much less when some fair friend was at my side,
And swear I thought her charming,—which I did.
I am not sure I'd have a rookery;
But sure I am I'd not live near the sea,
To view its great flat face, and have my sleeps
Filled full of shrieking dreams and foundering ships;
Or hear the drunkard, when his slaughter's o'er,
Like Sinbad's monster scratching on the shore.
I'd live far inland, in a world of glades,
Yet not so desert as to fright the maids:
A batch of cottages should smoke beside;
And there should be a town within a morning's ride."

Our Vice says, "My grounds should not be large." His grounds!—Leigh Hunt's grounds!—A gentleman of landed property!—A Surrey freeholder!—What do you mean by "not large," Vice? It is an indefinite expression. What think you of a couple of hundred acres?—"No low, broad house" should ever have less than an estate of that extent, at least in a ring-fence. Now, is not this rather exorbitant? Consider also the danger of losing yourself in a multitudinous sea of Swedish turnips—the dead certainty of being lost for ever—or found a skeleton, of several months' lying, in a potato-furrow. Besides, what a most idiotical style of farming you here chalk out for yourself! "One spot for flowers, and the rest all turf and trees." That would never pay. Do you intend to sell the birds'-nests at Covent-Garden market—eggs, or broods and all? If so, you must study nidification; for if you have only a "flower-garden, turf, and trees," and nothing else, devil a singing-bird will build his nest near your "low, broad house," except it be a barn-door fowl or a guinea-pig. Farther, what sort of a brook will that be, without ever a stone, or a rock, or an old rotten stump, to amuse itself with? Such a brook would be an object of the deepest compassion in dry weather; and, indeed, unless you had a draw-well, of which no mention is made, what is to become of the tea-kettle? You say, "I am not sure I'd have a rookery." There you are right; for when you and some fair friend were strolling through the grove, and you were swearing you thought her charming—"which you did"—down haply would plump an epaulette on each of our Vice-Laureate's shoulders, which would be no small nuisance to your fair friend, and stop the current of her ideas. But, my good soul, you speak doubtfully about the rookery, just as if you could order the rooks to build on any morning you chose to appoint. Take our advice, and have no rookery. Rook-pies are disgusting; and then a crowd of Cockneys would be firing away at the young hop-the-twigs every spring, to the great annoyance of yourself and fair friend, to say nothing of the positive danger of flying ramrods and split barrels. Let it be fixed, therefore, that there shall be no rookery. "Not so desert as to fright the maids." Do you mean here, simply, your brace of servant girls, or maids in general? "The maids" is an equivocal expression; so is "fair friend;" and really all these inuendoes set one's tooth on edge, and look more like Odoherty himself than his Vice. "A batch of cottages" is far more elegant than a batch of Peers, or a batch of bread;—and "within a morning's ride" leaves the distance of the town in a pleasing obscurity.—So you seriously intend keeping a horse? I am sorry to hear it, both on your account and his own. He will have poor picking on the turf among the trees, and will come down with you to a certainty. Keep a cuddy, and let him browse in the lanes; but on no account whatever venture upon horseback. Your fair friend would have nothing else to do but to make plasters; and we humbly conceive, that this "morning's ride" will furnish a fundamental objection to your villa. Take the coach at once, or borrow a shandrydan at the "batch of cottages," from the pig-dealer; and so jog into town in safety.

Aha! my friend! you are at your old tricks—we knew we should catch you at last. Next comes the old imageman, with his batch of gods and goddesses on his board; and Mr. Hunt purchases about a dozen nudities for the moderate sum of eighteen-pence a-pair, rough and smooth.

"And yet to show I had a taste withal,
I'd have some casts of statues in the hall,
Or rather entrance, whose sweet steady eyes
Shoud touch the comers with a mild surprise,
And so conduct them, hushing to my door,
Where, if a friend, the house should hear a roar.
The grateful beggar should peep in at these,
And wonder what I did with Popish images."

Next our Laureate says he could write and read,

> "Till it was time
> To ride or walk, or on the grass go rhyme."

Stop a moment, if you please—no riding. You forget that we already put our veto on that. It is not so easy a matter for a man at your time of life to learn to ride. Gracious heavens! are you mad?

> "I'd never hunt, EXCEPT THE Fox, and then
> Not much, for fear I should fall," &c.

Hunting the Fox a little! Only imagine him breaking cover. Why, you fly over your horse's ears at the first ditch, six inches wide. First of all, you talk of riding to town—on paper—your brain and your bottom warm—and nothing will satisfy you, but to HUNT THE FOX. O, Editor of the Annals of Sporting! what wouldst thou not give for a sight of our worthy Vice-Laureate leading the Surrey Hunt, Reynard in view, and Tims whipper-in! After HUNTING THE FOX, but "*not much*," Mr. Hunt thinks himself equal to any display of bodily vigor, and declares—

> "All manly games I'd play at: golf, and quoits,
> And cricket, to set all my limbs to rights,
> And make me conscious, with a due respect,
> Of muscles one forgets by long neglect.
> But as for prize-fights, with their butchering shows,
> And crowds of black-legs, I'd have none of those;—
> I am not bold in other people's blows.
> Besides, I should reside so far from town,
> Those human waves could never bear me down—
> Which would endear my solitude, I own.
> But if a neighbor, fond of his antiques,
> Tried to renew a bout or two at sticks,
> I'd do my best to force a handsome laugh
> Under a ruddy crack from quarter-staff;
> Nor think I had a right to walk my woods,
> Coy of a science that was Robin Hood's.
> 'Tis healthy, and a man's; and would assist
> To make me wield a falchion in my fist,
> Should foes arise who'd rather not be taught,
> And war against the course of truth-exploring thought."

This is a good passage. But what if Bill Gibbons snould some day pitch the ring for a fight between the Bush-Cove and Cabbage, with the ropes belonging to the P. C. in Mr. Hunt's Park? Fifty miles from town is no security against such an invasion; and surely Mr. Hunt would not countenance the Beaks. What would honest Robin Hood have thought of the expression, "coy of a science?" If our Vice would consider the matter for a minute or two, he would be sensible of the extreme ludicrousness of the most remote comparison between himself and Robin Hood. He—with his yellow breeches, silk hat, red slippers, and shabby-genteel surtout, picking his steps, within sound of the dinner-bell, among a few beds of tulips and peony-roses, or selecting a dry spot of his "turf and trees," that he might "on the grass go rhyme," or scribble a literary Examiner—and that immortal Bowman of the Forest! Tims, personating Bruce at Bannockburn in our Tent, was nothing to the King of the Cockneys, with a quarter-staff in his lily hand, enacting the Outlaw of Sherwood!

Such pastimes, however, would be but rare, and never allowed to interfere with our bard's severer studies. For

"I'd write, because I could not help it; read
Much more, but nothing to oppress my head;
For heads are very different things at ease,
And forced to bear huge loads for families.
Still I would think of others; use my pen,
As fits a man and lettered citizen,
And so discharge my duty to the state;
But as to fame and glory, fame might wait,
Nevertheless, I'd write a work in verse,
Full of fine dreams and natural characters;
Eastern, perhaps, and gathered from a shore
Whence never poet took his world before.
To this sweet sphere I would retire at will,
To sow it with delight, and shape with skill;
And should it please me, and be roundly done,
I'd launch it into light, to sparkle round the sun."

Now, high as our opinion is of our laureate's abilities and genius, we offer to lay six guineas of wirewove gilt to a pound of whitey-brown that not two hundred copies of this Eastern Tale are sold within the two years. Instead of "sparkling round the sun," it will lie a heavy bale in a dark warehouse; and if printed at his own risk, Mr. Hunt will find himself some twenty or thirty pounds out of pocket. Our Vice-Laureate must therefore give up all idea of "launching it into light," and confine himself to his Odes on our Birthday, and the Anniversary Hymn on the creation of the Magazine.

Pomfret, we are told, got into a row with some bishop or other, on account of a suspicious line in his poem, which was thought to recommend a kept mistress, in preference to a wife. Mr. Hunt is facetious on this in a note; but it puzzles us to know, from the following passage, whether he holds the opinion erroneously attached to the "Parson."

"In pleasure and in pain, alike I find
My face turn tenderly to womankind;
But then they must be truly women,—not
Shes by the courtesy of a petticoat,
And left without inquiry to their claims,
Like haunted houses with their devil's dams.
I'd mend the worst of women, if I could,
But for a constancy, give me the good;—
I do not mean the formal or severe,
Much less the sly, who's all for character;

But such as, in all nations and all times,
Would be good creatures, fit for loving rhymes,
Kind, candid, simple, yet of sterling sense,
And of a golden age for innocence.
Of these my neighbors should have choice relations;
And I (though under certain alterations)
I too would bring—(though I dislike the name;
The Reverend Mr. Pomfret did the same;
Let its wild flavor pass a line so tame;)—
A wife,—or whatsoever better word
The times, grown wiser, might by law afford
To the chief friend and partner of my board.
The dear, good she, by every habit then,—
Ties e'en when pleasant, very strong with men;
Though your wise heads first make one's system wrong,
And then insist that only theirs last long,—
Would finish, and make round in every part,
The natural harmony of her own wise heart;
And by the loss of something of her right
Of being jealous, consummate delight.
Gods! how I'd love her morning, noon, and night!"

Now, who and what the devil is this madam? How is she to be named? Miss, or Mistress? What alteration does our mysterious friend mean to make on the Marriage Law? Has he communicated with the Lord Chancellor, my Lord Ellenborough, Dr. Phillimore, and the blacksmith at Gretna-Green? What is there peculiarly odious, loathsome, and repulsive in the word "wife," that Mr. Hunt should publicly express his dislike of it, "in mild singing clothes?" What word would he prostitute in its place? Or what is the matter with the tympanum of his ear, or the core of his heart, that a word sacred to all the rest of his species, should, to him, sound unhallowed?

On he goes.

"I'd have my mornings to myself. Ev'n ladies
Should not prevent me this, except on May-days;
Unless we fairly struck our tents awhile,
To stroll, like gipsies, round about the isle;
A plan I might be bent on, I confess,
Provided colds would give us leave, and dress,
And twenty other inconveniences.
I'd give up even my house to live like them,
And have a health in every look and limb,
To which our best perceptions must be dim.
A gipsy's body, and a poet's mind,
Clear blood, quick foot, free spirit, and thought refined,
Perpetual airs to breathe, and loves to bind,—
Such were the last perfection of mankind."

It does not seem to us, that the difficulties in the way of putting this scheme into practice are at all insurmountable. What if some two or three of the party should have a cold, cannot they take with them a few boxes of lozenges, and a score of aperient powders? In a few days, all obstructions will be worked off; and the Blanket-Tent will murmur beneath the moon with a mellower and more subdued snore. In a Blanket-Tent, we presume, the gipsying party mean to shelter; and do not forget now to provide for yourselves a sufficient stock of horn for the manufactory of ornamental spoons. As to dress, about which Mr. Hunt seems to be so unhappy, let him boldly take with him his yellow breeches in a bandbox; and every day before dinner, he can put them on most rurally in a ditch by the roadside, exhibiting

"The last perfection of mankind,
A gipsy's body, and a poet's mind."

As to the "twenty other inconveniences," we consider them, whatever they are, quite imaginary; and the party will find both luxuries and necessaries in every wood.

On returning home from this pretty little wild excursion, Mr. Hunt once more "takes up house;" and he really gives himself the character of a very pleasant and amiable landlord.

"These mornings, with their work, should earn for me
My afternoon's content and liberty.
I'd have an early dinner, and a plain,
Not tempting much 'to cut and come again;'
A little wine, or not, as health allow'd,
But for my friends, a stock to make me proud;
Bottles of something delicate and rare,
Which I should draw, and hold up with an air,
And set them on the table, and say, 'There!'"

We were here most anxious to know the dimensions of Mr. Hunt's dining-room, and the prevailing color of its furniture. But we are only told,

"My dining-room should have some shelves of books,
If only for their grace and social looks—
Horace and Plutarch, Plato, and some more,
Who knew how to refine the tables' roar,
And sprinkled sweet philosophy between,
As meats are reconciled with slips of green.
I read infallibly, if left alone;
But after meat, an author may step down
To settle a dispute or talk himself:—
I seem to twitch him now with finger from his shelf."

Hitherto our opinions on all the principal questions in taste, manners, morals, and religion, have been in unison; but now Mr. Hunt and we cease to row in the same boat—for if we did, we should be pulling away, when he was backing water. What will Odoherty say to his Vice, when he reads,

"I would not sit in the same room to dine
And pass the evening; much less booze till nine,

And then with a white waistcoat and red face,
Rise, with some stupid, mumbling, common-place,
And 'join the ladies,' bowing, for some tea,
With nauseous looks, half lust, half irony."

The last line in this quotation speaks of something beyond our experience or observation—but may, nevertheless, show Mr. Hunt's familiar knowledge of the human heart. To prevent the possibility of such enormities, he suggests a very notable expedient.

"I'd have two rooms, in one of which, as weather
Or fancy chose, we all might come together,
With liberty for each one nevertheless
To wander in and out, and taste the lawns and trees.
One of the rooms should face a spot of spots,
Such as would please a squirrel with his nuts;
I mean a slope, looking upon a slope,
Wood-crown'd, and dell'd with turf, a sylvan cup.
Here, when our moods were quietest, we'd praise
The scenic shades, and watch the doves and jays."

Besides the ordinary and necessary out-houses, such as hen-house, pig-sty, dog-kennel, "and the rest," Mr. Hunt proposes to build a "chapel." This made us wink again; for nothing makes him so irritable as to be suspected of Christianity. But list—oh! list—if ever you did the dear Cockney love—

"Greek beauty should be there, and Gothic shade;
And brave as anger, gentle as a maid,
The name on whose dear heart my hope's worn cheek was laid.
Here, with a more immediate consciousness,
Would we feel all that blesses us, and bless;
And lean on one another's heart, and make
Sweet resolutions, ever, for love's sake;
And recognise the eternal Good and Fair,
Atoms of whose vast active spirit we are,
And try by what great yearnings we could force
The globe on which we live to take a more harmonious course."

But, gentle reader, out with your pocket-handkerchief—and if you have any tears, prepare to shed them now. For, woe is me! and alack! alack-a-day! poor dear Mr. Hunt has taken to his bed—is going to die—is dead.

"And when I died, 'twould please me to be laid
In my own ground's most solitary shade;
Not for the gloom, much less to be alone,
But solely as a room that still might seem my own.
There should my friends come still, as to a place
That held me yet, and bring me a kind face:
There should they bring me still their griefs and joys,
And hear in the swell'd breeze a little answering noise.
Had I renown enough, I'd choose to lie,
As Hafiz did, bright in the public eye,

With marble grace inclosed, and a green shade,
And young and old should read me, and be glad."

No—no—no. It must not—shall not be. Buried in your own grounds! No—no—no! It is too far from town—and the Wuster-Heavy would be perpetually overloaded with pilgrims seeking the shrine where thou wert laid. We insist on your submitting to a public funeral, and in WESTMINSTER ABBEY.

Tickler. After all, we must succumb, Odoherty. North is North. He is our master in all things, and above all in good humor.

Odoherty. An admirable lecture indeed. Put round the bottles, and I shall repay Great Christopher with a chant.

Omnes. Do—do—do.

Odoherty (*sings*).

THE TORIES—A NATIONAL MELODY.*

1.

'Tis with joy and exultation I look round about this nation,
And contemplate the sum of her glories;
You must share in my delight, for whoever IS is right—
Oh! the prime ones are every where Tories.
Start whatever game ye please, you'll be satisfied in these
The just pride of the Island reposes—
Whigs in ambushes may chaff, but the Tories have the laugh
When it comes to the counting of noses,
Dear boys!
When it comes to the counting of noses.

2.

Can the gentlemen of Brookes' show a nose, now, like the Duke's,
Who squabashed every Marshal of Boney's;
And at last laid Boney's self on yon snug outlandish shelf,
Just with three or four rips for his cronies?
When the Hollands and the Greys see the garniture of bays
Nodding o'er this invincible Tory,
Can they give the thing the by-go, by directing us to Vigo,
And parading their Corporal's story?
Poor Bob!†
Their negotiating Corporal's story!

3.

'Tis the same way in the law:—in the Chancellor's big paw,
What are all these Whig-praters but rushes?
With one knitting of his brows every whelp of them he cows,
With one sneer all their balaam he crushes.

* By Dr. Maginn.—M.

† Sir Robert Wilson.—M.

They got silkers from the Queen; but in ragged bombazeen
  They must all be contented to jaw, now.
Hence, the virulence that wags twenty clappers at "Old Bags,"
  And behind his back calls him "Bashaw" now—
                                        Poor dears!
  They behind his back call him "Bashaw" now!

4.

Stout Sir Walter in Belles Lettres has, I'm bold to say, no betters;
  Even the base Buff-and-Blue don't deny this—
Why?—Because their master, Constable, would be packing off for Dunstable,
  The first pup of the pack that durst try this.
"You shan't breakfast, dine, nor sup" ties their ugly muzzles up
  From the venture of such a vagary;
But a sulky undergrowl marks the malice of the foul,
  And we see and enjoy their quandary,
                                        Poor curs!
  We all see and enjoy their quandary.

5.

Thus, in Letters, Law, and Arms, we exhibit peerlees charms;
  We in Parliament equally triumph—
When to Canning we but point, Brougham's nose jumpeth out of joint,
  And Sir Jammy Macgerald* must cry "humph!"
Then we've Peel, too, and we've Croker, who upraised the "holy poker"
  O'er thy crockery, lately, Joe Hume!
'Neath our eloquence and wit, Duck-in-thunder-like they sit,
  And await the completion of doom—
                                        Poor things!
  They await the completion of doom.

6.

We've the President to paint—we've the Wilberforce for Saint—
  And our sculptors are Flaxman and Chantrey!
On the stage we've Young and Terry—ay, and Liston the arch-merry,
  And great Kitchener chants in our pantry!—
'Mong the heroes of the ring, we've a Jackson and a Spring—
  We've a Bull to gore all the Whig news-folk—
Among preachers we've a Phillpotts—an O'Doherty 'mong swill-pots—
  And Saul Rothschild to tower o'er the Jews-folk,
                                        Dear boys!
  Baron Rothschild to tower o'er the Jews-folk.

7.

What Review can Whig-sty furnish, but is sure to lose its burnish
  When our Quarterly's splendors we hang up?
Or what Magazine's to mention, of the slenderest pretension,
  Beside CHRISTOPHER's princely prime bang-up?
There's but ONE besides in Britain, I consider 'twould be fitting
  To name after and over that rare man,

* Sir James Mackintosh.—M.

'Tis the TORY on the throne—for his heart is all our own,
And 'tis this KEEPS their elbows so bare, man,
Poor souls!
Their hearts low, and their breeches so bare, man!

8.

Oh! with joy and exultation we look round about the nation,
And contemplate the sum of her glories.
Oh! how just is our delight! Oh! whoever IS is right,
Oh! the prime ones are every where TORIES!
Look whatever way you please, 'tis in these, and only these,
All the pride of the Island reposes—
We've the corn and they've the chaff,—they've the scorn and we've the laugh,—
They've the nettles and ours are the roses,
Dear boys!
They've the nettles and we have the roses.

No. XII.—OCTOBER, 1823.

SCENE I.—*The Chaldee Closet.*

Enter NORTH *and* MR. AMBROSE.

Mr. Ambrose. I hope, my dear sir, you will not be offended; but I cannot conceal my delight in seeing you lighten my door again, after two months' absence. God bless you, sir, it does my heart good to see you so strong, so fresh, so ruddy. I feared this wet autumn might have been too much for you in the country. But Heaven be praised—Heaven be praised—here you are again, my gracious sir! What can I do for you?—What will you eat?—What will you drink?—Oh dear! let me stir the fire; the poker is too heavy for you.

North. Too heavy!—Devil a bit. Why, Ambrose, I have been in training, out at Mr. Hogg's, you know. Zounds, I could fell a buffalo. Well, Ambrose, how goes the world?

Mr. Ambrose. No reason to complain, sir. Oysters never were better; and the tap runs clear as amber. Let me hang up your crutch, my dear sir. There now, I am happy. The house looks like itself now. Goodness me, the padding has had a new cover! But the wood-work has seen service.

North. That it has, Ambrose. Why, you rogue, I got a three-pronged fork fastened to the end on't, and I used it as a lister.

Mr. Ambrose. A lister, sir?—I ask your pardon.

North. Ay, a lister. I smacked it more than once into the side of a salmon; but the water has been so drumly, that Sandy Ballantyne himself could do little or nothing.

Mr. Ambrose. Nothing surprises me now, sir, that you do. We have a pretty pheasant in the larder. Shall I venture to roast him for your honor?

North. At nine o'clock I expect a few friends; so add a stubble-goose, some kidneys, and hodge-podge; for the night is chilly; and a delicate stomach like mine, Ambrose, requires coaxing. Glenlivet.

Mr. Ambrose. Here, sir, is your accustomed caulker.

(NORTH *drinks, while* MR. AMBROSE *keeps looking upon him with a smile of delighted deference, and exit.*)

North (*solus*). What paper have we here?—Morning Chronicle

Copyright sold for £40,000. A lie.*—Let me see; any little traitorous copy of bad verses? Not one. Tommy Moore and Jack Bowring are busy otherwise. Poor occupation for gentlemen, sneering at Church and King. "That wretched creature, Ballasteros!" Nay, nay; this won't do; I am getting drowsy.—(*Snores.*)

Enter MR. AMBROSE. *A sound of feet in the lobby.*

Mr. Ambrose. Mr. Tickler, sir—Mr. Mullion—and a strange gentleman. Beg your pardon, gentlemen; tread softly. He SLEEPS. *Bonus dormitat Homerus.*

Strange Gentleman. Wonderful city. Modern Athens indeed. Never heard a more apt quotation.

Tickler (*slap-bang on* NORTH'S *shoulder*). Awake, arise, or be for ever fallen! Mullion, shake him by the collar; or a slight kick on the shins. Awake, Samson; the Philistines are upon thee!

(NORTH *yawns; stretches himself; sits erect; stares about him; rises and bows.*)

Mullion. Capital subject, faith, for Wilkie. A choice bit. Odds safe us, what a head! Gie's your haun, my man. Hooly, hooly; your nieve's like a vice. You deevil, you hae jirted the bluid frae my finger-ends.

North. Mr. Tickler, you have not introduced me to the young gentleman.

Tickler. Mr. Vivian Joyeuse.†

North. Young gentleman—happy to take you by the hand. I hope you have no objections to smoking.

Joyeuse. I have no objections to any thing; but I shall hardly be on an equal footing with you Sons of the Mist.

North (*to Tickler*). Gentlemanly lad.—(*Re-enter* AMBROSE.)—

* Mr. James Perry, "a canny Scotchman," had made the *Morning Chronicle* one of the daily journals of London. It was the recognised organ of the Whig or Opposition party. He was on intimate terms with the leaders of that party, and had shown, more than once, that he was to be trusted. In his paper appeared the earliest, and some of the best, of Moore's political squibs. There, also, did Byron sometimes appear. The editorial part was ably performed, and the dramatic critic was no less a person than William Hazlitt. Perry was the founder of the European Magazine in 1782. He died in 1821, and the *Chronicle* was then sold to Mr. Clements, proprietor of the *Observer* and *Bell's Life*, which continue to have large circulation. Clements paid £40,000 for the copyright, presses and types. The paper gradually declined in his hands, until after having had it about thirteen years, he sold it to Sir John Easthope, a stock-broker, about the period (Nov. 1834) when *The Times* suddenly turned round, on Peel's accession to office, and became Conservative instead of Radical. The *Chronicle*, for a time, seemed likely to resume its position as a Liberal organ, but its proprietor was believed to have used part of its machinery (foreign correspondents) for stock-jobbing purposes, and the shadow settled on it again. It was purchased from him by a party of gentlemen possessed of much wealth, who forthwith gave it a Puseyite politico-religious leaning. This it retains, but it is said that Baron Rothschild, of London, has entered into the proprietorship. At present, its leading articles have no weight, but its foreign correspondence is generally admirable. The article in the *Edinburgh Review*, on the "Morning Chronicle," was written by Hazlitt.—M.

† In *Knight's Quarterly Magazine*, one of the best periodicals ever published in London, there was an imitation of the Noctes, lively, well written, and with the character of each speaker well individualized. Mr. Vivian Joyeuse was the *nom de plume* assumed by one of Knight's contributors. Macaulay, Praed, John Moultrie, Chauncey Hare Townshend, Charles Knight, (Editor and publisher,) were among the leading writers in this periodical.—M.

Hollo! Ambrose? What now? Have you seen a ghost? or has the cat run off with the pheasant? If so, I trust he has insured his lives.

Mr. Ambrose. Here is a gentleman in the lobby, inquiring for Mr. Tickler.

Tickler. Show him in. Hope it is not that cursed consignment of cotton from Manchester—raw-twist, and——THE ENGLISH OPIUM-EATER!—huzza! huzza! (*Three hearty cheers.*)

Enter THE ENGLISH OPIUM-EATER* *and* THE ETTRICK SHEPHERD.

The Shepherd. Thank ye, lads; that's me you're cheering. Haud your hauns, ye hallan-shakers, or my drums will split. Sit down, sit down; my kite's as toom as the Cornal's head. I've had nae four-hours, and only a chack wi' Tam Grieve, as I came through Peebles. You'll hae ordered supper, Mr. North?

North. My dear late English Opium-Eater, this is an unexpected, unhoped for happiness. I thought you had been in Constantinople.

The Opium-Eater. You had no reason whatever for any such thought. Nò doubt I *might* have been at Constantinople—and I wish that I had been—but I have not been; and I am of opinion that you have not been there since we last parted, any more than myself. Have you, sir?

The Shepherd. I dinna ken, sir, where you hae been; but, hech, sirs, yon bit Opium Tract's a desperate interesting confession. It's perfectly dreadfu', yon pouring in upon you o' oriental imagery. But nae wunner. Sax thousand draps o' lowdnam! It's as muckle, I fancy, as a bottle o' whusky. I tried that experiment mysel, after reading the wee wud wicked wark, wi' five hunner draps, and I couped ower, and continued in ae snore frae Monday night till Friday morning. But I had naething to confess; naething at least that wad gang into words; for it was a week-lang, dull, dim dwawm o' the mind, with a kind o' soun' bumming in my lugs; and clouds, clouds, clouds hovering round and round; and things o' sight, no made for the sight; and an awfu' smell, like the rotten sea; and a confusion between the right hand and the left; and events o' auld lang syne, like the torments o' the present hour, wi' naething to mark ony thing by; and doubts o' being quick or dead; and something rouch, rouch, like the fleece o' a ram, and motion as of everlasting earthquake; and nae re-

* Thomas de Quincey, whose "Confessions of an English Opium Eater," in the *London Magazine*, immediately obtained him high repute as a writer, has done nothing half as good, during his four and thirty years of authorship, as that, his first production, Well learned in ancient and modern tongues, he has written a vast quantity, but when his transcendental and unintelligible metaphysics are weeded out, the actual substance of his works will be in a small space. With the German school of philosophy he is well acquainted, and has endeavored, chiefly by translation, to make his countrymen familiar with it. He has written a great deal —chiefly for magazines. Sometimes he is extremely graphic and picturesque, but his great fault is diffuseness, want of concentration, and an inability to discuss a subject without digressions—*apropos* to nothing. His writings have been published in America in a collected form; this has not been done in England, where only a selection could obtain a sale.—M.

membrance o' my ain Christian name; and a dismal thought that I was converted into a quadruped cretur, wi' four feet; and a sair drowth aye sook, sooking awa' at empty win'; and the lift doukin down to smoor me; and the moon within half a yard o' my nose; but no just like the moon either. O Lord safe us! I'm a' grewing to think o't; but how could I CONFESS? for the sounds and the sights were baith shadows; and whare are the words for expressing the distractions o' the immaterial soul drowning in matter, and wastling wi' unknown power to get ance mair a steady footing on the greensward o' the waking world?

Mullion. Hear till him—hear till him. Ma faith, that's equal to the best bit in a' the Confessions.

The Shepherd. Haud your tongue, you sumph; it's nae sic things. Mr. Opium-Eater, I used aye to admire you, years sin syne; and never doubted you wad come out wi' some wark, ae day or ither, that wad gar the Gawpus glower.

The Opium-Eater. Gar the Gapus glower!—Pray, who is the Gapus?

The Shepherd. The public, sir; the public is the Gawpus. But what for are you sae metapheesical, man? There's just nae sense ava in metapheesics; they're a' clean nonsense. But how's Wudsworth?

The Opium-Eater. I have not seen him since half-past two o'clock on the 17th of September. As far as I could judge from a transitory interview, he was in good health and spirits; and I, think, fatter than he has been for some years. "Though that's not much."

The Shepherd. You lakers are clever chiels; I'll never deny that; but you are a conceited, upsetting set, ane and a' o' you. Great yegotists; and Wudsworth the warst o' ye a'; for he'll alloo nae merit to ony leevin cretur but himsel. He's a triflin cretur in yon Excursion; there's some bonny spats here and there; but nae reader can thole aboon a dozen pages o't at a screed, without whumbling ower on his seat. Wudsworth will never be popular. Naebody can get his blank poems aff by heart; they're ower wordy and ower windy, tak my word for't. Shackspear will say as muckle in four lines, as Wudsworth will say in forty.

The Opium-Eater. It is a pity that our great living poets cannot be more lavish of their praise to each other.*

The Shepherd. Me no lavish o' praise? I think your friend a great man—but——

North. I wish, my dear Shepherd, that you would follow Mr.

*** De Quincey has written a great deal about Wordsworth, apparently as his friend and admirer, but it may be noticed that a certain deprecatory tone runs through his description of the man and estimate of the poet. Wordsworth and his friends, I know, were ill-pleased with this, which—from early and extended kindnesses to De Quincey—Wordsworth had no reason to expect.—M.**

Wordsworth's example, and confine yourself to poetry. Oh! for another Queen's Wake.

The Shepherd. I'll no confine myself to poetry for ony man. Neither does he. It's only the other day that he published "A Guide to the Lakes," and he might as well have called it a Treatise on Church Music. And then his prose work about Spain* is no half as gude as a leading paragraph in Jamie Ballantyne's Journal. The sense is waur, and sae is the wording—and yet sae proud and sae pompous, as gin nane kent about peace and war but himsel, as gin he could fecht a campaign better than Wellington, and negotiate wi' foreign courts like anither Canning. Southey writes prose better than Wudsworth, a thousand and a thousand times. Wha's that glowering at me in the corner? Wha are ye, my lad?

Mr. Vivian Joyeuse. I am something of a nondescript.

The Shepherd. An Englisher—an Englisher—I've a gleg lug for the deealicks. You're frae the South—but nae Cockney. You're ower weel-spoken and ower weel-faured. Are ye married?

Mr. Joyeuse. I fear that I am. I am fresh from Gretna.

The Shepherd. Never mind—never mind—you're a likely laddie—and hae a blink in thae eyne o' yours that shows smeddum. What are all the people in England doing just the now?

Mr. Joyeuse. All reading No. II. of Knight's Quarterly Magazine.

North. A very pleasant miscellany. Tickler, you have seen the work. Mr. Joyeuse, your very good health, and success to Knight's Quarterly Magazine.† (*General breeze.*)

The Shepherd. Did ony body ever see siccan a blush? Before you hae been a contributor for a year, you'll hae lost a' power of reddening in the face. You may as weel try then to blush wi' the palm o' your hand.

Tickler. Mullion, who knows every thing and every body, brought Mr. Joyeuse to Southside, and I have only to hope that his fair bride will not read him a curtain-lecture to-night, when she hears where he has been, among the madcaps.

The Shepherd. Curtain-lecture! We are a' ower gude contributors to be fashed wi' any daft nonsense o' that sort. Na—na—but what's this Quarterly Magazine?—I never heard tell o't.

North. Why, I will speak for Mr. Joyeuse. It is a gentlemanly miscellany—got together by a clan of young scholars, who look upon the world with a cheerful eye, and all its ongoings with a spirit of hopeful kindness. I cannot but envy them their gay juvenile temper,

* In 1809, with an intention of urging that the Peninsular War be vigorously carried on, (with a view to checking the vast puissance of Napoleon,) Wordsworth published a prose pamphlet on the relations of Great Britain, Spain, and Portugal to each other.—M.

† *Knight's Quarterly Magazine* died after completing three volumes. It is very difficult to be obtained now, at any price, in England, and is curious as containing, among other things, as much of Macaulay's early poetry and prose as would fill a volume.—M.

so free from gall and spite; and am pleased to the heart's core with their elegant accomplishments. Their egotism is the joyous freedom of exulting life; and they see all things in a glow of enthusiasm which makes ordinary objects beautiful, and beauty still more beauteous. Do you wish for my advice, my young friend?

Mr. Joyeuse. Upon honor, Sir Christopher, I am quite overpowered. Forgive me, when I confess that I had my misgivings on entering your presence. But they are all vanished. Believe me that I value most highly the expression of your good-will and friendly sentiments towards myself and coadjutors.

North. Love freedom—continue, I ought to say, to love it; and prove your love, by defending all the old sacred institutions of this great land. Keep aloof from all association with base ignorance, and presumption, and imposture. Let all your sentiments be kind, generous and manly, and your opinions will be safe, for the heart and the head are the only members of the Holy Alliance, and woe unto all men when they are not in union. Give us some more of your classical learning—more of the sparkling treasures of your scholarship, for in that all our best miscellanies are somewhat deficient, (mine own not excepted,) and you may here lead the way. Are you not Etonians, Wykeamists, Oxonians, and Cantabs, and in the finished grace of manhood? Don't forget your classics.

The Shepherd. Dinna mind a single word that Mr. North says about classics, Mr. Joyous. Gin ye introduce Latin and Greek into your Magazine, you'll clean spoil't. There's naething like à general interest taken in the classics throughout the kintra; and I whiles jalouse that some praise Homer and Horace, and Polydore Virgil, and "the rest," that ken but little about them, and couldna read the crabbed Greek letters aff-hand without stuttering.

The Opium-Eater. All the magazines of the day are deficient; first, in classical literature, secondly, in political economy, and thirdly, in psychology.

The Shepherd. Tuts, tuts.

Tickler. Mr. Joyeuse, I agree with North in strenuously recommending you and your friends to give us classical dissertations, notes, notices, conjectures, imitations, translations, and what not. Confound the Cockneys! they will be prating on such points—and have smuggled their cursed pronunciation into Olympus. There is County Tims proceeding, step by step, from Robert Bruce to Jupiter Tonans; and addressing DianAR as familiarly as he would a nymph of Covent-Garden, coming to redeem two silver teaspoons.* There was John Keats enacting ApollAR, because he believed that personage to have

* The Scotch and the Irish very contemptuously regard the Cockney mispronunciation of words ending with a vowel. To say Julia*r*, Appolla*r*, sofa*r*, Anna*r*-Maria*r*, and lo*r*, for Julia, Apollo, sofa, Anna-Maria, law, &c., is true Cockney;—but they have not an idea*r* of the error they thus fall into. On the American stage, where so many English performers are to

been, like himself, an apothecary, and sickening, because the public was impatient of his drugs. There is Barry, quite beside himself with the spectacle of Deucalion and Psyche peopling the earth anew by chucking stones over their shoulders—in my humble opinion, I confess, a most miserable pastime;—and there is King Leigh absolutely enlisting Mars into the Hampstead heavy dragoons, and employing him as his own ORDERLY.

The Shepherd. Capital, Mr. Tickler, capital. I aye like you when you are wutty. Gang on—let me clap you on the back—slash awa at the Cockneys, for they are a squad I scunner at; and oh! but you hae in troth put them down wi' a vengeance!

Tickler. Hazlitt is the most loathsome, Hunt the most ludicrous. Pygmalion is so brutified and besotted now, that he walks out into the public street, enters a bookseller's shop, mounts a stool, and represents Priapus in Ludgate Hill.* King Leigh would not do this for the world. From such enormities he is preserved, partly by a sort of not unamiable fastidiousness, but chiefly by a passionate admiration of his yellow breeches, in which he feels himself satisfied with his own divine perfections. I do not dislike Leigh Hunt by any manner of means. By the way, Mr. Joyeuse, there are some good stanzas about him, in Knight—for example:

They'll say—I shan't believe 'em—but they'll say,
  That Leigh's become what once he most abhorr'd,
Has thrown his independence all away,
  And dubb'd himself toad-eater to a lord;
And though, of course, you'll hit as hard as they,
  I fear you'll find it difficult to ward
Their poisoned arrows off—you'd best come back,
Before the Cockney kingdom goes to wrack.

The Examiner's grown dull as well as dirty,
  The Indicator's sick, the Liberal dead—
I hear its readers were some six-and-thirty;†
  But really 'twas too stupid to be read.
'Tis plain your present partnership has hurt ye;
  Poor brother John "looks up, and is not fed,"
For scarce a soul will purchase, or get through one,
E'en of his shilling budgets of Don Juan.

North. Do you quote from memory? I remember a good stanza in Don Juan about John Keats, Hazlitt's Apollo and Apothecary.

be seen and heard, the Cockneys proper may at once be detected by this abuse of the consonant *r*.—M.

* William Hazlitt, so many years persecuted by *Blackwood*, was a quiet, reserved student, who seldom mingled in society, was rarely personal in his writings, and had broken down his nervous system by excessive fondness for strong tea.—M.

† Of Leigh Hunt's repeated efforts to establish a periodical, which it would pay him to continue, The Indicator was the best. It was crowded with affectations, (or worse, else it would not have been Hunt's,) but there was a freshness running through it which was real. Hunt loved books and nature, and liked to write on both subjects.—M.

John Keats, who was killed off by one critique,
  Just as he *really promised* something great,
If not intelligible—without Greek,
  Contrived to talk about the gods of late,
Much as they might have been supposed to speak.
  Poor fellow! his was an untoward fate;
'Tis strange, the mind, that very fiery particle,
Should let itself be snuff'd out by an article.

Tickler. Exactly so. Now, what a pretty fellow is the publisher of Don Juan! John Keats was the especial friend of himself and brother; and they both raved like bedlamites against all who were at all sharp upon the poor apothecary. But what will not the base love of filthy lucre!—Alas! his lordship is driven to degradation. And who but this crew would become parties to a libel on their own best-beloved dead friend?

The Shepherd. There's nae answering questions like these. The puir devil must be dumb. A crabbed discontented creature o' a neebor o' ours takes in the Examiner; and I see they are aye yammering and compleening upon you lads here, but canna speak out. They are a' tongue-tied, and can only girn, girn, girn.* Blackwood here, and Blackwood there, but nothing made out or specified. Bandy-legged Baldy Dinmont himself allows they are just like a parcel o' weans frighted at their dominie, when Christopher appears, and lose a' power to bar the maister out, when they see the taws ance mair, and begin dinglan in their doups in the very fever o' an imaginary skelping.

North. It is all very true, my dear Shepherd. I often think that our weak points have never yet been attacked, for is it not singular that no impression has ever yet been made on any part of our whole line? Good gracious! only think on our shameful violation of truth! Why, that of itself, if properly exposed, and held out to universal detestation, would materially diminish our sale in this great matter-of-fact age and country. Who, like us, has polluted the sources of history?

The Shepherd. Hush, hush!—We dinna ken Mr. Joyous weel aneuch yet to lippen to him. Perhaps he'll betray the sacred confidence o' private friendship! Isna that the way they word it?

Mr. Joyeuse. I shall make no rash promises. My reply to the Shepherd shall be in a quotation. Byron loquitur.

They err'd, as aged men will do; but by
  And by we'll talk of that; and if we don't,
'Twill be because our notion is not high
  Of politicians, and their double front,

* *Girn*—to grin.—M.

Who live by lies, yet dare not boldly lie:—
  Now, what I love in women is, they won't,
Or can't do otherwise, than lie; but do it
So well, the very truth seems falsehood to it.

And, after all, what is a lie? 'Tis but
  The truth in masquerade; and I defy
Historians, heroes, lawyers, priests, to put
  A fact without some leaven of a lie.
The very shadow of true truth would shut
  Up annals, revelations, poesy,
And prophecy—except it should be dated
Some years before the incidents related.

North. Well, well, we stand excused like our neighbors, the rest of the human race. But what say you to our gross inconsistency, in raising a mortal one day to the skies, and another pulling him an angel down? In one article you are so saluted in the nose with the bagpipe of our praise, "that you cannot contain, you ninny, for affection;" and at p. 36 you find yourself so vilified, vituperated, tarred and feathered, that you are afraid even to run for it, and would fain hide yourself for a month in a dark closet. Who can defend this?

Tickler. I can. The fault is not with us, but it lies in the constitution of human nature. For, to-day, a given man is acute, sensible, enlightened, eloquent, and so forth. We praise and pet him accordingly—smooth him down the back along with the hair—give him a sop —tell him he is a clever dog, and call him Trusty, or Help, or Neptune, or Jupiter. The very next day we see the same given man in a totally different predicament, that is to say, utterly senseless, worse than senseless, raving. What do we do then? We either eye him askance, and not wishing to be bitten, and to die of the hydrophobia, make the best of our way home, or to Ambrose's, without saying a word; or we take a sapling and drub him off; or if the worst come to the worst, we shoot him dead upon the spot. Call you this inconsistency? Not it indeed. Shall I illustrate our conduct by examples?

North. There is no occasion for that at present. But what do you say to our COARSENESS?

The Shepherd. Ay, ay, Mr. Tickler, what do you say to your coorseness?

Tickler. In the meantime, James, read that, and you will know what I say about yours. (*Gives him a critique on the Three Perils.*) But as to the occasional coarsenesses to be found in Maga, I am, from the very bottom (no coarseness in that, I hope) of my heart, sorry to see them, and much sorrier to think that I should myself have written too many of them. They must be disgusting occasionally to delicate minds; nay, even to minds not delicate. And I verily believe, that to Englishmen in general, this is our very greatest fault. With sincere sorrow, if not contrition, do I, for one, confess my fault; and should I ever write any more for the Magazine, I hope to keep myself within the limits of decorum. Intense wit will season intense coarseness; but then I am at times very coarse indeed, without being witty at all; and am convinced, that some passages in my letters, although these are on the whole popular, and deservedly so, have been read by not a few whom I would be most unwilling to offend, with sentiments of the deepest and most unalloyed disgust.

Mr. Joyeuse. Not at all, Mr. Tickler—not at all. Believe it not, my dear sir. Coarse you may occasionally be, but you are always witty.

The Opium-Eater. I have always admired Mr. Tickler's letters, there is such a boundless overflow of rejoicing fancies; and what if one particular expression, or sentence, even paragraph, be what is called coarse, (of coarseness as a specific, definite, and determinate quality of thought, I have no clear idea,) it is lost, swallowed up, and driven along in the ever-flowing tide; and he who should be drowned in trying to pick it up, could never, in my opinion, be a fit subject for resuscitation, but would deserve to be scouted not only by the humane, but by the Humane Society. If I were permitted to say freely what are your greatest faults, I should say that——

Enter MR. AMBROSE, *just in the nick of time.*

Mr. Ambrose. Gentlemen, supper's on the table.

North. Mr. Joyeuse, lend me your arm.

(*Exeunt, followed by the Opium-Eater, Tickler, the Shepherd, and Mullion.*)

SCENE II.—*Blue Parlor.*

Tickler. Now for the goose. A ten-pounder. All our geese are swans. There, saw ye ever a bosom sliced more dexterously?—Off go the legs—smack goes the back into shivers—so much for the doup. Reach me over the apple sauce. Mullion, give us the old pun upon the sage. Who chooses goose?

Mullion. I'll trouble you for the breast and legs, wi' a squash o' the apple crowdy. Ambrose, bread and potatoes, and a pot of porter.

The Opium-Eater. Mr. Ambrose, be so good as to bring me coffee.

Shepherd. Coffee——!! What the deevil are you gaun to do wi' coffee at this time o' night, man? Wha ever soops upon coffee? Come here, Mr. Ambrose, tak him ower this trencher o' het kidneys, I never hae touched them.

Tickler. Is your pullet tender, Kit? There be vulgar souls who prefer barn-door fowl to pheasants, mutton to venison, and cider to champagne. So there be who prefer corduroy to cassimere breeches, and

16*

the "Blue and Yellow" to green-gowned Maga.* To such souls, your smooth-shining transparent grape is not so sweet as your small red hairy gooseberry. The brutes cannot dine without potatoes to their fish——

The Shepherd. What say ye, Mr. Tickler? wadna you eat potatoes to sawmont? I thought he had kent better than to place gentility on sic like gruns. At the Duke's, every one did just as he liked best himself, and tell't the flunkies to take their plates to ilka dish that pleased their e'e, without ony restraint. But ye haena been muckle in hee life these last fifty years.

Tickler. My dear Mullion, I beseech you not to draw your knife through your mouth in that most dangerous fashion: you'll never stop till ye cut it from ear to ear. For the sake of our common humanity, use your fork.

The Shepherd. Never mind him, Mullion—he's speaking havers. I hae used my knife that way ever since I was fed upon flesh, and I never cut my mouth to any serious extent, above a score times in my life.

(MR. AMBROSE *sets down a silver coffee-pot, and a plate of muffins, before the Opium-Eater.*)

The Opium-Eater. I believe, Mr. Hogg, that it has been ascertained by medical men, through an experience of some thousand years, that no eater of hot and heavy suppers ever yet saw his grand climacteric. I do not mention this as any argument against hot and heavy suppers, except to those persons who are desirous of attaining a tolerable old age. You, probably, have made up your mind to die before that period; in which case, not to eat hot and heavy suppers, if you like them, would truly be most unreasonable, and not to be expected from a man of your acknowledged intelligence and understanding. I beg now to return your kidneys, with an assurance that I have not touched them, and they still seem to retain a considerable portion of animal heat.

The Shepherd. I dinna ken what's the matter wi' me the night, but I'm no half so hungry as I expeckit. Thae muffins look gaen inviting; the coffee comes gurgling out wi' a brown sappy sound. I wonder whare Mr. Ambrose got that ream.† A spider might crawl on't. I wush, sir, you would gie us a single cup, and a wheen muffins. (*The Opium-Eater benignantly complies.*)

North. Pray, Tickler, what sort of an eater do you suppose Barry Cornwall?

Tickler. The merry-thought of a chick—three tea-spoonfuls of peas, the eighth part of a French roll, a sprig of cauliflower, and an almost imperceptible dew of parsley and butter, would, I think, dine the author of "The Deluge." By the way, there is something surely

* Maga, as published in Edinburgh, is clothed in a covering which, if not exactly entitling it to the name of "green-gowned Maga," may be said to be the color of *sage*.—M.

† *Ream*—cream.—M.

not a little absurd in the notion of a person undertaking the "Flood," whom the slightest shower would drive under a balcony, or into a hackney-coach. I have no doubt that he carried "The Deluge" in his pocket to Colburn, under an umbrella.

North. My dear Tickler, you cannot answer the very simplest question without running into your usual personalities. What does Byron dine on, think ye?

Tickler. Byron!—Why, bull-beef and pickled salmon, to be sure. What else would he dine on? I never suspected, at least accused him, of cannibalism. And yet, during the composition of Cain, there is no saying what he may have done.

The Shepherd. I'm thinking, sir, when Tam Muir was penning his Loves of the Angels, that he fed upon calf-foot jeelies, stewed prunes, the dish they ca' curry, and oysters. These last are desperate for that.

Tickler. Did you ever hear it said that Mr. Rogers never eat animal food, nor drank spirits?

North. I have seen him do both.

Tickler. Well, you astonish me. I could not otherwise have believed it.

Mullion. Never, never, never in all my born days, did I eat such a glorious plateful of kidneys as that which Mr. Opium-Eater lately transmitted to me through the hands of our Ambrose. I feel as if I could bump my crown against the ceiling. I hae eaten the apple o' the tree of knowledge. I understand things I never had the least ettling of before. Will ony o' ye enter into an argument? Choose your subject, and I'm your man, in theology, morality, anatomy, chemistry, history, poetry, and the fine arts. My very language is English, whether I will or no, and I am overpowered with a power of words.

The Opium-Eater (*aside to* TICKLER). I fear that Mr. Mullion's excessive animation is owing to a slight mistake of mine. I carelessly allowed a few grains of opium to slide out of my box into the plate of kidneys which Mr. Hogg sent for my delectation; and ere I could pick them out, Mr. Ambrose wafted away the poisoned dish to Mr. Mullion, at a signal, I presume, understood between the parties.

Mullion. I say, Opium-Eater, or Opossum, or what do they call you, did you ever see a unicorn? What signifies an Egyptian ibis, or crocodile of the Nile? I have a unicorn at livery just now in Rose Street. Tickler, will you mount? Noble subject for John Watson.* No man paints a unicorn better.

North. John Watson paints every thing well. But (*aside to* THE SHEPHERD) saw ye ever such extraordinary eyes in a man's head as in Mullion's?

*** Now Sir John Watson Gordon, President of the Scottish Academy of the Fine Arts, and one of the best portrait-painters in Great Britain.—M.**

Mullion. Francis Maximus Macnab's Theory of the Universe is the only sensible book I ever read. Mr. Ambrose—Mr. Ambrose—bring me the Scotsman.

The Shepherd (*to* NORTH). I have heard there was something wrang wi' Mullion at school; and it's breaking out you see noo. He's gane clean wud. I wus he mayna bite.

Tickler. Sell your unicorn to Polito, Mullion.

Mullion. Polito!—ay, a glorious collection of wild beasts—a perfect House o' Commons; where each tribe of the beasts has its representative. Mild, majestic, towzy-headed, big-pawed, lean-hurdied lion, saw ye ever Mungo Park? Tiger, tiger, royal tiger—jungle-jumping, son-o'-Sir-Hector-Munro-devouring tiger! (*Rises.*)

The Shepherd. Whare are you gaun?—Wait an hour or twa, and I'll see ye hame.

Mullion. I am off to the Pier of Leith. What so beautiful as the sea at midnight! A glorious constellation art thou, O Great Bear! Hurra! Hurra! (*Exit, without his hat.*)

The Opium-Eater. I must give this case, in a note, to a new edition of my Confessions. If Mr. Mullion did really eat all the kidneys, he must now have in his stomach that which is about equal to five hundred and seventy drops of laudanum.

The Shepherd. Eat a' the kidneys!—That he did, I'll swear.

The Opium-Eater. Most probably, Mr. Mullion will fall into a state of utter insensibility in a couple of hours. Convulsions may follow, and then—death.

The Shepherd. Deevil the fears. Mullion 'ill dee nane. I'll wauger he'll be eating twa eggs to his breakfast the morn, and a shave o' the red roun'; lurking frae him a' the time wi' een as sharp as darnin' needles, and paunin' in his cup for mair sugar.

Tickler. Suppose now that the conversation be made to take a literary or philosophical turn. Mr. North, what is your opinion on the influence of literature on human life?

North. Why, after all, a love or knowledge of literature forms but a small and unimportant part of the character either of man or woman. Have we not all dear friends whom we admit to our most sacred confidence, who never take up a printed book (Maga excepted) from year's end to year's end? How few married women remember, or at least care a straw about, any thing they read in their maidenhood, when in search of husbands! Take any lady, young, old, or middle-aged, and examine the dear creature with a few cross-questions, and you will not fail to be delighted with her consummate ignorance of all that is written in books. But what of that? Do you like, love, esteem, despise, or hate her, the more or less?—Not a whit.*

* "And oh, ye lords of ladies intellectual,
Inform us truly, have they not hen-peck'd you all!"—M.

The Opium-Eater. The female mind knows intuitively all that is really worth knowing; and the performance of duty with women is simply an outward manifestation of an inward state agreeable to nature; both alike unconsciously, it may be, existing in perfect adaptation to the peculiar circumstances of life. Books may, or may not, cherish and direct the tendencies of a female character, naturally fine, delicate, pure, and also strong; but most certain is it that books are not the sine-quâ-non condition of excellence. The woman who never saw a book may be infinitely superior, even in all those matters of which books treat, to the woman who has read, and read intelligently, 10,000 volumes. For one domestic incident shall teach more wisdom than the catastrophes of a hundred novels; and one single smile from an infant at its mother's breast may make that mother wiser in love than even all the philosophy of Plato and the poetry of Wordsworth.

The Shepherd. There now—I just ca' that sound sense and a true apothegm. And what'll ye say to poets and sic like, that put meretricious thoughts into the nature of woman, and dazzle the puir innocent things' eyne till they can see naething like the path of duty, but gang ramstam and camstrairy, aiblins to the right hand and aiblins to the left? In that case, one might call his brother a fool, without danger of the fire.

Tickler. Well spoken, my dear James. I beg your pardon, once more, for having ever called you "a coorse tyke." You have a soul, James; and that is enough.

The Shepherd. We have all sowls, Mr. Tickler, and that some folks will come to know at last. But I am nae dour Calvinistic minister, to deal out damnation on my brethren. All I say is this, that if the lowest shepherd lad in a' Scotland were to compose poems just on purpose to seduce lasses, he would be kicked like a foot-ba' frae ae parish to anither. And will gentlemen o' education, wha can read Greek, and hae been at a college-university, do that and be cuddled for't, that would bring a loon like Jock Linton to the stang, the pond, or the pump?

North. You don't mean to tell me that there are no such songs among the old Scottish poetry, Shepherd?

The Shepherd. No half a dizzen in the hail byke—and them wrote, I jalouse, by lazy monks, losels, and gaberlunzie-men.* But what I say is true, that love-verses, composed wi' a wicked spirit o' deceit and corruption, are no rife in ony national poetry; and, least o' all, in that of our ain Scotland. Men are men—and, blessings on them, women are women; and mony a droll word is said, and droll thing done, among kintra folks. But they a' ettle at a kind o' innocence; and when they fa', it is the frailty of nature for the maist part, and there is

* *Gaberlunzie*—a mendicant; a poor guest who cannot pay for his entertainment.—M.

true repentance and reformation. But funny sangs are the warst o' poets' sins in lowly life; and if siccan a chiel as Tam Muir, bonny bonny writer as he is, were to settle in the Forest, he might hae a gowden fleece, but in faith he would soon be a wether.

The Opium-Eater. Amatory poetry is not only the least intellectual, but it is also the least imaginative and the least passionate of poetry.

The Shepherd. Hoots, man—I dinna understand you sae weel now. What say ye?

The Opium-Eater. In mere amatory poetry—that is, verse addressed to ladies in a spirit of complimentary flirtation, there is a necessary prostration or relinquishment of the intellect: the imaginative faculty cannot deal with worthless trifles; and passion, which cleaves to flesh and blood, dies and grows drowsy on a cold thin diet of words.

The Shepherd. That's better expressed; at least, it suits better the level o' my understanding, and that's the criterion we a' judge by. Now, sir, this I wull say for the Lake folk, that they, ane and a', without exceptions, excel in painting she-characters. Wudsworth, Wulson, Soothey, Coalrich, and yourself, sir, (for confound me gin you're no a poet,) make me far mair in love with the "Women-Folk—the Women-Folk," (wait a wee and you'll hear me sing that sang,) than Tam Muir and a' that crew. Wulson's gotten awfu' proud, they say, since he was made a Professor; but let him lecture as eloquently's he likes, frae Lammas to Lammas, for fifty year—and by the Isle o' Palms and the City o' the Plague wull he be remembered at last. They're baith fu' o' havers; but oh! man, every now and then, he is shublime, and for pawthos he beats a'. Wudsworth wunna alloo that; but it's true, and I hae pleasure in saying it.

The Opium-Eater. If, by pathos, you mean mere human feeling, as it exists unmodified by the imagination, then our opinions respecting the two poets coincide. But in "the thoughts that do often lie too deep for tears," I conceive William Wordsworth unequalled among the sons of song. Mark me—I do not say that the other poet has no imagination; he has a fine and powerful imagination. But——

The Shepherd. You may say ony thing against him ye like; but you needna ruze Wudsworth aboon every body, leevin or dead. Ae thing he does excel in—the making o' deep and true observations and reflections, that come in unco weel among dull and barren places, and wad serve for mottoes or themes. Wudsworth's likewise a capital discourser in a vivy-voce twa-handed crack, awa' frae his ain house. About yon Lakes, he's just perfectly intolerable.

Tickler. Come—have done with the Lakers.

North. I confess criticism is not what it ought to be, not what it might be. But am I a bad critic, sir?

The Opium-Eater. No, sir, you may justly be called a good critic. For, in the first place, you have a reverent, I had almost said a devout regard for genius, and not only unhesitatingly, but with alacrity and delight, pay it homage. You feel no degradation of self in the exaltation of others; and seem to me never to write such pure English, as when inspired by the divine glow of admiration. No other critic do I know since Aristotle, to compare with you in this great essential; and feeling that on all grand occasions you are cordial and sincere, I peruse your eloquent expositions, and your fervid strains of thought, not always with entire consentaneity of sentiment, yet, without doubt, always in a state approximating to mental unison; a state in which I am made conscious of the concord subsisting between the great strings of our hearts, even by the slight discords that I internally hear proceeding with an under tone, among the inferior notes of that mighty and mysterious instrument.

The Shepherd. Gude safe us!—that's grand—and it's better than grand, it's true. I forgie the lads a' their sins, for sake o' their free, out-spoken, open-handed praise, when they do mean to do a kind thing. They lauch far ower muckle at me in their Magazine; but I canna deny, I proudly declare't, that none o' a' the critics o' this age hae had sic an insight into my poetical genius, or roused me wi' sic fearsome eloquence. When they eulogize me in that gate, my blŏod gangs up like spirits o' wine, and I fin' myself a' gruin' wi' a sort o' courageous sense o' power, as if I could do ony thing, write a better poem than the Lay of the Last Minstrel, fecht Bonaparte gin he was leevin, and snap my fingers in the very face o' "The Gude Man."

The Opium-Eater. But farther; you, sir, and some of your coadjutors, possess a fineness of tact and a delicacy of perception, that I in vain look for in the critical compositions of your contemporaries. You see and seize the beautiful evanescences of the poet's soul; you know the regions and the race of those fair spectral apparitions that come and go before the "eye that broods on its own heart." Never can poet lament over your blindness to beauty, your deafness to the sounds singing for ever, loud or low, from the shrine of nature;—sir, *you have no common sense*, and that in this age is the highest praise that can be bestowed on the immortal soul of man.

The Shepherd. The deevil the like o' that heard I ever since I was born! The want o' common sense, the greatest praise o' a man's immortal sowl!

North. The Opium-Eater is in the right, James; there is no common sense in your Kilmeny, in Coleridge's Ancient Mariner, in Wordsworth's Ruth, in our eloquent friend's "Confessions." Therefore dolts and dullards despise them—and will do to the end of time.

Tickler. I am of the old school, gentlemen, and lay my veto on the complete exclusion of common sense from a critical journal. But I understand what Opium would be at; and verily believe that he speaks the truth, when he says, that the wildest creation of genius, and the fairest too, pure poetry in short, and not only pure poetry, but every species of impassioned or imaginative prose, is understood better, deeper, and more comprehensively, by Maga than Mrs. Roberts——

The Opium-Eater. Mrs. Roberts? Pray, who is she?

Tickler. Why, My Grandmother. She edits the British Review.* It was a whim of the proprietors to try a female; so they bought Mother Roberts a pair of spectacles, a black sarsnet gown, and an armchair; and made her a howdy. She delivers the contributors, and swathes their bantlings. However, she has been, it is said, rather unfortunate in her practice; for although most of the brats to whom she has lent a helping hand, have come into the world alive, and cried lustily, yet seldom have they survived the ninth day. Poor things! they have all had Christian burial; but resurrection-men have grown to a lamentable height; and several of the ricketty infant charges of Mrs. Roberts have been traced to the dissecting-table. Lord Byron, it is said, has bottled a brace; but there is no end of such shocking stories, so push about the toddy, Christopher.

North. Pray, is it true, my dear Laudanum, that your "Confessions" have caused about fifty unintentional suicides?

The Opium-Eater. I should think not. I have read of six only; and they rested on no solid foundation.

Tickler. What if fifty foolish fellows have been buried in consequence of that delightful little Tractate on Education? Even then it would be cheap. It only shows the danger that dunces run into, when they imitate men of genius. T'other day, a strong-headed annuitant drank to the King's health, standing upon his head, on the pinnacle of a church spire. He afterwards described his emotions as most delightful. Up goes his nephew (his sister's son) next morning before breakfast; and in the excess of his loyalty, loses his heading; and at the conclusion of a perpendicular descent of 180 feet by the quadrant, alights upon a farmer's wife going to market with a pig in a poke; and without any criminal intention, commits one murder and two suicides. Was his uncle to blame?

North. The exculpation of the Opium-Eater is complete. A single illustration has smashed the flimsy morality of all idle objectors. And now, my dear friend, that you have fed and flourished fourteen years on opium, will you be persuaded to try a course of arsenic?

The Opium-Eater. I have tried one; but it did not suit my consti-

* Mr. Roberts, a lawyer, was proprietor and editor of a quarterly periodical called the *British Review;* and, when Byron jocosely said, in "Don Juan,"

"I've bribed my grandmamma's Review, the British,"

Mr. Roberts was so silly as to take the matter seriously, challenge Byron to name how and when the bribe was given, and declare that the whole was a falsehood. Byron responded in an amusing prose-epistle, signed "Worthy Clutterbuck," and turned the laugh against his opponent. It is difficult to realize the idea of a man being so completely what Hogg would call "just a green guse."—M.

tution either of mind or body. I leave the experiment to younger men.

Tickler. Pray, North, tell us how you kissed the rosy hours at Hogg's? Had you any rain?

North. I presume Noah would have thought it dry weather; but we had a little moisture for all that. The lake rose ten feet during the month I sorned* upon the Shepherd. First Sunday morning we thought of going to the kirk; but looking through my snug bed-room window, I saw a hay-rick with Damon and Phœbe sailing down the Yarrow at about seven knots; so I shouted to them, that if they were going to divine service, they would please apologize for me to the minister.

The Shepherd. Lord, man, it was an awfu' spate!† The stirks and the stots came down the water like straes; and in maist o' the pools, sheep were thicker than sawmon. I heucked a toop wi' a grilsh-flee, and played him wi' the pirn till I had his head up the Douglas-Burn, but he gied a wallop in the dead-thraws, and brak my tackle.

North. On the twentieth day, the waters began to subside; and then how beautiful the green hill-tops!

The Shepherd. Ay, they were e'en sae. For the flocks on a hundred hills were snaw-white, and the pastures drenched and dighted by the rains and the winds, till they kithed brichter than ony emerald, and launched up to the bonny blue regions aboon, that had their flocks, too, as quate and as white as the silly sheep o' the earth.

Tickler. Did the Shepherd give you good prog, North?

North. Prime—choice—exquis. Short jigots of five year olds, taper-jointed and thick-thighed, furnished, but not overloaded, with brown, crisp fat, deep-red when cut into, and oozing through every pore with the dark richness of natural gravy that overflowed the trencher, with a tempting tincture not to be contemplated with a dry mouth by the most abstemious of the children of men.

Tickler. Go on, you dog—what else?—Please, Mr. Joyeuse, ring the bell. Mr. Ambrose must bring us a devil. Or what do you say to supping over again?

North. To such mutton, add potatoes, dry even in such a season; so great is the Shepherd's agricultural skill. Ay, dry and mouldering, at a touch, into the aforesaid gravy, till the potato was lost to the eye in a heap of sanguine hue, but felt on the palate, amalgamated with the mountain mutton into a glorious mixture of animal and vegetable matter; each descending mouthful of which kept regenerating the whole man, and giving assurance of a good old age.

Tickler. Why the devil don't Ambrose answer the bell?

North. Then the salmon. In the Forest, fish follows flesh. It is

* *Sorned*—sojourned; it sometimes means sponged.—M.
† *Spate*—a flood.

the shoulder cut. Each flake is clear as a cairngorum—clear and curdled—sappy—most sappy.

Tickler. I say, why the devil don't Ambrose answer the bell?

(*Rises and pulls the worsted rope till it snaps in twain.*)

North. But then the moorfowl! The brown-game! The delicious mulattoes! The dear pepper-backs! Savoriness that might be sucked without satiety by saint and sinner for three quarters of an hour! Oh! James, that old cock!

The Shepherd. He was as gude a beast as I ever pree'd;* but I did nae mair than pree him; for frae neb to doup did our editor devour him, as he had been a bit snipe—he crunched his very banes, Mr. Tickler; and the very marrow o' the cretur's spine trinkled down his chin frae ilk corner o' his mouth, and gied him, for the while being, a most terrible and truculent feesionomy.

Enter MR. AMBROSE.

Tickler. Bring in the cold round, a welsh-rabbit, and a devil.

(*Exit* AMBROSE.)

North. My dear Shepherd, you will be dubbing me of the Gormandizing School of Oratory.

The Shepherd. Oratory! Gude faith, ye never uttered a syllable till the cloth was drawn. To be sure, you were gran' company at the cheek o' the fire, out ower our toddy. I never heard you mair pleasant and satirical. You seemed to hate every body, and like every body, and abuse every body, and plaud every body; and yet, through a' your deevilry there ran sic a vein o' unendurable funniness, that, had you been the foul Fiend himsel, I maun hae made you welcome to every thing in the house. Watty Bryden has had a stitch in his side ever sin' syne; and Fahope swears you're the queerest auld tyke that ever girned by an ingle.

North. Read that aloud, James. It is an article Ebony put into my hand this afternoon. Let us hear if it will do for next Number.

ON THE GORMANDIZING SCHOOL OF ORATORY.

NO. II.—LAWLESS.

We were informed by an observing Whig friend, who sat within two or three of Mr. Lawless's right or left hand at "The Glasgow Dinner," that never in his life did he see such a knife-and-fork played as by the IRISHMAN.† No sooner had Professor Mylne said grace,

* *Pree*—to taste.—M.

† In the autumn of 1822, at what was called "The Great Glasgow Dinner," one of the guests was John Lawless, editor of a paper in Belfast, called *The Irishman*. He was a man to make any quantity of speeches, being always ready, with the true *copia facundi*, and sometimes

than Mr. Lawless began munching bread, till the table-cloth before him was all over crumbs. After demolishing his own roll, nothing would satisfy him but to clutch his neighbor's; in which act of aggression, (to our minds, as unjustifiable as the partition of Poland,) he was resisted by the patriotic and empty-stomached constitutionalist, to whom, by the law of nature and nations, the staff of life did, beyond all controversy, belong. At this critical juncture, a waiter clapped down before the IRISHMAN a profound platter of warm soup, and the vermicelli in a moment disappeared from the face of the earth. As good luck would have it, another waiter covered the emptied trencher with one of hotch-potch; and our informant expresses his conviction, that Mr. Lawless, while gobbling up the mess, retained not the most distant recollection of his own prior performance. A cut of salmon then went the way of all flesh. The fish was instantly pursued, "without stop or stay, down the narrow way," by the spawl of a turkey. It appeared to our astonished informant, that the IRISHMAN had swallowed the shank; but in that he had afterwards reason to believe himself mistaken. True it was, however, that a cold tongue, half as long as his own, but with a different twang, went down the throat of the distinguished stranger from the sister kingdom. A dumpling, like a beetle, followed instanter; an apple-tart, about eight inches square, barely turned the corner before a custard, and our last fat friend was speedily overtaken by six sprightly syllabubs. At this stage of proceedings, our excellent Whig thought it high time to look after himself; and hence he was unable to keep an eye on Orator Lawless. But he distinctly remembers seeing him at his cheese. Paddy had manifestly exchanged his own plate for one coming down the table with a full cargo; while ever and anon a gulp of Bell's Beer swept millions of mites into the great receptacle; and finally, a long delighted "pech," from the bottom of his stomach and his soul, told that No. II. of the Gormandizing School of Oratory, would ere long discharge a—Speech.

In this proud state of repletion did Mr. Lawless sit for about three hours, more or less, digesting his dinner and his harangue. The IRISHMAN, like most of his countrymen, has rather a pleasant appearance; and now, with his brow bedewed, his cheeks greased, his eyes starting in his head, and his stomach, God bless him! tight as a drum, HE AROSE. You might have heard the faintest eructation, so dead

rising into something very like eloquence. Lawless had studied the law, but, at the instance of Lord Clare, (the Irish Chancellor,) the benchers of the King's Inn, Dublin, refused to call him to the bar, because he had been the warm friend of Robert Emmett. He entered into business after that, but settled down into the editorship of the very liberal "Irishman." He was an original member of the first Catholic Association, but offended O'Connell in 1825, by opposing what were called "The Wings"—concessions from the Irish Catholics, in view of Catholic Emancipation. In 1832 he was defeated as a candidate for Parliament, and died in 1837. He was called "Honest Jack Lawless," from his courage in maintaining his own opinion, believing it to be well-founded, notwithstanding the opposition of O'Connell.—M.

was the silence of the Assembly Room. Except that he seemed rather a little pot-bellied—as well he might—his figure showed to no disadvantage after that of Mr. Brougham. Yes! "After Mr. Brougham had concluded, Mr. LAWLESS, proprietor of the *Irishman*, of Belfast, rose and addressed the Assembly in a most impressive and animated manner."

Conscious of his own great acquirements, which our readers have seen were great, the eloquent gormandizer exclaimed:

"I hope that I do not presume too much when I say, that I am proprietor of a press which has some claims to independence. I am an IRISHMAN; and in my native country I have the conducting of a press, which, to the inhabitants of that part of Ireland, IS ITS GREATEST GUARDIAN AND CONSOLATION!!"

Here Mr. Lawless put his hand to his stomach, and the room rang with applause. Well might he have said, "I feel it *here*, gentlemen." Soon afterwards he spoke of "a starving population," having himself, in one single half hour, devoured victuals that would have kept ten cabins in animal food from Mullingar to Michaelmas. But hear the glutton after deglutition and digestion!

"What is the situation of the Irish peasant? Goaded to madness by the law, he appeals for refuge to public opinion. That opinion is to be found in the press—IT IS FOUND IN THIS ROOM; it is found in the proverbial generosity of Englishmen; it is discoverable in the CHARITIES OF THE HUMAN HEART!" So the Irish peasant is, first of all, to read in Mr. Lawless's Belfast newspaper what is public opinion, as it exists in the Assembly Room of Glasgow, and what are the charities of the human heart as they breathe from the well-lined stomach of this most unconscionable gormandizer; and then he is to set fire to "haggards" far and wide over a blazing country, and murder families, father, mother, and son, in cold blood.

But now the dumpling begins to work, and the custard cries within him.

"Your illustrious guest has eloquently spoken of the wonders which he has witnessed in his tour through Scotland, this LAND OF CHIVALRY AND BEAUTY; but he has not touched on a much greater wonder *than this*, nor has it yet been mentioned, namely, an Irishman addressing a Scotch assembly, in defence of the civil and religious freedom of his native land, and that Scotch assembly, not only listening to him with the utmost toleration, but actually cheering him in his progress."

Now, Pat, you are indeed an Irishman. How the devil could Harry Brougham call the attention of the company to the miraculous fact of a speech from Mr. Lawless before you had opened your great bawling mouth? "It had not yet been mentioned," you say; and I again ask you, how the devil it could? But where is the wonder in an Irishman spouting before Scotch Whigs, upon the miseries of his country? Both O'Connors have done so a hundred times, and many other traitors, now hanged or expatriated. Did you expect to be hissed for your rhodomontade, after praising the "Chivalry and Beauty" of Glasgow? And was your oratory a "greater wonder than these?" Thou art a most ungrammatical gormandizer, Mr. Lawless, proprietor of the Irishman of Belfast; and yet so delightedly unconscious is the Devourer of Dumplings of the bulls and blunders that have come roaring out of his jaws, that he winds up his sage exordium thus; and then we have no doubt, after cracking and creaking, lolloping and laboring, stood still for a short pace of time, like an ill-appointed jack, that seems to get rusty as the weight is wound up, and then all at once re-commences operations, as if a brownie had got into the wheel, and was making a fool of the machinery.

"HERE, GENTLEMEN, IS THE TRIUMPH OF THE PRESS, AND OF REASON AND LIBERALITY."

Our gormandizer then goes to Paisley, and by way of a little variety, he dines instead of sups. At Paisley, however, he is a much greater character; for he is the Brougham of the Saracen Head. The Scotsman tells us, "that the band and the spirits were excellent." So, we know, from the best authority, were the tripes, the black puddings, the hot cockles, and the red herrings, a Dutch importation of the 1821. Mr. Lawless then made his expected speech—the sum and substance of which was this, in his own words—"What more does a radical reformer want than what Professor Mylne of Glasgow, in his own modest, softened phraseology, was pleased to call a substantial reform, at the late splendid dinner to Mr. Brougham? I have been long an advocate for radical reform, understanding the term *radical* exactly in the sense of Professor Mylne; and what then does radical mean? It means this, that every honest man of sound mind, should have the right to choose his representative. The election should be frequent, and that to secure the honesty of the constituent, and the independence of the representative, the suffrage should be universal." Such, according to the Scotsman, is the opinion of the Reverend James Mylne, Professor of Moral Philosophy in the University of Glasgow, as expounded by his gormandizing commentator, Mr. Lawless of Belfast. We can no more.

At the request of the President, Mr. Stewart, a friend and companion of Mr. Lawless, addressed the meeting thus: "Mr. Chairman, I am a Catholic. Here do I stand before you, with manacles on my hands, and chains on my legs!" He ought to have been recommitted on a new warrant.

The Shepherd. I hae read just aneuch o't. It will do for Balaam, and that fule Lawless for the ass.

North. James—James—you are getting personal.

Tickler. Why, this red-hot potato supposes itself something above common. Only think of his bouncing up after Brougham, and claiming both kindred and equality with that bird of passage. Brougham is not a phœnix, in my opinion; but as for this braying, bragging, bawling, bullying, brazen-faced blockhead, with his blundering blarney from Belfast, a greater goose never gabbled on a green, nor groaned on a gridiron, since the first introduction of that absurdest of all feathered fowls into the island of Great Britain.

The Shepherd. Stop Tickler, as weel's me, Mr. North.

Tickler. What brought the hound, with his Irish howl, into the Lanarkshire pack?

The Shepherd. What a confusion o' a' metaphors! First, this Mr. Lawless is a potawto—then a guse, syne a jowler—and forgie me, I mysel ca'd him an ass. What, what'll he be neist?

Tickler. What think ye, North, of the fellow's insolence in making free with Professor Mylne's name in that way?

North. It would be more interesting and instructive to know what Professor Mylne thinks of it, and also how he relishes it. Horrible degradation, indeed, to a man of genius, learning, and virtue! But if Pat would drag the Professor into the Saracen's Head, how could the Professor help it?

Tickler. He might have helped it by holding his tongue at the Glasgow dinner, and by being satisfied with saying grace, or, better still, by staying away. But this is not the first time the worthy Professor has been misrepresented; and let us believe that Pat's report of his speech is as incorrect as (in days of old) Barbara's note of his prayer, and commentary on his selection of Scriptural paraphases.

The Shepherd. That's a' utter darkness to me—some local allusion, I suppose—like so many jokes in your Magazine that nobody kens ony thing about, but some three or four o' yoursels; and yet the Magazine is read over all the world! I sometimes get sae angry at that, that I think you a set o' stupid sumphs thegither. I ken the English folk canna thole't. Gin Mr. Joyous werena sleeping, he wad tell you sae.

North. I acknowledge the justice of your reproof; and to show you that I mean to profit by it, there goes into the fire a long article of fourteen pages, and a good one too, written by myself on the Glasgow dinner. Tickler's fragment is enough.*

The Shepherd. Eh! what a bleeze. It's maist a pity to see the low. Nae doubt, you geed them an awfu' dressing; but far, far better to prent in its place yon gran article on Wallenstein, (is that right pronounced?) or even that ane on my own Perils; for I have observed,

* This was an article in *Blackwood* for October, 1823, (called "The Glasgow Dinner. A Fragment. By Mr. Tickler,") which undertook to be very severe on Mr. Lawless, as an orator, but was simply a strong tirade against Catholic Emancipation.—M.

that let the Whigs do or dine, or drivel as they choose, none but themsells recollect ony thing about it, aboon a week at the farthest; and therefore that article, now black in the awse, might, for ony novelty the public could hae seen in't, as weel been a description of Alexander's or Belshazzar's Feast.

North. Who, think ye, Tickler, is to be the new editor of the Quarterly? Coleridge?

Tickler. Not so fast. The contest lies, I understand, between him and Odoherty. That is the reason the Adjutant has not been with us to-night. He is up canvassing.

The Opium-Eater. Mr. Coleridge is the last man in Europe to conduct a periodical work. His genius none will dispute; but I have traced him through German literature, poetry, and philosophy; and he is, sir, not only a plagiary, but, sir, a thief, a *bonâ fide* most unconscientious thief. I mean no disrespect to a man of surpassing talents. Strip him of his stolen goods, and you will find good clothes of his own below. Yet, except as a poet, he is not original; and if he ever become Editor of the Quarterly, (which I repeat is impossible,) then will I examine his pretensions, and show him up as impostor. Of Shakspeare it has been said, in a very good song, that "the thief of all thiefs was a Warwickshire thief;" but Shakspeare stole from Nature, and she forbore to prosecute. Coleridge has stolen from a whole host of his fellow-creatures, most of them poorer than himself; and I pledge myself I am bound over to appear against him.* If he plead to the indictment, he is a dead man—if he stand mute, I will press him to death, under three hundred and fifty pound weight of German metaphysics.

North. Perhaps it is a young Coleridge—a son or a nephew.

The Opium-Eater. Perhaps. Mr. North, I was most happy to see you let Odoherty do something like justice to Don Juan. Why will you let political animosities prevent your Magazine being a real reflection of the literature of the Tories? I never saw poetry criticised except in Blackwood. The Edinburgh Reviewers know nothing about it. The Quarterly are hide-bound. The rest, with the exception of a stray writer or two, are both ignorant and hide-bound. Your criticisms on Shelley, in particular, did you immortal honor. Every body of liberality and feeling thanked you. Why not be always thus? Cut up the Whigs and Whiglings, (God knows they are vulnerable enough,) and the Radicals and Republicans, (God knows they are

* One of De Quincey's favorite hobbies was a pretence—it may have been a belief—that Coleridge stole *ideas* from German authors. So often did he charge the poet with this, (it is republished in the Boston edition of his works, brought out with his authority, and to a certain extent under his supervision,) that when Coleridge's family brought out an edition of the Biographia Literaria, a large space of the introduction was dedicated to a defence of the author from the Opium-Eater's accusations. Even if Coleridge *had* plagiarized, it was like stealing lead, to melt in the crucible of his own thought, and be reproduced as rich barbaric gold, pure as from the mines of Ophir.—M.

prostate enough,) to your soul's contentment. Only don't *mix* politics with literature; nor

> "To party give up what was meant for mankind."

North. We have got back to the old story. What, my dear sir, do you think of our personality?

The Opium-Eater. It is the only charge I have for a long time past heard urged against you. To me it seems a very trifling matter, and necessarily unconnected with the chief merits or demerits of a work so various and profound as your Magazine. Coarse attacks, if you have any such, and you know better than I do, fail in their effect, excepting upon animals too low for gentlemen's game. As a mere affair of taste, I should say, "use the dissecting-knife rather than the cleaver, and leave the downright butchering business of literature to those to whom the perquisite of the offal may be of consequence." As a general rule, I would say, fight a gentleman with a Damascus blade, tempered with perfume; with a blackguard, why, order your footman to knock him down; but if you want exercise, and now and then choose to turn to yourself, and drub him in his own way, where is the objection, I should like to know? This is my personality creed.

Tickler. And a clear creed it is, thou most orthodox Opium-Eater. One thing all must acknowledge, that people cannot help judging of personality according to their amiable prejudices. A Whig reads a libel on a Tory, and chuckles over it as a most midriff-moving jeu d'esprit worthy of Moore himself, or Pirie's Chronicle, while the pluckless Tory shows it to his friends, who tell him not to trouble his head about it, as it is evidently a piece of low blackguardism from some hungry hack of the Old Times.* A Tory reads a libel on a Whig, and instantly, in the joy of his heart, gets it off by heart, perhaps sets it to music, and sings it at Ambrose's; while the enraged Whig consults counsel, carries the Tory before a jury of his country, and bites his nails over farthing damages. All this is very perplexing to a simple man like Timothy Tickler.

North. In that perplexity I humbly beg leave to join. There is good Mr. Jeffrey, of whom I shall never speak but in terms of the highest respect, who calls Coplestone, the Provost of Oriel, a great, awkward, clumsy barn-door fowl, foolishly flapping himself into an unavailing effort at flight.† He even changes the Provost's sex, makes him a hen, swears he saw him lay an egg, and heard him cackle. There, on the other hand, is good Mr. Jeffrey, as fierce as a fiend upon me in a court of justice, because Dr. Olinthus Petre thought

* Dr. Stoddart, who had edited *The Times*, commenced *The New Times*, in opposition. The original paper was then usually named as the *Old Times*—or, as Cobbett loved to call it, "*The bloody Old Times*."—M.

† Dr. Edward Copleston was elected Bishop of Llandaff in 1827, and died in 1849.—M.

he perceived some resemblance, either in face, person, dress, habits, or conversation, between a friend of his and a parrot.* What am I to make of all this? Is a parrot an animal that ranks lower in the scale of creation than a pullet? Again, the same lively and most exceedingly candid and consistent Mr. Jeffrey, calls Mr. Davison, a clergyman, (also once of Oriel,) a rat in a gutter, and all the fellows of the same college, cats, or retromingent creatures, which Mr. Jeffrey will confess is a most incredible accusation, if he will only try to qualify himself for admission into that society. Now, for any thing that I care, Coplestone may be a barn-door fowl, Davison a rat, and Plumer a cat; but if so—you see the consequence logical.

Tickler. Clearly, most noble Festus. I have long observed that you never speak of Mr. Jeffrey but in terms of the highest respect. So do I. For example, Baron Lawerwinkel was somewhat severe on the late Professor Playfair, insinuating, or asserting, I forget which, that he had ceased to be true to his early profession of faith.† Up jumps Jeff., and sallies forth *cap-a-pie*, against the Baron, like Jack the Giant-Killer; but thinking better about it, he doffs his armor, buckles his enormous two-edged sword, half as long as himself, and betakes himself to railing as bitterly as a northeast wind on a sleepy morning. But soft, who comes here? Not a grenadier, but Jeff. himself, calling out upon Mr. Southey, "apostate," "renegade," and every other most opprobrious epithet. The Baron eyes him for a while with increased, but calm contempt, and then, like a noble-minded mastiff, lifts him up gently by the nape of the neck, and drops him into a pool, out of which he scrambles with ludicrous alacrity, and shaking his small sides, barks out "Personality." Now, Mr. North, ye may talk in high terms of respect of whomsoever you think proper to flatter; but of this priggish person, for this particular piece of priggery, I, Timothy Tickler, have chosen to speak in still higher terms of pity and contempt.

The Opium-Eater. I confess that my opinion of Mr. Jeffrey is altogether different. I am rather disposed to think with Wordsworth, "that he who feels contempt for any living thing, has faculties that he has never used." Mr. Jeffrey seems to me to be an amiable, ingenious man, without much grasp and of no originality; petulant

* Dr. Olinthus Petre was the name under which (in *Blackwood* for November, 1820) the late Dr. Maginn charged Professor Leslie, who had criticised the Hebrew language, with thorough ignorance on the subject. In this article Petre said, "Am I to bow to him because he is an Edinburgh Reviewer? I question the inspiration of that worthy oracle;—and as to the Professor's own part in its lucubrations, why, his impudent puffings of himself, and ignorant sneerings at others, have often made me liken Leslie the Reviewer to some enormous over-fed pet of the parrot species, stuck up at a garret-window, and occupied all day with saying, 'Pretty poll—pretty poll,' to itself; 'Foul witch—foul witch,' to every passer-by." This comparison gave great offence to the Edinburgh Whigs, of whom Leslie was one, and was set forth, I believe, in the law-prosecution of Blackwood by Leslie, as having brought him "into hatred, contempt, and ridicule."—M.

† Baron Lawerwinkel (like Kempferhausen, Mullion, Buller, Tims, and others) was one of Blackwood's *Messieurs de l'Imagination*.—M.

and fretted in his humors, but kind and cordial where he has a liking—not surely a bitter enemy, and, I can well believe, an attached friend. His great original error in life lay in his attempting to sway the mind of England: a giant could not do that, nor twenty giants; no wonder, then, that signal discomfiture befell one single dwarf. If I might be allowed to use an illustration, after the manner of Mr. Tickler, I should say that Mr. Jeffrey, being ambitious of notice, conceived the scheme of going up in a balloon—that the machine was constructed of the proper material, a light silk, and not untastily ornamented; but that unfortunately there was a deficiency of gas, so that the *globus aërostaticus* was never sufficiently inflated. The cords, however, were cut, and the enterprising voyager began to ascend. By and by, getting entangled somehow or other by the foot, there he hung with his head downwards, while the balloon cleared the roofs of the houses, but could make no approximation to the lowest strata of clouds. Finally, Mr. Jeffrey got released, and he and his balloon came to the earth almost together, and without any serious hurt to the aëronaut, but the vehicle was irremediably injured, and in all probability will never more be able to reach the chimney-top.

The Shepherd. Odd's my life! that simile's just unco like Tickler, wi' a great tinge o' eloquence; for, oh dear me! after all, a weel-educated Southron says things in a tosh and complete manner, that we modern and northern Athenians canna come up to for our lives. There's nae denying that.

The Opium-Eater. With regard to these ludicrous, and, as many persons may not unwarrantably call them, impertinent and insolent expressions of Mr. Jeffrey, more especially impertinent and insolent when applied to persons in the same rank of life as his own, and indeed somewhat superior, at least more dignified and authoritative, I should say, that most probably Mr. Jeffrey employed them without any very culpable feeling towards the parties, and merely in compliance with the spirit of that vituperative system of contention with our real or supposed opponents, which he did not originate, but which, nevertheless, he, by his popular abilities, and by the favor which the Edinburgh Review found with a great portion of the reading public, helped to make of very great prevalence in the periodical literature of this country. A high-minded, and high-facultied man, could scarcely, I think, have written as Mr. Jeffrey has too often done; but I do not wish rashly to assert that he might not, remembering the vulgar virulence of Milton not truly to his equals or superiors, for where were they, but to his inferiors indubitably, and without reference to individuals, to all that portion of mankind, or womankind, concerning whom he wrote in a controversial or polemical spirit.

North. Wisely spoken. But Mr. Tickler chiefly despises him, as it seems to me, for the hypocritical claim he advances to perfect freedom from this failing, and for the bitterness with which he arraigns that conduct in others of which he is himself more frequently guilty than any other man of eminence in this age.

The Opium-Eater. That is another matter, and therein he is without defence.

The Shepherd. Weel, then, Mr. Tickler, is party-spirit, think ye, likely to rin, like a great heavy sea, ower domestic intercourse in families, this winter?

Tickler. Why, James, I neither know nor care. My friends, for upwards of half a century, have been TORIES; and what is the sour sulky face of a captious Whig to me, any more than his portrait in a picture—falling from which, I turn in calm contempt, or deep disgust, to the well-pleased countenance of some staunch lover of his country and his King?

The Shepherd. But isna it a desperate pity to see mony clever chiels keepit apart just for mere difference o' opinion about the government?

Tickler. Pray, where are all these "clever chiels?" Take away about four Whigs, and are not all the rest confounded dogs? I cannot really be too grateful to party-spirit for keeping such gentry in their own circles. I hope, James, you are not going to join the PLUCKLESS?

North. I am more Whiggish than you, Tickler. What can be more amiable than the present zeal of the Whigs in the cause of Spain? They are doing all they can to wipe off the foul stain of their truckling to Bonaparte when he stormed Spain. They are crying shame upon their former selves; and why not believe them to be sincere?

Tickler. Hypocrites.

North. Then, have they not subscribed four thousand, three hundred, sixteen shillings, and eight-pence three farthings, for the Greeks?

Tickler. Scrubs.

North. Did they not wish us to go to war, like a brave people?

Tickler. Fools.

North. Did they not call Bonaparte the guardian of the liberties of the world?

Tickler. Liars.

North. Who but they would change our criminal law?

Tickler. Knaves.

North. Are they not for a "substantial reform?"

Tickler. Radicals.

North. Are they not adverse to the prosecution of the foes to Christianity?

Tickler. Deists.

North. Would they not fain overlook blasphemy?

Tickler. Atheists.

North. Are they not friends to the liberty of the Press?

Tickler. Libellers.

The Shepherd. You stopt me a while since, and I cry stop till baith o' you now. I kenna wha's the worst. I hae nae notion o' sic desperate bitterness in politics. What can Mr. Joyous be thinking a' this while? Mr. Vivian, you haena spoken muckle the nicht, but the little you did say was to the purpose. I dinna like folk ower furthy a' at ance. Besides, you are sadly knocked up, man. That Gretna Green is a sad business.

North (*laying his gold repeater on the table*). Twelve o'clock. Old Chronos smites clearly, and with a silver sound. My dear Vivian, we keep early hours, and your young bride will be in tears. I understand your silence, and know your thoughts. You are at Barry's Hotel. None better. Allow me to accompany you to the steps. Give me your arm, my good boy.

(*Exeunt omnes*—NORTH *leaning on* JOYEUSE *and the* OPIUM-EATER, *Mr.* AMBROSE *bustling before with the blazing branches, and* TICKLER, *arm-in-arm with the* SHEPHERD, *towering in the rear.*)

No. XIII.—MARCH, 1824.

Dram. Pers.—NORTH *and* TICKLER.

Tickler. Proper humbug!—but don't rail, North, for I remember his father——

North. I rail!—I like him better than most of them, for he *has* pluck—he has the old lad's blood in him. I was only wondering that he should again commit himself in such a way; but there really is no accounting for Whig conduct.

Tickler. Pooh! pooh! I was joking, man; he is in private a pleasant fellow enough, but in public, he is one of the hacks of the party, and of course obliged to get through such things. Yet it would be no harm, I think, if he remembered to what set of men, and what system, his people owed their honors; and, perhaps, although he *is* in the service of the Duke of Devonshire,* such a recollection might make him less rabid on the followers of Pitt.

North. Hang it! such a cheese-paring is not worth wasting a sentence about. Keep moving with the Review. The price of tea—I think we're that length——

Tickler. I leave to the swallowers of Souchong, Campoi, Hyson, Hymskin, Bohea, Congou, Twankay, and Gunpowder. This will be a favorite article with the Cockneys—with the leafy—that is, tea-leafy bards, who

> Te redeunte die, te decedente canebant.

It is nothing to us.

North. Nothing whatever. I leave it and the discussion on the Holy Alliance, to be swallowed by those whom it is meant for.

Tickler. The Jeremiade over the Italian traitors is vastly interesting; then it appears, that, after all, only one of the ruffians expiated his crimes on the gallows.

North. God bless the Jacobins, and their child and champion. They would have made cleaver work of it. It is, however, quite comfortable to hear Old Bailey lawyers, like Denman and Brougham, talking of

* It would appear from this that the delinquent was James Abercromby, the Duke's steward, and now Lord Dumferline, with a pension of £4000 a year for his own life, and that of his son, as ex-Speaker of the House of Commons!—M.

the savageness of the Austrian Government, when they must know, that in a population double our own, the executions are as one to five, if not in a still smaller proportion. A Vienna review, if there be such a thing, could finely retort that in our faces. With respect——

Odoherty (*outside*). The club-room — only Mr. North and Mr. Tickler.

Waiter (*outside*). That's all, sir. There's a trifle of a balance, sir, against you since——

Odoherty (*speaks as he enters*). Pshaw—don't bother me, man, with your balances. Do you think, when the interests of the world are going to be debated—Gentlemen, a pair, am right glad to see you.

North. Sit down.

Tickler. And here's a clean glass.

North. What will ye drink?

Tickler. Champagne, Chateau-Margot, Glenlivet, or Jamaica?

North. We have got to the hot stuff this *hour*. Will you try our jug, or make for yourself?

Tickler. I recommend the jug.

Odoherty. I am quite agreeable wherever I go. Here's a bumper to your health, and that of all good men and true.

Tickler. How long are you arrived?

Odoherty. Half an hour. Knew I'd meet somebody here. Where are the rest?

North. Hogg is at work with his epic poem.

Odoherty. His He-pig poem you mean. Queen Hynde, if I mistake not. A great affair, I suppose.

Tickler. Quite grand. The Shepherd has been reading it all over the hills and far away. There are fine bits in it, I assure you. I heard the exordium; it is splendid.

Odoherty. Do you remember any of it?

Tickler. No—not enough at least to spout.

Odoherty. I met Jemmy Ballantyne at York—we supped together —and he told me he had heard it was to open like the Æneid or Madoc.

North. The Æneid or Madoc! Just as you would say Blackwood's Magazine and the London! How do you mean?

Odoherty. Why, with a recapitulation of all his works—as thus—I quote from memory——

Tickler (*aside*). Or imagination.

Odoherty.

Come listen to my lay, for I am he
Who wrote Kilmeny's wild and wondrous song,
Likewise the famous Essay upon Sheep,
And Mador of the Moor; and then, unlike

Those men who fling their pearls before the Hog,
I, Hogg, did fling my Perils before men.*

North. A pun barbarous.

Odoherty.

But still more famous for the glorious work,
Which I, 'neath mask of oriental sage,
Wrote and concocted in auspicious hour—
THE CHALDEE MANUSCRIPT—which, with a voice
Of thundering sound, fulmined o'er Edinburgh,
Shook the old Calton from its granite base,
Made Arthur's Seat toss up its lion head,
And snuff the wind in wonder; while around,
Eastward and westward, northward, southward, all
The ungodly, struck with awe and ominous dread
Of the great ruin thence impending o'er them,
Fled frighted, leaving house and home behind,
In shameful rout—or, grovelling prostrate, showed
Their nether parts uncomely——

Tickler. I think you may stop there.

North. In all conscience: I shall not permit Hogg to be quizzed. He is too good a fellow, and I am sure his poem will do him credit. Sing a song, Ensign, for you seem to be in fine voice.

Odoherty (*sings*).

Would you woo a young virgin of fifteen years,
You must tickle her fancy with Sweets and Dears,
Ever toying and playing, and sweetly, sweetly,
Sing a love-sonnet and charm her ears—
Wittily, prettily, talk her down—
Phrase her and praise her, fair or brown—
Soothe her and smooth her,
And tease her and please her,
Ah! touch but her fancy, and all's your own

I must have a glass ere I take the next stanza.

Would you woo a stout widow of forty years—

Tickler. Come, stop, stop, Odorherty, none of your stuff. Any literary news in London town?

Odoherty. Not much. Lord Byron, you are aware, has turned Turk.

North. Greek, you mean.*

Odoherty. Ay, ay—Greek, I meant. I always confound these scoundrels together. But the Greeks in London have met with a sad defeat. That affair of Thurtell's was a bore.

* Two of Hogg's prose fictions were "Three Perils of Man," and "Three Perils of Woman.' They are amusing enough, but often improbable in incident, and sometimes too broad in language and sentiment.—M.

† Byron quitted Genoa the Proud in August, 1823, for Greece, where he died on the 19th April, 1824.—M.

Tickler. Curse the ruffian—the name ought not to be mentioned in decent society. But Weare was just as great a blackguard.

Odoherty. Yes; and Sam Rogers says that that is the only excuse for Thurtell. He did right, said Sam, to *cut* such an acquaintance.

North. Why, Sam is turning quite a Joe Miller. Have you seen the old gentleman lately?

Odoherty. About a fortnight ago—Tom Moore was with him.

North. I thought Tom was rusticating.

Odoherty. Yes, in general; but he is now in town, bringing out a new number of his Melodies.

North. Is it good?

Odoherty. Nobody except Power and his coterie has seen it yet;* but I understand it is very excellent. It will be out in a couple of months. There is one song in it to the tune of the Boyne Water; the great Orangemen tune, you know, which is making them nervous.

North. Why?

Odoherty. Because conciliation—curse the five syllables, as Sir Abraham King says—is carried to such a happy pitch in Ireland, that tune, toast, statue, picture, displeasing to the majority, are denounced as abominable.

North. A pretty one-sided kind of conciliation with a vengeance! but I am sorry Moore is so squeamish. Are the words Orange?

Odoherty. Not at all; some stuff about an angel or nymph rising out of the Boyne, and singing a song to pacify the natives.†

Tickler. And even this must not be published, for fear of offending the delicate ears of Sheilinagig‡ and Co.! Is not Moore doing a *jeu d'esprit* about your Irish Rugantino, Captain Rock?

* James Power, a music-publisher in London, employed Moore, from 1806 to 1836, (when Power died,) to write the Irish Melodies and other songs for him. For the Melodies alone, he paid him £500 a-year during those 30 years. There are 124 Melodies, and as the whole amount received by Moore was £15,000—to say nothing of loss of interest, which would more than quadruple it, by arithmetical progression—Moore actually received £121 for each of those songs. Their average length was twenty lines,—which would make the payment over £6 or $30 *a line!*—Moore's correspondence with Power, during thirty years, amounted to over 1200 letters, all of which were submitted by Power's daughters to Lord John Russell, editor of Moore's Memoir, Journal, and Correspondence. Russell selected only 57 out of these, which he printed with omissions. The whole collection was then sold by public auction in London, and thus dispersed for ever. A volume was prepared, giving the gist of this correspondence,—it was even printed. But Lord John Russell, thinking that it was not likely to exalt the character of Moore—whose conduct to Power, even while literally supported by him, was insolent and ungrateful—threatened to apply for an injunction to restrain the publication, (as had been successfully done, in 1824, by Byron's letters to his mother and to Mr. Dallas, on the legal ground that his executors alone had a publishing property in his correspondence,) and the appearance of the book in England was prevented. However, it has been published in this country, with an explanatory introduction by Crofton Croker, and unhappily shows that as no man is a hero to his *valet-de-chambre*, so a poet may be very "small deer" in his relations with his publisher.—M.

† The melody represents vanquished Erin weeping beside the river Boyne, into which Discord drops his quiver,—each year to return, recover, and disperse them through Ireland; and, when she asks the power of Good when this is to end, the Demon replies, "Never!" It was a puerile fancy feebly elaborated into song.—M

‡ There is an Irish air called Sheilinagig. Once upon a time, in Dublin, when one of the great Irish orators, who had accidentally injured one of his legs, was proceeding through Sackville-street in a Bath chair, a bystander, (viz. Mr. J. G. Maeder, the musical composer,

Odoherty. Yes—but he is nervous there too.* Longman & Co. are cautious folk, and it is submitted to Denman, or some other doer, who will bedevil it, as he did the Fables for the Holy Alliance.

Tickler. Well, Longman has published, however, one little book this year, that bears no marks of the knife—have you seen that clever thing—the "Stranger's Grave," I mean?

Odoherty. I have to be sure, so has all the world—but still upon the whole it is not to be denied, that the Divan have not half the spunk of their rival who rules in the west of the Empire of Cockaigne.

North. Joannes de Moravia? Have you seen him, Odoherty, in your travels?

Odoherty. Of course—of course—a most excellent fellow that said bibliopole is.

North. That I know. How does he carry on the war?

Odoherty. In the old style. Morier and his people are mad with you for your blackguard review of Hajji Baba.†

North. *My* blackguard review, Mr. Adjutant—it was *you* who wrote it.

Odoherty. *I!* Well, that beats Banagher.‡

Tickler. No matter who wrote it—it was a very fair quiz—better than any thing in the novel—though really I must say that I consider Hajji rather an amusing book after all.

North. N'importe. Has Murray much on hand?

Odoherty. A good deal. Croker is going to publish with him the Suffolk Papers.§

North. Heavy, I suppose.

now of New-York,) being asked by a friend from the country, who was that little man with the large flashing eyes, musically answered, "Sheil-in-a-gig."—M.

* Moore's Memoirs of Captain Rock appeared in April, 1824—was much abused by *Blackwood* and other Tory publications, but was very successful.—M.

† The Adventures of Hajji Baba of Ispahan; a novel, in three volumes," was published in London, by Murray, in 1824. It was reviewed in *Blackwood* for January, 1825. Oddly enough, Ebony, which had attributed "Anastasius" to Lord Byron, who did not write it, made another blunder in this review, by affiliating "Hajji Baba" upon Thomas Hope, the actual author of "Anastasius," and said, "The work is not merely as regards matter, interest, taste, and choice of subjects, three hundred per cent. at least under the mark of Anastasius, but the style is never forcible and eloquent; and, in many places, to say the truth, it is miserably bad." Again, "Of Anastasius, one would say that it seemed to have been written by some mighty hand, from a store, full, almost to overflowing, with rich and curious material: of Hajji Baba, that some imitator, of very little comparative force indeed, had picked up the remnant of the rifled note-book, and brought it to market in the best shape that he was able." It appeared, after all, that James Morier was the author. In early life he had travelled extensively in the East, and related his adventures in "Travels through Persia, Armenia, Asia Minor to Constantinople." In 1810, at the age of thirty, he was appointed British Envoy to the Court of Persia, where he remained until 1816, and soon after his return, published "A second Journey through Persia." This was followed by Hajji Baba, which (despite the *Blackwood* criticism) is very clever. In a second series, he brought his hero—a sort of Persian picaroon, on the Gil Blas model—into England. In Zohrab the Hostage, and other works of prose fiction, Mr. Morier showed great knowledge of Eastern life, manners and customs, and considerable skill in embodying it. He died in 1848, aged sixty-eight.—M.

‡ There is an Irish saying, "That beats Banagher, and Banagher beats the world."—M.

§ John Wilson Croker edited the Letters of Lord Hervey, the Suffolk Papers, and Lord Hervey's Memoirs of the Reign of George the Second.—M.

Odoherty. No—the contrary—at least so I am told. Croker could not do any thing heavy.

North. He is fond of editing old papers—Lord Hertford has placed the Conway Papers in his hands; and I perceive, by a note in the new edition of D'Israeli's Curiosities of Literature, that the old gentleman——

Tickler. An excellent judge.

North. Few better—declares that they will throw much light on our, that is, English history.

Odoherty. Apropos of Croker—a namesake of his, and a countryman of mine, a fine lad, one of my chiefest chums, indeed, has brought out with Murray a quarto on the South of Ireland.

North. I have not read it—just looked over the prints—very famous lithography, by my honor.

Odoherty. Oh, the Nicholsons are prime fists at that kind of work. The book has sold in great style, which is no bad thing for a lump of a quarto.* How does Maga get on?

North. As usual. Are our brother periodicals *in statu quo?*

Odoherty. Yes, heavy and harmless. Whittaker is going to start a new bang-up, to be called the Universal—a most comprehensive title.

North. It is, I understand, a second Avatar of the New Edinburgh, with some fresh hands. God send it a good deliverance!

Tickler. Was the Universal the name originally proposed?

Odoherty. No—the Bimensial—as it is to come out every two months. Rogers knocked up that name by a pun. "Ay," said he, "you may cry Bi-men-sial, but the question is, whether Men-shall-buy?" A bad pun, in my opinion.†

North. O hideous—(*aside*) it is his own.

Tickler. Abominable—(*aside*) evidently his. We'll spoil his fishing for compliments.

Odoherty. Why, look ye, gentlemen, I do not think it quite so bad as that—I can tell you I have heard worse at this table.

North. Ha! ha! ha! Caught, Ensign?—Empty your glass, man, and don't think to impose on *us*.

Odoherty. Well, so be it. Any thing for a quiet life. Here I have

* This "lump of a quarto" was called "Researches in the South of Ireland, illustrative of the Scenery, Architectural Remains, and the Manners and Superstitions of the Peasantry. By T. Crofton Croker." It was reviewed more than once, with high commendation, in *Blackwood*, who said it "consists in [of?] dissertations on the civil and ecclesiastical history; the scenery; the architectural antiquities; the romantic superstitions; and the literature of Ireland, connected by a slender thread of personal adventure, in a tour through the southern counties, in company with Miss Nicholson and Mr. Alfred Nicholson, whose illustrations increase the beauty and value of the work." The lady here mentioned afterwards became Mrs. Croker.—M.

† It is foolish to give a book a name which can be punned upon. Thus, even before No. 1 was published, a projected and since popular periodical was spoken of as Bentley's Miss-sell-any. That, by the way, was originaly announced as "The Wits' Miscellany," but finally appeared as "Bentley's Miscellany." Hood said, when he heard that the first name was abandoned, as too ambitious, "That may be a reason for not calling it the *Wits'* Miscellany, but, my dear Bentley, *why run into the opposite extreme?*"—M.

brought you Mr. Gleig's pamphlet about the Missionaries. I assure you few things have made more noise about town. 'Tis really a pithy performance—devilish well written too—a rising sprig of the Mitre this, sirs.

Tickler. Just the thing I was wanting to see—I saw it quoted in the John Bull. Such authors are much wanted now-a-days. Any thing else, Ensign?

Odoherty. Why, here's the new comedy, too—spick and span.

North. "Pride shall have a Fall." Whose is it?

Odoherty. Moore's—Luttrell's—Croly's—Jones's—Rogers's—Soane's. All of which names I saw in print.*

Tickler. But which is right?

Odoherty. Never dispute with the newspapers—all must be right. I only think it proper to mention that Soane is given on the authority of the Old Times.

Tickler. A lie, of course. Nothing more is needed to prove that it is *not* Soane. How did it run?

Odoherty. Like Lord Powerscourt's waterfall—full and fast. It is the most successful comedy since John Bull.

North. I shall read it in the morning. It seems to be elegantly written.

Odoherty. Very elegantly indeed—and the music is beautiful. Altogether it acts right well. You have heard of Shee's Alasco?

North. How George Colman suppressed it?

Odoherty. Yes, and on what grounds?

North. Something political, I understand; but I do not know exactly what.

Odoherty. Nor I very exactly;—but it is understood that the hero (to be enacted by Charles Kemble) was a Liberal.

Tickler. That is, a ruffian "*nulla virtute redemptus.*"

Odoherty. Exactly, and Shee, with no other meaning than to write dramatically—for Shee is a worthy and right-minded fellow†—gave this lad all the roaring, rumfustian, upper gallery, clap-trap, hullabaloos about liberty, emancipation, the cause of freedom all over the

* It was written by the Rev. George Croly, and was performed in London (at Covent Garden Theatre) with great success, partly owing to the merit of the comedy; partly to its being written to illustrate the airs and graces of a fashionable Cavalry Regiment, so that every line was applicable to the 10th Hussars, who had just made themselves the butt of London; and partly to Frederick Yates's extraordinary personation of Cornet Count Carmine.—M.

† Martin Archer Shee, who was at once Poet and Painter—a few degrees above mediocrity in both professions—published a Tragedy called "Alasco," with a preface, in which he severely rated George Colman, the licenser of plays, for having prohibited its performance without the omission of certain lines which he (the licenser) thought unfit for publication. On the death of Sir Thomas Lawrence, it was intimated that George IV. would be pleased if the Royal Academy would elect Sir David Wilkie to fill the Presidential chair, thus vacated. The Academicians, indignant at the idea of being dictated to, almost unanimously elected Shee, who was knighted, as a matter of course, on the occasion. The Presidents, since the formation of the Royal Academy, in 1768, have been Sir Joshua Reynolds, Mr. West, Sir Thomas Lawrence, Sir Martin Shee, and Sir Charles Eastlake. This last was elected on Shee's death, in 1850.—M.

world, and the other fine things, on which the Breeches-maker's Review——

North. What review, do you say?

Odoherty. The Westminster—but as Place, the snip of Charing-Cross, is the great authority in it, it is never called any thing in London but the Breeches-maker's Review. However, as I was saying, the effective part, acted by the effective actor, was this sort of gunpowder stuff, while the antagonizing principle, as his holiness Bishop Coleridge would say, was a fellow as humdrum as one of the pluckless Prosers of the Modern Athens, and to be performed by one Cooper or Carpenter. So the Benthamism had it all to itself—and in English too, a language which Jerry, you know, does not understand; and therefore cannot corrupt the nation by scribbling in it.

Tickler. If such be the case, Colman was quite right; though, after all, the country is so well disposed, that it might have been left to the decision of the House.

North. Which would, I think, in the present temper of the people, have damned any thing jacobinical or verging thereto.

Odoherty. Ay, ay, countryman O'Connell, with grief, is obliged to confess, that "Toryism is triumphant." Fill your glasses—Here's long may it so continue!

North and Tickler. Amen, amen.

Odoherty. Any news in Edinburgh?

North. Order up supper immediately. News in Edinburgh! Bless your heart, when had we news here?

Tickler. The old affair—Listen and you shall hear how it has gone, goeth, and shall go at Ambrose's. (*Sings.*)

1.

Ye sons of the platter give ear,
  Venter habet aures, they say,
The praise of good eating to hear,
  You'll never be out of the way;
But with knives sharp as razors, and stomachs as keen,
  Stand ready to cut through the fat and the lean—
      Through the fat and the lean—
Sit ready to cut through the fat and the lean.

2.

The science of eating is old,
  Its antiquity no man can doubt:
Though Adam was squeamish, we're told,
  Eve soon found a dainty bit out;
Then with knives sharp as razors and stomachs as keen,
Our passage let's cut through the fat and the lean—
      &c. &c.

3.

Through the world from the West to the East,
  Whether City, or Country, or Court,
There's no honest man, Laic or Priest,
  But with pleasure partakes in the sport,
And with knife sharp as razor, and stomach as keen,
His passage doth cut through the fat and the lean—
&c. &c.

4.

They may talk of their roast and their boiled,
  They may talk of their stew and their fry,
I am gentle simplicity's child,
  And I dote on a West Riding pie,
While with knife sharp as razor and stomach as keen,
I splash through the crust to the fat and the lean—
  To the fat and the lean,
&c. &c.

5.

Let the Whigs have sour bannocks to chew,
  And their dishwater namesake to swill;
But, dear boys, let the wet ruby flow
  For the comfort of Torydom still.
Be our dishes like mountains, our bumpers like seas,
Be the fatness with us, and the leanness with these—
&c. &c.

North. I like to hear you talk of leanness!—Well, well, after all, what an infernal bump of gluttony you must sport, Timotheus!—and you too, Odoherty. You are not aware, that the infernal idiots have got you into their hands.

Odoherty. The infernal idiots—who are they?—Oh, the Phrenologists! How have the asses got me?

North. It appears that you were lying on your old bench in the watch-house, after an evening's carouse here, when a party of Craniologists were committed for exercising the Organ of Destructiveness on the windows of somebody, whom they wanted to convince of the truth of the theory—and one of them took a cast of your head.

Odoherty. The devil he did!—What did he find there?

North. Imprimis, one huge bump on the top of the forehead, denoting extraordinary piety.

Odoherty. What, this bump here?—Piety with a vengeance!—To be sure I went on my knees immediately after getting it—for it is the mark of a rap of a shillela which I got in the days of my youth from Cornelius O'Callaghan, in a row at Ballyhooly. What else am I, besides being pious?

North. Oh, I forgot the entire—but it is to appear in the next volume of their transactions.

Tickler. They found the organ of punch-drinking very large, which tends, more than any other fact I have heard, to prove the truth of their wise science.

Odoherty. Where did they find it, pray?

Tickler. Somewhere above your eyebrow.

Odoherty. Oh! the asses—if they found it somewhere under my gullet, they would be nearer the mark. But come, here they go!—(*Sings.*)

1.

Of all the asses in the town
None's like the Phreno-lógers,—
They sport a braver length of ears
Than all the other codgers.
There's not a jackass in the land
Can bray so true and sweetly,
Nor prove a turnip is a head
As wise as theirs completely.

2.

'Tis they who write in learned words,
By no means long or braggart;
'Tis they who proved no saint e'er lived
If none was Davie Haggart.
For Davie is a favorite name
Among our northern witches;—
'Twas David Welsh who made the club,
Along with David Breeches.

I meant to say Bridges, but I could not think of a rhyme. Davie,* who is an excellent fellow in all other respects, is turned phrenologer, and has an interesting paper on a young thief of his acquaintance, in the Idiot Transactions, which is quite edifying to read.

3.

They prove that Chalmers' pate across†
Is half a foot and over;
Whereas in Joseph Hume, M. P.,
An inch less they discover;
And therefore they declare the one
A most poetic prancer,
While Joseph they pronounced to be
No mighty necromancer.

* David Bridges of Edinburgh, clothier, had a fine collection of paintings and sketches, and was Secretary to the Dilettanti Society.—M.

† See Combe's Letter to Dr. Barclay.—C. N.

4.

But Hume, you needna fash your thumb,
  Nor stint your* smuggled bottle;—
Still prove in style that three and three
  Make up fifteen in tottle.
For ev'n if what these wooden pates
  Have tried to prove were swallow'd,
Yet if it be a narrow skull,
  Your head's a perfect solid.

5.

They proved from Whig Jack Thurtell's head,
  That he was kind and gentle;
And though too fond of cutting throats,
  Yet still he never meant ill.
And now the seven-and-eighty wit's,†
  To all our satisfactions,
Have shown it takes no brains to print
  A volume of transactions.

Shall I go on?——

North. No—no—let the turnip-tops rot in quiet. (*Sings.*)

The Doncaster mayor, he sits in his chair—
  His mills they merrily go—
His nose it does shine with Oporto wine,
  And the gout is in his great toe.

And so it is in mine too. Oh! oh! O dear! what a cough I have! heigh, heigh, heigh! Come now, Tickler, one stave from your old mouse-trap, to conclude the ante-cœnal part of our symposium, for I hear the dishes rattling below.

Tickler (*sings à la Matthews*).

Young Roger came tapping at Dolly's window—
    Thumpaty, thumpaty, thump;
He begg'd for admittance—she answered him no—
    Glumpaty, glumpaty, glump.
No, no, Roger, no—as you came ye may go—
    Stumpaty, stumpaty, stump.
O what is the reason, dear Dolly, he cried—
    Humpaty, humpaty, hump—
That thus I'm cast off, and unkindly denied?—
    Trumpaty, trumpaty, trump—
Some rival more dear, I guess, has been here—
    Crumpaty, crumpaty, crump.

* Vide Hume's Speech of the 12th inst.—C. N.
† The number of prenologists in the club in Edinburgh.—C. N.

Suppose there's been two, sir, pray what's that to you, sir ?—
Numpaty, numpaty, nump.
Wi' a disconsolate look, his sad farewell he took—
Frumpaty, frumpaty, frump—
And all in despair jump'd into a brook—
Jumpaty, jumpaty, jump;
His courage did cool in a filthy green pool—
Slumpaty, slumpaty, slump—
So he swam to the shore, but saw Dolly no more—
Dumpaty, dumpaty, dump—
He did speedily find one more fat and more kind—
Plumpaty, plumpaty, plump—
But poor Dolly's afraid she must die an old maid—
Mumpaty, mumpaty, mump.

Enter AMBROSE *with his tail on.* (*Left eating.*)

No. XIV.—APRIL, 1824.

SCENE I.—*Sky-Blue Parlor.*

MR. NORTH, *the* ETTRICK SHEPHERD, *and* MR. AMBROSE.

North. Just so—just so, Mr. Ambrose. No man sets a cushion with more gentle dexterity. As my heel sinks into the velvet, my toe forgets to twinge. Now, my dear St. Ambrosio, for *l'eau médicinal!* (*Mr. Ambrose communicates a nutshell of Glenlivet, and exit.*) Now, my dear Shepherd, let us have a "twa-handed crack."

The Shepherd. What's the gout like,* Mr. North, sir? Is't like the stang o' a skep-bee? or a toothacky stoun? or a gumboil, when you touch't wi' het parritch? or a whitlow on ane's nose, thrab thrabbing a' the night through? or is't liker, in its ain way, till what ane drees after thretty miles o' a hard-trotting, barebacked beast, wi' thin breeks on ane's hurdies?

North. Gentle Shepherd, "Where ignorance is bliss, 'tis folly to be wise."

The Shepherd. I'se warrant now, sir, that your big tae's as red as a rose in June.

North. There spoke the poet—the author of the Queen's Wake. Mr. Hogg, I am happy to know that you are about to give us a new poem, Queen Hynde. Is it very fine?

The Shepherd. Faith, I'm thinking it's no muckle amiss. I've had great pleasure aye in the writing o't. The words came out, helter skelter, ane after the other, head to doup, like bees frae a hive on the first glimpse o' a sunny summer morn.

North. Again! Why, that is poetry, Mr. Hogg.

The Shepherd. Fie shame! That's just what Mr. Jaffray said to Coleridge, when walking in the wud wi' him at Keswick. And yet what does he do a towmont or twa after, but abuse him and his genius baith, like ony tinkler, in the Embro' Review. I canna say, Mr. North, that I hate flattery, but, oh man! I fear't, and at the very time I swallow't, I keep an e'e on the tyke that administers the cordial.

* The Frenchman's idea of the difference between gout and rheumatism would answer this query :—"You puts your fingeres in a vice and somebody does squeeze, squeeze, beyond what man can bear, dat is ze rumateeze: you get doo or dree squeeze more, and dat is ze gout."—M.

North. Queen Hynde will do, James. Tales, tales, tales, eternal prose tales—out with a poem, James. Your prose tales are but——

The Shepherd. What kind o' a pronunciation is that, man?

North. I seldom write verses myself, now-a-days, James, but as I have not bothered you much lately by spouting MSS. as I used to do long ago, pray, be so kind as to listen to me for a few stanzas.

1.

Hail, glorious dawning! hail, auspicious morn!
  APRIL THE FIRST! grand festival, all hail!
My soaring Muse on goosequill pinion borne,
  From that wide limbo, sung in Milton's tale,
Hastens to pay thee love and reverence due,
  For thou to me a day most sacred art;
And I shall call around a jovial crew,
  Who love and worship thee with single heart.
Come, crown'd in foolscap, rolling forth this lay,
Hail, mighty mother, hail!—hail, glorious ALL FOOLS' day!

2.

Which of you first shall press to show your love—
  To vail your bonnet to your patron saint?
I see you hasten from the earth above,
  And sea below, to pay your service quaint;
White, black and gray, in every livery decked,
  The stay-laced dandy, and the Belchered blood,
The grave divine of many a jangling sect—
  Lawyers and doctors, and the critic brood,
All singing out in concert, grave or gay,
Hail, mighty mother, hail!—hail, glorious ALL FOOLS' day!

3.

March in the foremost rank—'tis yours by right—
  March, grenadiers of folly—march, my Whigs—
Hoist the old tattered standard to the light,
  Grunting in chorus like Will Cobbett's pigs.
George Tierny holds it with unsteady paw,
  Looking right hungry on the golden hill
Of Place and Power, from which his ravening maw
  Hopes vainly for vittal its chinks to fill.
Dupe to himself he growls, but loud must say,
Hail, mighty mother, hail!—hail, glorious ALL FOOLS' day!

4.

Brougham, in a hated gown of stuff,* attends,
  His nose up-twitching like the devil's tail.

* Up to this time, although fully entitled to it by his standing at the bar, as well as high repute and large practice as a lawyer, the distinction of being made a King's Counsel (which entitles the holder to peculiar precedence at the bar) had been withheld from Brougham, by Lord Chancellor Eldon, because of the truly courageous and independent manner in which Brougham had defended Queen Caroline, in 1820–1. Ordinary (that is outer or utter) barristers wear black stuff gowns, and sit *outside* the bar in English courts of law. Queen's Counsel and persons holding patents of precedency sit *within* the bar and wear silken gowns.—M.

There Aberdeen her learnit Ractor sends,
Joseph, at whom great Cocker's self turns pale;
There's Scarlett Redivivus, whom the band
Of bloody gemmen of the press had slain,
And Wilson (once Sir Robert) hand in hand
With Nugent lading of the Falmouth Wain,
Joining right loudly in the grand huzza,
Hail, mighty mother, hail!—hail, glorious ALL FOOLS' day!

5.

Wise Hutchinson, and Wiser Peter Moore,
Great Holland, redolent of female fist;
Sir James, the faithful treasurer of the poor,
Mick Taylor, lord of cutlets and gin-twist;*
Frothy Grey Bennet, patron of the press,
Whose freedom is their toast in bumpers full,
And which they show, by crowding to caress
Fudge Tommy Moore, and actioning John Bull.
Shout, my old Coke!—shout, Albemarle!—shout, Grey!
Hail, mighty mother, hail!—hail, glorious ALL FOOLS' day!

6.

Apt are the emblems which the party shows—
Here's "Great Napoleon, victor over Spain,"
And "Wellington of war no science knows,"
And "Angoulême has touched his hilt in vain,"
And "We must perish if the gold's withdrawn,"
And "We must perish if the gold is paid,"
And "Chaste art thou, O Queen! as snow ere dawn,"
And "Princess Olive† is an injured maid;"
But shining over all, in alt still say,
Hail, mighty mother, hail!—hail, glorious ALL FOOLS' day!

7.

Close by their tails see Jeff's reviewers sneak
In buff and blue, an antiquated gang;
Jeffrey himself with penny-trumpet squeak,
Chimes with Jackpudding Sydney's jews-harp twang;
Hallam is there with blood of Pindar wet,
And there Macculloch bellows, gallant stot,

* Michael Angelo Taylor was a member of Parliament, wealthy, and with his residence very near the then St. Stephen's Chapel, in which the Commons used to sit. From 4 o'clock every day, until 12 at night, Taylor kept open house for such members of the Opposition as pleased to "eat, drink, and be merry." On one occasion, when Lord Durham (then Mr. Lambton) had brought in a bill—either for Catholic Emancipation or Parliamentary Reform—most of the Opposition had retired to take refreshments, at Taylor's, during Lambton's speech, and a tough debate and strong struggle was; expected the Government declined making a speech in reply, forcing on a division, before the other party could be collected from Taylor's "cutlets and gin-twist," and negatived the question, for that session, by a sudden vote. This trick was much complained of, by the Liberals, for a long time.—M.

† Mrs. Olive Serres claimed to be the legitimate daughter of Henry Frederick, Duke of Cumberland, (brother to George III.,) by a marriage with Miss Wilmot. She assumed the rank and title of Princess Olive of Cumberland, and had her case brought before Parliament, where her claims were not recognised. This was in 1822, and most of her remaining years were spent within the rules of a prison, for debt. She died in 1834.—M.

And Christian Leslie, to whom is set
  A bust of stone in Stockbridge shady grot.
In puppy chorus yelps the full array,
Hail, mighty mother, hail!—hail, glorious ALL FOOLS' day!

8.

Still impudent their gestures—still their mien
  Swaggers beneath the load of self-conceit;
Yet all in spite of vanity is seen
  Graven on each brow disorder and defeat;
Still BYRON'S canister, too deftly tied,
  Rings "kling-ling-ling," bedraggling at their tail!
Still NORTH'S stout cowhide, to each back applied,
  Makes even the stoutest of the crew to quail;
Yet boldly still they cry with brave hurra—
Hail, mighty mother, hail!—hail, glorious ALL FOOLS' day!

9.

Whom have we next?—I note the gesture trim,
  The throat unkerchiefed, and the jaunty air,
The yellow silk that wraps the nether limb,
  And all the singing robes that poets wear—
Hail, Bohea-bibbing monarch of Cockaigne!
  Who is more fit than thou to join the song
Of glory to Tom-foolery, the strain
  Thou and thy subject tribes have trolled so long?
Shout o'er thy bumpered dish, hip! hip! hurra!
Hail, mighty mother, hail!—hail, glorious ALL FOOLS' day!

10.

For the remainder of this rabble rout,
  Their names I know not, nor desire to know.
For aught I care, each long-eared lubber lout
  May march to Orcus on fantastic toe,
Save Barry Cornwall, milk-and-water bard,
  Lord of the flunky clad in livery green!
To send so sweet a poet 'twere too hard,
  To the chaise-percée of old Pluto's queen.
No, here as Cockney-Laureate let him stay,
Singing, hail, mother, hail!—hail, glorious ALL FOOLS' day!

11.

Make way, make way, in plenitude of paunch,
  See London's learned livery waddling on.
Lord Waithman heads the rumpled avalanche,*
  Tailed by Teautamen's hero—Whittington!
Oh, Huckaback the Great, alike sublime
  In measuring speech or gingham by the ell,

* Alderman Waithman, who was a strong Liberal, carried on the business of a linen-draper in the premises, corner of Fleet-street and Bridge-street, Blackfriars, now partly occupied by the *Sunday Times* newspaper office. He filled the office of Lord Mayor, and was elected four times to represent the city of London in Parliament. After his death, his friends erected an obelisk, in his honor, opposite that raised in commemoration of John Wilkes, at the foot of Ludgate Hill, and within view of the place where he long had kept a shop.—M.

Worthy alike of poet's lofty rhyme,
  The stuff you utter, and the stuff you sell!
Sing with that voice which can e'en kings dismay,
Hail, mighty mother, hail!—hail, April ALL FOOLS' day!

The Shephed. That'll do—*Ohe! jam satis.* I ken naething about tae half o' the chiels, and the little I do ken about the lave is na worth kenning. Bnt the verses sound weel, and seem fu' o' satire. They'll no be popular, though, about Ettrick.

North. I must occasionally consult the taste of the people in London, and the neighboring villages. They are fond of their little local jeers, and attach mighty importance to men and things, that in the Forest, James, are considered in the light of their own native insignificance.

The Shepherd. That's God's truth! In London you'll hear a soun', like laigh thunder, frae a million voices, growl-growling on ae subject, for aiblins a week thegither; a' else is clean forgotten, and the fate o' the world seems to hang on the matter in han';—but just wait you till the tips o' the horns o' the new moon hae sprouted, and the puir silly craturs recollec' naething ava', either o' their ain fear, or their ain folly, and are aff on anither scent, as idle and thochtless as before. In the kintra, we are o' a wiser, and doucer, and dourer nature; we fasten our feelings rather on the durable hills, than on the fleeting cluds; tomorrow kens something about yesterday, and the fifty-twa weeks in the year dinna march by like isolated individuals; but like a company strongly mustered, and on an expedition or enterprise o' pith and moment.

North. So with books. In a city they are read—flung aside—and forgotten like the dead.

The Shepherd. In the pure air o' the kintra, beuks hae an immortal life. I hae nae great leebrary—feck o't consists o' twenty volumes o' my ain writing; but, oh! man, it is sweet to sit down, on a calm simmer evening, on a bit knowe, by the lochside, and let ane's mind gang daundering awa down the pages o' some volume o' genius, creating thochts alang with the author, till, at last, you dinna weel ken whilk o' you made the beuk. That's just the way I aften read your Magazine, till I could believe that I hae written every article—Noctes and a'.

North. How did the Border games go off this Spring Meeting, Shepherd?

The Shepherd. The loupin' was gude, and the rinnin' was better, and the ba' was best. Oh, man! that ye had but been there!

North. What were the prizes?

The Shepherd. Bunnets. Blue bunnets—I hae ane o' them in my pouch, that wasna gien awa'. There—try it on.

(*The Shepherd puts the blue bonnet on Mr. North's head.*)

North. I have seen the day, James, when I could have leaped any man in Ettrick.

The Shepherd. A' but ane. The Flying Tailor would hae been your match ony day. But there's no denying you used to take awfu' spangs. Gude safe us, on springy meadow grun, rather on the decline. you were a verra grasshopper. But, wae's me—the crutches? *Eheu! fugaces, Posthume, Posthume, labuntur anni!*

North. Why, even yet, James, if it were not for this infernal gout here, I could leap any man living, at hop, step, and jump——

The Shepherd. Hech, sirs!—hech, sirs! but the human mind's a strange thing, after a'! Here's you, Mr. North, the cleverest man, I'll say't to your face, noo extant, a scholar and a feelosopher, vauntin' o' your loupin'! That's a great weakness. You should be thinkin' o' ither things, Mr. North. But a' you grit men are perfet fules either in ae thing or anither.

North. Come, James, my dear Hogg, draw your chair a little closer. We are a set of strange devils, I acknowledge, we human beings.

The Shepherd. Only luk at the maist celebrated o' us. There's Byron, braggin' o' his soomin', just like yourself o' your loupin'. He informs us that he swom through the streets of Venice, that are a' canals, you ken—nae very decent proceeding—and keepit ploutering on the drumly waves for four hours and a half, like a wild guse, diving, too, I'se warrant, wi' his tail, and treading water, and lying on the back o' him—wha' the deevil cares?

North. His lordship was, after all, but a sorry Leander?

The Shepherd. You may say that. To have been like Lander, he should hae swom the Strechts in a storm, and in black midnight, and a' by himself, without boats and gondolas to pick him up gin he tuk the cramp, and had a bonnie lass to dicht him dry,—and been drown'd at last—but that he'll never be.

North. You are too satirical, Hogg.

The Shepherd. And there's Tammas Mure braggin' after anither fashion o' his exploits amang the lasses. O man, dinna you think it rather contemptible, to sit in a cotch wi' a bonnie thochtless lassie, for twa three lang stages, and then publish a sang about it?* I ance heard a gran' leddie frae London lauching till I thocht she would hae split her sides, at Thomas Little, as she ca'd him. I could scarcely fadom her—but ye ken't by her face what she was thinking,—and it was a' quite right—a severe reproof.

North. Mr. Coleridge? Is he in the habit, Hogg, of making the Public the confidants of his personal accomplishments?

The Shepherd. I canna weel tell, for deevil the like o' sic books

* The Shepherd must here allude to one of Moore's songs, (*not* included in the collective edition of his poetry,) which commences thus:—

"Sweet Fanny of Timmol! when first I came in
To the dear little carriage in which you were hurled,
I thought to myself, if it were not a sin,
I could teach you the prettiest things in the world."—M.

as his did I ever see wi' my cen beneath the blessed licht. I'm no speakin' o' his Poems—I'll aye roose them—but the Freen* and the Lay Sermons are aneuch to drive ane to distraction. What's logic?

North. Upon my honor as a gentleman, I do not know; if I did, I would tell you with the greatest pleasure.

The Shepherd. Weel, weel, Coleridge is aye accusing folk o' haeing nae logic. The want o' a' things is owing to the want o' logic, it seems. Noo, Mr. North, gin logic be soun' reasoning, and I jalouse as much, he has less o't himself than ony body I ken, for he never sticks to the point twa pages; and to tell you the truth, I aye feel as I were fuddled after perusing Coleridge. Then he's aye speaking o' himsel—but what he says I can never mak out. Let him stick to his poetry, for, oh! man, he's an unyerthly writer, and gies Superstition sae beautifu' a countenance, that she wiles folk on wi' her, like so many bairns, into the flowery but fearfu' wildernesses, where sleeping and wauking seem a' ane thing, and the very soul within us wonders what has become o' the every-day warld, and asks hersel what creation is this that wavers and glimmers, and keeps up a bonnie wild musical sough, like that o' swarming bees, spring-startled birds, and the voice of a hundred streams, some wimpling awa' ower the Elysian meadows, and ithers roaring at a distance frae the clefts o' mount Abora. But is't true that they hae made him the Bishop of Barbadoes?

North. No, he is only Dean of Highgate.† I long for his "Wanderings of Cain," about to be published by Taylor and Hessey.‡ That house has given us some excellent things of late. They are spirited publishers. But why did not Coleridge speak to Blackwood? I suppose he could not tell if he were questioned.

The Shepherd. In my opinion, sir, the bishops o' the Wast Indies should be blacks.

North. Prudence, James, prudence,—we are alone, to be sure, but the affairs of the West Indies——

The Shepherd. The bishops o' the Wast Indies should be blacks. Naebody 'll ever mak me think itherwise. Mr. Wilberforce, and Mr. Macaulay,§ and Mr. Brougham, and a' the ither saints, have tell't us

* "The Friend" was a weekly periodical, edited by Coleridge, which lived through six months or so, and died from the irregularity of its issue, and the very unbusiness-like manner in which it was carried on. This was one of the many failures of S. T. C., (ες τε σε, he liked to write it,) and, De Quincey informs us, was chiefly made so by Coleridge's use of opium.—M.

† It was one of Coleridge's nephews who was made Bishop of Barbadoes, which he ceased to be, by resignation, in 1842. Coleridge resided at Highgate, near London.—M.

‡ "The Wanderings of Cain," a poem in prose, originally appeared in an Annual, I believe, and is now included in the Works of Coleridge.—M.

§ William Wilberforce, long the leader of the Anti-Slavery party in the House of Commons He died in 1833. His son, Dr. Samuel Wilberforce, is now Bishop of Oxford.—Zachary Macaulay was for forty years associated with Wilberforce in the British Anti-Slavery movement. He died in 1838, and was the father of Thomas Babington Macaulay, the poet, orator, critic, and historian.—M.

that blacks are equal to whites; and gin that be true, make bishops o' them—what for no?

North. James, you are a consistent poet, philosopher, and philanthropist. Pray, how would you like to marry a black woman? How would Mr. Wilberforce like it?

The Shepherd. I canna answer for Mr. Wilberforce; but as for myself, I scunner at the bare idea.

North. Why, a black skin, thick lips, grizzly hair, long heels, and convex shins—what can be more delightful?—But to be serious, James, do you think there is no difference between black and white?

The Shepherd. You're drawing me into an argument about the West Indies, and the neegars. I ken naething about it. I hate slavery as an abstract idea—but it's a necessary evil, and I canna believe a' thae stories about cruelty. There's nae fun or amusement in whipping women to death—and as for a skelp or twa, what's the harm?—Hand me ower the rum and the sugar, sir.

North. What would Buxton the Brewer say, if he heard such sentiments from the author of Kilmeny? But what were we talking about a little while ago?

The Shepherd. Never ask me siccan a like question. Ye ken weel aneuch that I never remember a single thing that passes in conversation. But may I ask gin you're comin' out to the fishing this season?

North. Apropos. Look here, James. What think you of these flies? Phin's, of course. Keep them a little farther off your nose, James, for they are a dozen of devils, these black heckles. You observe,—dark yellow body—black half heckle, and wings of the mallard, a beautiful brown—gut like gossamer, and the killing Kirby.

The Shepherd. I'll just put them into my pouch. But, first, let me see how they look sooming.

(*Draws out a fly and trails it slowly along the punch in his tumbler, which he holds up to the argand lamp—a present to Mr. Ambrose from Barry Cornwall.*)

O man! that's the naturallest thing ever I saw in a' my born days. I ken whare there's a muckle trout lying at this very moment, below the root o' an auld birk, wi' his great snout up the stream, drawing in slugs and ither animalculas, into his vortex, and no-caring a whisk o' his tail for flees; but you'se hae this in the tongue o' you, my braw fellow, before May-day. He'll sook't in saftly, saftly, without showing mair than the lip o' him, and then I'll streck him, and down the pool he'll gaung, snoring like a whale, as gin he were descending in a' his power to the bottomless pit, and then up wi' a loup o' lightning to the verra lift, and in again into the water wi' a squash and a plunge, like a man gaun in to the douking, and then out ae pool into anither, like a kelpie gaun a-coorting, through alang the furds and shallows, and ettling wi' a' his might at the waterfa' opposite Fahope's house.

Luk at him! luk at him! there he glides like a sunbeam strong and steady, as I give him the butt, and thirty yards o' the pirn—nae stane to stumble, and nae tree to fankle—bonnie green hills shelving down to my ain Yarrow—the sun lukin' out upon James Hogg, frae behint a cloud, and a breeze frae St. Mary's Loch chanting a song o' triumph down the vale, just as I land him on the gowany edge of that grassy-bedded bay,

> Fair as a star, when only one
> Is shining in the sky.

North. Shade of Isaac Walton!

The Shepherd. I'm desperate thirsty—here's your health. Oh, Lord! What's this? what's this? I've swallowed the flee!

North (*starting up in consternation*). Oh, Lord! What's this? what's this? I've trodden on a spike, and it has gone up to my knee-pan!—O my toe! my toe! But, James—James—shut not your mouth—swallow not your swallow—or you are a dead man. There—steady—steady—I have hold of the gut, and I devoutly trust that the hook is sticking in your tongue or palate. It cannot, must not be in your stomach, James. Oh!——

The Shepherd. Oh! for Liston,* wi' his instruments!

North. Hush—hush—I see the brown wings.

Enter AMBROSE.

Ambrose. Here, here is a silver spoon—I am all in a fluster. O dear, Mr. North, will this do to keep dear Mr. Hogg's mouth open, while you are——

North. It is the soup-ladle, sir. But a sudden thought strikes me. Here is my gold ring. I shall let it down the line, and it will disentangle the hook. Don't swallow my crest, my dear Shepherd. There—all's right—the black heckle is free, and my dear poet none the worse.

The Shepherd (*coughing out Mr. North's gold ring*). That verra flee shall grip the muckle trout. Mr. Ambrose, quick,—countermand Liston. (*Mr. Ambrose vanishes.*) I'm a' in a poor o' sweat. Do you hear my heart beating?

North. Mrs. Phin's tackle is so excellent that I felt confident in the result. Bad gut, and you were a dead man. But let us resume the thread of our discourse.

The Shepherd. I have a sore throat, and it will not be weel till we soop. Tak my arm, and we'se gang into the banqueting-room. Hush—there's a clampering in the trance. It's the rush o' critics frae the

* Robert Liston, then of Edinburgh, and the best operator there. He removed to London, where he established the highest character as a surgeon, and died in 1847.—M.

pit o' the theatre. They're coming for porter—and let's wait till they're a' in the tap-room, or ither holes. In five minutes you'll hear nae ither word than "Vandenhoff," "Vandenhoff."*

North. The shower is over, let us go; and never, James, would old Christopher North desire to lean for support on the arm of a better man.

The Shepherd. I believe you noo—for I ken when you're serious and when you're jokin', and that's mair than every ane can say.

North. Forgive, James, the testy humors of a gouty old man. I am your friend.

The Shepherd. I ken that fu' brawly. Do you hear the sound o' that fizzing in the pan? Let's to our wark. But, North, say nothing about the story of the flee in that wicked Magazine.

North. Mum's the word. *Allons.*

SCENE II.—*The Banqueting-Room.*

Enter MR. NORTH, *leaning on the arm of the* SHEPHERD, *and* MR. AMBROSE. MR. TICKLER *in the shade.*

North. By the palate of Apicius! What a board of oysters!—Ha, Tickler! Friend of my soul, this goblet sip, how art thou?

Tickler. Stewed—foul from the theatre. Ah, ha! Hogg—your paw, James.

The Shepherd. How's a' wi' ye?—how's a' wi' ye, Maister Tickler? Oh, man, I wish I had been wi' you. I'm desperate fond o' theatricals, and Vandenhoff's a gran' chiel—a capital actor.

Tickler. So I hear. But the Vespers of Palermo won't do at all at all; so I shan't criticise any actor or actress that strutted and spouted to-night. Mrs. Hemans, I am told, is beautiful—and she has a fine feeling about many things. I love Mrs. Hemans; but if Mrs. Hemans loves me, she will write no more tragedies.† My dear Christopher, fair play's a jewel—a few oysters, if you please.

North. These "whiskered Pandours," as Campbell calls them in his Pleasures of Hope, are inimitable.

The Shepherd. God safe us a', I never saw a man afore noo put-

* John Vandenhoff, the actor, was an especial favorite with Edinburgh play-goers. They cherished a fond recollection of John Kemble, something of whose style of acting Vandenhoff had adopted.—M.

† "The Vespers of Palermo," beautiful as a dramatic poem, made slight impression on the public mind either in London or Edinburgh. At the latter place it was brought out on the especial solicitation of Sir Walter Scott, who was urged to take an interest in it by Joanna Baillie. Before its production in Edinburgh, Scott wrote to say, "I trust the piece will succeed; but there is no promising, for Saunders is meanly jealous of being thought less critical than John Bull, and may, perhaps, despise to be pleased with what was less fortunate in London." He subsequently said, in allusion to this play, that, in Edinburgh, it was "situation, passion, and rapidity of action, which seem to be the principal requisites for securing the success of a modern drama."—M.

ting sax muckle oysters in the mouth o' him a' at aince, but yoursel, Mr. North.

Tickler. Pray, North, what wearisome and persevering idiot kept mumbling monthly and crying quarterly about Mrs. Hemans, in the 'Baillie's Guse," for four years on end?

The Shepherd. The Baillie's Guse!—wha's he that? Is't ane o' the periodicals you're misca'ing?

Tickler. Yes—Waugh's Old New Edinburgh Review.* It was called so, for the first time, by the Shepherd himself—and most aptly—as it waddled, flapped, and gabbled, out of the worthy Baillie's shop, through among the stand of coaches in Hunter Square.

North. It was indeed a bright idea to fight a gander against a game-cock—Pool *versus* Jeffrey!

The Shepherd. Weel, do you ken, I thought it a gay gude review—but it was unco late in noticing warks. The contributors, I jalouse, werena very original-minded lads, and lay back till they heard the general sugh. But when they did pronounce, I thought them, for the maist part, gude grammarians.

Tickler. The ninny I allude to, who must be a phrenologist, could utter not a syllable but "Hemans, Hemans, Hemans!" The lady must have been disgusted.

Shepherd. No she, indeed. What leddy was ever disgusted even by the flattery o' a fule?

Tickler. They were a base as well as a stupid pack. Low mean animosities peeped out in every page, and with the exception of our most excellent friend R., and two or three others, the contributors were scarcely fit to compile an obituary. The editor himself is a weak well-meaning creature, and when the Baillie's Guse breathed her last, he naturally became Taggar to the Phrenological Journal.

North. I should be extremely sorry to think that my friend Waugh, who is a well-informed gentlemanly man, has lost money in this ill-judged business. The Guse, as you call it, occasionally quacked, as if half afraid, half angry, at poor innocent Maga, but I never gave the animal a single kick. Was its keep expensive to the Baillie?

Tickler. Too much so, I fear. These tenth-raters are greedy dogs. Do you not remember Tims?

North. Alas! poor Tims! I had forgot his importunities. But I thought I saw his Silliness in Taylor and Hessey, a month or two ago—"a pen-and-ink sketch of the late trial at Hertford."

Tickler. Yes—yes—yes—Tims on Thurtell!! By the way, what a most ludicrous thing it would have been had Thurtell assassinated Tims! Think of Tims's face when he found Jack was serious. What small, mean, paltry, contemptible Cockney shrieks would he have emitted! 'Pon my honor, had Jack *bonâ fide* Thurtellized Tims, it

* The *New Edinburgh Review* was published by Waugh & Innes.—M.

would have been productive of the worst consequence to the human race; it would have thrown such an air of absurdity over murder.*

Shepherd. What! has that bit Cockney cretur Tims, that I frightened sae in the Tent at Braemar, when he offered to sing "Scots wha hae wi' Wallace bled," been writing about ae man murdering anither? He wasna blate.

Tickler. Yes, he has—and his account is a curiosity. Tims thinks, that the most appalling circumstance attending the said murder was, that every thing was "in clusters." "It is strange," quoth he, "that, solitary as the place was, and desperate as was the murder"—the actors—the witnesses—all but the poor helpless solitary thing that perished, "were in clusters!"

Shepherd. Hout, tout, Tims!

Tickler. "The murderers were in clusters," he continues—"the farmer that heard the pistol had his wife, and child, and nurse with him; there were two laborers at work in the lane, on the morning after the butcher-work; there was a merry party at the cottage on the very night, singing and supping, while Weare's mangled carcass was lying darkening in its gore in the neighboring field; there were hosts of publicans and hostlers witnesses of the gang's progress on their blood-journey; and the gigs, pistols, even the very knives ran in pairs." Quod Tims, in Taylor and Hessey,† for Feb. 1, 1824—for here is the page, with which I now light my pipe. By all that is miraculous, these candles are in clusters.

Shepherd. That's ae way, indeed, o' makin' murder ridiculous. But it's a lee. The gigs did not run in clusters. Only think o' ca'ing ae gig passing anither on the road, a cluster o' gigs! Neither did the actors run in clusters, for Thurtell was by himself when he did the job. And then the pistols! Did he never hear before o' a pair o' pistols? Tims, if you were here, I wad thraw your nose for you, ye conceited prig.

Tickler (*reading*). "It seems as though it were fated, that William Weare should be the only solitary object on that desperate night, when he clung to life in agony and blood, and was at last struck out of existence as a *thing*, *single*, valueless, and vile." He was, it seems, a bachelor.

Shepherd. The only solitary object on that desperate night. Was nae shepherd walking by himsel' on the mountains? But what kind o' a Magazine can that o' Taylor and Hessey be, to take sic writers as Tims? I hope they don't run in clusters.

North. Give me a bit of the sheet—for my cigar (Heaven defend

* The murder of William Weare, a London gambler, by Thurtell, Probert, and Hunt:—this last was brother of the late Henry Hunt, a dramatic vocalist in New-York, and father of Mrs. or Madame Thillon, the operatic singer.—M.

† The *London Magazine*.—M.

me, the cigars run in clusters) is extinct. Let me see. Hear Tims on Thurtell's speech.

"The solid, slow, and appalling tone in which he rang out these last words, can never be imagined by those who were not auditors of it. He had worked himself up into a great actor—and his eye, for the first time during the trial, became alive and eloquent; his attitude was expressive in the extreme. He clung to every separate word with an earnestness which we cannot describe, as though every syllable had the power to buoy up his sinking life—and that these were the last sounds that were ever to be sent unto the ear of those who were to decree his doom!

"The final word, God! was thrown up with an almost gigantic energy—and he stood, after its utterance,* with his arm extended, his face protruded, and his chest dilated, as if the spell of the sound were yet upon him, and as though he dared not move, lest he should disturb the still-echoing appeal! He then drew his hands slowly back—pressed them firmly to his breast, and sat down, half exhausted, in the dock."

Omnes. Ha! ha! ha! ha! ha! ha! ha! ha! ha! ha! ha! ha!

North (*gravely*). "When he first commenced his defence, he spoke in a steady, artificial manner, after the style of Forum orators—but as he warmed in the subject, and felt his ground with the jury, he became more unaffectedly earnest, and naturally solemn—and his mention of his mother's love, and his father's piety, drew the tear up to his eye almost to falling. He paused—and, though pressed by the judge to rest, to sit down, to desist, he stood up, resolute against his feelings, and finally, with one fast gulp, swallowed down his tears! *He wrestled with grief, and threw it!* When speaking of Barber Beaumont, the tiger indeed came over him, and his very voice seemed to escape out of his keeping. There was such a savage vehemence in his whole look and manner, as quite to awe his hearers. With an unfortunate quotation from a play, in which he long had acted too bitterly,—The Revenge!—he soothed his maddened heart to quietness, and again resumed his defence, and for a few minutes in a doubly artificial serenity. The tone in which he wished that he had died in battle *reminded me of Kean's farewell to the pomp of war in Othello*—and the following consequence of such a death was as grandly delivered by Thurtell as it was possible to be: 'Then my father and my family, though they would have mourned my loss, would have blessed my name; and shame would not have rolled its burning fires over my memory!' "†

* To strengthen his protestation of innocence, Thurtell closed with the common adjuration, "So help me God."—M.

† In 1824, when Thurtell was tried for the murder of Weare, the law expressly forbade that persons accused of such a crime should be allowed the privilege, extended to prisoners in all other cases, (except in courts-martial,) of being heard by counsel. The law has since been altered. It was stated and believed that Thurtell's defence, which he read remarkably well,

Omnes. Ha! ha! ha! ha! ha! ha! ha! ha! ha!

Shepherd. Weel, I dinna ken the time I hae laucht so muckle. I'm sair exhausted. Gie's a drink. The English folk gaed clean mad a'thegither about that fallow. I never could see ony thing very remarkable about his cutting Weare's craig. It was a puir murder yon. There was that deevil-incarnate Gordon, that murdered the bit silly callant o' a pedlar on Eskdale muir, the ither year, and nae sic sugh about it in a' the papers.

Tickler. I forget it. The particulars? .

Shepherd. Oh! man, it was a cruel deed. He foregathered wi' the laddie and his bit pack, trudging by himsel' among the hills, frae housie to housie; and he keepit company wi' him for twa hail days, ane o' them the Sabbath. Nae doubt he talked, and lauched, and joked wi' the puir creature, wha was a bonnie boy they say, but little better in his intellects than an innocent, only hafflins wise; and when the ane stapped, the ither stapped, and they eat bread thegither by different ingles, and sleepit twa nichts in ae bed. In a lanesome place he tuk the callant and murdered him wi' the iron-heel o' ane of his great wooden clogs. The savage-tramper smashed in the skull wi' its yellow hair, didna wait to shut the bonnie blue een, put the pack over his ain braid shouthers, and then, demented as he was, gaed into the verra next town as a packman, and selt to the lassies the bits o' ribbons, and pencils, and thumbles, and sic like, o' the murdered laddie. I saw him hanged. I gaed into Dumfries on purpose. I wanted them no to put ony night-cap over the ugly face o' him, that we might a' see his last girns, and am only sorry that I didna see him dissecked.

Tickler. A set of amusing articles might, I think, be occasionally compiled from the recorded trials of our best British murderers. We are certainly a blood-thirsty people; and the scaffold has been mounted, in this country, by many first-rate criminals.

North. One meets with the most puzzling malefactors, who perpetrate atrocious deeds upon such recondite principles, that they elude the scrutiny of the most perspicacious philosophers. Butlers, on good wages and easy work, rise out of comfortable warm beds, and cut the throats of their masters quite unaccountably; well-educated gentlemen of a thousand a-year, magistrates for the county, and præses of public meetings for the redress of grievances, throw their wives over bridges and into coal-pits; pretty blue-eyed young maidens poison whole families with a mess of pottage; matrons of threescore strangle their sleeping partners with a worsted garter; a decent well-dressed person meets you on your evening stroll, and after knocking out your brains with a bludgeon, pursues his journey; if you are an old bachelor, or a single lady advanced in years, you may depend upon being found

was written for him by Charles Phillips, the Irish Barrister.—The article in the *London Magazine* was attributed to Hazlitt.—M.

some morning stretched along your lobby with your eyes starting out of their sockets, the blue marks of finger-nails indented into your wizen, and your *os frontis* driven in upon your brain, apparently by the blow of a sledge-hammer.

Shepherd. Haud your tongues, haud your tongues, ye twa; you're making me a' grew.

Tickler. A beautiful variety of disposition and genius serves to divest of sameness the simple act of slaughter; and the benevolent reader never tires of details, in which knives, daggers, pistols, clubs, mallets, hatchets, and apothecaries' phials, "dance through all the mazes of rhetorical confusion." Nothing can be "more refreshing" than a few hours' sleep after the perusal of a bloody murder. Your dreams are such as Coleridge might envy. Clubs batter out your brains;—your throat is filled with mud, as three strong Irishmen (their accent betrays them) tread you down seven fathoms into a quagmire. "You had better lie quiet, sir," quoth Levi Hyams, a Jew, while he applies a pig-butcher's knife to the jugular vein; you start up like Priam at the dead of night, and an old hag of a housekeeper chops your nose off with a cleaver. "Oh! what a pain methinks it is to die," as a jolly young waterman flings you out of his wherry into the Thames, immediately below Wellington Bridge. "Spare—spare my life, and take all I have!" has no effect upon two men in crape, who bury you, half dead, in a ditch. "He still breathes," growls a square thickset ruffian in a fustian jacket, as he gives you the *coup-de-grace* with a hedge-stake.

Shepherd. Haud your tongues, I say. You'll turn my stomach at this dish o' tripe. The moniplies and the lady's hood are just excellent. Change the conversation.

Tickler. You are huddled out of a garret-window by a gang of thieves, and feel yourself impaled on the area spikes; or the scoundrels have set the house on fire, that none may know they have murdered you; you are gagged with a floor-brush till your mouth yawns like a barn-door, yet told, if you open your lips, you are a dead man; outlandish devils put you into a hot oven; you try to escape from the murderer of the Marrs, and other households, through a common-sewer, and all egress is denied by a catacomb of cats, and the offal of twenty dissecting-tables. "Hoize him into the boiler, and be d——d to him;" and no sooner said than done. "Leave off haggling at his windpipe, Jack, and scoop out his bloody eyes."

North. How do you like to be buried in quick-lime in your back-court, heaving all the while like a mole-hill, above your gashes, and puddled with your slow-oozing heart-blood? Is it a luxury to be pressed down, neck and crop, scarified like bacon, into a barrel below a water-spout, among dirty towels, sheets, and other napery, to be discovered, six weeks hence, in a state of putrefaction? What think you of being fairly cut up like a swine, and pickled, salted, barrelled, and shipped off at fourpence a pound, for the use of a blockading squadron? Or would you rather, in the shape of hams, circumnavigate the globe with Cook or Vancouver? Dreams—dreams—dreams. "I wake in horror, and dare sleep no more!"

Tickler. Could it have been believed, that in a country where murder has thus been carried to so high a pitch of cultivation, its fourteen million inhabitants would have been set agape and aghast by such a pitiful knave as Jack Thurtell killing and bagging one single miserable sharper? Monstrous!

North. There was Sarah Malcolm, a sprightly young charwoman of the Temple, that murdered, with her own hand, a whole household. Few spinsters, we think, have been known to murder three of their own sex; and Sarah Malcolm must ever stand in the first class of assassins. She had no accomplice; her own hand held down the gray heads of the poor old women, and strangled them with unflinching fingers. As for the young girl of seventeen, she cut her throat from ear to ear, while she was perhaps dreaming of her sweetheart. She silenced all the breath in the house, and shut by the dead bodies; went about her ordinary business, as sprightly as ever, and lighted a young Irish gentleman's fire at the usual hour.

Tickler. What an admirable wife would Sarah have made for Williams, who, some dozen years ago, began work as if he purposed to murder the metropolis! Sarah was sprightly and diligent, good-looking, and fond of admiration. Williams was called "Gentleman Williams," so genteel and amiable a creature did he seem to be; so pleasant with his chit-chat, and vein of trifling, peculiar to himself, and not to be imitated. He was very fond of children, used to dandle them with a truly parental air, and pat their curled heads, with the hand that cut an infant's throat in the cradle. Williams was a sober man, and no brawler; he preferred quiet conversation with the landlady and her family within the bar, to the brutal mirth of the tavern-boxes; and young and old were alike delighted with the suavity of his smile. But in his white great-coat—with his maul—or his ripping-chisel—or his small ivory-handled penknife, at dead of night, stealing upon a doomed family, with long silent strides, while, at the first glare of his eyes, the victims shrieked aloud, "We are all murdered!" Williams was then a different being indeed, and in all his glory. His ripping-chisel struck to the heart the person whose cheek he had patted two hours before. Charles Martell himself, or the Pounder, smashed not a skull like Williams, the Midnight Malletteer—and tidily and tenderly did he cover up the baby with its cradle-clothes, when he knew that he had pierced its gullet like a quill. He never allowed such trifles long to ruffle his temper. In the evening, he was seen smiling as before; even more gentle aud insinuating than usual; more tenderly did he kiss little Tommy, as he prepared to toddle to his crib; and, as he touched the bosom of the bar-maid in pleasing violence, he thought how at one blow the blood would spout from her heart.*

North. Sarah Malcolm was just the person to have been his bride. What a honey-moon! How soft would have been their pillow, as they recited a past, or planned a future murder! How would they have fallen asleep in each other's blood-stained arms! with the ripping-chisel below their pillow, and the maul upon the hearth!

The Shepherd. I wadna walk by myself through a dark wood the night, gin ony body were to gie me a thousand pounds. I never heard you in sic a key before. It's no right—it's no right!

North. What do the phrenologers say about Thurtell? I have not seen any of their Transactions lately.

Tickler. That he had the organ of Conscientiousness full, a large Benevolence, and also a finely-developed organ of Veneration, just as it might have been expected, they say, from his character. For the phrenologer thinks that Jack would not have cheated an honest man, that he was another Howard in benevolence, and had a deep sense of religion.

The Shepherd. I canna believe they would speak sic desperate havers as that.

Tickler (*ringing the bell, enters Ambrose*). Bring No. II. of the Phrenological Journal, Mr. Ambrose. You know where to find it. Perhaps the article I allude to may not yet be destroyed.

North. What can the *Courier* mean by talking such infernal nonsense, Tickler, about that murderous desperado, Surgeon Conolly?

Tickler. A puzzle. The *Courier* is an excellent paper—and I never before knew it, in a question of common sense and common morality, obstinately, singularly, and idiotically in the wrong.

North. Why, the cruel villain would have shot others besides poor Grainger—and after his blood was cooled, he exulted in the murder of that unfortunate man. The gallows was cheated of Conolly, by a quirk of the law.

Tickler. Judge Best saw the thing in its true light; and the country is indebted to him for his stubborn justice. Why, the *Courier* says, that not one man in a hundred, but would have done as Conolly did.†—Oh monstrous! is murder so very ordinary a transaction?

North. No more, no more. But to be done with it, listen to this:—"We are informed that this unfortunate gentleman has directed his friends to supply him with a complete set of surgical instruments, with

* There was no actual *proof*, but the strongest presumption, that Williams really was a wholesale murderer. He died before the time appointed for his trial, and the London populace, solemnly taking his corpse to the places where the murders had been committed, treated it there with unheard of ignominy, and then shot it into a hole dug in a ditch, pouring over it as much quicklime as would have built a moderate-sized house.—M.

† I am ignorant of the circumstances here referred to.—M.

all the new inventions, and a complete chamber medicine chest. There is no doubt that he will be of the greatest utility to the colony, from the great want of medical men there; but there is less doubt that he will be one of the first in the country, as he is covered with misfortunes, *and unpolluted by crime.*"

Tickler. That cannot be from the *Courier.*

North. Alas! it is—although quoted from the Medical Adviser.

Tickler. I shall row Mudford for this, first time I dine with him in town. Here is another folly, although of a different character, from the same excellent paper of our excellent friend,* an account of the Stot's Introductory Lecture on what is called Political Economy. The Ricardo Lecture!! "Mr. M'Culloch began his lecture by pointing out the importance of the study of Political Economy, and observed, that the accumulation of wealth could alone raise men from that miserable state of society, in which all were occupied in providing for their immediate physical wants, by affording them the means of subsistence when employed in the cultivation of mental powers, or in those pursuits which embellish life."

North. Most statistical of Stots! I had quite forgotten the stupid savage—but, look here, Tickler—here is a flaming account of his second display, in the *Morning Chronicle.* "He showed that objects derive their value from labor alone, and that they are more or less valuable in proportion as labor is expended on them; that the air, and the rays of the sun, however necessary and useful, possess no value; that water, which at a river's side is of no value, acquires a value when required by persons who are at some distance, in proportion to the labor employed in its conveyance."

Shepherd. I aye thocht M'Culloch a dull dour fellow,† but the like o' that beats a'. It's an awfu' truism. The London folk 'ill never thole sic havers frae sic a hallanshaker.

North. On Mr. Canning's appointment to the Secretaryship, the *Courier* honored us by gracing its chief column with a character of that distinguished person from our pages, but without acknowledgment. He never quotes us, therefore why did he steal?

Tickler. Poo! poo! be not so sensitive. Nothing uncommon in that. It's the way of the world; and I am sure if Odoherty were here, he would laud Mudford for knowing a good thing. Here's that gentleman's health—I respect and esteem him highly.—James, you are a most admirable carver. That leg will do.

Shepherd. No offence, sir, but this leg's no for you, but for mysel. I thought I wad never hae gotten't aff. Naething better than the roasted

* William Mudford was Editor of the London *Courier* for many years, and author of a romance called "Five Nights of St. Albans."—M.

† J. R. M'Culloch had been appointed Professor of Political Economy in London University, then just founded.—M.

leg o' a hen. Safe us! she's fu' o' eggs. What for did they thraw the neck o' an eerock when her kame was red, and her just gaen to fa' a-laying? Howsomever, there's no great harm done. Oh! man, this is a grand sooping-house. Rax ower the porter. Here's to you, lads, baith o' you. What's a' this bizziness that I heard them speaking about in Selkirk as I came through, in regard to the tenth company o' Hoozawrs?

Tickler. Why, I cannot think Battier a well-used man. They sent him to Coventry.*

Shepherd. I would just as soon gang to Coventry as to Dublin city. But what was the cause o' the rippet?

North. Why, the Tenth is a crack regiment, and not thinking Mr. Battier any ornament to the corps, they rather forgot their good manners a little or so, and made the mess mighty disagreeable to him; so, after several trifling occurrences too tedious to bore you with, Hogg, why, Mr. Battier made himself scarce, got himself rowed a good deal by the people at the Horse-guards, sold his horses, I presume, and now sports half-pay in the pedestrian service.

The Shepherd. But what for was he nae ornament to the corpse? Wasna he a gentleman?

North. Perfectly a gentleman; but somehow or another not to the taste of the Tenth; and then, such a rider!

The Shepherd. What! wasna he a gude rider upon horseback?

North. The worst since John Gilpin. In a charge, he "grasped fast the flowing mane," gave tongue,—and involuntarily deserted. So says his colonel; and Mr. Battier, although he has published a denial of being the son of a merchant, has not, so far as I have observed, avowed himself a Castor.

Shepherd. Na, if that be the case, the ither lads had some excuse. But what garr'd Mr. Battier gang into the Hoozawrs, gin he couldna ride? I hope, now that he has gaen into the Foot, that he may be able to walk. If not, he had better leave the service, and fin' out some genteel sedentary trade. He wadna like to be a tailor?

Tickler. Why, Battier, I am told, is a worthy fellow, and as I said before, he was ill used. But he ought not to have gone into the Tenth, and he ought not to have made use of threatening inuendos after leaving the regiment, and crossing the Channel.

North. Certainly not. No gentleman should challenge a whole regiment, especially through the medium of the public press.

Shepherd. If Mr. Battier were to challenge me, if I were ane o' the

* Mr. Battier obtained a Cornetcy in the 10th Hussars, a dandy regiment, commanded by a gallant soldier, the late Marquis of Londonderry. The officers, on finding that Mr. Battier's father had been in trade, agreed to *cut* him. Of course, he did not tamely submit to this, but his complaints being useless, he left the regiment, challenging Lord Londondery to the duello, on the plea that he was to be held responsible for, because he could and ought to have checked, the ill conduct of the officers. Shots were exchanged, and this ended the affair.—M.

offishers o' the Tenth, I wad fecht him on horseback—either wi' sword or pistol, or baith; and what wad my man do, then, wi' his arms around the neck o' his horse, and me hewing awa' at him, head and hurdies?

North. It was a silly business altogether, and is gone by—but, alas, poor Collier! That was a tragedy indeed.

Tickler. Confound that lubber, James. If he has feeling at all, he must be miserable.

North. His account of the affair at first was miserably ill-written—indeed, incomprehensible—and grossly contradictory—extremely insolent, and in many essential points false. All were to blame, it seems, commodore, captains, crews, and Admiralty. A pretty presumptuous prig!

Shepherd. Puir chiel! puir chiel! I saw't in a paper—and couldna help greeting; a' riddled wi' wouns in the service o' his country, and to come to that end at last! Has that fallow James bitterly lamented the death o' the brave sea-captain,* and deplored having caused sic a woful disaster?

North. Not as he ought to have done. But the whole country must henceforth despise him and his book. I could pardon his first offence, for no man could have foreseen what has happened; but his subsequent conduct has been unpardonable. He owed to the country the expression of deep and bitter grief, for having been the unintentional, but not altogether the innocent cause of the death of one of her noblest heroes.

Tickler. I see Phillimore has been bastinadoing James—imprudently, I opine. You have no right to walk into a man's house with your hat on, like a Quaker, supported by a comrade, and then in the most un-Friendly manner, strike your host over the pate with a scion from an oak-stump.

North. Certainly you have not. I am sorry that my friend Phillimore, as brave a fellow as ever walked a quarter-deck, did not consult his brother the doctor. But I believe the captain had no intention of assaulting the naval historian when he entered the premises; and that some gross impertinence on the part of the scribe, brought the switch into active service.

Tickler. The public will pardon Phillimore.† A Naval History is a very good thing, if written by a competent person, which James is not, although the man has some merit as a chronicler. But the very idea of criticising in detail every action, just as you would criticise a volume of poems, is not a little absurd. Southey's Life of Nelson is good.

'* Mr. James *not* the novelist) had written a Naval Biography in which he did less than justice to a brave officer—Collier. This led to the fearful catastrophe, which is alluded to here.

† James frequently received *striking* criticisms of this nature. Captain Phillimore was brother of Dr. Phillimore, Government Advocate in the Admiralty Court, London, and Chancellor of Worcester, Oxford, and Bristol.—M.

North. Excellent. Look at James's History after reading that admi rable Manual, and you will get sick.

Shepherd. He's just a wonderfu' man, Soothey; the best o' a' the Lakers.

Tickler. Bam the Lakers. Here's some of the best Hollands that ever crossed the Zuyder Zee. Make a jug, James.

Shepherd. Only look, what has become of the supper? Mr. Tickler, you've a fearsome appetite. Hear—hear—there's the alarm-bell—and the fire-drum! Saw na ye that flash o' licht? I hope it may turn out a gude conflagration. Hear till the ingines. I'm thinking the fire's on the North Bridge. I hope it's no in my freen' Mr. John Anderson's shop.

North. I hope not. Mr. Anderson is a prosperous bibliopole, and these little cheap editions of the Scottish Poets, Ramsay, and Burns, and Grahame, are admirable. The prefaces are elegantly and judiciously written—the text correct—type beautiful, and embellishments appropriate.

Tickler. The "Fire-Eater," lately published by Mr. Anderson, is a most spirited and interesting tale—full of bustle and romantic incidents. I intend to review it.

Shepherd. The "Fire-Eater" is a fearsome name for ony Christian; but how can you twa sit ower your toddy in that gait, discussing the merits o' beuks, when I tell you the whole range o' buildings yonder's in a bleeze?

Enter MR. AMBROSE *with the Phrenological Journal.*

Ambrose. Gentlemen, Old Levy the Jew's fur-shop is blazing away like a fury, and threatening to burn down the Hercules Insurance Office.

Tickler. Out with the candles. I call this a very passable fire. Why, look here, the small type is quite distinct. I fear the blockheads will be throwing water upon the fire, and destroying the effect. Mr. Ambrose, step over the way and report progress.

Shepherd. Can ye see to read thae havers, by the fire-flaughts, Mr. Tickler?

Tickler. What think ye, James, of the following touch? "Yet the organ of benevolence is very large; and this is no contradiction, but a confirmation of phrenology. Thurtell, with all his violence and dissipation, was a kind-hearted man!"

Shepherd. You're making that. Nae man can be sic a fule as write that down, far less edit it. Do they give any proofs of his benevolence?

Tickler. Yes—yes. He once gave half-a-sovereign to an old broken black-leg, and "upon witnessing a quarrel which had nearly ended in a fight, between Harry Harmer and Ned Painter, at the house of the former pugilist—the Plough in Smithfield—and which originated through Thurtell, he felt so much hurt, that he shed tears in reconciling them to each other!"

Shepherd. The blackguard's been greetin' fu'.

Tickler (reading). "His behaviour in prison was of so affecting and endearing a nature, that the account of the parting scene between him and the jailer, and others who had been in the habit of great intercourse with him, during his confinement, is affecting enough to draw tears from every one whose heart is not made of stone!"

Shepherd. Weel, then, mine is made o' stane. For it was to me just perfectly disgustful and loathsome. Sir James Mackintosh broached preceesely my sentiments in the House o' Commons. A man may weel greet, in a parting scene wi' a jailer, when he is gaun out to the open air to be hanged, without ony great benevolence.

Tickler. "His uniform kindness to Hunt, after Probert had escaped punishment as king's evidence, up to the moment of his execution, was of the warmest nature. Although Hunt was probably drawn into a share of the bloody transaction by Thurtell, the affectionate conduct of Thurtell towards him so completely overpowered him, that had Thurtell been the *most virtuous person upon earth, and he and* HUNT OF OPPOSITE SEXES, Thurtell could not have rendered himself more beloved than every action of Hunt proved he was."

Shepherd. A fool and a phrenologist is a' ae thing, Mr. Tickler—I admit that noo. Hunt did all he could to hang Thurtell—Thurtell abused Joe constantly in prison—and in his speech frightened him out of his wits by his horrid faces, as Hunt tells in his confession to Mr. Harmer. Ten minutes after Jack is hanged, Hunt declares that he richly deserved it—his whole confession is full of hatred (real or affected) towards Thurtell. During his imprisonment in the hulks, his whole behaviour is reckless, and destitute of all feeling for any human creature, and at last he sails off with curses in his throat, and sulky anger in his miserable heart. It's a shame for Dr. Pool to edit sic vile nonsense, and I'll speak to him about it mysel'.

Tickler. Hear the Doctor himself. "That Thurtell, with a large benevolence, should commit such a deed, was reckoned by many completely subversive of the science. Do such persons recollect the character of one Othello, drawn by William Shakspeare? Is there no adhesiveness, no generosity, no benevolence in that mind so portrayed by the poet? and was a more cool and deliberate murder ever committed?"

Shepherd. That beats Tims. Othello compared to Thurtell; and what's waur, wee Weare in the sack likened, by implication, to Desdemona! That's Phrenology, is't? I canna doubt noo the story o' the Turnip.

Tickler. This Phrenologist admires Thurtell as one of the bravest of men. "No murder," says he, "was ever committed with more daring." Do you think so, James?

Shepherd. Oh! the wretched coward! What bravery was there in a big strong man inveigling a shilly-shally feckless swindler into a gig, a' sweddled up in a heavy great-coat, and a' at aince, unawares, in a dark loan, shooting him in the head wi' a pistol? And then, when the puir devil was frighted, and stunned, and half dead, cutting his throat wi' a penknife. Dastardly ruffian!

Tickler. "The last organ stated as very large is Cautiousness. This part of his character was displayed in the pains he took to conceal the murder, to hide the body, &c."

Shepherd. What the devil! wad ony man that had murdered anither no try either to conceal the body, or to avoid suspicion? Was it ony mark of caution to confide in twa such reprobates as Hunt and Probert, both of whom betrayed the murderer? Was it ony mark o' caution to tell the Bow Street officer, when he was apprehended, that he had thrown Weare's watch over a hedge? Was it ony mark o' caution to lose his pistol and penknife in the dark? Was it ony mark o' caution to keep bluidy things on and about him, afterwards for days, in a public house? Fule and phrenologist are a' ane, sir, truly enough.

Tickler. "A martyr could not have perished more heroically."

Shepherd. That's no to be endured. Thurtell behaved wi' nae mair firmness than ony ither strong-nerved ruffian on the scaffold. Was his anxiety about the length o' rope like a martyr? Naebody behaved sae weel at the last as the honest hangman.

Tickler. The ass thus concludes: "I will not detain the reader any longer; but trust enough has been said to show, that if ever head confirmed Phrenology, it is the head of Thurtell."

Shepherd. Fling that trash frae you, and let us out-by to the fire. The roof of the house must be falling in belyve. Save us, what a hum o' voices, and trampling o' feet, and hissing o' ingines, and growling o' the fire! Let's out to the Brig, and see the rampaging element.

Tickler. You remind me, Hogg, of Nero surveying Rome on fire, and playing on the harp.

Shepherd. Do ye want a spring on the fiddle? See till him, North's sleeping! Let's out amang the crowd for an hour. He'll never miss us till we come back, and crutches are no for a crowd.

SCENE III.—*The North Bridge.*—MR. TICKLER *and the* SHEPHERD *incog. in the crowd.*

Tickler. Two to one on the fire.

Shepherd. That's a powerfu' ingine. I wad back the water, but there's ower little o't. (*Addressing himself generally to what Pierce Egan calls the audience.*)—" Lads, up wi' the causeway, and get to the water-pipes."

(*The hint is taken, and the engines distinguish themselves greatly.*)

Tickler. Hogg, you Brownie, I never thought you were the man to throw cold water on any night's good amusement.

Shepherd. I'll back the water, noo, for a gallon o' whisky.

Tickler. Young woman, it's no doubt a very pretty song of old Hector Macneil's,—

" Come under my plaidie, the night's gaun to fa',
There's room in't, dear lassie, believe me, for twa."

But still, if you please, you need not put your arm under mine, till I whisper into your private ear.

Shepherd. What's the limmer wanting?

Female. What!—Is that you, Mr. Hogg? Ken ye ocht o' your friend, Captain Odoherty?

Shepherd. There—there's half-a-crown for you—gang about your business, you slut—or I'll brain ye. I ken nae Captain Odoherties.

Tickler. I remember, James, that a subscription-paper was carried about a few years ago, to raise money for pulling down this very range of buildings, which had just been carried up at a considerable expense.

Shepherd. And you subscribed ten pounds?

Tickler. I should as soon have thought of subscribing ten pounds for Christianizing Tartary.

Shepherd. There's an awfu' wark in Embro' just now, about raising monuments to every body, great and small. Did you hear, sir, o' ane about to be raised to Dubisson the dentist?

Tickler. I did. It is to be a double statue. Dubisson is to be represented in marble, with one hand grasping a refractory patient by the jaw-bone, and with the other forcibly introducing his instrument into the mouth.—I have seen a sketch of the design, and it is equal to the Hercules and Antæus.

Shepherd. Whaur's it to be erected?

Tickler. In the Pantheon, to be sure.

Shepherd. Houts—it maun be a joke. But Mr. Tickler, have you seen a plan o' the monument built at Alloa to Robert Burns?

Tickler. Ay, James, there is some sense in that. My friend Thomas

Hamilton's design is most beautiful, simple, and impresive. It stands where it ought to stand, and the gentlemen of Coila deserve every praise. I have heard that a little money may be still needed in that quarter—very little, if any at all. And I will myself subscribe five pounds.

Shepherd. So will I. But the Monument no being in Embro', you see, nor Mr. Thomas Hamilton a man fond o' putting himself forward ane hears naething about it. I only wish he would design ane half as gude for mysel.

Tickler. Ah! my beloved Shepherd, not for these thirty years at least. Your worthy father lived to ninety odd—why not his son? Some half century hence, your effigy will be seen on some bonny green knowe in the Forest, with its honest brazen face looking across St. Mary's Loch, and up towards the Gray-mare's tail, while by moonlight all your own fairies will weave a dance round its pedestal.

Shepherd (*in amazement*). My stars! yonder's Odoherty!

Tickler. Who?—The Adjutant?

Shepherd. Odoherty!—look at him—look at him—see how he is handing out the furniture through the window, on the third flat of an adjoining tenement. How the deevil got he there! Weel, siccan a deevil as that Odoherty!—and him, a' the time, out o' Embro', as I hae't under his ain hand!

Tickler. There is certainly something very exhilarating in a scene of this sort. I am a Guebir, or Fire-worshipper. Observe, the crowd are all in most prodigious spirits. Now, had it been a range of houses tenanted by poor men, there would have been no merriment. But Mr. Levy is a Jew—rich probably—and no doubt insured. Therefore, all is mirth and jollity.

Shepherd. Insurance offices, too, are a' perfect banks, and ana canna help enjoying a bit screed aff their profits. My gallon o' whisky's gane; the fire has got it a' its ain way noo,—and as the best o' the bleeze is ower, we may return to Ambrose's.

Tickler. Steady—there was a pretty tongue of fire flickering out of the fourth story. The best is to come yet. What a contemptible affair is an illumination!

Shepherd. Ye may say that—wi' an auld hizzie at every window, left at hame to watch the candle-doups.

Stranger (*to the Shepherd*). Sir, I beg your pardon, but you seem to be an amateur?

Shepherd. No, sir, I am a married man, with two children.

Stranger. 'Tis a very so-so fire. I regret having left bed for it.

Shepherd. What! were you siccan a fule as leave your warm bed for a fire? I'm thinking you'll be nae mair an amateur than mysel, but a married man.

Stranger. I have seen, sir, some of the first fires in Europe. Drury-

Lane, and Covent-Garden Theatres, each burned down twice—Opera-house twice—property to the amount of a million at the West India Docks—several successful cotton-mill incremations of merit at Manchester—two explosions (one with respectable loss of life) of powder-mills—and a very fine conflagration of shipping at Bristol.

Shepherd. Mr. Tickler—heard ye ever the like?

Tickler. Never, Hogg.

Shepherd. I'm the Ettrick Shepherd—and this is Mr. Tickler, sir.

Stranger. What! can I trust my ears—am I in presence of two of the men who have set the whole world on fire?

Shepherd. Yes—you are, sir, sure enough, and yonder's the Adjutant Odoherty, wi' his face a' covered wi' coom, getting sport up yonder, and doing far mair harm than good, that's certain. But will you come with us to Ambrose's? Whare is he, Tickler?—whare is he? Whare's the gentleman gone?

Tickler. I don't know. Look at your watch, James. What is the hour?

Shepherd (*fumbling about his fob*). My watch is gone! my watch is gone!—he has picket my pocket o' her!—Deevil burn him!—I niffered wi' Baldy Bracken, in the Grass-market, the day before yesterday, and she didna lose a minute in the twenty-four. This is a bad job—let us back to Ambrose's. I'll never see her face again.

SCENE IV.—*The Banqueting-Room.*

NORTH (*solus, and asleep*).

Enter on tiptoe MR. AMBROSE.

Mr. Ambrose. This fire has made me anxious about my premises. All right. He is fast as a nail; and snores (first time I ever heard him) like the rest of his species. Bless my soul!—the window is open at his very ear. (*Pulls down the sash.*)

North (*awakening*). Ambrose! I have had a congelating dream. Ice a foot thick in my wash-hand basin, and an icicle six inches long at my nose!

Ambrose. I am glad to have awakened you, sir. Shall I bring you a little mulled port?

North. No—no—Ambrose. Wheel me towards the embers. I hear it reported, Ambrose, that you are going to gut the tenement.—Is it so?

Ambrose. It is an ancient building, Mr. North, and somewhat incommodious. During the summer months it will undergo a great change and thorough repair.

North. Well, well, Ambrose, I rejoice to know that a change is demanded by the increase of resort; but yet, methinks, I shall con template any alteration with a pensive and melancholy spirit. This very room, Mr. Ambrose, within whose four walls I have been so often lately, must its dimensions be changed? Will this carpet be lifted? That chimney-piece be removed? I confess that the thought affects me, Mr. Ambrose. Forgive the pensive tear.

(*Takes out his square of India, and blows his nose in a hurried and agitated manner.*)

Ambrose. Mr. North, I have frequently thought of all this, and rather than hurt your feelings, sir, I will let the house remain as it is. I beseech you, sir, be composed.

North. No! "Ambrose, thou reasonest well," it must be so. The whole city undergoeth change deep and wide, and wherefore should Gabriel's Road, and the Land of Ambrose, be alone immutable? Down with the partitions! The mind soon reconciles itself to the loss of what it most dearly loved. But the Chaldee Chamber, Ambrose! the Chaldee Chamber, Ambrose!—must it go—must it go, indeed, and be swallowed up in some great big wide unmeaning room, destitute alike of character and comfort, without one high association hanging on its blue or yellow walls?

Ambrose. No, Mr. North; rather than alter the Chaldee Chamber, would I see the whole of Edinburgh involved in one general conflagration.

North. Enough—enough—now my mind is at rest. With hammers, and with axes both, let the workmen forthwith fall to. You must keep pace, Mr. Ambrose, with the progress, the advancement of the age.

Ambrose. Sir, I have been perfectly contented, hitherto, with the accommodation this house affords, and so, I humbly hope, have been my friends; but I owe it to those friends to do all I can to increase their comforts, and I have got a plan that I think will please you, sir.

North. Better, Ambrose, than that of the British itself. But no more. Think you the lads will return? If not, I must hobble homewards.

Ambrose. Hearken, sir—Mr. Tickler's tread in the trance.

(*Exit susurrans.*)

Enter TICKLER *and the* SHEPHERD.

Tickler. Have you supped, North?

North. Not I, indeed. Ambrose, bring supper. (*Exit Ambrose.*)

The Shepherd. I think I wull rather take some breakfast. Mr. North, I'm thinking you're sleepy; for you're lookin' unco gash. Do you want an account o' the fire?

North. Certainly not. Mr. Ambrose and I were engaged in a very interesting conversation when you entered. We were discussing the merits of the Exhibition.

The Shepherd. O' the pictures? I was there the day. Oh! man, yon things o' Wulkie's are chief endeavoors. That ane frae the Gentle Shepherd, is just nature hersel. I wush he would illustrate in that gait, some o' the bonniest scenes in the Queen's Wake.

Tickler. Worth all the dull dirty daubs of all the Dutchmen that ever vomited into a canal. Nauseous ninnies! a coarse joke may pass in idle talk—a word and away—but think, James, of a human being painting filth and folly, dirt and debauchery, vulgarity and vileness, day after day, month after month, till he finally covered the canvas with all the accumulated beastliness of his most drunken and sensual imagination!

North. Stop, Tickler—remember Teniers, and——

The Shepherd. Remember nae sic fallow, Mr. Tickler; Wulkie's wee finger's worth the hail o' them. "Duncan Gray cam here to woo," is sae gude, that it's maist unendurable. Yon's the bonniest lass ever I saw in a' my born days. What a sonsy hawse! But indeed, she's a' alike parfite.

Tickler. Stop Shepherd, remember. I saw a Cockney to-day looking at that picture, and oh! what a contrast between the strapping figure of Duncan Gray, his truly pastoral physiognomy, well-filled top-boots, (not unlike your own,) and sinewy hands that seem alike ready for the tug of either love or war—and the tout-ensemble of that most helpless of all possible creatures!

North. John Watson is great this year. Happy man, to whom that beautiful creature (picture of a Lady) may be inditing a soft epistle! What innocence, simplicity, grace and gaieté du cœur! Why, if that sweet damosel would think of an old man like the——

The Shepherd. Haud your tongue. Why should she think o' an auld man? "Ye might be her gutcher, you're threescore and twa."

Tickler. Mr. Thomson of Duddingston is the best landscape-painter Scotland ever produced—better than either Nasmyth, or Andrew Wilson, or *Greek* Williams.

North. Not so fast, Tickler. Let us discuss the comparative merits——

The Shepherd. Then I'm aff. For o' a' the talk in this world, that about pictures is the warst. I wud say that to the face o' the Director-General himsel.

North. A hint from my Theocritus is sufficient. What think you, Bion, of this parliamentary grant of £300,000 for repairing old Windsor?

The Shepherd. I never saw the Great House o' Windsor Palace, but it has been for ages the howf o' kings, and it maunna be allowed to gang back. If £300,000 winna do, gie a million. Man, if I was but in Parliament, I would gie the niggarts their fairings. Grudge a king a palace!

North. What say you, my good Shepherd, to a half million more for churches?

Shepherd. Mr. North, you and Mr. Tickler is aiblins laughing at me, and speering questions at me, that you may think are out o' my way to answer; but, for a' that, I perhaps ken as weel's either o' you, what's due to the religious establishments of a great and increasing kintra, wi' a population o' twal millions, mair or less, in or owre. Isn't it sae?

North. Well said, James. This is not the place, perhaps, to talk much of these serious matters; but no ministry will ever stand the lower in the estimation of their country, for having enabled some hundred thousands more of the people to worship their Maker publicly once a-week.

Shepherd. I'm thinking no. Nane o' the Opposition wad oppose a grant o' half a million for bigging schools, the mair's their merit; and if sae, what for no kirks? Edication and religion should gang hand in hand. That's aye been my thocht. (*Enter Ambrose, with supper.*) Howsomever, here's sooper; and instead o' talking o' kirks, let us a' gang oftener till them. Put down the sassages afore me, Ambrose. Ye're looken unco weel the noo, man; I hardly ever saw ye sae fat. How is the mistress and the bairns?

Ambrose. All well, sir, I thank you, Mr. Hogg.

The Shepherd. Od, man, I wush you would come out at the preachings, when the town's thin, and see us at Altrive.

Ambrose. I fear it is quite impossible for me to leave town, Mr. Hogg; but I shall always be most happy to see you here, sir.

The Shepherd. I've been in your house a hunder and a hunder times, and you ken I lodged ance in the flat aboon; and never did I hear ony noise, or row, or rippet, below your rigging. I dinna repent a single hour I ever sat here; I never saw or heard naething said or done here that michtna been said or done in a minister's manse. But it's waxing early, and I ken you dinna keep untimeous hours; so let us devoor supper, and be aff. That fire taigled us.

North. I had been asleep for an hour, before mine host awakened me, and had a dream of the North Pole.

The Shepherd. North Pole! How often do you think Captain Parry intends howking his way through these icebergs, wi' the snout o' his discovery ships? May he never be frozen up at last, he and a' his crew, in thae dismal regions!

North. Have you read Franklin and Richardson?

The Shepherd. Yes, I hae. Yon was terrible. Day after day naething to eat but tripe aff the rocks, dry banes, auld shoon, and a godsend o' a pair of leathern breeches! What would they no hae given for sic a sooper as this here!

Tickler. Have you no intention, James, of going on the next land-expedition?

The Shepherd. Na, na; I canna do without vittals. I was ance for twenty hours without tasting a single thing but a bit cheese and half a bannock, and I was close upon the fainting. Yet I would like to see the North Pole.

Tickler. Where's your chronometer, James?

The Shepherd. Whisht, whisht; I ken that lang-nebbit word. Whisht, whisht. Safe us! is that cauld lamb?—We'll no hae lamb in Yarrow for a month yet.

Tickler. Come, North, bestir yourself, you're staring like an owl in a consumption. Tip us Δ, my old boy.

The Shepherd. Mr. Tickler, Mr. Tickler, what langish is that to use till Mr. North? Think shame o' yoursel'.

North. No editor, James, is a hero to his contributors.

The Shepherd. Weel, weel, I for ane will never forget my respect for Mr. Christopher North. He has lang been the support o' the literature, the pheelosophy, the religion, and what's o' as great importance as ony thing else, the gude manners o' the kintra.

Tickler. Forgive me, North,—forgive me, James. Come, I volunteer a song.

The Shepherd. A sang! Oh man, you're a bitter bad singer—timmer-tuned, though a decent ear. Let's hear the lilt.

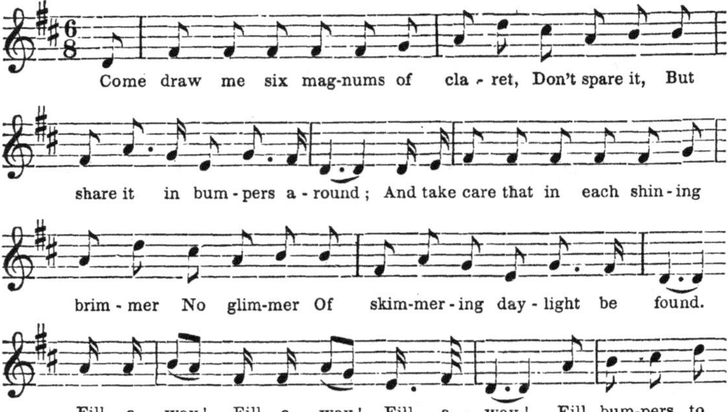

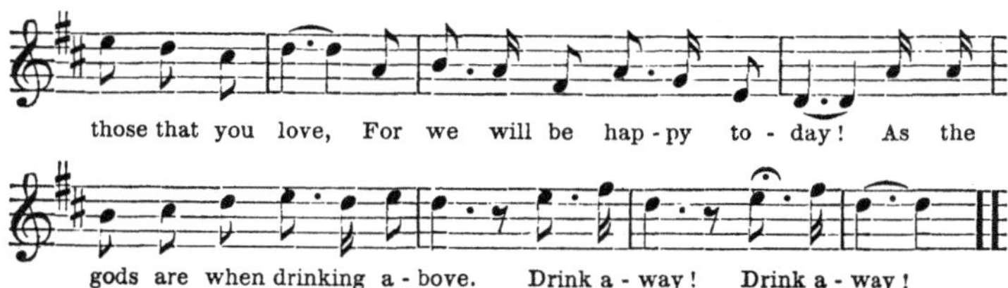

2.

Give way to each thought of your fancies,
That dances,
Or glances, or looks of the fair;
And beware that from fears of to-morrow
You borrow
No sorrow, nor foretaste of care.
Drink away, drink away, drink away!
For the honor of those you adore:
Come, charge! and drink fairly to-day,
Though you swear you will never drink more.

3.

I last night, *cut*, and quite melancholy,
Cried folly!
What's Polly to reel for her fame?
Yet I'll banish such hint till the morning,
And scorning
Such warning to-night, do the same.
Drink away, drink away, drink away!
'Twill banish blue devils and pain;
And to-night for my joys if I pay,
Why, to-morrow I'll go it again.

Enter MR. AMBROSE, *with alarm.*

Mr. Ambrose. As I live, sir, here's Mr. Odoherty. Shall I say you are here, for he is in a wild humor?

Enter ODOHERTY, *singing.*

I've kiss'd and I've prattled with fifty fair maids,
And changed them as oft, do ye see, &c.

(*North and Tickler rise to go.*)

Odoherty. What, bolting?

The Shepherd. Ay, ay, late hours disna agree wi' snawy pows. But I'se sit an hour wi' you.

(*The Adjutant and the Shepherd embrace. North and Tickler disappear.*)

No. XV.—JUNE, 1824.

Present—TIMOTHY TICKLER, ESQ., ENSIGN ODOHERTY, *the* ETTRICK SHEPHERD, *and* MR. JONATHAN SPIERS.

Odoherty. Yes, Tickler, you are, after all, quite in the right—I took the other side merely for the sake of conversation.

Tickler. Ay, and if my young friend here had happened to be called away half-an-hour ago—ay, or if I had happened not to be in the exact humor for squabashing, and particularly for squabashing *you*—what would have been the consequence, Mr. Morgan ?—what would have been the consequence, you care-me-devil ?

Odoherty. Why, I suppose, I should have helped to

"Give to the press one preux-chevalier more,"

as the old zig-zag of Twickenham says, or ought to say. Pope was decidedly the Z of Queen Anne's time*—his dunces were the progenitors of the present Cockneys.

Hogg. Wheesht—wheesht—for heaven's sake dinna name thae creatures again—I'm sure they're doon enough at ony rate. But really, Mr. Tickler, are ye no ower hasty ?—Od, man, (*whispering Timothy,*) the lad might have turned out a genius.

Tickler. No whispering at Ambrose's, Hogg. Here, Jonathan, boy—here's the Great Boar of the Forest grunting in my ear, that we may be spoiling a genius in your honorable person. What say ye to this, my hearty ?—Do you really now—but *sans phrase* now—do you really take yourself to be a genius ?

Hogg (*aside to Odoherty*). He takes his toddy brawlie, at ony rate.

Odoherty. Hogg remarks that our youthful friend is a promising punchifier. But this, even this, I fear, may still leave the matter a little dubious—*bibimus indocti doctique.*

Hogg. Jeering at me, I daursay—but what signifies that ? Here, Mr. Jonathan, you're a very fine douce lad—never ye heed what thae proud-nosed chiels tell you—put out the poem or the novell—whilk of them said ye it was ?

Mr. Spiers. A romantic tale, sir, interspersed with verses.

* The articles in *Blackwood* against Hunt, Hazlitt, &c., were signed "Z."—M.

Hogg. Is there a gay feck o' verses?

Mr. Spiers. A considerable number, sir. Several of the characters, sir, give vent to their feelings in a poetical form, sir.

Hogg. Ay, that's a gude auld fashion. A real novell young leddy has aye her keelavine in her pouch, and some bit back of a letter, or auld mantuamaker's count, or something or other, to put down her bit sonnet on, just after she's been stolen, or robbed, or, what's waur, maybe——

Tickler. Hold your tongue, Hogg. Jonathan Spiers' book is a very pretty book, I assure you—and his verses are very well introduced—very well indeed.

Odoherty. Why, Hogg himself, in one of his recent masterpieces, has given the finest example of the easy and unaffected introduction of the ornament of occasional verse, in a prose romance.

Tickler (aside to Odoherty). I forget what you are alluding to. Is this in the "Confessions of the Justified Sinner," which I see advertised?

Odoherty. No, 'tis in the "Three Perils of Man." One of the chief characters of that work is a *bonâ fide* poet, and this personage never opens his mouth, but out comes a *bonâ fide* regular psalm measure stanza of four lines. In the Pirate, to be sure, old Norna spouts most unconscionably; but even she must knock under to the poet of Hogg.

Tickler (rings—enter Ambrose). Mr. Ambrose, have you the Three Perils of Man in the house? If yea, bring them forthwith.

Ambrose (indignantly). Sir, Mr. Hogg's works form a part of the standing furniture of the tap-room.

Odoherty (aside). Standing furniture, I will be sworn.

Ambrose. I rather think Mr. Macmurdo, the great drover from Angus, has one of the volumes just now; but he seemed getting very drowsy, and I shall perhaps be able to extract it. (*Exit.*)

Hogg (aside). Honest man! he's surely been sair forfaughten the day at the market.

Odoherty. Hogg has another character in the same book—a priest; and what think ye is his dialect? Why, pure Chaldee, to be sure.

Tickler. Chaldee manuscript, you mean, I suppose. Well, I see no harm in this.

Hogg. It's a' perfect nature. If I liked I could speak nothing but poetry—deil a hait of prose—frae month's end to month's end. It would come like butter.

Odoherty. In a lordly dish, to be sure. Come, Hogg, I take you at your word. Stick to your psalm-tune then.

Hogg.

Now steadfastly adhere will I,
Nor swerve from this again,
But speak in measured melody
For ever more. Amen!

Tickler. Hurra! Hogg for ever! that's a thumping exordium, James. Could you match him there, Jonathan?

Hogg.

There is no poet, no, not one,
Nor yet no poetess,
Whose ready rhymes like those can run,
Which my lips do express.
Yea, all the day continually
Out from my mouth they go,
Like river that not waxeth dry,
But his waves still do flow.
Sith it be so that Og, the King
Of Bashan——

Tickler. Come, Hogg, in virtue of the power which Christopher gave me when he took the gout, you are absolved, and hereby I do absolve you. One rhyme more, you great pig, and I'll have you scalded on the spot.

Hogg. The pitcher's getting cauld, at ony rate. Ye had better ring, and bid Ambrose have on the big boiler at ance. And as for you, Jonathan Spiers, they were deaving us wi' saying there was nae opening in the literary world. Me away, that canna be said, my braw lad.

Odoherty. Come, Hogg, a joke's a joke—we've had enough of this. There *is* no opening in the literary world.

Hogg. Weel, Jonathan, if Byron and me canna make an opening between us, I'm thinking ye maun just ca' canny, and wait till ye see out Odoherty and the Author of Waverley—I reckon them about the next to Byron and me.

Tickler (*aside*). Either of their little fingers well worth you both. But, however—Come, Hogg, supposing Jonathan really to reject my poor advice, what would be your counsel? Come now, remember 'tis a serious concern:—so be for once the sagacious master of the sagacious Hector.

Hogg. I would be for Jonathan trying a good, rousing, independent Tory paper. Deil a paper I see's worth lighting one's pipe wi'. It would surely do.

Tickler. I dare say Jonathan's ambition aimed at rather higher concerns; but no matter, what have you to say against the papers, Jemmy?

Hogg. Just that they're a' clean trash—the Scots anes, I mean. There's the Scotsman—it was lang the only ane that had ony bit spice of the deevil in't, and it's noo turned as douce and as doited as the very warst of them, since that creature turned Ricardo Professor, or what ca' ye't. He was a real dour, ugly, sulky beast, but still he was a beast; now they're mere dirt the lave o' them—just the beast's leavings—perfect dirt.

Odoherty. What say ye to the Weekly Journal, James?

Hogg. Too—too—too—too—too! By'r Lady, good Master Lieutenant—too!—too!—too!—too!—too!—pheugh!

Tickler. The Courant, Hogg?

Hogg. An edificationing paper, I'll no deny. It has a' the farms and roups. I couldna do without the Courant.

Tickler. What sort of paper did you wish Jonathan to set up—a Beacon,* perhaps.

Hogg. A Beacon! Gude pity us, Timotheus,—are you gaun dementit a'thegither? I thought ye said Jonathan was a prudent, quiet, respectable laddie—wishing to make his way in the warld—and "your ain sense tells you," as Meg Dods says about the lad remaining in the room with Miss Mowbray, that, though your Antijacobins, and John Bulls, and Twopenny Post-Bags, and sae on, do very weel in the great Babel of Lunnun, the like o' thae things are quite heterogeneous in this small atmosphere of the Edinbro' meridian—the folk here canna thole't.

Tickler. Jonathan might try a good daily paper in London—that is much wanted at present. Indeed, a new one is wanted every three or four years; for the chaps that succeed soon get too rich and fat for their business. Stoddart is quite a Bourbon man now. The Courier is verging to conciliation.

Odoherty. By the by, some dandies always pronounce *Courier*, as if it were a French word, *Courié*. Did you hear our friend Peter's joke upon this at Inverness?

Tickler. Not I. What was it?

Odoherty. Why, a young Whig wit asked some witness before the venerable Jury Court, "Are you in the habit of taking in the *Courié*, sir?" Upon this, Patrick, in cross-examination, says, "Are you in the habit, sir, of taking in the Morning *Po—?*"

Tickler. Very well, Peter!—but enough of the papers. I wonder you, Odoherty, don't think of patching up the Memoirs of Byron—you could easily guess what sort of stuff they were; and, at any rate, an edition of 10,000 would sell ere the trick could be discovered.

Odoherty. Why, I flatter myself, if it were discovered, the book

* "*The Beacon*" was a newspaper, the publication of which commenced in Edinburgh in January, 1821, and was abruptly discontinued in August of the same year. The sympathy felt in Scotland for Queen Caroline, in 1820, would lead, it was feared, to the extension of antipathy towards her husband, George IV. and his ministers. The Edinburgh Tories subscribed money to establish a strong newspaper on their own side,—a publication even more personal and libellous than the London *John Bull* was produced, and when, at last—after being suddenly put an end to—*The Beacon* was noticed in Parliament, it was shown, that even the Law-officers of the Crown were part proprietors! On its ashes arose The *Glasgow Sentinel*, principally edited by the late Robert Alexander, (afterwards of the London *Morning Journal* and the *Liverpool Mail*,) a powerful, but indiscreet writer. More personalities than had made the *Beacon* notorious were introduced, and the end was that an editorial quarrel resulted in the betrayal or theft of a box of MSS., by which the late Sir Alexander Boswell of Auchinleck (son of Johnson's biographer) was discovered to be author of certain truculent pasquinades against James Stuart of Dunearn, who challenged and shot him.—M.

would still be good enough to sell on its own bottom.* But the booksellers are turning so deucedly squeamish now a-days, there's really no opening for a little fair quizzification. There was Hook went to Colburn about his Foote; Colburn remarked, it was a pity there was none of Foote's private correspondence to be got hold of. "Pooh, pooh!" quoth Theodore, "I'll make a volume of it in three weeks." Colburn took fright at this, and the thing stopped. What a pity now! Would not the letters have been all the better for being not Foote's but the Grand-Master's?

Tickler. To be sure they would; and, after the Memoirs of Byron that Colburn did publish—old paste-and-scissors work—he need not have been quite so sensitive, I would have thought. But there's no saying as to these people. Colburn's getting deuced rich upon the Literary Gazette, Lady Morgan, The Writer Tam, and the rest of these great Guns of his, I have a notion.

Odoherty. To be sure he is. But, as for Byron's Memoirs, why, I can tell you I have read the book myself, twice over; and, what is more, you will read it yourself within a month or six weeks' time of this present.

Tickler. Ay?—how?—indeed?—Well, you surprise me!

Odoherty. Why, the fact is, that the work had been copied, for the private reading of a great lady in Florence; and it is well known in London, that Galignani has bought the MS., and that it will be out in Paris forthwith.† But is this really news for you?

Hogg. It's news—and blythe news too—to me, for ane. But, I say, Ensign, speak truth now—am I mentioned?

Odoherty. Frequently.

Hogg. Dear me! what does he says of me?—nae ill, I'll be sworn—I aye took his part, I'm sure.

* At that time, had he been so minded, Maginn (Odoherty) could have got up a popular Life of Byron as well as most men in England. Immediately on the account of Byron's death being received in London, John Murray proposed that Maginn should bring out Memoirs, Journals, and Letters of Lord Byron, and, with this intent, placed in his hands every line that he (Murray) possessed of Byron's handwriting. Whatever, therefore, is here put into Odoherty's mouth, may be taken as authentic. The strong desire of Byron's family and executors that the Autobiography should be burned, to which desire Murray foolishly yielded, made such an *hiatus* in the materials that Murray and Maginn agreed it would not answer to bring out the work then. Eventually, Moore executed it.—M.

† The "great lady in Florence," for whose private reading Byron's Autobiography was copied, was the present Countess of Westmoreland, then Lady Burghersh. Her husband had been Envoy Extraordinary to the Court of Tuscany. Of the copy sent to her, I have heard that a transcript was made and retained. *No* copy was sent to Galignani by Murray. Lady Blessington had the Autobiography in her possession for weeks, and confessed to having transcribed every line of it. Moore remonstrated, and Lady B. committed her manuscript to the flames; but she did not tell him that her sister, Mrs. Home Purvis, (now Viscountess Canterbury,) had *also* made a copy. In fact, several people had been allowed the like opportunity, and it is hard to believe that, out of at least ten or twelve persons, only *three*, and these women, had taken the trouble of transcribing. From the quantity of "copy" which I have seen, (and others were more in the way of falling across it than myself,) I surmise that at least half a dozen copies were made, and that *five* of these are in existence. Some particular transactions—such as the marriage and the separation—were copied separately; but I think there cannot be less than five full copies yet to be found.—M.

Odoherty. Why, he takes your part on the whole—he puffs your Queen's Wake and Chaldee most stentoriously; and on the whole does you justice—you are in the Dictionary.

Hogg. The Dictionary!—was he at an English Dictionary too? Od, I would like to see myself quoted in the English Dictionary—a bit of Hogg in below a bit of bacon may be—it would look very well.

Odoherty. In the next Dictionary that appears, no question, you will be gratified with abundance of such compliments—but the Dictionary of Byron is quite another sort of thing. One volume of his Memoirs, in short, consists of a dictionary of all his friends and acquaintances, alphabetically arranged, with proper definitions of their characters—criticisms on their works (when they had any)—and generally a few specimens of their correspondence. To me this volume seemed, on the whole, the most amusing of the three.

Hogg. I dinna doubt it. Oh, the ne'er-do-weels, to gang awa and burn sic a book as this.

Odoherty. Pooh! I tell you 'tis *not* burnt*—you will see it in the course of the summer.

Tickler. After all, it could not well have been published by Murray. Galignani, or some foreigner or other, was the only plan.

Odoherty. Why, there may be two opinions as to this. It was at one time understood that Murray was to have employed my excellent friend Tegg to bring the thing forth—but perhaps Tom would have been over nice.

Tickler. O, as to that, you know Davison's name could have stood alone, as in the case of the first canto of the Don.

Odoherty. Hang it, you are forgetting that infernal narrow-minded old quiz of a Chancellor—his abominable punctilios about the injunctioning law, you know, have entirely done away with the temptation to publish improper books. There is an English judge and cabinet-man for you! Discountenancing Don Juan—strangling Byron's Memoirs, (so far as the English MS. was in question)—Fine doings—fine doings—we shall be a pretty nation soon, I calculate.

Hogg (*sings*)—

> My blessings on your auld pow,
> John Anderson, my joe, John.

And yet, I'm doom'd glad that the lady in Florence had had a copy of Byron's MS. I have a gay hantle letters o' Byron's in my ain dask. I

* Byron's "Dictionary" was *not* among the manuscripts burnt at the instance of Lord Byron's executors. It has been very fully described to me as written on long foolscap, bound together or stitched with narrow pink ribbon, and covered with stiff whitey-brown paper. What Odoherty calls "specimens of the correspondence," were actual letters from the parties treated of in the book, wafered upon the page opposite that on which Byron wrote. This "Dictionary," which was the bulkiest of these three volumes of manuscript, extended to nearly 250 written pages.—M.

wonder what the trade would give a body for a small volume of his epistolary correspondence wi' his friends?

Odoherty. Not one rap—his letters to John Murray will be quite a sufficient dose of themselves,—but, to be sure, they mayn't be printed just immediately.

Tickler. Not in my day, I calculate—you young dogs may expect to outlive both me and John Murray—you will see the whole of it, Ensign—and you, Jonathan. But I, long ere then, shall be enjoying the conversation of Byron himself

Ενθα γε Κιμμεριων ανδρων δημοστε πολιστε,
Ηερι και νεφελη κεκαλυμμενοι, ȣδε ποτ' αυτȣς
Ηελιος φαεθων επιδερκεται, ακτινε εσσιν
Ουδ' ὁποτ' αν στειχησι προς ȣ̓ρανον ἀϛεροεντα
Ουθ' ὁταν ἀψ επι γαιαν ἀπ' ȣ̓ρανοθεν προτραπηται—

Helas! helas! φεω, ϖοϖοι, ῳ!! och! och!

Hogg. Hech, sirs! what's a' this rumbleterow?—what's ailing Mr. Tickler?

Odoherty. You upon pale Cocytus' shore!—you old piece of whipcord!—I'll back you to ninety-five as readily as if you were a sinecurist. And besides, to be serious, I hope you don't mean to keep company with people down yonder, whom you've done nothing but abuse while εϖι χθονι δερκων.

Tickler. Come, Odoherty—I know very well you and I can never agree as to this. But, now that Lord Byron is dead, you must really stint in your gab, Morgan Odoherty. We have lost a great man, sir—a truly great man—one of the very few really great men of might that our age has witnessed.

Odoherty. Not at all, my dear youth—by no manner of means. Byron was a very clever man, and a very clever poet; but, as to his being either a truly great man, or a truly great poet, I must altogether differ from you. Why, sir, he has left no truly great work behind him; and his character was not *great.*

Tickler. I don't admit all that. But, taking the first thing you say to be so for a moment, what is the *great* work we have of Alcæus, of Sappho—even of Pindar, or of Sallust, or of Petronius? and yet these, I take it, *were* great people, and are so even in your estimation.

Hogg. I never heard tell of one of them afore since ever I was born. Did ye, Jonathan?

Mr. Spiers. O fie, Mr. Hogg!—never heard of Sallust?

Odoherty. Yes, Tickler, my good fellow, but you are not stating your case fairly. These people have left glorious fragments—enough to make us believe what other great people say of the works that have perished: but, misery on that infernal engine the press!—the next worst thing after gunpowder—Byron's fragments never can exist. Spite of fate, the whole mass of lumber exists, and will exist, and nobody, in modern times, will take the trouble to pick out the few fine bits Byron really may have produced, and place them before the eyes of the world, to the exclusion of his portentous balaam. This is the true devilry of your modern authorship.

Tickler. Has Candide, then, no separate existence of its own? Does any body, when they read that glorious thing, or the Princess of Babylon, or Zadig, trouble their heads with thinking of the existence of *Œdipe*, the Universal History, and all the rest of Voltaire's humbugging Tragedies and Histories? Not at all, my hearty. Or, when people read Manon Lescaut, does it diminish their delight that the Abbé wrote and published fifty volumes, or more, of *bad* novels, which no human creature above the calibre of a Turnipologist would now endure three pages of? Or do I, in reading Goldsmith's Essays, bother myself with his History of Animals, or his History of Rome? Or do any of us enjoy Tam o' Shanter the less, because Dr. Currie's edition contains all that stuff of Burns's Epistles to Mrs. Dunlop, George Thomson, &c.? Or who the devil has ever even heard the name of the five-hundredth part of the trashy productions which flowed from the pens of Fielding and Smollett, or their great masters, Le Sage and Cervantes? The critiques of the Doctor, the plays of the Justice, the many bitter bad plays and novels of the Author of Don Quixote, and the myriads of bad plays and bad books of all kinds, of the author of the Devil on Two Sticks—these matters are all pretty well forgotten, I suppose; and what signifies this to the student of Sancho Panza, Asmodeus, Commodore Trunnion, or Parson Trulliber? Come, come—own yourself beat now, like a fair man.

Odoherty. You spout nobly when your breath is once up; but, seriously, then, what are the works of Byron that you think will be remembered in honor? and what is the sort of name altogether that you think he will bear,

> "When we're all cold and musty,
> A hundred years hence?"

Tickler. I think Byron's Childe Harold, Corsair, Lara, and Don Juan (in part) will be remembered in the year of grace, 1924; and I think the name of Byron will then be ranked as the third name of one great era of the imaginative literature of England; and this I think is no trifle.

Hogg. After Sir Walter and me?

Tickler. No, Hogg, to be honest, before you, my dear creature. Yes, before you. Before every body else in the line, my dear James, except the author of the Bride of Lammermoor, and the author of Ruth.* I

* Scott and Wordsworth.—M.

name the two best and most pathetic works of the two best, and, to my feeling, most pathetic writers of our day—the only two—I speak with disparagement to no one—that have opened up absolutely new fields of their own. For, after all, I do not uphold Byron so much on the score of original invention, as on that of original energy.

Hogg. Original energy! what means that, being interpreted?

Tickler. Why, I mean to say, that mere energy of thought and language may be carried so far as to make, I do not say a poet of the very highest class, but a poet of a very high one—and I say that Byron's energy was of this kind—and I say that his place is immediately behind the all but Homeric magician of the North, and the all but Miltonic prophet of the Lakes. There's my apophthegm—for that, I think, Jemmy, is your name for any thing you don't understand.

Hogg. Many thousand thanks to you, Mr. Timothy Tickler, of Southside.

Odoherty. The fact is that Byron was a deuced good rattling fellow; a chap that could do most things he had seen any body else do before him, just as I could write five hundred first-rate songs, *à la* Tom Moore, or *à la* James Hogg, if I had a mind. The far greater part of his composition was decidedly of this class—his short narrative octosyllabic was as decidedly a copy of Walter Scott, as that of the Queen's Wake. His "deep feeling of nature"—ha! ha! ha!—in the third canto of Harold, and other subsequent concerns, was the result of his having read then—and a hint that he had not, more shame to him, read before—the poetry of that old Pan of the woods, W. W. His Beppo was the visible by-blow—a vigorous one, I admit—of Whistlecraft—his Manfred was a copy of Goethe—and his Deformed Transformed was at once a half-formed and a deformed transformation of the Devil and Doctor Faustus, of the same unintelligible, cloud-compelling, old Meerschaumite. Shall I go on?

Hogg. As lang as you like, my dear fellow—but you wunna make out Wordsworth to have written Parisina for a' that—no, nor Frere to have ever had one canto of Don Juan in his breeks. Pooh! pooh! Odoherty, you might as weel tell me that Shakspeare was the copyist of the auld idiots that wrote the original Henry Fifths, King Johns, and so forth. Byron *was* the great man, sir.

Odoherty. I'll give you this much—I do believe he might have been a great man, if he had cut verse fairly, and taken to prose. My humble opinion is, that verse will not thrive again in our tongue. Our tongue is, after all, not an over-melodious one. I doubt if even Shakspeare would not have done well to cut it—at least, it always appears to me, that when he writes what the critics call prose, he is most poetical What say you to Hamlet's talk with Rosencrantz and Gildenstern? "This overhanging vault, look ye, fretted with golden fires," &c. &c. &c. Is not that poetry, sir? At any rate, the fact is, that Byron never could versify, and that his Memoirs and his private letters are the only things of his that I have ever seen, that gave me, in the least degree, the notion of a fine creature enjoying the full and unconstrained swing of his faculties. Hang it! if you had ever seen that attack of his on Blackwood—or, better still, that attack of his on Jeffrey, for puffing Johnny Keats—or, best of all, perhaps, that letter on Hobhouse—or that glorious, now I think of it, that inimitable letter to Tom Moore, giving an account of the blow-up with Murray about the Don Juan concern—oh, dear! if you had seen these, you would never have thought of mentioning any rhymed thing of Byron's—no, not even his epigrams on Sam Rogers, which are well worth five dozen of Parisinas and Prisoners of Chillon, and——

Tickler. Stuff! stuff! stuff!—But I take it you're quizzing within the club—which you know is entirely *contra bonos mores*. Drop this, Ensign.

Odoherty. I am dead serious. I tell you, Byron's prose works, when they are printed, will decidedly fling his verse into total oblivion. You, sir, that have merely read his hide-bound, dry, barking, absurd, ungrammatical cantos of Don Juan, and judge from them of Byron's powers as a satirist, are in the most pitiable position imaginable. One thumping paragraph of a good honest thorough-going letter of his to Douglas Kinnaird, or Murray in the olden time, is worth five ton of that material. I tell you once again, he never wrote in verse with perfect ease and effect—verse never was his natural language, as it was with Horace or Boileau, or Pope or Spenser, or any of those lads that could not write prose at all. When he wrote verses, he was always translating—that is to say, beastifying—the prose that already existed in his pericranium. There was nothing of that rush and flow that speaks the man rhyming in spite of himself, as in the Battle of Marmion, or Hamilton's Bawn, or any other first-rate poem. No, no—he counted his feet, depend upon it—and, what is less excusable, he did not always count them very accurately. Of late, by Jupiter, he produced tooth-breakers of the most awful virulence. I take it the Odontists had bribed him.

Tickler. Why, whom *do* you call a good versifier, then?

Odoherty. We have not many of them. Frere and Coleridge are, I think, the most perfect, being at once more scientific in their ideas of the matter than any others now alive, and also more easy and delightful in their melody which they themselves produce. We have no better things in our language, looking merely to versification, than the psychological curiosity—

"A damsel, with a dulcimer,
In a vision once I saw,
It was an Abyssinian maid,
And on a dulcimer she played,
Singing of Mount Abora," &c.

Or Frere's translation of the Frogs, printed long ago in Ebony. Do you remember the verses, in particular, which old North used to read, with a few literal alterations, as a fine cut at Joseph Hume, Peter Moore, and the other grand leaders of the Whig party now?

"Foreign stamp and vulgar mettle raise them to command and place,
Brazen, counterfeit pretenders, flunkies of a flunky race;
Whom the Whigs of former ages scarce would have allowed to stand,
At the sacrifice of outcasts, as the scape-goats of their band."

Byron seldom or never made verses equal, merely *quâ* verses, to the like of these. When he did, it was by a strict imitation of something his ear had caught in the versification of some preceding poet. As for the Spenserian, you well know that whenever his sweep of stanza did not vividly recall Thomson or old Edmund himself, the stanza was execrably hard, husky, and unswallowable.

Tickler (*solemnly*).

"Tambourgi, tambourgi, thy larum afar
Gives hope to the valiant, and promise of war!"

Odoherty. Come, come, Timotheus, don't throw your chair back in that abominable Yankee-doodle fashion. Stick to the argument, sir—don't lounge and spout.

Tickler.

"It is the hour when from the boughs
The nightingale's high note is heard;
It is the hour when lover's vows
Seem sweet in every whispered word;—
And gentle winds and waters near
Make music to the lonely ear;—
Each flower the dews have lightly wet,
And in the sky the stars are met;
And on the waves a deeper blue,
And on the leaf a browner hue,
And in the heavens that clear obscure,
So softly dark and darkly pure,
Which follows the decline of day,
As twilight melts beneath the moon, away."

Hogg. Ay, ay, man, these *are* verses. (*Aside to Spiers.*) Do you think they're as good as Kilmeny?

Tickler. Listen to me one moment more, Odoherty. The fact, sir, stands simply thus:—It is obvious to any one who is capable of casting a comprehensive eye over things, that there are three different great veins of thought and sentiment prevalent in this age of the world; and I hold it to be equally clear, that England has furnished at least one great poetical expositor and interpreter for each of the three. This, sir, is the Age of Revolution. It is an age in which earth rocks to and fro upon its foundations—in which recourse is had to the elements of all things—in which thrones, and dominations, and principles, and powers, and opinions, and creeds, are all alike subjected to the sifting of the winds of Intellect, and the tossing and lashing of the waves of Passion. Now, there are three ways in which the mind of poetic power *may* look at all this—there are three parts among which it may choose. First, there is the spirit of scorn of that which is old—of universal distrust and derision, mingled up with a certain phrenzy of indignation and innovating fury—here is Byron. Then there is the high heroic spirit of veneration for that which has been—that still deeper, that infinitely more philosophical distrust, which has for its object this very rage and storm of coxcombical innovation which I have been describing. This is Scott—the noble bard of the noble—the prop of the venerable towers and temples, beneath which our fathers worshipped and did homage in the days of a higher, a purer, a more chivalric race. This is the voice that cries—*In defence!*—

'Faster come, faster come,
Faster and faster,—
Page, vassal, squire, and groom,
Tenant and master:
Come as the winds come,
When forests are rending;
Come as the waves come,
When navies are stranding!"

And there is yet a third spirit—the spirit of lonely, meditative, high-souled, and yet calm-souled men—of him who takes no part in sounding or obeying the war-pipe of either array—the far-off, philosophic contemplator, who, turning from the turmoil, out of which he sees no escape, and penetrated with a profound loathing of all this mighty clamor, about things, at the best, but fleeting and terrestrial, plunges, as it were, into the quiet, serene ocean-depths of solitary wisdom, there to forget the waves that boil upon the surface—there to brood over the images of eternal and undisturbed truth and beauty. This is Wordsworth; hear how *he* describes a poet's tomb—

"A convent—even a hermit's cell—
Would break the silence of this dell.
It is not quiet—is not ease,
But something deeper far than these.
The separation that is here
Is of the grave—and of *austere*
And happy feelings of the dead:
And therefore was it rightly said,
That Ossian, last of all his race,
Lies buried in this lonely place."

Hogg. Hech me!—I'll be buried beside Yarrow mysel!

Odoherty. And dug up, no doubt, quite fresh and lovely, like this new hero of yours, one hundred summers hence. I hope you will take care to be buried in the top boots, by the by—they will gratify the speculators of the year two thousand and two.

Tickler. So Byron is, after all, to be buried in Greece—quite right.* His suspiration was originally from thence—his muse always spread a broader pinion whenever she hovered over the blue Ægean. Proudly let him lie on Sunium! loftily let his spirit gaze at midnight npon the rocks of Salamis!

Odoherty. So be it. But I have still one word to say to you *ancnt* his lordship of Byron. Byron was by no means, Mr. Timothy, the Jacobin Bard that you seem to hold him. I'll be shot if he ever penned one stanza without feeling the coronet.—Ay, ay, sir, he was indeed "Byron my Baron," and that to the backbone.

Tickler. You are quite right, Odoherty, and I would have said the same thing if Hogg had not interrupted me. The fact is, that Byron took the walk I mentioned, but he did not take it in that singleness of heart and soul with which the two other gentlemen took to theirs. No, sir, he was too good by nature for what he wished to be—he could not drain the blood of the cavaliers out of his veins—he could not cover the coronet all over with the red nightcap—he could not forget that he was born a lord, a gentleman, an English gentleman, and an English lord;—and hence the contradictoriness which has done so much to weaken the effect of his strains—hence that self-reproaching melancholy which was eternally crossing and unnerving him—hence the impossibility of his hearing, without a quivering pulse, ay, even after all his thundering trumpets about Washington, America, republics, and fiddle-de-dees, the least echo of what he in his very last poem so sweetly alludes to—

——"The home
Heart ballads of green Erin or gray Highlands,
That bring Lochaber back to eyes that roam
O'er far Atlantic continents or islands—
The calentures of music that o'ercome
All mountaineers with dreams that they are nigh lands
No more to be beheld but in such visions."

Hence the dark heaving of soul with which he must have written in his Italian villezgiatura, that description of his own lost, forfeited, ancestral seat. I can repeat the glorious verses.

"It stood embosom'd in a happy valley,
Crown'd by high woodlands, where the Druid oak

* It was originally intended that Byron's heart, at least, should be retained in that Greece which he had loved so well, which obtained his early sympathy, and received his latest breath. This was not fulfilled. All that was mortal of him rests in the humble church of Hucknall, not far from that Newstead Abbey which he so exquisitely described.—M.

Stood like Caractacus in act to rally
His host, with broad arms, 'gainst the thunder-stroke;
And from beneath his boughs were seen to sally
The dappled foresters—as day awoke,
The branching stag swept down with all his herd,
To quaff a brook which murmur'd like a bird.

"Before the mansion lay a lucid lake,
Broad as transparent, deep, and freshly fed
By a river, which its soften'd way did take
In currents through the calmer water spread
Around: the wild fowl nestled in the brake
And sedges, brooding in their liquid bed;
The woods sloped downwards to its brink, and stood
With their green faces fix'd upon the flood.

"Its outlet dash'd into a deep cascade,
Sparkling with foam, until, again subsiding,
Its shriller echoes—like an infant made
Quiet—sank into softer ripples, gliding
Into a rivulet; and thus allay'd,
Pursued its course, now gleaming, and now hiding
Its windings through the woods; now clear, now blue,
According as the skies their shadows threw.

"A glorious remnant of the Gothic pile
(While yet the church was Rome's) stood half apart
In a grand arch, which once screened many an aisle.
These last had disappear'd—a loss to art:
The first yet frown'd superbly o'er the soil,
And kindled feelings in the roughest heart,
Which mourn'd the power of time's or tempest's march,
In gazing on that venerable arch.

"Within a niche, nigh to its pinnacle,
Twelve saints had once stood sanctified in stone;
But these had fallen, not when the friars fell,
But in the war which struck Charles from his throne,
When each house was a fortalice—as tell
The annals of full many a line undone,
The gallant cavaliers, who fought in vain
For those who knew not to resign or reign.

"But in a higher niche, alone, but crown'd,
The Virgin Mother of the God-born child,
With her Son in her blessed arms, look'd round,
Spared by some chance when all beside was spoil'd;
She made the earth below seem holy ground.
This may be superstition, weak or wild,
But even the faintest relics of a shrine
Of any worship, wake some thoughts divine.

"A mighty window, hollow in the centre,
Shorn of its glass of thousand colorings,

Through which the deepen'd glories once could enter,
  Streaming from off the sun like seraph's wings,
Now yawns all desolate: now loud, now fainter,
  The gale sweeps through its fretwork, and oft sings
The owl his anthem, where the silenced quire
Lie with their hallelujahs quench'd like fire.

"But in the noontide of the moon, and when
  The wind is wingèd from one point of heaven,
There moans a strange unearthly sound, which then
  Is musical—a dying accent driven
Through the huge arch, which soars and sinks again.
  Some deem it but the distant echo given
Back to the night wind by the waterfall,
And harmonized by the old choral wall.

"Others, that some original shape, or form
  Shaped by decay perchance, hath given the power
(Though less than that of Memnon's statue, warm
  In Egypt's rays, to harp at a fix'd hour)
To this gray ruin with a voice to charm.
  Sad, but serene, it sweeps o'er tree or tower:
The cause I know not, nor can solve; but such
The fact:—I've heard it,—once perhaps too much.

"Amidst the court a Gothic fountain play'd,
  Symmetrical, but deck'd with carvings quaint—
Strange faces, like to men in masquerade,
  And here perhaps a monster, there a saint:
The spring gush'd through grim mouths, of granite made,
  And sparkled into basins, where it spent
Its little torrent in a thousand bubbles,
Like man's vain glory, and his vainer troubles."

Hogg. It is there—it is nowhere but there, that Byron's ghost will linger. Ye may speak about Greece, and Rome, and America; but his heart was, after all, among the auld mouldering arches and oaks of his forefathers. I would not, for something, stand ae hour of black night below the shadow of that awful auld Abbey. Ghosts indeed! I could face the spectres of auld priests and monks enow, I daursay—but od, man, what a ghost of ghosts will Byron's be!

Tickler. Well said, James Hogg! Go on.

Hogg (*having drunk off a tumbler*). I canna express what my feelings are as to some things—but I have them, for a' that. I ken naething about your grand divisions and subdivisions, about old things and new things, and contemplative spirits and revolutionary spirits, and what not—but this I ken, sirs, that I canna bide to think that Byron's dead. There's a wonderful mind swallowed up somewhere. Gone! and gone so young!—and may be on the threshold of his truest glory, baith as a man and as a poet. It makes me wae, wae, to think o't. Ye'll laugh at me, Captain Odoherty; but it's as true as I'm telling ye,

I shall never see a grand blue sky fu' of stars, nor look out upon the Forest, when all the winds of winter are howling over the wilderness of dry crashing branches, nor stand beside the sea to hear the waves roaring upon the rocks, without thinking that the spirit of Byron is near me. In the hour of awe—in the hour of gloom—in the hour of sorrow, and in the hour of death, I shall remember Byron!

Tickler. Euge! Let no more evil be said of him. Μα τȣς εν Μαθαθωνι τορομαχευσαντας—Peace be to the illustrious dead!

Odoherty. By all means, gentlemen—by all manner of means. Here, then, fill your glasses to the brim—and rise up—To the Memory of Byron!

Omnes (rising). THE MEMORY OF BYRON!

Odoherty (sings)

*Air—The Last Rose of Summer.**

1.

Lament for Lord Byron,
In full flow of grief,
As a sept of Milesians
Would mourn o'er their chief!
With the loud voice of weeping,
With sorrow's deep tone,
We shall keen o'er our poet,
"All faded and gone."

2.

Though far in Missolunghi
His body is laid;
Though the hands of the stranger
His lone grave have made;
Though no foot from Old England
Its surface will tread,
Nor the sun of Old England
Shine over its head;

3.

Yet, bard of the Corsair,
High-spirited Childe;
Thou who sang'st of Lord Manfred
The destiny wild!
Thou star, whose bright radiance
Illumined our verse,
Our souls cross the blue seas,
To mourn o'er thy hearse.

4.

Thy faults and thy follies,
Whatever they were,
Be their memory dispersed
As the winds of the air;
No reproaches from me
On thy course shall be thrown;—
Let the man who is sinless
Uplift the first stone.

5.

In thy vigor of manhood
Small praise from my tongue
Had thy fame or thy talents,
Or merriment wrung;
For that church, and that state, and
That monarch I loved,
Which too oft thy hot censure
Or rash laughter moved.

6.

But I hoped in my bosom
That moment would come,
When thy feelings would wander
Again to their home.
For that soul, O lost Byron!
In brillianter hours,
Must have turn'd to its country—
Must still have been ours.

7.

Now slumber, bright spirit!
Thy body, in peace,
Sleeps with heroes and sages,
And poets of Greece;
While thy soul in the tongue of
Even greater than they,
Is embalm'd till the mountains
And seas pass away.

* Written by Maginn—as was the whole of this "Noctes."—M.

Tickler. Very well, indeed, Odoherty; I am glad to see that you really have some feeling about you still. Oh yes, man, that is what every body must feel.

Odoherty. Feel what?—why, what a proper old humbug you are, after all! (*Sings.*)

1.

Oh! when I am departed and passed away,
Let's have no lamentations or sounds of dismay—
Meet together, kind lads, o'er a three-gallon bowl,
And so toast the repose of Odoherty's soul.
Down, derry down.

2.

If my darling girl pass, gently bid her come in,
To join the libation she'll think it no sin;
Though she choose a new sweetheart, and doff the black gown,
She'll remember me kindly when down—down—down—
Down, derry down.

Were you deep in for it about the battle, Tickler? I won five ponies on Spring—that was all I had done.

Tickler. I have cut the pugilistic mania ever since the Thurtell business—it quite disgusted me with the ring.

Odoherty. Pooh! stuff of stuffs;—you're getting crazy, I believe. I suppose you shut Redgauntlet, whenever you came to that capital murder of Nanty Ewart and Master Nixon—the best thing in the book, in my humble opinion.

Hogg. An awfu' gruesome business, in truth. Weel, I think it's a very gude book, now, Redgauntlet. I consider it a very decent novel. I read him through without stopping; and it was after supper, too, ere I got haud o' the chiel.

Tickler. Why, that's not the worst way of judging of such affairs, James. My case was pretty much the same. 'Tis a very excellent book, a spirit-stirring one, and a spirit-sustaining one. It never flags.

Odoherty. I wish to God it had been written on in one even strain, no matter whether in the first or in the third person; but I hate all that botheration of Mr. Latimer's narrative, Mr. Fairford's narrative, and the Author of Waverley's narrative. Indeed it is obvious he had got sick of that stuff himself ere he reached the belly of the second volume, and had the sheets not gone to press, no doubt he would have altered it.

Hogg. I really never noticed that there was ony thing out of the ordinary in this particular. I read it clean on, till I got baith sair een and sair heart.

Tickler. Yes, yes—these are mere trifles. Give me such a stream of narrative, and give me one such glorious fellow as Auld Willie, and

I am pretty well off, I calculate. What a most terrific piece of diablerie that is, the story of the old Baron and his Baboon. By Jupiter, they may talk of their Sintrams and their Devil's Elixirs as long as they please. That's the best ghost story ever I read. I speak for myself—and how gloriously the Fiddler tells it, which, by the way, is, all things considered, not the smallest part of the feat. To make a cat-witted, old, blind creature like that tell such a tale, without for a moment using an expression out of his own character, and yet tell it with such portentous thrilling energy, and even sublimity of effect—this, sirs, is the perfection, not of genius merely, but of taste and consummate art.

Odoherty. Nanty Ewart for my money! Why, Byron might have written for fifty years without digging the fiftieth part so deep into the human heart—ay, even the blackguard human heart he is so fond of. The attempt to laugh—and the stammered "*Poor Jess!*"—and then that fearful sarcasm, "he is killing me—and I am only sorry he is so long about it." These, sir, are the undying *qu'il mouruts* that will keep this lad afloat, although he should write books enough to fill the James Watt steamboat.

Hogg. I kent Peter Peebles brawlies—I've seen the doited body gaun gaping about the Parliament-House five hundred times—I forget his real name though. Peter's really a weel-drawn character—he's a very natural delineation, to my fancy.

Tickler. Natural delineation! Well-drawn character, indeed!—Come, come, Jamie, he's a prince, a king, an emperor of characters. Give us one such a character, sir, and we will hoist you up till old Stodhard's ridiculous caricature be realized, and the top-boots of the Ettrick Shepherd are seen plaited in the most intimate and endearing familiarity with the point-hose of Will Shakspeare. He's quite as good, sir, as any Malvolio, or Slender, that was ever painted by the hand of man. I build, in the true Catholic phrase, *super hunc Petràm.*

Odoherty. Nothing is so disgusting to me as the chat of these cockneyfied critics about those books. Prating, prating about fallings off, want of respect for the public, absurd haste, repetitions of Meg Merrilies, &c. &c. &c.—I trouble them to show me the man that can give us a Meg Dods, or a Clara Mowbray, or one of these characters we have just been discussing. Till then, I spurn their Balaam with my heels. The only person I really was sorry to see joining in the beastly stuff was Tom Campbell—but to be sure, his dotage is sufficiently evident from many things besides that.

Tickler. Ay, ay, poor Ritter Bann!* He has gone down hill with a vengeance, to be sure.

Odoherty. Spurn we with our heels the Balaam and the Balaam-

* A very inferior ballad, by Campbell, so named.—M.

ites!—North, I suppose, will be squabashing them in the shape of a Review of Redgauntlet.

Tickler. Not he, i' faith. He was in a deuced rage with Ebony, for wanting him to have a review of it. He said he supposed the next thing would be to review Homer's Iliad, and the Psalms of David. And after all, Kit is so far right—every body has read a book of that sort as soon as yourself, and there being nothing new in the *kind* of talent it displays, most people are just as able as any of us to make a decent judgment. When another Ivanhoe, or any thing ranking as the commencement of another flight altogether, makes its appearance, then, no doubt, the old lad will touch the trumpet again—not, I think, till then.

Odoherty. He is getting crustier and crustier every day. One can scarcely get him to put in the least puff now, merely to oblige a friend. Ebony does not like to speak to him on the subject, particularly when his gout is flying about in this horrid way; but *entre nous*, he is by no means satisfied with old Christopher. He seldom or never mentions any of Blackwood's books, which to me, I must own, seems deuced unfair. But he's so capricious, the old cock. There is Gilbert Earle, now, a really clever thing too—but that ought to have been nothing, either here or there, when I asked him so small a favor,—I sent him one of the handiest little articles on Master Gilbert you ever saw, and, by Jupiter, back it came by return of the caddie, with just this scrawled on the top in red ink, or beet-root sauce, I rather think: "Out upon novels!"—these were the words of the curmudgeon.

Hogg. Out upon novels! keep us a'!

Tickler. Gad! I almost sympathize with Christopherus—there positively is too great a crop—but *sans phrase*, now, what sort of a concern is this same Gilbert Earle?

Odoherty. Why, it is a work of real talent—I assure you—'pon honor it is—a very clever work indeed—and besides, it is published by Knight, a lad for whom I have a particular regard. 'Tis a most melancholy tale—both the subject and the style are after Adam Blair, but that does not prevent the author's exhibiting great and original talent in many of the descriptions. By the by, he would suit you exactly in one thing, Hogg. Such a hand for describing a pretty woman, has not often fallen in your way, I calculate. Upon my soul, I'm not very inflammable, you know, and yet some of his pieces of this kind almost took away my breath. But read the book, lads, for yourselves—ask for "Some Account of the late Gilbert Earle, Esq.," written by himself, and published by Mr. Knight. You will find the author to be one of these true fellows who blend true pathos with true luxury. Some of his bits, by the by, may have caught your eye already, for he published one or two specimens of the affair in the Album.

Tickler. A clever and gentlemanlike periodical, which I am truly sorry to find stopped—at least I suppose it is so, for I have not lately heard the name. There were some capital contributors to that concern.

Odoherty. I believe North has now enlisted some of the best of them; but not the author of the said Gilbert Earle,* he being a Whig. He is a devilish nice lad, however, for all that.

Tickler. I perceive, Odoherty, that you have no notion of impartial criticism. You always sit down with a fixed resolution to abuse a fellow up hill and down dale, or else to laud him to the Empyrean. I suspect you are capricious as to these matters.

Odoherty. Not at all. I always abuse my enemies, and puff my friends. So do all the rest of the lads "of the WE," if they had the candor to confess things—but that they have not, wherefore let perdition be their portion. I, for my part, have no hesitation in avowing that I consider Burns's best, truest, and most touching line to be,

"They had been fu' for weeks together."

How could one hesitate about puffing him whose cigar-case has never been closed upon his fingers? Do you know why Jeffrey has been so severe of late upon Doctor Southey?

Tickler. Impertinence, that's all—though I admit there *is* a pretty considerable d—d deal of humbug about him (*ut Yankicè loquar*).

Odoherty. The reason of Jeffrey's spleen is obvious. The laureate invited him to *tea!*—invite a literary character of rank to a dish of catlap, and a thin, scraggy, dry, *butter-brodt*, as the Germans call it in their superb and now popularish dialect. Why, there's no saying what might have happened, had he set down the little man to a plate of hot kipper, or some nice fried trouts, and then a bowl of cold punch, or a bottle of sauterne or markebrunner. That is the way to treat an editor of that magnitude, when he calls on you in your country house in the evening of a fine summer's day—more particularly when, as I believe Jeffrey's case really was, the said editor has dined at an earlier hour than he is accustomed to, and when, as I also understood to have been the fact on this occasion, the lad is evidently quite sober. In such circumstances the notion of the tea was a real *bêtise.* Southey was always a spoon; but I wonder Coleridge could sit by without recollecting what sort of an appearance it would have, and tipping Betty a hint to bring in the broth.

Hogg. The broth! Het kail to the four-hours, Captain?

Odoherty. Was *broth* the word I used? I have been in Glasgow lately, you know. It has the same meaning there with punch—cold lime and rum punch, I mean—the best liquefier, perhaps, that has yet

* Barry St. Leger, an Irishman, was author of "Gilbert Earle," and of "Selections from Mr. Blount's MSS."—M.

been invented for this season of the year. I prefer it, I confess, both to Sangaree and Brandy Panny. These are morning tipples decidedly.

Tickler. Come, you're getting into your Maxim vein, I think. You are becoming a perfect Solomon of Soakers, Ensign. You should have called it the Code Odoherty, sir, and produced it at once in a handy, little, juridical-looking, punchy double duodecimo. The work would be much referred to.

Odoherty. I am great in my legislatorial capacity, I admit. Nothing equal to me in my own department. As Byron has expressed it, I am at present

> The Grand Napoleon of the realm of punch ;

or rather it should be of *paunch*, for of late I've been patronizing both sides of the victualling office.

Tickler. Yes, you've been poaching in every corner of Kitchener's preserve. By the way, how does the Doctor take up with your interference ?

Odoherty. Oh ! admirably. We understand each other thoroughly. Kitchener—his name, by the by, settles all disputes about the doctrine of predestination—Kitchener is a prime little fellow—an excellent creature as earth contains. Why, here's a man that has written three or four of the very best books our age has witnessed, as the puff-maker says ; and what's far better, my hearties, he gives one of the very best feeds going—quite the dandy—such sauces ! By jingo, I admire a man of this stamp.

Hogg. Deil doubts you. Wha doesna admire them that can give ye baith a gude book, and a gude dinner ? For my part, I admire a man that gives me the bare bit dinner, just itsell, without ony books.

Odoherty. The bare bit dinner ! Oh, you savage ! You have no more right, sir, to open that cod's-mouth of yours, for the purpose of uttering one syllable on any subject connected with eating or drinking, than Macvey Napier has to mention Bacon, or Professor Leslie to stand for the Hebrew chair,* or a Negro or a Phrenologist to be classed among the genus *rationale*.—The bare dinner ! Oh, ye beast !

Hogg. Some folk have a braw notion of themsells, Captain.

Odoherty. If I could choose now—if I had Fortunatus's cap in good earnest—I'll tell you how I would do—by Jericho, I would breakfast with Lord Fife at Marr Lodge. Such pasties ! such cakes ! what a glorious set out, to be sure !—I should then keep stepping southwards —take my basin of mulligatawny and glass of cherry-brandy at Mrs. Montgomery's here *en passant*—get on to Belvoir, or Burleigh,† or

* Napier's Essay on Bacon and Leslie's ignorance of Hebrew were *Blackwood's* standing subjects.—M.

† Belvoir Castle, Rutlandshire, the residence of the Duke of Rutland ; Burgley House, Lincolnshire, the mansion of the Marquis of Exeter.—M.

some of these grand places on the road, in time for dinner, and tap just about twelve at the door of the Blue Posts*—Prime whisky-punch there, sirs. If you were here, I might probably trace back a bit so as to drop in upon your third bowl.

Hogg. Hear to the craving ne'er-do-weel!—You'll not be a lang liver, I can tell you, Captain, if you go on at this rate. You ought to marry a wife, sir, and sit down for a decent, respectable head of a family—you've had your braw spell of devilry now. Marry some bit bonny body of an heiress, man, and turn over a new leaf.

Odoherty. With a gilt edge, you propose. Well, I have some thoughts of the thing ; the worst of it is, that I am getting oldish now, and deucedly nice—and I really distrust myself too. I have serious apprehensions that I might turn out rather a quisquis sort of a Benedict. Hang it! I've been too long on the hill—they could never break me now—but I'll try some day, that's obvious.

Hogg. You'll easily get an heiress, man, wi' that grand lang nose o' yours, and thae bonny, bonny legs, and that fine yellow curly head of hair.

Odoherty (*aside*). Bond Street growth—but no matter.

Hogg. And, aboon a', your leeterary name. Od, man, I ken twa leddies in the Cowgate that wad fain, fain have me to bring ye some night to tea. Bonny birds, Captain—will ye gang?

Odoherty. You be skinned!

Tickler. I'll tell you what my real views are, Odoherty.—Hang it, I don't see why you should not take up a Scots baronetcy as well as the Bishop of Winchester,† or, as Johnny Murray called him, Mr. Winton. I suppose this sort of concern don't stand one much higher than an Aberdeen degree. I really would have you think of it. Sir Morgan and Lady Odoherty request the honor——Lady Odoherty's carriage stops the way!—Sir Morgan Odoherty's cabriolet!!—By Jove, the thing is arranged!—You *must* be a baronet, my dear Signifer.

Odoherty. Hum!—Well, to oblige you, I shan't much object to such a trifle. How shall I set about it, then, Timothy?

Tickler. Poo!—Find out that there was some Odoherty, of course there were many—but no matter for that—in the army of M'Fadyen, the lad that flung his own head after Lieutenant-General Sir William Wallace, Baronet, K.T. and C.G.B.—or in the armies of Montrose—which, by the by, were almost all of them Irish armies; *secundo*, Find out that this glorious fellow—being, of course, (as all gentlemen in those days were,) a Knight-Bachelor—had been *once*—no matter from what beastly ignorance, or from what low, fawning vulgarity, *addressed*

* A well-known public house, in London, nearly opposite the Haymarket Theatre.—M.

† In 1823, Dr. Tomline, Bishop of Winchester, made a claim, which was allowed, to a Nova Scotia baronetcy, which had been conferred by Charles I. on one of his ancestors. His son, however, has not assumed the title.—M.

as a Baronet. Then, *tertio*, have a few of us assembled at Ambrose's some day at five o'clock, and the job is done.—I myself have frequently acted as Chancellor.—I am quite *au fait*.

Odoherty. Why, as to the first of these points, I have no doubt there must have been some Odoherties here in Montrose's time. As to the second, it obviously *must* be so; and as to the third, by Jupiter, name your day!

Tickler. This day three weeks—six o'clock sharp. I stipulate for a green goose, and a glass of your own genuine usquebaugh.*

Odoherty. Thou hast said it!—stinginess would ill beseem a man of my rank. I trust his Majesty the King of the Sandwich Islands will be here in time to join us. I am told he is a hearty cock.

Tickler. To be serious—I was really amazed to see John Bull, honest lad, going into the Prettyman humbug. It is very likely, indeed, that the worthy Bishop himself is by no means aware of the absurdity of the system under which he supposes himself to have acquired the orange ribbon of Nova Scotia. He has probably been led—but no matter, as to one particular case. The fact is, that if they wished to give us a real boon, they ought to look to this subject—the people above stairs, I mean. They ought to bring in a bill, requiring that the man who wishes to assume any title of honor in Scotland ought to do the same thing which the House of Lords demands when a man wishes to take up a peerage of Scotland. If that were done, the public would be satisfied, and the individual would be safe from that annoyance to which he must be subjected so long as matters are managed in the present ridiculous and most unlawyer-like method. Why, only consider what it is that the jury (Heaven bless the name!) does in such a case. The claimant appears, and demands to be recognised as the heir of such a man, who died two, three, or four centuries ago. Well, he proves himself to have *some blood relation* to the defunct. The *factio juris* is, that when a man makes such a claim, those, if there be any, that have a better title—a nearer propinquity—will of course appear and show fight; and, in the absence of any such appearance, the work of the said noble jury is at once finished.† Now, in the case of a man making a claim, which, if allowed, will give him a certain number of acres, no doubt the chances are infinitesimally small, that any person, concerned from his own interests in the redarguing of the said claim, will fail to come forth to give battle. Nay, even in the case of a Scotchman, of a Scotch family well known in the history, or at least in the records of the country, coming forward with a claim, the object of which is a mere honorary matter, such as a title of baronet, the chances are not very great, that, in a small nation

* From this date, the Adjutant is always mentioned in *Blackwood* as Sir Morgan Odoherty, Baronet!—M.

† It is from such a "source" as *this* that Mr. Humphreys has claimed the Earldom of Stirling.—M.

where every body knows every body, and where all are very much taken up about titular trifles—the chances are not great, that even a claimant of this order will be allowed to walk the course; but in the case of an Englishman, of whose family nobody in Scotland ever heard a word, coming down and wanting a title, to which nobody in Scotland can of couse have any claim—in this case, no doubt, the most perfect apathy must prevail. The Bishop *may* be in the right; but I, and all the world besides, must continue to regard with suspicion the assumption of a title, the patent for which is *not* produced, unless the clearest evidence as to the tenor of the patent be produced..

Odoherty. Then, what is the Bishop's way to get out of the scrape?

Tickler. Why, in the present state of matters, I see but one. He ought to bring an action before the Court of Sessions against some friend of his, no matter about what, assuming the style of baronet in his "summons," as we call it—that is, in his original writ. The friend may put in his objection to the style under which the Bishop sues, and then the Court will be open to hear him defend his right to use the said style. In this way the whole matter may be cleared up.

Hogg. There's naebody cares ae boddle about sic matters—they're a' just clean havers. I own I do like to hear of a real grand auld name like the house of Marr being restored to their ain. That is a thing to please a Scottish heart. The Earl of Marr! There's not a nobler sound in Britain.

Tickler. Quite so, Hogg. But was there ever such beastliness as Brougham's? Why, in seconding Peel's motion for dispensing with the personal appearance of an old gentleman of near ninety in London, what topic, think ye, does this glorious fellow dare to make the ground on which he (Brougham) solicits the indulgence of Parliament? Why, this—that Mr. Erskine of Marr is distinguished for his *liberal opinions!!!* Egregious puppy! what had old Marr's politics to do with the matter? They are Whig, and so much the worse for him; but conceive only the bad taste—the abominable taste—of this fellow's lugging in the old man's whiggery as a recommendation of him to the House of Commons, at the very moment when the House was about to pass a bill conferring high honors on the old man—a bill originating, no doubt, in the high personal feelings of the King, but still owing its existence there to the support of the King's Tory ministers. Such insolence is really below all contempt. I wonder Peel did not give him a wipe or two in return.

Odoherty. The sulky insolent ——!

Hogg. The born gowk!

Tickler. For cool, rancorous, deliberate impudence, give me, among all Whigs, Brougham! Only think of *his* daring, after all that has happened, to say one word in the House of Commons, when the topic before them referred, in any degree, however remote, to an act of generous and magnanimous condescension of that monarch whom, on the Queen's trial, he and his friend Denman dared to speak of as, we can never forget, they did!*

Odoherty. I confess Brougham is a fine specimen. By the way, what is all this piece of work about changes in your Scots Courts of Law?

Tickler. It is a piece of work originating in the by no manner of means unnatural aversion of the Chancellor to a law of which he is ignorant, and carried on by the base and fawning flattery (which he should have seen through) of certain low Scotch Whigs, who, nourishing the vile hope that, change once introduced, changes may be multiplied, are too happy to find, in the best Tory of England, their ally in a plan which has for its real object the destruction of all that is most dear and valuable to Scotland, and of course held and prized as such by the Tories of Scotland. But the low arts by which the whole affair has been got up and got on—the absurdity of the proposed innovations, and in particular, the pitiable imbecility with which the whole real concerns of the Jury Court—that *job*—are blinked—all these shall ere long be exposed in a full, and, I hope, a satisfactory manner. I shall demolish them in ten pages. Down—down—down shall they lie—never to rise again—or my name is not Timothy.

Odoherty. A letter to Jeffrey, I suppose?

Tickler. Even so let it be. My word, I'll give him a dose.

Hogg. It's aye a pleasure to you to be paiking at him—I wonder you're not wearied o't.

Tickler. I am wearied of it—but duty, Hogg, duty!

Hogg. It's my duty to tell you, that the bottom of the bowl has been visible this quarter of an hour. (*Rings.*)

* * * * * * *

* As "worse than the Roman Nero."—M.

No. XVI.—AUGUST, 1824.

Odoherty. By the way, North, have you seen a little book lately put forth by Hurst and Robinson, "On the Present State of the Periodical Press?" The subject is worth your notice, I should think.

North. Certainly, Ensign. I have considered the subject pretty seriously, I believe, and I have also seen the duodecimo you mention.* But I am not so well skilled in the minutiæ of these affairs as to be able to give any opinion as to its minute accuracy.

Odoherty. I don't mean to swear for all the particulars neither, for I have only dipped into it; but it seemed to me that there was an air of credibility over what little I read of it. How did you find it as to the Journals with which you are really acquainted?

North. Really, I cannot pretend to be really acquainted with many of them. Blackwood and the Quarterly are the only ones of the greater class that I always read; and as for the papers, you know, I have long been contented with the Courier, New Times, John Bull, and Cobbett. I used to take the Chronicle while Jamie Pirie lived,† and I took in the Examiner till his Majesty of Cockaigne went to Italy. Of late I see none of these trash.

Odoherty. Pooh! that's nonsense—you should see every thing.

North. Sir, I can't read without spectacles now-a-days; and I am very well pleased to let Tickler read the Edinburgh and Westminster for me, and you may do the same for me, if you have a mind, *quoad* the minor diurnals of the same faction. Cobbett I always must read, because Cobbett always must write. I enjoy my Cobbett.

* This *brochure*, published anonymously, was written by the late Robert Alexander, at one time connected with two scandalous Scottish papers, (*The Beacon*, in Edinburgh, and *The Sentinel*, in Glasgow,) and afterwards successively editor of *Flindell's Western Luminary*, in Exeter, the *Watchman*, in London, the London *Morning Journal*, the *Liverpool Standard*, and the *Liverpool Mail*. Alexander was conducting the *Morning Journal* when Wellington and Peel astonished their own Tory party by introducing and carrying the Catholic Relief Bill in 1829. He was bitterly personal on the Ministry, for what he called their "treachery." His animadversions must have deeply galled them, for it was determined to prosecute him for libel, whenever a good *casus belli* should occur. Alexander, who was audacious and imprudent, wrote an article accusing the Duke of Wellington of an intention of making himself Dictator, for the purpose of marrying his eldest son, then 24, to the present Queen Victoria, a child aged 11. For this he was tried, convicted, and imprisoned. The result was the suppression of the *Morning Journal*. In 1833, he went to Liverpool to conduct a local paper called *The Standard*. In 1836, he commenced the *Liverpool Mail*, on which he continued until his death, in February, 1854, aged fifty-eight. He was a strong, hard-hitting writer; a man of simple tastes; a faithful friend; a consistent politician; and extremely fond of the innocent prattle of children.—M.

† James Perry, proprietor of the London *Morning Chronicle*, was a native of Aberdeen, and his original name was *Pirie*.—M.

Odoherty. Surely, surely. But what think ye of the proposal which this new scribe sets forth? I mean his great plan for having the duties on the newspapers lightened? What will Robinson* say to that?

North. I have very little doubt that the Chancellor of the Exchequer will, in the course of a few sessions, bring in and carry through a bill for this purpose. It is the only way to level the arrogance of those great a-thousand-times-over-be-cudgelled monsters—I mean the Old Times and such like—the worst disgrace of the nation.

Odoherty. It would do that, to be sure, with a vengeance; but would not the revenue get some sore slaps?

North. Not one cuff, I honestly believe. These overgrown scampish concerns are, at present, enabled to brave, not merely the influence of government, for it is no evil, but a great good, that newspapers should be independent of this—no, no, that is not what I think of—but the general indignation of all honest men of all parties, the wide, the deep, the universal scorn with which the whole virtue and sense of the British people regard the unblushing, open, avowed, acknowledged, even boasted profligacy, of some of those establishments.

Odoherty. They are so to a certain extent, I admit; but, surely, the little book exaggerates their triumphs.

North. I don't know that, nor do I care for a few hundreds or thousands, more or less. But this I am certain of, that if the duty on the advertisements were considerably lowered, and also the duty on the newspapers themselves, two consequences would infallibly be the result. People would advertise in more papers than they do at present, and people would take in more papers. These are clear and obvious consequences, and from them I hold it scarcely less certain, that two others would ensue. I mean, that an honest new paper would contend on more equal terms with a dishonest old one, and that the far greater number of advertisements published, and the far greater number of newspapers circulated in the country, would more than atone to the Exchequer for the loss Mr. Robinson might at first sight apprehend, from a measure so bold and decided as that of striking off one-half of the newspaper tax, and of the tax on advertisements.

Odoherty. Which are——

North. Threepence-halfpenny on each copy of each newspaper—and three and sixpence on every thing, however trifling, that assumes the character of an advertisement.

Odoherty. I confess it appears a little hard to tax journals of one sort so heavily, and journals of another sort not at all. Why not tax a Magazine or a Review, as well?

North. Certainly. The excuse is, that newspapers are carried postage-free; but this is, of course, quite inapplicable to the enormous pro-

* Frederick Robinson, then Chancellor of the Exchequer, and now Earl of Ripon.—M.

portion of all papers circulated exclusively in London and its suburbs —and it is far too much to make a man living in Bond Street pay threepence-halfpenny, in order that a man living in the Orkney Islands may get his newspaper so much the cheaper.*

Odoherty. Viewed in one light it may seem so; but do you not see the policy in those days of trying to make the provinces balance the capital, by equalizing their condition as to all such things, in so far as it is by any means possible to do so?

North. Very true too, sir. But I can tell you this, Odoherty, that I see very great danger in this same balancing and equalizing you talk of, and nothing so likely to meet the danger as the adoption of the plan I am lauding. It is obvious, that the speedy conveyance of the papers published in the capital into every part of the empire, is gradually enabling those who influence the political feelings of the capital to influence also, and this almost in the same moment of time, the feelings of the remotest provincialists. Thus, in another way to be sure, London bids fair to become to Britain, what Paris has so long been to France;—and that London never can become, sir, without the whole character, not only of the Constitution, but of the nation, suffering an essential and most perilous change. To check the danger of this, I again tell you, I see nothing half so likely, as the adoption of a scheme which will at once deprive old hard determined villany of its exclusive means of lucre, and soon reduce all papers whatever under a decent measure of subjection to the general opinion of decent society. Sir, had there been no three-and-sixpence duty on advertisements, the thirty or forty traders who own the Times would not have dared to meet together in a tavern, and decide by a vote, whether that already infamous journal should, or should not, double its load of infamy, by fighting the battle of the late miserable Queen.† This *maximum opprobrium* had been spared.

* In 1824, upon every single newspaper there was a stamp which cost four pence, (eight cents,) less 20 per cent. discount. At that time, there was a duty of three shillings and sixpence (84 cents) upon each advertisement. A slight equivalent for the stamp-duty was afforded by allowing all newspapers to be carried, free of charge, through the post-office. In September, 1836, a remission of these duties, commonly called "Taxes upon Knowledge," came into effect. The newspaper duty was diminished to one penny (two cents) on each newspaper, and one cent for supplements. At the same time, the duty was reduced from 84 to 36 cents on each advertisement. In August, 1853, the advertisement duty was wholly abolished, and the supplement stamp further reduced. As *The Times* has not abated its charges, it thus gains 36 cents *extra* on each advertisement, and the reduction in the supplement duty has enabled it to extend its daily sale from 44,000 (beyond which it previously could not print, to sell at 10 cents each copy, without loss) to 73,000, which are its numbers at the present date [July, 1854]. These changes have put £100,000 per annum extra profit in the treasury of *The Times*, inasmuch as it has wholly appropriated to itself the benefits of the reduction legislatively intended for the public. All British newspapers continue to be carried free by the post-office, but it is probable that the law will be further amended, so as to provide that newspapers which do *not* pass through the post-office shall be unstamped, and that only those which are so conveyed shall bear a penny stamp, or be charged with a penny postage.—M.

† It was reported, and obtained many believers, that, early in 1820, on the accession of George IV., when a difficulty appeared likely to arise about his wife, the proprietors of *The Times* met and had a long discussion as to the part that journal should take in the coming

Odoherty. I don't follow you exactly—why?

North. I can't help it, if you can't see what is to me as plain as any pike-staff. A groom out of place advertises in only one paper, because he can't afford to pay two three-and-sixpences to the King—make the duty only one shilling and ninepence, and he will give himself the benefit of two advertisements, and a clever lad is he if he finds means to patronize another paper as blackguard as the Times. But I take much wider ground than all this, sir. If the newspaper press, particularly the Sunday one, were as free and unshackled (I mean as to taxes) as every other press is, we could not see it so infinitely above any other press that exists on the score of profligacy. We could not see it the daily, the hourly practice of a newspaper to take BRIBES, if the bribers were, in consequence of a greater competition, compelled to bribe many more than they at present have to do with. Thus, for example, we should see no more of the scandalous subjection to the interests of particular Stock-jobbers and brokers*—we should have no more of those egregious lies which every day shows and detects—we should have no more of those attacks on men who pay ten guineas next day or next week, to have their characters vindicated. This most crying evil of open venality would at least be greatly, very greatly diminished.

Odoherty. Well, I had rather see than hear tell of it, as Hogg's phrase is.

North. You remember what Clement of the Observer did about the trial of Thistlewood. The court prohibited in the most solemn manner the publication of any part of the evidence, in any one of that batch of trials, until the whole had been terminated. Mr. Clement was the only one who disobeyed this. Well, he was ordered into court, and fined £500 for the contempt—and what followed?

Odoherty. I can't charge my memory, i'faith, with such doings.

North. Why, he paid the money, and after he had done so, very coolly informed the public, that he had not only paid the fine out of the extra profits of the paper containing the offensive matter, but put, over and above, a very handsome sum into his own pocket.† This was as it should be!

Odoherty. Quite so.

contest. It was decided, by a majority of *one*, that it would side with the Queen, which it did, with great force and success, from the time her name was first mentioned in Parliament, in February, 1820, until and after her death in August, 1821.—M.

* It has never been attributed to *The Times* that it took advantage of its peculiar sources of information for stock-jobbing purposes. On the contrary, the *Morning Chronicle*, under Sir John Easthope, himself a member of the Stock Exchange, was strongly suspected as having been used by him to bull or bear particular stocks as his interests required.—M.

† Mr. Clement sold over 200,000 copies of the *Observer*, with the report of Arthur Thistlewood's trial for high treason. Taking the nett profit on each number to be three cents, the amount would be £1250 on that single issue, (to say nothing of its acting as the very best advertisement of the paper,) so that, by disobeying the order of the Court, he cleared £750.—M.

North. The second part of my plan would, however, tell quite as severely on many other quacks, as on the quacks of the Daily and Weekly papers. If it cost less to advertise, more would advertise. Your King Solomon would have brothers nearer the throne. In short, the thing by being egregiously overdone at the first would soon and effectually correct itself. This is very well argued in the little book you have tabled.

Odoherty. Be it so. But things will go on in the old way, notwithstanding. To tell you the truth, I skipped all that affair at once, as unquestionable balaam. What I looked to was the individual history of the different Journals—their comparative sales, &c. &c. &c.

North. All which, much distrusting, I scarcely gave one glance to.

Odoherty. Distrusting? Why?

North. Why? for this simple reason, sir, that there is no means of ascertaining the actual sale of any one newspaper in existence. They themselves, to be sure, pretend, that, when they refer you to the Stamp Office, which will prove incontestably the issuing of so many thousand stamps, for such and such a paper, it is impossible for any man in his senses to doubt that that number of the Times, the Chronicle, or whatever it be, was actually distributed among the British public on the day alleged. But this is all the merest bam. The fact, sir, is—and I know it—that it is the daily custom of the London papers to send and pay for a vast number of stamped sheets more than they want. Some provincial paper or other is happy to make use of their surplus paper, provided the London office will only save them the trouble of having a separate agent of their own in town, to get their stamps for them. One paper, one of the principal proprietors of which confessed the fact to me t'other day, supplies regularly no less than fifteen different provincial prints with their stamped paper in this way: but, although I did not exactly put that question, it cannot be doubted the whole aggregated sale of the said fifteen is made to figure as part and parcel of the circulation of my friend's own concern, in the yearly or half-yearly statements thereof, which you are in the habit of staring over.*

Odoherty. All this is, I confess, news to me. So you believe nothing, then, of the statements they all do put forth?

North. Nothing; unless I happen to know of my own knowledge, that the property and management of the paper (for I don't speak at present of either of these taken separately) are united in the hands of a man above having any connections with the promulgation of any

* No doubt this was done, and thus a fictitious circulation was claimed by some papers. To prevent this, a series of new dies came into use, in September, 1836, by which every newspaper stamp bore the name of the particular journal on which it was placed. This enabled the Stamp Office to make an annual return of the number of stamps actually taken out by each newspaper. After such return had been issued for years, causing perpetual disputes among rival journals, as to "comparative circulation," it was complained of as too inquisitorial, and has appeared only once during a long period.—M.

falsehood on any subject whatever. Such a man as Stoddart or Mudford, for example—nobody believes they would lie for any thing, far less for this sort of filth.

Odoherty. Certainly not. By the by, now you mention it, I was thunderstruck to find it laid down distinctly, that the total number of political journals circulated in the British islands has trebled—yes, trebled, within the last forty years.

North. No wonder. The American Revolution—the French Revolution—Bonaparte—Wellington—the stream of events, and the immense increase of readers of every thing else—when you take this into view, no wonder at the increase about the newspapers.

Odoherty. I suppose nobody ever heard of such editions of even the best books a hundred years ago, as we now daily hear of.

North. No; not at all. In Pope's time, sir, 500 copies was a great edition—you will find this taken for granted in all the books of the time. Even in Dr. Johnson's time, 750 was reckoned a very large edition of the most popular book, by the most popular author of his day. Even twenty years back, things were in a totally different condition from what we are now accustomed to. What would any body have said to an edition of 10,000 or 12,000 of a new novel? What would any body have said to a review selling 12,000 or 14,000 regularly every number, as I believe the Quarterly has done, for several years back? Sir, this business has *progressed* in the most astonishing ratio.

Odoherty. Ay, i'faith, and nobody has more reason to rub his hands thereupon than yourself.

North. So—well, well, let that pass—now that your cigar is out, pray have the kindness to unlock the balaam-box here, and let's see what's to go on; for the 12th draweth on, and my heart panteth for Brae-mar.

Odoherty. And that's what I will do, my hearty; and many's the time we have done more for each other before this night was born. Here, give me the key; you always keep it at your watch, I think.

North. There it is; take care of my grandmother's repeater;—'tis the little queer-looking fellow, with the B. B. B. B. woven in cipher upon it.

Odoherty. What, four B's?

North. Yes. Bailie—Blackwood's—Balaam—Box. 'Tis his box, you know,—because, according to our friend's verses long ago, out of every one of these bunches it is highly probable

> "Our worthy Publisher purloins a few
> About his roasting-mutton shanks to screw——"

Odoherty. Here's something in old Tickler's fist—shall we begin with overhauling that lad?

North. Certainly. Does he mean to stay all the summer in Dublin, I wonder? Read him, Morgan.

Odoherty (*reads*). "Letters of Timothy Tickler, Esq., to Eminent Literary Characters, Number —to Sir James Mackintosh, Knt., late Recorder of Bombay——"

North. What? what? what? Sir Jamie again?

Odoherty. Pooh! don't be alarmed—one would have thought you had seen Parr's wig or Gerald's ghost, or the Bonassus rampant—'tis only a letter to Sir Jamie, I perceive, about his articles on Brodie's History, and Croker's edition of the Suffolk Papers, in the last Edinburgh Review.

North. Come, that's rather too much, Timotheus. I thought he had sufficiently squabashed those two concerns in one of his late effusions to Jeffrey. But read on.

Odoherty. Excuse me—'tis a cursed small hand—I see it begins as usual with a philippic *anent* things in general—"Burke"—"Pitt"—"Gibbon"—"Hume"—"Brodie"—"Charles"—"Colonel Harrison"—ay, ay, we may hop over a little of this ground. "Your last Number, sir,"—here we are more likely to have something—"Flagrant"—"calumnious"—Pooh! pooh! what a pother about nothing! Come, here's something in double column, and one half in red ink, I swear. Listen to him here, North—(*reads*)—"It may be thought that the trivial punishment I have already inflicted on your critique was as much as the affair merited. It may be so, very probably. But it so happens, sir, that you have to do with a queer old gentleman, three-fourths of whose library is made up of old books, and one-half of whose time is spent in hunting up and down among them in quest of matters nearly as insignificant as the party spleen of an Edinburgh Reviewer, or the historical accuracy of a Sir James Mackintosh." Come, Timothy gets prosy.

North. Let me hear the double column part of it.

Odoherty. Oh! it is infernally long—I haven't wind for it, really.

North. A specimen, then—corrections of Sir James's corrections as to matters of fact, I presume?

Odoherty. Exactly—ay, he puts the sentence of blue and yellow on the first column, and his own in red ink opposite to it. Ha! I see where he had begun to write with a new pen. I can make him out here, I believe—here goes, then.

Thus reciteth and correcteth Sir J. Mackintosh, Knt.	*To which respondeth Timothy Tickler, Esq.*
"Henry Grey, only Duke of Kent, died in 1740," *for which read* 1741.	The Duke of Kent died the 5th June, 1740. See London Magazine for 1740, p. 301, and Gent. Mag. for 1740, p. 314.

North. Very well, Timothy!—Go on.

Odoherty.

Sir Jamie again.

"Her eldest son, (George,) afterwards *second* Lord Hervey." *There was John,* FIRST *Lord Hervey, afterwards created Earl of Bristol. Carr,* SECOND *Lord Hervey, his eldest son. John,* THIRD *Lord Hervey, his second son; consequently Lady Hervey's son, George, was the* FOURTH *Lord Hervey.*

To which again Timotheus.

These four Lord Herveys did really exist, and yet the editor of Lady Suffolk's Letters is right, and the critic egregiously wrong.

John, first Lord Hervey, so created in 1703, was created Earl of Bristol in 1714. His eldest son, Carr, was only a commoner, called Lord Hervey by courtesy. So was his second son John for many years; but in 1733, the latter was created a peer, (see Coxe,) by the title of Lord Hervey, and on his death, (old Lord Bristol being still alive,) his son George became the *second* peer of the creation of 1733, and on Lord Bristol's death, he became *also* the *second* peer of the creation of 1703. So that the critic is doubly wrong; and without any excuse; for all these facts may be gathered from the editor's notes, as well as from the Peerages.

North. Well hit again, Tim.

Odoherty. At it again, boys.

Sir James!

"Leonel, seventh Earl, and first Duke of Dorset, died in 1765."—*For* 1765, *read* 1763!

Southside!!!

The Duke of Dorset died 9th October, 1765. See London Magazine, p. 598, and Gentleman's Magazine, p. 491.

Odoherty. Round fourth!

The Recorder.

"Lord Scarborough put a period to his existence in 1739."—*For* 1739, *read* 1740.

Longshanks!!!

This is not mere inaccuracy on the part of the critic; it is ignorance. He has forgotten that the *style* was not yet changed, and Lord Scarborough died on the 4th February, 1739, old style.

North. A facer!—Does he come to time?

Odoherty. Round fifth. Here they go.

Jem!

"The Great Lord Mansfield died on the 20th of March, 1793, in the *eighty-eighth* year of his age."—*Lord Mansfield was born on the 2d March,* 1705, *and was therefore in the* EIGHTY-NINTH *year of his age.*

Tim!!!

I have already laughed at the value and importance of this *correction, if it even were one;* but unfortunately the erudite critic again forgets the change of the style. March, 1705, old style, would be March, 1706, new style; so that Lord Mansfield seems to have wanted some few days of completing his 88th year.

North. Enough, enough, man; such errors and such corrections are in themselves wholly inconsiderable, and not worth the notice of a pipe-stapple. It was ridiculous enough to see a solemn jackass set about such amendments; but to find that his grave amendments are, in fact, flagrant blunders, is as comical as any thing in Mathews's American judge. But we have other fish to fry. Just put Timothy into my portfolio, and see what comes to hand next.

Odoherty. "Remains of Robert Bloomfield." Ay, poor fellow! there was one genuine poet, though of the lowly breed.

North. He was so, indeed, Odoherty. I thought that book would be found in the box; for I had a letter not long ago mentioning the thing from his family. They sent me, by the way, most of the proof-sheets of the book, and a specimen of his handwriting. Should you like to see it?

Odoherty. Not I; give it to D'Israeli. He, you recollect, is one, not of the Bumpologists, but of the Fistologists; he will take it quite as a compliment.

North. I dare say they have sent him another letter and specimen of the same cut already. You must table your coin on this occasion, Odoherty. Bloomfield, from no fault of his own, has died poor, and left a worthy and amiable family in rather dependent condition.* You must take a few copies of the Remains at all events.

Odoherty. Why, as neither you nor I have any young ladies to put to school, I don't know in what other way we can do any thing for Bloomfield's daughters. Well, put me down, Editor.

North. I will, sir; but there is no school in the case. Miss Hannah Bloomfield, indeed, wishes to have a situation as a musical teacher in some respectable family; and as she is evidently, from what appears in these very volumes, possessed of very considerable musical taste and skill, I trust the worthy daughter of such a man will not be long in getting the establishment she wishes. The whole family have been brought up, I well know, in the most exemplary manner; as indeed what else could any body expect from the paternal solicitude of a man whose native strength of mind kept him at all times superior to the manifold temptations with which his lot naturally surrounded him, and who, in every line he wrote, showed himself the friend of virtue? Sir, we have had but few real poets from this class of people; and, alas! fewer still, who, like Bloomfield, adhered steadily to the virtuous feelings of their lowly youth, when circumstances had introduced him to the dazzle and bustle of the upper world. I honor the memory of Robert Bloomfield.

Odoherty. Yes, he was always one of your favorites. I see they have printed here your pretty verses on his death—this is right, too—

*** Robert Bloomfield, author of "The Farmer's Boy," a rural poem of great merit, died in 1823, aged fifty-seven. The latter part of his life was clouded with poverty and dejection.—M.**

and some verses of Montgomery's also, which I now recollect to have seen somewhere before.

North. In the Sheffield Iris, probably—or Alaric Watts' Leeds Intelligencer—which, by the way, is a paper of very high merit in a literary point of view; indeed the best of all the literary Gazettes.*

Odoherty. Literary Gazettes!—What a rumpus all that fry have been keeping up about Miss Landon's poetry—the Improvisatrice, I mean.

North. Why, I always thought you had been one of her greatest admirers, Odoherty. Was it not you that told me she was so very handsome?—A perfect beauty, I think you said.

Odoherty. And I said truly. She is one of the sweetest little girls in the world, and her book is one of the sweetest little books in the world; but Jerdan's extravagant trumpeting has quite sickened every body; and our friend Alaric has been doing rather too much in the same fashion. This sort of stuff plays the devil with any book. Sappho! and Corinna, forsooth! Proper humbug!

North. I confess you are speaking pretty nearly my own sentiments. I ran over the book—and I really could see nothing of the originality, vigor, and so forth, they all chatter about. Very elegant, flowing verses they are—but all made up of Moore and Byron.

Odoherty. Nay, nay, when you look over the Improvisatrice again, I am sure you will retract this. You know very well that I am no great believer in female genius; but nevertheless, there is a certain feminine elegance about the voluptuousness of this book, which, to a certain extent, marks it with an individual character of its own.†

North. I won't allow you to review this book, my dear Standard-

* The *Sheffield Iris*, and the *Leeds Intelligencer*, then edited by James Montgomery and Alaric Watts, were somewhat literary in 1824, when no other provincial newspapers ever contained an original critique upon a new book. It is different now, and there now is nearly as much talent, comparatively speaking, on the British provincial press, as there is on the London press. James Montgomery thought so well of his shorter literary articles in the *Sheffield Iris*, that he collected them, in two volumes, as "Prose by a Poet."—M.

† Odoherty very much flattered L. E. L., when he allowed North to describe her as "very handsome," and "a perfect beauty." She narrowly escaped being a dowdy. Her figure was *petite*, her manner natural and impulsive, her voice sweet and low, ("an excellent thing in women," if they would only recollect it!) and her whole bearing was that of a child-woman, (she was twenty-two in 1824, and looked seventeen,) delighted with society, and feeling bound to please. Graceful in motion—charming in repose,—yet by no means handsome,—Miss Landon was about the last person on earth whom, meeting in a drawing-room, you would suspect of authorship. Yet she composed poetry rapidly as her own Improvisatrice—writing her verses, scarcely ever with an emendation, in her small, neat, upright, old-fashioned hand. Quick, lively, and epigrammatic in conversation as she was, I never saw any woman, save one,—and she is the loveliest, in mind or person, whom I have ever known,—who was so solicitous to avoid scandal and mere gossip. "Letty Landon," as she used to like to be called, was the safest person in the world to whom a young author might speak of what he had in his mind to do, for her human sympathies were large, her judgment far riper than her years, and her grasp of mind vigorous and extended. Tell her the plot of a story, or the idea of a poem, and, at once, she would suggest how one might be better evolved in action, how the other might be exalted by particular treatment.—M. [On going over this note again, at the last moment, with the press—which, like time and tide, waits for no man—rattling in my ears, I am conscious that I have not done *full* justice to L. E. Landon. Said I that she was not beautiful? *C'est vrai*—but there is a beauty far beyond and far above mere loveliness of feature. There is the beauty of Expression, and if ever mortal possessed it, Letitia Landon did. It is

bearer, for I perceive you are half in love with the damsel concerned; and under such circumstances, a cool and dispassionate estimate is what nobody could be expected to give—least of all you, you red-hot monster of Munster.

Odoherty. No abuse, my old Bully-Rock!

North. Nay, 'tis you that must be called Bully-Rock, now—for I suppose you acknowledge the "Munster Farmer" now to be but another of your aliases. I knew you at the first page, man.* No drawing of straws before so old a cat.

Odoherty. The book is mine, sir. I need keep no secrets from you.

North. Gad-a-mercy! I now for the first time begin to suspect that you had nothing at all to do with it.

Odoherty. Even as you please, most worshipful. These trifles do not affect me or my equanimity.

North. Impenetrable, imperturbable brazen face!—But get on, man.

Odoherty. My eye! here's Gilray Redivivus. Here's the first number of the reprint of his caricatures; you must put on your spectacles, now, Mr. Christopher.

North. Ah! and that I will, my hearty. Well, this was really well thought on. What a pity that these things should have been sinking into the great gulf! Ha! ha! the old paper-money concerns once more! Here's Sherry ipsissimus. "Don't take the notes, John Bull; nobody takes notes now-a-days; they won't even take mine!" How good this view of the fine old sinner's phiz is—and Charlie, too, with his cockade tricolor! Well, these days are over.

Odoherty. What a capital Pitt!—The pen behind the ear, and all! —And John Bull, too—why, Liston never sported a better grin. Turn over—ay, ay, this will do.

North. "The Broad-bottomites getting into the grand costume!"—Long live the immortal memory of 1806. Glorious Charlie! in what a pother you are shaving!—Illustrious Lansdowne! in what majesty dost thou strut!—Profound Ego! what gravity is in thy self-adoration! —Oh dear! oh dear!—That face of Lord Henry Petty and that toe —they are enough to kill a horse!

Odoherty. This grand one of old George, with Bony on his hand,—how vividly it recalls to my memory the laughter of the years that were! Hang it! if I were to live a hundred years, I should never see any new thing to affect me in the same manner. How intensely familiar we all were made with the honest, open, well-larded counte-

mournful to think of her as she was when first I saw her, in 1828, and know that, in ten years from that time, she was lying, far away, in a grave in Africa. In 1828, when she was "the life, grace, and ornament of society," one would scarcely have been extravagant in anticipating that one so gifted and so courted would have worn a coronet, and been the mother of a line of nobles, whose ancestral glories would have been illumined by her wondrous genius.—M.]

* "Captain Rock Detected, by a Munster Farmer," was a reply, somewhat heavy and lumbering, from the pen of the Rev. Mortimer O'Sullivan.—M.

nance of Georgius Tertius! What a solemn, fatherly suavity in his goggling eyes! How reverend his bob-major! how grand his blue ribbon! how ample his paunch! What a sweet in-falling of the chin, honest old cock!

North. Excellent monarch! Pater patriæ truly, if ever there was one. Here, again, is a very worthy one; one of Gilray's very best things, Odoherty. Behold Nap, *en* gingerbread baker, thrusting a new batch of pie-crust kings into his oven. Ye glorious Josephs, Jeromes, Louises!—where are ye all now?—quite chop-fallen!—Bavaria! Wirtemburg! Baden!—Ah! Morgan, what queer times these were, my man!

Odoherty. Indeed they were, old royster; and may they that wish for the like of them find the short cut to Gehenna, say I. We have no political caricaturist now-a-days, North.*

North. Why, George Cruikshank does many things better; and yet it is impossible to deny great merit to many of his things about the time of the Queen's row. Alderman Wood was quite a hero for the pencil, and her Majesty was such a heroine.† Of late he, or whoever feeds the shop windows, has fallen off sadly. The whole batch of the Battier concerns was deplorably stupid, and as for the Windsor-Park sketches, saw ye ever such a leaden, laborious dulness of repetition?

Odoherty. Pooh! they're very well fitted to the time. Party spirit is very cool at present, and you would not have the party caricatures to be very pointed when that is the case. No, no, the public are taken up with other things, North.

North. True, Morgan; and, moreover, the great circulation lately of exquisite engravings of scenery among us shows decidedly a new and more polished sort of taste spreading among the people. Why, you cannot go into a print-shop now-a-days without seeing a whole swarm of new works coming out in numbers, any one leaf of which would have been looked on as a real wonder some dozen or ten years back. There's Hugh Williams's Greek Engravings, now, have you seen those?

Odoherty. To be sure I have; i'faith they are worthy of the drawings themselves, and that is compliment enough. Gad! what a fine thing we should have thought it, when we were young lads at our classics, to be able to get such divine views of all the scenes the old ones said and sung about, for such a mere trifle of money. The engraving of the Tombs of Platæa! Well, I really had no notion that the effect of

* James Gilray, the best caricaturist England has yet produced—for H. B. gave actual rather than burlesque portraits—died in 1815.—M.

† Cruikshank's sketches of Queen Caroline were admirably done. They represented her *en bon point*, as a royal lady of fifty might easily be; but they did not give her bold glance, nor her imperious frown, nor her *jolly* face. Their merit consisted in what they did *not* indicate.—M.

that most original and undescribable work of art could have been so nearly given in black and white, to say nothing of the great reduction of scale.

North. There are many others of the series not a whit less interesting. One, of the Temple of Jupiter Panhellenius in Ægina, particularly struck me—and Thebes! faith, I believe, that is, after all, the very chef-d'œuvre. But, perhaps, you don't know, Odoherty, what is one of my chiefest delights when I look over this work; and that is neither more nor less than this, sir, that Williams has had all his engravings done by native artists, and young, very young ones mostly. Sir, these things may show themselves by the side of the very best London can produce. The fortunes of Horsburg and Miller are made; for, as to James Stewart, he, you know, was up long enough before this job. His engraving of Allan's last picture is a grand thing. I never saw an artist who showed greater tact in preserving the minutiæ of his painter's peculiar touches.

Odoherty. Stewart is a fine handy lad, and a very modest one, too. So good luck to him,—and here's a bumper to Williams.*

North. Welshman though he be, he is an honor to Scotia—here he goes. His Views of Athens will live as long as her memory.

"Shall I unmoved behold the hallow'd scene
Which others rave of, though they know it not?
Though here no more Apollo haunt his grot,
And thou, the Muses' seat, art now their grave—
Some gentle spirit still pervades the spot,
Sighs in the gale, keeps silence in the cave,
And glides with glassy foot o'er yon melodious wave!"

Odoherty. Byron!—hum!

North. Come, come, none of your sneers. Hugh Williams's prints are certainly the best illustrations any one can bind up with Byron's poems. Others give you views, caricatures, (call them as you will,)

* Like Sir William Allan, Williams had lived much in foreign lands, and illustrated foreign subjects by his pencil. After travelling in Greece and Italy for some years, he fixed his residence in Edinburgh, in 1818. Lockhart, speaking of his views in Greece, says, "It is there,—I may be wrong in confessing it,—it is there, among the scattered pillars of Thebes or Corinth—or in full view of all the more glorious remains of more glorious Athens—or looking from the ivied or mouldering arches of Delphi, quite up through the mountain mists to the craggy summits of Parnassus, and the far-off windings of the Castalian brook—it is there, that the footsteps of men appear to have stamped a grander sanctity even on the most magnificent forms of nature. It is there that Williams seems first to have felt, and it is in his transcripts of these glorious scenes, that I myself have been sensible of feeling the whole fulness and awfulness of the works of the Creator—

'All this magnificent effect of power,
The earth we tread, the sky which we behold
By day, and all the pomp which night reveals.'"

A view of Athens, and another of Castri, were greatly praised by Lockhart, in 1819, who predicted, what was speedily accomplished, that Williams would take a high place as a landscape painter.—M.

of his personages, more or less happy, but this is nothing. Williams has been, like the poet, inspired by the sky, the mountains, the ruins of Greece, and the kindred stamp of their inspiration looks you in the face whichever way you turn among their works.

Odoherty. I was glad to see the prints were so small, for this was the purpose I at once thought of turning them to.

North. Upon the same principle I take Thomson of Duddingston's Fast Castle to be the finest and most satisfactory accompaniment for the story of Lammermoor—and Nasmyth's Old Prison of Edinburgh stands ditto, ditto, for the Heart of Mid-Lothian.*

Odoherty. I wish Williams would give us a series of his Italian things too—and particularly his Sicilian ones—for Agrigentum and Syracuse are, after all, less known to most people than any other old places of any thing like the same interesting character.

North. People may rail about boyish tastes, and what not, as long as they have a mind. I confess I like a book all the better for its being illustrated. Perhaps 'tis my imagination cooling, Ensign; but there, for example, was Basil Hall's book about South America: I confess I would fain have had a few cuts of his San Martins, O'Higginses, and the rest of them.

Odoherty. And I own I should have liked to see what sort of a figure old Cochrane cuts in his outlandish riggery. He was a rum one enough in that long blue tog, and low-browed, broad-brimmed castor, as we used to see him lounging about town.

North. By some accident I never saw Lord Cochrane in my life. He is a noble fellow—mad, of course—but that's what he can't help.

Odoherty. Was it madness that dished him!

North. Certainly, the only thing that dished him was the denying of the hoax, in the way he did, in the House of Commons. Had he stood firm on his feet, and said what was God's truth, that he was a sailor, and not a moral philosopher; and that if he had acted wrong, his error consisted merely in doing cleverly and successfully what thousands both of the most holy saints and the most hororable sinners in the land were trying to do every day; if he had stood up with a bold face, and spoken plain common sense after this fashion, I should like to know who would seriously have thought a pin the worse of him, at least for more than a week or two.† Not I, for one. But the

* Alexander Nasmyth, in 1824, was the venerable father of landscape painting in Scotland. Lockhart said, "There is a delightful sweetness in the old man's pencil, and assuredly there is in it as yet no want of vigor." The best portrait of Robert Burns was painted by Nasmyth. This fine old man died in 1840, aged eighty-three. His son Peter, who settled in London at the age of twenty, and had won the honorable title of "The English Hobbima," died in 1831. —M.

† Lord Cochrane, who had entered the British Navy at an early age, distinguished himself by his exploits in the war with France, particularly in the Basque Roads, for which he was created Knight of the Bath, was very popular on his return to London, and was elected member for Westminster. In February, 1814, he was accused of being concerned in a Stock-Exchange scheme, intended to raise the funds by spreading simultaneous reports of Napoleon's

truth is, that every one thing he ever did in this country after he began to think himself a politician, was a perfect proof of madness.

Odoherty. Well, 'tis lucky he has got into a walk, where, what you are pleased to call madness, does better than all the wisdom in the world would do. Will he ever come home again, think ye?

North. I don't know. Many queer stories are going about. Some say he has done things about the English shipping that would land him inextricably in lawsuits if he showed his nose here. Others, again, maintain that he has arranged all these concerns of late, and that it would be nothing strange if he should be seen parading Pall-Mall within this twelvemonth.* For my part, I know nothing of the matter. Captain Hall could tell, no doubt.

Odoherty. Ay, ay; but Hall was a great deal too knowing to tell half what he knew about some of those folks in his book.

North. To be sure he was; and, in particular, I have heard that his MS. Journal could furnish a very extraordinary bundle of Cochraniana, over and above what the book sets forth. Well, we can't quarrel with this reserve.

Odoherty. Bless your soul, I quarrel with nothing. I think Hall's book is a perfect model in its way. Great art in both the whole-speaking part of it, and the half-speaking.

death. He was indicted for complicity herein, in June, 1814, convicted, sentenced to stand in the pillory, opposite the Royal Exchange, for an hour, to be imprisoned for twelve months, and to pay a fine of £1000. All his efforts to obtain a new trial were in vain. On July 5th, a motion for his expulsion from the House of Commons was carried by a (ministerial) majority. On the 16th, he was re-elected. The indignity of putting him in the pillory was waived by the Government. Soon after, he was solemnly turned out of the Knightly Order of the Bath, and deprived of his rank in the Navy. After having been some time in prison, he escaped, (on March 15, 1815,) and went down to the House of Commons, to take his seat for Westminster; but before he could take the oaths, was re-captured by the Marshal of the prison. On the very day that his sentence expired, Lord Cochrane speeded to the House, and was just in time to defeat, by his single vote, an intended increase of £6000 a year to the Duke of Cumberland, one of his bitterest opponents. The £1000 fine was paid by a penny subscription among his constituents. He left Parliament in 1818, and went abroad on foreign service, first in South America, and afterwards in Greece. In 1829, he permanently fixed his abode in London. He succeeded to the Earldom of Dundonald, and William IV. (himself a sailor) had him restored to the station in the navy which he would have occupied had he remained in the service. He was also reinstated in his position as Knight of the Bath. In 1814, the King of Arms had proceeded to Henry the Seventh's Chapel, in Westminster Abbey, removed Lord Cochrane's banner and other insignia from his stall, kicked them down the chapel steps, and into the street. A popular writer says: Had he been there in person, the remainder of the degradation (hacking off his knight's spurs by a butcher with a cleaver) would most probably have been performed—or attempted. Oddly enough, the kicked-out banner was picked up, in the street, by one of Cochrane's friends, taken home, and carefully preserved. This was about forty years ago. Time rolled on—Cochrane eminently distinguished himself in South America and Greece—he had returned to England—he had become Earl of Dundonald, by the death of his father—it was felt that he had been harshly dealt with—the political asperities which prosecuted and persecuted him had subsided—a liberal king was on the throne—a liberal government ruled the country—and tardy justice was done, by restoring Cochrane to the honors from which he had been degraded. His banner was duly reinstated in its old place in Westminster Abbey, and it actually was the identical banneret which, two-and-twenty years ago, had been unceremoniously kicked out. Cochrane's friend who had picked it up, evidently acted on the old saw which says, "Keep a thing for seven years, and it will be sure to come in useful." He kept the document for treble that period, but was rewarded.—In 1854, when a commander was required for the British fleet in the Baltic, the Earl of Dundonald (Cochrane) solicited to be employed, but his seventy-nine years (he was born in 1775) were so many reasons against it.—M.

* He did return, four years after this date.—M.

North. The Edinburgh Reviewer of Basil, whether he was Sir Jamie or not,* devil cares, made a grand attempt to persuade the world that the weight of the Captain's authority lay entirely his own way as to the question of revolutions in South America, and, by implication, elsewhere; but as you have seen the work, I need not tell you this is just another trick of the old trade.

Odoherty. And what else should it be? He, of course, gave no opinion about any other revolution question except that on which all the world has all along been exactly of the same way of thinking. I mean the total impossibility and absurdity of every scheme for re-establishing the government of Spain over her great American colonies.

North. Exactly so—he speaks decidedly, as he should do, upon this head, and as to all the details of the different humbug constitutions that have been knocked up and down like so many nine-pins in that quarter during the last ten or twelve years, he says, in spite of Sir Jamie,—he says not one word but what is perfectly consistent with the truth and justice of the views which I have recently been putting forth as to those concerns. He, in fact, hints continually his total contempt for every thing connected with these new establishments, except only the individual merits (such he esteems them) of San Martin in Chili and Iturbide† in Mexico. The wild and cruel ruin which, with scarcely one exception, the insurgent party has everywhere heaped on the private and domestic fortunes of those opposed to them, or suspected of being opposed to them in opinion,—the brutal sulky rage with which every thing venerable for rank, station, refinement, and virtue, has, in a thousand instances, been sacrificed to the mean and jealous demon of Liberalism,—the outrages on age, elegance, loveliness,—the rash, remorseless villany which has trampled all that has ennobled the soil into the dust of degradation, nay, of absolute misery, —of all this, sir, Captain Hall, being a Scottish gentleman and a British officer, could not possibly think a whit differently from all the others of the same class of men I have ever happened to converse with on any of the topics in question, nor has he said one syllable that looks as if he had done so; though I have no sort of doubt the critique in the Edinburgh Review, and Sir James's puff parliamentary, were both of them dictated in some measure by a skulking sort of notion that the *brutum vulgus* might be bamboozled into the belief that Captain Hall had really written a Whiggish book touching South America.

* "Sir Jamie" was Sir James Mackintosh, of course. Basil Hall's book was his "Extracts from a Journal written on the Coasts of Chili, Peru, and Mexico, in the years 1820, 1821, and 1822."—M.

† Augustus Iturbide, who was Emperor of Mexico for a short period, (proclaimed May 18th, 1822, and abdicating in March, 1823,) retired to Italy on a large pension, conditional on his not returning to Mexico. He returned, after a year's absence, to attempt the recovery of power, was proscribed, betrayed, captured, and sentenced to death. He was shot, July 19th, 1822, aged forty.—M.

Odoherty. Does Sir James owe Constable any money?

North. Not knowing, can't say.

Odoherty. Well, well. The Captain should certainly have given us a few prints of his heroes. He had some grand affairs in his Loo-choo book.

North. Ay, and so he had. By the by, have you heard that it turns out that he was completely taken in by those petticoated prigs? That his primitive Loo-choo lads are now understood to be, without exception, the prettiest set of old rascally cunning swindlers that ever infested the Yellow Sea?

Odoherty. I had not heard of the humbug being ripped up. Well, I am sorry to hear this, for I really had been much affected with the simplicity of their manners.* The print of the leave-taking, in particular, was rather too much for my feelings—them *booing* and Basil *booing*—them doing him, and him Loo-chooing them. 'Twas a fine picture of humanity on the umbrella system.

North. Ay, ay. Well, he has got hold of people whom he could understand this time, and he has done himself justice. His book, sir, is, after all, one of the few sprigs of 1824, which won't wither with the season. I back Captain Hall's South America, and Captain Rock Detected, against any three octavos, or duodecimos either, of the growth.

Odoherty. Have you seen a Tour in Germany lately published by Constable's people? I hear 'tis rather a clever thing.

North. I was reading some parts of it over again this very evening. I like the book very well upon the whole. Who writes it?

Odoherty. A Mr. Russell, I hear; a young man who has just been called to the bar here.

North. I hoped it might turn out to be a very young man, for otherwise there would be something offensive in the style occasionally. Cursedly spruce and pointed—you understand me.

Odoherty. O ay; but I hear this is a genuine clever fellow, so one must overlook these little things, and expect better hereafter.

North. Why, as to that, I made no objection to any thing, but a little occasional false taste in style—a thing which, in an early work like this, is of no sort of consequence. The stuff of his book is good, and his feelings are good throughout. We must get Kempferhausen to bring him here some night—for being a German—*Nihil Germanici a se alienum*—you understand me?

Odoherty. Yes, yes, of course, the lad has laid his lugs in our friend's Steinwein long ere this time of day. Well, the Germanic faction is

* When Captain Basil Hall visited Napoleon at St. Helena, on his return from a voyage of discovery, in which he had visited the Loo-Choo Islands, he mentioned that the people had no offensive weapons. "*Mon Dieu!*" said the Emperor, "how do they fight?" When he afterwards spoke, in presence of Mr. Vansittart, then Chancellor of the Exchequer, of their having no money, the financier abruptly asked, "How can they pay the taxes?"—M.

getting on; this gentleman and young Carlyle*—he who translated Meister—are two pretty additions to Kempferhausen's battalion. To be serious, North, we shall run some risk of inundation. Have you seen the last London Magazine, how bitter they are on the poor William Meister?

North. Not I, i'faith—I see none of these concerns—not I. What are they saying?

Odoherty. Oh! abusing the Germans up-hill and down-dale, buzzing like fiery myriads of sand flies.

North. And stinging?

Odoherty. Not knowing, can't say.

North. Well, I should have thought my friend Opium would have kept them from this particular piece of nonsense—but that's true too, the whole may be one of his quizzes. He was always fond of a practical joke, hang him.

Odoherty. He says old Goethe is an idiot—this is pretty abuse, surely.

North. Ay, ay, about abuse as well as other things, 'tis a true saying enough that most people consider it as "no loss, that a friend gets."

Odoherty. You would disapprove, I suppose, of the attack on De Quincey in the John Bull Magazine?†

North. Disapprove!—I utterly despised it, and so, no doubt, did he. They say he is no scholar, because he has never published any verbal criticisms on any Greek authors‡—what stuff! then, I take it, the best

* In 1824 Thomas Carlyle was a young man, and if not a better, by all means a more intelligible writer than he has been for the last fifteen years. At one time, Carlyle could and did write plain English—how beautiful, in its Saxon simplicity, is his Life of Schiller!—but he has Germanized and spoiled his style, until it almost requires a glossary to turn it into English. —M.

† In *Blackwood*, for July, 1824, was a poetical epistle, by the renowned "Timothy Tickler," to the Editor of the *John Bull Magazine*, on an article in his first number. This article (not named by Maga, though sufficiently indicated) professed to be a portion of the veritable Autobiography of Byron, which was burnt, and was called "My Wedding Night." It appeared to relate, in detail, *every thing* that occurred in the twenty-four hours immediately succeeding that in which Byron was married. It had plenty of coarseness, and some to spare; it went into particulars such as hitherto had been given only by Faublas; and it had, notwithstanding, many phrases and some facts which evidently did not belong to a mere fabricator. Some years after, I compared this "Wedding Night" with what I had all assurance of having been transcribed from the actual MSS. of Byron, and was persuaded that the magazine writer must have had the *actual* statement before him, or have had a perusal of it. The writer in *Blackwood* declared his conviction that it really was Byron's own writing, and said—

"But that you, sir,—a wit, and a scholar like you,
Should not blush to produce what he blushed not to do—
Take your compliment, youngster—this doubles (almost)
The sorrow that rose when his honor was lost."

Why the *John Bull Magazine* should have been patted on the back by Maga, can only be accounted for by the belief that Maginn was chief writer in it—as he was, at the same time, in *Blackwood*. Murray is said to have declared that "My Wedding Night" could only have been supplied by Maginn. The *John Bull Magazine* was dropped after the sixth or seventh number.—M.

‡ In De Quincey's Literary Reminiscences (Boston edition, Vol. II.) is a chapter of 44 pages, called "Libellous Attack by a London Journal," which is a specimen of word-spinning and sentence-making, "full of sound and fury, but signifying nothing." De Quincey had been

scholars in the world are such creatures as Dr. Parr—rubbish that I honestly confess, I never used to think any sensible man would condescend to class much higher than a Petralogist or a——

Odoherty. I'll defy you to fill up that sentence—go on.

North. Parr indeed! Persuade me that that goggling ass knows any thing about the true spirit of Athenian antiquity! That egregious consumer of shag, a fit person to analyze the soul of Sappho!—that turnip-headed buffoon in a cassock, able to follow the wit of Aristophanes!—no, no, sir—no tricks upon travellers. What has he done? What has he done? That is the question.

Odoherty. Why, all the world knows what he has done—he has drunk a great deal of bad beer, smoked a great deal of bad tobacco, uttered a great deal of bad jokes, and published, thank Heaven! *not* a great deal of dull prose, out-caricaturing the pomposity of Dr. Johnson's first and worst style, accompanied with some score or two of notes in English, and *Notulæ* in Latin, of which it is entirely impossible for any human creature to decide which is the most contemptible—their strutting boldness of language, their blown-up inanity of thought, or the vile self-satisfied grin of their abominable pædogical republicanism—a disgusting old fellow, sir!

North. Old! Is that an epithet of contempt, Mr. Ensign?

Odoherty. Beg pardon—a disgusting fellow——

North. Thou hast said it. An excellent clergyman in his parish, an excellent schoolmaster in his school, but in his character of a wit and an author, one of the most genuine feather-beds of humbug that ever filled up a corner in the world—all which, however, is no matter of ours—wherefore pass we on. I would not have thought it worth while to name his name, even to you, had it not been that I lately remarked sundry attempts to bolster up his justly battered reputation, not in the writings of any of his own filthy party, for that would have been quite right, but in one of D'Israeli's recent works—which of them I at this moment forget—so help me, my memory, Morgan, even my memory begins to——

Odoherty. Stuff—stuff—stuff!! What's the use of what they call a good memory?

North. You will perhaps think more of that, young gentleman, when your hairs, like mine——

dished up in the *John Bull Magazine* as one of the "Humbugs of the Age," and the article had been republished in a newspaper in the provincial locality where his family were then residing, he being in London, honorably using his pen for their and his own subsistence. The chapter treats of nearly every topic except that which gave it a title—of Romish casuistry—of Wordsworth's imagery—of Paley's Moral Philosophy—of duelling—of the pain of being libelled—of courts of honor—of pugilistic contests—of the Duke of Wellington—of other matters. But it never mentioned *what* the "libellous attack" was, nor did he once name the journal which made it. All we learn is that he was attacked in *some* publication, of which he bought a copy in Smithfield. This is so thoroughly De Quinceyish, (like Mrs. Nickleby bringing in persons and things quite independent of the matter on the *tapis*,) that of course I cannot complain of his thus writing "an infinite deal of nothing."—M.

Odoherty. Pooh! pooh! I've worn falsities these five years. But what signifies your grand memory? Things really of importance to any man's concerns, are by that man remembered—other things are of no consequence. I, for my part, find it is always much less trouble to fill up the details of any piece of business from the creation of fancy, than by cudgelling one's brains for the minutiæ of fact—in fact, sir, I despise fact.

North. Aha! my lad, very pretty talking all this! But, as Coleridge says in his Friend, we always think the least about what we feel the most. In the heroic ages, they had not so many words as we have now for expressing the different shades and shapes of personal beauty or personal valor; there was less talk about chivalry among the Cœur-de-Lions than among a pack of dandy hussars;—and from what lips does one hear so much about honor as a puppy Whig's?—But I'm weary of talking to you, Ensign. Here, draw another cork. I desired our friend, the Ambrosian, to have him touched with the ice—just touched. Ay, that's your sort. What a satisfactory thing this is now!

Odoherty. Sam, I suppose*—ay, I thought so from the twist of your lips.

North. Now, take your pen in your hand like a good diligent lad, and touch me off a neat handy little article on this same Tour in Germany.

Odoherty. Me! Bless you, I have not read one word of it.

North. Never heed—begin with a sounding paragraph about things in general; at the close of each paragraph you shall have a bumper. Yea, stick we to the old bargain.

Odoherty. Pretty little pebbles of paragraphs we shall be having; well, here goes! But to save time and trouble, tell me, since you have read the book, what you really think of it—honestly, now, Kit.

North. Well, well—fill my glass again, boy. 'Tis an excellent little book, I assure you, Sir Morgan. The author appears to have spent some time at Jena, and after making himself well acquainted with the language, to have travelled considerably over the north of Germany, and a little in the south also. He has given, in what will probably be the most amusing part of his book to common readers, a very graphic account indeed of the mode of life prevalent among that apparently queerest of all queer orders of beings, the German students. He has entered into full and, *ex facie*, accurate details of their extravagant, enthusiastic, absurd, overbearing, hobbletehoy existence, their pride, their folly, their clubs, their duels, their whiskers, their tobacco-pipes, their schnaps, their shirt-collars, and their enormous jack-boots. All other bodies of students that I have seen or heard of, would ap-

* Mr. Samuel Anderson, then a wine-merchant in Edinburgh, afterwards, by favor of Lord Brougham, Registrar of the Court of Chancery in London.—M.

pear to be but milk-and-water shadows of their academical absurdity—and yet, strange to say, it appears to be by no means clear, that a German university is not at this moment the place where the most extensive and the most accurate learning may be acquired at the cheapest rate. Sir, this affair seems to be made up of one bundle of anomalies. You must, on reflection, read the whole of the chapters he has devoted to its consideration, ere you review them.

Odoherty. If their way of thinking be either more queer or more laudable than what we had to do with at old Trin. Coll. Dub., I shall consider myself as a rump and dozen in my victim's debt.

North. As to that, not knowing, can't say. But the really important part of the book is its politics, and it was this that made me wish you should do something for it in Maga. Sir, we have been much abused by the people who have written and spoken about Germany for the last five or six years.

Odoherty. As how?

North. Why, for example, we have been deaved with the hoarse cry, that the King of Prussia has behaved in all manner of beastly ways to his people. We have been told that he has promised to do every thing for them, and that he has done nothing: and this sort of thing has been repeated so often by all the regiment of bawlers, from Brougham the Bold downwards, that honest people have really been dinned into some sort of belief, that the thing must be so. But here we have the facts—Sir Morgan Odoherty, here we have the plain facts of the case; and I assure you, I think the author of this book would have deserved no slight commendation had his work consisted merely of this one excellent exposé. He has shown, sir, in the most complete and satisfactory manner, that in so far as it has been possible for the government of Prussia to increase the political privileges of the people of Prussia, the thing actually has been done.* The king and his ministers have reformed to a very great extent—but they have reformed like men of sense, wisdom and experience—not after the fashion of your Bolivars, your Riegos, your Robespierres, your Pepes, your Thistlewoods. Here is the rub.

Odoherty. A real defence of the Prussian government must be of high importance at present. Whereabouts is this subject taken up?

North. Give me the book—ay, here it is. I shall be happy to hear it once again; so read aloud—begin where you see the mark of my pencil.

Odoherty. Well, if it must be so—"The Prussian government is usually decried"——

* This was Frederick-William III., father of the present King. The convulsions which shook the Prussian throne to its foundations, in 1848, may in some small degree be traced to his refusal to grant those constitutional privileges which had long been promised to his people, and which they were well fitted to exercise.—M.

North. That's the passage I mean.

Odoherty. And a pretty long one it seems to be.

North. No matter; I assure you, you will find Mr. Russell's prose much more entertaining than my prosing. Get on.

Odoherty (*reads*).*

"The Prussian government is usually decried amongst us, as one of the most intolerant and illiberal of Germany, attentive only to secure the implicit and unthinking obedience of its subjects, and therefore encouraging every thing which may retain them in ignorance and degradation. Every Briton, from what he has heard, must enter Prussia with this feeling; and he must blush for his hastiness, when he runs over the long line of bold reforms, and liberal ameliorations, which were introduced into the whole frame of society and public relations in Prussia, from the time when the late Chancellor Prince Hardenberg was replaced, in 1810, at the head of the government. They began, in fact, with the battle of Jena; that defeat was, in one sense, the salvation of Prussia. The degradation and helplessness into which it plunged the monarchy, while they roused all thinking men to see that there must be something wrong in existing relations, brought likewise the necessity of stupendous efforts to make the resources of the diminished kingdom meet both its own expenditure, and the contributions levied on it by the conqueror. A minister was wanted; for dimineering France would not allow Hardenberg, the head of the Anti-Gallican party, and listened to only when it was too late to retain his office, and he retired to Riga. *Prenez Monsieur Stein*, said Napoleon to the king, *c'est un homme d'esprit;* and Stein was made minister. In spirit, he was a minister entirely suited to the times; but he wanted caution, and forgot that in politics, even in changing for the better, some consideration must be paid to what for centuries has been bad and universal. He was not merely bold, he was fearless; but he was thoroughly despotic in his character; having a good object once in his eye, he rushed on to it, regardless of the mischief which he might be doing in his haste, and tearing up and throwing down all that stood in his way, with a vehemence which even the utility of his purpose did not always justify.

"Stein was too honest a man long to retain the favor of France. An intercepted letter informed the cabinet of St. Cloud, that he was governing for Prussian, not for French purposes; and the king was requested to dismiss *le nommé Stein.* He retired to Prague, and amused himself with reading lectures on history to his daughters. His retirement was followed by a sort of interregnum of ministers, who could contrive nothing except the cession of Silesia to France, instead of paying the contributions. From necessity, Hardenberg was recalled; and whoever will take the trouble of going over the principal acts of his administration will acknowledge, not only that he was the ablest minister Prussia has ever possessed, but likewise that few statesmen, in the unostentatious path of internal improvement, have effected in so brief an interval, so many weighty and beneficial changes—interrupted as he was by a war of unexampled importance, which he began with caution, prosecuted with energy, and terminated in triumph. He received Prussia stripped of half its extent, its honors blighted, its finances ruined, its resources at once exhausted by foreign contributions, and depressed by ancient relations among the different classes of society, which custom had consecrated, and selfishness was vehement to defend. He has left it to his king, enlarged in extent, and restored to its

* See Tour in Germany, in 1820, 1821, 1822, (Edinburgh, Constable, 2 vols. 12mo.,) volume second, p. 110, *et seq.*—C. N.

fame; with a well-ordered system of finance, not more defective or extravagant than the struggle for the redemption of the kingdom rendered necessary; and, above all, he has left it freed from those restraints which bound up the capacities of its industry, and were the sources at once of personal degradation and national poverty. Nor ought it to be forgotten, that, while Hardenberg had often to contend, in the course of these reforms, now with the jealousies of town corporations, and now with the united influence and prejudices of the aristocracy, he stood in the difficult station of a foreigner in the kingdom which he governed, unsupported by family descent or hereditary influence. His power rested on the personal confidence of the king in his talents and honesty, and the confidence which all of the people who ever thought on such matters reposed in the general spirit of his policy.

"It was on agriculture that Prussia had chiefly to rely, and the relations between the peasantry who labored the soil and the proprietors, chiefly of the nobility, who owned it, were of a most depressing nature. The most venturous of all Hardenberg's measures was that by which he entirely new-modelled the system, and did nothing less than create a new order of independent landed proprietors. The *Erbunterthänigkeit*, or hereditary subjection of the peasantry to the proprietors of the estates on which they were born, had been already abolished by Stein: next were removed the absurd restrictions which had so long operated, with accumulating force, to diminish the productiveness of land, by fettering the proprietor not merely in the disposal, but even in the mode of cultivating his estate. Then came forth, in 1810, a royal edict, effecting, by a single stroke of the pen, a greater and more decisive change than has resulted from any modern legislative act, and one which a more popular form of government would scarcely have ventured. It enacted, that all the peasantry of the kingdom should in future be free, hereditary proprietors of the lands which hitherto they had held only as hereditary tenants, on condition that they gave up to the landlord a fixed proportion of them. The peasantry formed two classes. The first consisted of those who enjoyed what may be termed a hereditary lease, that is, who held lands to which the landlord was bound, on the death of the tenant in possession, to admit his successor, or, at least, some near relation. The right of the landlord was thus greatly inferior to that of unlimited property; he had not his choice of a tenant; the lease was likely to remain in the same family as long as the estate in his own; and, in general, he had not the power of increasing the rent, which had been originally fixed, centuries, perhaps, before, whether it consisted in produce or services. These peasants, on giving up *one-third* of their farms to the landlord, became unlimited proprietors of the remainder. The second class consisted of peasants whose title endured only for life, or a fixed term of years. In this case, the landlord was not bound to continue the lease, on its termination, to the former tenant, or any of his descendants; but still he was far from being unlimited proprietor; he was bound to replace the former tenant with a person of the same rank; he was prohibited to take the lands into his own possession, or cultivate them with his own capital.* His right, however, was clearly more absolute than in the former case, and it is difficult to see what claim the tenant could set up beyond the endurance of his lease. That such restrictions rendered

* This regulation has sometimes been ascribed to anxiety to keep up the numbers of the peasantry to fill the armies; a more probable explanation is to be found in the exemption of the nobility, that is, generally speaking, the landholders, from taxation. They established this exemption in favor of the property which they retained in their own hands, by abandoning to taxation the lands which they had given out to the peasantry *Bauernhöfe*. It thus became the interest of the Crown to prevent any diminution of the Bauernhöfe, the only taxable land in the country. To abolish this restriction, was one of Stein's first measures, in 1808; for he was determined to make all land taxable, without exception.—R.

the estate less valuable to the proprietor, may have been a very good reason for abolishing them entirely, but seems to be no reason at all for taking a portion of the lands from him who had every right to them, to give it to him who had no right whatever, but that of possession under his temporary lease. But this class of peasants, too, (and they are supposed to have been by far the more numerous,) on giving up *one-half* of their farms, became absolute proprietors of the remainder. The half thus taken from the landlords appears just to have been a price exacted from them for the more valuable enjoyment of the other;—as if the government had said to them, give up to our disposal a certain portion of your estates, and we shall so sweep away those old restrictions which render them unproductive to you, that what remains will speedily be as valuable as the whole was before.

"It cannot be denied, therefore, that this famous edict, especially in the latter of the two cases, was a very stern interference with the rights of private property; nor is it wonderful that those against whom it was directed should have sternly opposed it; but the minister was sterner still. He found the finances ruined, and the treasury attacked by demands, which required that the treasury should be filled; he saw the imperious necessity of rendering agriculture more productive; and though it may be doubted, whether the same end might not have been gained by new-modelling the relations between the parties, as landlord and tenant, instead of stripping the former to create a new race of proprietors, there is no doubt at all as to the success of the measure, in increasing the productiveness of the soil. Even those of the aristocracy, who have waged war most bitterly against Hardenberg's reforms, allow that, in regard to agriculture, this law has produced incredible good. 'It must be confessed,' says one of them, 'that, in ten years, it has carried us forward a whole century;'—the best of all experimental proofs how injurious the old relations between the proprietors and the laborers of the soil must have been to the prosperity of the country.

"The direct operation of this measure necessarily was to make a great deal of property change hands; but this effect was farther increased by its indirect operation. The law appeared at a moment when the greater part of the estates of the nobility were burdened with debts, and the proprietors were now deprived of their rentals. They indeed had land thrown back upon their hands; but this only multiplied their embarrassments. In the hands of their boors, the soil had been productive to them; now that it was in their own, they had neither skill nor capital to carry on its profitable cultivation, and new loans only added to the interest which already threatened to consume its probable fruits. The consequence of all this was, that besides the portion of land secured in free property to the peasantry, much of the remainder came into the market, and the purchasers were generally persons who had acquired wealth by trade or manufactures.* The sale of the royal domains, to supply

* It will scarcely be believed that, up to 1807, a person not noble could only by accident find a piece of land, whatever number of estates might be in the market, which he would be *allowed* to purchase. By far the greater portion of the landed property consisted of estates-noble; and if the proprietor brought his estate into the market, only a nobleman could purchase it. The merchant, the banker, the artist, the manufacturer, every citizen, in short, who had acquired wealth by industry and skill, lay under an absolute prohibition against investing it in land, unless he previously purchased a patent of nobility, or stumbled on one of those few spots which, in former days, had escaped the hands of a noble proprietor, small in number, and seldom in the market. Even Frederick the Great lent his aid to perpetuate this preposterous system, in the idea that he would best compel the investment of capital in trade and manufactures, by making it impossible to dispose of it, when realized, in agricultural pursuits,—a plan which led to the depression of agriculture, the staple of the kingdom, as certainly as it was directed in vain to cherish artificially a manufacturing activity, on which the country is much less dependent. This could not possibly last; the noble proprietors were regularly becoming poorer, and the same course of events which compelled so many of them

the necessities of the state, operated powerfully in the same way. These domains always formed a most important item in the revenue of a German prince, and one which was totally independent of any control, even that of the imperfectly constituted estates. In Prussia, they were estimated to yield annually nearly half a million sterling, even in the hands of farmers, and, under the changes which have so rapidly augmented the value of the soil all over the kingdom, they would soon have become much more profitable. But, while compelled to tax severely the property of his subjects, the king refused to spare his own; and, in 1811, an edict was issued, authorizing the sale of the royal domains at twenty-five years' purchase of the estimated rental. These, too, passed into the hands of the purchasers not connected with the aristocracy; for the aristocracy, so far from being able to purchase the estates of others, were selling their own estates to pay their debts. The party opposed to Hardenberg has not ceased to lament that the Crown should thus have been shorn of its native and independent glories; 'for it ought to be powerful,' say they, 'by its own revenues and possessions.' Our principles of government teach us a different doctrine.

"Beneficial as the economical effects of this division of property may have been, its political results are no less important. It has created a new class of citizens, and these the most valuable of all citizens; every trace, not merely of subjection, but of restraint, has been removed from the industrious, but poor and degraded peasants, and they have at once been converted into independent landed proprietors, resembling much the *petits proprietaires* created by the French Revolution. In Pomerania, for example, the estates of the nobility were calculated to contain 260 square miles; those of free proprietors, not noble, only five miles. Of the former, about 100 were *Bauernhofe*, in the hands of the peasantry; and, by the operation of the law, 60 of these would still remain the property of the boors who cultivated them. Thus there is now twelve times as much landed property, in this province, belonging to persons who are not noble, as there was before the appearance of this edict. The race of boors is not extinct; for the provisions of the law are not imperative, if both parties prefer remaining in their old relation; but this is a preference which, on the part of the peasant at least, is not to be expected. Care has been taken that no new relations of the same kind shall be formed. A proprietor might settle his agricultural servants upon his grounds, giving them land, instead of wages, and binding them to hereditary service: this would just have been the seed of a new race of boors to toil under the old personal services. Probably the thing had been attempted; for, in 1811, an edict appeared, which, while it allows the proprietor to pay his servants in whole or in part with the use of land, limits the duration of such a contract to twelve years. It prohibits him absolutely from giving these families land *heritably*, on condition of service; if a single acre is to be given in property, it must either be a proper sale, or a fixed rent must be stipulated in money or produce. Hardenberg was resolved that his measure should be complete.

"When to the peasants who have thus become landholders, is added the numerous class of citizens, not noble, who have come into the possession of landed property by the sales of the royal domains, and the necessities of so many of the higher orders, it is not difficult to foresee the political consequences of such a body of citizens gradually rising in wealth and respectabil-

to sell, disabled them generally from buying; destitute of capital to cultivate their own estates, it was not among *them* that the purchasers of the royal domains were to be looked for. In 1807, Stein swept away the whole mass of absurd restrictions, and every man was made capable of holding every kind of property.—R.

ity, and dignified by that feeling of self-esteem which usually accompanies the independent possession of property. Unless their progress be impeded by extraneous circumstances, they must rise to political influence, because they will gradually become fitting depositaries of it. It would scarcely be too much to say, that the Prussian government must have contemplated such a change; for its administration, during the last fourteen years, has been directed to produce a state of society in which pure despotism cannot long exist but by force; it has been throwing its subjects into those relations which, by the very course of nature, give the people political influence by making them fit to exercise it. Is there any thing in political history that should make us wish to see them in possession of it sooner? Is it not better that liberty should rise spontaneously from a soil prepared for its reception, and in which its seeds have gradually been maturing in the natural progress of society, than violently to plant it on stony and thorny ground, where no congenial qualities give strength to its roots, and beauty to its blossoms, where it does not throw wide its perennial shadow, under which the people may find happiness and refuge, but springs up, like the gourd of Jonah, in the night of popular tumult, and unnatural and extravagant innovation, to perish in the morning beneath the heat of reckless faction, or the consuming fire of foreign interference?

"This great, and somewhat violent measure, of creating in the state a new order of citizens possessing independent property, was preceded and followed by a crowd of other reforms, all tending to the same end, to let loose the energies of all classes of the people, and bring them into a more comfortable social relation to each other. While the peasantry were not only set free, but converted into landholders, the aristocracy were sternly deprived of that exemption from taxation which, more than any thing else, renders them odious in every country where it has been allowed to remain. They struggled hard to keep their estates beyond the reach of the land tax, but the king and Hardenberg were inflexible: 'We hope,' says the royal edict, 'that those to whom this measure will apply will reflect, that, in future, they will be free from the reproach of escaping public burdens at the expense of their fellow-subjects. They will likewise reflect, that the tax to be laid upon them will not equal the expense to which they would be put, if called on to perform the military services which originally burdened their estates.' The whole financial system acquired an uniformity and equality of distribution, which simplified it to all, and diminished the expense of collection, while it increased the revenue. Above all, that anomalous system, under which every province had its own budget, and its peculiar taxes, was destroyed, and Hardenberg, after much opposition, carried through one uniform and universal system for the whole monarchy. This enabled him to get rid of another monstrous evil. Under the miserable system of financial separation, every province and every town was surrounded with custom-houses, taxing and watching the productions of its neighbors, as if they came from foreign countries, and discouraging all internal communication, The whole was swept away. At the same time, the national expenditure in its various departments, the ways and means, the state of the public debt, and the funds for meeting it, were given forth with a publicity which produced confidence in Prussia, and alarm, as setting a bad example, in some less prudent cabinets. Those amongst ourselves who clamor most loudly against the misconduct of the Prussian government, will allow, that the secularization and sale of the church lands was a liberal and patriotic measure; those who more wisely think, that an arbitrary attack on any species of property endangers the security of all property, will lament that the public necessities should have rendered it advisable. The servitudes of thirlage,* of brewing beer, and distilling spirituous liquors, existed in their most oppressive form, discouraging agriculture, and fostering the ruinous spirit of monopoly. They were abolished with so unsparing a hand, that, though indemnification was not absolutely refused, the forms and modes of proof of loss sustained to found a claim to it were of such a nature, as to render it difficult to be procured, and trifling when made good. This was too unsparing.

"In the towns there was much less to be done; it was only necessary to release their arts and manufactures from old restraints, and rouse their citizens to an interest in the public weal. Hardenberg attempted the first by a measure on which more popular governments have not yet been bold enough to venture, however strongly it has been recommended by political economists; he struck down at one blow all guildries and corporations,—not those larger forms, which include all the citizens of a town, and constitute a *borough*, but those subordinate forms which regard particular classes and professions. But, whether it was from views of finance, or that he found himself compelled, by opposing interests, to yield something to the old principle, that the public is totally unqualified to judge who serves them well and who serves them badly, but must have some person to make the discovery for them, the chancellor seems to have lost his way in this measure. He left every man at liberty to follow every profession, free from the fetters of an incorporated body; but he converted the government into one huge, universal corporation, and allowed no man to pursue any profession without annually procuring and paying for the permission of the state. The *Gewerbsteuer*, introduced in 1810, is a yearly tax on every man who follows a profession, on account of that profession; it is like our ale and pedlar licenses, but it is universal. So far, it is only financial; but the license by no means follows as a matter of course, and here reappears the incorporation spirit; every member of those professions, which are held to concern more nearly the public weal, must produce a certificate of the provincial government, that he is duly qualified to exercise it. Doctors and chimney-sweeps, midwives and ship-builders, notaries-public and mill-wrights, booksellers and makers of water-pipes, with a host of other equally homogeneous professionalists, must be guaranteed by that department of the government within whose sphere their occupation is most naturally included, as perfectly fit to execute their professions. The system is cumbersome, but it wants, at least, the exclusive *esprit de corps* of corporations.

"The other and more important object, that of rousing the citizens to an active concern in the affairs of their own community, had already been accomplished by Stein in his *Stadteordnung*, or constitution for the cities, which was completed and promulgated in 1808. He did not go the length of annual parliaments and universal suffrage, for the magistracy is elected only every third year; but the elective franchise is so widely distributed among all resident householders, of a certain income or rental, that none are excluded whom it would be proper to admit. Nay, complaints are sometimes heard from persons of the upper ranks, that it compels them to give up paying any attention to civic affairs, because it places too direct and overwhelming an influence in the hands of the lower orders. There can be no doubt, however, of the good which it has done, were there nothing else than the publicity which it has bestowed on the management and proceedings of public and charitable institutions. The first merchant of Breslau, the second city of the monarchy, told me it was impossible to conceive what a change it had effected for the better, and what interest every citizen now took in the public affairs of the corporation, in hos-

* Let those who accuse the Prussian government of disregarding the improvement of its subjects reflect, that it was only in 1799, that the British Parliament thought of contriving means to rescue the agriculture of Scotland from this servitude.—R.

pitals and schools, in roads, and bridges, and pavements, and water-pipes. 'Nay,' added he, 'by our example, we have even compelled the Catholic charities to print accounts of their funds and proceedings; for, without doing so, they could not have stood against us in public confidence.' This is the true view of the matter; nor is there any danger that the democratic principle will be extravagant in the subordinate communities, while the despotic principle is so strong in the general government of the country.

"Such has been the general spirit of the administration of Prussia, since the battle of Jena; and it would be gross injustice to her government to deny, that in all this it has acted with an honest and effective view to the public welfare, and has betrayed any thing but a selfish or prejudiced attachment to old and mischievous relations; that was no part of the character of either Stein or Hardenberg. The government is in its forms a despotic one; it wields a censorship; it is armed with a strict and stern police; and, in one sense, the property of the subject is at its disposal, in so far as the portion of his goods which he shall contribute to the public service depends only on the pleasure of the government; but let not our just hatred of despotic forms make us blind to substantial good. Under these forms, the government, not more from policy than inclination, has been guilty of no oppressions which might place it in dangerous opposition to public feeling or opinion; while it has crowded its administration with a rapid succession of ameliorations, which gave new life to all the weightiest interests of the state, and brought all classes of society into a more natural array, and which only ignorance or prejudice can deny to have been equally beneficial to the people, and honorable to the executive. I greatly doubt, whether there be any example of a popular government doing so much real good in so short a time, and with so much continued effect. When a minister roots out abuses which impede individual prosperity, gives free course to the arts and industry of the country, throws open to the degraded the paths of comfort and respectability, and brings down the artificial privileges of the high to that elevation which nature demands in every stable form of political society; while he thus prepares a people for a popular government, while, at the same time, by this very preparation, he creates the safest and most unfailing means of obtaining it, he stands much higher as a statesman and philosopher, than the minister who rests satisfied with the easy praise, and the more than doubtful experiment, of giving popular forms to a people which knows neither how to value nor exercise them. The statesmen of this age, more than of any other, ought to have learned the folly of casting the political pearl before swine.

"This is no defence of despotism; it is a statement of the good which the Prussian government has done, and an elucidation of the general spirit of improvement in which it has acted; but it furnishes no reason for retaining the despotic forms under which this good has been wrought out, so soon as the public wishes require, and the public mind is, in some measure, capable of using more liberal and manly instruments. On the other hand, it is most unfair (and yet, in relation to Prussia, nothing is more common) to forget what a monarch has done for his subjects, in our hatred of the fact that he has done it without their assistance, and to set down his government as a mere ignorant, selfish, and debasing tyranny. The despotism of Prussia stands as far above that of Naples, or Austria, or Spain, as our own constitution stands above the mutilated Charter of France. The people are personally attached to their king; and, in regard to his government, they feel and recognise the real good which has been done infinitely more strongly than the want of the unknown good which is yet to be attained, and which alone can secure the continuance of all the rest. They have not enjoyed the political experience and education which would teach them the value of this security; and even the better informed classes tremble at the thought of exacting it by popular clamor, because they see it must speedily come of itself. From the Elbe to the Oder, I found nothing to make me believe in the existence of that general discontent and ripeness for revolt which have been broadly asserted, more than once, to exist in Prussia; and it would be wonderful to find a people to whom all political thinking is new, who knew nothing of political theories, and suffer no personal oppressions, ready to raise the shout of insurrection.

"To this it is commonly added, that the general discontent is only forcibly kept down by the large standing army. The more I understood the constitution of the Prussian army, the more difficult I found it to admit this constantly-repeated assertion. Not only is every male of a certain age, a regularly trained soldier, the most difficult of all populations to be crushed by force, when they are once warmed by a popular cause, but by far the greater part of this supposed despotic instrument consists of men taken, and taken only for a time, from the body of citizens against whom they are to be employed. There is always, indeed, a very large army on foot, and the foreign relations of Prussia render the maintenance of a large force indispensable; but it is, in fact, a militia. 'We have no standing army at all, properly speaking,' said an officer of the Guards to me; 'what may be called our standing army is, in reality, nothing but a school, in which all citizens, without exception, between twenty and thirty-two years of age, are trained to be soldiers. Three years are reckoned sufficient for this purpose. A third of our army is annually changed. Those who have served their three years are sent home, form what is called the War Reserve, and, in case of war, are first called out. Their place is supplied by a new draught from the young men who have not yet been out; and so it goes on.' Surely a military force so constituted is not that to which a despot can well trust for enchaining a struggling people; if popular feeling were against him, these men would bring it along with them to his very standard. I can not help thinking, that, if it were once come to this between the people and government of Prussia, it would not be in his own bayonets, but in those of Russia and Austria, that Frederick William would have to seek a trustworthy ally.

"It will never do to judge of the general feeling of a country from the mad tenets of academical youths, (who are despised by none more heartily than by the people themselves,) or from the still less pardonable excesses of hot-headed teachers. When I was in Berlin, a plot, headed by a schoolmaster, was detected in Stargard, in Pomerania; the object was, to proclaim the Spanish Constitution, and assassinate the ministers and other persons of weight who might naturally be supposed to be hostile to the innovation. This no more proves the Prussian people to be ripe for revolt, than it proves them to be ready to be murderers.

"In judging of the political feelings of a country, a Briton is apt to be deceived by his own political habits still more than by partial observation. The political exercises and education which we enjoy, are riches which we may well wish to see in the possession of others; but they lead us into a thousand fallacies, when they make us conclude, from what our feelings would be under any given institutions, that another people, whose very prejudices go with its government, must be just as ready to present a claim of right, bring the king to trial, or declare the throne to be vacant. Prussia is by no means the only country of Germany where the people know nothing of that love of political thinking and information which pervade ourselves. But Prussia is in the true course to arrive at it; the most useful classes of her society are gradually rising in wealth, respectability, and importance; and, ere long, her government, in the natural course of things, must admit popular elements. If foreign influence, and above all, that of Russia, whose leaden weight is said to hang too heavily already on the cabinet of Berlin, do not interfere, I shall be deceived if the change be either demanded with outrageous clamor from below, or refused with unwise and selfish obstinacy from above. No people of the continent better deserve political liberty than the Germans; for none will wait for it more patiently, receive it more thankfully, or use it with greater moderation."

North. Thank ye, Odoherty—that's a good boy.

Odoherty. May I take the book home with me? I must certainly read the rest of it.

North. By all means. I assure you you will find the writing throughout clever, the facts interesting, and the tone excellent. Ring, Morgan; I must have my chair.

* * * * * * *

END OF VOL. I.

www.ingramcontent.com/pod-product-compliance
Lightning Source LLC
LaVergne TN
LVHW021315110826
845150LV00003B/575